Arbitration

Arbitration

Cases, Problems, and Practice

SECOND EDITION

MATTHEW H. ADLER

Partner at Troutman Pepper Hamilton Sanders LLP
and Adjunct Professor at
George Washington University Law School

CAROLINA ACADEMIC PRESS
Durham, North Carolina

ISBN: 978-1-5310-1758-3
eISBN: 978-1-5310-1759-0
LCCN: 2021931281

Carolina Academic Press, LLC
700 Kent Street
Durham, NC 27701
Telephone (919) 489-7486
www.cap-press.com

Printed in the United States of America

For Loretta

Contents

Table of Principle Cases xix
Preface to the Second Edition xxiii
Preface to the First Edition xxvii
Acknowledgments xxix
Introduction and Overview xxxi

UNIT I | CREATING THE ARBITRATION

Chapter 1 | Why Study Arbitration? 3
I. Why Study Arbitration? 3
II. Roadmap 6
III. What Is Arbitration? 6
AMF, Inc. v. Brunswick Corp. 7
Notes and Questions 10
Advanced Bodycare Solutions, LLC v. Thione Int'l, Inc. 12
Notes and Questions 16
IV. Arbitration vs. Mediation 17
Business Law Monographs, Vol. L4—Using Arbitration in Commercial Disputes (2015) 17
Notes and Questions 22
Class Exercises 24
V. Drafting the Arbitration Clause 25
Exercise 26
VI. Practical Exercises 36

Chapter 2 | The Arbitration Presumption 39
I. Mandate and Consensus 39
II. The FAA's Commandment to Enforce Arbitration Agreements 40
A. *Moses Cone* and the Foundation of Modern Arbitration Law 41
Moses H. Cone Mem'l Hosp. v. Mercury Constr. Corp. 41
Notes and Questions 43
Problem 44
B. The "Saving Clause" in Section 2: How Far Does It Go? 45
Epic Systems Corp. v. Lewis 46
Notes and Questions 51
C. *Moses Cone* and Federalism 52
Southland Corp. v. Keating 53
Notes and Questions 56
Volt Info. Scis. v. Board of Trs. 57
Notes and Questions 61
Marmet Health Care Ctr., Inc. v. Brown 62
Notes and Questions 64
D. Arbitration, Sexual Harassment Cases, and Preemption 65
Mahmoud Latif v. Morgan Stanley & Co. LLC 65
Chamber of Commerce of the United States v. Becerra 69
E. Construction of Arbitration Agreements: How Heavy Is the Foot on the Scale? 73
Nguyen v. Barnes & Noble Inc. 74
Notes and Questions 79
Atalese v. U.S. Legal Services Grp., L.P. 79
Notes and Questions 82
Lamps Plus, Inc. v. Varela 84
Problem 89
F. The Scope of the Arbitration Clause 89
Problem 90
G. Failure to Arbitrate: Specific Remedies 91
1. The FAA's Remedies Sections 91
2. The Process Question: What Relief to Ask for on a Motion to Compel Arbitration? 93

Chapter 3 | Arbitrability, Severability, and Delegation 97
I. Who Decides Arbitrability? 97
Prima Paint Corp. v. Flood & Conklin Mfg. Co. 98
Notes and Questions 105

II. Federalism and Severability: *Buckeye* 108
Buckeye Check Cashing, Inc. v. Cardegna 108
Notes and Questions 112
III. Delegation Clauses: Letting Arbitrators Decide Arbitrability 113
First Options of Chi., Inc. v. Kaplan 113
Notes and Questions 117
Vergara v. Nintendo 120
Notes and Questions 123
Class Problem 123
IV. Recent Jurisprudence on Delegation Clauses 124
New Prime Inc. v. Oliveira 124
Henry Schein, Inc. v. Archer & White Sales, Inc. 128
Notes and Questions 131
A. Delegation Clauses and the Class Action Controversy 132
Green Tree Fin. Corp. v. Bazzle 132
Notes and Questions 138
Rent-A-Ctr., W., Inc. v. Jackson 139
Notes and Questions 150

Chapter 4 | Arbitration and Class Actions **153**
I. Overview of the Class Action Ban Debate 153
II. *Concepcion* and Its Progeny: The Supreme Court's Class Action Arbitration Jurisprudence 157
AT&T Mobility LLC v. Concepcion 157
Notes and Questions 167
Comment: How Important Is Efficiency? 169
Oxford Health Plans LLC v. Sutter 170
Notes and Questions 172
III. Effective Vindication, Federalism, and *Concepcion* Rolling On 173
Am. Express Co. v. Italian Colors Rest. 174
Notes and Questions 182
IV. Federalism and Preemption After *Concepcion* 183
DIRECTV, Inc. v. Imburgia 184
Notes and Questions 190
V. Pro-Consumer, Extra-Judicial Reaction to *Concepcion* 192
Comment: Consumer Arbitration Clauses in Institutional Arbitration 194
VI. The Life and Death of Administrative Agency Reform of Class Action Bans 195

UNIT II | CONDUCTING THE ARBITRATION

Chapter 5 | Choosing an Arbitrator **199**
I. The Selection Process: Various Options 199
A. The Parties Can Name the Arbitrator in the Arbitration Clause 199
B. The Parties Can Specify the Expertise of the Arbitrator 200
Class Problem 201
C. The Party-Appointed Arbitrators Can Choose a Third Arbitrator 201
Problem 202
D. The Parties Can Select Institutional Rules to Control the Appointment Process 202
II. Researching the Potential Arbitrator 203
III. Interviewing the Arbitrator Candidate 205
Class Problem 206
IV. Diversity in Arbitrator Selection 206
A. Institutional Rules: Producing Results or Just Rhetoric? 206
B. Improve Intelligence, Improve Diversity: Two Suggestions 207
Sarah R. Cole, *Arbitrator Diversity: Can It Be Achieved?* 208
Catherine A. Rogers, *The Key to Unlocking the Arbitrator Diversity Paradox?* 210
C. The *Jay-Z* Case and Beyond 213
Shawn C. Carter, et al. v. Iconix Brand Group, Inc., et al. 213
Comment 216
Rekha Rangachari, *Can't Knock the Hustle . . . [To Broaden Diversity in Arbitration]* 217
Notes and Questions 219

Chapter 6 | Challenging Arbitrator Selection **221**
I. The Experience vs. Conflict Dichotomy 221
Class Problems 221
II. The FAA's Treatment of Arbitrator Bias 222
III. Conflict Guidelines from Arbitrator Institutions 223
Class Problem 226
IV. The Importance of Disclosure 226
Commonwealth Coatings Corp. v. Continental Casualty Co. 228
Notes and Questions 232
Tenaska Energy, Inc. v. Ponderosa Pine Energy, LLC 235
Notes and Questions 241
Golden v. O'Melveny & Myers LLP 243
Problem: Arbitrator Conflicts of Interest 244

V. Timing Arbitrator Challenges: Balancing Waiver vs. Prematurity 245
Savers Prop. & Cas. Ins. Co. v. Nat'l Union Fire Ins. Co. 246
Monster Energy Co. v. City Bevs., LLC 250
Martin v. NTT Data, Inc. 252
Notes and Questions 253

Chapter 7 | Discovery in Arbitration **255**
I. Two Myths 255
Burton v. Bush 256
Comment: The Myths Exploded 257
II. Legal Bases of Discovery in Arbitration 258
A. The Arbitration Clause 258
B. Institutional Rules 259
Notes and Questions 261
Problem 262
Comment 263
Notes and Questions 263
Class Exercise 264
C. Procedural Orders 265
International Centre for Dispute Resolution 266
John Wilkinson, *Arbitration Discovery: Getting It Right* 274
Janice L. Sperow, *Discovery in Arbitration: Agreement, Plans, and Fairness: One arbitrator's view of how you can structure the discovery process* 279
Problem 283
III. The Growing Importance of e-Discovery 284
Richard Posell, *E-Discovery in Arbitration* 284
IV. Fairness and Efficiency 288

Chapter 8 | Third-Party Evidence **291**
I. "When" Question: When Can Third Parties Be Compelled to Give Evidence in Arbitration? 292
Class Problem 293
Hay Grp., Inc. v. E.B.S. Acquisition Corp 294
Sec. Life Ins. Co. of Am. v. Duncanson & Holt 299
Stolt-Nielsen Transp. Grp., Inc. v. Celanese AG 303
Note 309
Notes and Questions 311
II. Where Should a Section 7 Subpoena Be Enforced? 313
A. The Changes to the Federal Rules Regarding Third-Party Subpoenas in Litigation 313

Problem 314
Alliance Healthcare Servs. v. Argonaut Private Equity, LLC 315
Notes and Questions 320
In re Managed Care Litig. 320
Notes and Questions 322
Class Problem 323
III. Closing Note—An "Immodest Proposal" 324
Benjamin Eichel & Matthew H. Adler, *When, Where, and Whether: The Confusing Law of Third-Party Evidence* 324

Chapter 9 | Third Parties and Arbitration **327**
Arthur Andersen LLP v. Carlisle 328
Notes and Questions 330
N.A. Rugby Union LLC v. United States Rugby Football Union 331
Notes and Questions 336
I. Incorporation by Reference 339
Spinks v. Krystal Co. 339
Notes and Questions 342
II. Assumption 342
Gvozdenovic v. United Air Lines, Inc. 342
III. Agency 345
Grand Wireless, Inc. v. Verizon Wireless, Inc. 345
Ouadani v. TF Final Mile LLC 351
Comment 356
IV. Veil-Piercing/Alter Ego 356
Keystone Shipping Co. v. Textport Oil Co. 356
V. Third-Party Beneficiary 358
Flexi Van Leasing, Inc. v. Through Transp. Mut. Ins. Ass'n 358
N.A. Rugby Union LLC v. United States Rugby Football Union 361
A.D. v. Credit One Bank, N.A. 362
Nicosia v. Amazon.com, Inc. 367
Ouadani v. TF Final Mile LLC 376
Notes and Questions 378

Chapter 10 | Injunctions **381**
I. Early Judicial Hostility to Court-Imposed Injunctions in an Arbitration 382
Merrill Lynch, Pierce, Fenner & Smith, Inc. v. Hovey 383
Comment 385
Performance Unlimited v. Questar Publishers 385

II. Arbitration Clauses and Injunctions 391
American Express Fin. Advisors v. Thorley 391
III. Drafting and the Modern Approach to Injunction Carve-Out Clauses 394
Problem 394
A. Going Overboard on "Equitable" Relief 395
Benjamin J. Eichel & Matthew H. Adler, *Injunction Carve-Outs in Arbitration: Emergency Only, or All Equity Claims?* 395
B. How Far Can a Court Go? Mandatory vs. Permissive Injunctions 400
Practical Exercise 401
C. Injunction Orders by the Arbitrator 402
D. Is There a Conflict Between Arbitrator Injunctions and Court Injunctions? 404
Toyo Tire Holdings of Ams., Inc. v. Cont'l Tire N. Am., Inc. 404
Smart Techs v. Rapt Touch Ir. Ltd 407
A & C Disc. Pharm., L.L.C. v. Caremark, L.L.C. 408
E. How Far Should the "Emergency Arbitrator" Go? 413
Yahoo! Inc. v. Microsoft Corp. 414
Notes and Questions 418
F. Injunctions Limited to Specific Areas 419
Class Exercise 419
IV. Wrapping Up: The Drafting 421

Chapter 11 | Consolidation and Waiver **423**

I. Consolidation 423
A. Consolidation Scenarios 425
B. Consolidation: A Battle Between Efficiency and Consensus? 427
Specialty Bakeries v. RobHal, Inc. 428
Notes and Questions 431
C. Consolidation and Arbitrability: Who Decides? 431
Certain Underwriters at Lloyd's London v. Westchester Fire Ins. Co. 432
Comment 435
Champion Chrysler v. Dimension Serv. Corp. 436
Notes and Questions 439
D. Institutional Arbitration and Consolidation 442
E. Consolidation and the Arbitration Clause 444
II. Waiver 445
Solo v. United Parcel Service Company 446

Creative Solutions Group v. Pentzer Corp. 450
Example 454

Chapter 12 | The Arbitration: Before, During, and After the Hearing **457**
I. Overview 457
II. *BatPow v. GyScope:* A Hypothetical Complex Arbitration 459
A. Facts 459
Problem 462
B. Injunction 462
C. Arbitrator Selection 463
D. The Scheduling Conference 464
E. Procedural Order No. 1 466
F. Pre-Hearing Discovery 469
1. Third-Party Discovery 471
2. Depositions 472
3. Dispositive Motions 472
G. Procedural Order No. 2 473
H. The Liability Hearing 475
I. Partial Final Award on Liability 478
J. Confirmation and Vacatur Proceedings Under FAA Section 10 479
Comment 480
K. Procedural Order No. 3 480
L. The Quantum (Damages) Phase 481
1. Expert Reports 481
2. Expert Depositions 482
3. The Motion to Strike Claimant's Expert 482
4. The Damages Hearing 483
M. The Partial Final Award on Damages 484

UNIT III | ENFORCING THE ARBITRATION

Chapter 13 | Enforcing and Appealing Arbitration Awards **487**
I. The Differences Between Review of Court Decisions and Arbitral Awards 488
II. The Mechanics of Arbitration Enforcement 489
III. The Grounds for Vacating an Arbitration Award 491
Oxford Health Plans LLC v. Sutter 492
Comment: The Deferential Standard 495

A. "Procured by Fraud, Corruption, or Other Means" (Section 10(a)(1)) 496
Floridians for Solar Choice v. PCI Consultants, Inc. 496
Notes and Questions 502
Envtl. Chem. Corp. v. Coastal Envtl. Grp., Inc. 502
Comment 505
Class Problems 506
B. Evident Partiality (Section 10(a)(2)) 506
ErgoBilt, Inc. v. Neutral Posture Ergonomics, Inc. 507
Savers Prop. & Cas. Ins. Co. v. Nat'l Union Fire Ins. Co. 509
Morelite Constr. Corp. v. N.Y.C. Dist. Council Carpenters Ben. Funds 512
Notes and Questions 516
C. Failure to Allow Evidence (Section 10(a)(3)) 516
White v. Valero Ref. New Orleans, LLC 516
Notes and Questions 519
Floridians for Solar Choice v. PCI Consultants, Inc. 520
Comment 521
Hoteles Condado Beach, La Concha & Convention Ctr. v. Union de Tronquistas Local 901 521
D. "Exceeded Powers" (Section 10(a)(4)) 523
Barclays Capital Inc. v. Platt 524
Comment 525
Soaring Wind Energy, LLC v. Catic United States, Inc. 525
Hoteles Condado Beach, La Concha & Convention Ctr. v. Union de Tronquistas Local 901 528
Gherardi v. Citigroup Global Mkts., Inc. 530
Notes and Questions 534
IV. Section 10(a) and the COVID-19 Crisis: Will Virtual Hearings Be Subject to Challenge? 535
Al-Haddad Commodities Corp. v. Toepfer Int'l Asia Pta, Ltd. 536
Notes and Questions. 540
V. Next Steps During—and Following?—the COVID Era 541
Neal Eiseman, *Can a Commercial Arbitrator Demand a Virtual Hearing?* 543

Chapter 14 | Special Issues in Arbitration Enforcement 545
I. Section 11—When Is a Mistake Just a Mistake? 545
Class Exercise 546
A. Section 11 and the "Face of the Award" Test 546

Mid Atl. Capital Corp. v. Bien 546
Notes and Questions 556
B. Section 11 and New Evidence 557
Transnitro, Inc. v. M/V Wave 557
Notes and Questions 559
II. *Functus Officio* and Its Limits 560
Gen. RE Life Corp. v. Lincoln Nat'l Life Ins. Co. 561
Notes and Questions 563
Verizon Pa. LLC v. Communications Workers of Am., Local 1300 563
Notes and Questions 566
III. Confidentiality 567
Century Indem. Co. v. AXA Belgium 568
Contship Containerlines, Ltd. v. PPG Indus., Inc. 571

Chapter 15 | The Rise, Fall, and Uncertain Life of Manifest Disregard 575
Hall St. Assocs., L.L.C. v. Mattel, Inc. 576
Comment 582
I. Should the Grounds for Arbitration Review Be Exclusive? 582
Problem 582
A. *Hall Street* and Manifest Disregard: "Maybe" 583
B. Manifest Disregard Is Dead 584
Citigroup Global Mkts. Inc. v. Bacon 584
Paisley Park Enters. v. Boxill 588
Comment 589
C. Manifest Disregard Is Alive 590
ExxonMobil Oil Corp. v. TIG Ins., Co. 590
Dewan v. Walia 592
Notes and Questions 597
Comedy Club, Inc. v. Improv West Assocs. 598
Notes and Questions 602
Barzelatto v. Spire Sec., LLC 603
D. Some Courts Are Just Undecided 604
Prospect CCMC, LLC v. CCNA/Pa. Ass'n of Staff Nurses & Allied Prods. 604
Notes and Questions 605
E. *Daesang Corp. v. NutraSweet*: Manifest Disregard Comes to Life—Briefly 606
Matter of Daesang Corp. v. NutraSweet Co. 607
Notes and Questions 613

Chapter 16 | International Commercial Arbitration **615**
I. The Trend Toward International Arbitration 616
II. Getting the Arbitration Started 617
A. The International Arbitration Clause 617
B. Institutions in International Arbitration 618
C. The Law of the Seat 619
Example 620
William W. Park, *The* Lex Loci Arbitri *and International Commercial Arbitration* 620
D. Arbitrator Selection in International Arbitration 625
1. Institutional Rules 626
Comment 629
2. Nationality of International Arbitrators 629
Example 629
3. Conflicts of Interest in International Arbitrator Selection 630
Class Problems 631
Comment 631
4. Diversity in International Arbitration 631
III. Presenting the Case in International Arbitration 632
A. Pre-Hearing Discovery and Disclosure in International Arbitration 632
Class Problem 633
B. Witness Statements 634
C. Due Process Paranoia and the Prague Rules 634
Comment 637
D. Investment Arbitration: The Special Case of Suing the Sovereign 637
Example 637
Rusoro Mining Ltd. v. Bolivarian Republic of Venezuela 638
Comment 640
IV. Enforcement of International Arbitration Awards 641
A. The New York Convention 641
B. The New York Convention in United States Courts 643
Yusuf Ahmed Alghanim & Sons, W.L.L. v. Toys "R" Us, Inc. 643
Notes and Questions 647
Iran Aircraft Industries v. Avco Corp. 648
Notes and Questions 653
Aggarao v. MOL Ship Mgmt. Co. 653
Final Practice Problem 659

Index **661**

Table of Principle Cases

A & C Disc. Pharm., L.L.C. v. Caremark, L.L.C., 408
A.D. v. Credit One Bank, N.A., 362
Advanced Bodycare Solutions, LLC v. Thione Int'l, Inc., 12
Aggarao v. MOL Ship Mgmt. Co., 653
Al-Haddad Commodities Corp. v. Toepfer Int'l Asia Pta, Ltd., 536
Alliance Healthcare Servs. v. Argonaut Private Equity, LLC, 315
Am. Express Co. v. Italian Colors Rest, 174
American Express Fin. Advisors v. Thorley, 391
AMF, Inc. v. Brunswick Corp., 7
Arthur Andersen LLP v. Carlisle, 328
AT&T Mobility LLC v. Concepcion, 157
Atalese v. U.S. Legal Services Grp., L.P., 79

Barclays Capital Inc. v. Platt, 524
Barzelatto v. Spire Sec., LLC, 603
Buckeye Check Cashing, Inc. v. Cardegna, 108
Burton v. Bush, 256

Century Indem. Co. v. AXA Belgium, 568
Certain Underwriters at Lloyd's London v. Westchester Fire Ins. Co., 432
Chamber of Commerce of the United States v. Becerra, 69
Champion Chrysler v. Dimension Serv. Corp., 436
Citigroup Global Mkts. Inc. v. Bacon, 584
Comedy Club, Inc. v. Improv West Assocs., 598
Commonwealth Coatings Corp. v. Continental Casualty Co, 228
Contship Containerlines, Ltd. v. PPG Indus., Inc., 571
Creative Solutions Group v. Pentzer Corp., 450

Dewan v. Walia, 592
DIRECTV, Inc. v. Imburgia, 184

Envtl. Chem. Corp. v. Coastal Envtl. Grp., Inc., 502
Epic Systems Corp. v. Lewis, 46
ErgoBilt, Inc. v. Neutral Posture Ergonomics, Inc., 507

ExxonMobil Oil Corp. v. TIG Ins., Co., 590

First Options of Chi., Inc. v. Kaplan, 113
Flexi Van Leasing, Inc. v. Through Transp. Mut. Ins. Ass'n, 358
Floridians for Solar Choice v. PCI Consultants, Inc., 496, 520

Gen. RE Life Corp. v. Lincoln Nat'l Life Ins. Co., 561
Gherardi v. Citigroup Global Mkts., Inc., 530
Golden v. O'Melveny & Myers LLP, 243
Grand Wireless, Inc. v. Verizon Wireless, Inc., 345
Green Tree Fin. Corp. v. Bazzle, 132
Gvozdenovic v. United Air Lines, Inc., 342

Hall St. Assocs., L.L.C. v. Mattel, Inc., 576
Hay Grp., Inc. v. E.B.S. Acquisition Corp, 294
Henry Schein, Inc. v. Archer & White Sales, Inc., 128
Hoteles Condado Beach, La Concha & Convention Ctr. v. Union de Tronquistas Local 901 521, 528

In re Managed Care Litig., 320
Iran Aircraft Industries v. Avco Corp., 648

Keystone Shipping Co. v. Textport Oil Co., 356

Lamps Plus, Inc. v. Varela, 84

Mahmoud Latif v. Morgan Stanley & Co. LLC, 65
Marmet Health Care Ctr., Inc. v. Brown, 62
Martin v. NTT Data, Inc., 252
Matter of Daesang Corp. v. NutraSweet Co., 607
Merrill Lynch, Pierce, Fenner & Smith, Inc. v. Hovey, 383
Mid Atl. Capital Corp. v. Bien, 546
Monster Energy Co. v. City Bevs., LLC, 250
Morelite Constr. Corp. v. N.Y.C. Dist. Council Carpenters Ben. Funds, 512
Moses H. Cone Mem'l Hosp. v. Mercury Constr. Corp., 41

N.A. Rugby Union LLC v. United States Rugby Football Union, 331, 361
New Prime Inc. v. Oliveira, 124
Nguyen v. Barnes & Noble Inc., 74
Nicosia v. Amazon.com, Inc., 367

Ouadani v. TF Final Mile LLC, 351, 376
Oxford Health Plans LLC v. Sutter, 170
Oxford Health Plans LLC v. Sutter, 492

Paisley Park Enters. v. Boxill, 588
Performance Unlimited v. Questar Publishers, 385
Prima Paint Corp. v. Flood & Conklin Mfg. Co., 98
Prospect CCMC, LLC v. CCNA/ Pa. Ass'n of Staff Nurses & Allied Prods. 604

Rent-A-Ctr.,W., Inc. v. Jackson, 139
Rusoro Mining Ltd. v. Bolivarian Republic of Venezuela, 638

Savers Prop. & Cas. Ins. Co. v. Nat'l Union Fire Ins. Co., 246

Savers Prop. & Cas. Ins. Co. v. Nat'l Union Fire Ins. Co., 509
Sec. Life Ins. Co. of Am. v. Duncanson & Holt, 299
Shawn C. Carter, et al. v. Iconix Brand Group, Inc., et al., 213
Smart Techs v. Rapt Touch Ir. Ltd, 407
Soaring Wind Energy, LLC v. Catic United States, Inc., 525
Solo v. United Parcel Service Company, 446
Southland Corp. v. Keating, 53
Specialty Bakeries v. RobHal, Inc., 428
Spinks v. Krystal Co., 339
Stolt-Nielsen Transp. Grp., Inc. v. Celanese AG, 303
Tenaska Energy, Inc. v. Ponderosa Pine Energy, LLC, 235
Toyo Tire Holdings of Ams., Inc. v. Cont'l Tire N. Am., Inc., 404
Transnitro, Inc. v. M/V Wave, 557

Vergara v. Nintendo, 120
Verizon Pa. LLC v. Communications Workers of Am., Local 1300, 563
Volt Info. Scis. v. Board of Trs., 57

White v. Valero Ref. New Orleans, LLC, 516

Yahoo! Inc. v. Microsoft Corp., 414
Yusuf Ahmed Alghanim & Sons, W.L.L. v. Toys "R" Us, Inc., 643

Preface to the Second Edition

As with the introduction to the first edition of this book, this introduction to the Second Edition is written on the eve of a new Presidential Administration in the United States. It is a testament to the importance of arbitration in our society that these changes in government have so significant an impact on arbitration law. What was (and still remains) a means of dispute resolution among "merchants" has become a battleground on fundamental issues of access to courts. As a result, the law of arbitration is far more sensitive to political changes than is, for example, the law of contracts or property or civil procedure.

It therefore makes sense to prepare a second edition at this time and take stock of the last four years. In that time, the subjects in this book have been buffeted by many of the issues in our society. Battles over equality and individual rights have played out in arbitration law, including the entertainer Jay-Z's battle in a New York arbitration to expand arbitrator pools to persons of color. The #MeToo movement has had an impact in the efforts of several states to cut back on the availability of arbitration (and thus privacy and confidentiality) in sexual harassment cases.

Meanwhile, the elevation of arbitration as a basis for eliminating class actions, and its primacy when balanced against other statutes of arguably competing interest, continues—and, given the nature of judicial appointments over the past four years, has if anything accelerated. The exclusion hurdles to class actions and other multi-party proceedings in arbitration, which took on headwinds in Justice Scalia's seminal opinions in *Concepcion* and *Italian Colors*, both covered at length in the first edition, have been picked up by his ideological successors. Justices Kavanaugh and Gorsuch both rendered important arbitration decisions shortly after being sworn in.

These and other topical issues are treated here, all within the structure that this edition continues: the formation of the arbitration clause, the conduct of the arbitration, and its enforcement. It is my hope that students and professors using this book find this structure useful and accomplish in turn a three-party win: understanding arbitration law, mastering arbitration practice, and doing so against the background of the public policy issues we cover here.

In preparing this work I have had the great good fortune to work with a team of outstanding legal professionals. Their judgment was essential. It was, in many ways, easier to write the first edition on a blank slate than it was to decide which new materials merited inclusion in the second edition and which old materials had to walk the plank—especially since my wonderful editor then and now, the inestimable Carol McGeehan, wisely kept me to the same page limit. Here as always, from start of this project to its end, Carol's judgment, advice and friendship was not merely a reason for these books: she remains THE reason.

That task was made incredibly easier, and a lot more fun, by Sara Pitt and Danni Shanel. Sara was a colleague at Pepper Hamilton LLP where she and I worked on several arbitrations in which she repeatedly distinguished herself as an exceptional lawyer of any level and amazed people when they learned she was just a junior associate. When Sara moved on in firms, she asked to stay involved in the book. Sara's version of "involved," as always, was to run the project. I was touched by her wanting remain on the team, and elated at the result she helped produce. We then enlisted the particular help of Danni Shanel, a student in my first class at the George Washington Law School in Spring 2020. When the COVID-19 virus (itself a topic of coverage in the second edition) freed up Danni's summer, we jumped on that, and the result may be seen in the plethora of new and topical cases. Both Danni and Sara (helped by Craig Steen, to whom I also owe thanks) are on their way to glorious careers. That I got to work with them early in their distinctive road to come is a distinct thrill of my own career. They will forever have my gratitude and this book quite plainly would not have happened without them.

Two newcomers over the last four years also supported this work. First, with the arrival of my daughter as a student at the University of Virginia Law School, where I had been teaching, I elected that it might be better to switch schools. The George Washington University School of Law was kind enough to offer me an adjunct position, thereby cutting my train ride to school from Philadelphia (in the Land Before Zoom). I am particularly indebted to Jeremy Pam and Lisa Schenck for being so supportive in my first year and showing how valued adjuncts are to the School, and look forward to a long association. Second, my law firm of many years, Pepper Hamilton, merged this past summer with the Troutman Sanders firm, and we are now Troutman Pepper Hamilton Sanders LLP. The new firm was equally supportive of this work as was legacy Pepper, and I again look forward with gratitude to a long association.

The new edition benefited as well from critical and specific commentary from two outstanding former UVA students who took the class with the First Edition, Luke Zaro and Michael Atkins. Both offered extremely useful comments, especially in the Unit I chapters. A special thank you as well to Ben Eichel, who co-authored with me several of the articles excerpted in the book and who was kind enough to critically review those and other chapters in Unit II. Thanks also to my Troutman

Pepper colleagues Martha Guarnieri, Mia Rosati, Jeremy Heep and Will Taylor, who critically reviewed various portions of the work.

I wish to thank my family in particular for putting up with this during what was a challenging year for all for reasons both global and local. My daughter was home for much of this, not by choice, and ran the family during some challenging times, impeccably as she does everything.

Finally, and most importantly, I thank my students. At UVA and now at GW they continue to offer an enthusiastic and informed take on arbitration law which has elevated any presentation I could ever hope to make. They allow me to see everything in a fresh way that private practice could never replicate. It is a privilege to appear before them each week, and I hope this book is in some way reflective and deserving of their own work.

This field will continue to change, and I suspect at warp speed. Enjoy.

Matt
Voorhees, New Jersey
March 2021

Preface to the First Edition

I have been reading acknowledgments for books for most of my life. At the end the author usually thanks his or her spouse for being so supportive and without whom the book could not have been written. I never knew how true those words were until I tried my own hand at a book, and so my only addition is to move those parting words to the front. Loretta, you make everything possible, starting but hardly ending with this book. I would never have written it unless you had repeatedly urged me to do so, and once I started, you were as supportive as you have been with everything else in our blessed marriage. Thank you.

From there, I would like to thank my editor, Carol McGeehan, for believing in the idea of this book when it was just a thought and I was considerably less engaged. To say that she inspired this book is to make the real something trite. She literally brought this to life, and for that I shall always be grateful.

Ryan Peters, Chad Holtzman, Krysten Connon and Kate Puccio deserve something more than a mere acknowledgement. They provided thorough yet succinct case research and, from there, valuable substantive drafting and input. They are outstanding writers, advocates, and arbitration lawyers in their own rights, and this book reflects their distinct views and their expertise. Ryan and Krysten in particular have been at this for a long time with me, starting with their design of the syllabus for this course that I taught first at Rutgers (Camden) Law School and later at the University of Virginia Law School. It has been a privilege working with them, as well as with Chad and Kate, and it is nothing short of thrilling to anticipate the brilliant careers that lie ahead for all of them. You will hear their names, in and out of traditional legal practice, for decades to come.

Since this work is a product of my interest in both arbitration and in teaching, I wish to thank those who encouraged both. Stewart Baker of Steptoe & Johnson kicked in my door one day when I was a second-year associate, said "Uncle Stu wants you!" and put me on an Iran-US Claims Tribunal case that hooked me for life. His advice has continued from that day to this. Lucy Reed, my boss at the State Department, has been a consistent inspiration for how to combine advocacy with scholarship and how to elevate ethics above all else in arbitration practice. I was extremely lucky to have had the chance to work for her as a young lawyer. Gary Born, in whose wake any arbitration scholar can only hope to trail from a distance, gave me the needed push to at least try to imitate him. One day at lunch I asked him just how one can possibly write a book while running a busy legal practice. He replied that it was "just like building a snowman. You make one snowball at a time." I thank him for inspiring the rolling of those early snowballs.

Professor John Beckerman at Rutgers (Camden) Law School has a special place in my heart and my development for first encouraging me to teach. Professor Richard Hyland at Rutgers gave me repeated and valuable advice in those early years of teaching. Professor Kent Sinclair of the University of Virginia was instrumental in my becoming an adjunct at that great institution, and my old Pepper Hamilton colleague and now University of Virginia Professor Margaret Foster Riley has been a great resource since I was fortunate enough to start teaching in Charlottesville. Assistant Dean Jason Dugas, and the inimitable Emily Cockrell, have made me feel especially welcome at UVA, and created an environment that stimulated this book. My students at both schools played the greatest role in the formation, application and testing of much of the material laid out here. Many of the questions between these covers are theirs.

Lastly, I wish to acknowledge my legal home since 1989, the law firm of Pepper Hamilton LLP. Andy Fletcher, Jeremy Heep and Will Taylor, my arbitration partners, manage to be demanding and supportive at the same time, and nobody has taught me more. Jim Rosener never lets me forget the client perspective, and I hope some of his practical wisdom is in this book. Ben Eichel, TJ Griffin, Lydia Furst, Whitney Redding, and our former colleague Professor Brian Berkley have each sat at arbitration hearings with me for weeks on end, and have made the time practicing with them in this field a joy ride. Andy, Will, TJ and Ben each made extremely incisive comments on various chapter drafts of this book. My sister from another mother, Jan Levine, my former co-chair as head of the Commercial Litigation Practice Group, supported every step of this work and covered some extra meetings as a result. *Mensch* does not begin to describe Jan. Pepper Hamilton generally has my distinct gratitude for giving me the time to do this despite a myriad of other demands. Thank you, partners.

Matt
Union River Bay, Maine
June 2017

Acknowledgments

I gratefully acknowledge the following copyright holders for granting permission to use materials in this casebook: James Hosking, *Non-Signatories and International Arbitration in the United States: The Quest for Consent*, 20 Arb. Int'l 289 (2004); William W. Park, *Americanization of International Arbitration and Vice Versa Arbitration of International Business Disputes: Studies in Law and Practice* 8 (Oxford Press 2006); Alan S. Rau, *Evidence and Discovery in American Arbitration: The Problem of "Third Parties,"* 19 Am. Rev. Int'l Arb. 1 (2008); George M. von Mehren and Alana C. Jochum, *Is International Arbitration Becoming Too American?*, 2 Global Bus. L. Rev. 47 (2011).

Introduction and Overview

This book follows the same chronological approach to arbitration that faces practitioners in the field. That chronology has three distinct phases: creating the arbitration, conducting the arbitration, and enforcing the arbitration's result. The courts are most active in the first and third phases, because they frequently have to order (or prevent) an arbitration, and after the arbitration they have to enforce it (or not). The middle part is the arbitration itself.

The book devotes a unit to each of these phases. We will look at how courts, parties, commentators, and arbitration institutions address the following questions.

Unit I: Creating the Arbitration

What is arbitration? What is the difference between arbitration and mediation? How does an arbitration get created? What makes for a good arbitration clause, and how can one avoid a bad clause that plunges clients into court without resolving the merits of their dispute?

What happens when parties ignore an arbitration clause, and who decides — the court or the arbitrator — when and to what degree an arbitration takes place?

Are arbitrations compatible with class actions, and are class action waivers fair to consumers?

Unit II: Conducting the Arbitration

Once the parties have an arbitration clause and have agreed on the parameters of the arbitration, they need to conduct that exercise.

How do parties select an arbitrator? What conflicts and contacts between arbitrators and parties are permissible? What conflict rules should apply?

When can third parties be bound to, or allowed to participate in, arbitrations?

Are arbitration institutions like the American Arbitration Association advisable to use in arbitrations or do they add unnecessary expense?

What discovery rules are appropriate in arbitration? What evidence rules? When can discovery reach third parties?

What are the differences between arbitration and litigation in witness testimony and trial techniques?

Unit III: Enforcing the Arbitration

An arbitration award is merely a piece of paper until it is "confirmed" by a court. The Federal Arbitration Act has particular sections that speak to when arbitration awards should and should not be confirmed.

When should an arbitration award be modified?

When should it enforced as written?

Can "wrong" arbitration awards be enforced?

What is the present level of appellate review of arbitration awards?

How are arbitration awards enforced?

UNIT I

Creating the Arbitration

Chapter

Chapter 1
Why Study Arbitration?

I. Why Study Arbitration?

Arbitration is a study in contrasts. Like a college student living away from home who is both wholly dependent upon and independent from her parents, arbitration stands both apart from and within our court system. It is on the one hand an independent and private means of resolving legal disputes. The decisions are rendered by private citizens, not judges (and not even always lawyers). The proceedings are confidential rather than heard in open court. But because the arbitration process needs the judicial system in order both to begin and to end, arbitration is linked closely to our legislatures and our courts. The very essence of the private arbitration regime is found in public laws, in particular, state arbitration acts and the Federal Arbitration Act ("FAA"). The FAA commands the courts to enforce arbitration agreements. Courts will therefore step in where needed to compel a party who has agreed to arbitrate its dispute to follow through on that agreement, rather than force its opponent to litigate in court. At the other end of the process, when a dispute has been arbitrated and a decision rendered, the FAA commands courts to enforce the results of arbitration in all but the most extreme circumstances. Arbitration decisions—called "awards"—are given the force of law. Once approved in court "confirmed," in the language of the statutes—an arbitration award is as enforceable as any other judgment a party wins in court.

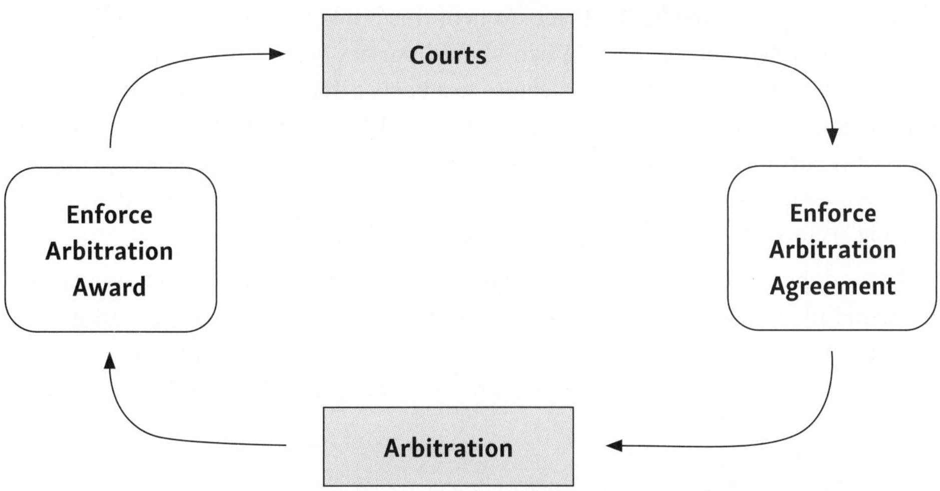

Because the courts are inevitably and necessarily involved in the arbitration process at both the start and the finish, a complicated and inconsistent relationship has developed between the courts and the arbitration process. In theory, the process should be entirely divorced from the courts because arbitration by its very nature is separate from the judicial system. The parties to an arbitration have, by definition, elected to resolve their dispute *outside* of the courtroom. Honoring their choice has the twin policy benefits of upholding contracts (since the choice to arbitrate is usually by contract) and relieving stress on judicial dockets. Since arbitration is generally about commercial disputes, courts view arbitration as a release valve while they are consumed with criminal and statutory matters that cannot as easily be outsourced. For this reason, judges need and want arbitration to succeed as an independent basis of dispute resolution.

Out of this has grown two judicial doctrines: (1) that arbitration agreements should be enforced, and (2) that the product of those agreements, the arbitral awards themselves, should also be enforced. So great is the pro-arbitration view of these decisions that, as we will see in the final section of this book, even legally "wrong" arbitration awards are upheld, and judges are commanded not to disturb them. The judicial review of decisions that you have seen in your other courses is, in arbitration, instead left largely to procedural irregularities rather than correcting legal error.

And yet . . . courts cannot leave arbitration alone. The number of arbitration decisions from courts grows every year. From 2006 through the end of the 2020 term, there were at least 26 United States Supreme Court decisions about arbitration. Compare that to just ten on personal jurisdiction, an issue which occupies more space in the everyday lives of most commercial litigators. Why does arbitration get so much judicial space relative to its popularity? The answer proposed and explored by this book is that arbitration receives so much judicial attention because of its inherent tensions. There is too much of a tug of war, every day, on multiple doctrines, for courts to let arbitrations proceed with no judicial oversight.

As a result, judicial decisions on arbitration touch on every matter of arbitration policy, as demonstrated by the three units of this book: the beginning, middle, and end of the arbitration process. When should parties be commanded to arbitrate? What is the reach of an arbitration clause to a party's dispute? When may, and must, third parties be joined in the arbitration process? What relationships can arbitrators have with parties, their counsel, and their counsel's lawyers before there is a conflict? What discovery is proper in arbitration? When should awards be upheld, and how "wrong" is too wrong for an award to be denied enforcement?

Beyond these basic structural and logistical arbitration questions loom issues fundamental to our social contract. Central to arbitration is the notion of "consensus," meaning that the parties have chosen to arbitrate their dispute and so courts must respect and uphold that decision, no matter its potential consequences as to fairness or access. Of late, however, that "consensus" has been open to considerable question and critique in the specific area of consumer contracts.

Businesses increasingly favor arbitration as a shield from jury verdicts and class action cases. In recent years, sustained by an ever-increasing and ideologically consistent number of United States Supreme Court decisions, that has resulted in an effective one-two punch: businesses first put form arbitration clauses into their standard contracts with consumers, then wrap a ban on class actions into the arbitration clauses. Consumers who may later find themselves in a dispute with that business might be surprised to learn that they "chose" arbitration and so will never see the inside of a courtroom in any fight (though there may be an exception for small claims court), nor will they ever be able to join with other plaintiffs to ratchet up the value of their claims and thus attract sophisticated plaintiff's bar lawyers to their otherwise low-dollar individual case. The "consensus" to arbitrate exists on paper only; in reality, the consumer either never read the agreement or had no chance to change it. In the terms of your first-year contracts class, arbitration clauses in consumer contracts are contracts of adhesion.

The result is that an entire category of commercial disputes—those between many businesses and their individual consumer customers—has been displaced from any effective dispute resolution process. The arbitration clause bars these disputes from the courts, and the class action ban makes arbitration less effective. There are simply fewer disputes. Some say that is a good thing and a reflection of arbitration's "efficiency." Consumer advocates disagree but have been met by a Supreme Court that consistently rejects challenges to class action bans in arbitration clauses. We will review these cases in Chapter 4 as well as efforts to circumvent this result through regulatory changes which did not survive the 2016 presidential election, but which may be revived in future administrations.

How this dispute plays out in the courts over the next decade will have significant implications not merely for the limited subject of arbitration studied in this book, but for the entire nature of class actions and consumer rights in the United States.

Beyond those issues of social policy, this book explores the broad and diverse common law decisions that have grown into the gap between a private consensual arbitration process and a public court system that breathes life into that process. The FAA was enacted in 1925, but the number of FAA decisions in the last two decades has significantly expanded. Rules and doctrines are being written at an increasing pace, yet, either despite or because of this increasing activity, substantial questions remain unanswered. In this gap and uncertainty, the accomplished arbitration practitioner can distinguish herself from just any litigator and derive substantial advantage from a knowledge of the emerging procedural rules and differing features of arbitration.

II. Roadmap

We begin this chapter with a look at what the word "arbitration" means, both practically and legally. As we will see, courts sometimes struggle with the definitional aspects of arbitration, which can be a critical problem when courts are charged with enforcing arbitration agreements.

We turn next to arbitration's placement within what is popularly called "ADR," meaning "Alternative Dispute Resolution," a term which refers to the various ways that disputes may be resolved outside of traditional courtroom litigation. Arbitration, as we will see, differs in important ways from litigation, but it is just as different from other ADR processes such as mediation, with which it is all-too-frequently confused. With those definitions and distinctions in mind, we conclude with examples of how to draft (and for illustrative measure, how *not* to draft) an arbitration clause. Since arbitration begins with an agreement to arbitrate, that drafting launches the rest of the book.

Finally, as you begin this study, keep firmly in mind the limited scope of the cases we will review. This book is dominated by cases on *commercial* arbitration. There are many other subject areas and fields of law where arbitration is also a preferred means of dispute resolution. These include brokerage disputes, where customers can sue their stockbrokers under the auspices of the National Association of Securities Dealers; matrimonial disputes, where custody or support issues can be arbitrated; and labor disputes, including well-publicized professional sports disputes. While this book includes a study of certain cases that directly intersect with some of these subject areas, the substantive body of those fields is beyond the scope of this text; we need only observe that, as with commercial arbitration, the requirements of party consensus and arbitrator mandate are equally as necessary as they are in general commercial contracts. We will use commercial arbitration as our laboratory for examining arbitration law.

III. What Is Arbitration?

Arbitration agreements are enforceable under a federal statute. Section 2 of the Federal Arbitration Act, 9 U.S.C. § 2 *et seq.*, provides:

> A written provision in any maritime transaction or a contract evidencing a transaction involving commerce to settle by arbitration a controversy thereafter arising out of such contract or transaction, or the refusal to perform the whole or any part thereof, or an agreement in writing to submit to arbitration an existing controversy arising out of such a contract, transaction or refusal, shall be valid, irrevocable and enforceable, save upon such grounds as exist at law or in equity for the revocation of any contract.

This unambiguous language commanding courts to enforce arbitration agreements comes with a latent ambiguity: nowhere does the FAA define the word "arbitration." As a result, the FAA instructs courts to enforce arbitration agreements without ever stating what is an arbitration agreement, or indeed what is arbitration. Courts have struggled with this more than one might expect. The struggle should not be that hard.

CASE PREVIEW. What happens when a party seeks to compel another to comply with their agreement to obtain a non-binding advisory opinion as a form of alternative dispute resolution regarding advertising claims? The judge in the following case, one of the more renowned jurists in the country (and author of a leading treatise on evidence), ruled that there is no rigid or formalistic approach to a definition of arbitration.

AMF, Inc. v. Brunswick Corp.

621 F. Supp. 456 (E.D.N.Y. 1985)

WEINSTEIN, C.J.

I. Facts

AMF and Brunswick compete nationally in the manufacture of electronic and automatic machinery used for bowling centers. In earlier litigation before this court, AMF alleged that Brunswick had advertised certain automatic scoring devices in a false and deceptive manner. Brunswick responded with counterclaims regarding advertisements for AMF's pinspotter, bowling pins and automatic scorer. In 1983 the parties ended the litigation with a settlement agreement filed with the court. Any future dispute involving an advertised claim of "data based comparative superiority" of any bowling product would be submitted to an advisory third party, the National Advertising Division ("NAD") of the Council of Better Business Bureaus, to determine whether there was experimental support for the claim.

Paragraph 9 of the agreement reads as follows:

> If either party shall hereafter publish or disseminate any claim by advertisement or promotional materials of any kind or nature, which expressly or impliedly refer to a comparative superiority of a bowling product manufactured, sold or distributed by either of them, as compared to a similar product manufactured, sold or distributed by the other, which claim shall expressly or impliedly be based on data, studies or tests (hereafter "data based comparative superiority") such claims shall be subject to the provisions of this paragraph. . . .

> Should either party make a claim to data based comparative superiority, the other may request that substantiation for the same be delivered to the agreed upon advisory third party, subject to the provisions of this agreement, whereupon the party who has made the claim shall promptly comply.
>
> Both parties agree to submit any controversy which they may have with respect to data based comparative superiority of any of their products over that of the other to such advisory third party for the rendition of an advisory opinion. Such opinion shall not be binding upon the parties, but shall be advisory only. . . .

NAD was created in 1971 by the American Advertising Federation, American Association of Advertising Agencies, Association of National Advertisers, and the Council of Better Business Bureaus "to help sustain high standards of truth and accuracy in national advertising." If NAD finds that the advertising claims are unsupported, and the advertiser refuses to modify or discontinue the advertising, the organization will complain to the appropriate governmental authority. Voluntary compliance with NAD's decisions has been universal. Reportedly no advertiser who has participated in the complete process of a NAD investigation and NARB appeal has declined to abide by the decision.

In March and April 1985, Brunswick advertised its product, Armor Plate 3000, in a trade periodical called *Bowler's Journal*. Armor Plate is a synthetic laminated material used to make bowling lanes. It competes with the wood lanes produced by AMF. "The wood lane. A relic of the past," claims the advertisement, under a sketch of a horse and buggy. It goes on to detail the advantages of Armor Plate; and, as indicated in the footnote to the advertisement, strongly suggests that research supports the claim of durability as compared to wood lanes: "By replacing your worn out wood lanes with Armor Plate 3000, Brunswick's high tech laminated surface, what you're doing is saving money. Up to $500.00 per lane per year in lost revenue and upkeep."

AMF, disputing the content of the advertisement, sought from Brunswick the underlying research data referred to in the footnote. Brunswick replied that having undertaken the expense of research it would not make the results available to AMF. Thereupon AMF informed Brunswick that it was invoking Paragraph 9 of the settlement agreement and requested that Brunswick provide substantiation to an independent third party. Brunswick responded that its advertisement did not fall within the terms of the agreement. AMF now brings this action to compel Brunswick to submit its data to the NAD for nonbinding arbitration.

II. Law

AMF characterizes the settlement agreement as one subject to the Federal Arbitration Act, 9 U.S.C. §1 *et seq.* The Act provides for enforcement of agreements to "settle" disputes arising after the agreement was entered into. In relevant part it reads:

> A written provision in . . . a contract evidencing a transaction involving commerce to *settle by arbitration* a controversy thereafter arising out of such contract or transaction, or the refusal to perform the whole or any part thereof . . . shall be valid, irrevocable, and enforceable, save upon such grounds as exist at law or in equity for the revocation of any contract.

The issue posed is whether "a controversy" would be "settled" by the process set forth in the agreement.

Brunswick argues that the parties did not contemplate the kind of arbitration envisaged by the Act because the opinion of the third party is not binding on AMF and Brunswick and the agreement cannot settle the controversy. Arbitration, Brunswick argues, must present an alternative to litigation; that is, it must provide "a final settlement of the controversy between the parties."

Arbitration is a term that eludes easy definition. One commentator has pointed out that "difficulty with terminology seems to have persisted throughout the entire development of arbitration." G. Taylor, Preface to E. Witte, Historical Survey of Labor Arbitration vi (1952).

The Federal Arbitration Act, adopted in 1925, made agreements to arbitrate enforceable without defining what they were. Contemporary cases provide a broad description of arbitration: "[A] form of procedure whereby differences may be settled." *Pacific Indemnity Co. v. Insurance Co. of North America*, 25 F.2d 930, 931 (9th Cir. 1928); *Berkovitz v. Arbib & Houlberg*, 230 N.Y. 261, 130 N.E. 288, 290 (1921). At no time have the courts insisted on a rigid or formalistic approach to a definition of arbitration. Case law following the passage of the Act reflects unequivocal support of agreements to have third parties decide disputes—the essence of arbitration. No magic words such as "arbitrate" or "binding arbitration" or "final dispute resolution" are needed to obtain the benefits of the Act. *See City of Omaha v. Omaha Water Co.*, 218 U.S. 180, 194, 30 S. Ct. 615, 54 L. Ed. 991 (1910) (dictum) ("a plain case of the sub- mission of a dispute or difference which had to be adjusted . . . was in fact an arbitration, though the arbitrators were called appraisers").

* * *

As the Supreme Court pointed out in *Dean Witter Reynolds, Inc. v. Byrd*, 470 U.S. 213, 105 S. Ct. 1238, 1243, 84 L. Ed. 2d 158 (1985), compelling arbitration "successfully protects the contractual rights of the parties and their rights under the Arbitration Act." As "a matter of federal law, any doubts concerning the scope of arbitrable issues should be resolved in favor of arbitration. . . ." *Moses H. Cone Memorial Hospital v. Mercury Construction Corp.*, 460 U.S. 1, 24–25, 103 S. Ct. 927, 941, 74 L. Ed. 2d 765 (1983). *See also Allegaert v. Perot*, 548 F.2d 432, 437 (2d Cir.) ("judicial hostility to the arbitration process is, and should remain, a thing of the past"), *cert. denied*, 432 U.S. 910, 97 S. Ct. 2959, 53 L. Ed. 2d 1084 (1977); *City of Meridian, Miss. v. Algernon Blair, Inc.*, 721 F.2d 525, 527–28 (5th Cir. 1983); *GAF Corporation v. Werner*, 66 N.Y.2d 97, 495 N.Y.S.2d 312, 485 N.E.2d 977, N.Y.L.J. Oct. 29, 1985, p. 20 ("the Act is 'a liberal federal policy favoring arbitration agreements, notwithstanding any state substantive or procedural problems to the contrary,'" *quoting Moses H. Cone Memorial Hospital, supra* 460 U.S. at 24).

An adversary proceeding, submission of evidence, witnesses and cross-examination are not essential elements of arbitration. *Cf.* P. Spiegelman, *An Introduction to the Lawyer's Role in Dispute Resolution* (unpublished manuscript attached to Petitioner's Supplemental Brief in Support of Its Petition for Arbitration as Exhibit 5) at 15. The Second Circuit has set a standard of "fundamental fairness" in arbitration; rules of evidence and procedure do not apply with the same strictness as they do in federal courts. *See Bell Aerospace Co. v. Local 516, UAW*, 500 F.2d 921 (2d Cir. 1974).

Arbitration is a creature of contract, a device of the parties rather than the judicial process. If the parties have agreed to submit a dispute for a decision by a third party, they have agreed to arbitration. The arbitrator's decision need not be binding in the same sense that a judicial decision needs to be to satisfy the constitutional requirement of a justiciable case or controversy. *Cf.* C.A. Wright, Law of Federal Courts 53 ff. (4th ed. 1983).

Notes and Questions

In the last paragraph of the excerpt, Judge Weinstein writes:

> Arbitration is a creature of contract, a device of the parties rather than the judicial process. If the parties have agreed to submit a dispute for a decision by a third party, they have agreed to arbitration. The arbitrator's decision need not be binding in the same sense that a judicial decision needs to be to satisfy the constitutional requirement of a judicial case or controversy.

There is something correct and something incorrect in this statement.

1. *Is Arbitration Really a "Creature of Contract"?* Yes. An agreement to arbitrate is necessarily an agreement between parties. Many of the elements of contract law, particularly the analysis of a party's contracting intent in interpreting ambiguous contracts, play a role in arbitration law. As we will see below, courts frequently resort to extrinsic evidence and other contract tools in deciding whether and to what extent parties agreed to arbitrate. The Federal Arbitration Act ("FAA") then federalizes that concept by making arbitration agreements not merely enforceable as contracts, but enforceable under color of federal law.
2. As we will further see in Chapter 2, courts are *commanded* to enforce arbitration agreements. Judge Weinstein writes that this is "unequivocal support" for arbitration. But what form should that "support" take? Arbitration is a contract. The Federal Arbitration Act instructs courts faced with a breach of that contract to provide a remedy that amounts to spe-

cific performance. A party who has contracted for arbitration in the event of a dispute but is faced with an opponent who refuses to arbitrate when the contemplated dispute occurs does not have to pursue traditional remedies for breach of contract. Instead, she can, and should, proceed directly to the FAA, at the *beginning* of the case, and pursuant to Section 4 (set out below) seek a judicial order compelling the other party to arbitrate. The FAA thus affords a speedy remedy rather than forcing a party to waste its time in court and then, only at the end of the case, receive a decision that the other party should have arbitrated in the first place. In this way the FAA federalizes the common law (and procedural remedy) as to this particular type of contract.

3. *Is Arbitration Not Binding?* Judge Weinstein writes that "the arbitrator's decision need not be binding in the same sense that a judicial decision needs to be to satisfy the constitutional requirement of a justiciable case or controversy." But if an arbitration agreement is NOT binding then is it arbitration at all? What is it? Just a conversation between disputing parties? See FAA Section 4:

> A party aggrieved by the alleged failure, neglect, or refusal of another to arbitrate under a written agreement for arbitration may petition any United States district court which, save for such agreement, would have jurisdiction under title 28, in a civil action or in admiralty of the subject matter of a suit arising out of the controversy between the parties, for an order directing that such arbitration proceed in the manner provided for in such agreement.
>
> Five days' notice in writing of such application shall be served upon the party in default.

How would a "non-binding arbitration" be reconciled with the FAA's requirements that a party who agrees to arbitrate can be compelled to do so? What is the point of "compelling" a party to arbitrate to a non-binding result?

4. If arbitration "need not be binding," then what purpose is served by the enforcement provision of FAA Section 9: "at any time within one year after the award is made any party to the arbitration may apply to the court so specified for an order confirming the award." *See generally infra* Chapter 13. How can a non-binding award be "confirmed," that is, given the force of law?

5. Arbitrations therefore need to be binding. The "binding" nature is again best understood within the three-part structure of this book. The agreement to arbitrate (stage 1) is itself binding because it is a contract. And the result of the arbitration (stage 2) is also binding and so enforced

(stage 3) by the courts pursuant to the FAA. One is bound to both the process and the result. An arbitration award is not an advisory opinion.

But while an arbitration award is as binding as a court judgment, the particular process of arbitration can be much less formal than a court proceeding. Therefore, Judge Weinstein is correct that "an adversary proceeding, submission of evidence, witnesses and cross-examination are not essential elements of arbitration." Arbitrations can take on any degree of formality or informality agreed to by the parties. Some arbitrations resemble full-blown trials, while others can be extremely informal. There is no magic or statutory formula. A "binding" result, however, is *not* discretionary. However structured or free-form the arbitration process might be, at the end, the decision—the arbitration "award"—is binding upon the parties.

6. How would you define arbitration to those not familiar with it?

CASE PREVIEW. Does the substance of the agreement overcome the particular label parties give to the dispute resolution process? If a dispute resolution procedure calls itself a "mediation," can it nonetheless be arbitration? What should a court do when the parties appear to commingle different types of ADR processes in their contract? The next case shows the importance of careful drafting and of courts seeing behind labels.

Advanced Bodycare Solutions, LLC v. Thione Int'l, Inc.

524 F.3d 1235 (11th Cir. 2008)

KRAVITCH, Circuit Judge.

I.

Advanced Bodycare International and Thione International Inc. are parties to a licensing agreement. The contract grants Advanced Bodycare exclusive rights to market and distribute Thione's nutritional supplements and a related testing kit, which purports to monitor the amount of free radical cells in the body. Pursuant to the contract, Advanced Bodycare ordered and paid for, and Thione shipped, a certain quantity of supplements and testing kits, which were delivered in September and December, 2004. According to the complaint, Advanced Bodycare discovered that many of the testing kits were defective. It raised the issue with Thione, which, according to the complaint, eventually acknowledged a manufacturing defect and shipped some replacement units in October 2005, but not enough to replace all the defective kits. Thus, Advanced Bodycare alleges Thione is in breach of the contract.

The contract contains a provision specifying the procedures to be followed in the event of a dispute. It provides as follows:

> A. The parties recognize that disputes as to certain matters may from time to time arise which relate to either party's rights and/or obligations hereunder. It is the objective of the parties to establish procedures to facilitate the resolution of such disputes in an expedient manner by mutual cooperation and without resort to litigation. To accomplish that objective, the parties agree to follow the procedures set forth below if and when such a dispute arises between the parties.
>
> B. If any dispute arises between the parties relating to the interpretation, breach[,] or performance of this Agreement or the grounds for the termination thereof, and the parties cannot resolve the dispute within thirty (30) days of a written request by either party to the other party, the parties agree to hold a meeting, attended by the Chief Executive Officer or President of each party, to attempt in good faith to negotiate a resolution of the dispute prior to pursuing other available remedies. If within sixty (60) days after such written request, the parties have not succeeded in negotiating a resolution of the dispute, such dispute shall be submitted to non-binding arbitration or mediation with a mutually agreed upon, independent arbitrator or mediator. The arbitration or mediation shall be held in Atlanta, Georgia. Each party shall bear its own costs and legal fees associated with such arbitration or mediation. If no resolution acceptable to both parties is reached through arbitration or mediation, either party may resort to instituting legal action against the other in court and all rights and remedies of the party shall be preserved in such action. This Agreement shall be interpreted in accordance with the laws of the state of Georgia.

Advanced Bodycare filed this suit in Florida state court in December 2006, alleging breach of contract and related state-law claims based on the defective test kits. It did not first seek arbitration or mediation. The complaint was amended and the case was then removed to the district court. After removal, Thione moved to stay the suit pending arbitration pursuant to § 3 of the Federal Arbitration Act, 9 U.S.C. § 3 (FAA). The motion was denied in an order which is the subject of this appeal.

II.

On the merits, we must decide if a contract under which disputes "shall be submitted to non-binding arbitration or mediation" is an agreement "to settle by arbitration a controversy," 9 U.S.C. § 2, thereby making the dispute "referable to arbitration,"

9 U.S.C. § 3. If so, the district court erred in denying a stay, because when a dispute is arbitrable, entry of a § 3 stay is mandatory. *See Klay v. Pacificare Health Sys., Inc.*, 389 F.3d 1191, 1204 (11th Cir. 2004).

This contract purports to require "mediation or non-binding arbitration." It is apparent that an aggrieved party had the option to initiate whichever procedure it preferred, because the contract contains no conditions requiring that one or the other procedure be invoked in certain circumstances. Although we could not locate any law on this point, we conclude that if either mediation or non-binding arbitration is not FAA "arbitration," this agreement is not enforceable under the FAA. When an aggrieved party has an unconditional right to choose between two or more dispute resolution procedures, and one of them is not FAA arbitration, the contract is not one "to settle by arbitration a controversy." 9 U.S.C. § 2. This is merely an application of the principle that arbitration is a creature of contract; a party may not be compelled to arbitrate if he did not agree to do so. *Klay*, 389 F.3d at 1201. When an aggrieved party may satisfy his contractual duties under a dispute resolution clause without undertaking arbitration, he has not obligated himself to settle the dispute by arbitration. So if either procedure specified in this contract is not "arbitration" under the FAA, we must affirm the order on appeal.

We come now to the substantive question: is mediation arbitration? When posed this way, the answer may seem obvious. But the FAA does not define its key term, "arbitration," and courts have had a difficult time defining just what types of procedures are enforceable under the statute. Because doubts about arbitrability are resolved in favor of arbitration, *see Klay*, 389 F.3d at 1201, and because a few district courts have decided on that basis that mediation contracts are enforceable under the FAA, the issue merits close scrutiny.

This circuit has not enunciated a test for resolving whether a particular dispute resolution procedure is FAA "arbitration." One widely-followed opinion asks whether the parties have agreed to submit a dispute to a third party for a decision. *AMF Inc. v. Brunswick Corp.*, 621 F. Supp. 456, 460 (E.D.N.Y. 1985) (Weinstein, J.). Other authority considers how closely the procedure chosen resembles "classic arbitration" and whether enforcing it serves the intuited purposes of Congress. *Fit Tech v. Bally Total Fitness*, 374 F.3d 1, 6–7 (1st Cir. 2004); *Salt Lake Tribune Publ'g Co. v. Mgmt. Planning Inc.*, 390 F.3d 684, 689–90 (10th Cir. 2004). These differing verbal formulations do not constitute a real disagreement, because submitting a dispute to a third party for a binding decision is quintessential "classic arbitration." *See Salt Lake Tribune*, 390 F.3d at 689 ("classic arbitration" is characterized by "empower[ing] a third party to render a decision settling [the] dispute"). Thus, when there is a dispute about whether any particular dispute resolution method chosen in a contract is FAA arbitration, we will look for the "common incidents" of "classic arbitration," including (i) an independent adjudicator, (ii) who applies substantive legal standards (i.e. the parties' agreement and background contract law), (iii) considers evidence and argument (however formally or informally) from each party, and (iv) renders a decision that purports to resolve the rights and duties of the parties, typically by awarding dam- ages or equitable relief. *See Fit Tech*, 374 F.3d at 7. The presence or absence of any one of these circumstances will not always be determinative, and parties have great flexibility under the FAA to select pre-packaged dispute resolution procedures, or to craft their own.

Although we acknowledge that there are few clear rules in delineating the bounds of FAA arbitration, we believe there is one that controls this case. The FAA clearly presumes that arbitration will result in an "award" declaring the rights and duties of the parties. Indeed, much of arbitration law is predicated on the existence of an award: the FAA provides that an award may be confirmed and judgment entered upon it if the parties have so agreed, 9 U.S.C. § 9, or if challenged it may be modified or vacated by the court on grounds established by law. *See* 9 U.S.C. § 10 (statutory grounds for vacatur); (statutory grounds for modification); *BL Harbert Int'l LLC v. Hercules Steel Co.*, 441 F.3d 905, 910 (11th Cir. 2006) (judicially-created grounds for vacatur). If a dispute resolution procedure does not produce some type of award that can be meaningfully confirmed, modified, or vacated by a court upon proper motion, it is not arbitration within the scope of the FAA.

This bright line rule makes sense not only in light of the FAA's statutory structure but its statutory purposes as well. The purpose of the FAA is to "relieve congestion in the courts and to provide parties with an alternative method of dispute resolution that is speedier and less costly than litigation." *AIG Baker Sterling Heights LLC v. Am. Multi-Cinema Inc.*, 508 F.3d 995, 1001 (11th Cir. 2007). But "[t]he laudatory goals of the FAA will be achieved only to the extent that courts ensure arbitration is an alternative to litigation, not an additional layer in a protracted contest." *BL Harbert Int'l*, 441 F.3d at 907. When, as here, a party has contractually preserved all its rights and remedies in court and is unwilling to undertake mediation voluntarily, the FAA's goal of minimizing the time and cost of litigation is ill-served by a prefatory round of motions practice. Unlike submitting a dispute to a private adjudicator, which the FAA contemplates, compelling a party to submit to settlement talks it does not wish to enter and which cannot resolve the dispute of their own force may well *increase* the time and treasure spent in litigation.

These principles lead clearly to the conclusion that mediation is not within the FAA's scope. Indeed, as a leading dispute resolution scholar explained, "the law of arbitration is in nearly every respect an illogical foundation for enforcement of mediation agreements." Thomas Stipanowich, *The Arbitration Penumbra: Arbitration Law and the Rapidly Changing Landscape of Dispute Resolution*, 8 Nev. L.J. 427, 446 (2007). Mediation, as that term is commonly understood, is a "method of nonbinding dispute resolution involving a neutral third party who tries to help the disputing parties reach a mutually agreeable solution," Black's Law Dictionary 996 (7th ed. 1999), or "a process in which a mediator facilitates communication and negotiation between parties to assist them in reaching a voluntary agreement regarding their dispute." Unif. Mediation Act § 2(1). Simply stated, mediation does not resolve a dispute, it merely helps the parties do so. In contrast, the FAA presumes that the arbitration process itself will produce a resolution independent of the parties' acquiescence—an award which declares the parties' rights and which may be confirmed with the force of a judgment. That a typical mediation produces no award is highly probative evidence that an agreement to mediate a dispute is not "an agreement to settle by arbitration a controversy." 9 U.S.C. § 2. Parties to a mediation contract have not "agreed to submit a dispute for decision by a third party," *AMF, Inc.*, 621 F. Supp. at 460, because the third party makes no decision.

In short, because the mediation process does not purport to adjudicate or resolve a case in any way, it is not "arbitration" within the meaning of the FAA. Accordingly, FAA remedies, including mandatory stays and motions to compel, are not appropriately invoked to compel mediation. Further, a dispute resolution clause that may be satisfied by arbitration or mediation, at the aggrieved party's option, is not "an agreement to settle by arbitration a controversy" and thus is not enforceable under the FAA either. Because we decide the case on this basis, we reserve for another day whether *non-binding* arbitration is within the scope of the FAA.

We emphasize the limited nature of our ruling. This opinion should not be read as denigrating mediation—quite the contrary. We encourage parties to make liberal use of it, and we encourage district courts to liberally employ any authority they have under local rules to order mediation *sua sponte* when doing so may expedite the resolution of a case. Nor do we hold that agreements to mediate are per se unenforceable. They might be specifically enforceable in contract or under other law; that issue is not before us. Finally, we emphasize that we do not hold that stays in aid of mediation are per se impermissible. To the contrary, district courts have inherent, discretionary authority to issue stays in many circumstances, and granting a stay to permit mediation (or to require it) will often be appropriate. We merely hold that the mandatory remedies of the FAA may not be invoked to compel mediation.

Notes and Questions

1. What was the dispute resolution clause in *Advanced Bodycare*? Was it an arbitration clause or some other form of dispute resolution clause?
2. The *Advanced Bodycare* clause sets up a two-step process. Step 1 is a meeting between officers "to attempt in good faith to negotiate a resolution of the dispute prior to pursuing other available remedies." What, precisely, were the parties to do in step 2? What would be the difference between non-binding arbitration and mediation? Would the non-binding arbitrator merely render an advisory opinion?

PRACTICE POINTER. How would you improve the dispute resolution clause in this case? Knowing that the parties wanted to attempt to resolve the difference by informal negotiations or by mediation before rushing to court or arbitration but also wanted a binding dispute resolution process in case informal negotiations (or mediation) did not work, how would you draft the dispute resolution clause? (*See infra* discussion of "hybrid" clauses.)

IV. Arbitration vs. Mediation

Both arbitration and mediation are often lumped together under the label "Alternative Dispute Resolution" or "ADR." It is true that both are means of "dispute resolution"—as, for that matter, is court litigation. It is true as well that, by definition, both are "alternatives" to litigation. Beyond those broad points, how similar are the two processes? Is the confusion we see in the above cases between the two merited? How can practitioners and drafters minimize that confusion? When is one process more suitable than the other? Can a dispute resolution clause call for both, perhaps in particular phases, first mediation and then arbitration if mediation is not successful? Or is this too expensive and time-consuming?

Business Law Monographs, Vol. L4—Using Arbitration in Commercial Disputes (2015)

§ 1.01 Mediation and Arbitration—The Leading Alternative Dispute Resolution ("ADR") Modalities

[1] The Threshold Question: Choosing an ADR Process.

Propelled by increasing litigation costs and increasingly crowded court dockets, the use of ADR continues to expand. Employed as a dispute-resolving mechanism. in a wide range of business and personal contexts, ADR has come to be used regularly not only in the business/commercial field (including international trade) with which this book primarily deals, but also in many other fields, including employment, insurance, automobile accident and other tort claims, and community and domestic relations problems.

The spectrum of commonly used ADR modalities includes:

- *Mediation.* A non-binding process that can be either voluntary, contractually-mandated or court-ordered, in which one or more neutral mediators facilitate communication between contesting parties to help them settle previously irreconcilable issues.
- *Early Neutral Evaluation.* Similar to mediation in that it is a non-binding voluntary, contractual or court-ordered process in which a neutral eval-

uator intervenes in a lawsuit to evaluate and narrow the issues and possibly to assist in settlement.

- *Arbitration.* Similar to mediation in that it is a voluntary, contractually-mandated or court-ordered process, but different in that one or more neutral arbitrators preside over case presentation and issue a decision which is generally binding and subject to court confirmation and limited court review.
- *Med-Arb.* A potentially binding but voluntary process that to some extent combines mediation and arbitration, in which a neutral facilitates negotiations and if no settlement results, receives a streamlined presentation of evidence and issues a decision.
- *Mini-Trial.* A sometimes binding but voluntary process in which lawyers and witnesses make an abbreviated case presentation to a panel, which renders a decision, in writing if requested, on the merits.
- *Summary Jury Trial.* A voluntary, non-binding process usually conducted after substantial discovery and when a trial date is near, in which lawyers and witnesses make an abbreviated case presentation to, and receive a verdict from, an advisory jury.

[2] The "Mediation Explosion."

In recent years, the use of mediation has expanded to a point where the literature in the field frequently refers to a "mediation explosion." This "explosion" has been fueled by a number of factors, including corporate America's insistence on the use of ADR as part of what have proved to be effective litigation cost-cutting programs; the courts' expanding embrace of ADR (and especially mediation) to pare down their overloaded dockets; and public policy at the state and the federal levels. Even litigators, often said to be traditionally hostile to mediation, are coming around in response to client demand: 1500 law firms have signed the CPR Institute's Law Firm Pledge, which requires them to ensure that lawyers responsible for litigation are knowledgeable about ADR and, where appropriate, will discuss its availability with their clients.

[3] Mediation and Arbitration: An Overview.

[a] Mediation.

As provided in the American Arbitration Association's ("AAA") Commercial Arbitration Rules and Mediation Procedures:

> Any party or parties to a dispute may initiate mediation under the AAA's auspices by making a request for mediation to any of the AAA's regional offices or case management centers via telephone, email, regular mail or fax. Requests for mediation may also be filed online via WebFile at www.adr.org.

The party initiating the mediation shall simultaneously notify the other party or parties of the request.

Where there is no preexisting stipulation or contract by which the parties have provided for mediation of existing or future disputes under the auspices of the AAA, a party may request the AAA to invite another party to participate in "mediation by voluntary submission." Upon receipt of such a request, the AAA will contact the other party or parties involved in the dispute and attempt to obtain a submission to mediation.

If counsel deem a case suitable for mediation, or if mediation is contractually mandated or court ordered, the parties then must select a mediator and may mutually agree upon ground rules for the mediation: Will documents be exchanged? Who will attend? Where will the mediation take place? In a commercial dispute, the mediation sessions themselves usually include:

- An opening statement by the mediator;
- An initial joint session with the mediator and both parties, in which the parties, often through counsel, make some sort of opening presentation;
- Private sessions, called "caucuses," between the mediator and each party;
- Further joint and private sessions as settlement terms are negotiated; and
- A joint session in which the mediator and the parties draft an agreement or memorandum of understanding.

Mediation differs from arbitration in that the mediator does not impose a solution upon the parties, but rather assists the parties in fashioning their own solution, which is binding only if they agree to make it binding. Unlike in arbitration, in mediation there is no "winner" and no "loser": the mediator's emphasis is on helping the parties to find a solution that advances both side's interests—a true win-win situation. Indeed, one of the advantages of mediation over more formal processes such as arbitration and litigation is that the parties, with the help of a mediator to whom they feel free to confide their real wishes and goals, can devise creative solutions to resolve even non-legal issues.

[b] Arbitration.

While scholars have offered varying definitions of arbitration, it is generally agreed that it is characterized by the following features:

- Arbitration is a method for dispute resolution generally employed as an alternative to court proceedings.
- Arbitration is similar to litigation in that it involves an adjudicative process including the presentation of proofs and arguments and the making of a decision by a third party. However, the parties may contractually structure certain features of the proceedings.
- Arbitration is grounded in contract. It is the parties themselves who voluntarily agree to submit their differences to an arbitrator, and it is the agreement of the parties which provides the arbitrator's authority to de-

cide the dispute and determines the scope of the arbitrator's authority and duties. With few exceptions, a party who has not contractually obliged himself to arbitrate a dispute cannot be forced to do so.

- The arbitrator is a neutral person (or a panel of more than one person, at least one of whom is a neutral), selected specifically for the dispute at hand, either directly by the parties or in accordance with procedures agreed upon by the parties.
- The arbitration procedure permits each party to present its case to the arbitrator, who hears and weighs the evidence presented.
- In hearing and deciding the dispute, the arbitrator is not obligated to comply strictly with rules of evidence or substantive principles of law.
- The arbitrator's decision is final, conclusive and binding upon the parties; it is subject to challenge only on extremely limited grounds, rarely bearing on the merits of the decision.
- The parties are bound to comply with the arbitral award, which usually may be confirmed and enforced in a court of appropriate jurisdiction.

[4] Mediation and Arbitration: A Comparison.

Both mediation and arbitration generally are said to offer substantial cost and time savings over traditional litigation. However, it is often claimed that arbitration "frequently fails to live up to its billing as a 'speedy and economical' substitute for litigation, especially in large or complex disputes." Moreover, some of the supposed traditional advantages of arbitration—the exclusion of costly, American-style discovery and the relative finality and insulation from appeal of arbitration awards—have come under substantial attack and may be eroding. Notwithstanding these criticisms, in contrast to mediation, arbitration confers upon a neutral third party the power to make a *final* and *binding* solution of a dispute. Although arbitration provides the parties with more control than traditional litigation—over whether to arbitrate, who will arbitrate, when, where and how the arbitration will occur—in many ways arbitration and litigation are similar. The parties' presentations to the arbitrator are usually formal and trial-like, and the arbitrator imposes a binding solution on the parties, a solution that may or may not address their real interests or allow them to continue any working relationship.

Mediation, on the other hand, unquestionably is quicker and less expensive than litigation or arbitration. Another advantage of mediation is greater party control: in mediation, the parties control who will mediate, when and where the mediation will take place, what the ground rules will be, whether to walk away from the process at any point, what the terms of any agreement will be, and whether to make that agreement legally binding. The result is a process that improves communication and allows parties to save face and work together in the future.

[a] Similarities and Differences.

The following chart outlines the similarities and differences between mediation and arbitration:

Summary: Mediation Compared to Arbitration

Mediation	Arbitration
Assisted negotiation	Adjudication
Parties decide if any settlement reached will be binding; mediator without authority to impose settlement	Arbitrator issues binding decision; parties have limited rights to appeal in court system
Parties control outcome	Parties relinquish control of outcome
Process is voluntary, parties may withdraw at any time	Although parties voluntarily agree to process, once commenced, parties may not withdraw
Role of mediator is to aid in identification of issues, clarify interests, explore alternatives, generate options and facilitate negotiations	Role of arbitrator is to listen to evidence and render an award
Parties able to vent feelings, tell story, engage in creative problem-solving	Parties may present case, testify under oath
Parties meet with mediator in joint and private meetings	Arbitrator conducts evidentiary hearings
Any agreement reached is based on the parties' interests	Arbitrator's decision based on evidence and law—the record
The process encourages and facilitates "win-win" solutions, mutually satisfactory outcomes that preserve or create relationships between the parties	Although arbitrations may, in some instances, "split the baby," the process tends to result in a "win-lose" award
Low-cost	Can be but is not always, less expensive than traditional litigation
Can be scheduled and completed quickly	Often quicker to schedule and complete than traditional litigation, but more time-consuming than mediation
Sessions, negotiations and agreements are private and confidential	Hearing is private but not necessarily confidential, and decisions and proceedings can be made public particularly if award must be confirmed
Uses professional neutral	Uses professional neutral
May be accessed independently at time of dispute by request of parties, mandated by contract provision, or ordered by court	May be accessed independently at time of dispute by request of parties, mandated by contract provision, or ordered by court

Notes and Questions

1. Modern case law makes plain that arbitrations are binding and mediations are not. This is the key difference between the two. Both are consensual processes in that both come about only if the parties agree to engage in them—unlike court litigation in which, if jurisdiction is otherwise present, no consent at all is needed. Arbitration and mediation both take the dispute out of the court system. But from there the similarity ends because, while both require consent at the beginning, only in arbitration is the final result mandated. Parties can ignore a mediator's recommendation; they cannot ignore an arbitrator's award. That award is given the force of law by the FAA, as we will see in Unit III of this book.
2. The differences may aptly be summed up in this chart:

	Consensual	**Binding**
Litigation	No	Yes
Arbitration	Yes	Yes
Mediation	Yes	No

3. *Confidentiality*. The author cited, as one advantage of litigation over arbitration, that litigation is public and therefore may be used to "send a message" in a manner that arbitration, which is a private process, cannot. Arbitration awards are not published (which is why you will not read many in this book). If a winning party issues a press release about its arbitration award, it can be liable for breach of the confidentiality portions of its contract. As arbitration has gained increased popularity in the past decade in business-to-consumer contracts (*see* Chapter 4 *infra*), businesses which might otherwise have wanted to "send a message" that they will fight litigation have lost this tool. When, however, arbitration awards become part of the confirmation process, and especially if the confirmation is contested under section 10 of the FAA, the material elements of the arbitration award frequently end up being incorporated into the court's opinion. We discuss that issue in Unit III.

PRACTICE POINTER. What if your client does NOT want confidentiality? What if you represent a consumer advocacy organization that wants to "teach corporations a lesson" by showing it is not intimidated by arbitration clauses? And should some cases, such as sexual harrassment, never be confidential? What if you represent a corporation that wants to show that it fights everything and is not going to roll over and settle cases? If your clients press for a waiver of confidentiality in the arbitration clause, how should you advise them?

---

4. *Cooling-Off Periods and "Hybrid" Dispute Resolution Clauses.* Can arbitration and mediation be combined? Yes, but they should not be confused, nor should (unless there are compelling circumstances suggesting otherwise) the order of the two processes be inverted. Parties can, and frequently do, agree to engage in some form of "cooling-off" period before they engage in a formal dispute resolution process (court litigation or arbitration). That cooling-off period can be, but does not have to be, a mediation process. Alternatively, it can be a requirement that no party can take formal action (filing a civil complaint or arbitration demand) until there is a meeting of the primary decision makers for each party. As the *Advanced Bodycare* case shows, parties should take care as to what process they want, and in what order. If mediation is commanded to take place before arbitration, then the best features of each of the processes come into play: the parties may resolve their dispute consensually through mediation, and if not, they then proceed to a binding process in which they lose control over the outcome but have certainty that there will be an outcome.

   Courts have treated the mediation or cooling-off phases of hybrid arbitration proceedings as a separate process that is a condition precedent to arbitration and have denied motions to compel arbitration on this ground. For example, in *HIM Portland, LLC v. Devito Builders Inc.*, the First Circuit held that "where contracting parties condition an arbitration agreement upon the satisfaction of some condition precedent, the failure to satisfy the specified condition will preclude the parties from compelling arbitration and staying proceedings under the FAA." 317 F.3d 41, 44 (1st Cir. 2003) (finding that, under the plain language of the contract, the arbitration provision was not triggered until a party requested mediation); *see also Kemiron Atlantic, Inc. v. Aguakem Int'l, Inc.*, 290 F.3d 1287, 1291 (11th Cir. 2002) (declining to stay litigation proceedings pending arbitration where the movant failed to meet the contractual prerequisites to arbitration).

   Cooling-off periods are not without their detriments. First, aggrieved parties ("plaintiffs" in court, "claimants" in arbitration) may want to get things moving quickly. They are aggrieved, they want a remedy, and they don't want to have to check boxes to get there. They instead want to file something that puts pressure on their opponents. Sitting around a campfire singing Kumbaya is frequently the furthest thing from their minds and strategic goals.

   Second, cooling-off-period clauses can also be overly specific as to the precise individuals who must participate in the process, as the following exercise demonstrates.

Class Exercises

1. Assume that the parties' arbitration clause requires the two Chief Financial Officers of the parties to negotiate for 30 days before any party files for arbitration, but:

    (i) Party A has performed a reorganization, since signing the original contract, that eliminates the CFO position, or

    (ii) Party B's CFO is in Latin America for the next 90 days negotiating a sale of a key corporate division. If he sends a delegate rather than rushing back for negotiations, is party B in breach of the clause? And if Party B then elects after the end of that cooling-off period to file an arbitration demand, is that demand subject to dismissal as premature because the contract's preliminary procedures, which can appropriately be viewed as conditions precedent to the arbitration, were not followed?

2. Consider a variant of the above exercise, where the CFO position still exists but one party simply does not show. More particularly, assume this dispute resolution clause: "*In the event of a Dispute, the party claiming a Dispute will send a Notice. The respective executive officers must meet within 10 days of the Notice to attempt in good faith to resolve the Dispute. If the executive officer meeting is not successful, then the parties agree to have their Dispute resolved by arbitration in Washington, DC, under the commercial rules of the American Arbitration Association.*" If the party sending the dispute resolution notice then does not send its executive officer for a good faith meeting, can that party file the arbitration? What if it is the other party, the one receiving the dispute resolution notice, who does not show? Can a party prevent an arbitration being filed against it by frustrating the condition precedent to that arbitration occurring? Is there a way to control for this problem in the effective drafting of the hybrid dispute resolution clause?

    Recall when considering the above the specific performance remedy afforded arbitration parties by section 4 of the FAA. Where a party who has agreed to a cooling-off clause skips directly to the arbitration, the court faced with a section 4 motion to compel arbitration would have to ignore a different part of the dispute resolution contract. More likely, that party would have its complaint (and therefore its companion motion for arbitration) subject to dismissal for failure to fulfill a condition precedent. *See, e.g., Kawasaki Heavy Indus. v. Bombardier Rec. Prods.*, 660 F.3d 988, 996 (7th Cir. 2011); *HIM Portland, LLC v. Devito Builders Inc.*, 317 F.3d 41, 44 (1st Cir. 2003); *Kemiron Atlantic, Inc. v. Aguakem Int'l, Inc.*, 290 F.3d 1287, 1291 (11th Cir. 2002).

What if the parties have a cooling-off period, perhaps coupled with a binding mediation process, but neither of them wants it? Consider a contract which requires multiple such stages before either party can file for arbitration: first a meeting of principals, then a mediation, and only then can the dispute be formalized. What if, after the meeting of principals, the parties decide that mediation at this stage of the game would be a waste of time and a delay of resolution? Can they agree to skip that stage? What if only one party feels that way? How would you draft a mutual agreement to proceed to arbitration?

3. When does the first part of the hybrid process end? Assume, again as in the above examples, that the parties have agreed to negotiate before arbitrating. What if one party wants to keep negotiating but the other party wants to move on with life and file the arbitration? A well-drafted dispute resolution clause anticipates this scenario and draws clear borders. One such example would be: "Either party may declare the meeting and negotiation state to be at an end and may then file a demand for arbitration not sooner than ten (days) after that declaration."

V. Drafting the Arbitration Clause

If arbitration is (a) a creature of contract and (b) binding, then the best way to create arbitration is through a binding arbitration clause in the parties' contract. Like any other contract clause, the parties should strive for clear and unambiguous language. This sounds obvious, but keep in mind that dispute resolution clauses are usually the afterthought of most contracts. They are analogous to a pre-nuptial agreement: when the parties agree, they only foresee a successful relationship. They don't think they will ever need it and may even find it embarrassing to talk about. Be it divorce or dispute, failure is the furthest thing from their minds. Clarity is often the first victim of such hope.

As a result, parties may spend many hours, weeks, or months negotiating the material terms of their transaction and then simply tack on a "boilerplate" dispute resolution clause without much thought. If a dispute arises, however, then this "boilerplate" clause will set the playing field for the parties' disagreement. It will dictate the when/where/how of the dispute resolution process. These clauses are thus worth significant attention. Parties who treat them as the equivalent of a standard integration clause or other such boilerplate risk unnecessary "litigation about litigation," in which the parties expend time and money arguing about process rather than pressing toward a resolution on the merits.

The dispute resolution clause should instead be seen as an opportunity to build one's own courthouse. Elements of litigation that are ordinarily thrust upon the parties by the rules of civil procedure can instead be negotiated, crafted, and chosen.

As you go through this book and class, focus on the particular dispute resolution clause on which most of the cases are based. Ask yourself if the lawyers involved in the drafting did the best possible job for their clients, by avoiding uncertainty and ambiguity and thereby cutting off any future litigation about the clause. As you see particular problems and ambiguities with dispute resolution clauses emerge in these cases, keep a checklist of how the dispute resolution clauses *you* will one day draft can improve on the clauses in the book, eliminate grey areas, and avoid your client having to spend money on litigation about litigation.

Challenge yourself as to how you would draft more tightly. Think about what you and your client want in a formal dispute resolution proceeding. Think even harder about what you absolutely need to make the clause effective and to avoid litigation about litigation. From there, you and your client need to decide how much you want to set out in advance versus how much you wish to leave for the dispute. The advantage of setting matters out in advance is that downstream disputes are eliminated. The disadvantage is that at the time of the contract, the parties cannot anticipate the nature of a potential dispute, and so overly specific rules can interfere with flexibility that may be needed at the time of the dispute in order to have an efficient process.

Exercise

Your client had a disastrous experience with litigation several years ago, when using another lawyer. She "won" the case but spent $100,000 in legal fees winning a $71,000 contract judgment. She has explained to you that should she ever face another dispute, she wants it to go to arbitration so as to avoid the expense of the legal system. Her business sells electrical parts, with the sizes of the contracts running from anywhere between $50,000 and $5 million, so the range of possible disputes is large. She wants the new clause inserted into all her future "form" contracts with buyers. Now that you know what an arbitration clause must contain, how much more would you add? How would you go about drafting that clause? With what level of detail would you approach it?

The choices are endless.

Sample Clause A

In the event of a dispute about this Agreement, the parties may elect to resolve it by resorting to non-binding arbitration. The arbitrator has discretion to award costs to the winning party.

Sample Clause B (Model AAA clause)

Any controversy or claim arising out of or relating to this contract, or the breach thereof, shall be settled by arbitration administered by the American Arbitration Association in accordance with its Commercial [or other] Arbitration Rules, and judgment on the award rendered by the arbitrator(s) may be entered in any court having jurisdiction thereof.

Sample Clause C

Any dispute arising under or relating to this Agreement shall be resolved by binding arbitration. The place of the arbitration shall be Philadelphia, Pennsylvania. The arbitration shall be governed by the laws of the Commonwealth of Pennsylvania. The arbitration shall be heard by a single arbitrator to be appointed by the parties. If the parties cannot agree on an arbitrator within thirty (30) days of the notice of dispute, then the arbitrator shall be appointed by the Chief Judge of the United States District Court for the Eastern District of Pennsylvania. The arbitration award may be enforced in any court of competent jurisdiction.

Sample Clause D

Any dispute or claim arising under or relating to this Agreement shall be resolved by arbitration in Philadelphia, Pennsylvania, in accordance with the Commercial Arbitration Rules of the American Arbitration Association, as modified through the provisions set forth: (1) The arbitration shall be heard by three arbitrators, with one arbitrator to be named by the party at the time of the service of the notice of claim, the second to be named by the responding party within thirty (30) days of that party's receipt of the notice of claim, and the third arbitrator to be appointed by the two party-appointed arbitrators within thirty (30) days of the appointment of the second party-appointed arbitrator. (2) The arbitrators shall permit reasonable discovery in their discretion and upon a party's application. (3) The arbitrators shall issue a reasoned award. (4) Judgment on the award may be entered in any court having jurisdiction. (5) The arbitrators shall determine which party, in their view, is the prevailing party and have the discretion to award that prevailing party its reasonable attorney's fees and costs. The arbitration award may be enforced in any court of competent jurisdiction.

Sample Clause E

Any dispute arising out of or relating to this Agreement shall be resolved through Arbitration before a single arbitrator pursuant to the rules of the American Arbitration Association. The arbitration award may be enforced in any court of competent jurisdiction.

Mandatory Is Mandatory, and Other Things Mandatory. What elements of an arbitration clause are absolutely essential?

a. An arbitration clause must, first of all, call for arbitration. It must use the "A" word.

   An arbitration clause must be mandatory. It should never leave any doubt as to the parties' intent in choosing arbitration as THE means of dispute resolution. Words like "may" must be avoided. Words like "shall" are favored. So: not "any dispute MAY be referred to arbitration," but rather "any dispute SHALL be resolved by arbitration."

b. An arbitration clause must be properly defined in scope. Even when there is an intent for all conceivable contractual disputes to be settled through arbitration, parties regularly try to avoid that outcome when it subsequently becomes to their advantage. In this regard, lawyers should be mindful of how arbitration clauses are construed under the law governing the contract. For example, in California, the phrase "arising under" is construed narrowly, while "arising out of or relating to" is construed broadly. *Compare Mediterranean Enters., Inc. v. Ssangyong Corp.*, 708 F.2d 1458, 1464 (9th Cir. 1983) ("The phrase 'arising under' has been called 'relatively narrow as arbitration clauses go'"), *and Cape Flattery Ltd. v. Titan Mar., LLC*, 647 F.3d 914, 921–23 (9th Cir. 2011) (adopting a narrow interpretation off the phrase "arising under" and holding that claims that relate "only peripherally" to the agreement will not be arbitrable under provisions containing such language), *with Simula, Inc. v. Autoliv, Inc.*, 175 F.3d 716, 721 (9th Cir. 1999) (agreement requiring arbitration of all disputes "arising in connection with this Agreement" covered "every dispute between the parties having a significant relationship to the contract and all disputes having their origin or genesis in the contract") (emphasis added), *and Chiron Corp. v. Ortho Diagnostic Sys.*, 207 F.3d 1126 (9th Cir. 2000) (arbitration clause requiring arbitration of any dispute "arising out of or relating to" the parties' agreement was "broad and far reaching"). Alternatively, if the parties only intend for arbitration to govern in certain circumstances, those circumstances should be clearly and unambiguously spelled out in the contract.

An arbitration clause should provide that the arbitration can be confirmed. There is particular language on this in the FAA. *See* Chapter 13.

Default Procedures. What happens if a party doesn't cooperate with the arbitration clause's agreed upon procedures?

A recurring issue is arbitrator appointment. Many clauses provide for party cooperation and working together in vetting and appointing arbitrator(s) within a given time (*see supra* sample clauses). If a party simply ignores the appointment deadline(s), however, the arbitration is stalled, which may be precisely what the ignoring party has in mind. A complete arbitration clause anticipates lack of cooperation and provides for so-called "default" measures that kick in where a party avoids its obligations. In the context of appointment, the default measures may either provide for direct appointment of arbitrator(s) by the other cooperating party (e.g., "In the event that the Responding party does not appoint its arbitrator within the above-referenced thirty days after receiving the Statement of Claim, the other arbitrator may be appointed by the party submitting the original claim.") or refer to institutional rules, which generally provide for default situations. For a further discussion of institutional rules, see below.

On the Federal Arbitration Act's authority for the court to intervene ultimately in appointments, see FAA section 5:

> If in the agreement provision be made for a method of naming or appointing an arbitrator or arbitrators or an umpire, such method shall be followed; but if no method be provided therein, or if a method be provided and any party thereto shall fail to avail himself of such method, or if for any other reason there shall be a lapse in the naming of an arbitrator or arbitrators or umpire, or in filling a vacancy, then upon the application of either party to the controversy the court shall designate and appoint an arbitrator or arbitrators or umpire, as the case may require, who shall act under the said agreement with the same force and effect as if he or they had been specifically named therein; and unless otherwise provided in the agreement the arbitration shall be by a single arbitrator.

Number of Arbitrators. Standard practice calls for disputes to be resolved by either one or three arbitrators. As a general matter, proceeding before one arbitrator is cheaper and more efficient. Unlike judges, arbitrators are compensated by the parties for their time, and paying one costs less than paying three. Additionally, many arbitrators are also working lawyers with their own busy schedules, so a three-arbitrator proceeding requires the coordination of those schedules. On the other hand, a three-arbitrator proceeding may be advisable in cases of greater complexity and/or amount in controversy, so there is a full vetting of the issues. Additionally, in three-arbitrator cases where one arbitrator is appointed by each party, the parties may derive comfort from thinking that they have an advocate on the panel. *See* Chapter 6 for a discussion of arbitrator independence. The number of arbitrators is wholly within the discretion of the parties.

Appointment Process. There is no fixed, standard way to appoint arbitrators. The parties can name an arbitrator in advance or identify one by title ("Chair of the local Board of CPAs"). They can agree to work together to pick a single arbitrator. They can agree to work together to appoint all three arbitrators. They can each name a party-appointed arbitrator and then negotiate between them as to the chair, or they can delegate to the party-appointed arbitrators the duty to select the chair. In considering the appointment process, consider also the "default procedures" and "institutional rules" portions of these notes.

Arbitration Institutions and Institutional Rules. **A threshold decision in drafting the arbitration clause is whether to select "institutional" arbitration or "ad hoc" (non-institutional) arbitration.** The obvious advantage of institutional arbitration is that it provides a standardized procedural framework to the arbitration and, as noted above, can contribute a roster of professional and vetted arbitrators as candidates to resolve the dispute. The disadvantage is the imposition of additional costs, which are often tied to the size of the claim.

In the arbitration world, there are a number of institutions that can act as a "host" for the arbitration. Among the better known of these institutions are the American Arbitration Association, the Center for Dispute Resolution, JAMS, and, for international arbitration cases, the International Chamber of Commerce and the London Court of International Arbitration. These institutions have their own sets of procedural rules and often have a roster of arbitrators from which the parties may select theirs. The roster is composed of arbitrators who have been screened by the institution and so are presumed to have experience, with good reviews, in serving as arbitrators. The procedural rules account for arbitrator selection, the location of the arbitrator, and, because of this, the default process referred to above. *See, e.g.*, American Arbitration Association, Commercial Arbitration Rules, R-12 (providing for "appointment from a national roster" where "the parties have not appointed an arbitrator and have not provided any other method of appointment"). Rules 12, 13, and 14 of the AAA Commercial Arbitration Rules provide for various of the scenarios considered in this section. *See also, e.g.*, JAMS Rule 15:

> (b) If the Parties do not agree on an Arbitrator, JAMS shall send the Parties a list of at least five (5) Arbitrator candidates in the case of a sole Arbitrator and ten (10) Arbitrator candidates in the case of a tripartite panel. JAMS shall also provide each Party with a brief description of the background and experience of each Arbitrator candidate. JAMS may replace any or all names on the list of Arbitrator candidates for reasonable cause at any time before the Parties have submitted their choice pursuant to subparagraph (c) below.
>
> (c) Within seven (7) calendar days of service upon the Parties of the list of names, each Party may strike two (2) names in the case of a sole Arbitrator and three (3) names in the case of a tripartite panel, and shall rank the remaining Arbitrator candidates in order of preference. The remaining Arbitrator candidate with the highest composite ranking shall be appointed the Arbitrator. JAMS may grant a reasonable extension of the time to strike and rank the Arbitrator candidates to any Party without the consent of the other Parties.
>
> (d) If this process does not yield an Arbitrator or a complete panel, JAMS shall designate the sole Arbitrator or as many members of the tripartite panel as are necessary to complete the panel.

By selecting institutional arbitration, the parties make these rules part of their contract (although those rules can be modified in the contract itself, *see* Sample Clause B).

But What Institutional Rules? Simply selecting an institution and incorporating its rules is not the end of the drafting road. Rules change. Parties who select institutional rules should be precise not only as to the particular institution's rules that they are selecting but also as to *what version* of those rules they are picking. The leading arbitration institutions enact changes to their rules in the same way that state and federal rules of civil procedure are on occasion amended to keep up with current developments and needs. *See, e.g., JAMS Announces Updated Arbitration Rules*, JAMS (July 9, 2014), https://www.jamsadr.com/news/2014/jams-announces-updated-arbitration-rules; American Arbitration Association, Summary of Changes, Commercial Arbitration Rules (2013).

Consider excerpts from three different arbitration clauses in which the respective parties had agreed in their negotiations to make their arbitration "institutional" rather than "ad hoc" (no institution).

- Clause A. "The arbitration shall take place under the Commercial Arbitration Rules of the American Arbitration Association."
- Clause B. "The arbitration shall take place under the Commercial Arbitration Rules of the American Arbitration Association in effect at the time of this Agreement."
- Clause C. "The arbitration shall take place under the Commercial Arbitration Rules of the American Arbitration Association in effect at the time of the Notice of Dispute under this Agreement."

If the rules do not change, then the differences among these three clauses are not material. But rules *do* change. Both the JAMS rules and the AAA rules provide for more discovery than in their original form. *See infra* Chapter 7. In California, employment arbitration rules which originally allocated arbitrator payment equally now provide that the employer must pay 100% of the arbitrator's (or arbitrators') costs and fees. The AAA rules were revised in 2013 to give arbitrators the power to order "appropriate sanctions" on account of a party's failure to follow AAA rules. If the parties made their (institutional) arbitration clause in their contract in year-1, the rules change in year-2, and the dispute arises in year-3, then absent specificity in date, the institutional selection will be ambiguous.

What if the rules change, but the parties have anticipated that there may be changes and so provide for language along the lines of Clause C above: that the rules in effect at the time of the dispute govern? That answer is easy on its face—but what if one party argues that the rule change is unconscionable and contract "assent" should not be found when the parties themselves did not agree to the specific material change? At least one court has held that this does not matter, and so if a party agrees to be bound by rule changes, so be it, materiality or not. *Lucas v. Gund*, 450 F. Supp. 2d 1125 (C.D. Cal. 2006).

Discovery. Few issues in arbitration are as misunderstood as discovery. We devote an entire chapter of this book to the subject. *See infra* Chapter 7. For the reasons discussed above, it is often difficult to get parties to consider addressing in their arbitration clause the scope of permissible discovery in advance in the contract. It may be even more difficult for the parties to reach agreement once a claim has been filed, due to the adversarial nature of the dispute—which can lead to more litigation about litigation. Do the parties want discovery at all? If yes, should full federal court discovery or more limited discovery be allowed (e.g., document production but no depositions)? Or would the parties simply rather wait until there is an actual dispute and, at that point, leave it to the arbitrator's discretion? Or—a variant of the two choices above—do they want to leave discovery to the arbitrator's discretion but with certain up-front limits or guidelines?

a. *Discovery and Institutional Arbitrations.* Note that the absence of a discovery provision will not necessarily foreclose the arbitrator from permitting limited, or otherwise, discovery—particularly if the parties have chosen institutional rules. *See, e.g.*, American Arbitration Association, Commercial Arbitration Rules, Rule 22(a) ("The arbitrator shall manage any necessary exchange of information among the parties with a view toward achieving an economical and efficient resolution of the dispute . . .").

b. *Sample Arbitration Clause for Discovery.* The Parties agree that each Party may take discovery of Parties and third parties related to any dispute or claim arbitrated under this Agreement, as follows:

Each Party may request that the other Party produce any and all non-privileged documents that are relevant to any claim or defense raised in the arbitration by either Party;

Except as set forth in subsection iv below, each Party may take no more than a total of [______] depositions, including depositions of the third parties;

Each Party shall, through subpoenas issued by the arbitrators, have the right to seek documents and deposition testimony from third parties who may have information relevant to a claim or defense raised in the arbitration by either Party; and

Each Party shall be permitted to depose any expert witness that the opposing Party intends to call at the arbitration hearing.

There shall be no other discovery permitted or required, including but not limited to initial disclosures, interrogatories or requests for admission. If the Parties disagree on any aspect of discovery, the Parties shall submit the dispute to the arbitrators who shall resolve the dispute in accordance with federal law.

Limiting the amount of permissible discovery in the initial contract has the additional advantage of controlling costs. That control comes with a cost, however, as a party may find itself in a dispute where it needs documents from the other party—or perhaps a third party—to prove its case. What looked like a sensible limitation of costs when agreeing to the contract now appears to be a terrible limitation of options.

Therefore, even when the contract sets out the rules of the road in advance, it remains advisable to provide the arbitrator some ability to vary them, as one never knows how a case may develop. The critical issue here will be whether to allow the arbitrator to vary *sua sponte* the discovery rules, vary them on the application of one party, or vary them on the application of both parties.

Injunctions. What happens when the facts on the ground outpace the process? For example, what if a party to an arbitration clause is faced with an ongoing infringement of its intellectual property as a result of the opposing party's alleged conduct? Can it go to court to enjoin that disclosure or does the arbitration clause preclude even that form of emergency and temporary relief? Like discovery, injunctions in arbitration are the subject of an entire chapter of this book. *See infra* Chapter 10. Here again, the parties should consider whether they want to empower the arbitrator to issue injunctions and whether they want to permit a court to issue an injunction to preserve the status quo. Note that irrespective of this choice, many circuits allow courts to issue injunctions to preserve the status quo even without the customary carve out language.

Form of Award. Arbitration decisions, called "awards," can take many forms. There is no overarching requirement under the law that an arbitrator set forth her reasons for decision, let alone make detailed findings of fact and conclusions of law—this is all the more so because of the general prohibition on merits appeals of arbitration decisions. *See infra* Chapter 13. Here again, the parties can set their own table, and specify whether they want simply a ruling ("I find for the Claimant on her breach of contract claims and award her $197,452 plus interest and costs"), detailed findings of fact and conclusions of law, or, as is the more recent custom, a "reasoned award." "Reasoned awards" set out in more detailed form the reason(s) for the arbitrator's decision, and they may be particularly valuable where the parties remain in some form of relationship and so need a charter for the future performance of their mutual obligations.

Choice of Law. The arbitration will be governed by the applicable law set forth in the contract, and so either in the arbitration clause itself, or elsewhere in the contract, parties should specify this law. A contract specifying Delaware as the governing law will therefore have Delaware's substantive law of, for example, contracts govern any dispute that may arise under this agreement. Parties who fail to specify the choice of law anywhere in the contract risk having a separate and additional dispute that the arbitrator will have to decide. The relevant law may then be that of the forum or based on where the arbitrator finds the "center of gravity." *See Allstate Ins. Co. v. Stolarz*, 81 N.Y.2d 219, 226 (1993) ("The 'center of gravity' or 'grouping of contacts' choice of law theory applied in contract cases enables the court to identify which law to apply without entering into the difficult, and sometimes inappropriate, policy thicket. Under this approach, the spectrum of significant contacts—rather than a single possibly fortuitous event-may be considered. Critical to a sound analysis, however, is selecting the contacts that obtain significance in the particular contract dispute.") (internal citations omitted).

Choice of Forum and Law of the "Seat." Parties do usually pay attention to where the arbitration must be held. The party with the greater bargaining power in the contract may wish to minimize travel costs in any dispute (and maximize the opponent's travel costs) by choosing a forum close to home. In contracts with more equal bargaining power, the parties may choose a neutral location. Here as elsewhere, specificity in advance is advisable. One does not want to have an arbitration without knowing where it will be.

The choice of forum can wind up having impacts beyond merely the logistical. There are certain procedural questions that can be governed by the law of the "seat," which generally is the formal arbitration term for forum. If, for example, there are allegations of corruption in the arbitration panel or other allegations of unfairness, then the challenge will be brought in the situs of the arbitration rather than in the courts of whatever jurisdiction provides the governing law. For example, if the parties choose to arbitrate in Los Angeles under Delaware law, any procedural disputes will be resolved by California law interpreting the FAA and not Delaware law. The law of the seat is a topic of considerable importance in international arbitration. Interested readers should see, as an example of the literature in this field, Henderson, Lex Arbitri, *Procedural Law and the Seat of the Arbitration—Unraveling the Law of the Arbitration Process*, 2014 SING. ACAD. LAW J. 886. In the domestic arbitration cases which form the bulk of this book, the law of the seat is less important a distinction because both seat law and the law of the contract, even of different states, will still be from the same country (the United States) and thus substantially similar. That said, there are situations—such as third-party discovery in arbitration, *see infra* Chapter 8—where the law of the specific jurisdiction can make a difference, and thus where this distinction will matter.

Special Qualifications for Arbitrator. Parties sometimes elect to set specific qualifications that an arbitrator must possess. They may decide that it is especially important that, for example, their dispute be decided by a professional accountant or engineer. There are decided advantages and disadvantages to such clauses. The advantage is the obvious one—that the arbitrator will come prepared with substantive expertise in the dispute. One potential disadvantage is the complication of the selection process, since it may be difficult to find a professional in a non-lawyer field who has the skill and the interest in the entirely separate field of dispute resolution. A second potential disadvantage is that the parties may differ on the candidate's expertise. A third potential disadvantage is that dispute resolution is a skill set unto itself, and so a person who is a very good engineer may not be the strongest at running a proceeding. A fourth is that, even if such persons have the interest and the ability to run a dispute resolution proceeding, they find themselves called upon to make legal determinations—for example, decisions on whether to admit evidence and whether to dismiss or allow claims based on legal sufficiency—for which they have no training. On account of the disadvantages, parties may elect to wait until a dispute arises and then attempt to agree on the ideal arbitrator's qualifications. This is particularly true when the parties have agreed to institutional arbitrations, as the institutions generally solicit each party's input on what qualifications the arbitrator should possess.

Other contracts bridge this gap by providing for different persons to resolve different kinds of disputes that may arise. A frequent example is that of so-called "earn-out clauses." A contract for a sale of a business may leave part of the purchase price open based on how the business performs after the purchase. Thus, some of the purchase price is held back and "earned" in the future. The financial performance of the new business may then be subject to dispute based on accounting issues. Anticipating such disputes, the parties provide that in the event of a dispute about the earn-out, the issue is to be resolved by a CPA, but in the event of any other dispute, the issue goes to arbitration or the courts.

a. Sample Earn-Out Clause.

> Following the Closing Date, the Executive shall be eligible to receive a cash payment of up to $10 million (the "Earn-out") upon the achievement by the Company of certain contribution margin benchmarks during the period commencing on January 1, 2015 and ending on December 31, 2015, (the "Earn-out Period") as outlined in Appendix A. Within forty-five (45) days after each scheduled benchmark event, the Company shall deliver to the Executive its assessment of the Earn-out due to him in connection therewith (the "Estimated Earn-out").
>
> In the event the Executive disagrees with the Company's assessment of the achievement of the contribution margin benchmarks, the Executive shall deliver a "Notice of Disagreement" to the Company within thirty (30) days following the Company's delivery of the Estimated Earn-out. During the fourteen (14) day period following the delivery of a Notice of Disagreement, the Company and the Executive shall seek in good faith to resolve in writing any differences that they may have with respect to the matters specified in the Notice of Disagreement. If at the end of such fourteen (14) day period the Company and the Executive have not resolved in writing the matters specified in the Notice of Disagreement, the Company and the Executive shall submit to the Independent Accountant for final and binding resolution, acting as an expert, and not an arbitrator, and in accordance with the standards set forth in this Section, only matters that remain in dispute (the "Disputed Items"). Judgment may be entered upon the determination of the Independent Accountant in any court having jurisdiction over the party against which such determination is to be enforced.

Arbitration Agreements Made After the Dispute Arises ("Post-Dispute Clauses"). Most of the arbitration clauses that we will study in this book were drafted and included as part of the parties' overall contract. As you will shortly see in succeeding chapters, courts therefore analyze an arbitration clause as a contract within a contract. The arbitration clause is considered a specific, stand-alone agreement to a particular form of dispute resolution (arbitration) that, because of the Federal Arbitration Act provisions we have just reviewed, is entitled to particular, rapid, and specific performance. But an arbitration clause does not *always* have to be included in the parties' contract. Parties can agree to arbitration however and whenever they want. It is entirely possible, for example, for parties who may have agreed in their contract to court litigation as a means of dispute resolution, or for that matter may not have agreed to any form of dispute resolution at all, to decide on arbitration after a dispute actually arises. It is equally possible for them to modify their arbitration clause in the wake of a dispute arising. They can decide that three arbitrators are too expensive and so elect to proceed before a single arbitrator. They can change the venue from Detroit to Las Vegas. They can decide that even though they originally had not selected an arbitration institution, it would be more efficient for the arbitration to take place according to American Arbitration Association rules. Skilled arbitration lawyers look closely at the parties' clause and should attempt, at the beginning of the process, to propose any changes that would be more in their clients' strategic and economic interest. These lawyers do not let the outbreak of a substantive dispute preclude potential agreement on process. It is never too late. Consensus rules.

VI. Practical Exercises

1. As part of your practice, you advise businesses on employment agreements. A small Maryland grocery store chain owner has come to you because he wants you to draw up a new employment agreement for every employee of his grocery stores to sign. The grocery store chain has done very well. There are 15 stores and over 200 employees. Knowing that litigation is expensive, he has asked you about requiring any employee suits to be settled by either arbitration or mediation. He is unsure of the differences between the two and wholly trusts your opinion. Explain to him the benefits and drawbacks of both arbitration and mediation. Then make a recommendation to him about which process he should specify in the employment agreements for employee disputes.
2. Several years later the owner of that grocery store chain has come back to you because he sold a number of his grocery stores to a company that he says has not paid him the full amount due. The owner is very wealthy and has considerable assets and access to cash. He says he wants "to go after them [the buyer company] for all they are worth." After calming him down, you formulate a plan and speak to the lawyer for the buyer company. The buyer company says that it is are willing to agree to either arbitration or mediation in order to avoid a lengthy lawsuit, but that if

your client refuses to agree to either, it will engage in an expensive lawsuit. Which would you recommend to your client—arbitration or mediation? Is the choice either/or?

3. That same year the grocery store chain owner comes to you with another predicament. He has had a falling out with the grocery store chain's longtime supplier of paper products. The supply agreement between the grocery store chain owner and the supplier contains an arbitration clause which specifies that disputes arising out of the supply agreement are to be subject to the AAA rules. The supply agreement also has a choice-of-forum clause—Pennsylvania—but the supply agreement does not have a choice of law clause. Where is the arbitration seated? That is, where do the parties go to arbitrate? Can they agree among themselves on the location? If they cannot, who decides, and on what basis? What law applies to the arbitration? Is it, quite simply, the law of the seat? Or, as in federal courts, should the arbitrator look to the seat's law for conflict of interest?

Chapter 2
The Arbitration Presumption

I. Mandate and Consensus

Two of the most important words in arbitration are *consensus* and *mandate*. "Consensus" reflects that arbitration is a creature of contract, and so without an agreement between the parties, there is no arbitration. This is a big difference from court proceedings. Assuming there is personal and subject matter jurisdiction, any party can be compelled to appear in court. By sharp contrast, one cannot be compelled to arbitrate without some pre-existing manifestation of consent to arbitrate. To be sure, there are disputes about as to whether that particular manifestation of consent to arbitrate exists in any given case. The existence of an arbitration agreement, plus the scope and range of that agreement, defines "consensus."

"Mandate" means the authority the parties give the arbitrator in their arbitration clause (or other agreement to arbitrate). The arbitrator's authority is only as great as that conferred upon her by the parties. The arbitrator's mandate is an inch wide and a mile deep. On one side of the equation, courts grant broad deference to arbitration. That is the scope of this chapter. On the other side, that deference can run only as far as the arbitrator's specific mandate. Consider this literally as an apples-and-oranges example. Assume that a grower and a wholesaler have a contract by which the grower sells apples to the wholesaler. The apples contract has an arbitration clause. Assume the grower and wholesaler have a separate contract for the sale and purchase of oranges. The oranges contract does not have an arbitration clause. If a dispute arises under the apples contract, that dispute most likely will have to be arbitrated, and a court deciding otherwise will have to stare down the barrel of a long line of federal case precedent—what the next case you are about to read famously calls "a body of federal substantive law of arbitrability commanding deference to the arbitration clause." If a dispute arises under the oranges contract, there is no express mandate for an arbitrator to act. The tension is between deference to arbitration and the absence of a mandate.

Mandate and consensus form an arbitration agreement. But what about when one party believes its dispute should be arbitrated and another does not? The party favoring arbitration argues that the parties agreed to a valid arbitration clause which now covers the dispute in which the parties are engaged. The party opposing arbitration may argue either that the clause is invalid or that, while valid, the scope of the clause does not extend to the present dispute.

These disputes are known as disputes about "arbitrability," meaning whether or not the case should be arbitrated. In deciding arbitrability questions, courts start with a substantial, admitted, and oft-proclaimed bias in favor of arbitration.

This chapter begins with that bias: the federal presumption in favor of finding arbitration agreements. We will then examine the courts' application of this presumption, from the tools they use to find whether arbitration agreements exist, to the scope given to arbitration agreements, to the remedies imposed when parties are found to be acting inconsistently with this presumption.

II. The FAA's Commandment to Enforce Arbitration Agreements

The FAA did not invent arbitration. It made arbitration enforceable.

Arbitration existed before the Federal Arbitration Act was enacted in 1925. But, odd as it may seem in today's age of turbocharged arbitration decisions that mow down anything our present courts deem to be "hostile" to arbitration, originally arbitration agreements were deemed to be something akin to discretionary. "It was a settled rule of the common law that a general agreement to submit to arbitration did not oust the courts of jurisdiction." *Haskell v. McClintic-Marshall Co.*, 289 F. 405, 409 (9th Cir. 1923). Looking back 70 years later, the Supreme Court commented on what had been the "longstanding judicial hostility to arbitration agreements that had existed at English common law and had been adopted by American courts." *Gilmer v. Interstate/Johnson Lane Corp.*, 500 U.S. 20, 24 (1991).

The Federal Arbitration Act changed that hostility and made it a congressional command that courts enforce arbitration agreements. Whether Congress meant to elevate arbitration to its present exalted state, and indeed meant to hold courts to enforce arbitration agreements between any parties other than merchants of common bargaining power, are hotly contested issues. We will review those cases. Congress, meanwhile, remains quiet on this point, as there has never been any significant, material amendment to the FAA.

The FAA's mandate to enforce arbitration agreements is found in Section 2:

> A written provision in any maritime transaction or a contract evidencing a transaction involving commerce to settle by arbitration a controversy thereafter arising out of such contract or transaction, or the refusal to perform the whole or any part thereof, or an agreement in writing to submit to arbitration an existing controversy arising out of such a contract, transaction, or refusal, **shall be valid, irrevocable, and enforceable**, [emphasis

> added—Ed.] save upon such grounds as exist at law or in equity for the revocation of any contract.

The operative words for this chapter are "shall be valid, irrevocable and enforceable." This statutory language has been interpreted, especially since the Supreme Court's landmark 1983 decision in *Moses Cone*, as creating a federal presumption in favor of enforcing arbitration clauses.

A. *Moses Cone* and the Foundation of Modern Arbitration Law

Moses H. Cone Mem'l Hosp. v. Mercury Constr. Corp.

460 U.S. 1, 103 S. Ct. 927 (1983)

JUSTICE BRENNAN delivered the opinion of the Court.

Petitioner Moses H. Cone Memorial Hospital (Hospital) is located in Greensboro, N. C. Respondent Mercury Construction Corp. (Mercury), a construction contractor, has its principal place of business in Alabama. In July 1975, Mercury and the Hospital entered into a contract for the construction of additions to the Hospital building. The contract, drafted by representatives of the Hospital, included provisions for resolving disputes arising out of the contract or its breach. All disputes involving interpretation of the contract or performance of the construction work were to be referred in the first instance to J. N. Pease Associates (Architect), an independent architectural firm hired by the Hospital to design and oversee the construction project. With certain stated exceptions, any dispute decided by the Architect (or not decided by it within a stated time) could be submitted by either party to binding arbitration under a broad arbitration clause in the contract:

> "All claims, disputes and other matters in question arising out of, or relating to, this Contract or the breach thereof, . . . shall be decided by arbitration in accordance with the Construction Industry Arbitration Rules of the American Arbitration Association then obtaining unless the parties mutually agree otherwise. This agreement to arbitrate shall be specifically enforceable under the prevailing arbitration law. The award rendered by the arbitrators shall be final, and judgment may be entered upon it in accordance with applicable law in any court having jurisdiction thereof."

The contract also specified the time limits for arbitration demands.

Construction on the project began in July 1975. Performance was to be completed by October 1979. In fact, construction was substantially completed in February 1979, and final inspections were made that June.

At a meeting in October 1977 (during construction), attended by representatives of Mercury, the Hospital, and the Architect, Mercury agreed, at the Architect's request, to withhold its claims for delay and impact costs (i.e., claims for extended overhead or increase in construction costs due to delay or inaction by the Hospital) until the work was substantially completed. On this record, the Hospital does not contest the existence of this agreement, although it asserts that the Architect lacked authority to agree to a delay in presentation of claims or to entertain claims after the contract work was completed.

In January 1980, Mercury submitted to the Architect its claims for delay and impact costs. Mercury and the Architect discussed the claims over several months, substantially reducing the amount of the claims. According to the Hospital, it first learned of the existence of Mercury's claims in April 1980; its lawyers assumed active participation in the claim procedure in May. The parties differ in their characterizations of the events of the next few months—whether there were "ongoing negotiations," or merely an "investigation" by the Hospital. In any event, it appears from the record that lawyers for the Hospital requested additional information concerning Mercury's claims. As a result, on August 12, 1980, Mercury gave a detailed presentation of its claims at a meeting attended by Mercury's representatives and lawyers, the Hospital's representatives and lawyers, and representatives of the Architect. Mercury agreed to send copies of its files to an expert hired by the Hospital, and the parties agreed to meet again on October 13.

On October 6, Mercury's counsel telephoned the Hospital's counsel to confirm that the scheduled meeting would go forward. The Hospital's counsel said he would call back the next day. When he did, he informed Mercury's counsel that the Hospital would pay nothing on Mercury's claim. He also said that the Hospital intended to file a declaratory judgment action in North Carolina state court.

True to its word, the Hospital filed an action on the morning of October 8 in the Superior Court of Guilford County, N. C., naming Mercury and the Architect as defendants. The complaint alleged that Mercury's claim was without factual or legal basis and that it was barred by the statute of limitations. It alleged that Mercury had lost any right to arbitration under the contract due to waiver, laches, estoppel, and failure to make a timely demand for arbitration. The complaint also alleged various delinquencies on the part of the Architect. As relief, the Hospital sought a declaration that there was no right to arbitration; a stay of arbitration; a declaration that the Hospital bore no liability to Mercury; and a declaration that if the Hospital should be found liable in any respect to Mercury, it would be entitled to indemnity from the Architect. The complaint was served on Mercury on October 9. On that same day, Mercury's counsel mailed a demand for arbitration.

The basic issue presented in Mercury's federal suit was the arbitrability of the dispute between Mercury and the Hospital. Federal law in the terms of the Arbitration Act governs that issue in either state or federal court. Section 2 is the primary substantive provision of the Act, declaring that a written agreement to arbitrate "in any maritime transaction or a contract evidencing a transaction involving commerce . . . shall be valid, irrevocable, and enforceable, save upon such grounds as exist at law or in equity for the revocation of any contract." 9 U. S. C. § 2. Section 2 is a congressional declaration of a liberal federal policy favoring arbitration agreements, notwithstanding any state substantive or procedural policies to the contrary. The effect of the section is to create a body of federal substantive law of arbitrability, applicable to any arbitration agreement within the coverage of the Act. In *Prima Paint Corp. v. Flood & Conklin Mfg. Corp.*, 388 U.S. 395 (1967), for example, the parties had signed a contract containing an arbitration clause, but one party alleged that there had been fraud in the inducement of the entire contract (although the alleged fraud did not go to the arbitration clause in particular). The issue before us was whether the issue of fraud in the inducement was itself an arbitrable controversy. We held that the language and policies of the Act required the conclusion that the fraud issue was arbitrable. *Id.*, at 402–404. Although our holding in *Prima Paint* extended only to the specific issue presented, the Courts of Appeals have since consistently concluded that questions of arbitrability must be addressed with a healthy regard for the federal policy favoring arbitration. We agree. The Arbitration Act establishes that, as a matter of federal law, any doubts concerning the scope of arbitrable issues should be resolved in favor of arbitration, whether the problem at hand is the construction of the contract language itself or an allegation of waiver, delay, or a like defense to arbitrability.

Notes and Questions

1. Fifty-eight years after the passage of the Federal Arbitration Act, *Moses Cone* gave arbitration a significant judicial push forward. *Moses Cone* instructed courts to put a heavy foot on the scale: "questions of arbitrability must be addressed with a healthy regard for the federal policy favoring arbitration" and so "any doubts as to the scope of arbitrable issues should be resolved in favor of arbitration."
2. Just how heavy should that foot on the scale be? To the point of extinguishing other rights? It is one thing to love all of one's children equally, and quite another to favor one child over another. When the *Moses Cone* court held that there was "a federal policy favoring arbitration," was that meant simply to reinforce the FAA's goal of enforcing arbitration agreements so that an arbitration clause would be treated with the same deference as a dispute resolution clause choosing, say, litigation in the courts of New York? Or did it mean something more: that the policy "favoring" arbitration means that an arbitration clause can act as a steamroller over any other federal statutes or public policies? In recent years, as arbitration clauses have been used to eradicate consumer pro-

tections and neuter the force of competing statutes, *see infra* Chapter 4, several of Justice Ginsburg's dissents have questioned the appropriate weight given these words. *See, e.g., Epic Sys. Corp. v. Lewis*, 138 S. Ct. 1612, 1643 (2018) (GINSBURG, J., dissenting) ("Congress, it bears repetition, envisioned application of the Arbitration Act to voluntary, negotiated agreements.... Congress never endorsed a policy favoring arbitration where one party sets the terms of an agreement while the other is left to 'take it or leave it.'"); *Lamps Plus, Inc. v. Varela*, 139 S. Ct. 1407, 1421 (2018) (GINSBURG, J., dissenting) ("The Court has relied on the FAA, not simply to overcome once-prevalent judicial resistance to enforcement of arbitration disputes between businesses. In relatively recent years, it has routinely deployed the law to deny to employees and consumers 'effective relief against powerful economic entities.'"). Justice Ginsburg repeatedly pressed that "[c]ongressional correction of the Court's elevation of the FAA over the rights of employees and consumers to act in concert remains urgently in order." *Lamps Plus, Inc.*, 139 S. Ct. at 1422 (GINSBURG, J., dissenting) (internal citations omitted).

Problem

Consider different ways in which arbitrability disputes arise:

a. Do the parties have an arbitration clause at all?
b. If so, does the arbitration clause cover this particular dispute? Or are the parties having a different dispute but "borrowing" the arbitration clause from an unrelated contract between them? (the apples/oranges situation)
c. If so, does the arbitration clause cover the particular claims asserted?

As you review these cases, get used to classifying the nature of the dispute. Is it about the existence of arbitration at all? Are the parties disputing that they agreed to arbitration? Are the parties disputing the validity of the clause and its applicability to the case? Did a party not line up its claim with the clause?

PRACTICE POINTER. Draft the Arbitration Demand to Match the Arbitration Clause.

The claims subject to arbitration can only be as broad as the arbitration clause provides or the parties otherwise agree. *See United Teachers of L.A. v. L.A. Unified Sch. Dist.*, 54 Cal. 4th 504 (2012) ("It is well established that a court will not grant a petition to compel arbitration . . . if the subject matter to be arbitrated is not within the scope of the arbitration agreement. Generally, a court will look to the arbitration agreement itself to determine its scope.") (internal citations omitted). If the arbitration clause states only that "any claims for breach of this contract are subject to arbitration," then that is all that can be arbitrated: claims for breach of contract. *See, e.g., Perez v. DirecTV, LLC*, 740 F. App'x 560 (9th Cir. 2018) (affirming the district court's denial of motion to compel arbitration, where the relevant arbitration clause specifically exempted disputes involving violations of the Communications Act and the plaintiff's claims involved alleged violations of the same); *Grand Summit Hotel Condo. Unit Owners' Ass'n v. L.B.O. Holding, Inc.*, 171 N.H. 343, 344, 350 (2018) (an agreement to arbitrate disputes over the "actual" amount of pass-through costs incurred by a manager in operating and maintaining a condominium did not require condo owners to arbitrate their claim for damages caused by the manager's misconduct in failing to maintain the building's heating and cooling systems). Since most commercial contract cases often also include non-contract and quasi-contract claims, such as for fraud, promissory estoppel, unjust enrichment, and/or misrepresentation, a narrow arbitration clause creates a risk of forum-splitting: a party can find itself having to arbitrate some of its claims and litigate others.

The skilled practitioner anticipates these objections. You are not in federal court. Arbitration is not a court of general jurisdiction. You cannot list in your arbitration demand any cause of action that strikes your fancy unless the arbitration clause is broad enough to cover that claim. If it is not, and you plead a broad claim anyway, you may find yourself subjecting your client to litigation about litigation, meaning months in court determining the reach of the clause to the case, before a second's progress is made on reaching the merits of the dispute the client hired you to resolve. *Read the clause. Draft the demand. And be sure that the former embraces the latter.*

B. The "Saving Clause" in Section 2: How Far Does It Go?

We begin with attacks on the validity of an arbitration clause. The source of these attacks comes in what is now known as the "saving clause" of Section 2 of the FAA.

Section 2 begins not by undermining, but by blessing, arbitration agreements. The federal presumption in favor of arbitration is made manifest in Section 2, which commands courts that an agreement to arbitrate "shall be valid, irrevocable, and enforceable." But while Section 2 gives, it also takes away. You learned in contracts class that not all written agreements are enforceable. Parties seeking to resist their alleged obligation to perform under a contract can attack the agreement's validity. They can raise validity defenses such as fraud, duress, lack of capacity, and illegality.

Since arbitration is a matter of contract, it stands to reason that these standard contract defenses are available to parties who want to contest their arbitration agreement. Congress recognized this in the proviso it added to the end of Section 2: "*save upon such grounds as exist at law or in equity for the revocation of any contract.*" (emphasis added).

These italicized words are the "saving clause." *See AT&T Mobility LLC v. Concepcion,* 563 U.S. 333, 339 (2011); *Gaffers v. Kelly Servs.,* 900 F.3d 293, 296 (6th Cir. 2018); *McInnes v. LPL Fin., LLC,* 466 Mass. 256, 262 (2013). Courts in recent years have struggled with their meaning. It is not a controversial position that an arbitration clause made with someone who is drunk, or a minor, should not be enforceable. In such cases, there are "grounds as exist at law or in equity"—state contract law, to be precise—"for the revocation of any contract."

But what about public policy arguments that touch on arbitration itself? If a state passes a law or rule that makes arbitration more difficult, perhaps for reasons of a consumer's lack of bargaining power, will a Section 2 defense to arbitration enforcement stand? The arbitration agreement would, after all, be arguably contrary to public policy and so subject to an "illegality" defense under the saving clause. Would those public policy reasons be ones that "exist at law or equity for the revocation" of the arbitration agreement? Or, given the federal presumption manifest in the FAA and reinforced by the *Moses Cone* line of decisions, must public policy arguments be excluded from the reach of Section 2? Courts have struggled with this issue for the past 25 years. Arbitration, as you will see, has emerged the clear victor.

> **CASE PREVIEW.** In the following opinion, a sharply divided Court ruled 5–4 that an arbitration agreement made between employer and employee was enforceable over the employee's challenge that the arbitration was "illegal" because it interfered with the employee's alleged rights to collective bargaining under the National Labor Relations Act (NLRA). The Court's opinion drew strict limits over the scope of the saving clause.

Epic Systems Corp. v. Lewis

138 S. Ct. 1612 (2018)

JUSTICE GORSUCH delivered the opinion of the Court.

Should employees and employers be allowed to agree that any disputes between them will be resolved through one-on-one arbitration? Or should employees always be permitted to bring their claims in class or collective actions, no matter what they agreed with their employers?

As a matter of policy these questions are surely debatable. But as a matter of law the answer is clear. In the Federal Arbitration Act, Congress has instructed federal courts to enforce arbitration agreements according to their terms—including terms providing for individualized proceedings. Nor can we agree with the employees' suggestion that the National Labor Relations Act (NLRA) offers a conflicting command. It is this Court's duty to interpret Congress's statutes as a harmonious whole rather than at war with one another. And abiding that duty here leads to an unmistakable conclusion. The NLRA secures to employees rights to organize unions and bargain collectively, but it says nothing about how judges and arbitrators must try legal disputes that leave the workplace and enter the courtroom or arbitral forum. This Court has never read a right to class actions into the NLRA—and for three quarters of a century neither did the National Labor Relations Board. Far from conflicting, the Arbitration Act and the NLRA have long enjoyed separate spheres of influence and neither permits this Court to declare the parties' agreements unlawful.

I

The three cases before us differ in detail but not in substance. *Take Ernst & Young LLP v. Morris.* There Ernst & Young and one of its junior accountants, Stephen Morris, entered into an agreement providing that they would arbitrate any disputes that might arise between them. The agreement stated that the employee could choose the arbitration provider and that the arbitrator could "grant any relief that could be granted by . . . a court" in the relevant jurisdiction. The agreement also specified individualized arbitration, with claims "pertaining to different [e]mployees [to] be heard in separate proceedings."

After his employment ended, and despite having agreed to arbitrate claims against the firm, Mr. Morris sued Ernst & Young in federal court. He alleged that the firm had misclassified its junior accountants as professional employees and violated the federal Fair Labor Standards Act (FLSA) and California law by paying them salaries without overtime pay. Although the arbitration agreement provided for individualized proceedings, Mr. Morris sought to litigate the federal claim on behalf of a nationwide class under the FLSA's collective action provision, 29 U. S. C. § 216(b). He sought to pursue the state law claim as a class action under Federal Rule of Civil Procedure 23.

Ernst & Young replied with a motion to compel arbitration. The district court granted the request, but the Ninth Circuit reversed this judgment. 834 F.3d 975 (2016). The Ninth Circuit recognized that the Arbitration Act generally requires courts to enforce arbitration agreements as written. But the court reasoned that the statute's "saving clause," *see* 9 U.S.C. §2, removes this obligation if an arbitration agreement violates some other federal law. And the court concluded that an agreement requiring individualized arbitration proceedings violates the NLRA by barring employees from engaging in the "concerted activit[y]," 29 U.S.C. § 157, of pursuing claims as a class or collective action.

Judge Ikuta dissented. In her view, the Arbitration Act protected the arbitration agreement from judicial interference and nothing in the Act's saving clause suggested otherwise. Neither, she concluded, did the NLRA demand a different result.

Rather, that statute focuses on protecting unionization and collective bargaining in the workplace, not on guaranteeing class or collective action procedures in disputes before judges or arbitrators.

Although the Arbitration Act and the NLRA have long coexisted—they date from 1925 and 1935, respectively—the suggestion they might conflict is something quite new. Until a couple of years ago, courts more or less agreed that arbitration agreements like those before us must be enforced according to their terms. *See, e.g., Owen v. Bristol Care, Inc.*, 702 F.3d 1050 (CA8 2013); *Sutherland v. Ernst & Young LLP*, 726 F.3d 290 (CA2 2013); *D. R. Horton, Inc. v. NLRB*, 737 F.3d 344 (CA5 2013); *Iskanian v. CLS Transp. Los Angeles, LLC*, 59 Cal. 4th 348, 173 Cal. Rptr. 3d 289, 327 P.3d 129 (2014); *Tallman v. Eighth Jud. Dist. Court*, 359 P.3d 113 (2015); 808 F.3d 1013 (CA5 2015) (case below in No. 16-307).

The National Labor Relations Board's general counsel expressed much the same view in 2010. Remarking that employees and employers "can benefit from the relative simplicity and informality of resolving claims before arbitrators," the general counsel opined that the validity of such agreements "does not involve consideration of the policies of the National Labor Relations Act." Memorandum GC 10-06, pp. 2, 5 (June 16, 2010).

But recently things have shifted. In 2012, the Board—for the first time in the 77 years since the NLRA's adoption—asserted that the NLRA effectively nullifies the Arbitration Act in cases like ours. *D. R. Horton, Inc.*, 357 N. L. R. B. 2277. Initially, this agency decision received a cool reception in court. *See D. R. Horton*, 737 F.3d, at 355–362. In the last two years, though, some circuits have either agreed with the Board's conclusion or thought themselves obliged to defer to it under *Chevron U.S.A. Inc. v. Natural Resources Defense Council, Inc.*, 467 U.S. 837, 104 S. Ct. 2778, 81 L. Ed. 2d 694 (1984). *See* 823 F.3d 1147 (CA7 2016) (case below in No. 16-285); 834 F.3d 975 (case below in No. 16-300); *NLRB v. Alt. Entm't, Inc.*, 858 F.3d 393 (CA6 2017). More recently still, the disagreement has grown as the Executive has disavowed the Board's (most recent) position, and the Solicitor General and the Board have offered us battling briefs about the law's meaning. We granted certiorari to clear the confusion. 580 U.S. ___, 137 S. Ct. 809, 196 L. Ed. 2d 595 (2017).

II

We begin with the Arbitration Act and the question of its saving clause.

Congress adopted the Arbitration Act in 1925 in response to a perception that courts were unduly hostile to arbitration. No doubt there was much to that perception. Before 1925, English and American common law courts routinely refused to enforce agreements to arbitrate disputes. *Scherk v. Alberto-Culver Co.*, 417 U.S. 506, 510, n. 4, 94 S. Ct. 2449, 41 L. Ed. 2d 270 (1974). But in Congress's judgment arbitration had more to offer than courts recognized—not least the promise of quicker, more informal, and often cheaper resolutions for everyone involved. *Id.*, at 511, 94

S. Ct. 2449, 41 L. Ed. 2d 270. So Congress directed courts to abandon their hostility and instead treat arbitration agreements as "valid, irrevocable, and enforceable." 9 U.S.C. § 2. The Act, this Court has said, establishes "a liberal federal policy favoring arbitration agreements." *Moses H. Cone Memorial Hospital v. Mercury Constr. Corp.*, 460 U.S. 1, 24, 103 S. Ct. 927, 74 L. Ed. 2d 765 (1983) (citing *Prima Paint Corp. v. Flood & Conklin Mfg. Co.*, 388 U.S. 395, 87 S. Ct. 1801, 18 L. Ed. 2d 1270 (1967)); *see id.*, at 404, 87 S. Ct. 1801, 18 L. Ed. 2d 1270 (discussing "the plain meaning of the statute" and "the unmistakably clear congressional purpose that the arbitration procedure, when selected by the parties to a contract, be speedy and not subject to delay and obstruction in the courts").

Not only did Congress require courts to respect and enforce agreements to arbitrate; it also specifically directed them to respect and enforce the parties' chosen arbitration procedures. *See* § 3 (providing for a stay of litigation pending arbitration "in accordance with the terms of the agreement"); § 4 (providing for "an order directing that . . . arbitration proceed in the manner provided for in such agreement"). Indeed, we have often observed that the Arbitration Act requires courts "rigorously" to "enforce arbitration agreements according to their terms, including terms that specify with whom the parties choose to arbitrate their disputes and the rules under which that arbitration will be conducted." *American Express Co. v. Italian Colors Restaurant*, 570 U.S. 228, 233, 133 S. Ct. 2304, 186 L. Ed. 2d 417 (2013).

On first blush, these emphatic directions would seem to resolve any argument under the Arbitration Act. The parties before us contracted for arbitration. They proceeded to specify the rules that would govern their arbitrations, indicating their intention to use individualized rather than class or collective action procedures. And this much the Arbitration Act seems to protect pretty absolutely. *See AT&T Mobility LLC v. Concepcion*, 563 U.S. 333, 131 S. Ct. 1740, 179 L. Ed. 2d 742 (2011); *Italian Colors, supra*; *DIRECTV, Inc. v. Imburgia*, 577 U.S. ____, 136 S. Ct. 463, 193 L. Ed. 2d 365 (2015). You might wonder if the balance Congress struck in 1925 between arbitration and litigation should be revisited in light of more contemporary developments. You might even ask if the Act was good policy when enacted. But all the same you might find it difficult to see how to avoid the statute's application.

Still, the employees suggest the Arbitration Act's saving clause creates an exception for cases like theirs. By its terms, the saving clause allows courts to refuse to enforce arbitration agreements "upon such grounds as exist at law or in equity for the revocation of any contract." § 2. That provision applies here, the employees tell us, because the NLRA renders their particular class and collective action waivers illegal. In their view, illegality under the NLRA is a "ground" that "exists at law . . .for the revocation" of their arbitration agreements, at least to the extent those agreements prohibit class or collective action proceedings.

The problem with this line of argument is fundamental. Put to the side the question whether the saving clause was designed to save not only state law defenses but also defenses allegedly arising from federal statutes. *See* 834 F.3d, at 991–992, 997 (Ikuta, J., dissenting). Put to the side the question of what it takes to qualify as a ground for "revocation" of a contract. *See Concepcion, supra,* at 352–355, 131 S. Ct. 1740, 179 L. Ed. 2d 742 (Thomas, J., concurring); post, at 1-2, 200 L. Ed. 2d, at 911–912 (Thomas, J., concurring). Put to the side for the moment, too, even the question whether the NLRA actually renders class and collective action waivers illegal. Assuming (but not granting) the employees could satisfactorily answer all those questions, the saving clause still can't save their cause.

It can't because the saving clause recognizes only defenses that apply to "any" contract. In this way the clause establishes a sort of "equal-treatment" rule for arbitration contracts. *Kindred Nursing Centers L. P. v. Clark*, 581 U.S. ___, ___, 137 S. Ct. 1421, 197 L. Ed. 2d 806, 812 (2017). The clause "permits agreements to arbitrate to be invalidated by 'generally applicable contract defenses, such as fraud, duress, or unconscionability.'" *Concepcion*, 563 U.S., at 339, 131 S. Ct. 1740, 179 L. Ed. 2d 742. At the same time, the clause offers no refuge for "defenses that apply only to arbitration or that derive their meaning from the fact that an agreement to arbitrate is at issue." Ibid. Under our precedent, this means the saving clause does not save defenses that target arbitration either by name or by more subtle methods, such as by "interfer[ing] with fundamental attributes of arbitration." *Id.*, at 344, 131 S. Ct. 1740, 179 L. Ed. 2d 742; *see Kindred Nursing, supra*, at ___, 137 S. Ct. 1421, 197 L. Ed. 2d 806, 814.

This is where the employees' argument stumbles. They don't suggest that their arbitration agreements were extracted, say, by an act of fraud or duress or in some other unconscionable way that would render any contract unenforceable. Instead, they object to their agreements precisely because they require individualized arbitration proceedings instead of class or collective ones. And by attacking (only) the individualized nature of the arbitration proceedings, the employees' argument seeks to interfere with one of arbitration's fundamental attributes.

The policy may be debatable but the law is clear: Congress has instructed that arbitration agreements like those before us must be enforced as written. While Congress is of course always free to amend this judgment, we see nothing suggesting it did so in the NLRA—much less that it manifested a clear intention to displace the Arbitration Act. Because we can easily read Congress's statutes to work in harmony, that is where our duty lies. The judgments in *Epic*, No. 16-285, and *Ernst & Young*, No. 16-300, are reversed, and the cases are remanded for further proceedings consistent with this opinion. The judgment in *Murphy Oil*, No. 16-307, is affirmed.

So ordered.

Notes and Questions

1. As you will see in greater detail in Chapter 4 on the controversy regarding class actions in arbitration, the Supreme Court has drawn strict limits around Section 2's public policy reach. The bright line is whether the particular public policy is found in the expression of a rule or statute that takes on arbitration itself. When that tipping point happens, presumption wins, and the saving clause loses. As you now review Section 2 in light of *Epic*, do you agree that the FAA strikes the balance correctly? Where should the Act strike that balance? What is the best way to enforce arbitration but still allow judicial policing of contractually invalid arbitration agreements?
2. Justice Ginsburg dissented in *Epic* on the basis that "illegality, like unconscionability, may be a traditional, generally applicable contract defense." *Epic Sys. Corp.*, 138 S. Ct. at 1623 (GINSBURG, J., dissenting). Because the arbitration agreement interfered with the collective bargaining rights granted by the NLRA, Justice Ginsburg reasoned that the arbitration agreement must be illegal—"the arbitration agreements' employer-dictated collective-litigation waivers are unlawful." *Id.* at 1645. But this was not an arbitration agreement that required ritual human sacrifice or payment in illegal drugs. There was nothing on its face "unlawful" about it. Rather, the alleged "illegality" was that the arbitration agreement collided, in the dissent's view, with another statute. This raises another issue considered in Chapter 4, "effective vindication": does the presumption in favor of arbitration run so strongly that it should overcome the ability to bring causes of action under *other* statutes? *See Italian Colors, infra* Chapter 4, p. 174.
3. Justice Thomas takes a rigid view of Section 2, holding repeatedly that the saving clause precludes arbitration *only* when a party successfully challenges the *formation* of an agreement to arbitrate—finding that "[i]t would be absurd to suggest that § 2 requires only that a defense apply to 'any contract.' If § 2 means anything, it is that courts cannot refuse to enforce arbitration agreements because of a state public policy against arbitration, even if the policy nominally applies to 'any contract.'" *Concepcion*, 563 U.S. at 352 (THOMAS, C., concurring); *see also Epic Sys. Corp.*, 138 S. Ct. at 1632 (THOMAS, C., concurring) ("As I have previously explained, grounds for revocation of a contract are those that concern 'the formation of the arbitration agreement.' Illegality is a public-policy defense, and because refusal to enforce a contract for public-policy reasons does not concern whether the contract was properly made, the saving clause does not apply."); *Am. Express Co. v. Italian Colors Rest.*, 570 U.S. 240 (2013) (THOMAS, C., concurring).

C. *Moses Cone* and Federalism

At the same time that it added a significant gloss to state law contract interpretation principles, *Moses Cone* created substantial questions of federalism. Consider two particular statements from *Moses Cone*, both specifically addressed to jurisdiction:

1. "The effect of . . . section [2] is to create a body of federal and substantive law of arbitrability, applicable to any arbitration agreement within the coverage of the Act."
2. "The Arbitration Act is something of an anomaly in the field of federal-court jurisdiction. It creates a body of federal substantive law establishing and relegating the duty to honor an agreement to arbitrate, *yet it does not create any independent federal-question jurisdiction*. . . . Section 4 [of the FAA] provides for an order compelling arbitration only when the federal district court would have jurisdiction over a suit on the underlying dispute; hence, there must be diversity of citizenship or some other independent basis for federal jurisdiction before the order can issue." (emphasis added).

The first statement acknowledges the creation of a substantive body of federal common law on arbitrability. That statement was to a great degree self-fulfilling, because once the Court stated the presumption, that "body of federal law" grew quickly and substantially. That growth extended beyond the federal courts: as you will shortly see below, the Supreme Court subsequently extended presumption to include a mandate that not only federal courts, but state courts as well, are to apply federal policy on arbitration.

The second statement makes clear that for all the talk of federal presumptions and new substantive law, the FAA did *not* create federal *jurisdiction*. Arbitration cases are contract cases. Contract cases do not generally raise federal question jurisdiction. Absent, then, an independent basis for federal jurisdiction founded upon diversity of citizenship and amount in controversy, an arbitration dispute will not reach federal court. The FAA is therefore that rare statute that creates federal law without also creating federal question jurisdiction.

The absence of federal question jurisdiction on occasion places arbitration directly in the crossroads of federalism principles. There may be aspects to arbitration of which state courts disapprove. Without federal jurisdiction, how much deference need states give the *Moses Cone* "presumption"?

The following cases explore that conflict. Following *Moses Cone*, in *Southland v. Keating*, 410 U.S. 1 (1984), and *Dean Witter Reynolds Inc. v. Byrd*, 470 U.S. 213 (1985), the Court further solidified the federal policy favoring arbitration and extended it to state law. State and lower federal courts now consistently apply the preemption principle that has emerged from this trilogy.

CASE PREVIEW. Does federal law preempt state law on arbitration issues?

Southland Corp. v. Keating

465 U.S. 1, 104 S. Ct. 852 (1984)

CHIEF JUSTICE BURGER delivered the opinion of the Court.

I.

Appellant Southland Corp. is the owner and franchisor of 7-Eleven convenience stores. Southland's standard franchise agreement provides each franchisee with a license to use certain registered trademarks, a lease or sublease of a convenience store owned or leased by Southland, inventory financing, and assistance in advertising and merchandising. The franchisees operate the stores, supply bookkeeping data, and pay Southland a fixed percentage of gross profits. The franchise agreement also contains the following provision requiring arbitration:

> Any controversy or claim arising out of or relating to this Agreement or the breach hereof shall be settled by arbitration in accordance with the Rules of the American Arbitration Association . . . and judgment upon any award rendered by the arbitrator may be entered in any court having jurisdiction thereof.

Appellees are 7-Eleven franchisees. Between September 1975 and January 1977, several appellees filed individual actions against Southland in California Superior Court alleging, among other things, fraud, oral misrepresentation, breach of contract, breach of fiduciary duty, and violation of the disclosure requirements of the California Franchise Investment Law, Cal. Corp. Code Ann. § 31000 et seq. (West 1977). Southland's answer, in all but one of the individual actions, included the affirmative defense of failure to arbitrate.

In May 1977, appellee Keating filed a class action against Southland on behalf of a class that assertedly includes approximately 800 California franchisees. Keating's principal claims were substantially the same as those asserted by the other franchisees. After the various actions were consolidated, Southland petitioned to compel arbitration of the claims in all cases, and appellees moved for class certification.

The Superior Court granted Southland's motion to compel arbitration of all claims except those claims based on the Franchise Investment Law. The court did not pass on appellees' request for class certification. Southland appealed from the order insofar as it excluded from arbitration the claims based on the California statute. Appellees filed a petition for a writ of mandamus or prohibition in the California Court of Appeal arguing that the arbitration should proceed as a class action.

The California Court of Appeal reversed the trial court's refusal to compel arbitration of appellees' claims under the Franchise Investment Law. *Keating v. Superior Court, Alameda County*, 167 Cal. Rptr. 481 (1980). That court interpreted the arbitration clause to require arbitration of all claims asserted under the Franchise Investment Law, and construed the Franchise Investment Law not to invalidate such agreements to arbitrate. Alternatively, the court concluded that if the Franchise Investment Law rendered arbitration agreements involving commerce unenforceable, it would conflict with § 2 of the Federal Arbitration Act, 9 U.S.C. § 2, and therefore be invalid under the Supremacy Clause. 167 Cal. Rptr., at 493–494. The Court of Appeal also determined that there was no "insurmountable obstacle" to conducting an arbitration on a classwide basis, and issued a writ of mandate directing the trial court to conduct class-certification proceedings. *Id.*, at 492.

The California Supreme Court, by a vote of 4–2, reversed the ruling that claims asserted under the Franchise Investment Law are arbitrable. *Keating v. Superior Court of Alameda County*, 31 Cal. 3d 584, 645 P. 2d 1192 (1982). The California Supreme Court interpreted the Franchise Investment Law to require judicial consideration of claims brought under that statute and concluded that the California statute did not contravene the federal Act. *Id.*, at 604, 645 P. 2d, 1203–1204. The court also remanded the case to the trial court for consideration of appellees' request for classwide arbitration.

We postponed consideration of the question of jurisdiction pending argument on the merits. 459 U.S. 1101 (1983). We reverse in part and dismiss in part.

As previously noted, the California Franchise Investment Law provides: "Any condition, stipulation or provision purporting to bind any person acquiring any franchise to waive compliance with any provision of this law or any rule or order hereunder is void." Cal. Corp. Code Ann. § 31512 (West 1977).

The California Supreme Court interpreted this statute to require judicial consideration of claims brought under the state statute and accordingly refused to enforce the parties' contract to arbitrate such claims. So interpreted the California Franchise Investment Law directly conflicts with § 2 of the Federal Arbitration Act and violates the Supremacy Clause.

In enacting § 2 of the federal Act, Congress declared a national policy favoring arbitration and withdrew the power of the states to require a judicial forum for the resolution of claims which the contracting parties agreed to resolve by arbitration. 9 U.S.C. § 2. Congress has thus mandated the enforcement of arbitration agreements.

We discern only two limitations on the enforceability of arbitration provisions governed by the Federal Arbitration Act: they must be part of a written maritime contract or a contract "evidencing a transaction involving commerce" and such clauses may be revoked upon "grounds as exist at law or in equity for the revocation of any contract." We see nothing in the Act indicating that the broad principle of enforceability is subject to any additional limitations under state law.

The Federal Arbitration Act rests on the authority of Congress to enact substantive rules under the Commerce Clause.

In *Moses H. Cone Memorial Hospital v. Mercury Construction Corp.*, 460 U.S., at 1, 25, and n. 32, we reaffirmed our view that the Arbitration Act "creates a body of federal substantive law" and expressly stated what was implicit in *Prima Paint*, i.e., the substantive law the Act created was applicable in state and federal courts. In holding that the District Court had abused its discretion, we found no showing of exceptional circumstances justifying the stay and recognized "the presence of federal-law issues" under the federal Act as "a major consideration weighing against surrender [of federal jurisdiction]." 460 U.S. at 26. We thus read the underlying issue of arbitrability to be a question of substantive federal law: "Federal law in the terms of the Arbitration Act governs that issue in either state or federal court." *Id.*, at 24.

Justice O'Connor argues that Congress viewed the Arbitration Act "as a procedural statute, applicable only in federal courts." If it is correct that Congress sought only to create a procedural remedy in the federal courts, there can be no explanation for the express limitation in the Arbitration Act to contracts "involving commerce." 9U.S.C. § 2. We therefore view the "involving commerce" requirement in § 2, not as an inexplicable limitation on the power of the federal courts, but as a necessary qualification on a statute intended to apply in state and federal courts.

In creating a substantive rule applicable in state as well as federal courts, Congress intended to foreclose state legislative attempts to undercut the enforceability of arbitration agreements. We hold that § 31512 of the California Franchise Investment Law violates the Supremacy Clause.

The judgment of the California Supreme Court denying enforcement of the arbitration agreement is reversed; as to the question whether the Federal Arbitration Act precludes a class-action arbitration and any other issues not raised in the California courts, no decision by this Court would be appropriate at this time. As to the latter issues, the case is remanded for further proceedings not inconsistent with this opinion.

It is so ordered.

JUSTICE O'CONNOR, with whom JUSTICE REHNQUIST joins, dissenting.

Section 2 of the Federal Arbitration Act (FAA) provides that a written arbitration agreement "shall be valid, irrevocable, and enforceable, save upon such grounds as exist at law or in equity for the revocation of any contract." Section 2 does not, on its face, identify which judicial forums are bound by its requirements or what procedures govern its enforcement. The FAA deals with these matters in §§ 3 and 4. Section 3 provides:

> If any suit or proceeding be brought in any of the courts of the United States upon any issue referable to arbitration ... the court ... shall on application of one of the parties stay the trial of the action until such arbitration has

> been had in accordance with the terms of the agreement . . .

Section 4 specifies that a party aggrieved by another's refusal to arbitrate

> may petition any United States district court which, save for such agreement, would have jurisdiction under title 28, in a civil action or in admiralty of the subject matter . . . for an order directing that such arbitration proceed in the manner provided for in such agreement. . . .

Today, the Court takes the facial silence of § 2 as a license to declare that state as well as federal courts must apply § 2. In addition, though this is not spelled out in the opinion, the Court holds that in enforcing this newly discovered federal right, state courts must follow procedures specified in § 3. The Court's decision is impelled by an understandable desire to encourage the use of arbitration, but it utterly fails to recognize the clear congressional intent underlying the FAA. Congress intended to require federal, not state, courts to respect arbitration agreements.

Today's decision is unfaithful to congressional intent, unnecessary, and, in light of the FAA's antecedents and the intervening contraction of federal power, inexplicable. Although arbitration is a worthy alternative to litigation, today's exercise in judicial revisionism goes too far. I respectfully dissent.

Notes and Questions

1. *Southland* repeated two of the foundational quotations of modern arbitration law: that the Federal Arbitration Act declared a "federal policy favoring arbitration" and that the Arbitration Act "creates a body of federal substantive law." The question remains whether the Act "favors" *arbitration* or simply approves enforcement of *arbitration agreements*. The difference between the two rests in the existence, or non-existence, of a presumption. A court can enforce an arbitration clause when confronted with one, or a court can *strain* to enforce that clause when it has to balance arbitration against other interests.
2. Which takes us to the second quotation: is there a body of federal *substantive* law created by the FAA concerning arbitration, or does arbitration remain merely one process among many available in the dispute resolution menu? The difference is again more than merely semantic, because when arbitration is balanced against indisputably "substantive" statutes—for example, antitrust statutes as considered in *Italian Colors*, *infra* at p.174 should the merely procedural take a back seat to advancement of the substantive law? Or do arbitration proponents avoid that

question by, as *Southland* puts it, viewing arbitration as "a body of federal substantive law"?

3. If the FAA does not create an independent basis of federal subject matter jurisdiction, then (a) how can it be "substantive," and (b) why should it be binding on the states per *Southland*?

CASE PREVIEW. In light of *Southland*, is there anything left of state law in arbitration? The next case carves out that answer.

Volt Info. Scis. v. Board of Trs.

489 U.S. 468, 109 S. Ct. 1248 (1989)

CHIEF JUSTICE REHNQUIST delivered the opinion of the Court.

Unlike its federal counterpart, the California Arbitration Act, Cal. Civ. Proc. Code Ann. § 1280 *et seq.* (West 1982), contains a provision allowing a court to stay arbitration pending resolution of related litigation. We hold that application of the California statute is not pre-empted by the Federal Arbitration Act (FAA or Act), 9 U.S.C. § 1 *et seq.*, in a case where the parties have agreed that their arbitration agreement will be governed by the law of California.

Appellant Volt Information Sciences, Inc. (Volt), and appellee Board of Trustees of Leland Stanford Junior University (Stanford) entered into a construction contract under which Volt was to install a system of electrical conduits on the Stanford campus. The contract contained an agreement to arbitrate all disputes between the parties "arising out of or relating to this contract or the breach thereof." The contract also contained a choice-of-law clause providing that "[t]he Contract shall be governed by the law of the place where the Project is located." App. 37. During the course of the project, a dispute developed regarding compensation for extra work, and Volt made a formal demand for arbitration. Stanford responded by filing an action against Volt in California Superior Court, alleging fraud and breach of contract; in the same action, Stanford also sought indemnity from two other companies involved in the construction project, with whom it did not have arbitration agreements. Volt petitioned the Superior Court to compel arbitration of the dispute. Stanford in turn moved to stay arbitration pursuant to Cal. Civ. Proc. Code Ann. § 1281.2(c) (West 1982), which permits a court to stay arbitration pending resolution of related litigation between a party to the arbitration agreement and third parties not bound by it, where "there is a possibility of conflicting rulings on a common issue of law or fact." The Superior Court denied Volt's motion to compel arbitration and stayed the arbitration proceedings pending the outcome of the litigation on the authority of § 1281.2(c). App. 59–60.

The California Court of Appeal affirmed. The court acknowledged that the parties' contract involved interstate commerce, that the FAA governs contracts in interstate commerce, and that the FAA contains no provision permitting a court to stay arbitration pending resolution of related litigation involving third parties not bound by the arbitration agreement. App. 64–65. However, the court held that by specifying that their contract would be governed by "'the law of the place where the project is located,'" the parties had incorporated the California rules of arbitration, including § 1281.2(c), into their arbitration agreement. *Id.*, at 65. Finally, the court rejected Volt's contention that, even if the parties had agreed to arbitrate under the California rules, application of § 1281.2(c) here was nonetheless pre-empted by the FAA because the contract involved interstate commerce. *Id.*, at 68–80.

The court reasoned that the purpose of the FAA was "'not [to] mandate the arbitration of all claims, but merely the enforcement . . . of privately negotiated arbitration agreements.'" *Id.*, at 70 (quoting *Dean Witter* Reynolds *Inc. v. Byrd*, 470 U.S. 213, 219 (1985)).While the FAA therefore pre-empts application of state laws which render arbitration agreements unenforceable, "[i]t does not follow, however, that the federal law has preclusive effect in a case where the parties have chosen in their [arbitration] agreement to abide by state rules." App. 71. To the contrary, because "[t]he thrust of the federal law is that arbitration is strictly a matter of contract," *ibid.*, the parties to an arbitration agreement should be "at liberty to choose the terms under which they will arbitrate." *Id.*, at 72. Where, as here, the parties have chosen in their agreement to abide by the state rules of arbitration, application of the FAA to prevent enforcement of those rules would actually be "inimical to the policies underlying state and federal arbitration law," *id.*, at 73, because it would "force the parties to arbitrate in a manner contrary to their agreement." *Id.*, at 65. The California Supreme Court denied Volt's petition for discretionary review. *Id.*, at 87. We postponed consideration of our jurisdiction to the hearing on the merits. 485 U.S. 976 (1988). We now hold that we have appellate jurisdiction and affirm.

Appellant devotes the bulk of its argument to convincing us that the Court of Appeal erred in interpreting the choice-of-law clause to mean that the parties had incorporated the California rules of arbitration into their arbitration agreement. Appellant acknowledges, as it must, that the interpretation of private contracts is ordinarily a question of state law, which this Court does not sit to review. But appellant nonetheless maintains that we should set aside the Court of Appeal's interpretation of this particular contractual provision for two principal reasons.

Appellant first suggests that the Court of Appeal's construction of the choice-of-law clause was in effect a finding that appellant had "waived" its "federally guaranteed right to compel arbitration of the parties' dispute," a waiver whose validity must be judged by reference to federal rather than state law. This argument fundamentally misconceives the nature of the rights created by the FAA. The Act was designed "to overrule the judiciary's longstanding refusal to enforce agreements to arbitrate," *Byrd*, *supra*, at 219–220, and place such agreements "'upon the same footing as other contracts,'" *Scherk v. Alberto-Culver Co.*, 417 U.S. 506, 511 (1974) (quoting H. R. Rep. No. 96, 68th Cong., 1st Sess., 1, 2 (1924)). Section 2 of the Act therefore declares that a written agreement to arbitrate in any contract involving interstate commerce or a maritime transaction "shall be valid, irrevocable, and enforceable, save upon such grounds as exist at law or in equity for the revocation of any contract," 9 U.S.C. § 2, and § 4 allows a party to such an arbitration agreement to "petition any United States district court . . . for an order directing that such arbitration proceed in the manner provided for in such agreement."

But § 4 of the FAA does not confer a right to compel arbitration of any dispute at any time; it confers only the right to obtain an order directing that "arbitration proceed in the manner provided for in [the parties'] agreement." 9 U.S.C. § 4 (emphasis added). Here the Court of Appeal found that, by incorporating the California rules of arbitration into their agreement, the parties had agreed that arbitration would not proceed in situations which fell within the scope of Calif. Code Civ. Proc. Ann. § 1281.2(c) (West 1982). This was not a finding that appellant had "waived" an FAA-guaranteed right to compel arbitration of this dispute, but a finding that it had no such right in the first place, because the parties' agreement did not require arbitration to proceed in this situation. Accordingly, appellant's contention that the contract interpretation issue presented here involves the "waiver" of a federal right is without merit.

Second, appellant argues that we should set aside the Court of Appeal's construction of the choice-of-law clause because it violates the settled federal rule that questions of arbitrability in contracts subject to the FAA must be resolved with a healthy regard for the federal policy favoring arbitration. Brief for Appellant 49–52, citing *Moses H. Cone Memorial Hospital v. Mercury Construction Corp.*, 460 U.S. 1, 24–25 (1983) (§ 2 of the FAA "create[s] a body of federal substantive law of arbitrability, applicable to any arbitration agreement within the coverage of the Act," which requires that "questions of arbitrability . . . be addressed with a healthy regard for the federal policy favoring arbitration," and that "any doubts concerning the scope of arbitrable issues . . . be resolved in favor of arbitration"); *Mitsubishi Motors Corp. v. Soler Chrysler-Plymouth, Inc.*, 473 U.S. 614, 626 (1985) (in construing an arbitration agreement within the coverage of the FAA, "as with any other contract, the parties' intentions control, but those intentions are generously construed as to issues of arbitrability"). These cases of course establish that, in applying general state-law principles of contract interpretation to the interpretation of an arbitration agreement within the scope of the Act, due regard must be given to the federal policy favoring arbitration, and ambiguities as to the scope of the arbitration clause itself resolved in favor of arbitration.

But we do not think the Court of Appeal offended the *Moses H. Cone* principle by interpreting the choice-of-law provision to mean that the parties intended the California rules of arbitration, including the § 1281.2(c) stay provision, to apply to their arbitration agreement. There is no federal policy favoring arbitration under a certain set of procedural rules; the federal policy is simply to ensure the enforceability, according to their terms, of private agreements to arbitrate. Interpreting a choice-of-law clause to make applicable state rules governing the conduct of arbitration—rules which are manifestly designed to encourage resort to the arbitral process—simply does not offend the rule of liberal construction set forth in *Moses H. Cone*, nor does it offend any other policy embodied in the FAA.

The question remains whether, assuming the choice-of-law clause meant what the Court of Appeal found it to mean, application of Cal. Civ. Proc. Code Ann. § 1281.2(c) is nonetheless pre-empted by the FAA to the extent it is used to stay arbitration under this contract involving interstate commerce. It is undisputed that this contract falls within the coverage of the FAA, since it involves interstate commerce, and that the FAA contains no provision authorizing a stay of arbitration in this situation. Appellee contends, however, that §§ 3 and 4 of the FAA, which are the specific sections claimed to conflict with the California statute at issue here, are not applicable in this state-court proceeding and thus cannot pre-empt application of the California statute.. While the argument is not without some merit, we need not resolve it to decide this case, for we conclude that even if §§ 3 and 4 of the FAA are fully applicable in state-court proceedings, they do not prevent application of Cal. Civ. Proc. Code Ann. § 1281.2(c) to stay arbitration where, as here, the parties have agreed to arbitrate in accordance with California law.

The FAA contains no express pre-emptive provision, nor does it reflect a congressional intent to occupy the entire field of arbitration. *See Bernhardt v. Polygraphic Co.*, 350 U.S. 198 (1956) (upholding application of state arbitration law to arbitration provision in contract not covered by the FAA). But even when Congress has not completely displaced state regulation in an area, state law may nonetheless be pre-empted to the extent that it actually conflicts with federal law—that is, to the extent that it "stands as an obstacle to the accomplishment and execution of the full purposes and objectives of Congress." *Hines v. Davidowitz*, 312 U.S. 52, 67 (1941). The question before us, therefore, is whether application of Cal. Civ. Proc. Code Ann. § 1281.2(c) to stay arbitration under this contract in interstate commerce, in accordance with the terms of the arbitration agreement itself, would undermine the goals and policies of the FAA. We conclude that it would not.

The FAA was designed "to overrule the judiciary's longstanding refusal to enforce agreements to arbitrate," *Dean Witter Reynolds Inc. v. Byrd*, 470 U.S. at 219–220, and to place such agreements "'upon the same footing as other contracts,'" *Scherk v. Alberto-Culver Co.*, 417 U.S. at 511 (quoting H. R. Rep. No. 96, 68th Cong., 1st Sess., 1, 2 (1924)). While Congress was no doubt aware that the Act would encourage the expeditious resolution of disputes, its passage "was motivated, first and foremost, by a congressional desire to enforce agreements into which parties had entered." *Byrd*, 470 U.S. at 220. Accordingly, we have recognized that the FAA does not require parties to arbitrate when they have not agreed to do so, *see id.*, at 219 (the Act "does not mandate the arbitration of all claims"), nor does it prevent parties who do agree to arbitrate from excluding certain claims from the scope of their arbitration agreement, *see Mitsubishi Motors Corp. v. Soler Chrysler-Plymouth, Inc.*, 473 U.S., at 628 (citing *Prima Paint Corp. v. Flood & Conklin Mfg. Co.*, 388 U.S. 395, 406 (1967)). It simply requires courts to enforce privately negotiated agreements to arbitrate, like other contracts, in accordance with their terms. *See Prima Paint*, *supra*, at 404, n. 12 (the Act was designed "to make arbitration agreements as enforceable as other contracts, but not more so").

Arbitration under the Act is a matter of consent, not coercion, and parties are generally free to structure their arbitration agreements as they see fit. Just as they may limit by contract the issues which they will arbitrate, so too may they specify by contract the rules under which that arbitration will be conducted. Where, as here, the parties have agreed to abide by state rules of arbitration, enforcing those rules according to the terms of the agreement is fully consistent with the goals of the FAA, even if the result is that arbitration is stayed where the Act would otherwise permit it to go forward. By permitting the courts to "rigorously enforce" such agreements according to their terms, we give effect to the contractual rights and expectations of the parties, without doing violence to the policies behind by the FAA.

The judgment of the Court of Appeals is Affirmed.

Notes and Questions

Justice Rehnquist dissented in *Southland* (in deference to the applicability of state arbitration law) and then wrote the majority opinion in *Volt* (which permitted the parties to invoke state rather than federal arbitration law). Plainly, there is a straight line between the two Rehnquist opinions—but can the majority opinions in the two cases be reconciled? If state law cannot be used to block arbitration (*Southland*), but the parties can defer to state law (*Volt*), what are the guardrails to state law preventing any arbitration at all? Does the answer rest on the procedural nature of the California rules that *Volt* let the parties choose—so that they were choosing arbitration either way, and it fell to them to choose the particular procedural path that would govern?

> **CASE PREVIEW.** The next case provides an answer: when the state law is overtly hostile to arbitration. West Virginia found that as a matter of public policy, nursing homes should not be able to shield themselves from jury verdicts by insisting on arbitration.

Marmet Health Care Ctr., Inc. v. Brown

132 S. Ct. 1201 (2012)

Per Curiam

State and federal courts must enforce the Federal Arbitration Act (FAA), 9 U.S.C. §1 et seq., with respect to all arbitration agreements covered by that statute. Here, the Supreme Court of Appeals of West Virginia, by misreading and disregarding the precedents of this Court interpreting the FAA, did not follow controlling federal law implementing that basic principle. The state court held unenforceable all predispute arbitration agreements that apply to claims alleging personal injury or wrongful death against nursing homes.

The decision of the state court found the FAA's coverage to be more limited than mandated by this Court's previous cases. The decision of the State Supreme Court of Appeals must be vacated. When this Court has fulfilled its duty to interpret federal law, a state court may not contradict or fail to implement the rule so established. *See* U.S. Const., Art. VI, cl. 2.

This litigation involves three negligence suits against nursing homes in West Virginia. The suits were brought by Clayton Brown, Jeffrey Taylor, and Sharon Marchio. In each case, a family member of a patient requiring extensive nursing care had signed an agreement with a nursing home on behalf of the patient. The relevant parts of the agreements in Brown's case and Taylor's case were identical. The contracts included a clause requiring the parties to arbitrate all disputes, other than claims to collect late payments owed by the patient. The contracts included a provision holding the party filing the arbitration responsible for paying a filing fee in accordance with the Rules of the American Arbitration Association fee schedules. The agreement in Marchio's case also included a clause requiring arbitration but made no exceptions to the arbitration requirement and did not mention filing fees.

In each of the three cases, a family member of a patient who had died sued the nursing home in state court, alleging that negligence caused injuries or harm resulting in death. A state trial court dismissed the suits by Brown and Taylor based on the agreements to arbitrate. The Supreme Court of Appeals of West Virginia consolidated those cases with Marchio's, which was before the court on other issues.

In a decision concerning all three cases, the state court held that "as a matter of public policy under West Virginia law, an arbitration clause in a nursing home admission agreement adopted prior to an occurrence of negligence that results in a personal injury or wrongful death, shall not be enforced to compel arbitration of a dispute concerning the negligence." *Brown v. Genesis Healthcare Corp.*, No. 35494, 228 W. Va. 646, 724 S.E.2d 250, 2011 W. Va. LEXIS 61 (W. Va., June 29, 2011), App. to Pet. for Cert. in No. 11-391, pp. 85a-86a (hereinafter Pet. App.). The state court considered whether the state public policy was pre-empted by the FAA. The state court found unpersuasive this Court's interpretation of the FAA, calling it "tendentious," *id.*, at 51a, and "created from whole cloth," *id.*, at 53a. It later concluded that "Congress did not intend for the FAA to be, in any way, applicable to personal injury or wrongful death suits that only collaterally derive from a written agreement that evidences a transaction affecting interstate commerce, particularly where the agreement involves a service that is a practical necessity for members of the public," *id.*, at 84a. The court thus concluded that the FAA does not pre-empt the state public policy against predispute arbitration agreements that apply to claims of personal injury or wrongful death against nursing homes.

The West Virginia court's interpretation of the FAA was both incorrect and inconsistent with clear instruction in the precedents of this Court. The FAA provides that a "written provision in . . . a contract evidencing a transaction involving commerce to settle by arbitration a controversy thereafter arising out of such contract or transaction . . . shall be valid, irrevocable, and enforceable, save upon such grounds as exist at law or in equity for the revocation of any contract." 9 U.S.C. § 2. The statute's text includes no exception for personal-injury or wrongful-death claims. It "requires courts to enforce the bargain of the parties to arbitrate."

As this Court reaffirmed last Term, "[w]hen state law prohibits outright the arbitration of a particular type of claim, the analysis is straightforward: The conflicting rule is displaced by the FAA." *AT&T Mobility LLC v. Concepcion*, 563 U.S. ___, ___, 131 S. Ct. 1740, 1747, 179 L. Ed. 2d 742 (2011). That rule resolves these cases. West Virginia's prohibition against predispute agreements to arbitrate personal-injury or wrongful-death claims against nursing homes is a categorical rule prohibiting arbitration of a particular type of claim, and that rule is contrary to the terms and coverage of the FAA. *See ibid. See also, e.g., Preston v. Ferrer*, 552 U.S. 346, 356, 128 S. Ct. 978, 169 L. Ed. 2d 917 (2008) (FAA pre-empts state law granting state commissioner exclusive jurisdiction to decide issue the parties agreed to arbitrate); *Mastrobuono v. Shearson Lehman Hutton, Inc.*, 514 U.S. 52, 56, 115 S. Ct. 1212, 131 L. Ed. 2d 76 (1995) (FAA pre-empts state law requiring judicial resolution of claims involving punitive damages); *Perry v. Thomas*, 482 U.S. 483, 491, 107 S. Ct. 2520, 96 L. Ed. 2d 426 (1987) (FAA pre-empts state-law requirement that litigants be provided a judicial forum for wage disputes); *Southland Corp. v. Keating*, 465 U.S. 1, 10, 104 S. Ct. 852, 79 L. Ed. 2d 1 (1984) (FAA pre-empts state financial investment statute's prohibition of arbitration of claims brought under that statute).

The West Virginia court proposed an "alternativ[e]" holding that the particular arbitration clauses in Brown's case and Taylor's case were unconscionable. It is unclear, however, to what degree the state court's alternative holding was influenced by the invalid, categorical rule discussed above, the rule against predispute arbitration agreements. For example, in its discussion of the alternative holding, the state court found the arbitration clauses unconscionable in part because a predispute arbitration agreement that applies to claims of personal injury or wrongful death against nursing homes "clearly violates public policy."

On remand, the West Virginia court must consider whether, absent that general public policy, the arbitration clauses in Brown's case and Taylor's case are unenforceable under state common law principles that are not specific to arbitration and preempted by the FAA.

The petition for certiorari is granted. The judgment of the Supreme Court of Appeals of West Virginia is vacated, and the cases are remanded for proceedings not inconsistent with this opinion.

It is so ordered.

Notes and Questions

1. Consider *Volt* again in light of *Marmet.* In *Volt*, the Court emphasized that the FAA did not favor arbitration but rather "agreements to arbitrate," whatever those agreements might be. Accordingly, the Court allowed the parties to effectively opt out of the FAA and choose California law. But what would happen if California law was hostile to arbitration? *See DirecTV*, *infra* Chapter 4.
2. By regulating food and drugs under the FDA Act, Congress created federal jurisdiction over this field. By regulating trade combinations under the Sherman Antitrust Act, Congress created federal jurisdiction over that field. And so on. Why should arbitration be any different? If Congress thought it was a good idea to promote arbitration, then why should not any arbitration agreement trigger Commerce Clause jurisdiction?
3. The *Marmet* court held that "when state law prohibits outright the arbitration of a particular type of claim, the analysis is straightforward: the conflicting rule is displaced by the FAA." Why was it considered acceptable under *Moses Cone* to defer to the California statute in *Volt* but not to the West Virginia statute in *Marmet*? What might be the principled distinctions? Wasn't the anti-piecemeal statute in California just as hostile to arbitration as the nursing home statute in *Marmet*?

PRACTICE POINTER: **Is There Federal Jurisdiction?** The arbitration novice may wrongly assume federal jurisdiction on the (incorrect) basis that the FAA confers federal question jurisdiction. We have seen that it does not. Courts faced with arbitration clauses instead apply the same jurisdiction testing principles as to other federal courts. Thus, in *Odeon Capital Group, LLC v. Ackerman*, No. 16 Civ. 274 (S.D.N.Y. Feb. 29, 2016), the court on a motion to vacate an arbitration award had to determine the date for measuring diversity, which differed as between the start of the arbitration and the day of the motion to vacate. *See also Grynberg v. Kinder Morgan Energy*, No. 14-1465 (10th Cir. Nov. 2, 2015). These rulings are not dissimilar from those you reviewed in civil procedure.

For practice purposes, if you bring a motion under the FAA to compel (or enforce) arbitration, be certain that your case otherwise satisfies federal jurisdiction. For defense purposes when faced with such a motion, be sure to test its jurisdictional sufficiency. The parties may instead belong in state court under a state's arbitration statute.

D. Arbitration, Sexual Harassment Cases, and Preemption

In recent years and in correspondence with the #MeToo movement, some states have enacted legislation that prohibits enforcement of arbitration clauses in sexual harassment suits. The theory behind the laws is that the defendant should be subject to publicity and the plaintiff entitled to a trial by jury.

If that is the public policy, then arbitration clauses that take cases out of court and place them behind closed doors conflict with that policy. But put differently, the harassment laws conflict with the arbitration cases you just read. Do these laws survive preemption? Are they any different than the nursing home prohibition in *Marmet*? Should there be a precise statutory carveout to the FAA which allows these lawsuits to avoid preemption? As this edition goes to press, these questions have yet to be addressed by higher courts. The following two case excerpts, one from New York and one from California, give a hint of what is to come.

Mahmoud Latif v. Morgan Stanley & Co. LLC

No. 18cv11528 (DLC), 2019 U.S. Dist. LEXIS 107020
(S.D.N.Y. June 26, 2019)

D. COTE, District Judge:

Mahmoud Latif ("Latif") has filed employment discrimination claims against his former employers Morgan Stanley & Co. LLC and Morgan Stanley Services Group, Inc. (collectively "Morgan Stanley") and seven individual employees of Morgan Stanley (collectively, with Morgan Stanley, "Defendants"). Defendants have moved to compel arbitration of Latif's claims. For the following reasons, that motion is granted.

Background

On June 5, 2017, Latif signed a written offer of employment with Morgan Stanley (the "Offer Letter"). The Offer Letter incorporated by reference Morgan Stanley's CARE Arbitration Program Arbitration Agreement (the "Arbitration Agreement"), which was also attached to the Offer Letter. The parties agree that Latif accepted the terms and conditions set forth in the Arbitration Agreement when he signed the Offer Letter.

The Arbitration Agreement provides that any "covered claim" that arises between Latif and Morgan Stanley "will be resolved by final and binding arbitration as set forth in this Arbitration Agreement and in the arbitration provisions of the CARE Guidebook," a copy of which was attached to the Arbitration Agreement. "Covered claims" are defined in the Arbitration Agreement to include, *inter alia*, common law claims and "statutory discrimination, harassment and retaliation claims." The Arbitration Agreement further provides that it "shall be governed by and interpreted in accordance with the Federal Arbitration Act ("FAA")."

Latif alleges that, beginning in the fall of 2017, he became the target of, *inter alia*, inappropriate comments regarding his sexual orientation, inappropriate touching, sexual advances, and offensive comments about his religion. He also alleges that around February 2018, a female supervisor sexually assaulted him. Beginning in February 2018, Latif reported these incidents to Morgan Stanley's human resources department. Following months of email exchanges and meetings between Latif and the human resources department, Latif's employment was terminated around August 1, 2018, which is just over a year after Latif executed the Offer Letter.

Latif filed this lawsuit on December 10, 2018, alleging discrimination, a hostile work environment, and retaliation in violation of Title VII of the Civil Rights Act of 1964, 42 U.S.C. § 2000a et seq., the New York State Human Rights Law, N.Y. Executive Law § 290 et seq., the New York City Human Rights Law, N.Y.C. Admin. Code § 8-101 et seq., and 42 U.S.C. § 1981; as well as assault and battery, aggravated sexual abuse, violation of the Gender Motivated Violence Protection Act, N.Y.C. Admin. Code § 8-902, and intentional and negligent infliction of emotional distress. The parties do not dispute the enforceability of the Arbitration Agreement generally nor its application to all but one category of Latif's claims. Accordingly, on March 21, the Honorable Robert W. Sweet, who then presided over this case, endorsed a stipulation between the parties in which they agreed that the Arbitration Agreement was enforceable as to all of Latif's claims except for his claims of sexual harassment.

Latif filed an amended complaint on May 3, 2019. Defendants filed the instant motion to compel arbitration and stay the proceedings on May 7. The only dispute between the parties is whether Latif's sexual harassment claims are subject to the Arbitration Agreement in light of a recently enacted New York Law, N.Y. C.P.L.R. § 7515 . The parties do not dispute that this issue is to be resolved by this Court. The motion to compel was fully submitted on May 31.

Discussion

"The Federal Arbitration Act requires courts to enforce covered arbitration agreements according to their terms." Lamps Plus, Inc. v. Varela, 139 S. Ct. 1407, 1412 (2019).

The Supreme Court has repeatedly instructed that the FAA reflects "both a liberal federal policy favoring arbitration and the fundamental principle that arbitration is a matter of contract." *AT&T Mobility LLC v. Concepcion*, 563 U.S. 333, 339 (2011) (citation omitted). Consistent with this policy, "[a] party to an arbitration agreement seeking to avoid arbitration generally bears the burden of showing the agreement to be inapplicable or invalid." *Harrington v. Atl. Sounding Co.*, 602 F.3d 113, 124 (2d Cir. 2010).

Under Section 2 of the Federal Arbitration Act ("FAA"),

> a written provision in . . . a contract evidencing a transaction involving commerce to settle by arbitration a controversy thereafter arising out of such contract or transaction . . . shall be valid, irrevocable, and enforceable, save upon such grounds as exist at law or in equity *for the revocation of any contract.*

9 U.S.C. § 2 (emphasis supplied). This "saving clause recognizes only defenses that apply to 'any' contract . . . establish[ing] a sort of 'equal-treatment' rule for arbitration contracts." *Epic Sys. Corp. v. Lewis*, 138 S. Ct. 1612, 1622 (2018). Thus, while arbitration agreements may be "invalidated by generally applicable contract defenses, such as fraud, duress, or unconscionability, . . . defenses that apply only to arbitration or that derive their meaning from the fact that an agreement to arbitrate is at issue" will not invalidate such an agreement. *Concepcion*, 563 U.S. at 339 (citation omitted). "[T]he saving clause does not save defenses that target arbitration either by name or by more subtle methods." *Epic Sys.*, 138 S. Ct. at 1622.

The FAA's policy favoring the enforcement of arbitration agreements is not easily displaced by state law. "[S]tate law is preempted to the extent it stands as an obstacle to the accomplishment and execution of the full purposes and objectives of the FAA." *Lamps Plus*, 139 S. Ct. at 1415 (citation omitted). "When state law prohibits outright the arbitration of a particular type of claim, the analysis is straightforward: The conflicting rule is displaced by the FAA." *Concepcion*, 563 U.S. at 341.

Section 7515 is titled "Mandatory arbitration clauses; prohibited." It was signed into law in April 2018 and became effective on July 11, 2018. The law was enacted as Part KK, Subpart B of the 2018–2019 New York budget bill. Part KK of this bill contains six subparts all addressing sexual harassment. These subparts address, among other things, certifications concerning sexual harassment in bids submitted to the state, "reimbursement of funds paid by state agencies, state entities and public entities for the payment of awards adjudicated in sexual harassment claims," and a model policy and training program for the prevention of sexual harassment. 2018 N.Y. Sess. L., ch. 57, at 4–5. The bill was described in Senate Floor debate as "sweeping legislation that deals with the scourge of sexual harassment" and that "handles all different kinds of sexual harassment situations." N.Y. State Senate, Stenographic Rec., 241st Leg., Reg. Sess., at 1855 (Mar. 30, 2018).

Section 7515(b) contains three subparts:

(i) Prohibition. *Except where inconsistent with federal law*, no written contract, entered into on or after the effective date of this section shall contain a prohibited clause as defined in paragraph two of subdivision (a) of this section.

(ii) Exceptions. *Nothing* contained in this section *shall* be construed to *impair* or prohibit an employer from incorporating a non-prohibited clause or other *mandatory arbitration provision* within such contract, *that the parties agree upon*.

(iii) Mandatory arbitration clause null and void. *Except where inconsistent with federal law*, the provisions of such prohibited clause as defined in paragraph two of subdivision (a) of this section shall be null and void. The inclusion of such clause in a written contract shall not serve to impair the enforceability of any other provision of such contract.

Under the terms of the Arbitration Agreement, Latif's sexual harassment claims are subject to mandatory arbitration. Section 7515 renders agreements to arbitrate sexual harassment claims null and void "[e]xcept where inconsistent with federal law." N.Y. C.P.L.R. 7515(b)(iii). Here, application of Section 7515 to invalidate the parties' agreement to arbitrate Latif's claims would be inconsistent with the FAA. The FAA sets forth a strong presumption that arbitration agreements are enforceable and this presumption is not displaced by § 7515.

Moreover, the FAA's saving clause does not render the parties' Arbitration Agreement unenforceable here. Section 7515(b) applies only to contract provisions that require "mandatory arbitration to resolve any allegation or claim of an unlawful discriminatory practice of sexual harassment." N.Y. C.P.L.R. § 7515(a)(2). This provision is not a "ground[] as exist[s] at law or in equity for the revocation of any contract," 9 U.S.C. § 2, but rather a "state law prohibit[ing] outright the arbitration of a particular type of claim," which, as described by the Supreme Court, is "displaced by the FAA." Concepcion, 563 U.S. at 341

Latif argues that, when read in conjunction with the bundle of sexual harassment provisions passed in the same bill, § 7515 reflects a general intent to protect victims of sexual harassment and not a specific intent to single out arbitration clauses for singular treatment. He points out that the statute affects a number of different types of contracts and contract provisions, and, as such, does not run afoul of the FAA's prohibition on arbitration-specific defenses. Latif similarly argues that because § 7515 does not disfavor all arbitration, but only arbitration of sexual harassment claims, it is not inconsistent with the FAA. These arguments are unavailing. The fact that § 7515 was enacted concurrently with other laws that address sexual harassment does not alter the plain language of the law. The bundle of laws that make up Part KK of the 2018–19 budget bill were clearly intended to address sexual harassment; nothing in the bill suggests that the New York legislature intended to create a generally applicable contract defense. Latif also suggests that because clauses mandating arbitration of sexual harassment claims interfere with New York's substantial state interest in transparently addressing workplace sexual harassment, § 7515 is a ground "in equity for the revocation of any contract" and thus not displaced by the FAA. 9 U.S.C. § 2. This argument again ignores the plain language of the FAA's saving clause and the Supreme Court's many decisions construing it, which require any ground providing an exception to arbitration, whether in law or equity, to be generally applicable. Section 7515 presents no generally applicable contract defense, whether grounded in equity or otherwise, and as such cannot overcome the FAA's command that the parties' Arbitration Agreement be enforced.

Conclusion

The Defendants' May 7, 2019 motion to compel arbitration is granted. The action is stayed pending the outcome of arbitration proceedings.

CASE PREVIEW. The next case similarly finds FAA pre-emption. Do you find its reasoning persuasive, or is this an area where public policy concerns should prevail? Is that possible without an FAA amendment?

Chamber of Commerce of the United States v. Becerra

438 F. Supp. 3d 1078 (E.D. Cal. 2020)

K. MUELLER, Chief United States District Judge

The Federal Arbitration Act ("FAA") provides that arbitration agreements are "valid, irrevocable, and enforceable, save upon such grounds as exist at law or in equity for the revocation of any contract." 9 U.S.C. § 2. The U.S. Supreme Court has interpreted this provision expansively, observing that it reflects "a liberal federal policy favoring arbitration agreements, notwithstanding any state substantive or procedural policies to the contrary." *Moses H. Cone Mem'l Hosp. v. Mercury Constr. Corp.*, 460 U.S. 1, 24 (1983). This case raises the question whether the FAA preempts a new law passed by the California Legislature and signed into law by the Governor in late 2019.

Specifically, on October 10, 2019, California Governor Gavin Newsom signed into law California Assembly Bill 51 ("AB 51"), which prohibits California employers from requiring prospective and current employees to "waive any right, forum, or procedure" for a violation of the California Fair Employment and Housing Act ("FEHA") or the California Labor Code. In so doing, the court explained that AB 51 "raise[s] serious questions regarding whether the challenged statute is preempted by the [FAA] as construed by the United States Supreme Court." *Id.* at 1.

II. FEDERAL ARBITRATION ACT ("FAA")

"The FAA was enacted in 1925 in response to widespread judicial hostility to arbitration agreements." *AT&T Mobility LLC v. Concepcion*, 563 U.S. 333, 339 (2011). The "primary substantive provision of the Act" is found in section 2. *Id.* (quoting *Moses H. Cone*, 460 U.S. at 24). That section provides:

> A written provision in any maritime transaction or a contract evidencing a transaction involving commerce to settle by arbitration a controversy thereafter arising out of such contract or transaction, or the refusal to perform the whole or any part thereof, or an agreement in writing to submit to arbitration an existing controversy arising out of such a contract, transaction, or refusal, shall be valid, irrevocable, and enforceable, save upon such grounds as exist at law or in equity for the revocation of any contract.

9 U.S.C. § 2. The Supreme Court has "described this provision as reflecting both a liberal federal policy favoring arbitration and the fundamental principle that arbitration is a matter of contract." *Id.* (internal quotation marks and citations omitted); *see also Ferguson v. Corinthian Colleges, Inc.*, 733 F.3d 928, 932 (9th Cir. 2013) ("[The FAA] reflects an 'emphatic federal policy' in favor of arbitration." (quoting *Marmet Health Care Ctr., Inc. v. Brown*, 565 U.S. 530, 533 (2012)).

III. ASSEMBLY BILL 51

California Assembly Bill 51 aims to make two additions to California's statutory scheme, section 12953 to the Government Code and section 432.6 to the Labor Code. AB 51, Labor and Employment—Discrimination—Waiver, 2019–2020 Reg. Sess. (Cal. 2019). The primary provisions of AB 51 appear in Labor Code section 432.6. That statute, as set forth in the bill, provides:

> (a) A person shall not, as a condition of employment, continued employment, or the receipt of any employment -related benefit, require any applicant for employment or any employee to waive any right, forum, or procedure for a violation of any provision of the California Fair Employment and Housing Act....
>
> (c) For purposes of this section, an agreement that requires an employee to opt out of a waiver or take any affirmative action in order to preserve their rights is deemed a condition of employment.

As reviewed above, § 2 of the FAA expressly makes agreements to arbitrate 'valid, irrevocable, and enforceable, save upon such grounds as exist at law or in equity for the revocation of any contract." 9 U.S.C. § 2. "Courts must place arbitration agreements on an equal footing with other contracts . . . and enforce them according to their terms." *Concepcion*, 563 U.S. at 339 (citations omitted). This "equal-footing," or "equal treatment" principle reflects the notion that "the FAA is 'at bottom a policy guaranteeing the enforcement of private contractual arrangements[.]" *E.E.O.C. v. Waffle House, Inc.*, 534 U.S. 279, 294 (2002) (quoting *Chrysler-Plymouth, Inc.*, 473 U.S. 614, 625(1985)).

In practical terms, equal treatment means "[a] court may invalidate an arbitration agreement based on 'generally applicable contract defenses like fraud or unconscionability, but not on legal rules that 'apply only to arbitration or that derive their meaning from the fact that an agreement to arbitrate is at issue.'" *Kindred Nursing Centers Ltd. P'ship v. Clark*, 137 S. Ct. 1421, 1426, (2017) (quoting *Concepcion*, 563 U.S. at 339). Therefore, if any state rule "singles out arbitration," it is preempted by the FAA. *Id.* at 1425.

In sum, unequal footing and interference with the fundamental attributes of arbitration are two ways in which a "state-law rule can be preempted by the FAA." *Blair v. Rent-A-Ctr., Inc.*, 928 F.3d 819, 825 (9th Cir. 2019).

Plaintiffs contend they are likely to succeed on the merits of their claims because AB 51 places arbitration agreements on unequal footing with other contracts. In opposition, defendants argue plaintiffs are unlikely to succeed on the merits because AB 51 does not regulate agreements; it only regulates employer attempts to "coerce agreements waiving employment and labor law rights."

Even when a state law puts arbitration agreements on equal footing, the law may nonetheless be subject to FAA preemption if it "interferes with fundamental attributes of arbitration." *Lamps Plus, Inc. v. Varela*, 139 S. Ct. 1407, 1418 (2019). This kind of interference implicates conflict preemption principles because the state law, in essence, "stand[s] as an obstacle to the Federal Arbitration Act." *Shroyer v. New Cingular Wireless Servs., Inc.*, 498 F.3d 976, 989 (9th Cir. 2007).

The equal-footing principle provides the foundation for determining whether a state law discriminates against arbitration agreements in some way. In *Kindred*, the Court found a Kentucky Supreme Court "clear-statement" rule preempted by the FAA because it failed to "put arbitration agreements on an equal plane with other contracts." 137 S. Ct. at 1427. The Kentucky rule, in essence, created an additional procedural safeguard before a party's representative, an attorney-in-fact, could contractually waive that party's right to resolve a dispute in court. *Id.* But the Court struck the rule down, saying this is "exactly what *Concepcion* barred: adopt[ing] a legal rule hinging on the primary characteristic of an arbitration agreement—namely, a waiver of the right to go to court and receive a jury trial." *Id.* Such a rule, "tailor-made to arbitration agreements," violates the equal footing principle and is incompatible with the FAA. *Id.* Similarly, in Doctor's *Assocs., Inc. v. Casarotto*, 517 U.S. 681, 683 (1996), the Court struck down a Montana law as preempted by the FAA because it required that any contract subject to arbitration provide notice, prominently displayed on the first page of the contract at issue. This "first-page notice requirement" was antithetical to FAA objectives because it "place[d] arbitration agreements in a class apart from 'any contract,' and singularly limits their validity." *Id.* at 688. The Court reiterated that "[a] state-law principle that takes its meaning precisely from the fact that a contract to arbitrate is at issue does not comport with [the text of § 2]." *Id.* at 685 (alteration in original) (quoting *Perry v. Thomas*, 482 U.S. 483, 492 n.9 (1987)).

It is AB 51's embodiment of a "legal rule hinging on the primary characteristic of an arbitration agreement," *Kindred*, 137 S. Ct. at 1427, and placing "arbitration agreements in a class apart from 'any contract,' " *Casarotto*, 517 U.S. at 688, that is the law's fatal flaw. AB 51's prohibition on California employers' use of "right, forum, or procedure" waivers as a condition of employment, Cal. Lab. Code § 432.6(a), "oh so coincidentally" disfavors contracts with the "defining features" of arbitration. *Kindred*, 137 S. Ct. at 1426. As in *Kindred*, defendants' attempt here to paint AB 51 in broader terms is unavailing. Defendants, again, argue AB 51 does not single out arbitration agreements; "[r]ather, for both arbitration and other types of employment agreements, it simply provides that employees cannot be forced to waive the rights and protections afforded them under the law." "But what other rights, really," as the Court in *Kindred* asked, is AB 51 designed to target? *Kindred*, 137 S. Ct. at 1427. When pressed at hearing on this question, defendants responded that the law applies equally to employment terms such as nondisclosure agreements, forum selection clauses, choice-of -law provisions and administrative exhaustion requirements. In response, plaintiffs argued that envisioning possible alternative applications cannot save an otherwise unlawfully crafted statute designed to inhibit arbitration agreements in particular. *Id.* at 6:24–8:17. Plaintiffs are correct. Other types of employment provisions may tangentially fall within AB 51's ambit, but the law's clear target is arbitration agreements, given the sponsors' concern regarding an overabundance of arbitration agreements in the California employment market. *See* S. Floor Analysis at 2–3 ("67.4% of all California employers mandate arbitration of employment disputes" (emphasis omitted)). Even if the law itself is artfully crafted to support the argument that it only regulates the behavior of employers, it cannot avoid being construed as law that in effect discriminates against arbitration agreements.

AB 51 also interferes with the FAA's goal as interpreted by the Supreme Court and is subject to preemption on this basis as well. The Supreme Court has declared as a bedrock principle "that the FAA was designed to promote arbitration," as it reflects a "national policy favoring arbitration." *Concepcion*, 563 U.S. at 345–46. Any law, therefore, that "stands as an obstacle to the accomplishment and execution of the full purposes and objectives of Congress . . . is pre-empted by the FAA." *Id.* at 352 (citations omitted). As noted above, AB 51 will likely have a deterrent effect on employers' use of arbitration agreements given the civil and criminal sanctions associated with violating the law.

For the reasons discussed above, plaintiffs meet their burden of showing they are likely to succeed on the merits of their claim that AB 51 is preempted by the FAA because it discriminates against arbitration and interferes with the FAA's objectives.

E. Construction of Arbitration Agreements: How Heavy Is the Foot on the Scale?

Having been told to enforce arbitration agreements (including by the cases above), how do courts go about that enforcement?

Without a contract calling for arbitration, all the presumption in the world will not create an arbitration. Consensus remains as important a touchstone as does mandate. Without consensus to arbitrate, one never gets to the arbitrator's mandate.

This takes us back to bias—and what degree of bias is appropriate. As you read these cases, consider whether the special features of arbitration agreements should lead to a different contract interpretation approach than if the subject matter were any other contract. Should the FAA's pro-arbitration policy insulate sloppy drafters? Why should courts stretch to find an arbitration agreement when there is no maxim instructing them to find, for example, an agreement on consequential damages, or choice of law, or any of the other countless features in a contract? The FAA was, to be sure, meant to allow parties who genuinely want to arbitrate a means to judicially enforce the preference. But what if it is not clear that this is what both parties want? Does *Moses Cone*'s presumption mean that a court must stretch to find a meeting of the minds where one might not otherwise exist?

CASE PREVIEW. Like other courts facing contract issues, courts addressing arbitration agreements in our digital age must grapple with issues of offer and acceptance made in non-traditional means. When arbitration terms are factored into "click wrap" or "browse wrap" contracts, these issues become even more acute. In the following case, a national company included on its website a terms-of-u se section that included a hyperlink to an arbitration provision. A consumer filed suit in court against the company relating to a dispute over his order and alleging deceptive business practices. The national company moved to compel arbitration and stay the proceedings pursuant to Section 3 of the FAA, which the lower court had denied.

Nguyen v. Barnes & Noble Inc.

763 F.3d 1171 (9th Cir. 2014)

NOONAN, Circuit Judge:

I. Background

The underlying facts are not in dispute. Barnes & Noble is a national bookseller that owns and operates hundreds of bookstores as well as the website <www.barnesandnoble.com>. In August 2011, Barnes & Noble, along with other retailers across the country, liquidated its inventory of discontinued Hewlett-Packard Touchpads ("Touchpads"), an unsuccessful competitor to Apple's iPad, by advertising a "fire sale" of Touchpads at a heavily discounted price. Acting quickly on the nationwide liquidation of Touchpads, Nguyen purchased two units on Barnes & Noble's website on August 21, 2011, and received an email confirming the transaction. The following day, Nguyen received another email informing him that his order had been cancelled due to unexpectedly high demand. Nguyen alleges that, as a result of "Barnes & Noble's representations, as well as the delay in informing him it would not honor the sale," he was "unable to obtain an HP Tablet during the liquidation period for the discounted price," and was "forced to rely on substitute tablet technology, which he subsequently purchased . . . [at] considerable expense."

In April 2012, Nguyen filed this lawsuit in California Superior Court on behalf of himself and a putative class of consumers whose Touchpad orders had been cancelled, alleging that Barnes & Noble had engaged in deceptive business practices and false advertising in violation of both California and New York law. Barnes & Noble removed the action to federal court and moved to compel arbitration under the Federal Arbitration Act ("FAA"), arguing that Nguyen was bound by the arbitration agreement in the website's Terms of Use.

The website's Terms of Use are available via a "Terms of Use" hyperlink located in the bottom left-hand corner of every page on the Barnes & Noble website, which appears alongside other hyperlinks labeled "NOOK Store Terms," "Copyright," and "Privacy Policy." These hyperlinks also appear underlined and set in green typeface in the lower left-hand corner of every page in the online checkout process.

Nguyen neither clicked on the "Terms of Use" hyperlink nor actually read the Terms of Use. Had he clicked on the hyperlink, he would have been taken to a page containing the full text of Barnes & Noble's Terms of Use, which state, in relevant part: "By visiting any area in the Barnes & Noble.com Site, creating an account, [or] making a purchase via the Barnes & Noble.com Site . . . a User is deemed to have accepted the Terms of Use." Nguyen also would have come across an arbitration provision, which states:

> **DISPUTE RESOLUTION**
>
> Any claim or controversy at law or equity that arises out of the Terms of Use, the Barnes & Noble.com Site or any Barnes & Noble.com Service (each a

> "Claim"), shall be resolved through binding arbitration conducted by telephone, online or based solely upon written submissions where no in-person appearance is required. In such cases, arbitration shall be administered by the American Arbitration Association under its Commercial Arbitration Rules (including without limitation the Supplementary Procedures for Consumer-Related Disputes, if applicable), and judgment on the award rendered by the arbitrator(s) may be entered in any court having jurisdiction thereof.
>
> . . . .
>
> Any claim shall be arbitrated or litigated, as the case may be, on an individual basis and shall not be consolidated with any Claim of any other party whether through class action proceedings, class arbitration proceedings or otherwise.
>
> . . . .
>
> Each of the parties hereby knowingly, voluntarily and intentionally waives any right it may have to a trial by jury in respect of any litigation (including but not limited to any claims, counterclaims, cross-claims, or third party claims) arising out of, under or in connection with these Terms of Use. Further, each party hereto certifies that no representative or agent of either party has represented, expressly or otherwise, that such a party would not in the event of such litigation, seek to enforce this waiver of right to jury trial provision. Each of the parties acknowledges that this section is a material inducement for the other party entering into these Terms of Use.

Nguyen contends that he cannot be bound to the arbitration provision because he neither had notice of nor assented to the website's Terms of Use. Barnes & Noble, for its part, asserts that the placement of the "Terms of Use" hyperlink on its website put Nguyen on constructive notice of the arbitration agreement. Barnes & Noble contends that this notice, combined with Nguyen's subsequent use of the website, was enough to bind him to the Terms of Use. The district court disagreed, and Barnes & Noble now appeals.

II. Discussion

A.

The FAA, 9 U.S.C. §1 *et seq.*, requires federal district courts to stay judicial proceedings and compel arbitration of claims covered by a written and enforceable arbitration agreement. *Id.* §3. The FAA limits the district court's role to determining whether a valid arbitration agreement exists, and whether the agreement encompasses the disputes at issue. *See Chiron Corp. v. Ortho Diagnostic Sys., Inc.*, 207 F.3d 1126, 1130 (9th Cir. 2000). The parties do not quarrel that Barnes & Noble's arbitration agreement, should it be found enforceable, encompasses Nguyen's claims. The only issue is whether a valid arbitration agreement exists.

For the reasons that follow, we hold that Nguyen did not enter into Barnes & Noble's agreement to arbitrate.

B.

"While new commerce on the Internet has exposed courts to many new situations, it has not fundamentally changed the principles of contract." *Register.com, Inc. v. Verio, Inc.*, 356 F.3d 393, 403 (2d Cir. 2004). One such principle is the requirement that "[m]utual manifestation of assent, whether by written or spoken word or by conduct, is the touchstone of contract." *Specht v. Netscape Commc'ns Corp.*, 306 F.3d 17, 29 (2d Cir. 2002) (applying California law).

Contracts formed on the Internet come primarily in two flavors: "clickwrap" (or "click-through") agreements, in which website users are required to click on an "I agree" box after being presented with a list of terms and conditions of use; and "browsewrap" agreements, where a website's terms and conditions of use are generally posted on the website via a hyperlink at the bottom of the screen. *See Register.com*, 356 F.3d at 428–30. Barnes & Noble's Terms of Use fall in the latter category.

"Unlike a clickwrap agreement, a browsewrap agreement does not require the user to manifest assent to the terms and conditions expressly . . . [a] party instead gives his assent simply by using the website." *Hines v. Overstock.com, Inc.*, 668 F. Supp. 2d 362, 366–67 (E.D.N.Y. 2009) (citation and quotation marks omitted) (alteration in original). Indeed, "in a pure-form browsewrap agreement, 'the website will contain a notice that—by merely using the services of, obtaining information from, or initiating applications within the website—the user is agreeing to and is bound by the site's terms of service.'" *Fteja v. Facebook, Inc.*, 841 F. Supp. 2d 829, 837 (S.D.N.Y. 2012) (quoting *United States v. Drew*, 259 F.R.D. 449, 462 n.22 (C.D. Cal. 2009)). Thus, "by visiting the website—something that the user has already done—the user agrees to the Terms of Use not listed on the site itself but available only by clicking a hyperlink." *Id.* "The defining feature of browsewrap agreements is that the user can continue to use the website or its services without visiting the page hosting the browsewrap agreement or even knowing that such a webpage exists." *Be In, Inc. v. Google Inc.*, No. 12-CV-03373-LHK, 2013 U.S. Dist. LEXIS 147047, 2013 WL 5568706, at *6 (N.D. Cal. Oct. 9, 2013). "Because no affirmative action is required by the website user to agree to the terms of a contract other than his or her use of the website, the determination of the validity of the browsewrap contract depends on whether the user has actual or constructive knowledge of a website's terms and conditions." *Van Tassell v. United Mktg. Grp.*, LLC, 795 F. Supp. 2d 770, 790 (N.D. Ill. 2011) (citing *Sw. Airlines Co. v. BoardFirst, LLC*, No. 06-CV-0891-B, 2007 U.S. Dist. LEXIS 96230, 2007 WL 4823761, at *4 (N.D. Tex. Sept. 12, 2007)); *see also* Mark A. Lemley, *Terms of Use*, 91 Minn. L. Rev. 459, 477 (2006) ("Courts may be willing to overlook the utter absence of assent only when there are reasons to believe that the [website user] is aware of the [website owner's] terms.").

Were there any evidence in the record that Nguyen had actual notice of the Terms of Use or was required to affirmatively acknowledge the Terms of Use before completing his online purchase, the outcome of this case might be different. Indeed, courts have consistently enforced browsewrap agreements where the user had actual notice of the agreement.

But where, as here, there is no evidence that the website user had actual knowledge of the agreement, the validity of the browsewrap agreement turns on whether the website puts a reasonably prudent user on inquiry notice of the terms of the contract. *Specht*, 306 F.3d at 30–31; *see also In re Zappos.com, Inc. Customer Data Sec. Breach Litig.*, 893 F. Supp. 2d 1058, 1064 (D. Nev. 2012). Whether a user has inquiry notice of a browsewrap agreement, in turn, depends on the design and content of the website and the agreement's webpage. *Google*, 2013 U.S. Dist. LEXIS 147047, 2013 WL 5568706, at *6. Where the link to a website's terms of use is buried at the bottom of the page or tucked away in obscure corners of the website where users are unlikely to see it, courts have refused to enforce the browsewrap agreement. *See, e.g., Specht*, 306 F.3d at 23 (refusing to enforce terms of use that "would have become visible to plaintiffs only if they had scrolled down to the next screen"); *In re Zappos.com*, 893 F. Supp. 2d at 1064 ("The Terms of Use is inconspicuous, buried in the middle to bottom of every Zappos.com webpage among many other links, and the website never directs a user to the Terms of Use."); *Van Tassell*, 795 F. Supp. 2d 792–93 (refusing to enforce arbitration clause in browsewrap agreement that was only noticeable after a "multi-step process" of clicking through non-obvious links); *Hines*, 668 F. Supp. 2d at 367 (plaintiff "could not even see the link to [the terms and conditions] without scrolling down to the bottom of the screen—an action that was not required to effectuate her purchase"). On the other hand, where the website contains an explicit textual notice that continued use will act as a manifestation of the user's intent to be bound, courts have been more amenable to enforcing browsewrap agreements. *See, e.g., Cairo, Inc. v. Crossmedia Servs., Inc.*, No. 04-04825, 2005 U.S. Dist. LEXIS 8450, 2005 WL 756610, at *2, *4–5 (N.D. Cal. Apr. 1, 2005) (enforcing forum selection clause in website's terms of use where every page on the website had a textual notice that read: "By continuing past this page and/or using this site, you agree to abide by the Terms of Use for this site, which prohibit commercial use of any information on this site"). *But see Pollstar v. Gigmania, Ltd.*, 170 F. Supp. 2d 974, 981 (E.D. Cal. 2000) (refusing to enforce browsewrap agreement where textual notice appeared in small gray print against a gray background). In short, the conspicuousness and placement of the "Terms of Use" hyperlink, other notices given to users of the terms of use, and the website's general design all contribute to whether a reasonably prudent user would have inquiry notice of a browsewrap agreement.

Barnes & Noble argues that the placement of the "Terms of Use" hyperlink in the bottom left-hand corner of every page on the Barnes & Noble website, and its close proximity to the buttons a user must click on to complete an online purchase, is enough to place a reasonably prudent user on constructive notice. It is true that the location of the hyperlink on Barnes & Noble's website distinguishes this case from *Specht*, the leading authority on the enforceability of browsewrap terms under New York law. There, the Second Circuit refused to enforce an arbitration provision in a website's licensing terms where the hyperlink to the terms was located at the bottom of the page, hidden below the "Download" button that users had to click to initiate the software download. *See Specht*, 306 F.3d at 30. Then-Second Circuit Judge Sotomayor, writing for the panel, held that "a reference to the existence of license terms on a submerged screen is not sufficient to place consumers on inquiry or constructive notice of those terms." *Id.* at 32. By contrast, here the "Terms of Use" link appears either directly below the relevant button a user must click on to proceed in the checkout process or just a few inches away.

But the proximity or conspicuousness of the hyperlink alone is not enough to give rise to constructive notice, and Barnes & Noble directs us to no case law that supports this proposition. The most analogous case the court was able to locate is *PDC Labs., Inc. v. Hach Co.*, an unpublished district court order cited by neither party. No. 09-1110, 2009 U.S. Dist. LEXIS 75378, 2009 WL 2605270 (C.D. Ill. Aug. 25, 2009). There, the "Terms [and Conditions of Sale] were hyperlinked on three separate pages of the online . . . order process in underlined, blue, contrasting text." 2009 U.S. Dist. LEXIS 75378, [WL] at *3. The court held that "[t]his contrasting text is sufficient to be considered conspicuous," thereby placing a reasonable user on notice that the terms applied. *Id.*

As in *PDC*, the checkout screens here contained "Terms of Use" hyperlinks in underlined, color-contrasting text. But *PDC* is dissimilar in that the final screen on that website contained the phrase "Review terms." *PDC Labs*, 2009 U.S. Dist. LEXIS 75378, 2009 WL 2605270, at *3. This admonition makes *PDC* distinguishable, despite the court's explanation that the blue contrasting hyperlinks were sufficiently conspicuous on their own.

In light of the lack of controlling authority on point, and in keeping with courts' traditional reluctance to enforce browsewrap agreements against individual consumers, we therefore hold that where a website makes its terms of use available via a conspicuous hyperlink on every page of the website but otherwise provides no notice to users nor prompts them to take any affirmative action to demonstrate assent, even close proximity of the hyperlink to relevant buttons users must click on—without more—is insufficient to give rise to constructive notice. While failure to read a contract before agreeing to its terms does not relieve a party of its obligations under the contract, *Gillman v. Chase Manhattan Bank, N.A.*, 73 N.Y.2d 1, 11, 534 N.E.2d 824, 537 N.Y.S.2d 787 (1988), the onus must be on website owners to put users on notice of the terms to which they wish to bind consumers. Given the breadth of the range of technological savvy of online purchasers, consumers cannot be expected to ferret out hyperlinks to terms and conditions to which they have no reason to suspect they will be bound.

We hold that Nguyen had insufficient notice of Barnes & Noble's Terms of Use, and thus did not enter into an agreement with Barnes & Noble to arbitrate his claims.

AFFIRMED.

Notes and Questions

1. Did *Nguyen v. Barnes & Noble* turn on arbitration principles or contract principles? Should it have included more arbitration law and less contract law? Can pro-arbitration policy conflict with "contract principles"?
2. How would you draft the arbitration agreement in *Barnes & Noble*? Is the issue notice? Consent? Clarity?
3. Take a moment and think of the last time you clicked, without thinking, on an agreement online. Go back and look—did it have an arbitration clause? Did you know it at the time? On review now with these cases and principles in mind, do you think it would stand up to a court challenge? *See also* cases cited *infra* 371–72.

CASE PREVIEW. Granted that consent is a required feature of any contract. Granted as well that these days, most of us do not look carefully before clicking our assent to that contract, arbitration clause or not. How bright must be the blinking lights that cry out ARBITRATION for the contract to be enforceable? The Supreme Court of New Jersey said "very bright indeed" in the following case.

Atalese v. U.S. Legal Services Grp., L.P.

219 N.J. 430, 99 A.3d 306 (N.J. 2014)

JUSTICE ALBIN delivered the opinion of the Court.

Arbitration provisions are now commonplace in consumer contracts. Consumers can choose to pursue arbitration and waive their right to sue in court, but should know that they are making that choice. An arbitration clause, like any contractual clause providing for the waiver of a constitutional or statutory right, must state its purpose clearly and unambiguously. In choosing arbitration, consumers must have a basic understanding that they are giving up their right to seek relief in a judicial forum.

Here, plaintiff, Patricia Atalese, contracted with defendant, U.S. Legal Services Group, L.P. (USLSG), for debt-adjustment services. The contract contained an arbitration provision for the resolution of any dispute between the parties, but the provision made no mention that plaintiff waived her right to seek relief in court. Plaintiff brought a lawsuit against USLSG in the Special Civil Part alleging violations of two consumer-protection statutes.

The trial court granted USLSG's motion to compel arbitration pursuant to the service contract. The Appellate Division affirmed, finding that "the lack of express reference to a waiver of the right to sue in court" did not bar enforcement of the arbitration clause.

We now reverse. The absence of any language in the arbitration provision that plaintiff was waiving her statutory right to seek relief in a court of law renders the provision unenforceable. An arbitration provision—like any comparable contractual provision that provides for the surrendering of a constitutional or statutory right—must be sufficiently clear to a reasonable consumer. The provision here does not pass that test. We therefore vacate the judgment of the Appellate Division and remand to the Special Civil Part for proceedings consistent with this opinion.

USLSG moved to compel arbitration based on an arbitration provision in the twenty-three-page service contract. The arbitration provision is located on page nine, paragraph sixteen, of the contract and states:

Arbitration: In the event of any claim or dispute between Client and the USLSG related to this Agreement or related to any performance of any services related to this Agreement, the claim or dispute shall be submitted to binding arbitration upon the request of either party upon the service of that request on the other party. The parties shall agree on a single arbitrator to resolve the dispute. The matter may be arbitrated either by the Judicial Arbitration Mediation Service or American Arbitration Association, as mutually agreed upon by the parties or selected by the party filing the claim. The arbitration shall be conducted in either the county in which Client resides, or the closest metropolitan county. Any decision of the arbitrator shall be final and may be entered into any judgment in any court of competent jurisdiction. The conduct of the arbitration shall be subject to the then current rules of the arbitration service. The costs of arbitration, excluding legal fees, will be split equally or be born by the losing party, as determined by the arbitrator. The parties shall bear their own legal fees.

The trial court granted USLSG's motion to compel arbitration and dismissed the complaint without prejudice. The court found the arbitration clause to be "minimally, barely sufficient to put the [plaintiff] on notice that if [the parties] have any sort of dispute arising out of [the] agreement, it's going to be heard in [a]rbitration."

Plaintiff appealed. Plaintiff contends that the arbitration clause does not comply with New Jersey law, because it "does not clearly and unequivocally state its purpose in depriving [plaintiff] of her time-honored right to sue." She asserts that New Jersey courts do not uphold "arbitration provisions that fail to: (1) indicate that the parties waive their right to sue; or (2) indicate that arbitration is the parties' exclusive remedy." Plaintiff does not suggest that an incantation of "magic words" is necessary for a waiver of rights but does assert that the language for such a waiver must be clear and unequivocal.

USLSG contends that the term "arbitration" is universally understood and that "[n]o reasonable consumer could have any doubt that arbitration is different than litigation." USLSG emphasizes that the Federal Arbitration Act (FAA) reflects a "liberal federal policy favoring arbitration" and requires courts to "place arbitration agreements on an equal footing with other contracts and enforce them according to their terms." USLSG submits that the arbitration clause is sufficiently clear and "adequately advised" plaintiff that her lawsuit would be resolved "in an arbitral forum."

Arbitration's favored status does not mean that every arbitration clause, however phrased, will be enforceable. An agreement to arbitrate, like any other contract, "must be the product of mutual assent, as determined under customary principles of contract law."

Mutual assent requires that the parties have an understanding of the terms to which they have agreed. "An effective waiver requires a party to have full knowledge of his legal rights and intent to surrender those rights." Moreover, because arbitration involves a waiver of the right to pursue a case in a judicial forum, "courts take particular care in assuring the knowing assent of both parties to arbitrate, and a clear mutual understanding of the ramifications of that assent." *Ibid.*

Arbitration clauses are not singled out for more burdensome treatment than other waiver-of-rights clauses under state law. Our jurisprudence has stressed that when a contract contains a waiver of rights—whether in an arbitration or other clause—the waiver "must be clearly and unmistakably established." *Garfinkel, supra*, 168 N.J. at 132 (citation and internal quotation marks omitted). Thus, a "clause depriving a citizen of access to the courts should clearly state its purpose." *Ibid.* (quoting *Marchak, supra*, 134 N.J. at 282). We have repeatedly stated that "[t]he point is to assure that the parties know that in electing arbitration as the exclusive remedy, they are waiving their time-honored right to sue." *Ibid.* (quoting *Marchak, supra*, 134 N.J. at 282); *Hirsch, supra*, 215 N.J. at 187 (same).

The requirement that a contractual provision be sufficiently clear to place a consumer on notice that he or she is waiving a constitutional or statutory right is not specific to arbitration provisions. "Rather, under New Jersey law, any contractual waiver-of-rights provision 'must reflect that [the party] has agreed clearly and unambiguously' to its terms."

With those principles in mind, we turn to the arbitration provision before us. The arbitration clause at issue appears on page nine of a twenty-three-page contract between plaintiff and USLSG.

Nowhere in the arbitration clause is there any explanation that plaintiff is waiving her right to seek relief in court for a breach of her statutory rights. The contract states that either party may submit any dispute to "binding arbitration," that "[t]he parties shall agree on a single arbitrator to resolve the dispute," and that the arbitrator's decision "shall be final and may be entered into judgment in any court of competent jurisdiction." The provision does not explain what arbitration is, nor does it indicate how arbitration is different from a proceeding in a court of law.

In the matter before us, the wording of the service agreement did not clearly and unambiguously signal to plaintiff that she was surrendering her right to pursue her statutory claims in court. That deficiency renders the arbitration agreement unenforceable.

Notes and Questions

1. Did *Atalese* honor the "federal policy favoring arbitration" in *Moses Cone*? Can you reconcile *Atlalese*'s decision not to enforce an arbitration clause with the sexual harassment cases you just read, in which the law took a back seat to arbitration?
2. In *Atalese*, was there any question that the parties agreed to arbitrate? What does "agreement" mean in this context other than the words on the contract?
3. Should there be a public policy exception to *Moses Cone*? Should it be written into the FAA?
4. As a matter of federalism, is it permissible to have less deference to arbitration in state court cases that do not touch on the FAA at all? If there is no diversity jurisdiction or federal question but there remains an arbitration clause, is the deference still required? *See* discussion *supra* page 57 regarding the lack of independent creation of subject matter jurisdiction by the FAA.
5. Parties waive rights all the time in contracts. Return to the earlier example of a contract clause that waives a claim to consequential damages, a not infrequent occurrence in commercial contracts. *See, e.g.*, Glen D. West & Sarah G. Duran, *Reassessing the "Consequences" of Consequential Damage Waivers in Acquisition Agreements*, 63 Bus. Lawyer 777 (2008) ("consequential damage waivers are a frequent part of merger and acquisition agreements involving private company targets. . ."). Parties would otherwise be entitled to seek consequential damages, assuming they so qualify under the governing state's contract law. The waiver clause thus gives up rights (to damages) just as an arbitration clause does (to a jury trial). Courts do not, however, require the consequential damages waiver to be in lights as bright red and blinking as the *Atalese* court does for arbitration clauses. Is that distinction and differing treatment correct?

PRACTICE POINTER. As a direct result of *Atalese*, the prudent practitioner should ensure they remove any questions as to whether the parties agree to arbitrate, especially in business to consumer ("B-to-C") agreements. The following draft arbitration clause was sent to this author by a colleague for review:

ARBITRATION AND WAIVER OF JURY TRIAL

This Agreement includes a binding Waiver of Jury Trial and Arbitration Provision. You may opt out of the Waiver of Jury Trial and Arbitration Provision by following the instructions below.

WAIVER OF JURY TRIAL AND ARBITRATION PROVISION. WE HAVE RETAINED AGENTS (PEOPLE WHO WORK FOR US BUT ARE NOT OUR EMPLOYEES) TO HELP US IN ORIGINATING AND SERVICING YOUR LOAN. YOU AGREE THAT ANY AGENTS RETAINED BY US, THE OPERATOR OF THE WEBSITE WHERE YOU SUBMITTED YOUR APPLICATION, AND THE PURCHASER(S) OF ANY BALANCES OF YOUR ACCOUNT ARE EXPRESS THIRD-PARTY BENEFICIARIES OF THIS WAIVER OF JURY TRIAL AND ARBITRATION PROVISION (THE "ARBITRATION PROVISION"), AND ARE ENTITLED TO ENFORCE IT TO THE SAME EXTENT IF THEY SIGNED THIS AGREEMENT.

FACTS ABOUT ARBITRATION. ARBITRATION IS A PROCESS IN WHICH A PERSON WITH A DISPUTE: (A) WAIVES THEIR RIGHTS TO FILE A LAWSUIT AND PROCEED IN COURT AND TO HAVE A JURY TRIAL TO RESOLVE THEIR DISPUTES; AND (B) AGREE, INSTEAD, TO SUBMIT THEIR DISPUTES TO A NEUTRAL THIRD PERSON (AN "ARBITRATOR") FOR DECISION. EACH PARTY TO THE DISPUTE HAS AN OPPORTUNITY TO PRESENT SOME EVIDENCE TO THE ARBITRATOR. PRE-ARBITRATION DISCOVERY MAY BE LIMITED. ARBITRATION PROCEEDINGS ARE PRIVATE AND LESS FORMAL THAN COURT TRIALS. THE ARBITRATOR WILL ISSUE A FINAL AND BINDING DECISION RESOLVING THE DISPUTE, WHICH MAY BE ENFORCED AS A COURT JUDGMENT. A COURT RARELY OVERTURNS AN ARBITRATION AWARD.

YOU ARE WAIVING YOUR RIGHT TO SERVE AS A REPRESENTATIVE, AS A PRIVATE ATTORNEY GENERAL, OR IN ANY OTHER REPRESENTATIVE CAPACITY, AND/OR TO PARTICIPATE AS A MEMBER OF A CLASS OF CLAIMANTS, IN ANY LAWSUIT FILED AGAINST US AND/OR RELATED THIRD PARTIES.

NO CLASS ACTIONS. ALL DISPUTES INCLUDING ANY REPRESENTATIVE CLAIMS AGAINST US AND/OR RELATED THIRD PARTIES SHALL BE RESOLVED BY BINDING ARBITRATION ONLY. DISPUTES SHALL BE RESOLVED ON AN INDIVIDUAL BASIS WITH YOU. THEREFORE, THE ARBITRATOR SHALL NOT HAVE THE POWER TO CONDUCT CLASS ARBITRATION OR TO CONSOLIDATE CLAIMS OF MULTIPLE PARTIES; THAT IS, THE ARBITRATOR SHALL NOT ALLOW YOU TO SERVE AS A REPRESENTATIVE, AS A PRIVATE ATTORNEY GENERAL, OR IN ANY OTHER REPRESENTATIVE CAPACITY FOR OTHERS IN THE ARBITRATION. NOT WITHSTANDING ANY OTHER PROVISION HEREIN, THE ARBITRATOR SHALL NOT HAVE THE POWER OR AUTHORITY TO DETERMINE IF THIS SECTION IS VALID AND ENFORCEABLE. ONLY A COURT SHALL HAVE SUCH POWER AND AUTHORITY.

ANY CLAIM, DISPUTE OR CONTROVERSY ("CLAIM") BY EITHER YOU OR US AGAINST THE OTHER, ARISING FROM OR RELATING IN ANY WAY TO THIS AGREEMENT OR YOUR ACCOUNT, OR THEIR

ESTABLISHMENT, OR ANY TRANSACTION OR ACTIVITY ON YOUR ACCOUNT, INCLUDING (WITHOUT LIMITATION) CLAIMS BASED ON CONTRACT, TORT (INCLUDING INTENTIONAL TORTS), FRAUD, AGENCY, NEGLIGENCE, STATUTORY OR REGULATORY PROVISIONS OR ANY OTHER SOURCE OF LAW AND (EXCEPT AS OTHERWISE SPECIFICALLY PROVIDED IN THIS AGREEMENT) SHALL BE SUBJECT TO ARBITRATION AS SET FORTH IN THIS SECTION.

* * *

The asterisks above indicate that the above clause went on for some length—in this case, for another 11 paragraphs. Did the justices in *Atalese* envision a clause of the above length when they announced their decision?

CASE PREVIEW. ***How Far Should the Presumption Go?*** The Supreme Court's 2019 *Lamps Plus* decision nicely crystalizes the debate between applying the principles of general contract interpretation and the "policy" in favor of arbitration. Applying state contract interpretation principles, the Ninth Circuit held that ambiguity in a contract "is construed against the drafter, a rule that applies with peculiar force in the case of a contract of adhesion." Chief Justice Roberts would have none of that.

Lamps Plus, Inc. v. Varela

139 S. Ct. 1407 (2019)

CHIEF JUSTICE ROBERTS delivered the opinion of the Court.

The Federal Arbitration Act requires courts to enforce covered arbitration agreements according to their terms. *See* 9 U.S.C. § 2. In *Stolt-Nielsen S. A. v. AnimalFeeds Int'l Corp.*, 559 U.S. 662 (2010), we held that a court may not compel arbitration on a classwide basis when an agreement is "silent" on the availability of such arbitration. Because class arbitration fundamentally changes the nature of the "traditional individualized arbitration" envisioned by the FAA, *Epic Systems Corp. v. Lewis*, 138 S. Ct. 1612 (2018), "a party may not be compelled under the FAA to submit to class arbitration unless there is a contractual basis for concluding that the party agreed to do so," *Stolt-Nielsen*, 559 U.S., at 684 (emphasis in original). We now consider whether the FAA similarly bars an order requiring class arbitration when an agreement is not silent, but rather "ambiguous" about the availability of such arbitration.

I

Petitioner Lamps Plus is a company that sells light fixtures and related products. In 2016, a hacker impersonating a company official tricked a Lamps Plus employee into disclosing the tax information of approximately 1,300 other employees. Soon after, a fraudulent federal income tax return was filed in the name of Frank Varela, a Lamps Plus employee and respondent here.

Like most Lamps Plus employees, Varela had signed an arbitration agreement when he started work at the company. But after the data breach, he sued Lamps Plus in Federal District Court in California, bringing state and federal claims on behalf of a putative class of employees whose tax information had been compromised. Lamps Plus moved to compel arbitration on an individual rather than classwide basis, and to dismiss the lawsuit. In a single order, the District Court granted the motion to compel arbitration and dismissed Varela's claims without prejudice. But the court rejected Lamps Plus's request for individual arbitration, instead authorizing arbitration on a classwide basis. Lamps Plus appealed the order, arguing that the court erred by compelling class arbitration.

The Ninth Circuit affirmed. The court acknowledged that *Stolt-Nielsen* prohibits forcing a party "to submit to class arbitration unless there is a contractual basis for concluding that the party agreed to do so" and that Varela's agreement "include[d] no express mention of class proceedings." But that did not end the inquiry, the court reasoned, because the fact that the agreement "does not expressly refer to class arbitration is not the 'silence' contemplated in Stolt-Nielsen." *Ibid.* In *Stolt-Nielsen*, the parties had stipulated that their agreement was silent about class arbitration. Because there was no such stipulation here, the court concluded that *Stolt-Nielsen* was not controlling.

The Ninth Circuit then determined that the agreement was ambiguous on the issue of class arbitration. On the one hand, as Lamps Plus argued, certain phrases in the agreement seemed to contemplate "purely binary claims." At the same time, as Varela asserted, other phrases were capacious enough to include class arbitration, such as one stating that "arbitration shall be in lieu of any and all lawsuits or other civil legal proceedings relating to my employment." The Ninth Circuit followed California law to construe the ambiguity against the drafter, a rule that "applies with peculiar force in the case of a contract of adhesion" such as this. Because Lamps Plus had drafted the agreement, the court adopted Varela's interpretation authorizing class arbitration. Judge Fernandez dissented. In his view, the agreement was not ambiguous, and the majority's holding was a "palpable evasion of *Stolt-Nielsen*."

Lamps Plus petitioned for a writ of certiorari, arguing that the Ninth Circuit's decision contravened *Stolt-Nielsen* and created a conflict among the Courts of Appeals.

The Ninth Circuit applied California contract law to conclude that the parties' agreement was ambiguous on the availability of class arbitration. In California, an agreement is ambiguous "when it is capable of two or more constructions, both of which are reasonable." Following our normal practice, we defer to the Ninth Circuit's interpretation and application of state law and thus accept that the agreement should be regarded as ambiguous.

We therefore face the question whether, consistent with the FAA, an ambiguous agreement can provide the necessary "contractual basis" for compelling class arbitration. *Stolt-Nielsen*, 559 U.S., at 684. We hold that it cannot—a conclusion that follows directly from our decision in *Stolt-Nielsen.* Class arbitration is not only markedly different from the "traditional individualized arbitration" contemplated by the FAA, it also undermines the most important benefits of that familiar form of arbitration. *Epic Systems*, 584 U.S., at ___, 138 S. Ct. 1612, 200 L. Ed. 2d 889, at 901; *see Stolt-Nielsen*, 559 U.S., at 686–687. The statute therefore requires more than ambiguity to ensure that the parties actually agreed to arbitrate on a classwide basis.

A

The FAA requires courts to "enforce arbitration agreements according to their terms." *Epic Systems*, 584 U.S., at ___, 138 S. Ct. 1612, 200 L. Ed. 2d 889, at 899 (quoting *American Express Co. v. Italian Colors Restaurant*, 570 U.S. 228, 233, 133 S. Ct. 2304, 186 L. Ed. 2d 417 (2013)). Although courts may ordinarily accomplish that end by relying on state contract principles, *First Options of Chicago, Inc. v. Kaplan*, 514 U.S. 938, 944 (1995), state law is preempted to the extent it "stands as an obstacle to the accomplishment and execution of the full purposes and objectives" of the FAA, *Concepcion*, 563 U.S., at 352 (internal quotation marks omitted). At issue in this case is the interaction between a state contract principle for addressing ambiguity and a "rule[ ] of fundamental importance" under the FAA, namely, that arbitration "is a matter of consent, not coercion." *Stolt-Nielsen*, 559 U.S., at 681 (internal quotation marks omitted).

"[T]he first principle that underscores all of our arbitration decisions" is that "[a]rbitration is strictly a matter of consent." *Granite Rock Co. v. Teamsters*, 561 U.S. 287, 299, 130 S. Ct. 2847, 177 L. Ed. 2d 567 (2010) (internal quotation marks omitted). We have emphasized that "foundational FAA principle" many times. *Stolt-Nielsen*, 559 U.S., at 684; *see also, e.g., Howsam v. Dean Witter Reynolds, Inc.*, 537 U.S. 79, 83, 123 (2002); *First Options*, 514 U.S., at 943; *Mastrobuono v. Shearson Lehman Hutton, Inc.*, 514 .S. 52, 57 (1995); *Volt Information Sciences, Inc. v. Board of Trustees of Leland Stanford Junior Univ.*, 489 U.S. 468, 479 (1989); *Mitsubishi Motors Corp. v. Soler Chrysler-Plymouth, Inc.*, 473 U.S. 614, 626 (1985).

Consent is essential under the FAA because arbitrators wield only the authority they are given. That is, they derive their "powers from the parties' agreement to forgo the legal process and submit their disputes to private dispute resolution." *Stolt-Nielsen*, 559 U.S., at 682. Parties may generally shape such agreements to their liking by specifying with whom they will arbitrate, the issues subject to arbitration, the rules by which they will arbitrate, and the arbitrators who will resolve their disputes. *Id.*, at 683–684. Whatever they settle on, the task for courts and arbitrators at bottom remains the same: "to give effect to the intent of the parties." Id., at 684.

In carrying out that responsibility, it is important to recognize the "fundamental" difference between class arbitration and the individualized form of arbitration envisioned by the FAA. *Epic Systems*, 584 U.S., at ___, 138 S. Ct. 1612, 200 L. Ed. 2d 889, at 900; *see also Concepcion*, 563 U.S., at 349, 351; *Stolt-Nielsen*, 559 U.S., at 686–687. In individual arbitration, "parties forgo the procedural rigor and appellate review of the courts in order to realize the benefits of private dispute resolution: lower costs, greater efficiency and speed, and the ability to choose expert adjudicators to resolve specialized disputes." *Id.*, at 685. Class arbitration lacks those benefits. It "sacrifices the principal advantage of arbitration—its informality—and makes the process slower, more costly, and more likely to generate procedural morass than final judgment." *Concepcion*, 563 U.S., at 348. Indeed, we recognized just last Term that with class arbitration "the virtues Congress originally saw in arbitration, its speed and simplicity and inexpensiveness, would be shorn away and arbitration would wind up looking like the litigation it was meant to displace." *Epic Systems*, 584 U.S., at ___, 138 S. Ct. 1612, 200 L. Ed. 2d 889, at 901. Class arbitration not only "introduce[s] new risks and costs for both sides," *ibid.*, it also raises serious due process concerns by adjudicating the rights of absent members of the plaintiff class—again, with only limited judicial review. *See Concepcion*, 563 U.S., 349; *see also Stolt-Nielsen*, 559 U.S., at 686.

Because of these "crucial differences" between individual and class arbitration, *Stolt-Nielsen* explained that there is "reason to doubt the parties' mutual consent to resolve disputes through classwide arbitration." 559 U.S., at 687, 685–686. And for that reason, we held that courts may not infer consent to participate in class arbitration absent an affirmative "contractual basis for concluding that the party agreed to do so." *Id.*, at 684. Silence is not enough; the "FAA requires more." *Id.*, at 687.

Our reasoning in *Stolt-Nielsen* controls the question we face today. Like silence, ambiguity does not provide a sufficient basis to conclude that parties to an arbitration agreement agreed to "sacrifice[ ] the principal advantage of arbitration." *Concepcion*, 563 U.S., at 348.

This conclusion aligns with our refusal to infer consent when it comes to other fundamental arbitration questions. For example, we presume that parties have not authorized arbitrators to resolve certain "gateway" questions, such as "whether the parties have a valid arbitration agreement at all or whether a concededly binding arbitration clause applies to a certain type of controversy." *Green Tree Financial Corp. v. Bazzle*, 539 U.S. 444, 452 (2003) (plurality opinion). Although parties are free to authorize arbitrators to resolve such questions, we will not conclude that they have done so based on "silence or ambiguity" in their agreement, because "doing so might too often force unwilling parties to arbitrate a matter they reasonably would have thought a judge, not an arbitrator, would decide." *First Options*, 514.S., at 945, (emphasis added); *see also Howsam*, 537 U.S., at 83–84. We relied on that same reasoning in *Stolt-Nielsen*, 559 U.S., at 686–687, and it applies with equal force here. Neither silence nor ambiguity provides a sufficient basis for concluding that parties to an arbitration agreement agreed to undermine the central benefits of arbitration itself.

B

The Ninth Circuit reached a contrary conclusion based on California's rule that ambiguity in a contract should be construed against the drafter, a doctrine known as contra proferentem. The rule applies "only as a last resort" when the meaning of a provision remains ambiguous after exhausting the ordinary methods of interpretation. 3 A. Corbin, Contracts § 559, pp. 268–270 (1960). At that point, contra proferentem resolves the ambiguity against the drafter based on public policy factors, primarily equitable considerations about the parties' relative bargaining strength. *See* 2 E. Farnsworth, Contracts § 7.11, pp. 300–304 (3d ed. 2004); *see also* 11 R. Lord, Williston on Contracts § 32:12, pp. 788–792 (4th ed. 2012) (stating that application of the rule may vary based on "the degree of sophistication of the contracting parties or the degree to which the contract was negotiated"); Restatement (Second) of Contracts § 206, pp. 80–81, 105–107 (1979) (classifying contra proferentem under "Considerations of Fairness and the Public Interest" rather than with rules for interpreting "The Meaning of Agreements"); 3 Corbin, Contracts § 559, at 270 (noting that contra proferentem is "chiefly a rule of public policy"). Although the rule enjoys a place in every hornbook and treatise on contracts, we noted in a recent FAA case that "the reach of the canon construing contract language against the drafter must have limits, no matter who the drafter was." *DIRECTV, Inc. v. Imburgia*, 577 U.S. ___, ___, 136 S. Ct. 463, 193 L. Ed. 2d 365, at 470 (2015). This case brings those limits into focus.

Unlike contract rules that help to interpret the meaning of a term, and thereby uncover the intent of the parties, contra proferentem is by definition triggered only after a court determines that it cannot discern the intent of the parties. When a contract is ambiguous, contra proferentem provides a default rule based on public policy considerations; "it can scarcely be said to be designed to ascertain the meanings attached by the parties." 2 Farnsworth, Contracts § 7.11, at 303. Like the contract rule preferring interpretations that favor the public interest, *see id.*, at 304, contra proferentem seeks ends other than the intent of the parties.

"[C]lass arbitration, to the extent it is manufactured by [state law] rather than consen[t], is inconsistent with the FAA." *Concepcion*, 563 U.S., at 348, 131 S. Ct. 1740, 179 L. Ed. 2d 742. We recently reiterated that courts may not rely on state contract principles to "reshape traditional individualized arbitration by mandating classwide arbitration procedures without the parties' consent." *Epic Systems*, 584 U.S., at ___, 138 S. Ct. 1612, 200 L. Ed. 2d 889, at 901. But that is precisely what the court below did, requiring class arbitration on the basis of a doctrine that "does not help to determine the meaning that the two parties gave to the words, or even the meaning that a reasonable person would have given to the language used." 3 Corbin, Contracts § 559, at 269–270. Such an approach is flatly inconsistent with "the foundational FAA principle that arbitration is a matter of consent." *Stolt-Nielsen*, 559 U.S., at 684, 130 S. Ct. 1758, 176 L. Ed. 2d 605.

* * *

Our opinion today is far from the watershed Justice Kagan claims it to be. Rather, it is consistent with a long line of cases holding that the FAA provides the default rule for resolving certain ambiguities in arbitration agreements. For example, we have repeatedly held that ambiguities about the scope of an arbitration agreement must be resolved in favor of arbitration. *See, e.g., Mitsubishi Motors Corp.*, 473 U.S., at 626;

Moses H. Cone Memorial Hospital v. Mercury Constr. Corp., 460 U.S. 1, 24–25 (1983). In those cases, we did not seek to resolve the ambiguity by asking who drafted the agreement. Instead, we held that the FAA itself provided the rule. As in those cases, the FAA provides the default rule for resolving ambiguity here.

* * *

Courts may not infer from an ambiguous agreement that parties have consented to arbitrate on a classwide basis. The doctrine of contra proferentem cannot substitute for the requisite affirmative "contractual basis for concluding that the part[ies] agreed to [class arbitration]." *Stolt-Nielsen*, 559 U.S., at 684.

We reverse the judgment of the Court of Appeals for the Ninth Circuit and remand the case for further proceedings consistent with this opinion.

It is so ordered.

Problem

Consider the following contract. Assume that it was drafted by the buyer of a business. The choice of law provision states: "This Agreement shall be governed by the laws of the State of Delaware. Any disputes arising under, concerning, or relating to this Agreement shall be resolved by litigation in the state or federal courts of Delaware." The dispute resolution provision states: "In the event of any dispute, the parties shall refer the dispute to binding arbitration in New York City under the Rules of the American Arbitration Association." (Lest you think this an absurd example invented for this casebook, the author saw such a contract in his practice in 2019.) The drafter made an obvious mistake, opting for court litigation in the choice of law clause and arbitration in the dispute resolution clause. The contract is thus ambiguous as to the parties' preferred means of dispute resolution: arbitration versus court. Now, assume there is a dispute, and the buyer/drafter wants the dispute resolved in arbitration but the seller wants it resolved in court. Under the "construe against the drafter" rule, normal contract rules of construction would allow for disregard of the arbitration clause, or at least present a strong argument in that direction as the court pondered how to construe the contract. In the wake of *Lamps Plus* is that still true?

F. The Scope of the Arbitration Clause

Just because federal courts are presumed to find that an arbitration clause exists does not necessarily mean that the case will go to arbitration. The particular clause must then be found to apply to the particular dispute. Should the rules in favor of the presumption of the arbitration agreement extend to a presumption that the arbitration clause applies to the particular dispute in question? Put differently: should the same presumptions apply to scope as they do to existence and formation?

Problem

1. In 2012, Buyer establishes a microbrewery in Northern California. Buyer wants to lock in prices of certain components and so travels to, negotiates, and concludes a contract with Louisiana Seller providing for delivery of 20 kegs per year for each of three years at a modest price escalation per year. The contract contains a binding arbitration clause that provides in relevant part that "any and all disputes arising under or relating to this Agreement shall be resolved by binding arbitration under the AAA Commercial Arbitration Rules. The arbitration shall take place in San Francisco, California." The contract expires in March 2015 and has no automatic renewal clause. In September 2015, Buyer sends an email to Seller stating: "Greetings. Business continues well. Can you send me another 10 kegs at the March 2015 price?" Seller writes back "Glad to hear from you. March 2015 price confirmed. Delivery will go out next Monday. Payment due in 30 days. Please confirm." Buyer replies: "Confirmed." Delivery does go out that next Monday together with an invoice calling for payment on the agreed 30-day terms. Buyer installs the kegs and claims to notice that seven of them leak and three have an unacceptable odor. Buyer thus refuses payment. Seller claims breach and sues in Louisiana. Buyer files motion under the FAA to stay the litigation and demands arbitration in San Francisco. Where should the dispute be heard and what are the arguments for and against it being arbitrated?

2. Buyer and Seller negotiate a contract for the sale and purchase of solar panels. The panels are manufactured in Italy, and a finished process is then applied in Germany. Buyer is located in Boston. Not wanting to litigate in the host courts of either country, the parties agree to the following dispute resolution clause:

   > In the event of any dispute arising under or relating to this contract, the party claiming breach shall send written notice of the dispute to the party accused of breach. The parties agree to hold negotiations between their principals, or persons designated by and having the authority of their principals, within 30 days of the notice in order to resolve the dispute. In the event that after 30 days the dispute remains unresolved, then the parties agree to resolve the dispute by arbitration to take place in Paris, France, under the Rules of the Paris Arbitration Society.

   There is no such organization or entity called the "Paris Arbitration Society," nor has there ever been such an organization. Have the parties agreed to arbitration? Where? What if the clause said Paris, Texas? How far should the courts go to "reform" the contract to find an arbitration clause? Where does deference to arbitration end and party intent begin? *See* Restatement of Contracts (Second) at §§ 151–158.

3. Seller is an established jewelry wholesaler and distributor. Buyer is a jewelry supplier but has long wanted to "vertically integrate" its business and have a foot in the wholesaling door. Buyer and Seller agree to the following structure: (a) Buyer purchases Seller's wholesaler business for $25 million under a document called Purchase Agreement; (b) Seller agrees, in a companion agreement entitled NonCompete Agreement, to exit the wholesaling business and not compete in it for three (3) years after the Purchase Agreement; and (c) because Buyer is a novice in wholesaling, Buyer agrees to employ Seller's son as the CEO of Buyer's new wholesaling entity, since Buyer recognizes that it needs expertise as it learns the wholesaling ropes. That hiring is memorialized in the Employment Agreement.

   The Purchase Agreement, NonCompete Agreement, and Employment Agreement are all executed on the same day. The Purchase and NonCompete Agreements call for resolution in the United States District Court for the District of Maine. The Employment Agreement calls for resolution under the Commercial Arbitration Rules of the American Arbitration Association (AAA).

   Within six months, Buyer's new wholesaling business is in shambles. Buyer blames Seller's son (who is now Buyer's CEO) for leaking information about the business and allowing his family to surreptitiously remain in the wholesaling business notwithstanding their three-year noncompete agreement. Buyer fires CEO son without notice or warning, leaving $938,000 in unpaid compensation. CEO son brings an arbitration, claiming breach of the Employment Agreement. Buyer wants to counterclaim for the full range of violations by CEO son and his family under the Purchase Agreement and the Noncompete Agreements. Can those counterclaims be heard in arbitration? Wouldn't that be more efficient? Wouldn't it favor the judicial presumption in favor of arbitration? What would be the obstacles? Who would be the parties?

G. Failure to Arbitrate: Specific Remedies

1. *The FAA's Remedies Sections*

Assume you have brought a motion to compel arbitration and won. Now what?

The FAA's presumption in favor of arbitration plays out in a number of specific ways provided by the statute. Consider three different situations in which a party may attempt to frustrate an arbitration agreement:

1. Although the parties have an arbitration clause, when a dispute arises, one party sues the other in federal court rather than instituting an arbitration.
2. Although the parties have an arbitration clause, when a dispute arises and one party institutes an arbitration, the other completely ignores it: no response, no reciprocal appointment of party arbitrator, nothing.
3. Although the parties have an arbitration clause, when a dispute arises and the two parties exchange early correspondence agreeing to arbitrate, one party then ignores it and refuses to appoint its arbitrator (or to agree with the other side on the selection of a sole arbitrator should the contract so require).

The FAA deals with each such contingency in short prescriptive language.

Section 3 applies to the first scenario, in which a party who had agreed to arbitrate instead sues in court. The court will stay the arbitration on application from the party objecting to court proceedings:

> If any suit or proceeding be brought in any of the courts of the United States upon any issue referable to arbitration under an agreement in writing for such arbitration, the court in which such suit is pending, upon being satisfied that the issue involved in such suit or proceeding is preferable to arbitration under such an agreement, shall on application of one of the parties stay the trial of the action until such arbitration has been had in accordance with the terms of the agreement, providing the applicant for the stay is not in default in proceeding with such arbitration.

Section 4 applies to the second scenario, in which a party simply ignores its prior agreement to arbitrate. In that instance the Court will command the imminent start of the arbitration:

> A party aggrieved by the alleged failure, neglect, or refusal of another to arbitrate under a written agreement for arbitration may petition any United States district court . . . for an order directing that such arbitration proceed in the manner provided for in such agreement. . . . The court shall hear the parties, and upon being satisfied that the making of the agreement for arbitration or the failure to comply therewith is not in issue, the court shall make an order directing the parties to proceed to arbitration in accordance with the terms of the agreement.

Section 5 applies to the third scenario. If there is no movement on arbitrator selection—either a party refuses to name its own arbitrator or refuses to join in the required consultations to pick an arbitrator—the court will do the picking for the recalcitrant party. Note that this assumes no reference by the parties to institutional rules which, as seen in Chapter 1, may themselves provide for such default procedures:

> If in the agreement provision be made for a method of naming or appointing an arbitrator or arbitrators or an umpire, such method shall be followed; but if no method be provided therein, or if a method be provided and any party thereto shall fail to avail himself of such method, or if for any other reason there shall be a lapse in the naming of an arbitrator or arbitrators or umpire, or in filling a vacancy, then upon the application of either party to the controversy the court shall designate and appoint an arbitrator or arbitrators or umpire, as the case may require, who shall act under the said agreement with the same force and effect as if he or they had been specifically named therein; and unless otherwise provided in the agreement the arbitration shall be by a single arbitrator.

See, e.g., Stop & Shop Supermarket Co. LLC v. UFCW Local 342, 246 Fed. App'x 7 (2d Cir. 2007) (appointing arbitrator for the parties, and commenting "Congress anticipated that breakdowns in the arbitrator selection process might indefinitely delay arbitration proceedings, and sought to cure this problem by granting parties access to a neutral forum, the courts, to correct such failures."

2. *The Process Question: What Relief to Ask for on a Motion to Compel Arbitration?*

A party faced with the first or second scenarios above may move a court to compel arbitration. A motion to compel asks the court to order an opposing party or a third party to a lawsuit to take some action. In this case, the moving party is asking the court to compel another party to submit to arbitration.

If a party files a lawsuit over claims that belong in arbitration, then your client's motion to compel may function as the answer to the complaint under Federal Rule of Civil Procedure 12. *See Lamkin v. Morinda Properties Weight Parcel, LLC*, 440 Fed. App'x 604 (10th Cir. 2011) (noting "a defendant in a pending lawsuit may file a petition to motion to compel arbitration in lieu of an answer to the complaint") (citing Jay A. Grenig, Alternative Dispute Resolution § 23:3 at 574 (3d ed. 2005)).

Currently, there is a split among the federal appeals courts regarding the specific relief to request when filing a motion to compel. This circuit split goes to a fundamental tactical choice a party must make in its papers: what should be the prayer for relief for the opposing party's failure to arbitrate? In some circuits, district courts are required to stay the lawsuit even when the entire dispute is sent to arbitration. In other circuits, district courts may dismiss the lawsuit when the dispute is referred to arbitration and there are no live controversies before the district court:

- The Second, Third, Seventh, and Tenth Circuits have held that when a case is properly referable to arbitration under § 3 of the FAA, the district court must stay rather than dismiss the lawsuit even if all the claims are sent to arbitration, and no trial will ever occur. *See Bernardino v. Barnes*

& Noble Booksellers, Inc., 763 F. App'x 101, 104 (2d Cir. 2019); *see also Devon Robotics, LLC v. DeViedma*, 798 F.3d 136, 144 (3d Cir. 2015) ("After reviewing the text of [FAA] § 3, we opted to 'side with those courts that take the Congressional text at face value' and reasoned that the statute's 'directive that the Court "shall" enter a stay simply cannot be read to say that the Court shall enter a stay in all cases except those in which all claims are arbitrable and the Court finds dismissal to be the preferable approach.'").

- Courts in the First, Fourth, Fifth, Sixth, Eighth, Ninth, and D.C. Circuits have stated that when claims can be fully heard and redressed in the arbitration, there is no purpose in staying the case. In these circumstances, the case is dismissed rather than stayed. *See Encore Ben. Mgmt. v. Phoenix Benefits Mgmt.*, LLC, No. 18-1821 (Member Case), 2019 U.S. Dist. LEXIS 197750, at *7 (D.P.R. Nov. 12, 2019). Courts have dismissed the cases under Rule 12(b)(1) and Rule 12(b)(6), respectively. *See Laver v. Credit Suisse Secs. (USA), LLC*, 2018 U.S. Dist. LEXIS 104358, at *11 (N.D. Cal. Jun. 21, 2018) (granting defendant's motions to dismiss litigation on the grounds that the claims are covered by a valid agreement to arbitrate, as "courts have held that a Rule 12(b)(1) motion to dismiss for lack of subject matter jurisdiction is a procedurally sufficient mechanism to enforce [an] [a]rbitration [p]rovision."); *Kapai v. Unified Bus. Techs.*, No. 4:19-CV-00749-RWS-CAN, 2020 U.S. Dist. LEXIS 101414 at *7 (E.D. Tex. May 8, 2020) ("once a court finds that arbitration is required, it must stay the underlying litigation to allow arbitration to proceed. 9 U.S.C. § 3. The Court, however, has the discretion to dismiss cases with prejudice when all the issues raised must be submitted to arbitration, but there is no obligation to do so . . . If the only *possible* role of the court once arbitration is complete is to review the arbitration award, then the case should be dismissed with prejudice.") (internal citations omitted); *Garcia v. MaoneGeneral Health*, No. 1:18-cv-00019-NT, 2018 U.S. Dist. LEXIS 197437, at *16 (D. Me. Nov. 20, 2018) ("In the First Circuit, federal courts have discretion to either dismiss or stay when all the issues before the court are arbitrable."); *Doe v. Déjà Vu Consulting Inc.*, No. 3:17-cv-00040, 2017 U.S. Dist. LEXIS 142019 (M.D. Tenn. Sep. 1, 2017) ("Because all of the plaintiff's claims are subject to arbitration under the very broadly worded arbitration agreement, the court will dismiss this action without prejudice rather than stay it. The plaintiff's Motion for Notice will be denied as moot."); *W&T Travel Servs., LLC v. Priority One Servs.*, 69 F. Supp. 3d 158, 174 (D.D.C. 2014) ("This Court will follow the majority rule regarding the propriety of dismissing a case where all of the claims are subject to resolution by the arbitrator."); *see also Jacobs Field Servs. N. Am., Inc. v. Wacker Polysilicon N. Am., LLC*, 375 F. Supp. 3d 898, 915 (E.D. Tenn. 2019)

> (finding that a dismissal is more appropriate than a stay, as the plaintiff did not ask the court to consider a stay if the court found the defendant's motion to be meritorious, and "[s]taying the action rather than dismissing it. . . would serve no purpose").

This circuit split is highly significant. An order dismissing the case in deference to arbitration is appealable, but a stay order is not. *See* FAA § 16(b)(1). This split dictates how a practitioner will draft her filings in federal court.

PRACTICE POINTER. In your motion resisting court resolution and seeking arbitration, consider your court and fashion your requested remedy accordingly. Don't ask for a "dismissal" in a "stay" court.

Chapter 3

Arbitrability, Severability, and Delegation

I. Who Decides Arbitrability?

We have seen that arbitration exists only where the parties agree to arbitrate, but who decides whether or not the agreement to arbitrate exists? Should it be the arbitrator who has been designated by the parties to resolve their disagreements? Or should it be the courts because that arbitrator cannot be tasked with resolving anything if there is no agreement in the first place? At what point, legally, does an arbitrator *exist*? This seemingly metaphysical question in fact requires consideration of when, and on what issues, courts may intervene at the start of the arbitration process. This question is referred to as "arbitrability," meaning, is the dispute arbitrable?

Courts resolve arbitrability by separating disputes into two categories: (i) disputes about the arbitration clause itself and (ii) disputes about the overall contract. This approach, known as *severability*, allocates the first category to the courts and the second to the arbitration process. So-called "gateway" issues as to the scope of the parties' agreement to arbitrate are for the courts, while disputes about contract interpretation are for the arbitrator. In theory, this allows courts to decide whether the dispute is arbitrable and arbitrators to decide everything else. In practice, the issues presented are never so neat and clean. Courts struggle with what is and is not a gateway issue, and with who (arbitrator or court) should decide what issue. The irony of this process is that parties who have agreed to arbitrate in order to avoid court litigation can spend a considerable portion of the early part of their dispute in court.

Roadmap. This chapter reviews cases in which one of the parties challenges either whether the case should be arbitrated at all, or whether it should be in arbitration in the particular manner stated in the arbitration clause. The cases call upon the courts to decide a *who* question and a *what* question: *who* should decide the matter at issue (courts or arbitrators), and *what* should be the scope of the dispute? Many of the cases provide acute lessons for the practitioner because the lawyers in each of these cases had to make a tactical decision as to what to challenge.

We begin the chapter with the seminal case that articulated the severability principle, and one you saw cited several times in cases in the preceding chapter: the United States Supreme Court's 1967 decision in *Prima Paint Corp. v. Flood & Conklin*

Manufacturing Co., 388 U.S. 395 (1967). That case answered the question of who decides whether a contract containing an arbitration clause was fraudulent. From there we move to examples of the severability principle in action, as articulated in a number of Supreme Court decisions that wrestle with whether courts or arbitrators should decide issues of contract unconscionability, and whether the arbitration clauses permit class actions. As in Chapter 2, we will touch again on the issues of federalism and preemption and when state court rules are displaced. We will also return to the saving clause in FAA Section 2, this time from the perspective of who decides whether the saving clause applies. Finally, we will examine so-called "delegation clauses" where the parties attempt to take into their own hands the question of "who decides" arbitrability.

As you read the cases, focus on two points: (1) how you would have drafted the arbitration clause, and (2) how you would have mounted the arbitrability challenge to the clause.

Prima Paint Corp. v. Flood & Conklin Mfg. Co.

388 U.S. 395, 87 S. Ct. 1801 (1967)

MR. JUSTICE FORTAS delivered the opinion of the Court.

This case presents the question whether the federal court or an arbitrator is to resolve a claim of "fraud in the inducement," under a contract governed by the United States Arbitration Act of 1925, where there is no evidence that the contracting parties intended to withhold that issue from arbitration.

The question arises from the following set of facts. On October 7, 1964, respondent, Flood & Conklin Manufacturing Company, a New Jersey corporation, entered into what was styled a "Consulting Agreement," with petitioner, Prima Paint Corporation, a Maryland corporation. This agreement followed by less than three weeks the execution of a contract pursuant to which Prima Paint purchased F & C's paint business. The consulting agreement provided that for a six-year period F & C was to furnish advice and consultation "in connection with the formulae, manufacturing operations, sales and servicing of Prima Trade Sales accounts." These services were to be performed personally by F & C's chairman, Jerome K. Jelin, "except in the event of his death or disability." F & C bound itself for the duration of the contractual period to make no "Trade Sales" of paint or paint products in its existing sales territory or to current customers. To the consulting agreement were appended lists of F & C customers, whose patronage was to be taken over by Prima Paint. In return for these lists, the covenant not to compete, and the services of Mr. Jelin, Prima Paint agreed to pay F & C certain percentages of its receipts from the listed customers and from all others, such payments not to exceed $225,000 over the life of the agreement. The agreement took into account the possibility that Prima Paint might encounter financial difficulties, including bankruptcy, but no corresponding reference was made to possible financial problems which might be encountered by F & C. The agreement stated that it "embodies the entire understanding of the parties on the subject matter." Finally, the parties agreed to a broad arbitration clause, which read in part: "Any controversy or claim arising out of or relating to this Agreement, or the breach thereof, shall be settled by arbitration in the City of New York, in accordance with the rules then obtaining of the American Arbitration Association. . . ."

The first payment by Prima Paint to F & C under the consulting agreement was due on September 1, 1965. None was made on that date. Seventeen days later, Prima Paint did pay the appropriate amount, but into escrow. It notified attorneys for F & C that in various enumerated respects their client had broken both the consulting agreement and the earlier purchase agreement. Prima Paint's principal contention, so far as presently relevant, was that F & C had fraudulently represented that it was solvent and able to perform its contractual obligations, whereas it was in fact insolvent and intended to file a petition under Chapter XI of the Bankruptcy Act, 52 Stat. 905, 11 U.S.C. § 701 et seq., shortly after execution of the consulting agreement. Prima Paint noted that such a petition was filed by F & C on October 14, 1964, one week after the contract had been signed. F & C's response, on October 25, was to serve a "notice of intention to arbitrate." On November 12, three days before expiration of its time to answer this "notice," Prima Paint filed suit in the United States District Court for the Southern District of New York, seeking rescission of the consulting agreement on the basis of the alleged fraudulent inducement. The complaint asserted that the federal court had diversity jurisdiction.

Contemporaneously with the filing of its complaint, Prima Paint petitioned the District Court for an order enjoining F & C from proceeding with the arbitration. F & C cross-moved to stay the court action pending arbitration. F & C contended that the issue presented—whether there was fraud in the inducement of the consulting agreement—was a question for the arbitrators and not for the District Court. Cross-affidavits were filed on the merits. On behalf of Prima Paint, the charges in the complaint were reiterated. Affiants for F & C attacked the sufficiency of Prima Paint's allegations of fraud, denied that misrepresentations had been made during negotiations, and asserted that Prima Paint had relied exclusively upon delivery of the lists, the promise not to compete, and the availability of Mr. Jelin. They contended that Prima Paint had availed itself of these considerations for nearly a year without claiming "fraud," noting that Prima Paint was in no position to claim ignorance of the bankruptcy proceeding since it had participated therein in February of 1965.

The District Court granted F & C's motion to stay the action pending arbitration, holding that a charge of fraud in the inducement of a contract containing an arbitration clause as broad as this one was a question for the arbitrators and not for the court. The Court of Appeals for the Second Circuit dismissed Prima Paint's appeal. It held that the contract in question evidenced a transaction involving interstate commerce; that a claim of fraud in the inducement of the contract generally—as opposed to the arbitration clause itself—is for the arbitrators and not for the courts; and that this rule—one of "national substantive law"—governs even in the face of a contrary state rule. We agree, albeit for somewhat different reasons, and we affirm the decision below.

The key statutory provisions are §§ 2, 3, and 4 of the United States Arbitration Act of 1925. Section 2 provides that a written provision for arbitration "in any maritime transaction or a contract evidencing a transaction involving commerce . . . shall be valid, irrevocable, and enforceable, save upon such grounds as exist at law or in equity for the revocation of any contract." Section 3 requires a federal court in which suit has been brought "upon any issue referable to arbitration under an agreement in writing for such arbitration" to stay the court action pending arbitration once it is satisfied that the issue is arbitrable under the agreement. Section 4 provides a federal remedy for a party "aggrieved by the alleged failure, neglect, or refusal of another to arbitrate under a written agreement for arbitration," and directs the federal court to order arbitration once it is satisfied that an agreement for arbitration has been made and has not been honored.

Having determined that the contract in question is within the coverage of the Arbitration Act, we turn to the central issue in this case: whether a claim of fraud in the inducement of the entire contract is to be resolved by the federal court, or whether the matter is to be referred to the arbitrators. The courts of appeals have differed in their approach to this question. The view of the Court of Appeals for the Second Circuit, as expressed in this case and in others, is that—except where the parties otherwise intend—arbitration clauses as a matter of federal law are "separable" from the contracts in which they are embedded, and that where no claim is made that fraud was directed to the arbitration clause itself, a broad arbitration clause will be held to encompass arbitration of the claim that the contract itself was induced by fraud. The Court of Appeals for the First Circuit, on the other hand, has taken the view that the question of "severability" is one of state law, and that where a State regards such a clause as inseparable a claim of fraud in the inducement must be decided by the court. *Lummus Co. v. Commonwealth Oil Ref. Co.*, 280 F.2d 915, 923–924 (C.A. 1st Cir.), *cert. denied*, 364 U.S. 911 (1960).

With respect to cases brought in federal court involving maritime contracts or those evidencing transactions in "commerce," we think that Congress has provided an explicit answer. That answer is to be found in § 4 of the Act, which provides a remedy to a party seeking to compel compliance with an arbitration agreement. Under § 4, with respect to a matter within the jurisdiction of the federal courts save for the existence of an arbitration clause, the federal court is instructed to order arbitration to proceed once it is satisfied that "the making of the agreement for arbitration or the failure to comply [with the arbitration agreement] is not in issue." Accordingly, if the claim is fraud in the inducement of the arbitration clause itself— an issue which goes to the "making" of the agreement to arbitrate—the federal court may proceed to adjudicate it. But the statutory language does not permit the federal court to consider claims of fraud in the inducement of the contract generally. Section 4 does not expressly relate to situations like the present in which a stay is sought of a federal action in order that arbitration may proceed. But it is inconceivable that Congress intended the rule to differ depending upon which party to the arbitration agreement first invokes the assistance of a federal court. We hold, therefore, that in passing upon a § 3 application for a stay while the parties arbitrate, a federal court may consider only issues relating to the making and performance of the agreement to arbitrate. In so concluding, we not only honor the plain meaning of the statute but also the unmistakably clear congressional purpose that the arbitration procedure, when selected by the parties to a contract, be speedy and not subject to delay and obstruction in the courts.

In the present case no claim has been advanced by Prima Paint that F & C fraudulently induced it to enter into the agreement to arbitrate "any controversy or claim arising out of or relating to this Agreement, or the breach thereof." This contractual language is easily broad enough to encompass Prima Paint's claim that both execution and acceleration of the consulting agreement itself were procured by fraud. Indeed, no claim is made that Prima Paint ever intended that "legal" issues relating to the contract be excluded from arbitration, or that it was not entirely free so to contract. Federal courts are bound to apply rules enacted by Congress with respect to matters—here, a contract involving commerce—over which it has legislative power. The question which Prima Paint requested the District Court to adjudicate preliminarily to allowing arbitration to proceed is one not intended by Congress to delay the granting of a § 3 stay.

Accordingly, the decision below dismissing Prima Paint's appeal is affirmed.

Dissent

MR. JUSTICE BLACK, with whom MR. JUSTICE DOUGLAS and MR. JUSTICE STEWART join, dissenting.

The Court here holds that the United States Arbitration Act, 9 U.S.C. §§ 1–14, as a matter of federal substantive law, compels a party to a contract containing a written arbitration provision to carry out his "arbitration agreement" even though a court might, after a fair trial, hold the entire contract—including the arbitration agreement— void because of fraud in the inducement. The Court holds, what is to me fantastic, that the legal issue of a contract's voidness because of fraud is to be decided by persons designated to arbitrate factual controversies arising out of a valid contract between the parties. And the arbitrators who the Court holds are to adjudicate the legal validity of the contract need not even be lawyers, and in all probability will be nonlawyers, wholly unqualified to decide legal issues, and even if qualified to apply the law, not bound to do so. I am by no means sure that thus forcing a person to forgo his opportunity to try his legal issues in the courts where, unlike the situation in arbitration, he may have a jury trial and right to appeal, is not a denial of due process of law. I am satisfied, however, that Congress did not impose any such procedures in the Arbitration Act. And I am fully satisfied that a reasonable and fair reading of that Act's language and history shows that both Congress and the framers of the Act were at great pains to emphasize that nonlawyers designated to adjust and arbitrate factual controversies arising out of valid contracts would not trespass upon the courts' prerogative to decide the legal question of whether any legal contract exists upon which to base an arbitration.

I.

The agreement involved here is a consulting agreement in which Flood & Conklin agreed to perform certain services for and not to compete with Prima Paint. The agreement contained an arbitration clause providing that "any controversy or claim arising out of or relating to this Agreement . . . shall be settled by arbitration in the City of New York." F & C, contending that Prima had failed to make a payment under the contract, sent Prima a "Notice of Intention to Arbitrate" pursuant to the New York Arbitration Act. Invoking diversity jurisdiction, Prima brought this action in federal district court to rescind the entire consulting agreement on the ground of fraud. The fraud allegedly consisted of F & C's misrepresentation at the time the contract was made, that it was solvent and able to perform the agreement, while in fact it was completely insolvent. Prima alleged that it would not have made any contract at all with F & C but for this misrepresentation. Prima simply contended that there was never a meeting of minds between the parties. F & C moved to stay Prima's lawsuit for rescission pending arbitration of the fraud issue raised by Prima. The lower courts held that, as a matter of "national substantive law," the arbitration clause in the contract is "separable" from the rest of the contract and that allegations that go to the validity of the contract in general, as opposed to the arbitration clause in particular, are to be decided by the arbitrator, not the court.

The Court holds that the language of § 4 of the Act provides an "explicit answer" to the question of whether the arbitration clause is "separable" from the rest of the contract in which it is contained. Section 4 merely provides that the court must order arbitration if it is "satisfied that the making of the agreement for arbitration . . . is not in issue." That language, considered alone, far from providing an "explicit answer," merely poses the further question of what kind of allegations put the making of the arbitration agreement in issue. Since both the lower courts assumed that but for the federal Act, New York law might apply and that under New York law a general allegation of fraud in the inducement puts into issue the making of the agreement to arbitrate (considered inseparable under New York law from the rest of the contract), the Court necessarily holds that federal law determines whether certain allegations put the making of the arbitration agreement in issue. And the Court approves the Second Circuit's fashioning of a federal separability rule which overrides state law to the contrary. The Court thus holds that the Arbitration Act, designed to provide merely a procedural remedy which would not interfere with state substantive law, authorizes federal courts to fashion a federal rule to make arbitration clauses "separable" and valid. And the Court approves a rule which is not only contrary to state law, but contrary to the intention of the parties and to accepted principles of contract law—a rule which indeed elevates arbitration provisions above all other contractual provisions. As the Court recognizes, that result was clearly not intended by Congress.

Fraud, of course, is one of the most common grounds for revoking a contract. If the contract was procured by fraud, then, unless the defrauded party elects to affirm it, there is absolutely no contract, nothing to be arbitrated. Sections 2 and 3 of the Act assume the existence of a valid contract. They merely provide for enforcement where such a valid contract exists. These provisions were plainly designed to protect a person against whom arbitration is sought to be enforced from having to submit his legal issues as to validity of the contract to the arbitrator.

That is precisely the issue that a general allegation of fraud in the inducement raises: Prima contended that it would not have executed any contract, including the arbitration clause, if it were not for the fraudulent representations of F & C. Prima's agreement to an arbitration clause in a contract obtained by fraud was no more "voluntary" than an insured's or employee's agreement to an arbitration clause in a contract obtained by superior bargaining power.

Finally, it is clear to me from the bill's sponsors' understanding of the function of arbitration that they never intended that the issue of fraud in the inducement be resolved by arbitration. They recognized two special values of arbitration: (1) the expertise of an arbitrator to decide factual questions in regard to the day-to-day performance of contractual obligations, and (2) the speed with which arbitration, as contrasted to litigation, could resolve disputes over performance of contracts and thus mitigate the damages and allow the parties to continue performance under the contracts. Arbitration serves neither of these functions where a contract is sought to be rescinded on the ground of fraud. On the one hand, courts have far more expertise in resolving legal issues which go to the validity of a contract than do arbitrators. On the other hand, where a party seeks to rescind a contract and his allegation of fraud in the inducement is true, an arbitrator's speedy remedy of this wrong should never result in resumption of performance under the contract. And if the contract were not procured by fraud, the court, under the summary trial procedures provided by the Act, may determine with little delay that arbitration must proceed. The only advantage of submitting the issue of fraud to arbitration is for the arbitrators. Their compensation corresponds to the volume of arbitration they perform. If they determine that a contract is void because of fraud, there is nothing further for them to arbitrate. I think it raises serious questions of due process to submit to an arbitrator an issue which will determine his compensation. *Tumey v. Ohio*, 273 U.S. 510.

Thus, 35 years after the passage of the Arbitration Act, the Second Circuit completely rewrote it. Under its new formulation, § 2 now makes arbitration agreements enforceable "save upon such grounds as exist at federal law for the revocation of any contract." And under § 4, before enforcing an arbitration agreement, the district court must be satisfied that "the making of the agreement for arbitration, as a matter of federal law, is not in issue."

The avowed purpose of the Act was to place arbitration agreements "upon the same footing as other contracts." The separability rule which the Court applies to an arbitration clause does not result in equality between it and other clauses in the contract. I had always thought that a person who attacks a contract on the ground of fraud and seeks to rescind it has to seek rescission of the whole, not tidbits, and is not given the option of denying the existence of some clauses and affirming the existence of others. Here F & C agreed both to perform consulting services for Prima and not to compete with Prima. Would any court hold that those two agreements were separable, even though Prima in agreeing to pay F & C not to compete did not directly rely on F & C's representations of being solvent? The simple fact is that Prima would not have agreed to the covenant not to compete or to the arbitration clause but for F & C's fraudulent promise that it would be financially able to perform consulting services.

IV.

The Court's summary treatment of these issues has made it necessary for me to express my views at length. The plain purpose of the Act as written by Congress was this and no more: Congress wanted federal courts to enforce contracts to arbitrate and plainly said so in the Act. But Congress also plainly said that whether a contract containing an arbitration clause can be rescinded on the ground of fraud is to be decided by the courts and not by the arbitrators. Prima here challenged in the courts the validity of its alleged contract with F & C as a whole, not in fragments. If there has never been any valid contract, then there is not now and never has been anything to arbitrate.

I would reverse this case.

PRACTICE POINTER. What did the lawyer representing Prima Paint attack in this case? Was the challenge to the entire contract? Or was the challenge to the arbitration clause in the contract? Going forward, if you represented a client who had agreed to arbitrate her dispute but thought she had been defrauded in the making of the contract, what would you challenge having now studied *Prima Paint*? What type of evidence would you seek to support your case? What would you ask your witnesses and what would you hope to see in the contract drafting? As you proceed in the cases in this chapter, ask yourself if the lawyers challenging arbitration picked the right battle and what might you have done differently.

Notes and Questions

1. Prima Paint *and the Saving Clause. Prima Paint* takes a great deal of Section 2 of the FAA—what we reviewed last chapter as the "saving clause"—right off of the table. Instead of being able to attack arbitration on the basis that the arbitration clause is contained inside a flawed vessel, such as a contract subject to fraud or other illegality, now parties resisting arbitration must instead demonstrate that the flaw is found solely in the arbitration clause itself. No matter how fraudulently procured or ripe with incapacity or illegal issues the underlying contract may be, those very issues must be decided by the arbitrator, not the courts, unless the flaw can be pinpointed within the arbitration clause itself. This is the essence of the Severability Doctrine. The majority in *Prima Paint* held that "in passing upon a Section 3 application for a stay while the parties arbitrate, a federal court may consider only issues relating to the making and performance of the agreement to arbitrate."

   Is this a practical standard? In the particular context of commercial contracts, fraud isolated in the arbitration clause would seem to be a rare event. Consider the negotiation of a contract for the sale and purchase of a business, as existed in *Prima Paint*. Of the various commercial issues to resolve—purchase price, customer lists, history of past revenues and profits, warranties, and the myriad of other details that make up a business transaction—how much attention is the dispute resolution clause likely to receive? And even then, what is the likelihood of fraud occurring in those negotiations about a dispute resolution clause? To prove fraud in the making of the dispute resolution clause, would a party need an admission such as, "You thought that we had agreed to arbitration with one arbitrator in Paris, but at the last minute I tricked you and slipped in a clause requiring a three-arbitrator panel in Bermuda"? Is there room for *Prima Paint*/severability analysis in the commercial context beyond this limited scenario? What would be other examples of fraud in the making of the arbitration clause?

   What about in the consumer-to-business context? There, as we have seen and will concentrate upon even more in Chapter 4, consumer advocates and the plaintiff's class action bar attempt to use severability analysis to show that the arbitration clause itself is "illegal" or otherwise contrary to public policy. This argument is often accompanied by the companion argument that either the overall contract or the arbitration clause that sits within that contract is a contract of adhesion. Severability analysis is therefore critical to understanding the class action controversy that has dominated arbitration jurisprudence for the past decade.

Does this leave as much as Congress intended to leave in FAA Section 2? We focused in Chapter 2 on the presumption in favor of arbitration and on arbitration being a creature of contract. FAA Section 2 embodies both points, creating the presumption and then including the saving clause as Section 2's concluding proviso: "save upon such grounds as exist at law or in equity for the revocation of any contract." But in the wake of *Prima Paint*, is the saving clause as strong as Congress originally intended it to be if that proviso applies only to the arbitration clause rather than to the entire contract? Justice Black's dissent focused heavily on this point: "An arbitration agreement is to be enforced by a federal court unless the court, not the arbitrator, finds grounds 'at law or in equity for the revocation of any contract.' If the contract was procured by fraud, then, unless the defrauded party elects to affirm it, there is absolutely no contract, [and therefore] nothing to be arbitrated." That much seems indisputable, but should it affect who—arbitrator or judge—decides whether there was fraud in the making of the contract as a whole? Justice Black thought it a perversion of Section 2 to relegate to the courts only what he variously called "tidbits" and "fragments."

2. *The Dissent: Overtaken by Events, or More Relevant than Ever?* In 1967, when Justice Black penned his *Prima Paint* dissent, arbitration was less widespread (indeed, *Prima Paint* is one of the landmark cases ushering in arbitration to greater popularity), and so there was less of a professional arbitration bar. Arbitrators were not as likely to be lawyers. This led Justice Black to take a two-handed swat.

   First, Justice Black's dissent asserted his incredulity at the "fantastic" result that "the arbitrators who the court holds are to adjudicate the legal validity of the contract need not even be lawyers, and in all probability will be nonlawyers, wholly unqualified to decide legal issues." Are arbitrators "in all probability nonlawyers" today? The answer is much less so, but still sometimes, especially in particular situations. Consider so-called "earnout arbitrations," in which part of the purchase price for a business is held back until the financial performance of the acquired business can be measured after the sale. Frequently, the parties provide that any dispute about the post-closing adjustment should be decided by an accountant, not a lawyer. Assume that in such an arbitration, issues of fraud in the issuance of the financial statements arises. Should that fraud issue be decided by the accountant or the court? For examples of cases dealing with earnout arbitration, see *Hebbronville Lone Star Rentals, LLC v. Sunbelt Rentals Indus. Servs., LLC*, No. 1:16-CV-856-RP, 2017 U.S. Dist. LEXIS 37265 (W.D. Tex. Mar. 15, 2017) ("Had they been agreeing to arbitrate technical legal issues such as mutual mistake, it is unlikely they would have chosen an accountant to arbitrate those issues. Rather, the fact that they contracted for an accountant to be the arbitrator is consistent with Lone Star's position that the only issues reserved for arbitration were accounting issues, not legal ones."); *Roadrunner Intermodal Servs., LLC v. T.G.S. Transp., Inc.*, 2019 U.S. Dist. LEXIS 142355 (E.D. Cal., Aug. 21, 2019); *Sapp v. Indus Action Servs., LLC*, No. 19–912-RGA, 2020 U.S. Dist. LEXIS 94066 (D. Del. May 29, 2020); *HBMA Holdings, LLC v. LSF9 Stardust Holdings LLC*, No. 12806-VCMR, 2017 Del. Ch. LEXIS 841 (Dec. 8, 2017) (dealing with earnout arbitration); *SGS N. Am., Inc. v. Mullholand*, 135 N.E.3d 646 (Ind. Ct. App. 2019).

Second, Justice Black commented that even if non-lawyer arbitrators were for whatever reason qualified to decide a dispute, they would be cynically self-interested: "The only advantage of submitting the issue of fraud to arbitration is for arbitrators. Their compensation corresponds to the volume of arbitration they perform. If they determine that a contract is void because of fraud, there is nothing further for them to arbitrate." Is this criticism as valid today, assuming an arbitration bar of qualified and experienced lawyers who have an interest in reputational honesty beyond the paycheck for their latest arbitration? Or does this defense place lawyers on an undeserving pedestal? Put more bluntly: what is the likelihood that an arbitrator will throw a case out on the basis that the arbitration clause is fraudulent under section 2 and thereby end the arbitration—and his payment for that arbitration?

Moses Cone and *Prima Paint* stand as two of the most important cases in modern arbitration law. Their combination has made arbitration considerably more widespread. The former states the presumption in favor of enforcing arbitration clauses. The latter states that arbitrators themselves will have considerable say in determining their own existence unless the challenge to them is narrowly drawn and confined only to the arbitration clause. Much of the jurisprudence we will review springs from the combined force of these two decisions.

II. Federalism and Severability: *Buckeye*

CASE PREVIEW. We have seen that the Supreme Court made clear the pro-arbitration policy set out in *Moses Cone* is not merely a creature of federal law but is applicable in state courts as well. *See Southland, supra* Chapter 2, page 53. The same general principle applies to severability. If there was any question as to whether *Prima Paint*'s severability rule left any wiggle room in state court, the following case slammed that door shut.

Buckeye Check Cashing, Inc. v. Cardegna

546 U.S. 440, 126 S. Ct. 1204 (2006)

JUSTICE SCALIA delivered the opinion of the Court.

I.

Respondents John Cardegna and Donna Reuter entered into various deferred-payment transactions with petitioner Buckeye Check Cashing (Buckeye), in which they received cash in exchange for a personal check in the amount of the cash plus a finance charge. For each separate transaction they signed a "Deferred Deposit and Disclosure Agreement" (Agreement), which included the following arbitration provisions:

> "1. *Arbitration Disclosure* By signing this Agreement, you agree that if a dispute of any kind arises out of this Agreement or your application therefore or any instrument relating thereto, then either you or we or third-parties involved can choose to have that dispute resolved by binding arbitration as set forth in Paragraph 2 below. . . .
>
> 2. *Arbitration Provisions* Any claim, dispute, or controversy . . . arising from or relating to this Agreement . . . or the validity, enforceability, or scope of this Arbitration Provision or the entire Agreement (collectively 'Claim'), shall be resolved, upon the election of you or us or said third-parties, by binding arbitration. . . . This arbitration Agreement is made pursuant to a transaction involving interstate commerce, and shall be governed by the Federal Arbitration Act ('FAA'), 9 U.S.C. Sections 1–16. The arbitrator shall apply applicable substantive law constraint *[sic]* with the FAA and applicable statutes of limitations and shall honor claims of privilege recognized by law. . . .

Respondents brought this putative class action in Florida state court, alleging that Buckeye charged usurious interest rates and that the Agreement violated various Florida lending and consumer-protection laws, rendering it criminal on its face.

Buckeye moved to compel arbitration. The trial court denied the motion, holding that a court rather than an arbitrator should resolve a claim that a contract is illegal and void ab initio. The District Court of Appeal of Florida for the Fourth District reversed, holding that because respondents did not challenge the arbitration provision itself, but instead claimed that the entire contract was void, the agreement to arbitrate was enforceable, and the question of the contract's legality should go to the arbitrator.

Respondents appealed, and the Florida Supreme Court reversed, reasoning that to enforce an agreement to arbitrate in a contract challenged as unlawful " 'could breathe life into a contract that not only violates state law, but also is criminal in nature."

II.

A.

To overcome judicial resistance to arbitration, Congress enacted the Federal Arbitration Act (FAA), 9 U.S.C. §§1–16. Section 2 embodies the national policy favoring arbitration and places arbitration agreements on equal footing with all other contracts:

> "A written provision in . . . a contract . . . to settle by arbitration a controversy thereafter arising out of such contract . . . or an agreement in writing to submit to arbitration an existing controversy arising out of such a contract . . . shall be valid, irrevocable, and enforceable, save upon such grounds as exist at law or in equity for the revocation of any contract."

Challenges to the validity of arbitration agreements "upon such grounds as exist at law or in equity for the revocation of any contract" can be divided into two types. One type challenges specifically the validity of the agreement to arbitrate. The other challenges the contract as a whole, either on a ground that directly affects the entire agreement (e.g., the agreement was fraudulently induced), or on the ground that the illegality of one of the contract's provisions renders the whole contract invalid. Respondents' claim is of this second type. The crux of the complaint is that the contract as a whole (including its arbitration provision) is rendered invalid by the usurious finance charge.

In *Prima Paint Corp. v. Flood & Conklin Mfg. Co.*, 388 U.S. 395, 87 S. Ct. 1801, 18 L. Ed. 2d 1270 (1967), we addressed the question of who—court or arbitrator—decides these two types of challenges. The issue in the case was "whether a claim of fraud in the inducement of the entire contract is to be resolved by the federal court, or whether the matter is to be referred to the arbitrators." Guided by § 4 of the FAA, we held that "if the claim is fraud in the inducement of the arbitration clause itself—an issue which goes to the making of the agreement to arbitrate—the federal court may proceed to adjudicate it. But the statutory language does not permit the federal court to consider claims of fraud in the inducement of the contract generally." We rejected the view that the question of "severability" was one of state law, so that if state law held the arbitration provision not to be severable a challenge to the contract as a whole would be decided by the court.

Subsequently, in *Southland Corp.*, we held that the FAA "created a body of federal substantive law," which was "applicable in state and federal courts." We rejected the view that state law could bar enforcement of § 2, even in the context of state-law claims brought in state court.

B.

Prima Paint and *Southland* answer the question presented here by establishing three propositions. First, as a matter of substantive federal arbitration law, an arbitration provision is severable from the remainder of the contract. Second, unless the challenge is to the arbitration clause itself, the issue of the contract's validity is considered by the arbitrator in the first instance. Third, this arbitration law applies in state as well as federal courts. The parties have not requested, and we do not undertake, reconsideration of those holdings. Applying them to this case, we conclude that because respondents challenge the Agreement, but not specifically its arbitration provisions, those provisions are enforceable apart from the remainder of the contract. The challenge should therefore be considered by an arbitrator, not a court.

In declining to apply *Prima Paint*'s rule of severability, the Florida Supreme Court relied on the distinction between void and voidable contracts. "Florida public policy and contract law," it concluded, permit "no severable, or salvageable, parts of a contract found illegal and void under Florida law." *Prima Paint* makes this conclusion irrelevant. That case rejected application of state severability rules to the arbitration agreement without discussing whether the challenge at issue would have rendered the contract void or voidable. Indeed, the opinion expressly disclaimed any need to decide what state-law remedy was available.

Likewise in *Southland*, which arose in state court, we did not ask whether the several challenges made there—fraud, misrepresentation, breach of contract, breach of fiduciary duty, and violation of the California Franchise Investment Law—would render the contract void or voidable. We simply rejected the proposition that the enforceability of the arbitration agreement turned on the state legislature's judgment concerning the forum for enforcement of the state-law cause of action. So also here, we cannot accept the Florida Supreme Court's conclusion that enforceability of the arbitration agreement should turn on "Florida public policy and contract law," 894 So. 2d, at 864.

C.

Respondents assert that *Prima Paint*'s rule of severability does not apply in state court. They argue that *Prima Paint* interpreted only §§ 3 and 4—two of the FAA's procedural provisions, which appear to apply by their terms only in federal court—but not § 2, the only provision that we have applied in state court. This does not accurately describe *Prima Paint*. Although § 4, in particular, had much to do with Prima Paint's understanding of the rule of severability, this rule ultimately arises out of § 2, the FAA's substantive command that arbitration agreements be treated like all other contracts. The rule of severability establishes how this equal-footing guarantee for "a written [arbitration] provision" is to be implemented. Respondents' reading of *Prima Paint* as establishing nothing more than a federal-court rule of procedure also runs contrary to *Southland*'s understanding of that case. One of the bases for *Southland*'s application of § 2 in state court was precisely *Prima Paint*'s "reliance for [its] holding on Congress' broad power to fashion substantive rules under the Commerce Clause." ... Southland itself refused to "believe Congress intended to limit the Arbitration Act to disputes subject only to federal-court jurisdiction." ...

Respondents point to the language of § 2, which renders "valid, irrevocable, and enforceable" "a written provision in" or "an agreement in writing to submit to arbitration an existing controversy arising out of" a "contract." Since, respondents argue, the only arbitration agreements to which § 2 applies are those involving a "contract," and since an agreement void ab initio under state law is not a "contract," there is no "written provision" in or "controversy arising out of" a "contract," to which § 2 can apply. This argument echoes Justice Black's dissent in *Prima Paint*: "Sections 2 and 3 of the Act assume the existence of a valid contract. They merely provide for enforcement where such a valid contract exists.

We do not read "contract" so narrowly. The word appears four times in § 2. Its last appearance is in the final clause, which allows a challenge to an arbitration provision "upon such grounds as exist at law or in equity for the revocation of any contract." There can be no doubt that "contract" as used this last time must include contracts that later prove to be void. Otherwise, the grounds for revocation would be limited to those that rendered a contract voidable—which would mean (implausibly) that an arbitration agreement could be challenged as voidable but not as void. Because the sentence's final use of "contract" so obviously includes putative contracts, we will not read the same word earlier in the same sentence to have a more narrow meaning. We note that neither *Prima Paint* nor *Southland* lends support to respondents' reading; as we have discussed, neither case turned on whether the challenge at issue would render the contract voidable or void.

It is true, as respondents assert, that the *Prima Paint* rule permits a court to enforce an arbitration agreement in a contract that the arbitrator later finds to be void. But it is equally true that respondents' approach permits a court to deny effect to an arbitration provision in a contract that the court later finds to be perfectly enforceable. *Prima Paint* resolved this conundrum—and resolved it in favor of the separate enforceability of arbitration provisions. We reaffirm today that, regardless of whether the challenge is brought in federal or state court, a challenge to the validity of the contract as a whole, and not specifically to the arbitration clause, must go to the arbitrator.

The judgment of the Florida Supreme Court is reversed, and the case is remanded for further proceedings not inconsistent with this opinion.

It is so ordered.

Notes and Questions

1. Up to this point, you may have been thinking what the *Buckeye* court at the end of the case finally acknowledged: severability means that an arbitrator may arbitrate a case that ultimately fails because the arbitration clause violates Section 2. But the *Buckeye* court saw this as the lesser of two evils. To repeat:

   > It is true, as respondents assert, that the *Prima Paint* rule permits a court to enforce an arbitration agreement in a contract that the arbitrator later finds to be void. But it is equally true that respondents' approach permits a court to deny effect to an arbitration provision in a contract that the court later finds to be perfectly enforceable. *Prima Paint* resolved this conundrum—and resolved it in favor of the separate enforceability of arbitration provisions.

   Something has to give: either the arbitrator arbitrates a case without there being ultimate jurisdiction or the court denies effect to an arbitration clause that is ultimately proper. The Court made an election in favor of arbitration. Do you agree? What would happen if the Court had gone the other way, letting judges go first without imposing on the severability rule? Would it affect arbitration's use overall? Would it be more or less efficient?

2. Does the result in *Buckeye* come down to basic lawyering skills rather than the language of the agreement? *Buckeye* was issued 39 years after *Prima Paint*, which made clear the severability doctrine: that the only challenges courts (rather than arbitrators) would hear would be those based on the validity of the arbitration clause itself. Yet the lawyers in *Buckeye* chose to attack the entire contract: "[R]espondents did not challenge the arbitration provision itself *but instead claimed that the entire contract was void*." (emphasis added). The distinction the majority articulated between challenges to the contract "either on a ground that directly affects the entire agreement. . . . or on the ground that the illegality of one of the contract's provisions renders the whole contract invalid" made no difference—both were contract challenges rather than arbitration challenges. This made application of the *Prima Paint* rule

virtually automatic once the Supreme Court disposed of the federalism objection (*see* note 3 *infra*). Would the result have been different if the lawyers had pitched their attack on the clause itself? *Should* it have made a difference? Could this have been done on these facts?

3. *Buckeye* extended *Southland* and *Prima Paint* to all of the FAA, notably including Section 2. Does this mean that Section 2 is effectively dead, and state law invalidity claims cannot defeat arbitration? Or does it mean only that it falls to arbitrators and not courts to decide the Section 2 issues?

III. Delegation Clauses: Letting Arbitrators Decide Arbitrability

As much as the severability doctrine cut back on the court's role and elevated the arbitrator's role in determining when a dispute goes to arbitration, to some it did not go far enough. Disputes about the validity of the arbitration clause still went to the courts. **Absent express consent by the parties, arbitrability is a decision for the courts.** *Howsam v. Dean Witter Reynolds*, 537 U.S. 79, 83 (2002) (emphasis added). This leaves it to a judge to wade through the severability questions, including whether the attack was on the overall contract or the arbitration clause, and whether any of the saving clause factors were triggered.

Those are a lot of court questions for parties who presumably chose arbitration. And those questions can create a lot of procedural litigation and thus a lot of litigation costs—again, ironically, for parties who chose arbitration.

To deal with this problem, lawyers drafted so-called "delegation clauses," which "delegated" to an arbitrator the power to decide everything. Under a delegation clause, all issues of arbitrability are to be determined by the arbitrator. A party claiming that there is no arbitration because the underlying contract was procured by fraudulent inducement would, in a contract containing a delegation clause, have that dispute determined by the arbitrator. Most modern arbitration clauses, especially those in commercial contracts, now contain this form of clause, known variously as a "delegation clause" or "severability clause" or, taking its name from the next case, a *First Options* clause.

First Options of Chi., Inc. v. Kaplan

514 U.S. 938, 115 S. Ct. 1920 (1995)

JUSTICE BREYER delivered the opinion of the Court.

In this case we consider two questions about how courts should review certain matters under the federal Arbitration Act, 9 U.S.C. §1 et seq.: (1) how a district court should review an arbitrator's decision that the parties agreed to arbitrate a dispute, and (2) how a court of appeals should review a district court's decision confirming, or refusing to vacate, an arbitration award.

I.

The case concerns several related disputes between, on one side, First Options of Chicago, Inc., a firm that clears stock trades on the Philadelphia Stock Exchange, and, on the other side, three parties: Manuel Kaplan; his wife, Carol Kaplan; and his wholly owned investment company, MK Investments, Inc. (MKI), whose trading account First Options cleared. The disputes center on a "workout" agreement, embodied in four separate documents, which governs the "working out" of debts to First Options that MKI and the Kaplans incurred as a result of the October 1987 stock market crash. In 1989, after entering into the agreement, MKI lost an additional $1.5 million. First Options then took control of, and liquidated, certain MKI assets; demanded immediate payment of the entire MKI debt; and insisted that the Kaplans personally pay any deficiency. When its demands went unsatisfied, First Options sought arbitration by a panel of the Philadelphia Stock Exchange.

MKI, having signed the only workout document (out of four) that contained an arbitration clause, accepted arbitration. The Kaplans, however, who had not personally signed that document, denied that their disagreement with First Options was arbitrable and filed written objections to that effect with the arbitration panel. The arbitrators decided that they had the power to rule on the merits of the parties' dispute, and did so in favor of First Options. The Kaplans then asked the Federal District Court to vacate the arbitration award, see 9 U.S.C. § 10, and First Options requested its confirmation, see § 9. The court confirmed the award. Nonetheless, on appeal the Court of Appeals for the Third Circuit agreed with the Kaplans that their dispute was not arbitrable; and it reversed the District Court's confirmation of the award against them. 19 F.3d 1503 (1994).

We granted certiorari to consider the standards that the Court of Appeals used to review the determination that the Kaplans' dispute with First Options was arbitrable. First, the Court of Appeals said that courts "should independently decide whether an arbitration panel has jurisdiction over the merits of any particular dispute." 19 F.3d at 1509 (emphasis added). First Options asked us to decide whether this is so (i.e., whether courts, in "reviewing the arbitrators' decision on arbitrability," should "apply a de novo standard of review or the more deferential standard applied to arbitrators' decisions on the merits") when the objecting party "submitted the issue to the arbitrators for decision."

II.

The first question—the standard of review applied to an arbitrator's decision about arbitrability—is a narrow one. To understand just how narrow, consider three types of disagreement present in this case. First, the Kaplans and First Options disagree about whether the Kaplans are personally liable for MKI's debt to First Options.

That disagreement makes up the merits of the dispute. Second, they disagree about whether they agreed to arbitrate the merits. That disagreement is about the arbitrability of the dispute. Third, they disagree about who should have the primary power to decide the second matter. Does that power belong primarily to the arbitrators (because the court reviews their arbitrability decision deferentially) or to the court (because the court makes up its mind about arbitrability independently)? We consider here only this third question.

Although the question is a narrow one, it has a certain practical importance. That is because a party who has not agreed to arbitrate will normally have a right to a court's decision about the merits of its dispute (say, as here, its obligation under a contract). But, where the party has agreed to arbitrate, he or she, in effect, has relinquished much of that right's practical value. The party still can ask a court to review the arbitrator's decision, but the court will set that decision aside only in very unusual circumstances. Hence, who—court or arbitrator—has the primary authority to decide whether a party has agreed to arbitrate can make a critical difference to a party resisting arbitration.

We believe the answer to the "who" question (i.e., the standard-of-review question) is fairly simple. Just as the arbitrability of the merits of a dispute depends upon whether the parties agreed to arbitrate that dispute, so the question "who has the primary power to decide arbitrability" turns upon what the parties agreed about that matter. Did the parties agree to submit the arbitrability question itself to arbitration? If so, then the court's standard for reviewing the arbitrator's decision about that matter should not differ from the standard courts apply when they review any other matter that parties have agreed to arbitrate. *See AT&T Technologies, Inc. v. Communications Workers*, 475 U.S. 643, 649 (1986) (parties may agree to arbitrate arbitrability); *Steelworkers v. Warrior & Gulf Nav. Co.*, 363 U.S. 574, 583, n. 7 (1960) (same). That is to say, the court should give considerable leeway to the arbitrator, setting aside his or her decision only in certain narrow circumstances. *See, e.g.*, 9 U.S.C. § 10.

If, on the other hand, the parties did not agree to submit the arbitrability question itself to arbitration, then the court should decide that question just as it would decide any other question that the parties did not submit to arbitration, namely, independently. These two answers flow inexorably from the fact that arbitration is simply a matter of contract between the parties; it is a way to resolve those disputes—but only those disputes— that the parties have agreed to submit to arbitration.

We agree with First Options, therefore, that a court must defer to an arbitrator's arbitrability decision when the parties submitted that matter to arbitration. Nevertheless, that conclusion does not help First Options win this case. That is because a fair and complete answer to the standard-of-review question requires a word about how a court should decide whether the parties have agreed to submit the arbitrability issue to arbitration. And, that word makes clear that the Kaplans did not agree to arbitrate arbitrability here.

When deciding whether the parties agreed to arbitrate a certain matter (including arbitrability), courts generally (though with a qualification we discuss below) should apply ordinary state-law principles that govern the formation of contracts.

This Court, however, has (as we just said) added an important qualification, applicable when courts decide whether a party has agreed that arbitrators should decide arbitrability: Courts should not assume that the parties agreed to arbitrate arbitrability unless there is "clea[r] and unmistakabl[e]" evidence that they did so. . . . In this manner the law treats silence or ambiguity about the question "who (primarily) should decide arbitrability" differently from the way it treats silence or ambiguity about the question "whether a particular merits-related dispute is arbitrable because it is within the scope of a valid arbitration agreement"—for in respect to this latter question the law reverses the presumption. *See Mitsubishi Motors, supra*, at 626 (" 'Any doubts concerning the scope of arbitrable issues should be resolved in favor of arbitration' ") (*quoting Moses H. Cone Memorial Hospital v. Mercury Constr. Corp.*, 460 U.S. 1, 24–25 (1983)).

But, this difference in treatment is understandable. The latter question arises when the parties have a contract that provides for arbitration of some issues. In such circumstances, the parties likely gave at least some thought to the scope of arbitration. And, given the law's permissive policies in respect to arbitration, one can understand why the law would insist upon clarity before concluding that the parties did not want to arbitrate a related matter. On the other hand, the former question—the "who (primarily) should decide arbitrability" question—is rather arcane. A party often might not focus upon that question or upon the significance of having arbitrators decide the scope of their own powers. And, given the principle that a party can be forced to arbitrate only those issues it specifically has agreed to submit to arbitration, one can understand why courts might hesitate to interpret silence or ambiguity on the "who should decide arbitrability" point as giving the arbitrators that power, for doing so might too often force unwilling parties to arbitrate a matter they reasonably would have thought a judge, not an arbitrator, would decide. *Ibid. See generally Dean Witter Reynolds Inc. v. Byrd*, 470 U.S. 213, 219–220 (1985) (Arbitration Act's basic purpose is to "ensure judicial enforcement of privately made agreements to arbitrate").

On the record before us, First Options cannot show that the Kaplans clearly agreed to have the arbitrators decide (i.e., to arbitrate) the question of arbitrability. First Options relies on the Kaplans' filing with the arbitrators a written memorandum objecting to the arbitrators' jurisdiction. But merely arguing the arbitrability issue to an arbitrator does not indicate a clear willingness to arbitrate that issue, i.e., a willingness to be effectively bound by the arbitrator's decision on that point. To the contrary, insofar as the Kaplans were forcefully objecting to the arbitrators deciding their dispute with First Options, one naturally would think that they did not want the arbitrators to have binding authority over them. This conclusion draws added support from (1) an obvious explanation for the Kaplans' presence before the arbitrators (i.e., that MKI, Mr. Kaplan's wholly owned firm, was arbitrating workout agreement matters);

and (2) Third Circuit law that suggested that the Kaplans might argue arbitrability to the arbitrators without losing their right to independent court review.

First Options makes several counterarguments: (1) that the Kaplans had other ways to get an independent court decision on the question of arbitrability without arguing the issue to the arbitrators (e.g., by trying to enjoin the arbitration, or by refusing to participate in the arbitration and then defending against a court petition First Options would have brought to compel arbitration, see 9 U.S.C. § 4); (2) that permitting parties to argue arbitrability to an arbitrator without being bound by the result would cause delay and waste in the resolution of disputes; and (3) that the Arbitration Act therefore requires a presumption that the Kaplans agreed to be bound by the arbitrators' decision, not the contrary. The first of these points, however, while true, simply does not say anything about whether the Kaplans intended to be bound by the arbitrators' decision. The second point, too, is inconclusive, for factual circumstances vary too greatly to permit a confident conclusion about whether allowing the arbitrator to make an initial (but independently reviewable) arbitrability determination would, in general, slow down the dispute resolution process. And, the third point is legally erroneous, for there is no strong arbitration-related policy favoring First Options in respect to its particular argument here. After all, the basic objective in this area is not to resolve disputes in the quickest manner possible, no matter what the parties' wishes, but to ensure that commercial arbitration agreements, like other contracts, "are enforced according to their terms," and according to the intentions of the parties. That policy favors the Kaplans, not First Options.

We conclude that, because the Kaplans did not clearly agree to submit the question of arbitrability to arbitration, the Court of Appeals was correct in finding that the arbitrability of the Kaplan/First Options dispute was subject to independent review by the courts.

The judgment of the Court of Appeals is affirmed.

Notes and Questions

1. *Of Presumptions and Delegation Clauses.* Presuming arbitration is one thing, but presuming delegation is quite another. Justice Breyer was frank in *First Options* that he was not following the standard pro-arbitration presumptions that flow from *Moses Cone* when he considered the particular issue of a delegation clause. To Justice Breyer, a presumption in favor of delegation of severability to the arbitrator would be unfair, because it would presume that parties have struck a bargain that he assumed the parties never even thought about. Parties may consider arbitration itself, but the separate question of delegating arbitrability to an arbitrator was, as Justice Breyer put it, "rather arcane" and so "[a]

party often might not focus upon that question or upon the significance of having arbitrators decide the scope of their own powers."

Thus, a mere presumption will not suffice, and hence, the "clear and convincing" test for delegation clauses was born. Return, with this in mind, to the Supreme Court's 2019 decision in *Lamps Plus*, which rejected standard contract presumptions like "construe against the drafter" and instructed courts to presume in favor of arbitration, contract interpretation tools notwithstanding.

As a result, a party is taken *doubly* out of court, first in the arbitration itself and then in that arbitration clause's delegation clause. The delegation clause is a jurisdiction-divesting rule. The guard against this remains Justice Breyer's admonition that the evidence in favor of the delegation must be clear and unambiguous.

The present state of play on presumptions, and their occasional absence, may be summed up with the following:

- arbitration is a contract (multiple SCOTUS cases)
- use contract tools to find in favor of arbitration (*Moses Cone*)
- but don't use those interpretive tools where they will find against arbitration (*Lamps Plus*)
- and in any event erect a higher standard for delegation clauses (*First Options*)

Does a consistent interpretive strategy emerge from the above?

2. *Drafting the Delegation Clause.* The result of a delegation clause in an agreement to arbitrate is the creation of three separate contracts, each within the other:

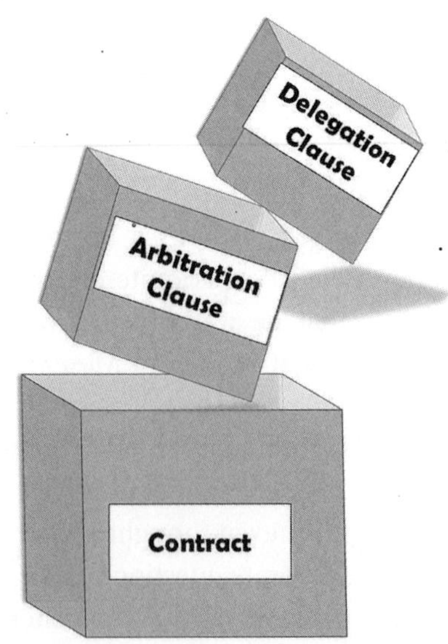

Once the Supreme Court gave its stamp of approval to delegation clauses in *First Options*, they became a common feature in arbitration practice (and drafting). The practical and real-life effect is that a consumer who likely never read the fine print of his arbitration clause may be surprised to learn that he cannot contest his cell phone bill in small claims court, and that if he has a problem with *that* fact, he may be all the more surprised and disturbed to learn that he cannot even challenge that delegation in court, because his cell phone agreement contains a delegation clause within the arbitration agreement that lets an arbitrator decide her own jurisdiction.

The high standard plays out in practice because courts apply the *First Options* test with extreme scrutiny. Consider the following excerpt: "[T]he arbitrators shall be empowered to interpret and determine the applicability of all provisions under this Code which interpretation shall be final and binding upon the parties." *Securities Serv. Network v. Cromwell*, No. 94–5778, 1995 U.S. App. LEXIS 22540, at *7 (6th Cir. Aug. 1, 1996). Though the arbitration clause here appears to empower the arbitrators to determine all "applicability," the Sixth Circuit Court of Appeals ruled this language alone was not enough to constitute the "requisite clear and unmistakable evidence" needed to prove "the parties intended and agreed to arbitrate the issue of arbitrability." *Id.* (citing *Edward D. Jones & Co. v. Sorrells*, 957 F.2d 509, 514, n.7 (7th Cir. 1992)) (internal quotations omitted).

So, what, exactly, is clear enough? Plainly, there must be some reference to arbitration itself or at least to "this arbitration clause." Consider this Airbnb contract delegation clause: "[I]f there is a dispute about whether this Arbitration Agreement can be enforced or applies to our Dispute, you and Airbnb agree that the arbitrator will decide that issue." *Dunbar v. Airbnb, Inc.*, No. 19–00648 JMS-WRP,, 2020 U.S. Dist. LEXIS 56828, at *7 (D. Haw. Apr. 1, 2020). The court found this to be a proper delegation clause since the language was "neither silent nor ambiguous," as it "specifically designates the arbitrator to decide disputes about whether the arbitration agreement is enforceable or applicable (that is, arbitrable)." *Id.* at *8.

3. *Delegation Clauses Within Institutional Rules.* We saw in Chapter 1 that parties can elect to have their arbitrations take place under the auspices of arbitration "institutions" such as the American Arbitration Association or JAMS. We saw as well that these institutions have a set of procedural rules.

   The selection of these rules can amount to a delegation clause in itself, because within these rules are provisions that allow an arbitrator to decide her jurisdiction:

American Arbitration Association, Commercial Arbitration Rules

R-7. Jurisdiction (a) The arbitrator shall have the power to rule on his or her own jurisdiction, including any objections with respect to the existence, scope, or validity of the arbitration agreement or to the arbitrability of any claim or counterclaim.

JAMS Comprehensive Arbitration Rules & Procedures

Rule 11. Interpretation of Rules and Jurisdictional Challenges

(b) Jurisdictional and arbitrability disputes, including disputes over the formation, existence, validity, interpretation or scope of the agreement under which Arbitration is sought, and who are proper Parties to the Arbitration, shall be submitted to and ruled on by the Arbitrator. The Arbitrator has the authority to determine jurisdiction and arbitrability issues as a preliminary matter.

Should this be enough? Keeping in mind *First Options*' commandment that a delegation of arbitrability to an arbitrator must be "clear and unmistakable," does a reference in an arbitration clause to institutional rules—which themselves contain the delegation—sufficient? Return to the example of the consumer with a cell phone contract whose contract provides for arbitration and now, this time, instead of stating that all disputes about arbitrability shall be decided by the arbitrator, states simply that the arbitration shall be governed by the Commercial Arbitration Rules of the American Arbitration Association. Is this a clear and unmistakable delegation?

The circuit courts have answered this question with a striking degree of unanimity. They embrace the proposition that reference to institutional rules that themselves delegate arbitrability to the arbitrator is sufficient to satisfy the *First Options* standard—even if the arbitration clause itself is silent as to arbitrability disputes. The following case summarizes that authority.

Vergara v. Nintendo

No. 19 C 6374, 2020 U.S. Dist. LEXIS 89412
(N.D. Ill. May 21, 2020)

FEINERMAN, United States District Judge.

Zachary Vergara brought this putative class action in the Circuit Court of Cook County, Illinois, against Nintendo of America Inc., alleging various state law torts. Nintendo's motion to compel arbitration is granted, with the understanding that Vergara may pursue his claims in this court if the arbitrator finds that they are not arbitrable, and Vergara's motion for leave to amend is denied without prejudice as moot.

On behalf of himself and a putative class, Vergara alleges that he bought Nintendo's "Switch" videogame console and that the "Joy-Con" controllers included with his purchase are defective. In conjunction with the purchase, Vergara and Nintendo entered into an End-User License Agreement ("EULA").

Two provisions are pertinent here. Section 7(A) provides: "Any matter we are unable to resolve and all disputes or claims arising out of or relating to this Agreement, including its formation, enforceability, performance, or breach (each, a 'Claim'), with the exception of the matters described in section 7(C) below, shall be finally settled by binding arbitration administered by the American Arbitration Association [("AAA")] in accordance with the provisions of its Commercial Arbitration Rules and the supplementary procedures for consumer-related disputes. "Section 7(C), in turn, provides in relevant part that "Section 7(A) does not apply to any Claim . . . that may be brought in small-claims court."

Vergara does not dispute that Section 7(A) of the EULA is a valid, written arbitration provision. Vergara instead maintains that Section 7(A) does not extend to this suit because his claims fall within the Section 7(C) carve-out for claims that could have been brought in small claims court. Nintendo responds that it is up to the arbitrator, not the court, to interpret Sections 7(A) and 7(C) and to determine whether Vergara's claims must be arbitrated.

As a general rule, courts rather than arbitrators decide "[t]he question whether the parties have submitted a particular dispute to arbitration, *i.e.*, the '*question of arbitrability*.'" *Howsam v. Dean Witter Reynolds, Inc.*, 537 U.S. 79, 83 (2002) An exception to the general rule applies where there is a "clear[] and unmistakabl[e]" agreement between the parties that the arbitrator will resolve disputes about arbitrability.

Nintendo argues that the EULA's arbitration clause, by incorporating the AAA's Commercial Arbitration Rules, expressly delegates to the arbitrator the parties' disputes concerning the arbitrability of particular claims. Vergara does not respond to the argument, thereby forfeiting the point. *See G & S Holdings LLC v. Cont'l Cas. Co.*, 697 F.3d 534, 538 (7th Cir. 2012) ("We have repeatedly held that a party waives an argument by failing to make it before the district court. That is true whether it is an affirmative argument in support of a motion to dismiss or an argument establishing that dismissal is inappropriate").

Nintendo is correct on the merits in any event. As noted, Section 7(A) of the EULA states that claims within its scope "shall be finally settled by binding arbitration administered by the [AAA] in accordance with the provisions of its Commercial Arbitration Rules and the supplementary procedures for consumer-related disputes." AAA Rule 7(a), in turn, expressly delegates to the arbitrator questions of arbitrability: "The arbitrator shall have the power to rule on his or her own jurisdiction, including any objections with respect to the existence, *scope*, or validity of the arbitration agreement or to *the arbitrability of any claim or counterclaim*." American Arbitration Association, *AAA Commercial Rule 7(a)*, http://www.adr.org/sites/default/files/CommercialRules_Web.pdf (last visited May 20, 2020) (emphasis added).

The Seventh Circuit has not decided whether an arbitration agreement's incorporation of the AAA Rules qualifies as a "clear and unmistakable" agreement to arbitrate arbitrability. The eight circuits to have directly addressed the question, though, all answered that question in the affirmative. *See Dish Network L.L.C. v. Ray*, 900 F.3d 1240, 1246 (10th Cir. 2018); *Brennan v. Opus Bank*, 796 F.3d 1125, 1130 (9th Cir. 2015); *Petrofac, Inc. v. DynMcDermott Petrol. Ops. Co.*, 687 F.3d 671, 675 (5th Cir. 2012); *Fallo v. High-Tech Inst.*, 559 F.3d 874, 878 (8th Cir. 2009); *Awuah v. Coverall* N. *Am., Inc.*, 554 F.3d 7, 11–12 (1st Cir. 2009); *Qualcomm Inc. v. Nokia* Corp., 466 F.3d 1366, 1373 (Fed. Cir. 2006), *abrogated* on *other* grounds by *Henry Schein, Inc. v. Archer & White Sales, Inc.*, 139 S. Ct. 524 (2019); *Terminix Int'l Co. v. Palmer Ranch Ltd. P'ship*, 432 F.3d 1327, 1332 (11th Cir. 2005); *Contec Corp. v. Remote Sol. Co.*, 398 F.3d 205, 211 (2d Cir. 2005). This court agrees with the consensus. *See Allscripts Healthcare, LLC v. Etransmedia Tech., Inc.*, 188 F. Supp. 3d 696, 701–02 (N.D. Ill. 2016).

Accordingly, by entering into an arbitration agreement that incorporates the AAA Rules, the parties delegated to the arbitrator the question whether Vergara's claims must be arbitrated.

Vergara correctly observes that a party cannot be required to arbitrate a dispute that he has not agreed to submit to arbitration. Doc. 24 at 3 (citing *AT&T Techs.*, 475 U.S. at 648). That principle, however, does not mandate that the court, rather than the arbitrator, decide whether his claims must be arbitrated. Vergara's observation elides the distinction between two separate questions: (1) whether the EULA's arbitration provision covers his claims; and (2) whether that arbitrability question must be decided by the court or the arbitrator. The answer to the second question is that the arbitrator decides—that is, Vergara agreed to arbitrate the scope of the arbitration provision—which means that it is up to the arbitrator to answer the first question. *See Local 744, Int'l Bhd. of Teamsters v. Hinckley & Schmitt, Inc.*, 76 F.3d 162, 165 (7th Cir. 1996) ("We do not mean to say that situations do not exist where it is proper for an arbitrator, and not a court, to decide whether a dispute is arbitrable. The Supreme Court has expressly recognized that parties may agree to 'arbitrate the arbitrability issue.'") (quoting *AT&T Techs.*, 475 U.S. at 648).

Conclusion

Nintendo's motion to compel arbitration is granted. The parties must submit Vergara's claims to arbitration administered by the AAA. This suit is stayed pending resolution of the arbitration. If the arbitrator decides that Vergara's claims are not arbitrable, the court will reopen these judicial proceedings on Vergara's motion. Because the amendments Vergara proposes to make to his complaint would not alter this result, his motion for leave to file an amended complaint is denied without prejudice as moot.

Notes and Questions

1. Since delegation clauses can be grafted onto an arbitration agreement simply by the selection of institutional rules, this becomes a further decision in the question we covered in Chapter 1, regarding whether you should make your arbitration "institutional" or "ad hoc" (non-institutional). Can a party who otherwise wants an institution to run the arbitration but who does not want an arbitration clause opt out of that portion of the rules? How does this affect the question we have now seen multiple times regarding the treatment of arbitration as a contract? Can a contract to arbitrate be a mixture of party-drafted clauses and piecemeal selections from the institution's rules? *See also* William Park, *Challenging Arbitral Jurisdiction: The Role of Institutional Rules*, No. 15–40 B.U. SCH. L., PUB. L. RES. PAPER, https://scholarship.law/bu.edu/faculty_scholarship/11.
2. What happens if an institution changes its rules after the parties adopt those rules? Which rules govern: those existing at the time the contract was made or at the time the dispute arose?

PRACTICE POINTER. In choosing institutional rules, parties may wish to guard against unwanted or unknown changes by specifying "the Rules of [institution] in effect as of the execution of this Agreement."

Class Problem

FruitCo purchases from FarmCo a large quantity of cherries every year. Two years ago, a blight on cherry trees caused significant damage to both quality and quantity.

FruitCo sued for fraud under the parties' contractual arbitration clause, alleging that FarmCo was fraudulent in not disclosing the fruit's condition before shipment. FarmCo argued that because the suit was for fraud rather than for breach of contract, the narrow arbitration clause ("any suits arising under this contract") did not extend to fraud claims. It took six months, and a six-figure legal bill, before a judge finally ordered the case to arbitration.

The parties then settled their dispute under a confidential settlement agreement that included as consideration (a) FarmCo making a payment to FruitCo and (b) the parties doing business for another two years. That period is now over, and the parties are negotiating a new contract. Suspicion remains in the air. FruitCo has asked you to draft the arbitration clause and to include a delegation clause because "the last thing I want is to be in court again for six months without the dispute moving forward." Given this history, how would you draft the clause?

IV. Recent Jurisprudence on Delegation Clauses

First Options has had a significant impact on modern arbitration practice. It did not carve out new ground that was not expressly in the FAA, such as was done in *Prima Paint* and *Moses Cone*. But it did affect the way lawyers draft arbitration clauses and, in the process, insulate arbitration cases all the more from judicial review. If arbitration is a contract—as the cases you have just reviewed repeat over and over—and that contract says that any review of it, as to any portion and involving any issue, must be resolved by an arbitrator and not the courts, then the seal around arbitration becomes all the tighter. There are almost metaphysical dimensions to this—how can an arbitrator juridically "exist" if the clause that creates her role is itself legally infirm? But such are the impacts of the severability doctrine.

Yet the central question explored in this book—the tug-of-war between courts and arbitrators over the life of an arbitration—returns. One might reasonably think that with severability enshrined such that courts look only at whether there was fraud in the arbitration clause, and then with delegation clauses enshrined such that an arbitrator can be delegated that inquiry as well, there would be no room left for courts. If a delegation clause places upon the arbitrator the entire arbitrability inquiry—whether the parties agreed to arbitrate the dispute, the limits of the clause, and whether any part of the clause or its "host" contract is objectionable—then what is left for a court? Have we not "severed" any role at all for the courts in this, the initial phase of an arbitration, when the pieces are being set up on the board?

Apparently not. In two recent cases, the United States Supreme Court considered delegation clauses in situations where there was a question as to whether the arbitration was legitimate at all. Both cases had delegation clauses of a sort, yet in both cases the Court's ruling rendered the clause irrelevant and seized control of the threshold jurisdictional question itself. As you read these cases, consider where the limits of an arbitrator's power even under the clearest of delegation clauses now lie.

New Prime Inc. v. Oliveira

139 S. Ct. 532 (2019)

JUSTICE GORSUCH delivered the opinion of the Court.

The Federal Arbitration Act requires courts to enforce private arbitration agreements. But like most laws, this one bears its qualifications. Among other things, §1 says that "nothing herein" may be used to compel arbitration in disputes involving the "contracts of employment" of certain transportation workers. 9 U.S.C. §1. And that qualification has sparked these questions: When a contract delegates questions of arbitrability to an arbitrator, must a court leave disputes over the application of §1's exception for the arbitrator to resolve? And does the term "contracts of employment" refer only to contracts between employers and employees, or does it also reach contracts with independent contractors? Because courts across the country have disagreed on the answers to these questions, we took this case to resolve them.

I.

New Prime is an interstate trucking company and Dominic Oliveira works as one of its drivers. But, at least on paper, Mr. Oliveira isn't an employee; the parties' contracts label him an independent contractor. Those agreements also instruct that any disputes arising out of the parties' relationship should be resolved by an arbitrator—even disputes over the scope of the arbitrator's authority.

Eventually, of course, a dispute did arise. In a class action lawsuit in federal court, Mr. Oliveira argued that New Prime denies its drivers lawful wages. The company may call its drivers independent contractors. But, Mr. Oliveira alleged, in reality New Prime treats them as employees and fails to pay the statutorily due minimum wage. In response to Mr. Oliveira's complaint, New Prime asked the court to invoke its statutory authority under the Act and compel arbitration according to the terms found in the parties' agreements.

That request led to more than a little litigation of its own. Even when the parties' contracts mandate arbitration, Mr. Oliveira observed, the Act doesn't *always* authorize a court to enter an order compelling it. In particular, §1 carves out from the Act's coverage "contracts of employment of . . . workers engaged in foreign or interstate commerce." And at least for purposes of this collateral dispute, Mr. Oliveira submitted, it doesn't matter whether you view him as an employee or independent contractor. Either way, his agreement to drive trucks for New Prime qualifies as a "contract[ ] of employment of . . . [a] worker[ ] engaged in . . . interstate commerce." Accordingly, Mr. Oliveira argued, the Act supplied the district court with no authority to compel arbitration in this case.

Naturally, New Prime disagreed. Given the extraordinary breadth of the parties' arbitration agreement, the company insisted that any question about §1's application belonged for the arbitrator alone to resolve. Alternatively and assuming a court could address the question, New Prime contended that the term "contracts of employment" refers only to contracts that establish an employer-employee relationship. And because Mr. Oliveira is, in fact as well as form, an independent contractor, the company argued, §1's exception doesn't apply; the rest of the statute does; and the district court was (once again) required to order arbitration.

Ultimately, the district court and the First Circuit sided with Mr. Oliveira. 857 F. 3d 7 (2017). The court of appeals held, first, that in disputes like this a court should resolve whether the parties' contract falls within the Act's ambit or §1's exclusion before invoking the statute's authority to order arbitration. Second, the court of appeals held that §1's exclusion of certain "contracts of employment" removes from the Act's coverage not only employer-employee contracts but also contracts involving independent contractors. So under any account of the parties' agreement in this case, the court held, it lacked authority under the Act to order arbitration.

II.

In approaching the first question for ourselves, one thing becomes clear immediately. While a court's authority under the Arbitration Act to compel arbitration may be considerable, it isn't unconditional. If two parties agree to arbitrate future disputes between them and one side later seeks to evade the deal, §§3 and 4 of the Act often require a court to stay litigation and compel arbitration "accord[ing to] the terms" of the parties' agreement. But this authority doesn't extend to *all* private contracts, no matter how emphatically they may express a preference for arbitration.

Instead, antecedent statutory provisions limit the scope of the court's powers under §§3 and 4. Section 2 provides that the Act applies only when the parties' agreement to arbitrate is set forth as a "written provision in any maritime transaction or a contract evidencing a transaction involving commerce." And §1 helps define §2's terms. Most relevant for our purposes, §1 warns that "nothing" in the Act "shall apply" to "contracts of employment of seamen, railroad employees, or any other class of workers engaged in foreign or interstate commerce." Why this very particular qualification? By the time it adopted the Arbitration Act in 1925, Congress had already prescribed alternative employment dispute resolution regimes for many transportation workers. And it seems Congress "did not wish to unsettle" those arrangements in favor of whatever arbitration procedures the parties' private contracts might happen to contemplate. *Circuit City Stores, Inc.* v. *Adams*, 532 U.S. 105, 121, 121 S. Ct. 1302, 149 L. Ed. 2d 234 (2001).

Given the statute's terms and sequencing, we agree with the First Circuit that a court should decide for itself whether §1's "contracts of employment" exclusion applies before ordering arbitration. After all, to invoke its statutory powers under §§3 and 4 to stay litigation and compel arbitration according to a contract's terms, a court must first know whether the contract itself falls within or beyond the boundaries of §§1 and 2. The parties' private agreement may be crystal clear and require arbitration of every question under the sun, but that does not necessarily mean the Act authorizes a court to stay litigation and send the parties to an arbitral forum.

Nothing in our holding on this score should come as a surprise. We've long stressed the significance of the statute's sequencing. In *Bernhardt* v. *Polygraphic Co. of America*, 350 U.S. 198, 201–202, 76 S. Ct. 273, 100 L. Ed. 199 (1956), we recognized that "Sections 1, 2, and 3 [and 4] are integral parts of a whole. . . . [Sections] 1 and 2 define the field in which Congress was legislating," and §§3 and 4 apply only to contracts covered by those provisions. In *Circuit City*, we acknowledged that "Section 1 exempts from the [Act] . . . contracts of employment of transportation workers." 532 U.S., at 119. And in *Southland Corp.* v. *Keating*, 465 U.S. 1, 10–11, 104 S. Ct. 852, 79 L. Ed. 2d 1, and n. 5 (1984), we noted that "the enforceability of arbitration provisions" under §§3 and 4 depends on whether those provisions are "part of a written maritime contract or a contract 'evidencing a transaction involving commerce'" under §2—which, in turn, depends on the application of §1's exception for certain "contracts of employment."

To be sure, New Prime resists this straightforward understanding. The company argues that an arbitrator should resolve any dispute over §1's application because of the "delegation clause" in the parties' contract and what is sometimes called the "severability principle." A delegation clause gives an arbitrator authority to decide even the initial question whether the parties' dispute is subject to arbitration. *Rent-A-Center, West, Inc.* v. *Jackson*, 561 U.S. 63, 68–69, 130 S. Ct. 2772, 177 L. Ed. 2d 403 (2010). And under the severability principle, we treat a challenge to the validity of an arbitration agreement (or a delegation clause) separately from a challenge to the validity of the entire contract in which it appears. *Id.*, at 70–71. Unless a party specifically challenges the validity of the agreement to arbitrate, both sides may be required to take all their disputes—including disputes about the validity of their broader contract—to arbitration. *Ibid.* Applying these principles to this case, New Prime notes that Mr. Oliveira has not specifically challenged the parties' delegation clause and submits that any controversy should therefore proceed only and immediately before an arbitrator.

But all this overlooks the necessarily antecedent statutory inquiry we've just discussed. A delegation clause is merely a specialized type of arbitration agreement, and the Act "operates on this additional arbitration agreement just as it does on any other." *Id.*, at 70. So a court may use §§3 and 4 to enforce a delegation clause only if the clause appears in a "written provision in . . . a contract evidencing a transaction involving commerce" consistent with §2. And only if the contract in which the clause appears doesn't trigger §1's "contracts of employment" exception. In exactly the same way, the Act's severability principle applies only if the parties' arbitration agreement appears in a contract that falls within the field §§1 and 2 describe. We acknowledged as much some time ago, explaining that, before invoking the severability principle, a court should "determine[ ] that the contract in question is within the coverage of the Arbitration Act." *Prima Paint Corp.* v. *Flood & Conklin Mfg. Co.*, 388 U.S. 395, 402, 87 S. Ct. 1801, 18 L. Ed. 2d 1270 (1967).

Epilogue. The Court in *New Prime* went on to affirm the lower courts' decisions, finding that Mr. Oliveira's agreement fell within Section 1's exception and therefore the courts lacked authority to order arbitration. While Section 1 of the Act excludes "contracts of *employment* of . . . workers engaged in foreign or interstate commerce" (emphasis added), and while New Prime argued that contracts with independent contractors do not qualify for this exclusion because independent contractors are not *employees*, the Court disagreed with New Prime's position. The Court reiterated "the fundamental canon of statutory construction" that statutory terms must be interpreted in accordance with their ordinary meaning *at the time Congress enacted the statute*. The Court then traced the etymological history of words such as "employer," "employee," and "employment" to find that, at the time the FAA was enacted in 1925, those terms were not as specific as "many lawyerly ears today" would interpret them and did not yet operate to exclude other types of work agreements. Accordingly, the Court held that the term "contracts of employment" as used in Section 1 of the FAA refers to "agreements to work" in general, not just "employer-employee" agreements.

Henry Schein, Inc. v. Archer & White Sales, Inc.

139 S. Ct. 524 (2019)

JUSTICE KAVANAUGH delivered the opinion of the Court.

Under the Federal Arbitration Act, parties to a contract may agree that an arbitrator rather than a court will resolve disputes arising out of the contract. When a dispute arises, the parties sometimes may disagree not only about the merits of the dispute but also about the threshold arbitrability question—that is, whether their arbitration agreement applies to the particular dispute. Who decides that threshold arbitrability question? Under the Act and this Court's cases, the question of who decides arbitrability is itself a question of contract. The Act allows parties to agree by contract that an arbitrator, rather than a court, will resolve threshold arbitrability questions as well as underlying merits disputes. *First Options of Chicago, Inc.* v. *Kaplan*, 514 U.S. 938, 943–944, 115 S. Ct. 1920, 131 L. Ed. 2d 985 (1995).

Even when a contract delegates the arbitrability question to an arbitrator, some federal courts nonetheless will short-circuit the process and decide the arbitrability question themselves if the argument that the arbitration agreement applies to the particular dispute is "wholly groundless." The question presented in this case is whether the "wholly groundless" exception is consistent with the Federal Arbitration Act. We conclude that it is not. The Act does not contain a "wholly groundless" exception, and we are not at liberty to rewrite the statute passed by Congress and signed by the President. When the parties' contract delegates the arbitrability question to an arbitrator, the courts must respect the parties' decision as embodied in the contract. We vacate the contrary judgment of the Court of Appeals.

I.

Archer and White is a small business that distributes dental equipment. Archer and White entered into a contract with Pelton and Crane, a dental equipment manufacturer, to distribute Pelton and Crane's equipment. The relationship eventually soured. As relevant here, Archer and White sued Pelton and Crane's successor-in-interest and Henry Schein, Inc. (collectively, Schein) in Federal District Court in Texas. Archer and White's complaint alleged violations of federal and state antitrust law, and sought both money damages and injunctive relief.

The relevant contract between the parties provided:

> "*Disputes.* This Agreement shall be governed by the laws of the State of North Carolina. Any dispute arising under or related to this Agreement (except for actions seeking injunctive relief and disputes related to trademarks, trade secrets, or other intellectual property of [Schein]), shall be resolved by binding arbitration in accordance with the arbitration rules of the American Arbitration Association [(AAA)]. The place of arbitration shall be in Charlotte, North Carolina." App. to Pet. for Cert. 3a.

After Archer and White sued, Schein invoked the Federal Arbitration Act and asked the District Court to refer the parties' antitrust dispute to arbitration. Archer and White objected, arguing that the dispute was not subject to arbitration because Archer and White's complaint sought injunctive relief, at least in part. According to Archer and White, the parties' contract barred arbitration of disputes when the plaintiff sought injunctive relief, even if only in part.

The question then became: Who decides whether the antitrust dispute is subject to arbitration? The rules of the American Arbitration Association provide that arbitrators have the power to resolve arbitrability questions. Schein contended that the contract's express incorporation of the American Arbitration Association's rules meant that an arbitrator—not the court—had to decide whether the arbitration agreement applied to this particular dispute. Archer and White responded that in cases where the defendant's argument for arbitration is wholly groundless—as Archer and White argued was the case here—the District Court itself may resolve the threshold question of arbitrability.

Relying on Fifth Circuit precedent, the District Court agreed with Archer and White about the existence of a "wholly groundless" exception, and ruled that Schein's argument for arbitration was wholly groundless. The District Court therefore denied Schein's motion to compel arbitration. The Fifth Circuit affirmed.

In light of disagreement in the Courts of Appeals over whether the "wholly groundless" exception is consistent with the Federal Arbitration Act, we granted certiorari.

II.

In 1925, Congress passed and President Coolidge signed the Federal Arbitration Act. As relevant here, the Act provides:

> "A written provision in. . . . a contract evidencing a transaction involving commerce to settle by arbitration a controversy thereafter arising out of such contract . . . shall be valid, irrevocable, and enforceable, save upon such grounds as exist at law or in equity for the revocation of any contract." 9 U.S.C. §2.

Under the Act, arbitration is a matter of contract, and courts must enforce arbitration contracts according to their terms. Applying the Act, we have held that parties may agree to have an arbitrator decide not only the merits of a particular dispute but also "'gateway' questions of 'arbitrability,' such as whether the parties have agreed to arbitrate or whether their agreement covers a particular controversy." We have explained that an "agreement to arbitrate a gateway issue is simply an additional, antecedent agreement the party seeking arbitration asks the federal court to enforce, and the FAA operates on this additional arbitration agreement just as it does on any other."

Even when the parties' contract delegates the threshold arbitrability question to an arbitrator, the Fifth Circuit and some other Courts of Appeals have determined that the court rather than an arbitrator should decide the threshold arbitrability question if, under the contract, the argument for arbitration is wholly groundless. Those courts have reasoned that the "wholly groundless" exception enables courts to block frivolous attempts to transfer disputes from the court system to arbitration.

We conclude that the "wholly groundless" exception is inconsistent with the text of the Act and with our precedent.

We must interpret the Act as written, and the Act in turn requires that we interpret the contract as written. When the parties' contract delegates the arbitrability question to an arbitrator, a court may not override the contract. In those circumstances, a court possesses no power to decide the arbitrability issue. That is true even if the court thinks that the argument that the arbitration agreement applies to a particular dispute is wholly groundless.

That conclusion follows not only from the text of the Act but also from precedent. We have held that a court may not "rule on the potential merits of the underlying" claim that is assigned by contract to an arbitrator, "even if it appears to the court to be frivolous." *AT&T Technologies, Inc.* v. *Communications Workers*, 475 U.S. 643, 649–650, 106 S. Ct. 1415, 89 L. Ed. 2d 648 (1986). A court has "'no business weighing the merits of the grievance'" because the "'agreement is to submit all grievances to arbitration, not merely those which the court will deem meritorious.'"

That *AT&T Technologies* principle applies with equal force to the threshold issue of arbitrability. Just as a court may not decide a merits question that the parties have delegated to an arbitrator, a court may not decide an arbitrability question that the parties have delegated to an arbitrator.

In sum, we reject the "wholly groundless" exception. The exception is inconsistent with the statutory text and with our precedent. It confuses the question of who decides arbitrability with the separate question of who prevails on arbitrability. When the parties' contract delegates the arbitrability question to an arbitrator, the courts must respect the parties' decision as embodied in the contract.

We express no view about whether the contract at issue in this case in fact delegated the arbitrability question to an arbitrator. The Court of Appeals did not decide that issue. Under our cases, courts "should not assume that the parties agreed to arbitrate arbitrability unless there is clear and unmistakable evidence that they did so." *First Options.*

The judgment of the Court of Appeals is vacated, and the case is remanded for further proceedings consistent with this opinion.

Notes and Questions

1. *First Options* stated what is now an oft-quoted arbitration rule as to delegation clauses: that the delegation must be "clear and convincing." This is ultimately a question of fact rather than of law, dependent for resolution on the testimony, documents and other evidence. Did either the *New Prime* or the *Schein* Court question or rule on the sufficiency of this evidence? If not, then why wasn't the question of the validity of the "wholly groundless" exception (*Schein*) or the impact of Section 1's exception (*New Prime*) left to the arbitrator? Why did the courts—and the Supreme Court to boot—rule on these questions? Why were they not arbitrability questions that the delegation clauses gave to the arbitrator to decide?
2. At issue in *Schein* was a purported exception to arbitration that is nowhere in the Act but, rather, judicially created. We will come back to another such doctrine in Unit III, when we examine the judicially created exception to enforcement called "manifest disregard." *See* Chapter 15 *infra*. Where should the Court begin, and end, in creating extra-Act doctrines?

   i. The *Schein* Court found that the "wholly groundless" exception was invalid. In a sense, this flipped what had been typical in wholly groundless cases, where a court would throw a kill switch on a case proceeding further in arbitration irrespective of what an arbitrator might say and irrespective of a delegation clause. Assume the Court instead had decided that the wholly groundless exception was valid but that so was the delegation clause. Would this have been intellectually possible? If so, would it have then been appropriate for the arbitrator to make a ruling on whether the wholly groundless exception applied here?

   ii. Although Justice Gorsuch's opinion in *New Prime* cut off the inquiry before any question reached the arbitrator to whom arbitrability had been delegated, the Court still took the opportunity to reinforce delegation clauses and where they sit within arbitrability:

   > A delegation clause gives an arbitrator authority to decide even the initial question whether the parties' dispute is subject to arbitration . . . [U]nder the severability principle, we treat a challenge to the validity of an arbitration agreement (or a delegation clause) separately from a challenge to the validity of the entire contract in which it ap-

> pears.... Unless a party specifically challenges the validity of the agreement to arbitrate, both sides may be required to take all their disputes—including disputes about the validity of their broader contract—to arbitration.

139 S. Ct. 532, 538 (2019). In years to come, this portion of *New Prime* may become the most frequently cited section of this opinion, wholly aside from the specialized and relatively rare context of a Section 1 challenge in which it appears. Delegation clauses thus remain alive and well.

A. Delegation Clauses and the Class Action Controversy

We will study in the following chapter the social and public policy questions inherent in arbitration and class actions. These have been the subject of vigorous court battles over the past 25 years and raise important questions about access to court, and this merits a chapter unto itself.

But because class action questions have often been the test cases and fact patterns on the reach of the saving clause in Section 2 of the FAA, these cases are also important precedent for the law of delegation clauses generally. It is one thing to say that a delegation clause allows an arbitrator to decide arbitrability, but quite another to say which issues are arbitrability questions and which are not. What should be the test? If the parties agree to arbitrate, does that resolve any question of arbitrability? Or does the *form* of the arbitration—and in particular, whether or not the arbitration can take the form of a class action—itself raise an arbitrability question? How do we break down responsibilities between the courts and the arbitrator?

As you read the following case, keep two questions in mind. First, was the question here genuinely one of arbitrability? Second, should the already high *First Options* evidentiary standard for delegation clauses be even higher when issues of access to court and social justice arise?

Green Tree Fin. Corp. v. Bazzle

539 U.S. 444, 123 S. Ct. 2402 (2003)

JUSTICE BREYER announced the judgment of the Court and delivered an opinion, in which JUSTICE SCALIA, JUSTICE SOUTER, and JUSTICE GINSBURG join.

This case concerns contracts between a commercial lender and its customers, each of which contains a clause providing for arbitration of all contract-related disputes. The Supreme Court of South Carolina held (1) that the arbitration clauses are silent as to whether arbitration might take the form of class arbitration, and (2) that, in that circumstance, South Carolina law interprets the contracts as permitting class arbitration. We granted certiorari to determine whether this holding is consistent with the Federal Arbitration Act.

In 1995, respondents Lynn and Burt Bazzle secured a home improvement loan from petitioner Green Tree. The Bazzles and Green Tree entered into a contract, governed by South Carolina law, which included the following arbitration clause:

> ARBITRATION—All disputes, claims, or controversies arising from or relating to this contract or the relationships which result from this contract . . . shall be resolved by binding arbitration by one arbitrator selected by us with consent of you. This arbitration contract is made pursuant to a transaction in interstate commerce, and shall be governed by the Federal Arbitration Act at 9 U.S.C. section 1 [9 U.S.C.S. § 1]. . . . THE PARTIES VOLUNTARILY AND KNOWINGLY WAIVE ANY RIGHT THEY HAVE TO A JURY TRIAL, EITHER PURSUANT TO ARBITRATION UNDER THIS CLAUSE OR PURSUANT TO COURT ACTION BY US (AS PROVIDED HEREIN). . . . The parties agree and understand that the arbitrator shall have all powers provided by the law and the contract. These powers shall include all legal and equitable remedies, including, but not limited to, money damages, declaratory relief, and injunctive relief.

Respondents Daniel Lackey and George and Florine Buggs entered into loan contracts and security agreements for the purchase of mobile homes with Green Tree. These agreements contained arbitration clauses that were, in all relevant respects, identical to the Bazzles' arbitration clause. (Their contracts substitute the word "you" with the word "Buyer[s]" in the italicized phrase.)

At the time of the loan transactions, Green Tree apparently failed to provide these customers with a legally required form that would have told them that they had a right to name their own lawyers and insurance agents and would have provided space for them to write in those names. The two sets of customers before us now as respondents each filed separate actions in South Carolina state courts, complaining that this failure violated South Carolina law and seeking damages.

In April 1997, the Bazzles asked the court to certify their claims as a class action. Green Tree sought to stay the court proceedings and compel arbitration. On January 5, 1998, the court both (1) certified a class action and (2) entered an order compelling arbitration. App. 7. Green Tree then selected an arbitrator with the Bazzles' consent. And the arbitrator, administering the proceeding as a class arbitration, eventually awarded the class $10,935,000 in statutory damages, along with attorney's fees. The trial court confirmed the award, and Green Tree appealed to the South Carolina Court of Appeals claiming, among other things, that class arbitration was legally impermissible.

Lackey and the Buggses had earlier begun a similar court proceeding in which they, too, sought class certification. Green Tree moved to compel arbitration. The trial court initially denied the motion, finding the arbitration agreement unenforceable, but Green Tree pursued an interlocutory appeal and the State Court of Appeals reversed. The parties then chose an arbitrator, indeed the same arbitrator who was subsequently selected to arbitrate the Bazzles' dispute.

In December 1998, the arbitrator certified a class in arbitration. App. 18. The arbitrator proceeded to hear the matter, ultimately ruled in favor of the class, and awarded the class $9,200,000 in statutory damages in addition to attorney's fees. The trial court confirmed the award. Green Tree appealed to the South Carolina Court of Appeals claiming, among other things, that class arbitration was legally impermissible.

The South Carolina Supreme Court withdrew both cases from the Court of Appeals, assumed jurisdiction, and consolidated the proceedings. That court then held that the contracts were silent in respect to class arbitration, that they consequently authorized class arbitration, and that arbitration had properly taken that form. We granted certiorari to consider whether that holding is consistent with the Federal Arbitration Act.

II.

The South Carolina Supreme Court's determination that the contracts are silent in respect to class arbitration raises a preliminary question. Green Tree argued there, as it argues here, that the contracts are not silent—that they forbid class arbitration. And we must deal with that argument at the outset, for if it is right, then the South Carolina court's holding is flawed on its own terms; that court neither said nor implied that it would have authorized class arbitration had the parties' arbitration agreement forbidden it.

Whether Green Tree is right about the contracts themselves presents a disputed issue of contract interpretation. The Chief Justice believes that Green Tree is right; indeed, that Green Tree is so clearly right that we should ignore the fact that state law, not federal law, normally governs such matters. The Chief Justice points out that the contracts say that disputes "shall be resolved . . . by one arbitrator selected by us [Green Tree] with consent of you [Green Tree's customer]," [and] finds that class arbitration is clearly inconsistent with this requirement. After all, class arbitration involves an arbitration, not simply between Green Tree and a named customer, but also between Green Tree and other (represented) customers, all taking place before the arbitrator chosen to arbitrate the initial, named customer's dispute.

We do not believe, however, that the contracts' language is as clear as The Chief Justice believes. The class arbitrator was "selected by" Green Tree "with consent of" Green Tree's customers, the named plaintiffs. And insofar as the other class members agreed to proceed in class arbitration, they consented as well.

Of course, Green Tree did not independently select this arbitrator to arbitrate its disputes with the other class members. But whether the contracts contain this additional requirement is a question that the literal terms of the contracts do not decide. The contracts simply say (I) "selected by us [Green Tree]." And that is literally what occurred. The contracts do not say (II) "selected by us [Green Tree] to arbitrate this dispute and no other (even identical) dispute with another customer." The question whether (I) in fact implicitly means (II) is the question at issue: Do the contracts forbid class arbitration? Given the broad authority the contracts elsewhere bestow upon the arbitrator, *see, e.g.*, App. to Pet. for Cert. 110a (the contracts grant to the arbitrator "all powers," including certain equitable powers "provided by the law and the contract"), the answer to this question is not completely obvious.

At the same time, we cannot automatically accept the South Carolina Supreme Court's resolution of this contract-interpretation question. Under the terms of the parties' contracts, the question—whether the agreement forbids class arbitration—is for the arbitrator to decide. The parties agreed to submit to the arbitrator "*all* disputes, claims, or controversies arising from or relating to this contract or the relationships which result from this contract." *Ibid.* (emphasis added). And the dispute about what the arbitration contract in each case means (i.e., whether it forbids the use of class arbitration procedures) is a dispute "relating to this contract" and the resulting "relationships." Hence the parties seem to have agreed that an arbitrator, not a judge, would answer the relevant question. *See First Options.* And if there is doubt about that matter—about the "'scope of arbitrable issues'—we should resolve that doubt in favor of arbitration.

In certain limited circumstances, courts assume that the parties intended courts, not arbitrators, to decide a particular arbitration-related matter (in the absence of "clear and unmistakable" evidence to the contrary). *AT&T Technologies, Inc. v. Communications Workers*, 475 U.S. 643, 649, 89 L. Ed. 2d 648, 106 S. Ct. 1415 (1986). These limited instances typically involve matters of a kind that "contracting parties would likely have expected a court" to decide. *Howsam v. Dean Witter Reynolds, Inc.*, 537 U.S. 79, 83, 154 L. Ed. 2d 491, 123 S. Ct. 588 (2002). They include certain gateway matters, such as whether the parties have a valid arbitration agreement at all or whether a concededly binding arbitration clause applies to a certain type of controversy. *See generally Howsam, supra. See also John Wiley & Sons, Inc. v. Livingston*, 376 U.S. 543, 546–547, 11 L. Ed. 2d 898, 84 S. Ct. 909 (1964) (whether an arbitration agreement survives a corporate merger); *AT&T, supra*, at 651–652, 89 L. Ed. 2d 648, 106 S. Ct. 1415 (whether a labor-management layoff controversy falls within the scope of an arbitration clause).

The question here—whether the contracts forbid class arbitration—does not fall into this narrow exception. It concerns neither the validity of the arbitration clause nor its applicability to the underlying dispute between the parties. Unlike *First Options*, the question is not whether the parties wanted a judge or an arbitrator to decide whether they agreed to arbitrate a matter. Rather, the relevant question here is what kind of arbitration proceeding the parties agreed to. That question concerns contract interpretation and arbitration procedures. Arbitrators are well situated to answer that question. Given these considerations, along with the arbitration contracts' sweeping language concerning the scope of the questions committed to arbitration, this matter of contract interpretation should be for the arbitrator, not the courts, to decide.

CHIEF JUSTICE REHNQUIST, with whom JUSTICE O'CONNOR and JUSTICE KENNEDY join, dissenting.

The parties entered into a contract with an arbitration clause that is governed by the Federal Arbitration Act (FAA), 9 U.S.C. §1 et seq. The Supreme Court of South Carolina held that arbitration under the contract could proceed as a class action even though the contract does not by its terms permit class-action arbitration. The plurality now vacates that judgment and remands the case for the arbitrator to make this determination. I would reverse because this determination is one for the courts, not for the arbitrator, and the holding of the Supreme Court of South Carolina contravenes the terms of the contract and is therefore pre-empted by the FAA.

The agreement to arbitrate involved here, like many such agreements, is terse. Its operative language is contained in one sentence:

> "All disputes, claims, or controversies arising from or relating to this contract or the relationships which result from this contract . . . shall be resolved by binding arbitration by one arbitrator selected by us with consent of you." App. 34.

The decision of the arbitrator on matters agreed to be submitted to him is given considerable deference by the courts. But the decision of what to submit to the arbitrator is a matter of contractual agreement by the parties, and the interpretation of that contract is for the court, not for the arbitrator. As we stated in *First Options of Chicago, Inc. v. Kaplan*, 514 U.S. 938, 945, 131 L. Ed. 2d 985, 115 S. Ct. 1920 (1995):

> Given the principle that a party can be forced to arbitrate only those issues it specifically has agreed to submit to arbitration, one can understand why courts might hesitate to interpret silence or ambiguity on the 'who should decide arbitrability' point as giving the arbitrators that power, for doing so might too often force unwilling parties to arbitrate a matter they reasonably would have thought a judge, not an arbitrator would decide.

Just as fundamental to the agreement of the parties as what is submitted to the arbitrator is to whom it is submitted. Those are the two provisions in the sentence quoted above, and it is difficult to say that one is more important than the other. I have no hesitation in saying that the choice of arbitrator is as important a component of the agreement to arbitrate as is the choice of what is to be submitted to him.

Thus, this case is controlled by *First Options* and not by our more recent decision in *Howsam v. Dean Witter Reynolds, Inc.*, 537 U.S. 79, 154 L. Ed. 2d 491, 123 S. Ct. 588 (2002). There, this Court held that it was for the arbitrator to interpret that limitation provision:

> "Procedural questions which grow out of the dispute and bear on its final disposition' are presumptively not for the judge, but for an arbitrator, to

> decide. . . . So, too, the presumption is that the arbitrator should decide 'allegations of waiver, delay, or a like defense to arbitrability.' "

I think that the parties' agreement as to how the arbitrator should be selected is much more akin to the agreement as to what shall be arbitrated, a question for the courts under *First Options*, than it is to "allegations of waiver, delay, or like defenses to arbitrability," which are questions for the arbitrator under *Howsam*.

Under the FAA, "parties are generally free to structure their arbitration agreements as they see fit." *Volt, supra*, at 479, 103 L. Ed. 2d 488, 109 S. Ct. 1248. Here, the parties saw fit to agree that any disputes arising out of the contracts "shall be resolved by binding arbitration by one arbitrator selected by us with consent of you." App. 34. Each contract expressly defines "us" as petitioner, and "you" as the respondent or respondents named in that specific contract. *Id.*, at 33 ("'We' and 'us' means the Seller *above*, its successors and assigns"; "'You' and 'your' means each Buyer *above* and guarantor, jointly and severally" (emphasis added)). The contract also specifies that it governs all "disputes . . . arising from . . . *this* contract or the relationships which result from *this* contract." *Id.*, at 34 (emphasis added). These provisions, which the plurality simply ignores, see ante, 156 L. Ed. 2d, at 421–422, make quite clear that petitioner must select, and each buyer must agree to, a particular arbitrator for disputes between petitioner and that specific buyer.

While the observation of the Supreme Court of South Carolina that the agreement of the parties was silent as to the availability of class-wide arbitration is literally true, the imposition of class-wide arbitration contravenes the just-quoted provision about the selection of an arbitrator. To be sure, the arbitrator that administered the proceedings was "selected by [petitioner] with consent of" the Bazzles, Lackey, and the Buggses. *Id.*, at 34–36. But petitioner had the contractual right to choose an arbitrator for each dispute with the other 3,734 individual class members, and this right was denied when the same arbitrator was foisted upon petitioner to resolve those claims as well. Petitioner may well have chosen different arbitrators for some or all of these other disputes; indeed, it would have been reasonable for petitioner to do so, in order to avoid concentrating all of the risk of substantial damages awards in the hands of a single arbitrator. As petitioner correctly concedes, Brief for Petitioner 32, 42, the FAA does not prohibit parties from choosing to proceed on a class-wide basis. Here, however, the parties simply did not so choose.

"Arbitration under the Act is a matter of consent, not coercion." *Volt, supra*, at 479, 103 L. Ed. 2d 488, 109 S. Ct. 1248. Here, the Supreme Court of South Carolina imposed a regime that was contrary to the express agreement of the parties as to how the arbitrator would be chosen. It did not enforce the "agreement to arbitrate . . . according to [its] terms." *Mastrobuono, supra*, at 54, 131 L. Ed. 2d 76, 115 S. Ct. 1212 (internal quotation marks omitted). I would therefore reverse the judgment of the Supreme Court of South Carolina.

Notes and Questions

1. *Green Tree* shows that it is far easier to define a concept than it is to apply it. Having established that certain issues are "gateway" ones left for the courts, the Supreme Court sharply divided as to whether the case should proceed as a class action or gateway issue. Is "gateway" a helpful classification standard for when a particular type of dispute should be heard by an arbitrator instead of by a court?
2. There was no doubt in *Green Tree* that the parties had agreed that their disputes "shall be resolved by binding arbitration." Once (a) the courts are clear that a binding arbitration clause exists, and (b) there is an agreement to let the arbitrator decide arbitrability, is any further judicial role appropriate?
3. Did the arbitrator's authority to rule on arbitrability in *Green Tree* come from the arbitration agreement or in a post-dispute agreement between the parties? Should that make a difference?
4. In *First Options*, Justice Breyer identified what he called a "who question." There are also "what" questions. Chief Justice Rehnquist's dissent classifies the following as a "what" question: "the decision of what to submit to an arbitrator is a matter of contractual agreement by the parties, and the interpretation of that contract is for the court, not the arbitrator." But was the question in *Green Tree* one of "what" or one of "who"?
5. How is "intent" supposed to be measured under *Green Tree*? The Court writes that in certain limited circumstances, courts *assume* that the parties intended courts, not arbitrators, to decide a particular arbitration-related matter in the "absence of clear and unmistakable evidence to the contrary." On what evidentiary basis is that assumption met? The Court provides no guidance other than the *absence* of "clear and unmistakable evidence to the contrary." This takes us back to the question we just considered after *Prima Paint*: what evidence will exist as to the parties' making of the dispute resolution clause? In the absence of such evidence, how will and should courts be guided? Since arbitration is, as the courts continually remind us, "a question of contract," should standard contract interpretation rules apply? Or should more specialized, and perhaps more weighted, rules apply that guide the court (or arbitrator) interpreting that contract toward a pro-arbitration result?
6. Return to Justice Black's dissent in *Prima Paint*, wherein he opined that leaving procedural disputes to arbitrators would result in decisions driven primarily by arbitrator greed for fees. *Green Tree*'s result presented the arbitrator with the opportunity not merely to keep fees alive in one

case before him but instead to decide on class-wide arbitration that would dramatically expand fees. Should that be a consideration in allocating who decides gateway questions or even what "gateway" should be under *Green Tree*?

CASE PREVIEW. In the next case, the Supreme Court had to decide *who* should make the arbitration vs. court decision, and *what* precisely was at issue.

Rent-A-Ctr., W., Inc. v. Jackson

561 U.S. 63, 130 S. Ct. 2772 (2010)

JUSTICE SCALIA delivered the opinion of the Court.

We consider whether, under the Federal Arbitration Act (FAA or Act), 9 U.S.C. §§1–16, a district court may decide a claim that an arbitration agreement is unconscionable, where the agreement explicitly assigns that decision to the arbitrator.

On February 1, 2007, the respondent here, Antonio Jackson, filed an employment-discrimination suit under Rev. Stat. §1977, 42 U.S.C. §1981, against his former employer in the United States District Court for the District of Nevada. The defendant and petitioner here, Rent-A-Center, West, Inc., filed a motion under the FAA to dismiss or stay the proceedings, 9 U.S.C. §3, and to compel arbitration, §4. Rent-A-Center argued that the Mutual Agreement to Arbitrate Claims (Agreement), which Jackson signed on February 24, 2003, as a condition of his employment there, precluded Jackson from pursuing his claims in court. The Agreement provided for arbitration of all "past, present or future" disputes arising out of Jackson's employment with Rent-A-Center, including "claims for discrimination" and "claims for violation of any federal . . . law." It also provided that "[t]he Arbitrator, and not any federal, state, or local court or agency, shall have exclusive authority to resolve any dispute relating to the interpretation, applicability, enforceability or formation of this Agreement including, but not limited to any claim that all or any part of this Agreement is void or voidable."

Jackson opposed the motion on the ground that "the arbitration agreement in question is clearly unenforceable in that it is unconscionable" under Nevada law. Rent-A-Center responded that Jackson's unconscionability claim was not properly before the court because Jackson had expressly agreed that the arbitrator would have exclusive authority to resolve any dispute about the enforceability of the Agreement. It also disputed the merits of Jackson's unconscionability claims.

The District Court granted Rent-A-Center's motion to dismiss the proceedings and to compel arbitration. The court found that the Agreement " 'clearly and unmistakenly [*sic*]' gives the arbitrator exclusive authority to decide whether the Agreement is enforceable," . . . and, because Jackson challenged the validity of the Agreement as a whole, the issue was for the arbitrator, App. to Pet. for Cert. 4a (citing *Buckeye Check Cashing, Inc. v. Cardegna*, 546 U.S. 440, 444–445, 126 S. Ct. 1204, 163 L. Ed. 2d 1038 (2006)). The court noted that even if it were to examine the merits of Jackson's unconscionability claims, it would have rejected the claim that the agreement to split arbitration fees was substantively unconscionable under Nevada law. It did not address Jackson's procedural or other substantive unconscionability arguments.

Without oral argument, a divided panel of the Court of Appeals for the Ninth Circuit reversed in part, affirmed in part, and remanded. The court reversed on the question of who (the court or arbitrator) had the authority to decide whether the Agreement is enforceable. It noted that "Jackson does not dispute that the language of the Agreement clearly assigns the arbitrability determination to the arbitrator," but held that where "a party challenges an arbitration agreement as unconscionable, and thus asserts that he could not meaningfully assent to the agreement, the threshold question of unconscionability is for the court." The Ninth Circuit affirmed the District Court's alternative conclusion that the fee-sharing provision was not substantively unconscionable and remanded for consideration of Jackson's other unconscionability arguments. Judge Hall dissented on the ground that "the question of the arbitration agreement's validity should have gone to the arbitrator, as the parties 'clearly and unmistakably provide[d]' in their agreement."

II.

A.

The FAA reflects the fundamental principle that arbitration is a matter of contract. Section 2, the "primary substantive provision of the Act," *Moses H. Cone Memorial Hospital v. Mercury Constr. Corp.*, 460 U.S. 1, 24, 103 S. Ct. 927, 74 L. Ed. 2d 765 (1983), provides:

> "A written provision in . . . a contract evidencing a transaction involving commerce to settle by arbitration a controversy thereafter arising out of such contract . . . shall be valid, irrevocable, and enforceable, save upon such grounds as exist at law or in equity for the revocation of any contract." 9 U.S.C. § 2.

The FAA thereby places arbitration agreements on an equal footing with other contracts, *Buckeye, supra*, and requires courts to enforce them according to their terms. Like other contracts, however, they may be invalidated by "generally applicable contract defenses, such as fraud, duress, or unconscionability."

The Act also establishes procedures by which federal courts implement § 2's substantive rule. Under § 3, a party may apply to a federal court for a stay of the trial of an action "upon any issue referable to arbitration under an agreement in writing for such arbitration." Under § 4, a party "aggrieved" by the failure of another party "to arbitrate under a written agreement for arbitration" may petition a federal court "for an order directing that such arbitration proceed in the manner provided for in such agreement." The court "shall" order arbitration "upon being satisfied that the making of the agreement for arbitration or the failure to comply therewith is not in issue." *Ibid.*

The Agreement here contains multiple "written provision[s]" to "settle by arbitration a controversy," § 2. Two are relevant to our discussion. First, the section titled "Claims Covered By The Agreement" provides for arbitration of all "past, present or future" disputes arising out of Jackson's employment with Rent-A-Center. Second, the section titled "Arbitration Procedures" provides that "[t]he Arbitrator . . . shall have exclusive authority to resolve any dispute relating to the . . . enforceability . . . of this Agreement including, but not limited to any claim that all or any part of this Agreement is void or voidable." *Id.*, at 32, 34. How does this clause address severability? The current "controversy" between the parties is whether the Agreement is unconscionable. It is the second provision, which delegates resolution of that controversy to the arbitrator, that Rent-A-Center seeks to enforce. Adopting the terminology used by the parties, we will refer to it as the delegation provision.

The delegation provision is an agreement to arbitrate threshold issues concerning the arbitration agreement. We have recognized that parties can agree to arbitrate "gateway" questions of "arbitrability," such as whether the parties have agreed to arbitrate or whether their agreement covers a particular controversy. *See, e.g., Howsam*, 537 U.S., at 83–85, 123 S. Ct. 588, 154 L. Ed. 2d 491; *Green Tree Financial Corp. v. Bazzle*, 539 U.S. 444, 452, 123 S. Ct. 2402, 156 L. Ed. 2d 414 (2003) (plurality opinion). This line of cases merely reflects the principle that arbitration is a matter of contract. *See First Options of Chicago, Inc. v. Kaplan*, 514 U.S. 938, 943, 115 S. Ct. 1920, 131 L. Ed. 2d 985 (1995). An agreement to arbitrate a gateway issue is simply an additional, antecedent agreement the party seeking arbitration asks the federal court to enforce, and the FAA operates on this additional arbitration agreement just as it does on any other. The additional agreement is valid under § 2 "save upon such grounds as exist at law or in equity for the revocation of any contract," and federal courts can enforce the agreement by staying federal litigation under § 3 and compelling arbitration under § 4. The question before us, then, is whether the delegation provision is valid under § 2.

B.

There are two types of validity challenges under § 2: "One type challenges specifically the validity of the agreement to arbitrate," and "[t]he other challenges the contract as a whole, either on a ground that directly affects the entire agreement (e.g., the agreement was fraudulently induced), or on the ground that the illegality of one of the contract's provisions renders the whole contract invalid." *Buckeye*, 546 U.S., at 444, 126 S. Ct. 1204, 163 L. Ed. 2d 1038. In a line of cases neither party has asked us to overrule, we held that only the first type of challenge is relevant to a court's determination whether the arbitration agreement at issue is enforceable. *See Prima Paint*. That is because § 2 states that a "written provision" "to settle by arbitration a controversy" is "valid, irrevocable, and enforceable" without mention of the validity of the contract in which it is contained. Thus, a party's challenge to another provision of the contract, or to the contract as a whole, does not prevent a court from enforcing a specific agreement to arbitrate. "[A]s a matter of substantive federal arbitration law, an arbitration provision is severable from the remainder of the contract." *Buckeye.*

But that agreements to arbitrate are severable does not mean that they are unassailable. If a party challenges the validity under § 2 of the precise agreement to arbitrate at issue, the federal court must consider the challenge before ordering compliance with that agreement under § 4. In *Prima Paint*, for example, if the claim had been "fraud in the inducement of the arbitration clause itself," then the court would have considered it. To immunize an arbitration agreement from judicial challenge on the ground of fraud in the inducement would be to elevate it over other forms of contract. In some cases the claimed basis of invalidity for the contract as a whole will be much easier to establish than the same basis as applied only to the severable agreement to arbitrate. Thus, in an employment contract many elements of alleged unconscionability applicable to the entire contract (outrageously low wages, for example) would not affect the agreement to arbitrate alone. But even where that is not the case—as in *Prima Paint* itself, where the alleged fraud that induced the whole contract equally induced the agreement to arbitrate which was part of that contract—we nonetheless require the basis of challenge to be directed specifically to the agreement to arbitrate before the court will intervene.

Here, the "written provision . . . to settle by arbitration a controversy," 9 U.S.C. § 2, that Rent-A-Center asks us to enforce is the delegation provision— the provision that gave the arbitrator "exclusive authority to resolve any dispute relating to the . . . enforceability . . . of this Agreement." The "remainder of the contract" is the rest of the agreement to arbitrate claims arising out of Jackson's employment with Rent-A-Center. To be sure this case differs from *Prima Paint, Buckeye*, and *Preston*, in that the arbitration provisions sought to be enforced in those cases were contained in contracts unrelated to arbitration—contracts for consulting services, *see Prima Paint*; check-cashing services, *see Buckeye*; and "personal management" or "talent agent" services, *see Preston*. In this case, the underlying contract is itself an arbitration agreement. But that makes no difference. Application of the severability rule does not depend on the substance of the remainder of the contract. Section 2 operates on the specific "written provision" to "settle by arbitration a controversy" that the party seeks to enforce. Accordingly, unless Jackson challenged the delegation provision specifically, we must treat it as valid under § 2, and must enforce it under §§ 3 and 4, leaving any challenge to the validity of the Agreement as a whole for the arbitrator.

C.

The District Court correctly concluded that Jackson challenged only the validity of the contract as a whole. Nowhere in his opposition to Rent-A-Center's motion to compel arbitration did he even mention the delegation provision. *See* App. 39–47.

Rent-A-Center noted this fact in its reply: "[Jackson's response] fails to rebut or otherwise address in any way [Rent-A-Center's] argument that the Arbitrator must decide [Jackson's] challenge to the enforceability of the Agreement. *Thus, [Rent-A-Center's] argument is uncontested." Id.*, at 50 (emphasis in original).

The arguments Jackson made in his response to Rent-A-Center's motion to compel arbitration support this conclusion. Jackson stated that "the *entire agreement* seems drawn to provide [Rent-A-Center] with undue advantages should an employment related dispute arise." At one point, he argued that the limitations on discovery "further suppor[t] [his] contention that the *arbitration agreement as a whole* is substantively unconscionable." And before this Court, Jackson describes his challenge in the District Court as follows: He "opposed the motion to compel on the ground that the *entire arbitration agreement*, including the delegation clause, was unconscionable." Brief for Respondent 55 (emphasis added). That is an accurate description of his filings.

As required to make out a claim of unconscionability under Nevada law, Jackson contended that the Agreement was both procedurally and substantively unconscionable. It was procedurally unconscionable, he argued, because it "was imposed as a condition of employment and was non-negotiable." But we need not consider that claim because none of Jackson's substantive unconscionability challenges was specific to the delegation provision. First, he argued that the Agreement's coverage was one sided in that it required arbitration of claims an employee was likely to bring—contract, tort, discrimination, and statutory claims—but did not require arbitration of claims Rent-A-Center was likely to bring—intellectual property, unfair competition, and trade secrets claims. This one-sided-coverage argument clearly did not go to the validity of the delegation provision.

Jackson's other two substantive unconscionability arguments assailed arbitration procedures called for by the contract—the fee-splitting arrangement and the limitations on discovery—procedures that were to be used during arbitration under both the agreement to arbitrate employment-related disputes and the delegation provision. Jackson, however, did not make any arguments specific to the delegation provision; he argued that the fee-sharing and discovery procedures rendered the entire Agreement invalid.

Jackson's appeal to the Ninth Circuit confirms that he did not contest the validity of the delegation provision in particular. His brief noted the existence of the delegation provision, Brief for Appellant in No. 07-16164, p. 3, but his unconscionability arguments made no mention of it, *id.*, at 3–7. Jackson repeated that argument before this Court. At oral argument, counsel stated: "There are certain elements of the arbitration agreement that are unconscionable and, under Nevada law, which would render the *entire arbitration agreement* unconscionable." Tr. of Oral Arg. 43 (emphasis added). And again, he stated, "we've got both certain provisions that are unconscionable, that under Nevada law render the entire agreement unconscionable . . ., and that's what the Court is to rely on." *Id.*, at 43–44 (emphasis added).

In his brief to this Court, Jackson made the contention, not mentioned below, that the delegation provision itself is substantively unconscionable. He brought this challenge to the delegation provision too late, and we will not consider it. *See 14 Penn Plaza LLC v. Pyett*, 556 U.S. 247, 273–274, 556 U.S. 247, 129 S. Ct. 1456, 173 L. Ed. 2d 398, 419–20 (2009).

We reverse the judgment of the Court of Appeals for the Ninth Circuit.

It is so ordered.

JUSTICE STEVENS, with whom JUSTICE GINSBURG, JUSTICE BREYER, and JUSTICE SOTOMAYOR join, dissenting.

Neither petitioner nor respondent has urged us to adopt the rule the Court does today: Even when a litigant has specifically challenged the validity of an agreement to arbitrate he must submit that challenge to the arbitrator unless he has lodged an objection to the particular line in the agreement that purports to assign such challenges to the arbitrator—the so-called "delegation clause."

The Court asserts that its holding flows logically from *Prima Paint Corp. v. Flood & Conklin Mfg. Co.*, 388 U.S. 395, 87 S. Ct. 1801, 18 L. Ed. 2d 1270 (1967), in which the Court held that consideration of a contract revocation defense is generally a matter for the arbitrator, unless the defense is specifically directed at the arbitration clause, *id.*, at 404, 87 S. Ct. 1801, 18 L. Ed. 2d 1270. We have treated this holding as a severability rule: When a party challenges a contract, "but not specifically its arbitration provisions, those provisions are enforceable apart from the remainder of the contract." *Buckeye*[.] The Court's decision today goes beyond *Prima Paint*. Its breezy assertion that the subject matter of the contract at issue—in this case, an arbitration agreement and nothing more—"makes no difference," *ante*, at 72, 177 L. Ed. 2d, at 413, is simply wrong. This written arbitration agreement is but one part of a broader employment agreement between the parties, just as the arbitration clause in *Prima Paint* was but one part of a broader contract for services between those parties. Thus, that the subject matter of the agreement is exclusively arbitration makes all the difference in the *Prima Paint* analysis.

I.

Under the Federal Arbitration Act (FAA), 9 U.S.C. §§ 1–16, parties generally have substantial leeway to define the terms and scope of their agreement to settle disputes in an arbitral forum. "[A]rbitration is," after all, "simply a matter of contract between the parties; it is a way to resolve those disputes—but only those disputes—that the parties have agreed to submit to arbitration." *First Options of Chicago, Inc. v. Kaplan*, 514 U.S. 938, 943, 115 S. Ct. 1920, 131 L. Ed. 2d 985 (1995). The FAA, therefore, envisions a limited role for courts asked to stay litigation and refer disputes to arbitration.

Certain issues—the kind that "contracting parties would likely have expected a court to have decided"—remain within the province of judicial review. *Howsam v. Dean Witter Reynolds, Inc.*, 537 U.S. 79, 83, 123 S. Ct. 588, 154 L. Ed. 2d 491 (2002); *see also Green Tree Financial Corp. v. Bazzle*, 539 U.S. 444, 452, 123 S. Ct. 2402, 156 L. Ed. 2d 414 (2003) (plurality opinion); *AT&T Technologies, Inc. v. Communications Workers*, 475 U.S. 643, 649, 106 S. Ct. 1415, 89 L. Ed. 2d 648 (1986). These issues are "gateway matter[s]" because they are necessary antecedents to enforcement of an arbitration agreement; they raise questions the parties "are not likely to have thought that they had agreed that an arbitrator would" decide. *Howsam*, 537 U.S., at 83, 123 S. Ct. 588, 154 L. Ed. 2d 491. Quintessential gateway matters include "whether the parties have a valid arbitration agreement at all," *Bazzle*, 539 U.S., at 452, 123 S. Ct. 2402, 156 L. Ed. 2d 414 (plurality opinion); "whether the parties are bound by a given arbitration clause," *Howsam*, 537 U.S., at 84, 123 S. Ct. 588, 154 L. Ed. 2d 491; and "whether an arbitration clause in a concededly binding contract applies to a particular type of controversy," *ibid.* It would be bizarre to send these types of gateway matters to the arbitrator as a matter of course, because they raise a "'question of arbitrability.'" *See, e.g., ibid.; First Options*, 514 U.S., at 947, 115 S. Ct. 1920, 131 L. Ed. 2d 985.

"[Q]uestion[s] of arbitrability" thus include questions regarding the existence of a legally binding and valid arbitration agreement, as well as questions regarding the scope of a concededly binding arbitration agreement. In this case we are concerned with the first of these categories: whether the parties have a valid arbitration agreement. This is an issue the FAA assigns to the courts. Section 2 of the FAA dictates that covered arbitration agreements "shall be valid, irrevocable, and enforceable, save upon such grounds as exist at law or in equity for the revocation of any contract." 9 U.S.C. § 2. "[S]uch grounds," which relate to contract validity and formation, include the claim at issue in this case, unconscionability. *See Doctor's Associates, Inc. v. Casarotto*, 517 U.S. 681, 687, 116 S. Ct. 1652, 134 L. Ed. 2d 902 (1996).

Two different lines of cases bear on the issue of who decides a question of arbitrability respecting validity, such as whether an arbitration agreement is unconscionable. Although this issue, as a gateway matter, is typically for the court, we have explained that such an issue can be delegated to the arbitrator in some circumstances. When the parties have purportedly done so, courts must examine two distinct rules to decide whether the delegation is valid.

The first line of cases looks to the parties' intent. In *AT&T Technologies*, we stated that "question[s] of arbitrability" may be delegated to the arbitrator, so long as the delegation is clear and unmistakable. We reaffirmed this rule, and added some nuance, in *First Options*. Against the background presumption that questions of arbitrability go to the court, we stated that federal courts should "generally" apply "ordinary state-law principles that govern the formation of contracts" to assess "whether the parties agreed to arbitrate a certain matter (including arbitrability)."

But, we added, a more rigorous standard applies when the inquiry is whether the parties have "agreed to arbitrate arbitrability": "Courts should not assume that the parties agreed to arbitrate arbitrability unless there is clear and unmistakable evidence that they did so." Justice Breyer's unanimous opinion for the Court described this standard as a type of "revers[e]" "presumption"—one in favor of a judicial, rather than an arbitral, forum. Clear and unmistakable "evidence" of agreement to arbitrate arbitrability might include, as was urged in *First Options*, a course of conduct demonstrating assent, or, as is urged in this case, an express agreement to do so. In any event, whether such evidence exists is a matter for the court to determine.

The second line of cases bearing on who decides the validity of an arbitration agreement, as the Court explains, involves the *Prima Paint* rule. That rule recognizes two types of validity challenges. One type challenges the validity of the arbitration agreement itself, on a ground arising from an infirmity in that agreement. The other challenges the validity of the arbitration agreement tangentially—via a claim that the entire contract (of which the arbitration agreement is but a part) is invalid for some reason. *See Buckeye*, 546 U.S., at 444, 126 S. Ct. 1204, 163 L. Ed. 2d 1038. Under *Prima Paint*, a challenge of the first type goes to the court; a challenge of the second type goes to the arbitrator. *See* 388 U.S., at 403–404, 87 S. Ct. 1801, 18 L. Ed. 2d 1270; *see also Buckeye*. The *Prima Paint* rule is akin to a pleading standard, whereby a party seeking to challenge the validity of an arbitration agreement must expressly say so in order to get his dispute into court.

In sum, questions related to the validity of an arbitration agreement are usually matters for a court to resolve before it refers a dispute to arbitration. But questions of arbitrability may go to the arbitrator in two instances: (1) when the parties have demonstrated, clearly and unmistakably, that it is their intent to do so; or (2) when the validity of an arbitration agreement depends exclusively on the validity of the substantive contract of which it is a part.

II.

We might have resolved this case by simply applying the *First Options* rule: Does the arbitration agreement at issue "clearly and unmistakably" evince petitioner's and respondent's intent to submit questions of arbitrability to the arbitrator? The answer to that question is no. Respondent's claim that the arbitration agreement is unconscionable undermines any suggestion that he "clearly" and "unmistakably" assented to submit questions of arbitrability to the arbitrator. *See* Restatement (Second) of Contracts § 208, Comment d (1979) ("[G]ross inequality of bargaining power, together with terms unreasonably favorable to the stronger party, may confirm indications that the transaction involved elements of deception or compulsion, or may show that the weaker party had no meaningful choice, no real alternative, or did not in fact assent or appear to assent to the unfair terms"); *American Airlines, Inc. v. Wolens*, 513 U.S. 219, 249, 115 S. Ct. 817, 130 L. Ed. 2d 715 (1995) (O'Connor, J., concurring in judgment and dissenting in part) ("[A] determination that a contract is 'unconscionable' may in fact be a determination that one party did not intend to agree to the terms of the contract"). The fact that the agreement's "delegation" provision suggests assent is beside the point, because the gravamen of respondent's claim is that he never consented to the terms in his agreement.

In other words, when a party raises a good-faith validity challenge to the arbitration agreement itself, that issue must be resolved before a court can say that he clearly and unmistakably intended to arbitrate that very validity question. This case well illustrates the point: If respondent's unconscionability claim is correct—i.e., if the terms of the agreement are so one-sided and the process of its making so unfair—it would contravene the existence of clear and unmistakable assent to arbitrate the very question petitioner now seeks to arbitrate. Accordingly, it is necessary for the court to resolve the merits of respondent's unconscionability claim in order to decide whether the parties have a valid arbitration agreement under § 2. Otherwise, that section's preservation of revocation issues for the Court would be meaningless.

This is, in essence, how I understand the Court of Appeals to have decided the issue below. *See* 581 F.3d 912, 917 (CA9 2009) ("[W]e hold that where, as here, a party challenges an arbitration agreement as unconscionable, and thus asserts that he could not meaningfully assent to the agreement, the threshold question of unconscionability is for the court"). I would therefore affirm its judgment, leaving, as it did, the merits of respondent's unconscionability claim for the District Court to resolve on remand.

III.

Rather than apply *First Options*, the Court takes us down a different path, one neither briefed by the parties nor relied upon by the Court of Appeals. In applying *Prima Paint*, the Court has unwisely extended a "fantastic" and likely erroneous decision. 388 U.S., at 407, 87 S. Ct. 1801, 18 L. Ed. 2d 1270 (Black, J., dissenting).

As explained at the outset, this case lies at a seeming crossroads in our arbitration jurisprudence. It implicates cases such as *First Options*, which address whether the parties intended to delegate questions of arbitrability, and also those cases, such as *Prima Paint*, which address the severability of a presumptively valid arbitration agreement from a potentially invalid contract. The question of "Who decides?"—arbitrator or court—animates both lines of cases, but they are driven by different concerns. In cases like *First Options*, we are concerned with the parties' intentions. In cases like *Prima Paint*, we are concerned with how the parties challenge the validity of the agreement.

Under the *Prima Paint* inquiry, recall, we consider whether the parties are actually challenging the validity of the arbitration agreement, or whether they are challenging, more generally, the contract within which an arbitration clause is nested. In the latter circumstance, we assume there is no infirmity per se with the arbitration agreement, i.e., there are no grounds for revocation of the arbitration agreement itself under § 2 of the FAA. Accordingly, we commit the parties' general contract dispute to the arbitrator, as agreed.

The claim in *Prima Paint* was that one party would not have agreed to contract with the other for services had it known the second party was insolvent (a fact known but not disclosed at the time of contracting). There was, therefore, allegedly fraud in the inducement of the contract— a contract which also delegated disputes to an arbitrator. Despite the fact that the claim raised would have, if successful, rendered the embedded arbitration clause void, the Court held that the merits of the dispute were for the arbitrator, so long as the claim of "fraud in the inducement" did not go to validity of "the arbitration clause itself." Because, in *Prima Paint*, "no claim ha[d] been advanced by Prima Paint that [respondent] fraudulently induced it to enter into the agreement to arbitrate," and because the arbitration agreement was broad enough to cover the dispute, the arbitration agreement was enforceable with respect to the controversy at hand.

The *Prima Paint* rule has been denominated as one related to severability. Our opinion in *Buckeye*, set out these guidelines:

> "First, as a matter of substantive federal arbitration law, an arbitration provision is severable from the remainder of the contract. Second, unless the challenge is to the arbitration clause itself, the issue of the contract's validity is considered by the arbitrator in the first instance."

Whether the general contract defense renders the entire agreement void or voidable is irrelevant. All that matters is whether the party seeking to present the issue to a court has brought a "discrete challenge[] to the validity of the . . . arbitration clause." *Buckeye*.

Prima Paint and its progeny allow a court to pluck from a potentially invalid contract a potentially valid arbitration agreement. Today the Court adds a new layer of severability—something akin to Russian nesting dolls—into the mix: Courts may now pluck from a potentially invalid arbitration agreement even narrower provisions that refer particular arbitrability disputes to an arbitrator. I do not think an agreement to arbitrate can ever manifest a clear and unmistakable intent to arbitrate its own validity. But even assuming otherwise, I certainly would not hold that the *Prima Paint* rule extends this far.

In my view, a general revocation challenge to a standalone arbitration agreement is, invariably, a challenge to the "'making'" of the arbitration agreement itself, and therefore, under *Prima Paint*, must be decided by the court. A claim of procedural unconscionability aims to undermine the formation of the arbitration agreement, much like a claim of unconscionability aims to undermine the clear-and-unmistakable-intent requirement necessary for a valid delegation of a "discrete" challenge to the validity of the arbitration agreement itself. Moreover, because we are dealing in this case with a challenge to an independently executed arbitration agreement—rather than a clause contained in a contract related to another subject matter—any challenge to the contract itself is also, necessarily, a challenge to the arbitration agreement. They are one and the same.

The Court, however, reads the delegation clause as a distinct mini-arbitration agreement divisible from the contract in which it resides—which just so happens also to be an arbitration agreement. Although the Court simply declares that it "makes no difference" that the underlying subject matter of the agreement is itself an arbitration agreement, . . . that proposition does not follow from—rather it is at odds with—*Prima Paint*'s severability rule.

Had the parties in this case executed only one contract, on two sheets of paper—one sheet with employment terms, and a second with arbitration terms—the contract would look much like the one in *Buckeye*. There would be some substantive terms, followed by some arbitration terms, including what we now call a delegation clause—i.e., a sentence or two assigning to the arbitrator any disputes related to the validity of the arbitration provision. *See Buckeye*. If respondent then came into court claiming that the contract was illegal as a whole for some reason unrelated to the arbitration provision, the *Prima Paint* rule would apply, and such a general challenge to the subject matter of the contract would go to the arbitrator. Such a challenge would not call into question the making of the arbitration agreement or its invalidity per se.

Before today, however, if respondent instead raised a challenge specific to "the validity of the agreement to arbitrate"— for example, that the agreement to arbitrate was void under state law—the challenge would have gone to the court. That is what *Buckeye* says. But the Court now declares that *Prima Paint*'s pleading rule requires more: A party must lodge a challenge with even greater specificity than what would have satisfied the *Prima Paint* Court. A claim that an entire arbitration agreement is invalid will not go to the court unless the party challenges the particular sentences that delegate such claims to the arbitrator, on some contract ground that is particular and unique to those sentences.

It would seem the Court reads *Prima Paint* to require, as a matter of course, infinite layers of severability: We must always pluck from an arbitration agreement the specific delegation mechanism that would—but for present judicial review—commend the matter to arbitration, even if this delegation clause is but one sentence within one paragraph within a standalone agreement. And, most importantly, the party must identify this one sentence and lodge a specific challenge to its validity. Otherwise, he will be bound to pursue his validity claim in arbitration.

The notion that a party may be bound by an arbitration clause in a contract that is nevertheless invalid may be difficult for any lawyer—or any person—to accept, but this is the law of *Prima Paint*. It reflects a judgment that the "national policy favoring arbitration," outweighs the interest in preserving a judicial forum for questions of arbitrability—but only when questions of arbitrability are bound up in an underlying dispute. *Prima Paint*. When the two are so bound up, there is actually no gateway matter at all: The question "Who decides" is the entire ball game. Were a court to decide the fraudulent inducement question in *Prima Paint*, in order to decide the antecedent question of the validity of the included arbitration agreement, then it would also, necessarily, decide the merits of the underlying dispute. Same, too, for the question of illegality in *Buckeye*; on its way to deciding the arbitration agreement's validity, the court would have to decide whether the contract was illegal, and in so doing, it would decide the merits of the entire dispute.

In this case, however, resolution of the unconscionability question will have no bearing on the merits of the underlying employment dispute. It will only, as a preliminary matter, resolve who should decide the merits of that dispute. Resolution of the unconscionability question will, however, decide whether the arbitration agreement itself is "valid" under "such grounds as exist at law or in equity for the revocation of any contract." 9 U.S.C. § 2. As *Prima Paint* recognizes, the FAA commits those gateway matters, specific to the arbitration agreement, to the court. Indeed, it is clear that the present controversy over whether the arbitration agreement is unconscionable is itself severable from the merits of the underlying dispute, which involves a claim of employment discrimination. This is true for all gateway matters, and for this reason *Prima Paint* has no application in this case.

Notes and Questions

1. *Rent-A-Center* contains a delegation clause. It provided that "the Arbitrator shall have exclusive authority to resolve any disputes relating to the enforceability of this Agreement"—which would go to arbitrability—and then went even further, granting the arbitrator power to rule on "any claim that all or any part of this Agreement is void or voidable." Thus, the arbitrator was granted, by the parties, the full power to decide not just whether the arbitration clause itself was valid but whether any part of the contract was invalid enough to defeat arbitration. By so doing, the parties answered up front the "who" question. What was left to litigate?
2. Didn't the plaintiff here do exactly what the Court instructed be done in *Prima Paint*? He attacked the arbitration clause, not the contract. This is the essence of severability—at which point Justice Scalia, writing for the majority, held that this was not enough. Because there was a delegation clause, then for *Prima Paint* purposes, the plaintiff should have attacked *that* clause and not the arbitration clause itself. Justice Scalia landed squarely on plaintiff's lawyer's choice of attack: "Accordingly, unless Jackson challenged the delegation provision specifically, we must treat it as valid under sec. 2, and just enforce it under secs. 3 and 4, leaving any challenge to the validity of the Agreement as a whole for the arbitrator." Why should it matter whether the challenge is to the delegation clause or the arbitration clause if both (obviously) apply to arbitration? Shouldn't either satisfy *Prima Paint*?
3. All this was too much for Justice Stevens, who saw in this precisely the dangers Justice Black foretold in *Prima Paint* ("In applying *Prima Paint*,

the Court has unwisely extended a 'fantastic' and likely erroneous decision. . .") (citing Justice Black's *Prima Paint* dissent)). Justice Stevens accused the majority of reducing this to a game of "Russian nesting dolls."

4. Return again to the issue of proof: if *Prima Paint* shifted to the arbitration challenger the burden of establishing fraud in the arbitration clause, is Justice Stevens correct that it is too far a leap to now shift that burden to showing fraud or other invalidity in the delegation clause? And isn't this precisely the difficult burden the arbitration bar was trying to impose on challengers? What types of evidence would you now seek to gather in mounting a challenge?

Chapter 4
Arbitration and Class Actions

I. Overview of the Class Action Ban Debate

"What rational lawyer would have signed on to represent the Concepcions in litigation for the possibility of fees stemming from a $30.22 claim?" So wrote Justice Breyer in dissent in the Supreme Court's 2011 decision in *AT&T Mobility v. Concepcion*, 563 U.S. 333, 365 (2011), which upheld an arbitration clause's ban on class actions despite an express state rule invalidating such bans. Voicing the same sentiment in similar circumstances, another judge wrote that "only a lunatic or fanatic sues for $30," *Carnegie v. Household Int'l, Inc.*, 376 F.3d 656, 661 (7th Cir. 2004), and was cited in Justice Ginsburg's 2015 *DIRECTV* dissent, *DIRECTV, Inc. v. Imburgia*, 136 S. Ct. 463, 476 (2015). Behind these one-liners is the serious notion that small-dollar consumer cases need a class action structure if they are to proceed at all, because no consumer would sign on for the possibility of such a small verdict and no lawyer would sign on for the possibility of such a small fee. Go big, or don't go at all. "The realistic alternative to a class action is not 17 million individual suits, but zero individual suits." *Carnegie*, at 661.

Yet five years after *Concepcion*, Justice Breyer wrote the majority opinion in *DIRECTV, Inc. v. Imburgia*, 136 S. Ct. 463 (2015), in which the parties had agreed that the class action ban in their arbitration clause could be invalidated if their state law would not enforce that ban. The majority found that allowing parties to contract around Supreme Court decisions in that matter was overtly hostile to the purposes of the Federal Arbitration Act. Justice Breyer wrote that while parties to arbitration were free to choose whatever law they wanted, including "the law of Tibet" or "the law of pre-revolutionary Russia," they were not free to choose the law of California as it existed before the Supreme Court's *Concepcion* ruling.

The pro-arbitration, anti-class action posture taken by the courts became a political issue. Ultimately, the Obama administration proposed regulatory reforms. These died on the vine in the early days of the Trump administration. Whether future administrations revive these efforts is open to the question, but for now the law remains settled and distinctly in favor of allowing arbitration clauses to ban class actions. What has lost is the ban on the ban, rather than the ban itself. Justice Gorsuch was blunt at the end of his 2018 majority opinion in *Epic*, concluding that the pro-arbitration views in the Court may not be popular in all circles, but will remain the law absent a legislative solution:

> The respective merits of class actions and private arbitration as means of enforcing the law are questions constitutionally entrusted not to the courts to decide but to the policy makers in the political branches where those questions remain hotly contested. Just recently, for example, one federal agency banned individualized arbitration agreements it blamed for under enforcement of certain laws, only to see Congress respond by immediately repealing that rule. This Court is not free to substitute its preferred economic policies for those chosen by the people's representatives. The policy may be debatable but the law is clear: Congress has instructed that arbitration agreements like those before us must be enforced as written. Congress is of course always free to amend this judgment.

Epic Sys. Corp. v. Lewis, 138 S. Ct. 1612, 1632 (2018).

No subject in arbitration has received more attention—from the courts, from commentary, and from the legislature—than the intersection of arbitration and class actions. On one side of the debate are those who say that a deal is a deal, a contract is a contract, and arbitration agreements—as you have just reviewed over the past two chapters—must be enforced as written, no matter their impact. On the other side are those who say that these "contracts" are not fairly made; that at the consumer level there is no real "assent," and therefore concepts of mandate and consensus are illusory; and, most important of all, that the impact of enforcing arbitration agreements as written is to displace ordinary people not just from court but from any remedy at all while at the same time distorting the market in favor of bad actors, who are able to avoid massive liability by avoiding class-wide liability in favor of piecemeal individual litigation (or no litigation at all).

This chapter studies that conflict. The following materials summarize the present state of the law and give an insight into the legal/administrative/political battle that is likely to rage on beyond your graduation. These cases apply and therefore shed further light upon concepts we have already studied, including arbitrability, the pro-arbitration presumption, severability, and federalism. We explore as well, in the context of this dispute, the notion of arbitration as "efficient," and consider too the impact arbitration agreements have on competing statutory regimes—the so-called "effective vindication" debate.

We begin with the basic question, *what is a class action*? As you may recall from civil procedure, a class action allows an individual or small group of persons to sue on behalf of a representative class. Not all class members have to be named or even participate in the suit. Class actions have specific requirements, laid out in Rule 23 of the Federal Rules of Civil Procedure, including that the class be definable, that it is numerous, that the class action representatives are typical of the class, that the class representative and the attorney seeking to represent the class are adequate to perform their functions, and that a class action is superior to individual actions.[1] In practice, class actions can be far more lucrative for the lawyers of the class, who can reap substantial fees, than for individual class members, who may receive relatively low, unsatisfactory, or non-compensatory awards. The flip side of this argument is that unless a case had a class action structure, it would not exist at all, and the defendant would be free to continue its conduct, essentially immune from any reckoning. Wholly apart from the arbitration focus of this chapter, class actions themselves are a controversial procedural tool.

The cases considering class actions under the FAA have shifted in their focus. Originally, as we have just seen in Chapter 3, most class action cases arose as effective test cases for the question of arbitrability: who decides—the court or the arbitrator—whether the arbitration should be a class action or an individual action? The underlying question of whether an arbitration should be a class action at all was subsumed. *See, e.g.*, *Buckeye Check Cashing, Inc. v. Cardegna*, 546 U.S. 440 (2006). As these cases continued to be brought, the real issue simmering behind them emerged: if an arbitration agreement contains a class action ban, is it enforceable?

Consider two arbitration clauses:

A. Any and all disputes under, relating to, or concerning this contract must be resolved by arbitration by a sole arbitrator.

B. Any and all disputes under, relating to, or concerning this contract must be resolved by binding arbitration according to the Commercial Arbitration Rules of the American Arbitration Association in effect at the time of the execution of this contract. The arbitrator shall have the power to decide any disputes as to his or her power including but not limited to the arbitrability of this dispute. In no event shall a dispute hereunder be resolved by a class action process or procedure, in arbitration or elsewhere, and by executing this agreement the parties both agree to waive any right to or participation in a class action proceeding relative to this contract and this dispute.

Clause A is a straight-forward arbitration clause with no other bells or whistles. Clause B contains both a delegation clause and a class action ban. Which would you prefer to execute? Which should the courts enforce? Which would a client unable to afford a lawyer prefer? Which would a large commercial defendant eager to cap its risk prefer?

The past decade has seen a distinct shift to Option B. The *Greentree* and *Buckeye* questions of who decides, reviewed in Chapter 3, gradually assumed less importance

1. In addition to these four core criteria applicable to all class actions, depending on the facts of the case and the type of relief sought, additional requirements are imposed by subsections (b)(1)–(4) of F.R.C.P. 23.

as the Bar grew more sophisticated in how to draft arbitration clauses. Lawyers read cases. "Adhesion arbitration contract drafters can easily avoid having arbitrability issues decided by a court rather than by an arbitrator." Ronald G. Aronovsky, *The Supreme Court and the Future of Arbitration*, 42 Sw. L. Rev. 131, 160 (2012). After *First Options* permitted lawyers to insert a clause that allows arbitrators to decide arbitrability, and *Green Tree* held that the validity of a class action procedure was up to the arbitrator absent language one way or the other in the arbitration clause, it was but a short leap to the formulation of clauses that (a) delegate arbitrability to the arbitrator and (b) expressly prohibit class actions in that arbitration. In a fell swoop, class actions were eliminated from arbitration.

Nor did it end there. If all consumer cases must be heard in arbitration, and no arbitration cases can be class actions, then all consumer cases must be one-on-one, solitary actions. That takes us back to the opening lines of this chapter: very few consumers will bring such cases and very few lawyers will sign on for them. By layering a delegation clause on top of an arbitration clause and sprinkling in a class action ban, arbitration lawyers created a triple punch that has been sustained by the cases in this chapter: wrap all consumers in an arbitration, ensure that any questions about that clause are themselves resolved in arbitration, and then ban class actions from that arbitration. The consumer never sees court and can never proceed collectively in *any* forum.

Was this Congress' intent in passing the FAA in 1925? The debate on this question triggered a war in three steps. First, responding to arguments that class action bans are unconscionable, a number of states passed laws that invalidated class action waivers in dispute resolution clauses, both in arbitration and litigation. These state laws quickly found a federal administrative ally: near the end of the Obama administration, a federal agency called the Consumer Financial Protection Bureau proposed a rule that would have invalidated class action bans in arbitration clauses in consumer financial services contracts. Third, the commercial interests on the other side of the clause—the ones imposing the ban in the first place—struck back with arguments that ignoring the ban was contrary to post-*Moses Cone*, pro-contract, pro-arbitration interpretations of the FAA.

The result in the period from 2010 through 2019 was a rout. In case after case, an uncommon number of which reached the Supreme Court, challenges to arbitration clauses with class action bans failed. Justice Ginsburg observed in her 2015 *DIRECTV* dissent that "it has become routine, in a large part due to this Court's decisions, for powerful economic enterprises to write into their form contracts with consumers and employees no-class-action arbitration clauses." 136 S. Ct. at 471. Plaintiffs tried everything: arguments of unconscionability, federalism, "effective vindication," adhesion, and other attacks. While state courts have continued to try and lay down pro-consumer rules, federal common law has been strikingly one-sided and consistent. The consistent holding from the Supreme Court has been that if a particular rule or statute interferes with an as-written arbitration clause, the statute or rule defers to the clause. Meanwhile, the Obama administration agency rule did not survive the transition to the Trump administration and never became final.

The class action ban stands. We review those cases below, starting with the judicial decisions that set the stage for the conflict.

II. *Concepcion* and Its Progeny: The Supreme Court's Class Action Arbitration Jurisprudence

AT&T Mobility LLC v. Concepcion

563 U.S. 333, 131 S. Ct. 1740 (2011)

JUSTICE SCALIA delivered the opinion of the Court.

I.

Section 2 of the Federal Arbitration Act (FAA) makes agreements to arbitrate "valid, irrevocable, and enforceable, save upon such grounds as exist at law or in equity for the revocation of any contract." 9 U.S.C. § 2. We consider whether the FAA prohibits States from conditioning the enforceability of certain arbitration agreements on the availability of classwide arbitration procedures.

II.

The FAA was enacted in 1925 in response to widespread judicial hostility to arbitration agreements. *See Hall Street Associates, L. L. C. v. Mattel, Inc.*, 552 U.S. 576, 581 (2008). Section 2, the "primary substantive provision of the Act," *Moses H. Cone Memorial Hospital v. Mercury Constr. Corp.*, 460 U.S. 1, 24 (1983), provides, in relevant part, as follows:

> "A written provision in any maritime transaction or a contract evidencing a transaction involving commerce to settle by arbitration a controversy thereafter arising out of such contract or transaction . . . shall be valid, irrevocable, and enforceable, save upon such grounds as exist at law or in equity for the revocation of any contract." 9 U.S.C. § 2.

We have described this provision as reflecting both a "liberal federal policy favoring arbitration," *Moses H. Cone, supra,* at 24, 103 S. Ct. 927, 74 L. Ed. 2d 765, and the "fundamental principle that arbitration is a matter of contract," *Rent-A-Center, West, Inc.* v. *Jackson*, 561 U.S. 63, 67 (2010). In line with these principles, courts must place arbitration agreements on an equal footing with other contracts, *Buckeye Check*

Cashing, Inc. v. *Cardegna*, 546 U.S. 440, 443 (2006), and enforce them according to their terms. *Volt Information Sciences, Inc. v. Board of Trustees of Leland Stanford Junior Univ.*, 489 U.S. 468, 478 (1989).

The final phrase of § 2, however, permits arbitration agreements to be declared unenforceable "upon such grounds as exist at law or in equity for the revocation of any contract." This saving clause permits agreements to arbitrate to be invalidated by "generally applicable contract defenses, such as fraud, duress, or unconscionability," but not by defenses that apply only to arbitration or that derive their meaning from the fact that an agreement to arbitrate is at issue The question in this case is whether § 2 pre-empts California's rule classifying most collective-arbitration waivers in consumer contracts as unconscionable. We refer to this rule as the *Discover Bank* rule.

Under California law, courts may refuse to enforce any contract found "to have been unconscionable at the time it was made," or may "limit the application of any unconscionable clause." Cal. Civ. Code Ann. § 1670.5(a) (West 1985). A finding of unconscionability requires "a 'procedural' and a 'substantive' element, the former focusing on 'oppression' or 'surprise' due to unequal bargaining power, the latter on 'overly harsh' or 'one-sided' results." *Armendariz* v. *Foundation Health Psychcare Servs.*, 24 Cal. 4th 83, 114 (2000); accord, *Discover Bank*, 36 Cal. 4th, at 159–161.

In *Discover Bank*, the California Supreme Court applied this framework to class-action waivers in arbitration agreements and held as follows:

> "[W]hen the waiver is found in a consumer contract of adhesion in a setting in which disputes between the contracting parties predictably involve small amounts of damages, and when it is alleged that the party with the superior bargaining power has carried out a scheme to deliberately cheat large numbers of consumers out of individually small sums of money, then . . . the waiver becomes in practice the exemption of the party 'from responsibility for [its] own fraud, or willful injury to the person or property of another.' Under these circumstances, such waivers are unconscionable under California law and should not be enforced." *Id.*, at 162–163 (quoting Cal. Civ. Code Ann. § 1668).

California courts have frequently applied this rule to find arbitration agreements unconscionable. See, *e.g.*, *Cohen* v. *DIRECTV, Inc.*, 142 Cal. App. 4th 1442, 1451–1453 (2006); *Klussman* v. *Cross Country Bank*, 134 Cal. App. 4th 1283, 1297 (2005); *Aral* v. *EarthLink, Inc.*, 134 Cal. App. 4th 544, 556–557 (2005).

III.

A.

The Concepcions argue that the *Discover Bank* rule, given its origins in California's unconscionability doctrine and California's policy against exculpation, is a ground that "exist[s] at law or in equity for the revocation of any contract" under FAA § 2. Moreover, they argue that even if we construe the *Discover Bank* rule as a prohibition on collective-action waivers rather than simply an application of unconscionability, the rule would still be applicable to all dispute-resolution contracts, since California prohibits waivers of class litigation as well. See *America Online, Inc.* v. *Superior Court*, 90 Cal. App. 4th 1, 17–18 (2001).

When state law prohibits outright the arbitration of a particular type of claim, the analysis is straightforward: The conflicting rule is displaced by the FAA. *Preston* v. *Ferrer*, 552 U.S. 346, 353 (2008). But the inquiry becomes more complex when a doctrine normally thought to be generally applicable, such as duress or, as relevant here, unconscionability, is alleged to have been applied in a fashion that disfavors arbitration. In *Perry* v. *Thomas*, 482 U.S. 483 (1987), for example, we noted that the FAA's pre-emptive effect might extend even to grounds traditionally thought to exist " 'at law or in equity for the revocation of any contract.' *Id.*, at 492, n. 9 (emphasis deleted). We said that a court may not "rely on the uniqueness of an agreement to arbitrate as a basis for a state-law holding that enforcement would be unconscionable, for this would enable the court to effect what . . . the state legislature cannot." *Id.*, at 493, n. 9.

The Concepcions suggest that all this is just a parade of horribles, and no genuine worry. "Rules aimed at destroying arbitration" or "demanding procedures incompatible with arbitration," they concede, "would be preempted by the FAA because they cannot sensibly be reconciled with Section 2." The "grounds" available under § 2's saving clause, they admit, "should not be construed to include a State's mere preference for procedures that are incompatible with arbitration and 'would wholly eviscerate arbitration agreements.' " *Id.*, at 33 (quoting *Carter* v. *SSC Odin Operating Co., LLC*, 237 Ill. 2d 30, 50 (2010)).

We largely agree. Although § 2's saving clause preserves generally applicable contract defenses, nothing in it suggests an intent to preserve state-law rules that stand as an obstacle to the accomplishment of the FAA's objectives. As we have said, a federal statute's saving clause "cannot in reason be construed as [allowing] a common law right, the continued existence of which would be absolutely inconsistent with the provisions of the act. In other words, the act cannot be held to destroy itself.

We differ with the Concepcions only in the application of this analysis to the matter before us. We do not agree that rules requiring judicially monitored discovery or adherence to the Federal Rules of Evidence are "a far cry from this case." The overarching purpose of the FAA, evident in the text of §§ 2, 3, and 4, is to ensure the enforcement of arbitration agreements according to their terms so as to facilitate streamlined proceedings. Requiring the availability of classwide arbitration interferes with fundamental attributes of arbitration and thus creates a scheme inconsistent with the FAA.

B.

The "principal purpose" of the FAA is to "ensur[e] that private arbitration agreements are enforced according to their terms." *Volt*, 489 U.S., at 478; *see also Stolt-Nielsen S. A.* v. *AnimalFeeds Int'l Corp.*, 559 U.S. 662, 681–682 (2010). This purpose is readily apparent from the FAA's text. Section 2 makes arbitration agreements "valid, irrevocable, and enforceable" as written (subject, of course, to the saving clause); § 3 requires courts to stay litigation of arbitral claims pending arbitration of those claims "in accordance with the terms of the agreement"; and § 4 requires courts to compel arbitration "in accordance with the terms of the agreement" upon the motion of either party to the agreement (assuming that the "making of the arbitration agreement or the failure . . . to perform the same" is not at issue). In light of these provisions, we have held that parties may agree to limit the issues subject to arbitration.

The point of affording parties discretion in designing arbitration processes is to allow for efficient, streamlined procedures tailored to the type of dispute. It can be specified, for example, that the decisionmaker be a specialist in the relevant field, or that proceedings be kept confidential to protect trade secrets. And the informality of arbitral proceedings is itself desirable, reducing the cost and increasing the speed of dispute resolution.

The dissent quotes *Dean Witter Reynolds Inc. v. Byrd*, 470 U.S. 213, 219 (1985), as "'reject[ing] the suggestion that the overriding goal of the Arbitration Act was to promote the expeditious resolution of claims.'? *Post*, at ___, 179 L. Ed. 2d, at 764 (opinion of Breyer, J.). That is greatly misleading. After saying (accurately enough) that "the overriding goal of the Arbitration Act was [not] to promote the expeditious resolution of claims," but to "ensure judicial enforcement of privately made agreements to arbitrate," 470 U.S., at 219, *Dean Witter* went on to explain: "This is not to say that Congress was blind to the potential benefit of the legislation for expedited resolution of disputes. Far from it."

In the present case, of course, those "two goals" do not conflict—and it is the dissent's view that would frustrate *both* of them.

Contrary to the dissent's view, our cases place it beyond dispute that the FAA was designed to promote arbitration. They have repeatedly described the Act as "embod[ying] [a] national policy favoring arbitration," *Buckeye Check Cashing*, 546 U.S., at 443, and "a liberal federal policy favoring arbitration agreements, notwithstanding any state substantive or procedural policies to the contrary," *Moses H. Cone*, 460 U.S., at 24.

California's *Discover Bank* rule interferes with arbitration. Although the rule does not *require* classwide arbitration, it allows any party to a consumer contract to demand it *ex post*. The rule is limited to adhesion contracts, *Discover Bank*, 36 Cal. 4th, at 162–163, but the times in which consumer contracts were anything other than adhesive are long past.

The rule also requires that damages be predictably small, and that the consumer allege a scheme to cheat consumers. *Discover Bank*, *supra*, at 162–163. The former requirement, however, is toothless and malleable (the Ninth Circuit has held that damages of $4,000 are sufficiently small, see *Oestreicher* v. *Alienware Corp.*, 322 Fed. Appx. 489, 492 (2009) (unpublished)), and the latter has no limiting effect, as all that is required is an allegation. Consumers remain free to bring and resolve their disputes on a bilateral basis under *Discover Bank*, and some may well do so; but there is little incentive for lawyers to arbitrate on behalf of individuals when they may do so for a class and reap far higher fees in the process. And faced with inevitable class arbitration, companies would have less incentive to continue resolving potentially duplicative claims on an individual basis.

Although we have had little occasion to examine classwide arbitration, our decision in *Stolt-Nielsen* is instructive. In that case we held that an arbitration panel exceeded its power under § 10(a)(4) of the FAA by imposing class procedures based on policy judgments rather than the arbitration agreement itself or some background principle of contract law that would affect its interpretation. 559 U.S., at 684–687. We then held that the agreement at issue, which was silent on the question of class procedures, could not be interpreted to allow them because the "changes brought about by the shift from bilateral arbitration to class-action arbitration" are "fundamental." *Id.*, at 686. This is obvious as a structural matter: Classwide arbitration includes absent parties, necessitating additional and different procedures and involving higher stakes. Confidentiality becomes more difficult. And while it is theoretically possible to select an arbitrator with some expertise relevant to the class-certification question, arbitrators are not generally knowledgeable in the often-dominant procedural aspects of certification, such as the protection of absent parties. The conclusion follows that class arbitration, to the extent it is manufactured by *Discover Bank* rather than consensual, is inconsistent with the FAA.

First, the switch from bilateral to class arbitration sacrifices the principal advantage of arbitration—its informality—and makes the process slower, more costly, and more likely to generate procedural morass than final judgment. "In bilateral arbitration, parties forgo the procedural rigor and appellate review of the courts in order to realize the benefits of private dispute resolution: lower costs, greater efficiency and speed, and the ability to choose expert adjudicators to resolve specialized disputes." 559 U.S., at 685, 130 S. Ct. 1758, 1776, 176 L. Ed. 2d 605, 625. But before an arbitrator may decide the merits of a claim in classwide procedures, he must first decide, for example, whether the class itself may be certified, whether the named parties are sufficiently representative and typical, and how discovery for the class should be conducted. A cursory comparison of bilateral and class arbitration illustrates the difference. According to the American Arbitration Association (AAA), the average consumer arbitration between January and August 2007 resulted in a disposition on the merits in six months, four months if the arbitration was conducted by documents only. AAA, Analysis of the AAA's Consumer Arbitration Caseload, online at http://www.adr.org/si.asp?id=5027 (all Internet materials as visited Apr. 25, 2011, and available in Clerk of Court's case file). As of September 2009, the AAA had opened 283 class arbitrations. Of those, 121 remained active, and 162 had been settled, withdrawn, or dismissed. Not a single one, however, had resulted in a final award on the merits. Brief for AAA as *Amicus Curiae* in *Stolt-Nielsen*, O.T. 2009, No. 08-1198, pp.

22–24. For those cases that were no longer active, the median time from filing to settlement, withdrawal, or dismissal—not judgment on the merits—was 583 days, and the mean was 630 days. *Id.*, at 24.

Second, class arbitration *requires* procedural formality. The AAA's rules governing class arbitrations mimic the Federal Rules of Civil Procedure for class litigation. Compare AAA, Supplementary Rules for Class Arbitrations (effective Oct. 8, 2003), online at http://www.adr.org/sp.asp?id=21936, with Fed. Rule Civ. Proc. 23. And while parties can alter those procedures by contract, an alternative is not obvious. If procedures are too informal, absent class members would not be bound by the arbitration. For a class-action money judgment to bind absentees in litigation, class representatives must at all times adequately represent absent class members, and absent members must be afforded notice, an opportunity to be heard, and a right to opt out of the class. *Phillips Petroleum Co.* v. *Shutts*, 472 U.S. 797, 811–812 (1985). At least this amount of process would presumably be required for absent parties to be bound by the results of arbitration.

We find it unlikely that in passing the FAA Congress meant to leave the disposition of these procedural requirements to an arbitrator. Indeed, class arbitration was not even envisioned by Congress when it passed the FAA in 1925; as the California Supreme Court admitted in *Discover Bank*, class arbitration is a "relatively recent development." 36 Cal. 4th, at 163, 113 P. 3d, at 1110. And it is at the very least odd to think that an arbitrator would be entrusted with ensuring that third parties' due process rights are satisfied.

Third, class arbitration greatly increases risks to defendants. Informal procedures do of course have a cost: The absence of multilayered review makes it more likely that errors will go uncorrected. Defendants are willing to accept the costs of these errors in arbitration, since their impact is limited to the size of individual disputes, and presumably outweighed by savings from avoiding the courts. But when damages allegedly owed to tens of thousands of potential claimants are aggregated and decided at once, the risk of an error will often become unacceptable. Faced with even a small chance of a devastating loss, defendants will be pressured into settling questionable claims. Other courts have noted the risk of "in terrorem" settlements that class actions entail, see, *e.g.*, *Kohen* v. *Pac. Inv. Mgmt. Co. LLC & PIMCO Funds*, 571 F.3d 672, 677–678 (CA7 2009), and class arbitration would be no different.

Arbitration is poorly suited to the higher stakes of class litigation. In litigation, a defendant may appeal a certification decision on an interlocutory basis and, if unsuccessful, may appeal from a final judgment as well. Questions of law are reviewed *de novo* and questions of fact for clear error. In contrast, 9 U.S.C. § 10 allows a court to vacate an arbitral award *only* where the award "was procured by corruption, fraud, or undue means"; "there was evident partiality or corruption in the arbitrators"; "the arbitrators were guilty of misconduct in refusing to postpone the hearing . . . or in refusing to hear evidence pertinent and material to the controversy[,] or of any other misbehavior by which the rights of any party have been prejudiced"; or if the "arbitrators exceeded their powers, or so imperfectly executed them that a mutual, final, and definite award.

The Concepcions contend that because parties may and sometimes do agree to aggregation, class procedures are not necessarily incompatible with arbitration. But the same could be said about procedures that the Concepcions admit States may not superimpose on arbitration: Parties *could* agree to arbitrate pursuant to the Federal Rules of Civil Procedure, or pursuant to a discovery process rivaling that in litigation. Arbitration is a matter of contract, and the FAA requires courts to honor parties' expectations. *Rent-A-Center, West*, 561 U.S., at 67–69. But what the parties in the aforementioned examples would have agreed to is not arbitration as envisioned by the FAA, lacks its benefits, and therefore may not be required by state law.

The dissent claims that class proceedings are necessary to prosecute small-dollar claims that might otherwise slip through the legal system. But States cannot require a procedure that is inconsistent with the FAA, even if it is desirable for unrelated reasons. Moreover, the claim here was most unlikely to go unresolved. As noted earlier, the arbitration agreement provides that AT&T will pay claimants a minimum of $7,500 and twice their attorney's fees if they obtain an arbitration award greater than AT&T's last settlement offer. The District Court found this scheme sufficient to provide incentive for the individual prosecution of meritorious claims that are not immediately settled, and the Ninth Circuit admitted that aggrieved customers who filed claims would be "essentially guarantee[d]" to be made whole. Indeed, the District Court concluded that the Concepcions were *better off* under their arbitration agreement with AT&T than they would have been as participants in a class action, which "could take months, if not years, and which may merely yield an opportunity to submit a claim for recovery of a small percentage of a few dollars." *Laster*, 2008 U.S. Dist. LEXIS 103712, at *12.

Because it "stands as an obstacle to the accomplishment and execution of the full purposes and objectives of Congress," *Hines* v. *Davidowitz*, 312 U.S. 52, 67 (1941), California's *Discover Bank* rule is pre-empted by the FAA. The judgment of the Ninth Circuit is reversed, and the case is remanded for further proceedings consistent with this opinion.

It is so ordered.

JUSTICE BREYER, with whom JUSTICE GINSBURG, JUSTICE SOTOMAYOR, and JUSTICE KAGAN join, dissenting.

The Federal Arbitration Act says that an arbitration agreement "shall be valid, irrevocable, and enforceable, *save upon such grounds as exist at law or in equity for the revocation of any contract.*" 9 U.S.C. § 2 (emphasis added). California law sets forth certain circumstances in which "class action waivers" in *any* contract are unenforceable. In my view, this rule of state law is consistent with the federal Act's language and primary objective. It does not "stan[d] as an obstacle" to the Act's "accomplishment and execution." *Hines* v. *Davidowitz*, 312 U.S. 52, 67 (1941). And the Court is wrong to hold that the federal Act pre-empts the rule of state law.

I.

The California law in question consists of an authoritative state-court interpretation of two provisions of the California Civil Code. The first provision makes unlawful all contracts "which have for their object, directly or indirectly, to exempt anyone from responsibility for his own . . . violation of law." Cal. Civ. Code Ann. § 1668 (West 1985). The second provision authorizes courts to "limit the application of any unconscionable clause" in a contract so "as to avoid any unconscionable result." § 1670.5(a).

The specific rule of state law in question consists of the California Supreme Court's application of these principles to hold that "some" (but not "all") "class action waivers" in consumer contracts are exculpatory and unconscionable under California "law." *Discover Bank* v. *Superior Court*, 36 Cal. 4th 148, 160 (2005). In particular, in *Discover Bank* the California Supreme Court stated that, when a class-action waiver

> "is found in a consumer contract of adhesion in a setting in which disputes between the contracting parties predictably involve small amounts of damages, and when it is alleged that the party with the superior bargaining power has carried out a scheme to deliberately cheat large numbers of consumers out of individually small sums of money, then . . . the waiver becomes in practice the exemption of the party 'from responsibility for [its] own fraud, or willful injury to the person or property of another.' *Id.*, at 162–163, 113 P. 3d, at 1110.

In such a circumstance, the "waivers are unconscionable under California law and should not be enforced." *Idz.*, at 163.

The *Discover Bank* rule does not create a "blanket policy in California against class action waivers in the consumer context." *Provencher* v. *Dell, Inc.*, 409 F. Supp. 2d 1196, 1201 (CD Cal. 2006). Instead, it represents the "application of a more general [unconscionability] principle." *Gentry* v. *Superior Court*, 42 Cal. 4th 443, 457 (2007). Courts applying California law have enforced class-action waivers where they satisfy general unconscionability standards. And even when they fail, the parties remain free to devise other dispute mechanisms, including informal mechanisms, that, in context, will not prove unconscionable. See *Volt Information Sciences, Inc.* v. *Board of Trustees of Leland Stanford Junior Univ.*, 489 U.S. 468, 479 (1989).

II.

A.

The *Discover Bank* rule is consistent with the federal Act's language. It "applies equally to class action litigation waivers in contracts without arbitration agreements as it does to class arbitration waivers in contracts with such agreements." 36 Cal. 4th, at 165–166, 113 P. 3d, at 1112. Linguistically speaking, it falls directly within the scope of the Act's exception permitting courts to refuse to enforce arbitration agreements on grounds that exist "for the revocation of *any* contract." 9 U.S.C. § 2 (emphasis added). The majority agrees.

B.

The *Discover Bank* rule is also consistent with the basic "purpose behind" the Act. We have described that purpose as one of "ensur[ing] judicial enforcement" of arbitration agreements. 'The purpose of this bill is to make *valid and enforcible* agreements for arbitration' " H. R. Rep. No. 96, 68th Cong., 1st Sess., 1 (1924); emphasis added)); 65 Cong. Rec. 1931 (1924) ("It creates no new legislation, grants no new rights, except a remedy to enforce an agreement in commercial contracts and in admiralty contracts"). As is well known, prior to the federal Act, many courts expressed hostility to arbitration, for example, by refusing to order specific performance of agreements to arbitrate. The Act sought to eliminate that hostility by placing agreements to arbitrate " '*upon the same footing as other contracts*.' *Scherk* v. *Alberto-Culver Co.*, 417 U.S. 506, 511, 94 S. Ct. 2449, 41 L. Ed. 2d 270 (1974) (quoting H. R. Rep. No. 96, at 2; emphasis added).

Thus, insofar as we seek to implement Congress' intent, we should think more than twice before invalidating a state law that does just what § 2 requires, namely, puts agreements to arbitrate and agreements to litigate "upon the same footing."

III.

The majority's contrary view that *Discover Bank* stands as an "obstacle" to the accomplishment of the federal law's objective rests primarily upon its claims that the *Discover Bank* rule increases the complexity of arbitration procedures, thereby discouraging parties from entering into arbitration agreements, and to that extent discriminating in practice against arbitration. These claims are not well founded.

For one thing, a state rule of law that would sometimes set aside as unconscionable a contract term that forbids class arbitration is not (as the majority claims) like a rule that would require "ultimate disposition by a jury" or "judicially monitored discovery" or use of "the Federal Rules of Evidence." Unlike the majority's examples, class arbitration is consistent with the use of arbitration. It is a form of arbitration that is well known in California and followed elsewhere. Indeed, the AAA has told us that it has found class arbitration to be "a fair, balanced, and efficient means of resolving class disputes." Brief for AAA as *Amicus Curiae* in *Stolt-Nielsen S. A.* v. *AnimalFeeds Int'l Corp.*, O. T. 2009, No. 08-1198, p. 25 (hereinafter AAA *Amicus* Brief). And unlike the majority's examples, the *Discover Bank* rule imposes equivalent limitations on litigation; hence it cannot fairly be characterized as a targeted attack on arbitration.

Where does the majority get its contrary idea—that individual, rather than class, arbitration is a "fundamental attribut[e]" of arbitration? The majority does not explain. And it is unlikely to be able to trace its present view to the history of the arbitration statute itself.

When Congress enacted the Act, arbitration procedures had not yet been fully developed. Insofar as Congress considered detailed forms of arbitration at all, it may well have thought that arbitration would be used primarily where merchants sought to resolve disputes of fact, not law, under the customs of their industries, where the parties possessed roughly equivalent bargaining power.

Regardless, if neither the history nor present practice suggests that class arbitration is fundamentally incompatible with arbitration itself, then on what basis can the majority hold California's law pre-empted?

For another thing, the majority's argument that the *Discover Bank* rule will discourage arbitration rests critically upon the wrong comparison. The majority compares the complexity of class arbitration with that of bilateral arbitration. And it finds the former more complex. See *ibid.* But, if incentives are at issue, the *relevant* comparison is not "arbitration with arbitration" but a comparison between class arbitration and judicial class actions. After all, in respect to the relevant set of contracts, the *Discover Bank* rule similarly and equally sets aside clauses that forbid class procedures—whether arbitration procedures or ordinary judicial procedures are at issue.

The majority's related claim that the *Discover Bank* rule will discourage the use of arbitration because "[a]rbitration is poorly suited to . . . higher stakes" lacks empirical support. Indeed, the majority provides no convincing reason to believe that parties are unwilling to submit high-stake disputes to arbitration. And there are numerous counterexamples. Loftus, Rivals Resolve Dispute Over Drug, *Wall Street Journal*, Apr. 16, 2011, p. B2 (discussing $500 million settlement in dispute submitted to arbitration); Ziobro, Kraft Seeks Arbitration In Fight With Starbucks Over Distribution, *Wall Street Journal*, Nov. 30, 2010, p. B10 (describing initiation of an arbitration in which the payout "could be higher" than $1.5 billion); Markoff, Software Arbitration Ruling Gives I.B.M. $833 Million From Fujitsu, *N. Y. Times*, Nov. 30, 1988, p. A1 (describing both companies as "pleased with the ruling" resolving a licensing dispute).

Because California applies the same legal principles to address the unconscionability of class arbitration waivers as it does to address the unconscionability of any other contractual provision, the merits of class proceedings should not factor into our decision. If California had applied its law of duress to void an arbitration agreement, would it matter if the procedures in the coerced agreement were efficient?

Regardless, the majority highlights the disadvantages of class arbitrations, as it sees them. But class proceedings have countervailing advantages. Agreements that forbid the consolidation of claims can lead small-dollar claimants to abandon their claims rather than to litigate. I suspect that it is true even here, for as the Court of Appeals recognized, AT&T can avoid the $7,500 payout (the payout that supposedly makes the Concepcions' arbitration worthwhile) simply by paying the claim's face value, such that "the maximum gain to a customer for the hassle of arbitrating a $30.22 dispute is still just $30.22."

What rational lawyer would have signed on to represent the Concepcions in litigation for the possibility of fees stemming from a $30.22 claim? See, *e.g.*, *Carnegie* v. *Household Int'l, Inc.*, 376 F.3d 656, 661 (CA7 2004) ("The *realistic* alternative to a class action is not 17 million individual suits, but zero individual suits, as only a lunatic or a fanatic sues for $30").

Federalism is as much a question of deeds as words. It often takes the form of a concrete decision by this Court that respects the legitimacy of a State's action in an individual case. Here, recognition of that federalist ideal, embodied in specific language in this particular statute, should lead us to uphold California's law, not to strike it down. We do not honor federalist principles in their breach.

With respect, I dissent.

Notes and Questions

1. Concepcion *and the Saving Clause.* Let's return to our discussion in Chapter 2 of the "saving clause" in Section 2 of the FAA. After *Concepcion*, is there anything left of this clause? Is anything "unconscionable"? And even if so, can state law do anything about it? The majority grappled with Section 2, first acknowledging that which is plainly written in the statute: that a rule that "applies the general principle of unconscionability or public-policy disapproval of exculpatory agreements . . . is applicable to 'any' contract and thus preserved by § 2." But the majority then made short work of this argument when it held that "[a]lthough § 2's saving clause preserved generally applicable contract defenses, nothing in it suggests an intent to preserve state-law rules that stand as an obstacle to the accomplishment of the FAA's objectives." That is a stark limitation of Section 2 and in particular of the "unconscionability" language in that statute. Courts supposedly remain free to invalidate arbitration clauses for general unconscionability, but the rule that emerged out of *Concepcion* is that "unconscionable" cannot mean any grounds that discriminate against arbitration itself. There is an inherent circularity to that argument which leaves precious little ground for Section 2 arguments, since by definition any arbitration clause struck down for unconscionability will foreclose the arbitration of that dispute. The majority would presumably respond that this reads *Concepcion* too broadly, and Section 2 remains but cannot be used to enforce rules, policies, or cases overtly anti-arbitration in construct and intent—such

as the *Discover Bank* rule. The Supreme Court would shortly return to that balance.

2. Did the arbitration clause at issue in *Concepcion* strike you as particularly friendly or unfriendly to the consumer? The arbitrator was given the power to award punitive damages; the arbitration could take place by phone; the consumer retained the right to go to small claims court; and a consumer who recovered more in the arbitration than AT&T offered would receive an automatic minimum award of $7,500 (likely far more than the amount of the claim) and full attorney's fees. Those pro-consumer features were, ironically, designed specifically to withstand judicial scrutiny for unfairness and adhesion. Why didn't this make a difference? Should it have? Conversely, consider a clause in which any consumer turning down AT&T's offer and then receiving less in the arbitration would have to pay AT&T a penalty and all AT&T's attorney's fees. Such a clause very likely would be viewed as unconscionable and one of adhesion—so why did it then not make any difference in *Concepcion*?
3. Was the ban in *Concepcion* targeted just to arbitration? Compare this case to *Marmet*, the West Virginia nursing home case we studied in Chapter 2. There, the Supreme Court held that a West Virginia statute that invalidated arbitrations against nursing homes was prohibited because it was arbitration-specific in its target. Did the *Discover Bank* rule invalidated by *Concepcion* target arbitration in particular? Or did it instead invalidate class action waivers in *any* dispute resolution clause, irrespective of whether that clause provided for litigation *or* arbitration? If arbitration is indisputably adversely affected by a state law but not *uniquely* affected, should that make a difference? Put differently: how was the *Discover Bank* rule uniquely targeted to arbitration for Section 2 purposes?
4. Justice Scalia candidly acknowledged that modern arbitration clauses in consumer contracts are not negotiated at all: "[T]he times in which consumer contracts were anything but adhesive are long past." He was equally candid about the difficulty individual consumers have in finding a lawyer: "[T]here is little incentive for lawyers to arbitrate on behalf of individuals when they may do so for a class and reap far higher fees." If even the majority acknowledged the adhesive nature of these contracts *and* the resulting representational impact, then is *Concepcion* consistent with the FAA's goals in enforcing consensual arbitration agreements? Is it legitimate jurisprudence to enforce an arbitration "agreement" after admitting that it is not an agreement at all but rather a unilateral cram down? How does that square with the concepts we discussed in Chapter 2 regarding mandate and consensus?

Comment: How Important Is Efficiency?

Just as *Moses Cone* announced a "liberal federal policy favoring arbitration" where no court had previously so stated, so did *Concepcion* suddenly elevate "efficiency" as a fundamental principle of arbitration. As Justice Scalia wrote for the majority, that "informality" was a "principle advantage" of arbitration. More formal procedures "make[] the process slower, more costly, and more likely to generate procedural morass than final judgment." *Concepcion*, 563 U.S. at 348.

Was this correct? Is efficiency a principle advantage of arbitration? If so, to what effect? What should give way in order to further efficiency?

To the *Concepcion* court (and its progeny), it was and remains a short step between bowing to efficiency and then mowing down anything, like class actions, that are seen to get in efficiency's way. But is efficiency really such a fundamental principle of arbitration? We can examine that question from a standpoint both of fact and of law.

As a factual proposition, Justice Breyer's dissent suggests that class arbitrations are *not* any more "inefficient" than class actions in court. That said, there can of course be no doubt that a litigant in a class action will move toward a result less quickly than a litigant in a single-plaintiff (or claimant) case. Class actions indisputably come with more process. But even leaving class actions aside, is arbitration really that much more efficient? The dollar costs and extended times of arbitration have been the focus of increasing concern. Edna Sussman & Christi Underwood, *Time and Cost Solutions for Commercial Arbitration: Highlights from the College of Commercial Arbitrators' Four Protocols for Parties, Counsel, Arbitrators and Arbitral Institutions*, 66(1) DISP. RESOL. J. 22–24 (Feb.-Apr. 2011); Michael A. Doornweerd & Andrew F. Merrick, *Strategies for Controlling Discovery Costs in Commercial Arbitration*, 12 COM. & BUS. LITIG. 4 (2011).

As a legal proposition, are efficiency and arbitration joined at the hip? Is that merely a matter of common sense? Or is this a judicially created presumption?

Efficiency is nowhere mentioned in the FAA or the legislative history; it was only in the modern arbitration era that courts ascribed this motivation to Congress. This progression happened gradually over three steps. First, in *Mitsubishi Motors Corp. v. Soler Chrysler Plymouth*, 473 U.S. 614, 628 (1985), the Court described arbitration as a "trade" in which a party "trades the procedures and opportunity for review of the courtroom for the simplicity, informality, and expedition of arbitration." Writing a few years later in *Stolt-Nielsen, S.A. v. Animal Feeds Int'l Corp.*, 559 U.S. 662 (2010), Justice Alito's majority opinion modified this description slightly but significantly: "In bilateral arbitration, parties forego the procedural rigor and appellate review of the courts *in order to realize* the benefits of private dispute resolution: lower costs, greater efficiency and speed, and the ability to choose expert adjudicators to resolve specialized disputes." *Id.* at 685 (emphasis added). Justice Scalia took the *Stolt-Nielsen* wording one step further in *Concepcion*, holding that parties agreed to arbitration *because of* efficiency concerns: "The point of affording parties discretion in designing arbitration processes is to allow for efficient, streamlined procedures tailored to the type of the dispute." 560 U.S. at 344. On Justice Scalia's reasoning, since the parties agreed to arbitration, they must have had efficiency on their mind.

This is a reasonable presumption, since removing procedural hurdles should reduce the amount of time and money parties need to spend to resolve their dispute. But is an efficient result always a just result? And do parties choose arbitration in order to obtain just results or speedy ones? *See* Hiro N. Aragaki, *Constructions of Arbitration's Informalism: Autonomy, Efficiency and Justice*, 2016 J. DISP. RESOL. 141, 150 (2016) (arguing that at the time of FAA's passage, proponents of arbitration viewed informalism as a method of obtaining just results, not speedy ones); Wesley A. Sturges, *Commercial Arbitration or Court Application of Common Law Rules of Marketing*, 34 YALE L.J. 480, 486–89 (1925) (arguing that evidentiary rules drove witnesses to yes-or-no answers which could detract from the merits). Efficiency may therefore not even have been on the minds of FAA proponents.

Despite these factual and legal questions as to the proper deference to be given "efficiency," the judicial ship has sailed. In the wake of *Concepcion*, courts now apply a legal presumption that efficiency is part of the arbitration contract, and any obstacle to that efficiency must be swept away. *See, e.g., Kindred Healthcare Operating, Inc. v. Boyd*, 403 P.3d 1014, 1016 (Wyo. 2017); *Richmond Health Facilities-Madison LP v. Curry*, 2017 WL 2211081 (Ky. Ct. App. May 19, 2017).

Is ascribing efficiency as an arbitration virtue simple common sense, or is it a further excuse for letting arbitration run amok over other rights?

CASE PREVIEW. The Supreme Court turned back to class actions in arbitration in two cases announced in June 2013: *Oxford Health* and *Italian Colors*. *Oxford Health* was a unanimous opinion authored by Justice Kagan. *Italian Colors* was a split decision, with Justice Kagan writing the dissent, and it introduced the concept of "effective vindication," to which the Supreme Court returned in 2018 in its *Epic Systems* decision.

Oxford Health Plans LLC v. Sutter

133 S. Ct. 2064 (2013)

JUSTICE KAGAN delivered the opinion of the Court.

Class arbitration is a matter of consent: An arbitrator may employ class procedures only if the parties have authorized them. See *Stolt-Nielsen S. A. v. AnimalFeeds Int'l Corp.*, 559 U.S. 662, 684 (2010). In this case, an arbitrator found that the parties' contract provided for class arbitration. The question presented is whether in doing so he "exceeded [his] powers" under §10(a)(4) of the Federal Arbitration Act (FAA or Act), 9 U. S. C. §1 *et seq.* We conclude that the arbitrator's decision survives the limited judicial review §10(a)(4)allows.

[T]he sole question for us is whether the arbitrator (even arguably) interpreted the parties' contract, not whether he got its meaning right or wrong. The arbitrator's first ruling recited the "question of construction" the parties had submitted to him: "whether [their] Agreement allows for class action arbitration." To resolve that matter, the arbitrator focused on the arbitration clause's text, analyzing (whether correctly or not makes no difference) the scope of both what it barred from court and what it sent to arbitration. The arbitrator concluded, based on that textual exegesis, that the clause "on its face . . . expresses the parties' intent that class action arbitration can be maintained." When Oxford requested reconsideration in light of *Stolt-Nielsen*, the arbitrator explained that his prior decision was "concerned solely with the parties' intent as evidenced by the words of the arbitration clause itself." He then ran through his textual analysis again, and reiterated his conclusion: "[T]he text of the clause itself authorizes" class arbitration. Twice, then, the arbitrator did what the parties had asked: He considered their contract and decided whether it reflected an agreement to permit class proceedings. That suffices to show that the arbitrator did not "exceed[ ] [his] powers." §10(a)(4).

In *Stolt-Nielsen*, the arbitrators did not construe the parties' contract, and did not identify any agreement authorizing class proceedings. So in setting aside the arbitrators' decision, we found not that they had misinterpreted the contract, but that they had abandoned their interpretive role. Here, the arbitrator did construe the contract (focusing, per usual, on its language), and did find an agreement to permit class arbitration. So to overturn his decision, we would have to rely on a finding that he misapprehended the parties' intent.

The arbitrator thought that clause sent to arbitration all "civil action[s]" barred from court, and viewed class actions as falling within that category. But Oxford points out that the provision submits to arbitration not any "civil action[s]," but instead any "dispute arising under" the agreement. And in any event, Oxford claims, a class action is not a form of "civil action," as the arbitrator thought, but merely a procedural device that may be available in a court. At bottom, Oxford maintains, this is a garden-variety arbitration clause, lacking any of the terms or features that would indicate an agreement to use class procedures.

We reject this argument because, and only because, it is not properly addressed to a court. In sum, Oxford chose arbitration, and it must now live with that choice. Oxford agreed with Sutter that an arbitrator should determine what their contract meant, including whether its terms approved class arbitration. The arbitrator did what the parties requested: He provided an interpretation of the contract resolving that disputed issue. His interpretation went against Oxford, maybe mistakenly so. But still, Oxford does not get to rerun the matter in a court. We accordingly affirm the judgment of the Court of Appeals.

Notes and Questions

1. The *Oxford* court opens by repeating the mantra about arbitration and consent: "Class arbitration is a matter of consent." In *Oxford*, the parties did not memorialize any such consent regarding class actions. Their mandatory arbitration clause neither selected nor waived class arbitration. The clause instead was silent. The parties left that decision to the arbitrator. Fair enough, but since *Concepcion* had already found that arbitrations are incompatible with class actions, then why was the arbitrator's decision to allow class actions sustained in *Oxford*? Couldn't the Court have simply applied *Concepcion* to fill the gap and hold class arbitration as contrary to the *Concepcion* interpretation of the FAA? Didn't Justice Scalia say precisely that in *Concepcion?*
2. The *Oxford* parties manifested consensus at two separate times. First, at the time of their original contract, they agreed to an arbitration clause. Second, after their dispute arose, they agreed to allow the arbitrator to decide whether or not the dispute should be heard as a class action. The parties therefore delegated specific power to the arbitrator. In the same manner in which a *First Options* clause allows an arbitrator to decide arbitrability, the *Oxford* clause allowed the arbitrator to decide whether the arbitration would be a class action. This additional layer of consensus worked. If there had been no "second" consensus and express delegation of the class action question, and the arbitrator had ruled in favor of a class action anyway, then the arbitrator's decision would have run headlong into the Supreme Court's decision in *Stolt-Nielsen v. Animal-Feeds Int'l Corp*, 559 U.S. 662 (2010), where, as the *Oxford* Court summarized, the Supreme Court invalidated an arbitrator's ruling that the matter could proceed as a class action. The distinguishing factor between *Oxford* and *Stolt-Neilsen* was the second consensus. But has the Supreme Court been consistent in its approach to consensus? The parties in *DIRECTV*, *infra*, reached consensus that they *would* permit class actions if state law so provided. Why did consensus appear to matter more in *Oxford* than in those other cases?
3. *Post-Dispute Arbitration Clauses*. We have considered arbitration clauses so far in the context of the original commercial contract between the parties; recall our "boxes" illustration when we studied delegation clauses, and Justice Stevens' allusion to "Russian dolls" in that same chapter. But an arbitration clause does not always have to be part of that original commercial contract. The parties can agree to arbitrate at any time, and sometimes they may not get around to this until a dispute actually arises. *Oxford* was such an example. The parties' freedom to modify their dispute resolution form—change it, for example, from

litigation to arbitration, or vice versa—extends to narrow issues as well as broad ones. As examples,

a. Parties who have agreed to ad hoc arbitration in their original clause can decide to arbitrate under AAA rules when their dispute arises.

b. Parties who have agreed to arbitrate before three arbitrators in their original clause can instead agree to have a single-arbitrator hearing when the dispute arises—or vice versa.

c. Parties can change the city in which they may have originally agreed to arbitrate.

d. Parties can decide—as did the parties in *Oxford*—to commit particular issues to an arbitrator that might otherwise not fall to her.

Consensus may therefore be expressed at any time, and the arbitrator's mandate follows from that consensus. *See, e.g., Mayo v. Dean Witter Reynolds, Inc.*, 258 F. Supp. 2d 1097, 1113 (N.D. Cal. 2003) (noting the parties entered into a post-dispute arbitration agreement); *Dobson Bros. Constr. v. Ratliff, Inc.*, No. 4:08CV3103, 2009 U.S. Dist. LEXIS 53876, *8–9 (D. Neb. Feb. 27, 2009) (evaluating the scope of a post-dispute arbitration agreement).

PRACTICE POINTER. *Oxford* again demonstrates the importance of strategy and pleading in arbitration procedure. We saw in *Rent-A-Center* the effects of the lawyer's choice in attacking the entire clause rather than the specific delegation clause. *Oxford* presents a similar situation: "We would face a different issue if Oxford had argued below that the availability of class arbitration is a so-called 'question of arbitrability,' but this case gives us no opportunity to do so because Oxford agreed that the arbitrator should determine whether its contract authorized class procedures. Indeed, Oxford submitted this issue to the arbitrator not once but twice." Should the decision in *Oxford* have turned on pleading when Justice Kagan was candid that the gateway issue remains open as to class actions?

III. Effective Vindication, Federalism, and *Concepcion* Rolling On

Up to this point, we have reviewed cases in which class action bans in arbitration go to war with contrary state rules. But what happens when the counterargument to enforcing the parties' class action ban is not a state policy but the pursuit of rights under another *federal* law? The courts then have to balance not state versus federal policy, which involves issues of federalism and preemption, but instead whether one federal policy must defer to another. Is the "liberal federal policy in favor of arbitration" announced by *Moses Cone* so powerful that it should overcome federal policies furthered by other acts of Congress?

This situation arose in the Supreme Court's 2013 term, when the Court considered a challenge to a class action arbitration ban by a party who argued that the ban would prevent the "effective vindication" of that party's ability to pursue a claim under the federal antitrust laws.

Am. Express Co. v. Italian Colors Rest.

570 U.S. 228, 133 S. Ct. 2304 (2013)

JUSTICE SCALIA delivered the opinion of the Court.

We consider whether a contractual waiver of class arbitration is enforceable under the Federal Arbitration Act when the plaintiff's cost of individually arbitrating a federal statutory claim exceeds the potential recovery.

I.

Respondents are merchants who accept American Express cards. Their agreement with petitioners—American Express and a wholly owned subsidiary—contains a clause that requires all disputes between the parties to be resolved by arbitration. The agreement also provides that "[t]here shall be no right or authority for any Claims to be arbitrated on a class action basis." *In re American Express Merchants' Litigation*, 667 F. 3d 204, 209 (CA2 2012).

Respondents brought a class action against petitioners for violations of the federal antitrust laws. According to respondents, American Express used its monopoly power in the market for charge cards to force merchants to accept credit cards at rates approximately 30% higher than the fees for competing credit cards. This tying arrangement, respondents said, violated §1 of the Sherman Act. They sought treble damages for the class under §4 of the Clayton Act.

Petitioners moved to compel individual arbitration under the Federal Arbitration Act (FAA), 9 U.S.C. §1 *et seq.* In resisting the motion, respondents submitted a declaration from an economist who estimated that the cost of an expert analysis necessary to prove the antitrust claims would be "at least several hundred thousand dollars, and might exceed $1 million," while the maximum recovery for an individual plaintiff would be $12,850, or $38,549 when trebled. App. 93. The District Court granted the motion and dismissed the lawsuits. The Court of Appeals reversed and remanded for further proceedings. It held that because respondents had established that "they would incur prohibitive costs if compelled to arbitrate under the class action waiver," the waiver was unenforceable and the arbitration could not proceed.

We granted certiorari, vacated the judgment, and remanded for further consideration in light of *Stolt-Nielsen S. A.* v. *AnimalFeeds Int'l Corp.*, 559 U.S. 662 (2010), which held that a party may not be compelled to submit to class arbitration absent an agreement to do so. *American Express Co.* v. *Italian Colors Restaurant*, 559 U.S. 1103,

559 U.S. 1103 (2010). The Court of Appeals stood by its reversal, stating that its earlier ruling did not compel class arbitration. *In re American Express Merchants' Litigation*, 634 F. 3d 187, 200 (CA2 2011). It then *sua sponte* reconsidered its ruling in light of *AT&T Mobility LLC* v. *Concepcion*, 131 S. Ct. 1740 (2011), which held that the FAA pre-empted a state law barring enforcement of a class-arbitration waiver. Finding *AT&T Mobility* inapplicable because it addressed pre-emption, the Court of Appeals reversed for the third time. We granted certiorari, to consider the question "[w]hether the Federal Arbitration Act permits courts . . . to invalidate arbitration agreements on the ground that they do not permit class arbitration of a federal-law claim."

Congress enacted the FAA in response to widespread judicial hostility to arbitration. As relevant here, the Act provides:

> "A written provision in any maritime transaction or contract evidencing a transaction involving commerce to settle by arbitration a controversy thereafter arising out of such contract or transaction . . . shall be valid, irrevocable, and enforceable, save upon such grounds as exist at law or in equity for the revocation of any contract." 9 U.S.C. §2.

This text reflects the overarching principle that arbitration is a matter of contract. *See Rent-A-Center, West, Inc.* v. *Jackson*, 561 U.S. 63 (2010). And consistent with that text, courts must "rigorously enforce" arbitration agreements according to their terms, including terms that "specify *with whom* [the parties] choose to arbitrate their disputes," *Stolt-Nielsen*, *supra*, at 683, and "the rules under which that arbitration will be conducted," *Volt Information Sciences, Inc.* v. *Board of Trustees of Leland Stanford Junior Univ.*, 489 U.S. 468, 479 (1989). That holds true for claims that allege a violation of a federal statute, unless the FAA's mandate has been "'overridden by a contrary congressional command.'"

III.

No contrary congressional command requires us to reject the waiver of class arbitration here. Respondents argue that requiring them to litigate their claims individually—as they contracted to do—would contravene the policies of the antitrust laws. But the antitrust laws do not guarantee an affordable procedural path to the vindication of every claim. Congress has taken some measures to facilitate the litigation of antitrust claims—for example, it enacted a multiplied-damages remedy. See 15 U.S.C. §15 (treble damages). In enacting such measures, Congress has told us that it is willing to go, in certain respects, beyond the normal limits of law in advancing its goals of deterring and remedying unlawful trade practice. But to say that Congress must have intended whatever departures from those normal limits advance antitrust goals is simply irrational. "[N]o legislation pursues its purposes at all costs." *Rodriguez* v. *United States*, 480 U.S. 522, 525–526 (1987) (*per curiam*).

We have specifically rejected the assertion that one of those requirements (the class-notice requirement) must be dispensed with because the "prohibitively high cost" of compliance would "frustrate [plaintiff's] attempt to vindicate the policies underlying the antitrust" laws. *Eisen* v. *Carlisle & Jacquelin*, 417 U.S. 156, 166–168, 175–176 (1974). One might respond, perhaps, that federal law secures a nonwaivable *opportunity* to vindicate federal policies by satisfying the procedural strictures of Rule 23 or invoking some other informal class mechanism in arbitration. But we have already rejected that proposition in *AT&T Mobility*.

IV.

Our finding of no "contrary congressional command" does not end the case. Respondents invoke a judge-made exception to the FAA which, they say, serves to harmonize competing federal policies by allowing courts to invalidate agreements that prevent the "effective vindication" of a federal statutory right. Enforcing the waiver of class arbitration bars effective vindication, respondents contend, because they have no economic incentive to pursue their antitrust claims individually in arbitration.

The "effective vindication" exception to which respondents allude originated as dictum in *Mitsubishi Motors*, where we expressed a willingness to invalidate, on "public policy" grounds, arbitration agreements that "operat[e] . . . as a prospective waiver of a party's *right to pursue* statutory remedies." 473 U.S., at 637, n. 19 (emphasis added). Dismissing concerns that the arbitral forum was inadequate, we said that "so long as the prospective litigant effectively may vindicate its statutory cause of action in the arbitral forum, the statute will continue to serve both its remedial and deterrent function." *Id.*, at 637. Subsequent cases have similarly asserted the existence of an "effective vindication" exception, *see, e.g., 14 Penn Plaza LLC* v. *Pyett*, 556 U.S. 247, 273–274 (2009); *Gilmer* v. *Interstate/Johnson Lane Corp.*, 500 U.S. 20, 28 (1991), but have similarly declined to apply it to invalidate the arbitration agreement at issue.

And we do so again here. As we have described, the exception finds its origin in the desire to prevent "prospective waiver of a party's *right to pursue* statutory remedies," *Mitsubishi Motors, supra*, at 637, n. 19 (emphasis added). That would certainly cover a provision in an arbitration agreement forbidding the assertion of certain statutory rights. And it would perhaps cover filing and administrative fees attached to arbitration that are so high as to make access to the forum impracticable. See *Green Tree Financial Corp.-Ala.* v. *Randolph*, 531 U.S. 79, 90 (2000) ("It may well be that the existence of large arbitration costs could preclude a litigant . . . from effectively vindicating her federal statutory rights"). But the fact that it is not worth the expense involved in *proving* a statutory remedy does not constitute the elimination of the *right to pursue* that remedy.

The class-action waiver merely limits arbitration to the two contracting parties. It no more eliminates those parties' right to pursue their statutory remedy than did federal law before its adoption of the class action for legal relief in 1938. Or, to put it differently, the individual suit that was considered adequate to assure "effective vindication" of a federal right before adoption of class-action procedures did not suddenly become "ineffective vindication" upon their adoption.

Truth to tell, our decision in *AT&T Mobility* all but resolves this case. There we invalidated a law conditioning enforcement of arbitration on the availability of class procedure because that law "interfere[d] with fundamental attributes of arbitration." "[T]he switch from bilateral to class arbitration," we said, "sacrifices the principal advantage of arbitration—its informality—and makes the process slower, more costly, and more likely to generate procedural morass than final judgment." We specifically rejected the argument that class arbitration was necessary to prosecute claims "that might otherwise slip through the legal system."

The regime established by the Court of Appeals' decision would require—before a plaintiff can be held to contractually agreed bilateral arbitration—that a federal court determine (and the parties litigate) the legal requirements for success on the merits claim-by-claim and theory-by-theory, the evidence necessary to meet those requirements, the cost of developing that evidence, and the damages that would be recovered in the event of success. Such a preliminary litigating hurdle would undoubtedly destroy the prospect of speedy resolution that arbitration in general and bilateral arbitration in particular was meant to secure. The FAA does not sanction such a judicially created superstructure.

The judgment of the Court of Appeals is reversed.

It is so ordered.

JUSTICE KAGAN, with whom JUSTICE GINSBURG and JUSTICE BREYER join, dissenting.

Here is the nutshell version of this case, unfortunately obscured in the Court's decision. The owner of a small restaurant (Italian Colors) thinks that American Express (Amex) has used its monopoly power to force merchants to accept a form contract violating the antitrust laws. The restaurateur wants to challenge the allegedly unlawful provision (imposing a tying arrangement), but the same contract's arbitration clause prevents him from doing so. That term imposes a variety of procedural bars that would make pursuit of the antitrust claim a fool's errand. So if the arbitration clause is enforceable, Amex has insulated itself from antitrust liability—even if it has in fact violated the law. The monopolist gets to use its monopoly power to insist on a contract effectively depriving its victims of all legal recourse.

And here is the nutshell version of today's opinion, admirably flaunted rather than camouflaged: Too darn bad.

That answer is a betrayal of our precedents, and of federal statutes like the antitrust laws. Our decisions have developed a mechanism—called the effective-vindication rule—to prevent arbitration clauses from choking off a plaintiff's ability to enforce congressionally created rights. That doctrine bars applying such a clause when (but only when) it operates to confer immunity from potentially meritorious federal claims. In so doing, the rule reconciles the Federal Arbitration Act (FAA) with all the rest of federal law—and indeed, promotes the most fundamental purposes of the FAA itself. As applied here, the rule would ensure that Amex's arbitration clause does not foreclose Italian Colors from vindicating its right to redress antitrust harm.

The majority barely tries to explain why it reaches a contrary result. It notes that we have not decided this exact case before—neglecting that the principle we have established fits this case hand in glove. And it concocts a special exemption for class-arbitration waivers—ignoring that this case concerns much more than that. Throughout, the majority disregards our decisions' central tenet: An arbitration clause may not thwart federal law, irrespective of exactly how it does so. Because the Court today prevents the effective vindication of federal statutory rights, I respectfully dissent.

I

Start with an uncontroversial proposition: We would refuse to enforce an exculpatory clause insulating a company from antitrust liability—say, "Merchants may bring no Sherman Act claims"—even if that clause were contained in an arbitration agreement. Congress created the Sherman Act's private cause of action not solely to compensate individuals, but to promote "the public interest in vigilant enforcement of the antitrust laws." *Lawlor* v. *National Screen Service Corp.*, 349 U.S. 322, 329 (1955). Accordingly, courts will not enforce a prospective waiver of the right to gain redress for an antitrust injury, whether in an arbitration agreement or any other contract. But its necessity is nowhere more evident than in the antitrust context. Without the rule, a company could use its monopoly power to protect its monopoly power, by coercing agreement to contractual terms eliminating its antitrust liability.

If the rule were limited to baldly exculpatory provisions, however, a monopolist could devise numerous ways around it. Consider several alternatives that a party drafting an arbitration agreement could adopt to avoid antitrust liability, each of which would have the identical effect. On the front end: The agreement might set outlandish filing fees or establish an absurd (*e.g.*, one-day) statute of limitations, thus preventing a claimant from gaining access to the arbitral forum. On the back end: The agreement might remove the arbitrator's authority to grant meaningful relief, so that a judgment gets the claimant nothing worthwhile. And in the middle: The agreement might block the claimant from presenting the kind of proof that is necessary to establish the defendant's liability—say, by prohibiting any economic testimony (good luck proving an antitrust claim without that!). Or else the agreement might appoint as an arbitrator an obviously biased person—say, the CEO of Amex. The possibilities are endless—all less direct than an express exculpatory clause, but no less fatal. So the rule against prospective waivers of federal rights can work only if it applies not just to a contract clause explicitly barring a claim, but to others that operate to do so.

And sure enough, our cases establish this proposition: An arbitration clause will not be enforced if it prevents the effective vindication of federal statutory rights, however it achieves that result. The rule originated in *Mitsubishi*, where we held that claims brought under the Sherman Act and other federal laws are generally subject to arbitration. 473 U.S., at 628. By agreeing to arbitrate such a claim, we explained, "a party does not forgo the substantive rights afforded by the statute; it only submits to their resolution in an arbitral, rather than a judicial, forum." *Ibid.* But crucial to our decision was a limiting principle, designed to safeguard federal rights: An arbitration clause will be enforced only "so long as the prospective litigant effectively may vindicate its statutory cause of action in the arbitral forum." *Id.*, at 637. If an arbitration provision "operated . . . as a prospective waiver of a party's right to pursue statutory remedies," we emphasized, we would "condemn[ ]" it. *Id.*, at 637, n. 19. Similarly, we stated that such a clause should be "set[ ] aside" if "proceedings in the contractual forum will be so gravely difficult" that the claimant "will for all practical purposes be deprived of his day in court." *Id.*, at 632. And in the decades since *Mitsubishi*, we have repeated its admonition time and again, instructing courts not to enforce an arbitration agreement that effectively (even if not explicitly) forecloses a plaintiff from remedying the violation of a federal statutory right.

Our decision in *Green Tree* confirmed that this principle applies when an agreement thwarts federal law by making arbitration prohibitively expensive. The plaintiff there (seeking relief under the Truth in Lending Act) argued that an arbitration agreement was unenforceable because it "create[d] a risk" that she would have to "bear prohibitive arbitration costs" in the form of high filing and administrative fees. We rejected that contention, but not because we doubted that such fees could prevent the effective vindication of statutory rights. To the contrary, we invoked our rule from *Mitsubishi*, making clear that it applied to the case before us. See 531 U.S., at 90. Indeed, we added a burden of proof: "[W]here, as here," we held, a party asserting a federal right "seeks to invalidate an arbitration agreement on the ground that arbitration would be prohibitively expensive, that party bears the burden of showing the likelihood of incurring such costs." *Id.*, at 92. Randolph, we found, had failed to meet that burden: The evidence she offered was "too speculative." *Id.*, at 91. But even as we dismissed Randolph's suit, we reminded courts to protect against arbitration agreements that make federal claims too costly to bring.

Applied as our precedents direct, the effective-vindication rule furthers the purposes not just of laws like the Sherman Act, but of the FAA itself. That statute reflects a federal policy favoring actual arbitration—that is, arbitration as a streamlined "method of resolving disputes," not as a foolproof way of killing off valid claims. Put otherwise: What the FAA prefers to litigation is arbitration, not *de facto* immunity. The effective-vindication rule furthers the statute's goals by ensuring that arbitration remains a real, not faux, method of dispute resolution. With the rule, companies have good reason to adopt arbitral procedures that facilitate efficient and accurate handling of complaints. Without it, companies have every incentive to draft their agreements to extract backdoor waivers of statutory rights, making arbitration unavailable or pointless. So down one road: More arbitration, better enforcement of federal statutes. And down the other: Less arbitration, poorer enforcement of federal statutes.

Which would you prefer? Or still more aptly: Which do you think Congress would?

The answer becomes all the more obvious given the limits we have placed on the rule, which ensure that it does not diminish arbitration's benefits. The rule comes into play only when an agreement "operate[s] . . . as a prospective waiver"—that is, forecloses (not diminishes) a plaintiff's opportunity to gain relief for a statutory violation. Moreover, the plaintiff must make that showing through concrete proof: "[S]peculative" risks, "unfounded assumptions," and "unsupported statements" will not suffice. With the inquiry that confined and the evidentiary requirements that high, courts have had no trouble assessing the matters the rule makes relevant. And for almost three decades, courts have followed our edict that arbitration clauses must usually prevail, declining to enforce them in only rare cases. The effective-vindication rule has thus operated year in and year out without undermining, much less "destroy[ing]," the prospect of speedy dispute resolution that arbitration secures.

And this is just the kind of case the rule was meant to address. Italian Colors, as I have noted, alleges that Amex used its market power to impose a tying arrangement in violation of the Sherman Act. The antitrust laws, all parties agree, provide the restaurant with a cause of action and give it the chance to recover treble damages. Here, that would mean Italian Colors could take home up to $38,549. But a problem looms. As this case comes to us, the evidence shows that Italian Colors cannot prevail in arbitration without an economic analysis defining the relevant markets, establishing Amex's monopoly power, showing anticompetitive effects, and measuring damages. And that expert report would cost between several hundred thousand and one million dollars. So the expense involved in proving the claim in arbitration is ten times what Italian Colors could hope to gain, even in a best-case scenario. That counts as a "prohibitive" cost, in *Green Tree*'s terminology, if anything does. No rational actor would bring a claim worth tens of thousands of dollars if doing so meant incurring costs in the hundreds of thousands.

An arbitration agreement could manage such a mismatch in many ways, but Amex's disdains them all. As the Court makes clear, the contract expressly prohibits class arbitration. But that is only part of the problem. The agreement also disallows any kind of joinder or consolidation of claims or parties. And more: Its confidentiality provision prevents Italian Colors from informally arranging with other merchants to produce a common expert report. And still more: The agreement precludes any shifting of costs to Amex, even if Italian Colors prevails. And beyond all that: Amex refused to enter into any stipulations that would obviate or mitigate the need for the economic analysis. In short, the agreement as applied in this case cuts off not just class arbitration, but any avenue for sharing, shifting, or shrinking necessary costs. Amex has put Italian Colors to this choice: Spend way, way, way more money than your claim is worth, or relinquish your Sherman Act rights.

So contra the majority, the court below got this case right. Italian Colors proved what the plaintiff in *Green Tree* could not—that a standard-form agreement, taken as a whole, renders arbitration of a claim "prohibitively expensive." 531 U.S., at 92. The restaurant thus established that the contract "operate[s] . . . as a prospective waiver," and prevents the "effective[ ] . . . vindicat[ion]" of Sherman Act rights. *Mitsubishi*, 473 U.S., at 637, and n. 19. I would follow our precedents and decline to compel arbitration.

II.

Still, the majority takes one last stab: "Truth to tell," it claims *Concepcion* "all but resolves this case." In that decision, the majority recounts, this Court held that the FAA preempted a state "law conditioning enforcement of arbitration on the availability of class procedure." According to the majority, that decision controls here because "[w]e specifically rejected the argument that class arbitration was necessary."

Where to begin? Well, maybe where I just left off: Italian Colors is not claiming that a class action is necessary—only that it have *some* means of vindicating a meritorious claim. And as I have shown, non-class options abound. The idea that *AT&T Mobility* controls here depends entirely on the majority's view that this case is "class action or bust." Were the majority to drop that pretense, it could make no claim for *AT&T Mobility*'s relevance.

And just as this case is not about class actions, *Concepcion* was not—and could not have been—about the effective-vindication rule. Here is a tip-off: *Concepcion* nowhere cited our effective-vindication precedents. That was so for two reasons. To begin with, the state law in question made class-action waivers unenforceable even when a party *could* feasibly vindicate her claim in an individual arbitration. The state rule was designed to preserve the broad-scale "deterrent effects of class actions," not merely to protect a particular plaintiff's right to assert her own claim. Indeed, the Court emphasized that the complaint in that case was "most unlikely to go unresolved" because AT&T's agreement contained a host of features ensuring that "aggrieved customers who filed claims would be essentially guaranteed to be made whole." So the Court professed that *Concepcion* did not implicate the only thing (a party's ability to vindicate a meritorious claim) this case involves.

And if that is not enough, *Concepcion* involved a *state* law, and therefore could not possibly implicate the effective-vindication rule. When a state rule allegedly conflicts with the FAA, we apply standard preemption principles, asking whether the state law frustrates the FAA's purposes and objectives. If the state rule does so—as the Court found in *Concepcion*—the Supremacy Clause requires its invalidation. We have no earthly interest (quite the contrary) in vindicating that law. Our effective-vindication rule comes into play only when the FAA is alleged to conflict with another *federal* law, like the Sherman Act here. In that all-federal context, one law does not automatically bow to the other, and the effective-vindication rule serves as a way to reconcile any tension between them. Again, then, *Concepcion* had no occasion to address the issue in this case. The relevant decisions are instead *Mitsubishi* and *Green Tree*.

The Court today mistakes what this case is about. To a hammer, everything looks like a nail. And to a Court bent on diminishing the usefulness of Rule 23, everything looks like a class action, ready to be dismantled. So the Court does not consider that Amex's agreement bars not just class actions, but "other forms of cost-sharing . . . that could provide effective vindication." In short, the Court does not consider—and does not decide—Italian Colors's (and similarly situated litigants') actual argument about why the effective-vindication rule precludes this agreement's enforcement.

As a result, Amex's contract will succeed in depriving Italian Colors of any effective opportunity to challenge monopolistic conduct allegedly in violation of the Sherman Act. The FAA, the majority says, so requires. Do not be fooled. Only the Court so requires; the FAA was never meant to produce this outcome. The FAA conceived of arbitration as a "method of *resolving* disputes"—a way of using tailored and streamlined procedures to facilitate redress of injuries. In the hands of today's majority, arbitration threatens to become more nearly the opposite—a mechanism easily made to block the vindication of meritorious federal claims and insulate wrongdoers from liability. The Court thus undermines the FAA no less than it does the Sherman Act and other federal statutes providing rights of action. I respectfully dissent.

Notes and Questions

1. Was it factually correct that the "effective vindication" of the antitrust laws required the court to permit something other than a strictly individual, arbitrated claim? How would you respond, if you were opposing counsel, to the following argument: "Respondents submitted a declaration from an economist who estimated that the cost of an expert analysis necessary to prove the antitrust claims would be at least several hundred thousand dollars and might exceed $1 million while the maximum recovery for an individual plaintiff would be $12,580, or $38,549 when trebled." In *Concepcion*, noted the *Oxford* Court, "we specifically rejected the argument that class arbitration was necessary to prosecute claims that might otherwise slip through the system." But if one accepts the testimony of the economist (the *Italian Colors* Court cited no contrary testimony or facts), then would the antitrust claim here in fact "slip through the system"? Should that affect the result?
2. Return to a fundamental question we looked at in *Concepcion* and then later in *Oxford Health*: is arbitration compatible with class actions? After zigging negatively on this issue in *Concepcion*, then zagging positively in *Oxford Health*, the *Italian Colors* majority held that the ban on class action waivers "interferes with fundamental attributes of arbitration" (citing *Concepcion*). Is the problem with the limitation on party choice or with the ban itself? Can you reconcile these differing positions?

3. Justice Kagan's scathing dissent opens with: "The monopolist gets to use its monopoly power to insist on a contract effectively depriving its victims of all legal recourse. And here is the nutshell version of today's opinion, admirably flaunted rather than camouflaged: Too darn bad." She elaborates later, still in blunt language: "Amex has put Italian Colors to this choice: Spend way, way, way more money than your claim is worth, or relinquish your Sherman Act claim." This hearkens back to the *Concepcion* points about how only a fanatic would spend money to vindicate a $30 claim. Should there be some factual threshold by which the percentage of a claim's cost should drive whether the claim could go to class arbitration?
4. Why should a procedural statute that does not even presumptively create federal question jurisdiction trump the effective vindication of substantive federal laws?

IV. Federalism and Preemption After *Concepcion*

Italian Colors' approach to *Concepcion* differed substantially between the majority and the dissent. The majority found *Concepcion* dispositive ("Truth to tell, our decision in *Concepcion* all but resolves this case."). The dissent found it completely irrelevant:

> *AT&T Mobility* involved a *state* law, and therefore could not possibly implicate the effective-vindication rule. When a state rule allegedly conflicts with the FAA, we apply standard preemption principles, asking whether the state law frustrates the FAA's purposes and objectives. If the state rule does so—as the Court found in *AT&T Mobility*—the Supremacy Clause requires its invalidation. We have no earthly interest (quite the contrary) in vindicating that law.

This is a significant difference. It has a direct impact on the debate over class action bans in arbitration. If *Concepcion* is properly limited to *state* law restrictions on class action bans, then, as in *Brown ex rel. Brown v. Genesis Health Care Corp.*, 724 S.E.2d 250 (W.Va. 2011), the matter is indeed one simply of preemption. But the majority in *Italian Colors* plainly believed *Concepcion* to have reach beyond preemption issues, since—to Justice Kagan's great consternation—the majority extended *Concepcion* to a case exclusively concerning federal law. The upcoming CFPB debate will have to address this issue.

The ironies of justices who otherwise proclaimed "federalism" (and founded the Federalist Society) allowing a federal policy on arbitration to control over state law can be left for another day. For present purposes, should there be any difference between the enforcement of class action bans in the federal versus the state courts? Or, as we saw in *Southland*, is the playing field now equal between the two and arbitration reigns supreme in both? Does the presumption in favor of arbitration that now exists in both the federal and state courts extend as well to hostility to class action bans throughout our federalist system?

> **CASE PREVIEW.** After *Concepcion*, it became clear that a class action ban by itself would have difficulty surviving. In an attempt to avoid that, the parties came up with a baby-and-bathwater approach: if they could not have class arbitration, then they would not have any arbitration at all. In *DIRECTV*, the Supreme Court considered an arbitration clause which contained a class action waiver but which further provided that if the "law of your state" would make the waiver of class actions unenforceable, then there would be no arbitration at all.

The divergent views of *Concepcion* played out in *DIRECTV*. Plainly, the clause in *DIRECTV* hearkened back to the pre-*Concepcion* law in California, when the *Discover Bank* rule governed state law and class action bans were not enforceable. Just as plainly, the parties achieved consensus on this point. There was no genuine dispute that they meant clearly to state that if a California court found that *Discover Bank* (and not *Concepcion*) was the true "law of the state," then the arbitration clause would be nullified. Despite this consensus, the court struck down the clause—with Justice Breyer, the author of the minority opinion in *Concepcion*, this time writing for the majority.

DIRECTV, Inc. v. Imburgia

136 S. Ct. 463 (2015)

JUSTICE BREYER delivered the opinion of the Court.

The Federal Arbitration Act states that a "written provision" in a contract providing for "settle[ment] by arbitration" of "a controversy . . . arising out of" that "contract . . . shall be valid, irrevocable, and enforceable, save upon such grounds as exist at law or in equity for the revocation of any contract." 9 U.S.C. §2. We here consider a California court's refusal to enforce an arbitration provision in a contract. In our view, that decision does not rest "upon such grounds as exist . . . for the revocation of any contract," and we consequently set that judgment aside.

I.

DIRECTV, Inc., the petitioner, entered into a service agreement with its customers, including respondents Amy Imburgia and Kathy Greiner. Section 9 of that contract provides that "any Claim either of us asserts will be resolved only by binding arbitration." App. 128. It then sets forth a waiver of class arbitration, stating that "[n]either you nor we shall be entitled to join or consolidate claims in arbitration."

Id., at 128–129. It adds that if the "law of your state" makes the waiver of class arbitration unenforceable, then the entire arbitration provision "is unenforceable." *Id.*, at 129. Section 10 of the contract states that §9, the arbitration provision, "shall be governed by the Federal Arbitration Act." *Ibid.*

In 2008, the two respondents brought this lawsuit against DIRECTV in a California state court. They seek damages for early termination fees that they believe violate California law. After various proceedings not here relevant, DIRECTV, pointing to the arbitration provision, asked the court to send the matter to arbitration. The state trial court denied that request, and DIRECTV appealed.

The California Court of Appeal thought that the critical legal question concerned the meaning of the contractual phrase "law of your state," in this case the law of California. Does the law of California make the contract's class-arbitration waiver unenforceable? If so, as the contract provides, the entire arbitration provision is unenforceable. Or does California law permit the parties to agree to waive the right to proceed as a class in arbitration? If so, the arbitration provision is enforceable.

The California Court of Appeal subsequently held in this case that, despite this Court's holding in *Concepcion*, "the law of California would find the class action waiver unenforceable." 225 Cal. App. 4th 338, 342 (2014). The court noted that *Discover Bank* had held agreements to dispense with class-arbitration procedures unenforceable under circumstances such as these. 225 Cal. App. 4th, at 341. It conceded that this Court in *Concepcion* had held that the Federal Arbitration Act invalidated California's rule. 225 Cal. App. 4th, at 341. But it then concluded that this latter circumstance did not change the result—that the "class action waiver is unenforceable under California law." *Id.*, at 347.

In reaching that conclusion, the Court of Appeal referred to two sections of California's Consumers Legal Remedies Act, §§1751, 1781(a), rather than *Discover Bank* itself. *See* 225 Cal. App. 4th, at 344. Section 1751 renders invalid any waiver of the right under §1781(a) to bring a class action for violations of that Act. The Court of Appeal thought that applying "state law alone" (that is, those two sections) would render unenforceable the class-arbitration waiver in §9 of the contract. *Id.*, at 344. But it nonetheless recognized that if it applied federal law "then the class action waiver is enforceable and any state law to the contrary is preempted." *Ibid.* As far as those sections apply to class-arbitration waivers, they embody the *Discover Bank* rule. We shall consequently refer to the here-relevant rule as the *Discover Bank* rule.

The court reasoned that just as the parties were free in their contract to refer to the laws of different States or different nations, so too were they free to refer to California law as it would have been without this Court's holding invalidating the *Discover Bank* rule. The court thought that the parties in their contract had done just that. And it set forth two reasons for believing so.

First, §10 of the contract, stating that the Federal Arbitration Act governs §9 (the arbitration provision), is a *general* provision. But the provision voiding arbitration if the "law of your state" would find the class-arbitration waiver unenforceable is a *specific* provision. The court believed that the specific provision "is paramount to" and must govern the general.

Second, the court said that "a court should construe ambiguous language against the interest of the party that drafted it." DIRECTV had drafted the language; to void the arbitration provision was against its interest. Hence the arbitration provision was void. The Court of Appeal consequently affirmed the trial court's denial of DIRECTV's motion to enforce the arbitration provision.

The California Supreme Court denied discretionary review. DIRECTV then filed a petition for a writ of certiorari, noting that the Ninth Circuit had reached the opposite conclusion on precisely the same interpretive question decided by the California Court of Appeal. We granted the petition.

II.

No one denies that lower courts must follow this Court's holding in *Concepcion*. The fact that *Concepcion* was a closely divided case, resulting in a decision from which four Justices dissented, has no bearing on that undisputed obligation.

The Federal Arbitration Act allows parties to an arbitration contract considerable latitude to choose what law governs some or all of its provisions, including the law governing enforceability of a class-arbitration waiver. In principle, they might choose to have portions of their contract governed by the law of Tibet, the law of pre-revolutionary Russia, or (as is relevant here) the law of California including the *Discover Bank* rule and irrespective of that rule's invalidation in *Concepcion*. The Court of Appeal decided that, as a matter of contract law, the parties did mean the phrase "law of your state" to refer to this last possibility. Since the interpretation of a contract is ordinarily a matter of state law to which we defer, *Volt Information Sciences, Inc.* v. *Board of Trustees of Leland Stanford Junior Univ.*, 489 U.S. 468, 474 (1989), we must decide not whether its decision is a correct statement of California law but whether (assuming it is) that state law is consistent with the Federal Arbitration Act.

III.

Although we may doubt that the Court of Appeal has correctly interpreted California law, we recognize that California courts are the ultimate authority on that law. While recognizing this, we must decide whether the decision of the California court places arbitration contracts "on equal footing with all other contracts." *Buckeye Check Cashing, Inc.* v. *Cardegna*, 546 U.S. 440, 443 (2006). And in doing so, we must examine whether the Court of Appeal's decision in fact rests upon "grounds as exist at law or in equity for the revocation of any contract." 9 U.S.C. §2. That is to say, we look not to grounds that the California court might have offered but rather to those it did in fact offer. Neither this approach nor our result "steps beyond *Concepcion*" or any other aspect of federal arbitration law.

We recognize, as the dissent points out, that when DIRECTV drafted the contract, the parties likely believed that the words "law of your state" included California law that then made class-arbitration waivers unenforceable. But that does not answer the legal question before us. That is because this Court subsequently held in *Concepcion* that the *Discover Bank* rule was invalid. Thus the underlying question of contract law at the time the Court of Appeal made its decision was whether the "law of your state" included *invalid* California law. We must now decide whether answering *that* question in the affirmative is consistent with the Federal Arbitration Act. After examining the grounds upon which the Court of Appeal rested its decision, we conclude that California courts would not interpret contracts other than arbitration contracts the same way. Rather, several considerations lead us to conclude that the court's interpretation of this arbitration contract is unique, restricted to that field.

Taking these considerations together, we reach a conclusion that, in our view, falls well within the confines of (and goes no further than) present well-established law. California's interpretation of the phrase "law of your state" does not place arbitration contracts "on equal footing with all other contracts," *Buckeye Check Cashing, Inc.*, 546 U.S., at 443. For that reason, it does not give "due regard to the federal policy favoring arbitration." *Volt Information Sciences*, 489 U.S., at 476. Thus, the Court of Appeal's interpretation is pre-empted by the Federal Arbitration Act. Hence, the California Court of Appeal must "enforc[e]" the arbitration agreement. 9 U.S.C. §2.

The judgment of the California Court of Appeal is reversed, and the case is remanded for further proceedings not inconsistent with this opinion.

It is so ordered.

JUSTICE GINSBURG, with whom JUSTICE SOTOMAYOR joins, dissenting.

It has become routine, in a large part due to this Court's decisions, for powerful economic enterprises to write into their form contracts with consumers and employees no-class-action arbitration clauses. The form contract in this case contains a Delphic provision stating that "if the law of your state" does not permit agreements barring class arbitration, then the entire agreement to arbitrate becomes unenforceable, freeing the aggrieved customer to commence class-based litigation in court. This Court reads that provision in a manner most protective of the drafting enterprise. I would read it, as the California court did, to give the customer, not the drafter, the benefit of the doubt. Acknowledging the precedent so far set by the Court, I would take no further step to disarm consumers, leaving them without effective access to justice.

II.

The Court today holds that the California Court of Appeal interpreted the language in DIRECTV's service agreement so unreasonably as to suggest discrimination against arbitration in violation of the FAA. As I see it, the California court's interpretation of the "law of your state" provision is not only reasonable, it is entirely right.

Arbitration is a matter of "consent, not coercion." *Stolt-Nielsen S. A.* v. *AnimalFeeds Int'l Corp.*, 559 U.S. 662, 681. The FAA "requires courts to enforce privately negotiated agreements to arbitrate, like other contracts, in accordance with their terms." "[T]he interpretation of private contracts is ordinarily a question of state law, which this Court does not sit to review." Historically, this Court has respected state-court interpretations of arbitration agreements. Indeed, in the more than 25 years between *Volt* and this case, not once has this Court reversed a state-court decision on the ground that the state court misapplied state contract law when it determined the meaning of a term in a particular arbitration agreement. Today's decision is a dangerous first.

Beyond genuine debate, DIRECTV originally meant the "law of your state" clause to refer to its customer's home state law untouched by federal preemption. As DIRECTV explained in a state-court filing, the clause prevented enforcement of the arbitration agreement in those States, California among them, where the class-arbitration proscription was unenforceable as a matter of state law, while requiring bilateral arbitration in States that did not outlaw purported waivers of class proceedings. App. 52 ("The Customer Agreement between DIRECTV and its customers provides that the customer's home state laws will govern the relationship, and that any disputes will be resolved in individual arbitration *if* the customer's home state laws enforce the parties' arbitration agreement." (emphasis added)).

According to DIRECTV, because the class-arbitration ban, post-*Concepcion*, is enforceable in all States, this case must now be resolved, if at all, in bilateral arbitration. The Court agrees. After *Concepcion*, the Court maintains, it no longer matters whether DIRECTV meant California's "home state laws" when it drafted the 2007 version of its service agreement. But *Concepcion* held only that a State cannot *compel* a party to engage in class arbitration when the controlling agreement unconditionally prohibits class procedures. Just as a contract itself may provide for class arbitration, so the parties may *choose* to be bound by a particular state law, in this case, the CLRA, even if the FAA would otherwise displace that state law. "In principle," the Court acknowledges, parties "might choose to have portions of their contract governed by the law of Tibet, [or] the law of pre-revolutionary Russia." Pre-revolutionary Russian law, but not California's "home state laws" operative and unquestionably valid in 2007? Makes little sense to me.

III.

Today's decision steps beyond *Concepcion* and *Italian Colors*. There, as here, the Court misread the FAA to deprive consumers of effective relief against powerful economic entities that write no-class-action arbitration clauses into their form contracts. In *Concepcion*, customers brought a class action claiming that AT&T Mobility had improperly charged $30.22 in sales tax while advertising cellular telephones as free. AT&T Mobility's form consumer contract contained a mandatory arbitration clause and a class-arbitration proscription. Because consumers lacked input into the contractual terms, and because few rational consumers would go through the hassle of pursuing a $30.22 claim in bilateral arbitration, the California courts deemed the arbitration agreement unenforceable as unconscionable. *See* 131 S. Ct. 1740 (Breyer, J., dissenting) ("'[T]he maximum gain to a customer for the hassle of arbitrating a $30.22 dispute is still just $30.22.'"); *Carnegie* v. *Household Int'l, Inc.*, 376 F. 3d 656, 661 (CA7 2004) ("The *realistic* alternative to a class action is not 17 million individual suits, but zero individual suits, as only a lunatic or a fanatic sues for $30."). Nonetheless, the Court held that the FAA mandated enforcement of the entire arbitration agreement, including the class-arbitration ban. *Concepcion.* Two years later, in *Italian Colors*, the Court reaffirmed that class-arbitration prohibitions are enforceable even where claimants "have no economic incentive to pursue their . . . claims individually in arbitration." Today, the Court holds that consumers lack not only protection against unambiguous class-arbitration bans in adhesion contracts. They lack even the benefit of the doubt when anomalous terms in such contracts reasonably could be construed to protect their rights.

These decisions have predictably resulted in the deprivation of consumers' rights to seek redress for losses, and, turning the coin, they have insulated powerful economic interests from liability for violations of consumer-protection laws. *See* N.Y. Times, Nov. 1, 2015, p. A1, col. 5 ("By inserting individual arbitration clauses into a soaring number of consumer and employment contracts, companies [have] devised a way to circumvent the courts and bar people from joining together in class-action lawsuits, realistically the only tool citizens have to fight illegal or deceitful business practices."). Studies confirm that hardly any consumers take advantage of bilateral arbitration to pursue small-dollar claims. Resnik, Diffusing Disputes: The Public in the Private of Arbitration, the Private in Courts, and the Erasure of Rights, 124 Yale L.J. 2804, 2900–2910 (2015) (Resnik, Diffusing Disputes). Because consumers lack bargaining power to change the terms of consumer adhesion contracts *ex ante*, "[t]he providers [have] won the power to impose a mandatory, no-opt-out system in their own private 'courts' designed to preclude aggregate litigation." Resnik, Fairness in Numbers: A Comment on *AT&T* v. *Concepcion*, *Wal-Mart* v. *Dukes*, and *Turner* v. *Rogers*, 125 Harv. L. Rev. 78, 133 (2011). *See also* Miller, Simplified Pleading, Meaningful Days in Court, and Trials on the Merits: Reflections on the Deformation of Federal Procedure, 88 N.Y.U. L. Rev. 286, 323 (2013) ("[P]owerful economic entities can impose no-class-action-arbitration clauses on people with little or no bargaining position—through adhesion contracts involving securities accounts, credit cards, mobile phones, car rentals, and many other social amenities and necessities."). The proliferation of take-it-or-leave-it agreements mandating arbitration and banning class procedures, and this Court's readiness to enforce such one-sided agreements, have disabled consumers from "shop[ping] to avoid arbitration mandates." Resnik, Diffusing Disputes 2839. *See also id.*, at 2872 ("[T]he numbers of clauses mandating arbitration are soaring across many sectors.").

The Court has suggested that these anticonsumer outcomes flow inexorably from the text and purpose of the FAA. But Congress passed the FAA in 1925 as a response to the reluctance of some judges to enforce commercial arbitration agreements between merchants with relatively equal bargaining power. Moses, Arbitration Law: Who's in Charge? 40 Seton Hall L. Rev. 147, 170–171 (2010). *See also id.*, at 170 (contract disputes between merchants have been a proper subject of arbitration since the 1600's). The FAA's purpose was to "make the contracting party live up to his agreement." H. R. Rep. No. 68–96, at 1 (1924). Congress in 1925 could not have anticipated that the Court would apply the FAA to render consumer adhesion contracts invulnerable to attack by parties who never meaningfully agreed to arbitration in the first place.

Nor does the text of the FAA compel this result. Section 2, on which the Court relied in *Concepcion*, *Italian Colors*, and this case, prescribes simply that arbitration provisions are to be treated the same as other contractual terms: "[a] written provision in . . . a contract evidencing a transaction involving commerce to settle by arbitration a controversy . . . shall be valid, irrevocable, and enforceable, save upon such grounds as exist at law or in equity for the revocation of any contract." 9 U.S.C. § 2. As Justice O'Connor observed when the Court was just beginning to transform the FAA into what it has become, "the Court has abandoned all pretense of ascertaining congressional intent with respect to the Federal Arbitration Act, building instead, case by case, an edifice of its own creation." *Allied-Bruce Terminix Cos.* v. *Dobson*, 513 U.S. 265, 283 (1995) (concurring opinion). *See also* Miller, *supra,* at 324 ("[O]ver the years the Act has been transformed by the Supreme Court through constant expansion into an expression of a 'federal policy' favoring arbitration, whether it involves a bilateral business dispute or not.").

The California Court of Appeal appropriately applied traditional tools of state contract law to interpret DIRECTV's reference to the home state laws of its customers. Demeaning that court's judgment through harsh construction, this Court has again expanded the scope of the FAA, further degrading the rights of consumers and further insulating already powerful economic entities from liability for unlawful acts. I resist the Court's bent, and would affirm the judgment of the California Court of Appeal.

Notes and Questions

1. *What's All This About Pre-Revolutionary Russia?* Justice Breyer wrote that the parties "In principle. . . . might choose to have portions of their contract governed by the law of Tibet, the law of pre-revolutionary Russia, or (as is relevant here) the law of California including the *Discover Bank* rule and irrespective of that rule's invalidation in *Concepcion*." That proved to be distinctly untrue. The parties *did* choose to have their dispute governed by the *Discover Bank* rule, and the Court invalidated that choice. As Justice Ginsburg put it in dissent, "Pre-revolutionary Russian law, but not California's 'home state laws' operative and unquestionably

valid in 2007? Makes little sense to me." Presumably, though, if the law of Tibet, pre-revolutionary Russia, or any other jurisdiction also failed to respect class action waivers then those choices too would be unenforceable even if "in principle" acceptable. On this basis, what is left of consensus? What box are the parties operating in when they draft their arbitration clauses? Is it now the law that once they take any step toward arbitration they cannot place any limits upon it at all?

2. The majority's invalidation of the clause relied primarily on the "equal footing" language from *Buckeye* ("we must decide whether the decision of the California court places arbitration contacts on equal footing with other contracts"). But the *Discover Bank* rule found that class action waivers were contrary to California policy whether those waivers were in litigation clauses or arbitration clauses, meaning that the invalidation of such a waiver was not an exclusively anti-arbitration action. Why would this not have saved the equal footing argument?

3. Justice Ginsburg aptly phrases the consensus question: can parties "choose consumer protective law to govern their arbitration agreements?" Note the verb "choose." She laments the negative answer: "After *Concepcion*, the Court maintains, it no longer matters whether *DIRECTV* meant California's 'home state laws' when it drafted the 2007 version of its service agreement. But *Concepcion* held only that a State cannot *compel* a party to engage in class arbitration when the controlling agreement unconditionally prohibits class procedures." Where does that leave consensus? Arbitration is all about contract law, the courts tell us, and consensus of course informs contract—but is it proper to pay such lip service to arbitration as contractual if the parties are on unequal footing and so cannot achieve true, arms-length consensus?

4. What is the future of state law limitations on arbitration after *DIRECTV*? Justice Ginsburg would say that state law is now left by the side of the road. "Historically, this Court has respected state-court interpretations of arbitration agreements. *See Mastrobuono*, 514 U.S., at 60, n. 4; *Volt*, 489 U.S., at 484. Indeed, in the more than 25 years between *Volt* and this case, not once has this Court reversed a state-court decision on the ground that the state court misapplied state contract law when it determined the meaning of a term in a particular arbitration agreement. Today's decision is a dangerous first." Is there—and should there be—room for state law invalidation of any form of any arbitration agreement after *DIRECTV*?

5. Recall that in her *Italian Colors* dissent, Justice Kagan criticized the majority for protecting something other than what she called "actual arbitration." Justice Ginsburg returns to this theme, finding that the recent wave of Supreme Court arbitration decisions "have predictably resulted

in the deprivation of consumer's rights to seek redress for losses, and turning the coin, they have insulated powerful interests from liability." She draws a sharp contrast between this result and what she finds to be the legislative intent of the act, concluding that the intent of the FAA was to put *commercial* arbitration agreements "between merchants" on the same footing as other contracts, and that these were true "*consensual* agreements." (italics in original). Is there any room for this classification in today's arbitration world? Should Congress parse out which types of arbitration should and should not be governed by these decisions? Should, for example, there be a definitional section inserted into the FAA by which "arbitration" is defined and the scope of these decisions confined to that type of defined "arbitration"? And should there be specific (consumer?) exclusions from that definition? *See generally* Matt Adler, Chad B. Holtzman, & Krysten L. Connon, *How Arbitration Swallowed Up Consumers' Ability to Bring Lawsuits*, LAW.COM/N.J. LAW. J. (Feb. 12, 2016), https://www.law.com/njlawjournal/almID/1202749672327/.

V. Pro-Consumer, Extra-Judicial Reaction to *Concepcion*

By the time *DIRECTV* drove the third nail in the coffin of class action bans in arbitration, opponents of this line of cases had begun their counterattack. In government and in the press, "pro-consumer" advocates had taken up the challenge. Justice Ginsburg's dissent summarizes these views. One such critique came in a three-part, front-page, above-the-fold series issued by the *New York Times* in October and November 2015. The overall series was called "Beware the Fine Print." The title of the first article was an accurate indication of the series' overall view: *Arbitration Everywhere: Stacking the Decks of Justice*. The *Times* interviewed many arbitration participants and questioned whether they received a fair shake. The result merits greater quotation.

As *The New York Times* observed:

> By inserting individual arbitration clauses into a soaring number of consumer an employment contracts, companies like American Express devised a way to circumvent the courts and bar people from joining together in class-action lawsuits, realistically the only tool citizens have to fight illegal or deceitful business practices.
>
> * * *
>
> Some state judges have called the class action bans a "get out of jail free" card, because it is nearly impossible for one individual to take on a corporation with vast resources.

* * *

> By banning class actions, companies have essentially disabled consumer challenges to practices like predatory lending, wage theft and discrimination, court records show.
>
> "This is among the most profound shifts in our legal history," William G. Young, a federal judge in Boston who was appointed by President Ronald Reagan, said in an interview. "Ominously, business has a good chance of opting out of the legal system altogether and misbehaving without reproach."
>
> [Not all agree with these characterizations:]
>
> Andrew J. Pincus, a law partner at Mayer Brown in Washington who has represented companies that use arbitration, said class actions yielded little relief for plaintiffs. "Arbitration provides a way for people to hold companies accountable without spending a lot of money," Mr. Pincus said. "It's a system that can work."
>
> Alan Kaplinsky, from Philadelphia-based Ballard Spahr, told *The New York Times*, "Clients were telling me they were getting killed by frivolous lawsuits [brought by consumers] and asking me what on earth could be done about it."

Jessica Silver-Greenberg & Robert Gebeloff, *Arbitration Everywhere, Stacking the Deck of Justice*, New York Times (Oct. 31, 2015), http://www.nytimes.com/2015/11/01/business/dealbook/arbitration-everywhere-stacking-the-deck-of-justice.html.

Numerous articles also noted the demise of consumer power in the wake of increasing use of arbitration clauses. *See, e.g.*, Shelly Smith, *Mandatory Arbitration Clauses in Consumer Contracts: Consumer Protection and the Circumvention of the Judicial System*, 50 DePaul L. Rev. 1191 (2001); Peter B. Rutledge & Christopher R. Drahozal, *Contract and Choice*, 2013 B.Y.U. L. Rev. 1 (2013); Jeff Sovern, Elyane E. Greenberg, Paul F. Kirgis, & Yuxiang Liu, *"Whimsy Little Contracts" with Unexpected Consequences: An Empirical Analysis of Consumer Understanding of Arbitration Agreements*, 75 Md. L. Rev. 1 (2015); Brenna A. Sheffield, *Pre-Dispute Mandatory Arbitration Clauses in Consumer Financial Products: The CFPB's Proposed Regulation and its Consistency with the Arbitration Study*, 20 N.C. Banking Inst. 219 (2016).

The California courts then mounted a new attack to the enforceability of class action waivers—invalidating consumer arbitration clauses and class action waivers on the grounds that they purport to waive a consumer's statutory *remedies*, including the right to seek injunctive relief for the benefit of the general public. *See McGill v. Citibank, N.A.*, 2 Cal. 5th 945, 966 (2017). In *McGill*, the California Supreme Court invalidated a Citibank arbitration clause on the grounds that its class action waiver purported to waive the consumer's statutory right to seek public injunctive relief in any forum under California consumer protection laws, including California's

Consumers Legal Remedies Act (CLRA), unfair competition law (UCL), and false advertising law (FAL)—a result the court determined was contrary to public policy and thus rendered the provision unenforceable.

McGill, and subsequent Ninth Circuit authority upholding its findings, square their holdings with *Concepcion* on the basis that a class action waiver implicates *procedural rights*, whereas a waiver of a statutory right to seek injunctive relief in the public interest is a *substantive right* to a specific remedy that cannot be waived. *See also Blair v. Rent-A-Center, Inc.*, 928 F.3d 819, 823 (9th Cir. 2019). Importantly, *McGill* does not preclude drafters of arbitration agreements from forcing consumers to *arbitrate* these claims, but rather only forbids provisions that purport to require consumers to waive this relief all together.

Comment: Consumer Arbitration Clauses in Institutional Arbitration

Mindful that many businesses include institutional arbitration clauses in their standard form contracts, the leading arbitration institutions have adopted minimum standards for consumer arbitration clauses that are designed to protect consumers. As noted in Chapter 1, two of the larger and well-known domestic arbitration institutions are the American Arbitration Association (AAA) and JAMS. The AAA requires all consumer arbitration clauses to adhere to its "Consumer Due Process Protocol," while JAMS has adopted "Consumer Arbitration Minimum Standards." In each instance, the institution will refuse to administer a consumer arbitration that fails to meet these standards. Some of the unique and common features of the AAA and JAMS consumer rules are as follows:

1. Both parties must be permitted to opt-out of arbitration and proceed in small claims court if the amount in controversy falls within a small claims court's jurisdiction. By way of example, this would include any claim up to $10,000 in California or New York.
2. The costs to the consumer must be limited to roughly the filing fee the consumer would pay to bring an action in court. For AAA, the cost to the consumer is $200, and for JAMS it is $250. The business otherwise bears the cost of the proceeding (including the arbitrator's fees). The consumer bears no costs if the business initiates the arbitration.
3. The business cannot dictate the location of the arbitration. The hearing must be held in a location convenient to the consumer.

Additionally, both AAA and JAMS review the form of contract to determine whether the consumer had adequate notice of the arbitration clause and information sufficient to locate the institutional rules. Thus, in each instance, the cost to consumer is roughly equal to litigating in court, and any hearing is held near the consumer's residence. Moreover, the right to proceed in small claims court is preserved. In light of these rules, is requiring a consumer to proceed to arbitration in and of itself unfair? Why or why not? Contrastingly, businesses that elect to include institutional arbitration clauses take the risk of incurring significant costs in arbitration hearings across the country. What are the benefits to the business?

VI. The Life and Death of Administrative Agency Reform of Class Action Bans

In the wake of the 2008 financial crisis, Congress passed the Dodd-Frank Act, which created a new federal agency called the Consumer Financial Protection Bureau (CFPB). Section 1028(a) of the Dodd Frank Act instructed the new agency to "conduct a study of, and provide a report to Congress concerning, the use of agreements providing for arbitration of any future dispute between covered persons and consumers in connection with the offering or providing of consumer financial products or services."

The CFPB issued its study in 2015, see Arbitration Study: Report to Congress, pursuant to Dodd-Frank Wall Street Reform and Consumer Protection Act § 1028(a) (available at https://files.consumerfinance.gov/f/201503_cfpb_arbitration-study-report-to-congress-2015.pdf), which gave a scathing review of the anti-consumer impact of arbitration clauses plus class action bans. According to the CFBP, "since most consumer contracts now contain arbitration clauses, the result of eliminating class actions from arbitrations was to eliminate class actions from most consumer cases. If all consumer cases have to be heard in arbitration and all arbitration cases eliminate class actions, then most consumers are foreclosed from court." See, e.g. Press Release, Consumer Financial Protection Bureau, CFPB Study Finds That Arbitration Agreements Limit Relief for Consumers (March 10, 2015), http://www.consumerfinance.gov/about-us/newsroom/cfpb-study-finds-that-arbitration-agreements-limit-relief-for-consumers/ (quoting CFPB Direct Richard Corday):

> Our study found that these arbitration clauses restrict consumer relief in disputes with financial companies by limiting class actions that provide millions of dollars in redress each year. The CFPB study specifically examined credit cards, checking accounts, general purpose reloadable prepayment accounts, private student loans, storefront payday loans, and mobile wireless third-party billing services. According to the study, nearly 100% of the market share covered by arbitration agreements in these industries include no-class arbitration provisions.

The CFPB followed this study with a Proposed Rule on Arbitration Agreements on May 3, 2016. 12 C.F.R. 1040. The proposed rule applied to providers of consumer financial products and services. The proposal prohibited these providers from using pre-dispute arbitration agreements to block consumer class actions in court. That proposal, however, never became law. It was revoked by the new Congress that took office after the 2016 election. 82 F.R. 55500 (Nov. 22, 2017).

Had the proposed rule actually been issued, there likely would have emerged an interesting court fight that weighed the pro-arbitration SCOTUS cases against the body of precedent on administrative deference. *See Chevron, U.S.A., Inc. v. NRDC, Inc.*, 467 U.S. 837, 842–44 (1984). The rule was, after all, an administrative rulemaking and not an amendment to the FAA. We were spared that constitutional drama when the rule failed to progress into law as a consequence of the change in administrations. Whether the issue emerges in future administrations or is otherwise pursued beyond the judicial level may rest with the future lawyers now reading this book.

As this book goes to press in the early days of the Biden Administration, there are predictions that the new President will seek to change the law of arbitrations, class actions and waivers as examined in this chapter. President Biden has announced his support for the "Forced Arbitration Injustice Repeal Act" or the "FAIR Act," which would amend the Federal Arbitration Act to provide that "no predispute arbitration agreement or predispute joint-action waiver shall be valid or enforceable with respect to an employment dispute, consumer dispute, antitrust dispute, or civil rights dispute." Whether this bill would get through a sharply divided Congress, and/or whether the Biden Administration will instead attempt regulatory reform in the manner of the Obama Administration as studied above, all remains to be seen. Early predictions are that the law is likely to change somehow. *See, e.g.*, http://indisputably.org/2021/01/arbitration-scholars-what-do-you-think-biden-approach-to-arbitration/ ("Having regained control of the Senate, Congressional Democrats are expected to pass the Forced Arbitration Injustice Repeal Act, and Biden has indicated his support. The act, which has already passed the House, would invalidate pre-dispute arbitration agreements in the employment, civil rights, consumer, and antitrust contexts, and would require employers to litigate workplace disputes in court.... Notwithstanding Epic Systems, President-elect Biden has stated that he would sign legislation prohibiting employers from seeking such waivers."; https://www.jdsupra.com/legalnews/biden-s-first-100-days-a-check-in-for-7247720/)

UNIT II
Conducting the Arbitration

It is a distinct anomaly in assembling arbitration cases for a course or a book that the majority of such cases are not "arbitration" cases at all. They are, to be sure, about arbitration, but they are not cases directly from the arbitration. They are written by judges, not arbitrators. Such cases demonstrate one of the central themes of this book and chief characteristics of arbitration: that however separate a process arbitration is from the courts, it remains inextricably tied to the judicial system, especially at its beginning and end.

That leaves a great middle, and it is to that middle we next turn. What happens in the arbitration itself after all the judicial skirmishing is done? After a lawyer surmounts all of the challenges in Unit I of this book, and finds herself with a valid arbitration clause, an arbitration undisturbed by the judicial branch, and an opponent willing to arbitrate, what to do?

This unit considers those mechanics, with a particular focus on what makes arbitration distinctive. At its core, there are overwhelming similarities between trying a case before an arbitration tribunal and a court. Witnesses must still be presented and examined, documents introduced, and briefs written. Governing precedents must be addressed, satisfied, or distinguished, although as we will see in Unit III, an arbitrator is not necessarily obligated to follow those precedents. Requested relief must be stated specifically. Burdens of proof must be met. The similarities are such that most litigators likely view with confidence their ability to conduct an arbitration. Frequently they will be correct—unless they run into procedural minefields unique to an arbitration, which can hamper the ability of the uninitiated lawyer to conduct (and win) the case.

How does one pick an arbitrator? How does one challenge an arbitrator? How should modern arbitration practice, and in particular arbitrator selection procedures, reflect greater societal trends toward diversity and inclusion? How does one gather evidence in arbitration from one's opponent, and from third parties? Can parties still obtain an injunction? And can parties avoid duplication by consolidating arbitrations?

We address those stages in the succeeding chapters. As you study them, reflect on the concepts of "consensus" and "mandate" that we explored in the last unit. Both retain central importance. The parties' consensus does not end with the agreement to arbitrate the dispute. There continue to be repeated opportunities for consensus going forward in the case. That consensus—the agreement of the parties as to how to proceed in the arbitration itself—usually forms the procedural backbone of their arbitration. The mandate that results from this consensus dictates the arbitrator's authority to manage the case.

Chapter 5
Choosing an Arbitrator

One of the most significant distinctions between arbitration and litigation is the opportunity to choose—or at least to have input in choosing—the person deciding the case. As we saw briefly in the opening chapter on drafting the arbitration clause, there are a number of different ways to create this input. Most of them will have been fixed in the dispute resolution clause itself, often starting with the parties' decision to select institutional vs. *ad hoc* arbitration.

Keep in mind, however, that the parties can vary this choice once a dispute actually arises. What was perhaps an afterthought to the transactional lawyers drafting an overall purchase agreement will suddenly become of central importance to the litigators now handling a dispute. As a result, consensus remains a potent tool. Arbitration lawyers can do what their "deal" colleagues did not, negotiating more particular parameters of the dispute resolution process.

I. The Selection Process: Various Options

There are a number of different ways for the parties to pick an arbitrator.

A. The Parties Can Name the Arbitrator in the Arbitration Clause

Parties may decide in their arbitration clause, or in a post-dispute agreement, that their issues are best resolved by a particular person. The person may be someone well known to the community as a highly competent arbitrator. The person may have arbitrated disputes for one or both parties in the past. If the person is available, that selection can end any selection issues then and there in efficient manner: one party gives notice of the dispute, the designated person in the clause takes the reins, and off the parties go. Nothing could be more efficient.

Unless the person is busy. Or now conflicted (*see* Chapter 6). Or no longer competent. Or dead. The time gap between the contract's execution and a dispute later arising under that contract could lead to any of these unwelcome events. What, then, are the parties to do?

B. The Parties Can Specify the Expertise of the Arbitrator

Parties may not know precisely *who* they want, but they may have a very particular idea of *what* they want: an expert in a particular subject. Subject matter expertise does not even necessarily mean a lawyer. Parties to an intellectual property dispute may want a software engineer, or at least a patent or other form of IP lawyer. Parties to a machinery contract may want an engineer. Increasingly, parties to financial disputes may wish the dispute to be decided by an accountant.

We saw an example of this in the opening chapter: in recent years, so called "earn-out" arbitrations have become common in sales of businesses. In such cases, a buyer holds back part of the purchase price, to release it only after seeing how the business performs in a particular negotiated time period (for example, one year) after the sale. The higher the business' earnings in that "earn out" period, the greater the subsequent payment, and vice versa. But what if the parties dispute the financial records? Parties to such earn-out agreements frequently include arbitration clauses calling on accountants to make these final assessments since the arbitration's result will be dictated almost entirely by how the buyer of the business chooses to account for revenues.

The downside of this approach is that non-lawyer arbitrators can find themselves in a position that requires them to make "legal" rulings. This downside can be particularly acute in dealing with evidentiary objections. Should an accountant hearing an earn-out dispute disqualify evidence as "hearsay" or lacking foundation? How would he have the expertise to do so? The result can be a trade-off in which the arbitrator may have substantive expertise in the particular field in dispute but does not have expertise in the legal points that may be called on to decide the dispute. What if, wrapped within accounting-based arguments about proper financial adjustments, one party also raises legal arguments, such as a breach of the representations and warranties, or fraud? Will the non-lawyer expert be competent to resolve those matters? Should the arbitration be segmented between "legal" and "non-legal" issues? Is that efficient?

These issues can be avoided, without sacrificing the arbitrator's expertise, by having a roster of lawyers committed to a particular subject. There are a number of arbitration institutions that advertise precisely this expertise. The American Health Lawyers Association has a set of arbitration rules and a roster of arbitrators with distinct health care, rather than necessarily legal, expertise. *See Arbitration,* AHLA, https://www.americanhealthlaw.org/dispute-resolution-services/arbitration. The Financial Industry Regulatory Authority (FINRA) takes this even further and allows non-lawyers to serve as arbitrators in securities disputes provided that they have sufficient industry experience. FINRA's FAQ page regarding arbitrator qualification states: "The Applicants should have at least five years of paid business and/or professional experience—inside or outside of the securities industry—and at least two years of college-level credits."

See Become an Arbitrator Frequently Asked Questions (FAQ), FINRA, https://www.finra.org/arbitration-mediation/become-arbitrator-frequently-asked-questions-faq.

Class Problem

In a sales agreement for a machine that cuts baseball cards with precision, the parties agree that any dispute shall be resolved by a sole arbitrator who shall be a mechanical engineer. Buyer is a national brand of sports cards. Seller is an innovative small manufacturer who contracted with buyer to cut the cards on its custom machine. Buyer alleges that the cards came back with measurements off, corners cut, the white area obscured, and other flaws that damaged the cards' worth in the baseball card trading market and ruined Buyer's reputation. Seller introduces testimony from a reputed expert on machines. The arbitrator declares the witness an expert before the buyer has the opportunity to *voir dire* the expert on prior testimony. Should this make a difference to the result? Or is this precisely the kind of lack of procedural formality that arbitration *should* avoid? How would you try to get your client the best of both worlds, in which you have an expert hearing the case but that expert needs to be educated in case management and evidence admissibility?

C. The Party-Appointed Arbitrators Can Choose a Third Arbitrator

The parties can agree to an arbitration before three arbitrators, where each party chooses a "party-appointed" arbitrator and the two party-appointed arbitrators choose the third arbitrator (the "chair"). In this instance, how much input should the parties have in the selection of the chair? Should they filter through their views on the criteria and their preferences through the arbitrator they appointed, or is such communication prohibited?

It is generally accepted arbitration practice, and mandated by most institutional rules, that once the arbitration begins in earnest, no arbitrator shall have *ex parte* contact with a party, irrespective of whether that party appointed her or not. *See* AAA R-19(a) ("[n]o party and no one acting on behalf of any party shall communicate *ex parte* with an arbitrator or a candidate for arbitrator concerning the arbitration"); *Daiichi Hawaii Real Estate Corp. v. Lichter*, 82 P. 3d 411 (2003) (arbitrator's failure to disclose an *ex parte* communication with one of the parties' attorneys regarding the possibility of serving as a mediator in an unrelated case constituted "evident partiality" under the FAA); *Star Ins. Co. v. Nat'l Union Fire Ins. Co. of Pittsburgh, PA*, 656 F. App'x 240, 253–54 (6th Cir. 2016) (vacating a $20 million arbitration award in light of *ex parte* communications with party-appointed arbitrator, and holding that the operative question is whether the *ex parte* contact violated parties' agreement to arbitrate); *but see Cox v. Bonni*, 30 Cal. App. 5th 287, 310 (2018) (arbitrator's *ex parte* communications with a party about purely administrative matters were insufficient to warrant vacating the arbitration award).

Problem

What happens when a party's appointed arbitrator has an *ex parte* communication with a neutral arbitrator? *See Maaso v. Singer*, 203 Cal. App. 4th 362 (2012) (vacating arbitration award because defense's appointed arbitrator sent a five-page letter to neutral arbitrator).

Three arbitrators may give the parties more opportunity to have direct input into at least one of the arbitrators. The flip side is increased time and expense. The three arbitrators will present three bills for legal services and have three schedules around which the arbitration must be planned. Any party who does not appreciate that up front is doomed to disappointment and sticker shock. The parties need to decide—and counsel drafting the arbitration clause needs to advise—whether it is worth it. Parties may select a neutral arbitrator jointly and then, notwithstanding the contract language calling for three arbitrators, be sufficiently satisfied with that neutral that they elect (jointly, of course) to modify the contract and proceed with the neutral as sole arbitrator.

This is particularly the case in smaller-dollar value arbitrations, where the expense is not worth it. Arbitration costs should not be permitted, by skilled counsel advising their clients at all stages of the process, to become a significant and material percentage of the amount in controversy.

D. The Parties Can Select Institutional Rules to Control the Appointment Process

Parties who choose institutional arbitration essentially delegate some or all of the selection process to the institution. The leading arbitration institutions each have rosters of arbitrators available to hear arbitrations in the particular region where the dispute arises. The parties then have limited, but more than zero, input into the appointment process. As one example, the AAA will issue a list of arbitrators that are geographically desirable for the dispute, and the parties can then "strike" (exclude) those choices they do not like, then rank in order of preference those they prefer. The AAA administrator reviews the strike-outs and rankings and selects the arbitrator based on the highest mutual ranking of the non-stricken arbitrator(s).

American Arbitration Association, Rule 16: Number of Arbitrators.

(a) If the arbitration agreement does not specify the number of arbitrators, the dispute shall be heard and determined by one arbitrator, unless the AAA, in its discretion, directs that three arbitrators be appointed. A party may request three arbitrators in the Demand or Answer, which request the AAA will consider in exercising its discretion regarding the number of arbitrators appointed to the dispute.

(b) Any request for a change in the number of arbitrators as a result of an increase or decrease in the amount of a claim or a new or different

> claim must be made to the AAA and other parties to the arbitration no later than seven calendar days after receipt of the R-6 required notice of change of claim amount. If the parties are unable to agree with respect to the request for a change in the number of arbitrators, the AAA shall make that determination.

There are also particular institutions with particular expertise. For example, with the increased role of health care in the U.S. economy, there has not surprisingly emerged more and more disputes related to the health care business. There is now a specialized arbitration institution, called the American Health Lawyers Association, with its own sets of rules for commercial, employment, and consumer arbitrations related to healthcare. *See Rules of Procedure for Arbitration*, AHLA, https://sharepoint.healthlawyers.org/dr/Pages/Arbitration-Rules.aspx. Their homepage proclaims that the AHLA has developed the "first national roster of arbitrators, mediators, and hearing officers with health care expertise. It remains the only national service dedicated exclusively to resolving dispute in the health care industry." *See* AHLA, https://www.americanhealthlaw.org/dispute-resolution-services.

In picking an arbitrator—or an institution—the lawyer should not forget that dispute resolution is an expertise in and of itself. The most well-known expert in the world on a particular subject may still struggle to arbitrate it. Doing so requires imposing procedure, order, discipline, and a schedule on the parties and their counsel. For all the advantages of substantive familiarity with a type of dispute, it is this author's view after several decades of arbitration practice that it is far easier to teach a lawyer the facts and law of a particular dispute than to teach that same lawyer (or qualified non-lawyer) how to run an arbitration fairly and efficiently. Specialization in dispute resolution procedure—in getting the arbitration train to run on time—should not lightly be discounted.

II. Researching the Potential Arbitrator

Inherent in the above discussion of the manner of "choosing" one's arbitrator assumes that the parties have information that enables them to make an educated choice. Input into a process is worthless if the voter is uneducated.

There is no magic bullet for obtaining this information. It requires old-fashioned detective work. No discovery task is more important. Counsel can make a substantial difference here. It is critical that you work hard on your client's behalf to learn all you can about the arbitrator(s). Experienced arbitration counsel treat this task as importantly as they do any other development of the facts in the case.

The process should, to be sure, focus on eliciting any information that would disclose conflicts or potential conflicts—and indeed, as we will see in more detail in the following chapter, a candidate's failure to disclose even *potentially* conflicting information can itself be a disqualifying factor even if the information itself might not rise to the level of a conflict. But conflicts aside, the advocates should focus at this stage not only on potentially "negative" information such as conflicts but also on the attributes they need: substantive intelligence, flexibility and availability in schedules, and, above all, the ability to conduct a fair and efficient proceeding.

Intelligence, fairness, and experience all sound like obvious and reasonable criteria for arbitrator selection. Schedules and workload may not as readily come to mind—until one has been in several arbitrations where financially and emotionally exhausted clients are asking why this is taking so long, and the arbitrator does not have time on his schedule for the next hearing until six months from now. Parties, and certainly clients, may forget that most arbitrators are working lawyers themselves. They have their own cases to move along. Where they are (as is to be preferred) also working arbitrators, they have an additional burden on their calendars. Where there are three arbitrators rather than one, the scheduling and availability issues are exacerbated because now the parties have to deal with three busy lawyers' schedules (in addition to their own). One of the most material perceived advantages of arbitration is its relative speed compared to litigation. When arbitrators' schedules compromise that feature, everybody becomes unhappy. Accordingly, candor in the selection process is essential—on both sides of the discussion. Advocates should not underemphasize the complexity of the dispute and the time they believe it will take to appropriately resolve it. Arbitrator candidates should not understate their workloads just to add one more arbitration feather to their experience cap.

Input is accordingly a two-edged sword. The lawyer will be glad to have a role in shaping who decides his dispute but then bears some responsibility for the arbitrator's foibles—even beyond a merits decision. It is not realistically possible to pick an arbitrator who will decide your case in your favor, but it is far more possible to pick an arbitrator who can at least run and decide a case in the right way. That goes a long way to helping the lawyer along and is invaluable for client relations.

How, then, to go about picking an arbitrator? Larger law firms have the advantage of their internal databases and, more often than not, mass emails that ask colleagues whether they have ever arbitrated before or if they know Arbitrator Candidate X. Affirmative answers then lead to further digging. Phone calls to colleagues at other firms, Internet articles and biographies, and bar association contacts are all appropriate (and often necessary) tools. Detailed analysis here can turn out to be one of the greatest services that the lawyer can render her client.

But this is a rather archaic way of choosing arbitrators. Word of mouth and anecdotal evidence are perfectly good methods of performing due diligence, but they should no longer be the only, or even the principal, methods. We live in an age of commercial transparency, with information about most products we buy available with a few keystrokes. If we are thinking of buying a car, we would not simply ask which of our friends might have that car. We could look at hundreds of reviews within seconds.

In recent years there have been efforts to bring arbitration selection into the twenty-first century by creating databases that share details about arbitrators from consumers: namely, lawyers who have had direct experience with these arbitrators in the past. This allows insight into areas such as intellect, judgment, judicial temperament, fairness, management ability, and the degree to which an arbitrator keeps to a schedule.

There are two inherent and related limitations on this method, which likely account for their limited availability and adoption to date. One is the concern about confidentiality. The other is that the databases are only as extensive as the legal community's participation in them. The more people participate, the more the reviews get converted from mere anecdotal evidence to something approaching a statistical consensus. Because of the stakes involved, lawyers may not wish to issue negative, harsh reviews to an independent rating service, saving those views instead—if shared at all—for a confidential conversation.

This is an ongoing battle, but some progress has been made. One solution, put into practice by information-aggregator Arbitrator Intelligence (AI), has been to adopt a market strategy by which lawyers receive reviews in exchange for giving reviews. Reviews are strictly protected, and the access to reviews from others should, theoretically, lead to greater participation. AI "aims to promote transparency, accountability, and diversity in arbitrator selection by increasing access to critical information about arbitrators and their decision-making." *Our Values*, ARBITRATOR INTELLIGENCE, https://arbitratorintelligence.com/ (last visited Sep. 10, 2020).

III. Interviewing the Arbitrator Candidate

Since this is a selection process, can the parties interview the candidate for the job? Can the arbitrator candidate meet with the parties and discuss the case? Here again, institution rules may speak to the issue, assuming parties agree to proceed under those rules. As an example, the rules of the American Arbitration Association allow limited interviews of "neutral" arbitrators:

> **American Arbitration Association, Rule 19(a).**
>
> No one party and no one acting on behalf of any party shall communicate ex parte with an arbitrator or a candidate for arbitrator concerning the arbitration, except that a party, or someone acting on behalf of a party, may communicate ex parte with a candidate for direct appointment pursuant to R-13 in order to advise the candidate of the general nature of the controversy and of the anticipated proceedings and to discuss the candidate's qualifications, availability, or independence in relation to the parties or to discuss the suitability of candidates for selection as a third arbitrator where the parties or party-designated arbitrators are to participate in that selection.

For three-arbitrator cases, where the parties have agreed that the "party-appointed" arbitrators do not have to preserve neutrality, the prohibitions of R-19(a) do not apply.

> **American Arbitration Association, Rule 19(b):**
>
> R-19(a) does not apply to arbitrators directly appointed by the parties who, pursuant to Section R-18(b), the parties have agreed in writing are non-neutral. Where the parties have so agreed under Section R-18(b), the AAA shall as an administrative practice suggest to the parties that they agree further that Section R-19(a) should nonetheless apply prospectively.

Class Problem

Buyer is a New York-based, sophisticated perfume company that requires an extensive database to track shipments, customers, budgets, and other attributes of its multi-national business. Seller is a five-year-old Silicon Valley software company. Seller convinces Buyer to purchase a "custom" software platform that will reorganize and modernize Buyer's entire perfume business. The negotiation of this project takes one year. Implementation is supposed to take a further six months, but that period drags on to a full year, during which Buyer accuses Seller of missing interim deadlines, and Seller accuses Buyer of not making available required information on time. Buyer ultimately invokes a clause in the contract calling for termination for lateness. Seller counterclaims for progress-payments past due. The parties' contract includes an arbitration clause calling for resolution by a single arbitrator chosen under AAA Commercial Arbitration Rules.

As lawyer for Seller, what type of arbitrator do you want? Does this change if you are the lawyer Buyer? Do you want computer-skills qualifications? Software platform experience? Experience running a complex arbitration? Perfume industry expertise? Diversity? Someone from the East or West coast? Which criteria are most important?

IV. Diversity in Arbitrator Selection

The old-school manner of finding and choosing an arbitrator has problems beyond lack of transparency. It also exacerbates an already-acute diversity problem in arbitration. For a very long time, the "best" arbitrators were those who arbitrated the most, and therefore had the most exposure and the most easily accessible recommendations. They were (and are), to be sure, qualified—but the process risked becoming an insular "old boys club."

A. Institutional Rules: Producing Results or Just Rhetoric?

Lack of diversity in arbitration has been recognized among arbitral institutions and commentary. As a result, most of the leading arbitration institutions included diversity commitments in their rules and policies. By way of example:

JAMS, Diversity and Inclusion Arbitration Clause

Businesses increasingly recognize that diverse workforces produce better results, and many have robust initiatives to promote inclusivity in terms of gender, ethnicity and sexual orientation. Parties may choose to include diversity as a consideration when selecting an arbitrator or arbitration panel. The following clause, modeled after the Equal Representation in Arbitration pledge, attempts to promote diversity while recognizing that other qualifications are also important when selecting an arbitrator.

The below sample clause may be inserted into a contract to promote diversity in the selection of an arbitrator or arbitration panel.

The parties agree that, wherever practicable, they will seek to appoint a fair representation of diverse arbitrators (considering gender, ethnicity and sexual orientation), and will request administering institutions to include a fair representation of diverse candidates on their rosters and list of potential arbitrator appointees.

AAA, Recruiting Diverse Arbitrators and Increasing Diverse Arbitrator Appointments

The AAA continues its multi-year undertaking to increase the gender and ethnic diversity of its Roster. Executives across every division and region of the organization actively recruit women and minority candidates who meet the criteria established for the AAA and ICDR panels.

The AAA Roster currently consists of 24% women and minorities, and this figure is increasing. To provide parties with lists of arbitrators that comprise at least 20% diverse panelists where party qualifications are met, the AAA has incorporated an algorithmic tool in its case-management system.

B. Improve Intelligence, Improve Diversity: Two Suggestions

The lack of diversity has also been the subject of extensive commentary, much of which notes the gap between word and deed. But the arbitration community did seem to recognize that, too often, arbitrators were "male and pale" and that nobody was doing very much about it.

To some extent, the diversity problem merges with the issue we just examined in the previous section of this chapter: the relative lack of available information about arbitrators. In the absence of information, there is a tendency to revert to what people know, which is of course the opposite of an expanding palate of arbitrators no matter the societal preference.

Two leading commentators note the connection between the relative lack of intelligence on arbitrators and the resulting lack of diversity in choices. The policy recommendations they both offer raise the hope of solving two problems at once:

Sarah R. Cole, *Arbitrator Diversity: Can It Be Achieved?*

98 Wash. U. L. Rev. Issue 3 (2021)

Rather than relying on arbitral organizations to provide information about arbitrators, given their interest in continuing to allow parties the freedom to select the arbitrator they prefer, it may make sense to develop a separate website, something akin to arbitralwomen.org, an international arbitration website focused on providing greater information about international commercial arbitrators who are women. Such a website might make available pictures, videos, and blogs written by arbitrators as well as, potentially, a party review area. Rather than just positive quotes about the dispute resolution neutral, this website could have a series of questions available to parties and counsel following an arbitration including questions like: did the arbitrator issue the award by the deadline? Was the award complete? Did the arbitrator offer reasons for the decision? Did the arbitrator manage the hearing efficiently? Did the arbitrator have special requests (for example, asking for every document to be mailed as well as e-mailed; including any case cited in the parties' briefs)? Did the arbitrator pay attention during the hearing? Did the arbitrator "split the baby"?

A website of this type already exists for federal district court judges and magistrates. Known as "The Robing Room," this monitored website allows lawyers to rate, on a scale from 1–10, federal judges and magistrates on a variety of criteria, including: temperament, scholarship, industriousness, ability to handle complex litigation, punctuality, evenhandedness in civil and criminal litigation, flexibility in scheduling, involvement in settlement discussions, and varied categories related to criminal cases. The website also permits lawyers to make comments and give the judges an overall star rating. The website operators, North Law Publishers, reserve the right not to publish a comment or rating if it determines that it was not made in good faith or was libelous.

In addition, arbitral organizations could begin creating evaluation programs for arbitrators similar to those some states have adopted for monitoring judicial performance. The National Center for State Courts states that seventeen states and the District of Columbia have official programs for evaluating judicial performance. Of the seventeen states, seven share judicial performance reviews with the voters when a particular judge is subject to a retention election. For example, Iowa adopted a merit system for selecting judges in 1962. Since that time, the Iowa State Bar Association has conducted a Judicial Performance Review as a means to convey to voters relevant information about those judges who are subject to a retention vote during that year. In order to rate a judge, attorneys must appear in front of that judge frequently. The attorneys rate the judges on 6–8 questions relevant to their professional competence; including knowledge and application of the law, perception of factual issues, attentiveness to arguments and testimony, management and control of the courtroom, and promptness of rulings and decisions. The ratings range from 1–5 with 5 being "excellent" and 1 being "very poor." Attorneys also rate, on the scale of 1 to 5, the demeanor of the judges subject to a retention vote. The demeanor questions include "whether the judge avoids undue personal observations or criticisms of litigants, judges, and lawyers from the bench or in written orders; decides cases on the basis of applicable law and fact, not affected by outside influence; is courteous and patient with litigants, lawyers, and court personnel; and treats people equally regardless of race, gender, age, national origin, religion, sexual orientation, socio-economic status, or disability."

A similar system could be put into place by any of the arbitral organizations or by an independent organization. The system could be comparable to the JPEs, which are intended to provide information about individual judges based on characteristics that the Institute for the Advancement of the American Legal System and the ABA have deemed relevant. These criteria include: command of relevant substantive law and procedural rules, impartiality and freedom from bias, clarity of oral and written communications, judicial temperament that demonstrates appropriate respect for everyone in the courtroom, administrative skills, including competent docket management, and appropriate public outreach. Of course, in creating a system for arbitrator performance review, any organization should be mindful of the criticisms levied at these systems. Several commentators have reported on criticisms that the performance review process (based on an ABA model) is systematically biased against women and minority judges.

Conclusion

Organized plaintiffs' lawyers and increased use of direct arbitrator appointment and arbitrator panels may well lead to increased diversity among arbitrators actually appointed to hear consumer and employment, and other, disputes. If increasing diversity among arbitrators is integral to ensuring the procedural integrity of the arbitration process, then arbitral organizations should continue efforts to push businesses to draft arbitration clauses that authorize arbitrator appointment or permanent panels. As long as arbitral organizations are committed to developing and maintaining diverse rosters of arbitrators, this approach will ensure that a much larger percentage of arbitrators from diverse backgrounds are appointed to hear cases, rather than simply languish on the arbitrator rosters, never to be chosen.

The following article similarly suggests that the problem is the "same old, same old" and that the root of the problem is a false dichotomy between an altruistic desire to aid diversity and picking the best arbitrator. The author shows that a Machiavellian approach is just as useful to achieving diversity as is a social utilitarian approach.

Catherine A. Rogers, *The Key to Unlocking the Arbitrator Diversity Paradox?*

KLUWER ARBITRATION BLOG (Dec. 27, 2017)
http://arbitrationblog.kluwerarbitration.com/2017/12/27/on-arbitrators/?doing_wp_cron=1595779964.1416029930114746093750

A strange paradox marks the debate about international arbitrator diversity.

Public consensus increasingly reflects a pervasive concern about the lack of diversity among international arbitrators. ArbitralWomen can claim much credit for focusing attention on the lack of gender diversity, as evidenced by now more than 2500 signatures on The Pledge. Meanwhile, many corporate users now insist that firms include diverse candidates on lists of proposed arbitrators.

Concern about the lack of diversity is also reflected in the results of a survey on diversity by Berwin Leighton Paisner (BLP). In that survey, 80% of respondents believe that tribunals contain too many white arbitrators, while 84% believe that they contain too many men, and 64% felt that there were too many arbitrators from Western Europe or North America.

The good news is that these efforts seem to have nudged arbitral institutions toward greater diversity in institutional appointments. In 2016, women constituted, on average, around 17% or institutionally appointed arbitrators, considerably up from 12% just a year earlier in 2015, and dramatically up from the mere 6% in 2012.

The bad news is that institutions account for only a fraction of all arbitrator appointments. And concerns about lack of diversity are not having a similar effect in the estimated 75% of cases in which parties appoint arbitrators. As Lucy Greenwood cautions, there is a "stark disconnect between the rate at which institutions appoint women and the willingness of the parties to do so."

This lack of "willingness" is underscored in other findings from the BLP survey. While 84% responded that tribunals had too many men, only 50% of respondents thought that it was desirable to have gender balance on arbitral tribunals, and 41% thought that "it makes no difference." Responses on ethnicity and national background followed a similar pattern. 80% and 64%, respectively, said too many arbitrators were white or from Western Europe and North America, but only 54% responded that ethnic balance on a tribunal was desirable, with 31% saying that "it makes no difference."

These responses reveal an apparent contradiction. On the one hand, they demonstrate widespread concern about the lack of diversity. On the other hand, they suggest an apparent inability to translate those concerns into actual appointments in individual cases. This gap is captured not only in the BLP statistics cited above, but also in the comments of an anonymous commentator, who explained "when asked by a client to select an arbitrator, the desirability of promoting diversity is the last feature on anyone's mind. 'We are not being asked to make a statement' he said, 'we are asked to pick the best person for the job.'"

Therein lies the diversity paradox.

The key to resolving this paradox is to close the gap between the altruism that animates abstract concerns about diversity, and the strategic pragmatism that dominates arbitrator selection in individual cases. To achieve a more representative pool of arbitrators, in other words, we should appeal not only to the "better angels of our nature," but also to the more Machiavellian instincts that inform our case-specific arbitrator appointments.

Our better angels do not have to be strangers to our inner Machiavellis—they meet in the many contexts in which we "do right by doing good." With respect to diversity, for example, a robust and growing body of literature demonstrates that group decision making can be markedly improved when decisional bodies have a diverse composition. Other studies have long confirmed, not surprisingly, that representativeness of judges improves perceived legitimacy of adjudicatory apparatus. These studies suggest we would all benefit from greater diversity among arbitrators.

These studies have limited impact on actual behavior, however, because they measure the benefits of diversity in the abstract. Arbitrator selection, by contrast, is hyper-individualized and highly personal—both in the process and substance of assessing potential arbitrators. So, to unlock the diversity paradox, let's look more closely at parties' actual practices and priorities when they are selecting individual arbitrators.

If not diversity, what are parties looking for when they appoint arbitral tribunals? Going back to the BLP survey, 93% of respondents identified "expertise" and 91% identified "efficiency" as the most important features in appointing arbitrators. In the words of our anonymous commentator cited above, they are looking for "the best person for the job."

As we all know, this information is generally not available on arbitrators' CVs. Given the confidential nature of arbitration, the traditional (and still only) way to collect this information is through personal phone calls with individuals who have appeared before a potential arbitrator or, better yet, sat as a co-arbitrator with that person.

For those concerned about diversity, there are two main problems with this approach.

The first problem with arbitrator research based only on person-to-person inquiries is that it creates an information bottleneck. The limited number of individuals who can provide such information stifles the ability of newer and more diverse arbitrators to develop international reputations that the BLP statistics tell us are key to getting appointments.

To illustrate, let's take a hypothetical.

Imagine a young Brazilian woman has been appointed by arbitral institutions in three sizable and complex arbitrations. And she was simply AWESOME. The parties were wowed. Her co-arbitrators were impressed. And the institutions were delighted. How many attorneys worldwide now know about her exceptional abilities? Maybe

20? 30? 40 tops? And what are the chances that one of those 40 people will receive a phone call about her future appointment? To borrow from the philosophical question about a tree silently falling in the woods: What happens if an arbitrator has a fantastic reputation, but no one knows about it?

The second problem with ad hoc person-to-person research is that such research largely confines assessment of potential arbitrators to subjective evaluation by a limited number of individuals. This research technique functions more as a telephonic lottery than systematic evaluation. Workplace research in the United States suggests that cognitive biases—those implicit biases we all have but are often unaware of—most easily translate into employment discrimination when hiring is premised on subjective evaluations and processes that do not involve systematic evaluation.

Arbitrator Intelligence seeks to promote diversity both by breaking the information bottleneck, and by providing an alternative to the highly subjective, ad hoc nature of arbitrator assessments.

The means to these ends is our Arbitrator Intelligence Questionnaire, or AIQ. If parties and counsel complete an AIQ at the end of each arbitration, Arbitrator Intelligence will compile the collected about arbitrators, analyze it, and compile it into AI Reports on individual arbitrators. These reports will then be made available (for a fee) through our partner, Wolters Kluwer.

The content of the AIQ was developed to replicate the same kinds of information currently sought, and available only, through personal phone calls. Unlike phone calls, however, the AIQ seeks to disaggregate the abstract qualities of "expertise" and "efficiency" into objective, measurable data points. For example, to paraphrase a few questions from the AIQ: Did the arbitrators grant document production? Did they ask questions that demonstrated familiarity with the record? Based on data collected through the AIQ, Arbitrator Intelligence will also be able to determine the overall duration of arbitrations and time to issue the award, and numerous other valuable objective data.

Can the Arbitrator Intelligence, through data from the AIQ, promote diversity in international arbitration? We are optimistic for two reasons.

First, we hope to tap into arbitration specialists' self-interest (not, or not only, their commitment to improving arbitrator diversity). Looking again to the BLP survey, there is reason to be optimistic. A staggering 92% of respondents indicated that they would welcome more information about new and less well-known candidates whom they could appoint. To generate this information, we need parties and counsel (and third-party funders) to complete AIQs. Lots of them! This may seem like a big ask for busy lawyers, but again looking to the BLP survey, 82% of respondents indicated an interest in providing feedback about arbitrators.

Second, by increasing information and reducing subjectivity in arbitrator assessment and selection, Arbitrator Intelligence undertakes to promote a more robust meritocracy. With more information, newer arbitrators can be more fairly evaluated based on their actual performance and more effectively compared to other arbitrators based on objective criteria. They can also develop reputations for excellence and efficiency that are independent of personal vouching through ad hoc phone calls that currently impedes their progress.

AI's ability to succeed, of course, depends on parties and counsel submitting AIQs at the end of each arbitration. So, as the 2018 New Year begins, consider taking the few minutes necessary to complete AIQs at the end of each case. Join the several law firms that have agreed to provide retrospective AIQs on cases completed in the past few years. Sign the Arbitrator Intelligence Pact, promising to support our mission of promoting transparency, accountability and diversity.

In other words, in 2018, do your part to solve the diversity paradox—both by acting both in your (and your clients') own self-interests and by answering to the better angels of your nature.

C. The *Jay-Z* Case and Beyond

The alleged gap between the words of these pledges and the actual results in arbitrator diversity received a dose of national attention in 2018 when the artist Jay-Z claimed that the AAA did not give him a sufficiently racially-balanced roster of arbitrators. He brought suit in New York state court in the middle of a pending arbitration to compel a more diverse panel.

Shawn C. Carter, et al. v. Iconix Brand Group, Inc., et al.

Sup. Ct., N.Y. County, Nov. 11, 2018, Index No. 655894/2018

Petitioner's Memorandum of Law in Support of the Order to Show Cause for A Temporary Restraining Order and Preliminary Injunction

Petitioners Shawn C. Carter, S. Carter Enterprises, Marcy Media Holdings, LLC and Marcy Media, LLC, submit this memorandum of law in support of their application for a temporary restraining order and preliminary injunction against Respondents Iconix Brand Group, Inc. ("Iconix") and Icon DE Holdings, LLC ("Icon DE," and together with Iconix, the "Respondents") pending resolution of the Article 75 Petition for a stay of arbitration.

PRELIMINARY STATEMENT

Through this proceeding, Petitioners seeks a preliminary and permanent stay of an ongoing arbitration before the American Arbitration Association (the "AAA") necessitated by AAA procedures that violate New York law and render the otherwise applicable arbitration clause void as against public policy.

Petitioner Shawn C. Carter is the celebrated rap artist known worldwide as JAY-Z and one of the most successful African-American male entrepreneurs in history. This dispute centers on one of his businesses, which was named after the Marcy Houses, a housing project in Brooklyn with predominantly black residents where Mr. Carter grew up.

Respondent Iconix is a publicly traded corporation that seeks to profit by licensing brands built by others, such as Mr. Carter. Facing serious financial distress, with its stock now trading at pennies on the dollar, Iconix has engaged in a series of desperate litigation gambits of which this is merely the latest installment. In addition to an unmeritorious trademark lawsuit pending in the Southern District of New York, Iconix separately commenced an arbitration against Petitioners on October 1, 2018, presumably seeking to put pressure on certain parties—who are also defendants in the trademark action—by suddenly demanding financial information about the businesses that they had not received in the ordinary course of performance.

After a preliminary conference with the AAA, Mr. Carter and his companies sought to choose an arbitrator pursuant to the parties' agreement, which required consultation of a list of more than 200 prospective neutrals who specialize in "Large and Complex Cases." When Mr. Carter began reviewing arbitrators on the AAA's Search Platform, however, he was confronted with a stark reality: he could not identify a single African-American arbitrator on the "Large and Complex Cases" roster, composed of hundreds of arbitrators, that had the background and experience to preside over the Arbitration. After repeated requests to the AAA for diverse arbitrators with expertise in complex commercial law, the AAA was able to provide only three neutrals it identified as African-American: two men—one of whom was a partner at the law firm representing Iconix in this arbitration and thus had a glaringly obvious conflict of interest—and one woman.

The AAA's lack of African-American arbitrators with the expertise necessary to arbitrate "Large and Complex Cases" came as a surprise to Petitioners, in part because of the AAA's advertising touting its diversity. This blatant failure of the AAA to ensure a diverse slate of arbitrators for complex commercial cases is particularly shocking given the prevalence of mandatory arbitration provisions in commercial contracts across nearly all industries, which undoubtedly include minority owned and operated businesses. The AAA's arbitration procedures, and specifically its roster of neutrals for large and complex cases in New York, deprive black litigants like Mr. Carter and his companies of the equal protection of the laws, equal access to public accommodations, and mislead consumers into believing that they will receive a fair and impartial adjudication..

When an arbitration provision violates public policy, New York courts routinely stay the arbitration. The AAA's failure to provide a venire of arbitrators that includes more than a token number of African-Americans renders the arbitration provision in the contract void as against public policy. Accordingly, Petitioners seek a preliminary injunction staying the pending arbitration.

STATEMENT OF FACTS

Petitioner Shawn C. Carter, professionally known as JAY-Z, is an African-American entrepreneur and business owner, born in Brooklyn, New York. Mr. Carter has seen great success in both his music and business careers.

The arbitration clause specifically calls for three arbitrators, "unless the Parties are able to agree on a single arbitrator." If the parties cannot agree, AAA's commercial panel will appoint a panel of three arbitrators of its choosing. After an administrative conference call with the AAA, the parties agreed that if they could not mutually agree on an arbitrator, they would each submit four names from the AAA's "Large and Complex Cases" roster, which is narrower than AAA's National Roster. Then, the AAA would add four names and send that larger list to the parties, who would then commence striking names. The parties agreed to use the AAA's Arbitrator Search Platform to select an arbitrator, and the AAA provided search tips for using the Platform. The Platform also allowed the parties to access AAA's National Roster of Arbitrators.

In its attempt to find a suitable list of arbitrators to submit to the AAA, Petitioners' counsel reviewed more than 200 potential arbitrators in the New York area from the Large and Complex Cases roster. Of these 200 potential arbitrators, however, Petitioners' counsel were unable to identify a single African-American arbitrator with the necessary expertise. After Petitioners raised their concerns with the AAA, noting that Mr. Carter is black, and asked the AAA to provide the names of "neutrals of color," AAA responded by providing the names of six individuals it described as arbitrators "of color." Of those six candidates, one appears to be Asian-American, another South Asian, and a third Latino. Only three of the proposed neutrals appear to be African-American—two men, and one woman. Worse yet, one of the African-American men suggested is a partner at the law firm that represents Iconix in the underlying Arbitration, Blank Rome, creating a blindingly obvious conflict of interest. Presently, Petitioners cannot determine whether the only two proposed African-American candidates have conflicts that would similarly disqualify them. Moreover, using the AAA's search tips, Petitioners were unable to identify whether all of these individuals actually belong to AAA's Large and Complex Cases Roster.

The lack of African-American arbitrator candidates stands in stark contrast to the proclamation on the AAA's website that the AAA prioritizes engaging arbitrators from diverse backgrounds. In reality, the AAA lacks any meaningful selection of African-American arbitrators who specialize in complex commercial disputes. A further breakdown by area of dispute reveals even less diversity in certain areas: commercial cases have only 17 percent "diverse" arbitrators—which refers to both women and minorities, without specifying the number of African-American arbitrators—while insurance and construction law "diversity" falls to just 10 percent, which again includes both women and minorities.

Rather than address Petitioners' concern that they were never given an adequate choice of arbitrators, the AAA presented Petitioners with an ultimatum: either Petitioners make selections from the existing sample they reviewed (plus the individuals the AAA identified in response to Petitioners' concerns), or the AAA would make selections for Petitioners. The following day, the AAA did just that. Implicitly recognizing the legitimacy of Petitioners' complaint, the AAA included the lone

African-American man and woman in the list of twelve individuals it sent to the parties.

Now, AAA insists that Petitioners select from the list of twelve arbitrator candidates. Indeed, AAA has imposed a deadline of November 30, 2018 for the parties to strike up to four of the twelve candidates. As the AAA warned, "[i]f the list of arbitrators is not returned by the date specified," they will proceed to appoint an arbitrator without ever giving Petitioners a meaningful and representative choice.

ARGUMENT

The AAA's procedures are particularly harmful in light of AAA's misleading statements on its website about the diversity of its slate of arbitrators, which violate the New York Deceptive Practices Act, N.Y. G.B.L. § 349. That statute makes it unlawful for "[d]eceptive acts or practices in the conduct of any business, trade or commerce or in the furnishing of any services." *See also Small v. Lorillard Tobacco Co.*, 94 N.Y.2d 43, 55 (1999) (holding that a claim under N.Y. G.B.L. requires a showing that a business engaged "in an act or practice that is deceptive or misleading in a material way and that plaintiff has been injured by reason thereof") (internal quotation marks omitted). The AAA advertises on its website that it prioritizes diversity and promotes "the inclusion of those individuals who historically have been excluded from meaningful and active participation in the alternative dispute resolution (ADR) field." American Arbitration Association, AAA Diversity Initiative, last visited Nov. 28, 2018, https://www.adr.org/DiversityInitiative. The AAA boasts that women and minority arbitrators make up 24% of its roster of neutrals. American Arbitration Association, Roster Diversity and Inclusion, last visited Nov. 28, 2018, https://www.adr.org/RosterDiversity. In reality, however, the AAA only provided two eligible African-American arbitrator candidates when prompted, who may or may not be qualified to adjudicate a complex commercial dispute.

Comment

The *Jay-Z* case settled on the particular point of arbitrator diversity, but the artist's point was made. Diversity received considerable additional attention. The leading institutions redoubled their pledges to promote diversity. The statistics suggest that while progress is being made on gender diversity, there remain substantial challenges on racial diversity. According to a May 2019 report in Bloomberg Law, "[t]he roster of arbitrators at JAMS is 28% women. The roster for the International Institute for Conflict Prevention & Resolution (CPR) is made up of 17% women, 13% of individuals who identify as ethnically or racially diverse; 31% of CPR panelists selected to serve as arbitrators are diverse. The American Arbitration Association said its roster consists of 25% women and people of color. The service providers didn't further break down their diversity figures." Paige Smith, *Lack of Arbitrator Diversity Is an Issue of*

Supply and Demand, BLOOMBERG LAW (May 15, 2019), https://biglawbusiness.com/lack-of-arbitrator-diversity-is-an-issue-of-supply-and-demand.

Much remains to be done, as the following commentator noted:

Rekha Rangachari, *Can't Knock the Hustle . . . [To Broaden Diversity in Arbitration]*

KLUWER ARBITRATION BLOG (Jan. 15, 2019)
http://arbitrationblog.kluwerarbitration.com/2019/01/15/cant-knock-the-hustle-to-broaden-diversity-in-arbitration/

On November 28, Rapper Jay-Z filed a petition in Manhattan Supreme Court pertaining to an ongoing arbitration administered by the AAA-ICDR. He sought (i) a temporary restraining order to halt Iconix from pursuing claims in arbitration; (ii) a preliminary injunction staying arbitration for a period of ninety days for the parties to find *suitable* African-American arbitrator candidates; and (iii) a permanent stay of the arbitration.

A flurry of press reported on the matter, of arbitration under fire.

* * *

The Transcript of the proceedings on November 28 begins with Judge Scarpulla's reminder of the supremacy of party autonomy in arbitration:

> *You voluntarily choose AAA, you know what AAA has . . . why are you alleging now something that you chose, that you've agreed to, and now you're dissatisfied because you think that African-American arbitrators are somehow going to decide a commercial dispute differently than Asian-Americans, than women, than gay arbitrators, than all of the other protected classes? What is that about?*

* * *

This unfinished story hits at the crux of working definitions of diversity and unconscious bias. Put a different way, are clients of arbitration modifying the system from alternative *dispute* resolution to alternative *diversity* resolution?

The issue of diversity or lack thereof is a collective action problem. While much pressure has been placed on arbitral institutions in ensuing years, it is a shared burden amongst all practitioners.

Empire State of Mind: There's Nothing You Can't Do

Most arbitral institutions have implemented diversity initiatives to respond to the perceived gaps within the arbitrator pool. This is a starting point. A snapshot of these innovations is provided from an institution operating within Jay-Z's Empire State and under fire by Jay-Z, the AAA-ICDR, their Mission and Vision Statement demonstrating a "shared commitment" to diversity with arbitrator lists "that comprise at least 20% diverse panelists where party qualifications are met" (AAA-ICDR Roster Diversity & Inclusion). For example, "87% of lists sent to parties [in 2017] met that goal" (NYSCEF Doc. Nos. 31, 50—Letter p. 4). The list provided by the AAA-ICDR to the aforementioned parties included 7 of 12 arbitrator candidates from diverse categories of gender, race, ethnicity, and sexual orientation, or 58%.

* * *

The larger arbitral community must also buttress the case for diversity and encourage apt candidates. Distinct from the arbitral institutions, many affinity groups have suggested solutions to address diversity in the practice. One example tethered to the Empire State was the inaugural launch of the "ArbitralWomen DiversityToolkit™" on November 8, in commemoration of ArbitralWomen's jubilee celebration of 25 years bringing together global women of dispute resolution. The Toolkit is noteworthy in defining a training module whereby trainers lead participants through various exercises to recognize the moral, equal access, and business case for diversity, problem solve in dialogue, and brainstorm ideas for critical change.

* * *

Where Do We Go from Here?

The Jay-Z arbitration headlines created undue hysteria. Now, in the aftermath, the arbitration community must come together thoughtfully and productively in response, to change the rules of the game. The lack of diversity falls on global communities, to recharge and reinvigorate for market demands. Gender parity is one case for diversity gaining momentum, but what of the other diversity categories that also need support and community leadership to flourish?

International lawyer Gary Born aptly noted during his 2018 Freshfields Lecture that "the ending [to arbitration] hasn't been written yet—it depends on us; it depends on you." This applies equally to the state of diversity in arbitration and the perpetual query: are we getting there? Does our system improve diversity at a sufficient rate across fluid categories each quarter, each year, each decade? Our ending is far from being written, as new law graduates join the practice and redefine how we look at education, the law, and representation. A famous quote of Jay-Z's parlays opportunely here, as a reminder to be "hungry for knowledge. The whole thing is to learn every day, to get brighter and brighter." With the calls for change growing ever louder, learn we will, and change we will enact, together.

See also Lucy Greenwood, *Unblocking the Pipeline: Achieving Greater Gender Diversity on International Arbitration Tribunals*, 42 ABA Int'l L. News (Spring 2013); Paige Smith, *Lack of Arbitrator Diversity Is an Issue of Supply and Demand*, Bloomberg Law (May 15, 2019), https://biglawbusiness.com/lack-of-arbitrator-diversity-is-an-issue-of-supply-and-demand; Michael Z. Green, *Fact or Fiction?: Arbitrarily Selecting Black Arbitrators*, 88 Fordham L. Rev. 2255 (2020).

Notes and Questions

1. As noted by one of the commentators above, the trial judge in the *Jay-Z* case invoked "party autonomy," which is a fundamental principle of arbitration that holds that parties themselves control the nature of the proceedings—the "build your own courthouse" mantra we began exploring in Chapter 1. The arbitral institution JAMS, as also seen above, has a provision that brings autonomy to diversity: the parties' arbitration clause commits them to diversity and so instructs the institution to find diverse arbitrators. But what if the parties' arbitration clause lacks that language? If they buy into institutional rules then, as with the delegation doctrine reviewed in Chapter 3, are they also buying into the institution's diversity programs? What if the institution lacks such a program or commitment?
2. Return yet again to Section 2 of the FAA, the "saving clause." Are arbitration clauses invalid if, as Jay-Z's lawyers alleged, they further discrimination by not being inclusive as to arbitrator selection? Is this a new ground for arguing "illegality" under Section 2? Is this an attack better made at the beginning of the arbitration (as to formation of the agreement) or at the end on the basis that the award should not be enforced? *See infra* Chapter 13.

   The ongoing intervention by courts in arbitration may continue in this subject and is one more example of the hands-on, hands-off judicial policy toward arbitration that is a theme of this book.

Chapter 6

Challenging Arbitrator Selection

I. The Experience vs. Conflict Dichotomy

Arbitrators are working lawyers. They do not lead the relatively monastic lives of those appointed to the bench. They attend the same conferences as the advocates. They have gone to law school with the advocates. They may have worked in law firms with the advocates. They may have represented one of the parties or been adverse to one of the lawyers, potentially quite recently. Their firms may still represent a party even if they do not know this personally.

Arbitration has struggled with this inherent conflict. On the one hand, the process demands competent and experienced arbitrators. There has emerged in recent years an informal group, often named on the rosters of institutional arbitration organizations, who are professional arbitrators. They have repeated appointments and so by definition will be familiar to parties, lawyers, and/or the law firm at which the lawyer practices. On the other hand, the Federal Arbitration Act makes arbitrator bias one of the very few bases upon which an arbitration award can be challenged. Section 10(a)(2) of the Act allows a district court to vacate an award "where there was evident partiality or corruption in the arbitrators." As one court we study below put it, "inherent in the arbitration process are two principles that are often in tension: expertise and impartiality." How does one strike this balance? How much contact is too much? And finally, what contact rises to a disclosure level even if not to a disqualifying level?

Class Problems

Let's start with some examples of the kinds of conflicts that can arise in twenty-first century practice:

- Arbitrator Jones is one of the leading patent attorneys in the country. After turning 65, he was forced by his law firm's policies to retire from partnership and become "of counsel." He is now paid a salary by the firm but no longer shares in its equity gains or losses. At the same time, Jones became an arbitrator, and due to his reputation, is frequently selected to arbitrate patent disputes. Can Arbitrator Jones sit as an arbitrator in a case in which his firm is counsel for Respondent?

- Can Arbitrator Jones sit in a case where Respondent is represented by a different firm than the one in which Arbitrator Jones is of counsel, but which still gives Arbitrator Jones' firm $2 million in business a year? Does the answer change if that amount is $20,000? Does it change if the business was this past year? Does it change if the last business was two years ago?
- Can Arbitrator Jones sit in a case where, long ago and far away in law school, he and lead counsel for the claimant dated? What if they were social friends after law school and their kids were in the same play group? What if they attend the same church?
- Can Arbitrator Jones sit in a case where a partner in his firm was the former general counsel of one of the parties in the arbitration? What if that was not the case when the arbitration began, but his firm since merged and the former general counsel is now a partner in the merged firm? And how is Arbitrator Jones supposed to learn of this?
- Can Arbitrator Jones sit as an arbitrator for the fifth arbitration in two years asserted against a leading tech company, where that company has nominated him as their party-appointed arbitrator in three of those previous four cases?

This chapter explores the rules from courts and arbitration institutions that help lawyers navigate through these areas. Some are black and white, but others are merely grey. The most important Supreme Court case is over a half-century old, and so this is an area where lower court decisions, and the institutional guidelines, play a particularly involved role. We begin with the FAA and institutional rules.

II. The FAA's Treatment of Arbitrator Bias

We start with the Federal Arbitration Act. While we will study in Chapter 13 all the grounds that the FAA prescribes for not enforcing an arbitration award, one of them merits advance consideration because it goes to the heart of this chapter. Congress stated that an arbitrator's "partiality" or "corruption" is grounds for a court vacating an arbitration award. Section 10(a)(2) of the Act reads,

> In any of the following cases the United States court in and for the district wherein the award was made may make an order vacating the award upon the application of any party to the arbitration . . .
>
> (2) where there was evident partiality or corruption in the arbitrators.

The statute says nothing about "conflicts of interest." The obvious question in the cases interpreting this section focuses on the point that a conflict becomes "partiality or corruption."

III. Conflict Guidelines from Arbitrator Institutions

Most arbitration institutions have ethical canons. The American Arbitration Association has issued the following canons to ensure impartiality by an arbitrator:

- Canon I: An Arbitrator Should Uphold the Integrity and Fairness of the Arbitration Process
- Canon II: An Arbitrator Should Disclose Any Interest or Relationship Likely to Affect Impartiality or Which Might Create an Appearance of Partiality
- Canon III: An Arbitrator Should Avoid Impropriety or the Appearance of Impropriety in Communicating with Parties
- Canon IV: An Arbitrator Should Conduct the Proceedings Fairly and Diligently
- Canon V: An Arbitrator Should Make Decisions in a Just Independent and Deliberate Manner
- Canon VI: An Arbitrator Should be Faithful to the Relationship of Trust and Confidentiality Inherent in that Office
- Canon VII: An Arbitrator Should Adhere to Standards of Integrity and Fairness When Making Arrangements for Compensation and Reimbursement of Expenses

The Code of Ethics for Arbitrators in Commercial Disputes (effective Mar. 1, 2004), AAA, https://www.adr.org/sites/default/files/document_repository/Commercial_Code_of_Ethics_for_Arbitrators_2010_10_14.pdf.

The concern is every bit as strong in international arbitration, and so the International Bar Association (IBA) has issued guidelines on this difficult subject. The IBA derived three levels of conflicts, which it classified as falling into a Green List (no conflict), an Orange List (disclose and discuss further), and a Red List (contact so material to the dispute as to be disqualifying). *See IBA Guidelines on Conflicts of Interest in International Arbitration* (2014).

The Red List consists of two parts: "a Non-Waivable Red List" and "a Waivable Red List." These lists are non-exhaustive and detail specific situations that, depending on the facts of a given case, give rise to justifiable doubt as to the arbitrator's impartiality and independence. In these circumstances, an objective conflict of interest exists from the point of view of a reasonable third person having knowledge of the relevant facts and circumstances. The Non-Waivable Red List includes situations deriving from the overriding principle that no person can be his or her own judge. The Waivable Red List covers situations that are serious but not as severe.

a. Non-Waivable Red List

- There is an identity between a party and the arbitrator, or the arbitrator is a legal representative or employee of an entity that is a party in the arbitration.
- The arbitrator is a manager, director or member of the supervisory board, or has a controlling influence on one of the parties or an entity that has a direct economic interest in the award to be rendered in the arbitration.
- The arbitrator has a significant financial or personal interest in one of the parties, or the outcome of the case.
- The arbitrator or his or her firm regularly advises the party, or an affiliate of the party, and the arbitrator or his or her firm derives significant financial income therefrom.

b. Waivable Red List

- The arbitrator has given legal advice, or provided an expert opinion, on the dispute to a party or an affiliate of one of the parties.
- The arbitrator holds shares, either directly or indirectly, in one of the parties, or an affiliate of one of the parties, this party or an affiliate being privately held.
- A close family member of the arbitrator has a significant financial interest in the outcome of the dispute.
- The arbitrator currently represents or advises one of the parties, or an affiliate of one of the parties.
- The arbitrator currently represents or advises the lawyer or law firm acting as counsel for one of the parties.
- The arbitrator is a lawyer in the same law firm as the counsel to one of the parties.
- The arbitrator regularly advises one of the parties, or an affiliate of one of the parties, but neither the arbitrator nor his or her firm derives a significant financial income therefrom.

The Orange List is a non-exhaustive list of specific situations that, depending on the facts of a given case may give rise to doubts as to the arbitrator's impartiality or independence. In all these situations, the parties are deemed to have accepted the arbitrator if, after disclosure, no timely objection is made.

- The arbitrator has, within the past three years, served as counsel for one of the parties, or an affiliate of one of the parties, or has previously advised or been consulted by the party, or an affiliate of the party, making the appointment in an unrelated matter, but the arbitrator and the party, or the affiliate of the party, have no ongoing relationship.

- The arbitrator has, within the past three years, served as counsel against one of the parties, or an affiliate of one of the parties, in an unrelated matter.
- The arbitrator has, within the past three years, been appointed as arbitrator on two or more occasions by one of the parties, or an affiliate of one of the parties.
- The arbitrator's law firm has, within the past three years, acted for or against one of the parties, or an affiliate of one of the parties, in an unrelated matter without the involvement of the arbitrator.
- The arbitrator's law firm is currently rendering services to one of the parties, or to an affiliate of one of the parties, without creating a significant commercial relationship for the law firm and without the involvement of the arbitrator.
- The arbitrator or his or her firm represents a party, or an affiliate of one of the parties to the arbitration, on a regular basis, but such representation does not concern the current dispute.
- The arbitrator was, within the past three years, a partner of, or otherwise affiliated with, another arbitrator or any of the counsel in the arbitration.
- A lawyer in the arbitrator's law firm is an arbitrator in another dispute involving the same party or parties, or an affiliate of one of the parties.
- A close family member of the arbitrator is a partner or employee of the law firm representing one of the parties but is not assisting with the dispute.
- The arbitrator has, within the past three years, been appointed on more than three occasions by the same counsel, or the same law firm.
- The arbitrator's law firm is currently acting adversely to one of the parties, or an affiliate of one of the parties.
- The arbitrator has been associated with a party, or an affiliate of one of the parties, in a professional capacity, such as a former employee or partner.

A close personal friendship exists between an arbitrator and a manager or director or a member of the supervisory board of: a party; an entity that has a direct economic interest in the award to be rendered in the arbitration; or any person having a controlling influence, such as a controlling shareholder interest, on one of the parties or an affiliate of one of the parties or a witness or expert.

The Green List is a non-exhaustive list of specific situations where no appearance and no actual conflict of interest exists from an objective point of view. Thus, the arbitrator has no duty to disclose situations falling within the Green List.

- The arbitrator has previously expressed a legal opinion (such as in a law review article or public lecture) concerning an issue that also arises in the arbitration (but this opinion is not focused on the case).
- A firm, in association or in alliance with the arbitrator's law firm, but that does not share significant fees or other revenues with the arbitrator's law firm, renders services to one of the parties, or an affiliate of one of the parties, in an unrelated matter.
- The arbitrator has a relationship with another arbitrator, or with the counsel for one of the parties, through membership in the same professional association, or social or charitable organization, or through a social media network.

These are international rules, but nothing prohibits the parties from adopting them in their contract. They are outside bodies' rules— nothing more and nothing less. They do not have the force of law (unlike the cases we will shortly turn to) unless adopted by the parties in a particular case.

Class Problem

Go back to the Arbitrator Jones examples at the top of this chapter. Apply the IBA Rules. Are your answers different from when you first answered these questions?

IV. The Importance of Disclosure

Beyond the broad commandments of these canons is the most important conflict concept of all: disclosure. If you take nothing else out of this chapter, take this: Disclose. *Disclose.* Disclose. If in doubt as to whether or not a fact you learn may be a disqualifying conflict, your instinctive reaction and response should be to disclose this fact to opposing counsel. As you will see below, many of the lawyers in these cases find themselves in difficulty, not necessarily because of an actual, bright-line, out-and-out conflict, but instead because these lawyers sat on information rather than exposing it to the light. The non-disclosure winds up looking worse than the actual conflict. Additionally, disclosure creates waiver problems for your opposing counsel: if you disclose and they take no action in response, then the disclosed fact can usually not be raised months later, after you have won the arbitration, as a disqualifying "conflict." So: Disclose. Disclose. Disclose.

Disclosure is required by most institutions' rules.

American Arbitration Association, Rule 17. Disclosure:

(a) Any person appointed or to be appointed as an arbitrator, as well as the parties and their representatives, shall disclose to the AAA any circumstance likely to give rise to justifiable doubt as to the arbitrator's impartiality or independence, including any bias or any financial or personal interest in the result of the arbitration or any past or present relationship with the parties or their representatives. Such obligation shall remain in effect throughout the arbitration. Failure on the part of a party or a representative to comply with the requirements of this rule may result in the waiver of the right to object to an arbitrator in accordance with Rule R-41.

(b) Upon receipt of such information from the arbitrator or another source, the AAA shall communicate the information to the parties and, if it deems it appropriate to do so, to the arbitrator and others.

(c) Disclosure of information pursuant to this Section R-17 is not an indication that the arbitrator considers that the disclosed circumstance is likely to affect impartiality or independence.

Assume you have made a disclosure, and the opposing counsel believes this to be a conflict. Alternatively, assume you have *not* disclosed a fact, but opposing counsel learns of it anyway and believes it to be a conflict. This takes us back to now-familiar concepts from Unit I of this book: *who, what,* and *when*? *Who* decides the challenge—the court or the arbitrator(s)? *What* conflicts are so material as to be disqualifying? *When* in the process—at the time a conflict is discovered or after the award is rendered—should the conflict issue be decided?

As to the issue of *who*, prudent practice dictates that a challenge to an arbitrator be made in the first instance to that arbitrator. This can no doubt be uncomfortable, but it has the dual advantage of addressing the issue before having to proceed with the entire case and thus avoiding charges later of waiver or gamesmanship—since, after the fact, only unsuccessful parties are the likely challengers.

The "what" question is an unfortunately unclear mix of doctrines. There can be as many as three ingredients to it. First, there is the pure statutory standard under FAA Section 10(a) of "evident partiality or corruption." Query, though, how courts should define "partiality" or "corruption." Second, there are the institutional rules reviewed above—in cases where the parties have selected those rules. They are inapplicable where the parties proceed *ad hoc*. Third, there is case law addressing arbitrator corruption and non-disclosure.

We begin with the "what." What actions constitute a conflict? What actions trigger disclosure?

CASE PREVIEW. The following case is over a half-century old but remains the leading, indeed the only, Supreme Court decision on arbitrator bias, partiality, and misconduct. At bottom, arbitrators must disclose previous interactions with any of the parties in order to preserve the partiality of the process. As you read the case, keep its 1968 date in mind. Is the guidance and law here still appropriate in twenty-first century practice?

Commonwealth Coatings Corp. v. Continental Casualty Co.

393 U.S. 145 (1968)

JUSTICE BLACK delivered the opinion of the Court.

At issue in this case is the question whether elementary requirements of impartiality taken for granted in every judicial proceeding are suspended when the parties agree to resolve a dispute through arbitration.

The petitioner, Commonwealth Coatings Corporation, a subcontractor, sued the sureties on the prime contractor's bond to recover money alleged to be due for a painting job. The contract for painting contained an agreement to arbitrate such controversies. Pursuant to this agreement petitioner appointed one arbitrator, the prime contractor appointed a second, and these two together selected the third arbitrator. This third arbitrator, the supposedly neutral member of the panel, conducted a large business in Puerto Rico, in which he served as an engineering consultant for various people in connection with building construction projects. One of his regular customers in this business was the prime contractor that petitioner sued in this case. This relationship with the prime contractor was in a sense sporadic in that the arbitrator's services were used only from time to time at irregular intervals, and there had been no dealings between them for about a year immediately preceding the arbitration. Nevertheless, the prime contractor's patronage was repeated and significant, involving fees of about "12,000 over a period of four or five years, and the relationship even went so far as to include the rendering of services on the very projects involved in this lawsuit. An arbitration was held, but the facts concerning the close business connections between the third arbitrator and the prime contractor were unknown to petitioner and were never revealed to it by this arbitrator, by the prime contractor, or by anyone else until after an award had been made. Petitioner challenged the award on this ground, among others, but the District Court refused to set aside the award. The Court of Appeals affirmed, 382 F.2d 1010 (C.A. 1st Cir. 1967), and we granted certiorari, 390 U.S. 979 (1968).

In 1925 Congress enacted the United States Arbitration Act, 9 U.S.C. §§1–14, which sets out a comprehensive plan for arbitration of controversies coming under its terms, and both sides here assume that this Federal Act governs this case. Section 10, quoted below, sets out the conditions upon which awards can be vacated. The two courts below held, however, that § 10 could not be construed in such a way as to justify vacating the award in this case.

We disagree and reverse. Section 10 does authorize vacation of an award where it was "procured by corruption, fraud, or undue means" or "where there was evident partiality . . . in the arbitrators." These provisions show a desire of Congress to provide not merely for *any* arbitration but for an impartial one. It is true that petitioner does not charge before us that the third arbitrator was actually guilty of fraud or bias in deciding this case, and we have no reason, apart from the undisclosed business relationship, to suspect him of any improper motives. But neither this arbitrator nor the prime contractor gave to petitioner even an intimation of the close financial relations that had existed between them for a period of years. We have no doubt that if a litigant could show that a foreman of a jury or a judge in a court of justice had, unknown to the litigant, any such relationship, the judgment would be subject to challenge. This is shown beyond doubt by *Tumey v. Ohio*, 273 U.S. 510 (1927), where this Court held that a conviction could not stand because a small part of the judge's income consisted of court fees collected from convicted defendants. Although in *Tumey* it appeared the amount of the judge's compensation actually depended on whether he decided for one side or the other, that is too small a distinction to allow this manifest violation of the strict morality and fairness Congress would have expected on the part of the arbitrator and the other party in this case. Nor should it be at all relevant, as the Court of Appeals apparently thought it was here, that "the payments received were a very small part of [the arbitrator's] income." For in *Tumey* the Court held that a decision should be set aside where there is "the slightest pecuniary interest" on the part of the judge, and specifically rejected the State's contention that the compensation involved there was "so small that it is not to be regarded as likely to influence improperly a judicial officer in the discharge of his duty."

Since in the case of courts this is a *constitutional* principle, we can see no basis for refusing to find the same concept in the broad statutory language that governs arbitration proceedings and provides that an award can be set aside on the basis of "evident partiality" or the use of "undue means." It is true that arbitrators cannot sever all their ties with the business world, since they are not expected to get all their income from their work deciding cases, but we should, if anything, be even more scrupulous to safeguard the impartiality of arbitrators than judges, since the former have completely free rein to decide the law as well as the facts and are not subject to appellate review. We can perceive no way in which the effectiveness of the arbitration process will be hampered by the simple requirement that arbitrators disclose to the parties any dealings that might create an impression of possible bias.

While not controlling in this case, § 18 of the Rules of the American Arbitration Association, in effect at the time of this arbitration, is highly significant. It provided as follows:

> Section 18 Disclosure by Arbitrator of Disqualification—At the time of receiving his notice of appointment, the prospective Arbitrator is requested to disclose any circumstances likely to create a presumption of bias or which he believes might disqualify him as an impartial Arbitrator Upon receipt of such information, the Tribunal Clerk shall immediately disclose it to the parties, who if willing to proceed under the circumstances disclosed, shall,

> in writing, so advise the Tribunal Clerk. If either party declines to waive the presumptive disqualification, the vacancy thus created shall be filled in accordance with the applicable provisions of this Rule.

And based on the same principle as this Arbitration Association rule is that part of the 33d Canon of Judicial Ethics which provides:

> 33 Social Relations. . . . [A judge] should, however, in pending or prospective litigation before him be particularly careful to avoid such action as may reasonably tend to awaken the suspicion that his social or business relations or friendships, constitute an element in influencing his judicial conduct.

This rule of arbitration and this canon of judicial ethics rest on the premise that any tribunal permitted by law to try cases and controversies not only must be unbiased but also must avoid even the appearance of bias. We cannot believe that it was the purpose of Congress to authorize litigants to submit their cases and controversies to arbitration boards that might reasonably be thought biased against one litigant and favorable to another.

Reversed.

JUSTICE WHITE, with whom JUSTICE MARSHALL joins, concurring.

While I am glad to join my Brother BLACK'S opinion in this case, I desire to make these additional remarks. The Court does not decide today that arbitrators are to be held to the standards of judicial decorum of Article III judges, or indeed of any judges. It is often because they are men of affairs, not apart from but of the marketplace, that they are effective in their adjudicatory function. *Cf. United Steelworkers of America v. Warrior & Gulf Navigation Co.*, 363 U.S. 574 (1960). This does not mean the judiciary must overlook outright chicanery in giving effect to their awards; that would be an abdication of our responsibility. But it does mean that arbitrators are not automatically disqualified by a business relationship with the parties before them if both parties are informed of the relationship in advance, or if they are unaware of the facts but the relationship is trivial. I see no reason automatically to disqualify the best informed and most capable potential arbitrators.

The arbitration process functions best when an amicable and trusting atmosphere is preserved and there is voluntary compliance with the decree, without need for judicial enforcement. This end is best served by establishing an atmosphere of frankness at the outset, through disclosure by the arbitrator of any financial transactions which he has had or is negotiating with either of the parties. In many cases the arbitrator might believe the business relationship to be so insubstantial that to make a point of revealing it would suggest he is indeed easily swayed, and perhaps a partisan of that party.* But if the law requires the disclosure, no such imputation can arise. And it is far better that the relationship be disclosed at the outset, when the parties are free to reject the arbitrator or accept him with knowledge of the relationship and continuing faith in his objectivity, than to have the relationship come to light after the arbitration, when a suspicious or disgruntled party can seize on it as a pretext for invalidating the award. The judiciary should minimize its role in arbitration as judge of the arbitrator's impartiality. That role is best consigned to the parties, who are the architects of their own arbitration process, and are far better informed of the prevailing ethical standards and reputations within their business.

Of course, an arbitrator's business relationships may be diverse indeed, involving more or less remote commercial connections with great numbers of people. He cannot be expected to provide the parties with his complete and unexpurgated business biography. But it is enough for present purposes to hold, as the Court does, that where the arbitrator has a substantial interest in a firm which has done more than trivial business with a party, that fact must be disclosed. If arbitrators err on the side of disclosure, as they should, it will not be difficult for courts to identify those undisclosed relationships which are too insubstantial to warrant vacating an award.

JUSTICE FORTAS, with whom JUSTICE HARLAN and JUSTICE STEWART join, dissenting.

I dissent and would affirm the judgment.

The facts in this case do not lend themselves to the Court's ruling. The Court sets aside the arbitration award despite the fact that the award is unanimous and no claim is made of actual partiality, unfairness, bias, or fraud.

The arbitration was held pursuant to provisions in the contracts between the parties. It is not subject to the rules of the American Arbitration Association. It is governed by the United States Arbitration Act, 9 U.S.C. §§1–14.

Each party appointed an arbitrator and the third arbitrator was chosen by those two. The controversy relates to the third arbitrator.

The third arbitrator was not asked about business connections with either party. Petitioner's complaint is that he failed to volunteer information about professional services rendered by him to the other party to the contract, the most recent of which were performed over a year before the arbitration. Both courts below held, and petitioner concedes, that the third arbitrator was innocent of any actual partiality, or bias, or improper motive. There is no suggestion of concealment as distinguished from the innocent failure to volunteer information.

The third arbitrator is a leading and respected consulting engineer who has performed services for "most of the contractors in Puerto Rico." He was well known to petitioner's counsel and they were personal friends. Petitioner's counsel candidly admitted that if he had been told about the arbitrator's prior relationship "I don't think I would have objected because I know Mr. Capacete [the arbitrator]."

Clearly, the District Judge's conclusion, affirmed by the Court of Appeals for the First Circuit, was correct, that "the arbitrators conducted fair, impartial hearings; that they reached a proper determination of the issues before them, and that plaintiff's objections represent a 'situation where the losing party to an arbitration is now clutching at straws in an attempt to avoid the results of the arbitration to which it became a party.'"

The Court nevertheless orders that the arbitration award be set aside. It uses this singularly inappropriate case to announce a *per se* rule that in my judgment has no basis in the applicable statute or jurisprudential principles: that, regardless of the agreement between the parties, if an arbitrator has any prior business relationship with one of the parties of which he fails to inform the other party, however innocently, the arbitration award is always subject to being set aside. This is so even where the award is unanimous; where there is no suggestion that the nondisclosure indicates partiality or bias; and where it is conceded that there was in fact no irregularity, unfairness, bias, or partiality. Until the decision today, it has not been the law that an arbitrator's failure to disclose a prior business relationship with one of the parties will compel the setting aside of an arbitration award regardless of the circumstances.

I agree that failure of an arbitrator to volunteer information about business dealings with one party will, prima facie, support a claim of partiality or bias. But where there is no suggestion that the nondisclosure was calculated, and where the complaining party disclaims any imputation of partiality, bias, or misconduct, the presumption clearly is overcome.

I do not believe that it is either necessary, appropriate, or permissible to rule, as the Court does, that, regardless of the facts, innocent failure to volunteer information constitutes the "evident partiality" necessary under § 10 (b) of the Arbitration Act to set aside an award. "Evident partiality" means what it says: conduct—or at least an attitude or disposition—by the arbitrator favoring one party rather than the other. This case demonstrates that to rule otherwise may be a palpable injustice, since all agree that the arbitrator was innocent of either "evident partiality" or anything approaching it.

Arbitration is essentially consensual and practical. The United States Arbitration Act is obviously designed to protect the integrity of the process with a minimum of insistence upon set formulae and rules. The Court applies to this process rules applicable to judges and not to a system characterized by dealing on faith and reputation for reliability. Such formalism is not contemplated by the Act nor is it warranted in a case where no claim is made of partiality, of unfairness, or of misconduct in any degree.

Notes and Questions

1. *Fortas vs. Black: The Rematch. Commonwealth Coatings* dates from the 1968 *Prima Paint* era where modern arbitration law was being fought out in that period's Supreme Court. The Justice Fortas vs. Justice Black battle in *Prima Paint* (Fortas writing for the majority) had a rematch in

Commonwealth Coatings a few months later, this time with Justice Black writing the majority opinion. The skepticism that Justice Black expressed in *Prima Paint* about an arbitrator's ability to assess fraud finds its way into his *Commonwealth* Court opinion that the prior relationship in *Commonwealth* should have been disclosed. Justice Fortas took a more relaxed approach, emphasizing "that the award was unanimous and no claim is made of actual partiality, unfairness, bias, or fraud." In the modern arbitration era, with an arbitrator's duties and powers more accepted by the courts, does the stricter approach of Justice Black make sense? Is it workable? Does it remain an admirable goal?

2. *Disclosure vs. Disqualification.* Was Justice Fortas accurate in his dissent? He wrote that the majority's ruling meant that "if an arbitrator has any prior business relationship with one of the parties of which he fails to inform the other party, however innocently, the arbitration award is always subject to being set aside." That suggests that the trigger for setting aside the award under FAA Section 10 is any "prior business relationship." That characterization washes away from the analysis concept of disclosure, yet disclosure is precisely what Justice Black's majority opinion focused upon: "We can perceive no way in which the effectiveness of the arbitration process will be hampered by the simple requirement that arbitrators *disclose* to the parties any dealings that might create an impression of possible bias." (emphasis added). If the "prior business relationship" (Justice Fortas' words) had been "disclosed" (Justice Black's words), would *Commonwealth Coatings* have come out the same way? The lesson: disclose, as Justice White's concurring opinion especially recommends:

    > It is enough for present purposes to hold, as the Court does, that where the arbitrator has a substantial interest in a firm which has done more than trivial business with a party, that fact must be disclosed. If arbitrators err on the side of disclosure, as they should, it will not be difficult for courts to identify those undisclosed relationships which are too insubstantial to warrant vacating an award.

3. *Contacts by the Law Firm.* Law firm size has increased dramatically since the *Commonwealth/Prima Paint* era. Fifty-seven of the 100 largest firms, when ranked by head count, have at least 1,000 lawyers. *The 2019 Global 100: Ranked by Head Count*, LAW.COM/ THE AMERICAN LAWYER (Sep. 24, 2019), https://www.law.com/americanlawyer/2019/09/24/the-2019-global-100-ranked-by-head-count/. As of 2018, the largest law firm (by number of attorneys), Baker McKenzie, had 4,809 lawyers. Two other firms, DLA Piper and Norton Rose Fulbright, had over 3,000 lawyers. Three others—Jones Day, Latham, and White & Case—had over 2,000.

The 500 Largest Law Firms In America (2020), ABOVE THE LAW (June 23, 2020), https://abovethelaw.com/2020/06/the-500-largest-law-firms-in-america-2020/. (On a point of personal knowledge and experience: during the time between the first and second editions of this book, the author's law firm merged with another comparably sized firm, and the number of lawyers more than doubles to over 1,100 lawyers.)

This is a long way from the days of *Commonwealth Coatings*. Firms must, and do, employ sophisticated conflicts tracking mechanisms, but these generally measure client relationships, not whatever personal or professional relationships a lawyer may have had with an arbitrator. To say that lawyers may not be aware of their colleagues' contacts with a party or arbitrator is wholly understandable when in many mega-firms, the lawyers may not even know one another—much less which of their hundreds of colleagues may have been in a college band with which arbitrator. Nor can the answer entirely be "leave that to the arbitrator to disclose," because compounding the mega-firm problem is the fluidity of lawyer job changes. So frequent are lawyer moves from firm to firm that *The American Lawyer* has for many years published a section entitled "On the Move." An arbitrator who thought that a particular lawyer in Los Angeles was at Firm A may not know that one year ago, that lawyer decamped to Firm B which is now handling a major arbitration in front of that arbitrator, led by one of that firm's New York partners. The two lawyers have never met one another. On whom does the disclosure burden fall? At common law? Under the IBA rules? In an ideal world?

4. *No Harm, No Foul.* We come now to a "when" question. When should the analysis of the conflict be undertaken? Should the reviewing court look to whether the alleged conflict of interest made a difference in the result? Or is the lack of disclosure so heinous that it triggers the "evident partiality" standard in the Act irrespective of result? Justice Fortas advocated for a backwards looking test that focused on impact rather than (non-)disclosure. He argued that since the award was unanimous, it was not possible to argue that the undisclosed contacts played any material role. Should that be the test, with the factfinder looking to the proximate cause and ultimate result of an arguably tainted arbitration award? Or does that risk masking the potentially pervasive influence of a rogue arbitrator? What if, for example, an arbitrator with close (but undisclosed) financial ties to one of the parties had determined from the outset that a certain party should win and so worked in the arbitrators' conferences to persuade his fellow arbitrators? Would the result be any less tainted for being unanimous?

Somewhat surprisingly, given both the expansion of arbitration since 1968 and the U.S. Supreme Court's repeated consideration of arbitration cases, *Commonwealth Coatings* remains the only U.S. Supreme Court case on arbitrator conflicts. In the years since, state and federal courts have had to apply its holding in a number of distinct factual circumstances. One strain of law that has developed is that the evident partiality standard in Section 10 of the FAA can be demonstrated *prima facie* by faulty disclosure. "Faulty" here means non-existent, or partial, or misleading. This faulty disclosure can smack of the arbitrator having something to hide. The Supreme Court of Texas in the next case confronted exactly that situation in 2014.

CASE PREVIEW. What happens when an arbitrator only partially discloses his dealings with the lawyers for the party who appointed him?

Tenaska Energy, Inc. v. Ponderosa Pine Energy, LLC

437 S.W.3d 518 (Tex. 2014)

JUSTICE GUZMAN delivered the opinion of the Court.

Evident partiality of an arbitrator is a ground for vacating an arbitration award under both the Federal Arbitration Act and the Texas Arbitration Act. Adhering to United States Supreme Court precedent, we held almost two decades ago that a neutral arbitrator is evidently partial if she fails to disclose facts that might, to an objective observer, create a reasonable impression of her partiality. And we have held that a party does not waive an evident partiality challenge if it proceeds to arbitrate without knowledge of the undisclosed facts.

Today, we are asked to evaluate these standards in light of a partial disclosure. Here, the neutral arbitrator in question disclosed that the law firm representing one party to the arbitration had recommended him as an arbitrator in three other arbitrations. He also disclosed that he was a director of a litigation services company and attended a meeting at the law firm, but there was no indication the firm and company would ever do business. The trial court found the arbitrator failed to disclose that all of his contacts at the 700-lawyer firm were with the two lawyers that represented the party to the arbitration at issue; he owned stock in the litigation services company that was pursuing business opportunities with the firm; he served as the president of the company's United States subsidiary; he conducted significant marketing in the United States for the company; he had additional meetings or contacts with the two lawyers in question to solicit business from the firm for the company; and he allowed one of the two lawyers to edit his disclosures to minimize the contact. The trial court vacated the arbitration award, but the court of appeals reversed, concluding the party waived its evident partiality claim by failing to object or inquire further when the disclosures occurred. We hold the failure to disclose this additional information might yield a reasonable impression of the arbitrator's partiality to an objective observer. We further hold that because the party making the evident partiality challenge was unaware of the undisclosed information, it did not waive the claim. Accordingly, we reverse the court of appeals' judgment and reinstate the trial court's order vacating the award and requiring a new arbitration.

I. Background

The Tenaska Companies sold their interests in a power plant in Cleburne, Texas to Ponderosa Pine Energy, LLC (Ponderosa). The purchase agreement contained a broad arbitration clause requiring the parties to arbitrate any dispute arising from or related to the agreement. The clause provided for a three-arbitrator panel, with each party selecting one arbitrator and those two arbitrators selecting the third. The parties conceded in the court of appeals that all three arbitrators were required to be neutral, which follows the current default protocol in arbitration.

After the transaction closed, the parties disputed whether the agreement required Tenaska to indemnify Ponderosa for breaching certain representations and warranties in the agreement. Ponderosa demanded arbitration and sought more than $200 million in indemnity rights. Lawyers from Nixon Peabody LLP's New York office represented Ponderosa, which designated Samuel A. Stern as its arbitrator. Stern's curriculum vitae was attached to his designation, which indicated he was a director of twelve closely held companies with third-world involvement—including a company in India named LexSite. At the time, the AAA Commercial Arbitration Rules provided: "Any person appointed or to be appointed as an arbitrator shall disclose . . . any circumstance likely to give rise to justifiable doubt as to the arbitrator's impartiality or independence, including any bias or any financial or personal interest in the result of the arbitration or any past or present relationship with the parties or their representatives. Such obligation shall remain in effect throughout the arbitration."

Stern disclosed that Nixon Peabody had designated him as an arbitrator in three other proceedings, and that he—on behalf of LexSite—had a discussion at Nixon Peabody's offices about Nixon Peabody outsourcing litigation discovery tasks to LexSite. But the disclosures noted that "Nixon-Peabody and LexSite have done no business, and it is not clear that Nixon-Peabody would ever have any business to give Lexsite." In response, Tenaska asked if Stern had a relationship with any of the sixteen bank entities that own Ponderosa, and Stern replied that he had no such relationships.

Tenaska designated Thomas S. Fraser as its arbitrator, and Fraser and Stern selected James A. Baker as the third arbitrator. Tenaska asked Baker the same question it asked Stern, and Baker replied that his firm had represented some of the banks that own Ponderosa. At Baker's suggestion, the panel issued a scheduling order that contained a provision stating the parties had made full disclosures of actual and potential conflicts and knowingly waived actual and potential conflicts of interest. After extensive discovery, Ponderosa proposed a $125 million settlement and

Tenaska proposed a $1.25 million settlement. A divided panel composed of Baker and Stern selected Ponderosa's $125 million settlement amount.

Ponderosa moved to confirm the award in state district court, and Tenaska moved to vacate it, asserting that Stern was neither impartial nor free from bias. After extensive discovery, the trial court held a hearing on the motions, where the parties admitted almost 500 exhibits. Those exhibits included the depositions of Stern, as well as Frank Penski and Constance Boland—the two lawyers at Nixon Peabody who represented Ponderosa.

The evidence showed that Stern was on the advisory board for LexSite, a legal outsourcing company in India that was seeking to obtain business from law firms in the United States. Stern gave LexSite business and legal advice, and owned 3,000 shares of LexSite stock. He was given options for an additional 10,000 shares, which he had not exercised. Stern contacted Penski in April 2006 to discuss the possibility of Nixon Peabody using LexSite's services Stern arranged for Penski to meet LexSite's CEO that month. At the subsequent May 3 meeting at Nixon Peabody that Stern did disclose, he made several remarks, mostly asking the firm's associates for their impressions of performing discovery work. After the meeting concluded, Stern told Penski "if you have any arbitrations that would be fun, keep me in mind."

On June 16, Penski asked Stern to serve as a neutral party arbitrator in a matter involving Ada Co-Generation. Stern responded by accepting the appointment and asked if there was "[a]ny movement there" with LexSite. Penski replied that he had talked to numerous partners at Nixon Peabody in an effort to find something to send to LexSite but had "no luck so far." On the suggestion of Boland, another Nixon Peabody partner recommended Stern as an arbitrator in another arbitration on June 19. And on June 26, Penski recommended Stern as an arbitrator in this matter.

Boland later edited Stern's disclosures in two ways. First, she added the AdaCogeneration arbitration. Second, she added the disclaimer that "Nixon-Peabody and Lexsite have done no business, and it is not clear that Nixon-Peabody would ever have any business to give Lexsite."

After the parties agreed on the arbitrators, the scheduling order of October 23 established a waiver of conflicts. Three days later, Nixon Peabody changed its fee agreement with Ponderosa from an hourly rate to a contingency fee of 15% of the first $50 million and 12.5% of any amount over "50 million."

LexSite later changed its name to Exactus. Stern incorporated Exactus U.S. and was the chairman of its board. Stern charged LexSite $1,000 for use of his office and $5,000 per month for services. He also met with LexSite's CEO twice a month to discuss such topics as marketing.

LexSite's CEO continued to correspond with Boland during the arbitration. Boland informed LexSite's CEO in April 2007 that "we need to wait about one more month or so until we can continue our discussions. Would you be so kind as to send an email to me again on or about May 15?" LexSite's CEO agreed and noted he had recently met a lawyer from Nixon Peabody's Boston office, who Boland responded was "a good person to know and we can include him, or one of his team, in our meetings later on." On May 7, the panel issued its opinion and award LexSite's CEO contacted Boland again at the end of May.

After the hearing on the motions, the trial court granted Tenaska's motion to vacate the award on the ground that Stern exhibited evident partiality due to "a calculated, deliberate attempt to minimize the relationship" between Stern and Penksi and Boland. Specifically, the trial court held that Stern did not disclose additional information it summarized as follows:

> When viewed in the totality of circumstances, including the fact that Arbitrator Stern failed to disclose that his contact[s] with Nixon Peabody were all with Mr. Penski or Ms. Boland, failed to disclose additional meetings or contacts regarding Lexsite with Ponderosa[]'s counsel, failed to disclose the true extent of his ties to Lexsite and his activities for Lexsite, and allowed Ponderosa[]'s counsel to modify his disclosures in a way that minimized the contact, . . . Stern's disclosures were intentionally incomplete and inaccurate.

The trial court concluded that the Nixon Peabody/LexSite relationship was material rather than trivial and the undisclosed information might yield a reasonable impression that Stern was not impartial. Accordingly, the trial court granted the motion to vacate the arbitration award.

The court of appeals reversed, 376 S.W.3d at 360. It held that Stern's disclosures regarding LexSite and the Ada Co-Generation arbitration were sufficient to put Tenaska on notice of potential partiality to require Tenaska to object or seek additional information. *Id.*

II. Discussion

A. Evident Partiality

The parties agree the Federal Arbitration Act (FAA) governs this case and allows courts to vacate arbitration awards "where there was evident partiality." 9 U.S.C. § 10(a)(2). The United States Supreme Court has observed that "these provisions show a desire of Congress to provide not merely for any arbitration but for an impartial one." *Commonwealth Coatings Corp. v. Cont'l Cas. Co.*, 393 U.S. 145, 147 (1968). In *Commonwealth Coatings*, a subcontractor sued a prime contractor's surety, and the neutral third arbitrator failed to disclose he obtained approximately $12,000 in business from the prime contractor over a four to five year period (but had done no business with the contractor in the year preceding the arbitration). *Id.* at 146. The Court likened arbitrator impartiality to the impartiality the constitution requires of judges, and observed that even the slightest pecuniary interest in an arbitration could be grounds to set aside the award. *Id.* at 148. Although it recognized arbitrators are not expected to sever their ties with the business world, the Court concluded it must be scrupulous in safeguarding the impartiality of arbitrators because they "have completely free rein to decide the law as well as the facts and are not subject to appellate review." *Id.* at 148–49. To further that goal, the Court imposed "the simple requirement that arbitrators disclose to the parties any dealings that might create an impression of possible bias." *Id.* at 149. Despite the fact that the Court found no evidence of actual bias, it found the arbitrator evidently partial due to his failure to disclose his relationship with the prime contractor, justifying vacatur of the award. *Id.* at 146–47, 150.

We addressed evident partiality in *Burlington Northern Railroad Co. v. TUCO Inc.*, where we held that under *Commonwealth Coatings*, a neutral arbitrator exhibits evident partiality "if the arbitrator does not disclose facts which might, to an objective observer, create a reasonable impression of the arbitrator's partiality." 960 S.W.2d 629, 630 (Tex. 1997). And "while a neutral arbitrator need not disclose relationships or connections that are trivial, the conscientious arbitrator should err in favor of disclosure." *Id.* at 637. There, TUCO Inc. and two carriers arbitrated a dispute over a rate adjustment in their contracts. *Id.* at 630. Unlike the present case (which follows the current default protocol to require impartiality or neutrality of all three arbitrators), only the third arbitrator in TUCO was required to be neutral. *Id.* The parties agreed to a neutral third arbitrator, George Beall, after he disclosed he had twice served as an expert witness for the law firm of the carriers' arbitrator. *Id.* Those matters had concluded and involved a relatively small amount of time and fees. *Id.*

The evident partiality standard the Supreme Court announced in *Commonwealth Coatings*, which we followed in *TUCO*, applies in the context of party appointed arbitrators. *See TUCO*, 960 S.W.2d at 637. We need not decide what standard applies when an arbitration agreement does not allow parties the ability to select arbitrators.

We observed that inherent in the arbitration process are two principles that are often in tension: expertise and impartiality. *Id.* at 635. Parties may prefer to resolve disputes through arbitration because they may choose arbitrators with extensive experience in the field related to the dispute. *Id.* But this heightened experience level may well result in an arbitrator having had previous business dealings with a party. *Id.* And while these dealings should not disqualify the arbitrator per se, disclosing the information can help the parties attain the impartiality they seek by evaluating potential bias at the outset of the arbitration. *Id.* This approach also preserves the independence and integrity of arbitration by allowing a party to assess potential bias before arbitrating rather than having a trial court weigh bias when a dissatisfied party challenges an award. *Id.* at 635–36. Accordingly, *TUCO* makes clear that "evident partiality is established from the nondisclosure itself, regardless of whether the nondisclosed information necessarily establishes partiality or bias." *Id.* at 636. Whether the undisclosed information actually establishes partiality or bias is a matter "better left to the parties." *Id.*

We held in *TUCO* that the referral "might have conveyed an impression of Beall's partiality to a reasonable person." *Id.* at 637. Notwithstanding the fact that the lawyer who suggested the referral was unaware of the arbitration and the carrier's arbitrator was unaware of the referral, we concluded that an objective observer could reasonably believe that Beall, grateful for the referral, would favor the firm and thus ultimately favor the carriers in the arbitration. *Id.*

In short, the standard for evident partiality in *Commonwealth Coatings* and *TUCO* requires vacating an award if an arbitrator fails to disclose facts which might, to an objective observer, create a reasonable impression of the arbitrator's partiality, but information that is trivial will not rise to this level and need not be disclosed. *Commonwealth Coatings*, 393 U.S. at 149; *TUCO*, 960 S.W.2d at 630, 637.

We next apply the standard for evident partiality to these facts. Tenaska asserts the information the trial court found Stern did not disclose (which Ponderosa does not challenge on appeal) might create a reasonable impression of partiality to an objective observer because the extent of Stern's relationship with LexSite and Nixon Peabody were more significant and concerning than what he disclosed. Ponderosa counters that, unlike in Commonwealth Coatings and TUCO, Stern disclosed every relationship Tenaska now complains of We agree with Tenaska.

Stern disclosed that Nixon Peabody recommended him to three arbitrations in addition to the one at issue, and he met with Nixon Peabody on behalf of LexSite about outsourcing litigation discovery tasks, but stated that "Nixon-Peabody and Lexsite have done no business, and it is not clear that Nixon-Peabody would ever have any business to give Lexsite." The trial court found that Stern did not disclose additional information, and our review of the record confirms this additional information is supported by some evidence:

When we examine this undisclosed information together against what Stern actually disclosed, we conclude the information is not trivial and might have conveyed an impression of Stern's partiality toward Penski and Boland's client to a reasonable person. The parties do not dispute that—beyond what he disclosed—Stern owned shares of LexSite, was being paid for office space and services given to LexSite, marketed LexSite in the United States, was actively soliciting business for LexSite from Nixon Peabody (specifically through Penski and Boland), and discussed in communications with Penski regarding the arbitrations the possibility of LexSite and Nixon Peabody doing business. Taken together, this undisclosed information might cause a reasonable person to view Stern as being partial toward Penski and Boland's client, Ponderosa, to gain their favor in securing business for LexSite from Nixon Peabody. And when compared to the information Stern did disclose (that Nixon Peabody recommended him for four arbitrations and he attended one meeting between LexSite and Nixon Peabody), we cannot say this undisclosed information is trivial. Accordingly, Stern's failure to disclose the extent of his relationship with LexSite and his attempts to secure business for LexSite from Nixon Peabody through Penski and Boland demonstrate evident partiality and support the trial court's vacatur of the award. *See Commonwealth Coatings*, 393 U.S. at 149; *TUCO*, 960 S.W.2d at 630, 636.

Ponderosa contends that disclosure of each relationship suffices under Commonwealth Coatings and *TUCO*. But if disclosing each relationship were sufficient, the

Supreme Court in *Commonwealth Coatings* and this Court in *TUCO* would have simply established that threshold as the operative test. Instead, the test for evident partiality asks whether the undisclosed "information" might convey an impression of the arbitrator's partiality to an objective observer. *TUCO*, 960 S.W.2d at 635–36 (also referring to disclosing "any dealings" and "facts" that might convey an impression of partiality). Adopting Ponderosa's reformulation of the test would serve to encourage partial disclosures. Such a standard for evident partiality negates the Supreme Court's directive to be "scrupulous to safeguard the impartiality of arbitrators" in a process not subject to appellate review. *Commonwealth Coatings*, 393 U.S. at 149.

As a final matter, we reiterate that our holding should not be read as indicating that Stern was actually biased. Reasonable people could debate whether Stern's relationship with Nixon Peabody was likely to affect his partiality in the arbitration. But such a debate is for the parties after a full disclosure—which did not occur here. *See TUCO*, 960 S.W.2d at 638.

III. Conclusion

We have long held that an arbitrator is evidently partial, and an award may be vacated, if the arbitrator fails to disclose facts which might, to an objective observer, create a reasonable impression of the arbitrator's partiality. *Id.* at 630. As we have observed, the most capable arbitrators often have ties to the business community. *Id.* at 639. Regardless of whether such ties demonstrate actual bias here, Stern's failure to disclose the extent of his relationship with LexSite and the two lawyers who represented Ponderosa in this arbitration might yield a reasonable impression of the arbitrator's partiality to an objective observer. Thus, Stern had a duty to disclose the additional information, and his failure to do so constitutes evident partiality. Accordingly, we reverse the court of appeals' judgment and reinstate the trial court's order vacating the award and requiring a new arbitration.

Notes and Questions

1. *Disclose, Disclose, Disclose.* Return to note 2 following *Commonwealth Coatings*. As noted, Justice Black, for the majority, observed that the Court could "perceive no way in which the effectiveness of the arbitration process will be hampered by the simple requirement that arbitrators disclose to the parties any dealings that might create an impression of possible bias." The concurring opinion emphasized that "it is far better that the relationship be disclosed at the outset." The IBA Rules summarized earlier in this chapter focus in particular on disclosures, and as you just saw, the lower courts have run with this standard. *Tenaska* leaves little doubt that the greater sin here was the lack of disclosure. The Texas Supreme Court concluded by "reiterat[ing] that our holding should not

be read as indicating that Stern was actually biased." The court acknowledges that "reasonable people could differ" as to whether Stern's contacts with Nixon Peabody "was likely to affect his partiality in the arbitration." The lack of overt evidence in favor of partiality is all the more striking given that the parties engaged in particularized discovery about the alleged conflict. That said, the *Tenaska* court landed exactly where the *Commonwealth Coatings* concurring opinion stated should be the standard: *non-disclosure equals evident partiality*. "The standard for evident partiality in *Commonwealth Coatings* . . . requires vacating an award if an arbitrator refuses to disclose facts which might, to an objective observer, create a reasonable impression of the arbitrator's partiality."

2. *"Any" Triviality and Materiality*. Now, to a "what" question: precisely *what* should be disclosed? In *Tenaska*, the parties expressly chose to proceed under AAA Rules, not only as to disclosure but as to the selection process for the neutral arbitrator (with the two party-appointed arbitrators choosing the neutral). The Texas court thus looked to the AAA Rules, including the repeated use of the word "any" in the relevant disclosure rule. Is "any" a workable standard? Does it dwarf any concept of materiality? Should "any dealings" be restricted to commercial dealings? Should there be a numerical threshold? A temporal limit? *Tenaska* addressed this directly, stating that "information that is trivial will not rise to this level and need not be disclosed." How is "trivial" best to be assessed?
3. *Lying*. There is non-disclosure, and then there is the simple misstatement of fact. What happens when the disclosure form cannot kindly be characterized as incomplete and instead contains an indisputable falsehood? *See Goldman Sachs & Co v. Athena Venture Partners*, No. 13-MC-130,, 2013 U.S. Dist. LEXIS 107966 (E.D. Pa. Aug. 1, 2013) (arbitrator failed to disclose that he had been indicted for unauthorized practice of law).
4. *Discovery, Disclosures, and Conflicts*. Arbitrators who contemplate incomplete disclosures might want to reflect on the "extensive discovery" that ensued at the challenge stage in *Tenaska*. The arbitrators themselves wound up being deposed. Is this "efficient" arbitration? Who do you think paid for that additional discovery stage? Parties contemplating cutting corners by not disclosing may wish to reflect on the odds that their strategic choice may ultimately cost more, not less, time, expense, and delay.
5. *More on Big Firms*. The law firm in *Tenaska* had over 700 lawyers at the time of the case. What might the result have been if the challenged arbitrator's contacts had been with lawyers at that mega-firm other than the ones directly involved in the arbitration? And what would be the disclosure requirement?

CASE PREVIEW. In the next case, a law firm decided *not* to interview the son of a party. The party claimed this was prejudice. Do you agree?

Golden v. O'Melveny & Myers LLP

No. 2:14-cv-08725-CAS(AGRx),
2019 U.S. Dist. LEXIS 191158 (C.D. Cal. Nov. 1, 2019)

SNYDER, Judge.

Golden seeks vacatur of the Final Award on the basis of arbitrator bias. The FAA permits vacatur "where there was evident partiality or corruption in the arbitrators, or either of them[.]" 9 U.S.C. § 10(a)(2). "The party challenging the arbitration decision has the burden of showing partiality." *Woods v. Saturn Distribution Corp.*, 78 F.3d 424, 427 (9th Cir. 1996).

1. Potential Employment of the Arbitrator's Son

Golden asserts that vacatur of the Final Award is warranted because the Arbitrator "made up his mind against [Golden's] case on the basis of bias after O'Melveny and its counsel, [Gibson Dunn], barred [his] son from employment while he was preparing [for] on-campus interviews with both firms, blaming their decisions on" Golden. The Court finds this argument unavailing.

Golden does not dispute that neither O'Melveny, a party in the arbitration, nor its counsel, Gibson Dunn, ever employed the Arbitrator's son. To the contrary, after the Arbitrator disclosed to the parties that his son, then a law student, was seeking employment with a number of law firms including Gibson Dunn and O'Melveny, and after Golden raised the issue of possible bias, both Gibson and O'Melveny decided that, out of an abundance of caution, neither would extend an offer of employment to the Arbitrator's son. Ex. 13 at 454. Golden contends that the firms' decision to eliminate the possibility of an appearance of impartiality by declining to consider the Arbitrator's son for employment served to exacerbate the possibility of bias because, "in turn, the Arbitrator refused to recuse himself." The Court finds this argument unpersuasive. *See Union Carbide Corp. v. U.S. Cutting Serv., Inc.*, 782 F.2d 710, 713–16 (7th Cir. 1986) (affirming denial of recusal where movant contended that judge "may be harboring a grudge" where movant originally moved to disqualify judge for holding stock in party and, in response, judge sold stock to eliminate conflict); *see also* Charles A. Wright & Arthur R. Miller, 13D Fed. Prac. & Proc. Juris. § 3542 (3d ed.) ("A litigant cannot force disqualification by attacking the judge and claiming that the attacks must have caused the judge to be biased against him.").

Nor would the actual hiring of the Arbitrator's son by either O'Melveny, a party, or Gibson Dunn, O'Melveny's counsel, have necessarily required the Arbitrator's recusal pursuant to either of the two federal statutes governing recusal of judicial officers, 28 U.S.C. § 144 or 28 U.S.C. § 455(a). *See Datagate, Inc. v. Hewlett-Packard Co.*, 941 F.2d 864, 871 (9th Cir. 1991) ("an employment relationship between a judge's child and a party to the suit has not generally been held to merit per se disqualification."); *U.S. ex rel. Weinberger v. Equifax, Inc.*, 557 F.2d 456, 463–64 (5th Cir. 1977) (recusal not required where judge's son was an associate of the law firm representing defendant and son did not actively participate in the case). Because the standard for determining partiality for arbitrators is more stringent than that for judges, Golden therefore fails to establish the "evident partiality" required for vacatur. *See Schmitz v. Zilveti*, 20 F.3d 1043, 1047 (9th Cir. 1994) (noting differences in standards)); *see also Transportes Coal Sea de Venezuela C.A. v. SMT Shipmanagement & Transp. Ltd.*, 2007 U.S. Dist. LEXIS 1802, 2007 WL 62715, at *4 (S.D.N.Y. Jan. 9, 2007) ("an arbitrator may not be deemed partial simply because he presides over an arbitration in which one party employs an arbitrator's family member's law firm").

Problem: Arbitrator Conflicts of Interest

Acadia, Inc., a Maine distributor, orders mouthwash from Visterine, a New York manufacturer. Visterine is a subsidiary of Dohnson & Dohnson. The parties periodically conclude supply contracts to account for such orders. The latest such contract contains a dispute resolution clause calling for arbitration in New York City under the American Arbitration Association's Commercial Rules.

Acadia files a demand for arbitration, alleging that Respondent Visterine shipped it 3,000 boxes of Artic Mint mouthwash flavor instead of the Soft Mint mouthwash flavor it allegedly specified in the supply contract. Acadia alleges further that it attempted to mitigate but its customers do not like this flavor, as a result of which it could not sell the goods. It alleges breach of contract and seeks both cover damages and lost profits.

Upon receiving the notice of claim, the parties agreed to a sole arbitrator.

The parties then selected Elliot Preston as their arbitrator. Mr. Preston filed disclosure papers under Rule 17, stating as follows: "He is the managing partner of Franklin Topez and Watson LLP (FTW), a law firm with 95 lawyers and offices in New York City, Chicago, and Philadelphia. The firm recently opened a small office in St. Louis, Missouri. Mr. Preston practices in the area of commercial litigation, with a focus on antitrust work. However, his firm handles a variety of matters, including labor and employment, intellectual property, family law, and immigration." Mr. Preston's R-17 disclosures included facts about the previous cases he and his firm were involved in on behalf of the named parties. After further review of these disclosures, the parties confirmed his selection and the AAA formalized that approval.

It is now day 9 of the 14-day arbitration. The day before, the arbitrator heard experts testify that there was no discernible taste difference in the mouthwash flavors. Two days before that, Visterine put on evidence that Acadia had been in a cash crunch and so was looking to conserve cash by rejecting contract orders. Visterine argued that the termination of the contract on the basis of nonconforming goods is a pretext. The expert testimony appears to bear that out, and so far, the arbitration is going badly for Acadia.

The morning of day 9, Acadia claims that its lead counsel has just learned, through her business contacts, that a lawyer who now works for Arbitrator Preston's law firm (FTW) represented Dohnson & Dohnson (as stated above, Visterine's parent) in a patent infringement law suit last year. This lawyer now works out of FTW's relatively new St. Louis office. The law clerk to Mr. Preston for the arbitration, who is a mid-level associate in his firm, worked on the patent case. Mr. Preston himself billed four hours to the case (which involved many thousands of hours) when he reviewed one contract issue at that associate's request.

You represent Acadia, who now wishes to challenge Mr. Preston and, if successful in that challenge, start the whole arbitration over. Draft Acadia's R-18 challenge. What additional questions would you ask Arbitrator Preston? Who should win and why?

V. Timing Arbitrator Challenges: Balancing Waiver vs. Prematurity

Timing is everything. Disclosure up front would restrict disqualification proceedings to those where the party articulates a conflict *before* any arbitral decision is reached and the party cannot point to an award allegedly tainted by the conflict. Disclosure up front also avoids the waiver issue discussed in *Tenaska* and which is the feature of many disqualification cases.

The fact-based nature of the challenge exacerbates the issues faced by any party contemplating a challenge to an arbitrator. The adage, "if you shoot at the King, be sure not to miss," is easier to repeat than to implement, especially when the outcome is so unclear. The temptation is to hold back rather than anger an arbitrator unless one thinks that the outcome is a slam-dunk—but how can one ever think a challenge will be a slam-dunk when in *Tenaska*, the Texas appellate and Supreme courts split?

Parties who hold back the challenge and are then met with a waiver defense will face an entirely different but still fact-based question: what did they know and when did they know it? In *Tenaska*, the court deflected the waiver challenge on this basis: "Tenaska did not waive its evident partiality challenge by proceeding to arbitration based upon information it was unaware of at the time." The alternative is to object before the arbitrator—or, in what would be an easier situation, the arbitrators. Initially, challenges are ruled upon by the arbitrators and not by the court. There is statutory support for this. The review contemplated by Section 10 of the Federal Arbitration Act takes place only at the confirmation stage, subsequent to an arbitration award.

What if the challenge is brought to the arbitration tribunal and rejected? Must a party then go through with the entire arbitration? Or, particularly where the arbitration is in stages, can the party call a time-out and have the courts consider the challenge? The next case shows the difficulties of that approach.

CASE PREVIEW. The holding below by a panel of the Sixth Circuit concluded that the longstanding policy favoring enforcement of arbitration provisions set forth in the Federal Arbitration Act, and the limited review of awards provided by Section 10 of the statute, permitted a court to intervene in an arbitration proceeding *only*: (i) at the initial stages involving questions of arbitrability and enforceability of the agreement to arbitrate, or (ii) after an award is entered. *See also Morelite Construction, infra* Chapter 13.

Savers Prop. & Cas. Ins. Co. v. Nat'l Union Fire Ins. Co.

748 F.3d 708 (6th Cir. 2014)

COLE, Circuit Judge.

National Union Fire Insurance Company ("National Union") appeals the grant of a preliminary injunction that halted an ongoing arbitration proceeding with Savers Property and Casualty Insurance Company. Because arbitration's essential virtue is resolving disputes straightaway, judicial review of arbitral awards is extremely narrow and exceedingly deferential. In the absence of a final arbitration award, the district court should not have interjected itself into this private dispute. Accordingly, we reverse the judgment, dissolve the injunction, and remand for dismissal.

A. Factual Background

The underlying dispute that gave rise to this arbitration stems from a contract for reinsurance (the "Treaty") between National Union and Meadowbrook. The Treaty required both parties to submit any reinsurance disputes to a three-member arbitration panel that would "make its decision with regard to the custom and usage of the insurance and reinsurance business" after entertaining evidence and conducting a hearing. The majority decision of the panel was to be final and binding upon all parties to the proceeding, and either side could seek judicial confirmation in any court of competent jurisdiction. Meadowbrook initiated this arbitration in February 2011 to settle matters surrounding its alleged practice of overbilling National Union for certain reinsurance programs.

As is customary in the reinsurance industry, the arbitration clause from the Treaty established a tripartite method of arbitration. Under this system, the panel was to be comprised of "two arbitrators and an umpire" who were "active or retired disinterested officials of the insurance or reinsurance companies, or Underwriters at Lloyd's,

London, not under the control of either party to this Agreement." Each party was to appoint its own arbitrator, and then the two party-appointed arbitrators would select a neutral umpire. In the event that the party-appointed arbitrators disagreed in selecting an umpire, each side was to submit a list of three candidates, from which the opposing arbitrator would strike two. The umpire would then be chosen by lot from the remaining name on each list.

National Union named Jonathan Rosen as its arbitrator, and Meadowbrook named Rex Schlaybaugh. After the two men deadlocked in selecting an umpire, the parties exchanged slates of candidates and asked them to complete a questionnaire detailing their experience and connections with the parties and their arbitrators Thomas Greene—who was ultimately selected as umpire—disclosed that he was a personal friend of National Union's arbitrator. Greene also disclosed that, like Rosen, he was a member of the reinsurance industry group ARIAS, a not-for-profit corporation that publishes guidelines and best practices for reinsurance arbitrations. Despite Greene's connections to Rosen, Meadowbrook selected Greene from the slate of individuals put forward by National Union, and after casting lots, he was named umpire.

The panel held an organizational meeting on August 1, 2012, at which it adopted the first of two scheduling orders with identical language regarding ex parte communications. Those orders stated, "Ex parte communications with any member of the Panel shall cease upon the filing of the parties' initial pre-hearing briefs."

The panel conducted a hearing, and on July 23 issued a unanimous "Interim Final Award" resolving all issues of liability in favor of National Union. The panel did not, however, calculate a final damages award at that time. Instead, the panel ordered Meadowbrook to pay National Union $1,950,680.48 for damages that were "capable of immediate calculation," and, in an effort to mete out a final award, ordered Meadowbrook to provide supporting documentation with respect to other reinsurance programs and their retained risk. The panel also ordered Meadowbrook to reimburse National Union for its attorneys' fees and costs. The panel denied all other requests for relief, ordered Meadowbrook to pay the sum-certain damages within fourteen days, and retained jurisdiction only to "adjudicat[e] those items requiring additional submissions"—*i.e.*, to calculate National Union's damages prior to issuing a final arbitration award.

B. Procedural Background

Unsatisfied with the panel's procedural orders, Meadowbrook filed a complaint in Michigan state court seeking to vacate the Interim Final Award on the grounds that Umpire Greene and Arbitrator Rosen exceeded their authority under the Treaty and that Rosen displayed evident partiality. The crux of Meadowbrook's complaint was that Rosen failed to disclose that he had been a guest speaker at a conference with National Union's attorney during the course of the arbitration. Meadowbrook alleged it would have moved to disqualify Rosen and Greene had it known of Rosen's speaking engagements. When Meadowbrook learned that Rosen and National

Union's attorney had resumed their ex parte communications following issuance of the Interim Final Award, Meadowbrook amended its state-court complaint to reflect those facts.

Simultaneously, Meadowbrook protested the panel's orders within the arbitration proceeding itself by filing a motion for reconsideration and a motion to stay all proceedings. Meadowbrook raised the same arguments it pressed in state court—namely, that Rosen failed to disclose his participation in a reinsurance industry educational seminar held at the law offices of National Union's attorney, and that Rosen and National Union's attorney engaged in improper ex parte communications following issuance of the Interim Final Award.

By a 2–1 vote, the arbitration panel denied both motions. As to Meadowbrook's first argument, regarding disclosure of Rosen's speaking engagements, Greene and Rosen ruled for the panel as follows:

The Panel sees no merit in Meadowbrook's complaint that Arbitrator Rosen did not disclose his participation at the AIRROC regional education seminar held at Foley & Lardner's offices earlier this year. That [National Union's attorney] also participated at AIRROC's invitation as a panelist at that seminar in a segment separate and distinct from Mr. Rosen's segment is of absolutely no moment or relevance in relation to this proceeding and did not, in the Panel's view, constitute a matter requiring disclosure.

Greene and Rosen also rejected Meadowbrook's claim that Rosen violated the rules governing ex parte communications, ruling as follows:

> The Panel sees no merit in Meadowbrook's complaint that Arbitrator Rosen's communications with [National Union's attorney] and his colleagues after issuance of the Interim Final Award constituted a breach of the rules governing ex parte contact in this proceeding. A review of the Organizational Meeting transcript and Scheduling Orders entered in connection with this proceeding readily establish that the prohibition on ex parte contact came to an end upon the Panel ruling on the merits of this dispute. That was occasioned upon the issuance of the Interim Final Award, which fully and finally resolved all liability aspects attendant to this dispute. . . .This conclusion not only comports with the parties' expressed intentions relative to ex parte contact with the party appointed arbitrators, but is consistent with the Panel's intent and understanding of its orders governing ex parte contact as well as the customs and practices existing in the conduct of reinsurance arbitrations.

Judicial Review was Improper Before Issuance of a Final Arbitration Award.

Based upon the text, structure, and purpose of the FAA, which all foster a speedy and less formal method of dispute resolution, we conclude that the district court erred in entertaining this interlocutory challenge to an ongoing arbitration proceeding. Parties to an arbitration generally may not challenge the fairness of the proceedings or the partiality of the arbitrators until the conclusion of the arbitration and the rendition of a final award. Because Meadowbrook's arbitration was ongoing, and because the panel had not yet issued a final award, the district court erred by prematurely interjecting itself into this private dispute.

"The point of affording parties discretion in designing arbitration processes is to allow for efficient, streamlined procedures tailored to the type of dispute." *AT&T Mobility*, 131 S. Ct. at 1749. Moreover, the informality of arbitration "is itself desirable" because it "reduc[es] the cost and increase[es] the speed of dispute resolution." *Id.* (citing *14 Penn Plaza LLC v. Pyett*, 556 U.S. 247, 257 (2009)).

To maintain "arbitration's essential virtue of resolving disputes straightaway," courts may vacate an arbitration award "only in very unusual circumstances." The FAA and Michigan's arbitration law contemplate only two stages at which courts may become involved in arbitration proceedings. At the outset of any dispute, the laws authorize courts to decide certain "gateway matters" of arbitrability, "such as whether the parties have a valid arbitration agreement at all or whether a concededly binding arbitration clause applies to a certain type of controversy." *Id.* at 2068 n.2 (internal quotation marks omitted). Then, at the conclusion of an arbitration proceeding, courts are authorized to enter an order confirming, vacating, or modifying the award, but even so, awards may be disrupted only under narrow circumstances. *See* 9 U.S.C. §§ 9–11; Mich. Ct. R. 3.602(I)–(K); *Oxford Health Plans*, 133 S. Ct. at 2068.

Between these two stages, however, the laws are largely silent with respect to judicial review. Over the years, our court and several of our sister circuits have interpreted that silence and the overall structure of the FAA to preclude the interlocutory review of arbitration proceedings and decisions. *See Quixtar, Inc. v. Brady*, 328 F. App'x 317, 320 (6th Cir. 2009) ("[C]ourts generally should not entertain interlocutory appeals from ongoing arbitration proceedings."); *see also, e.g., Blue Cross Blue Shield of Mass., Inc. v. BCS Ins. Co.*, 671 F.3d 635, 638 (7th Cir. 2011) (observing "that judges must not intervene in pending arbitrations" and noting that "[r]eview comes at the beginning or the end, but not in the middle" of arbitration); *Gulf Guar. Life Ins. Co. v. Conn. Gen. Life Ins. Co.*, 304 F.3d 476, 488 (5th Cir. 2002) ("We find no authority under the FAA for a court to entertain such challenges [to the arbitrator selection process or the unfairness of an arbitration] prior to [the] issuance of the arbitral award.").

In addition to these textual and structural considerations, there are sound policy reasons—all of which support the purposes underlying the FAA—for generally withholding judicial review until the conclusion of an arbitration proceeding. *See, e.g., Trustmark Ins. Co. v. John Hancock Life Ins. Co.*, 631 F.3d 869, 874 (7th Cir. 2011) (observing that if parties could obtain interlocutory review of arbitral decisions, "[t]hat would be the end of arbitration as a speedy and (relatively) low-cost alternative to litigation"); *Gulf Guar. Life Ins.*, 304 F.3d at 492 ("[A] prime objective of arbitration law is to permit a just and expeditious result with a minimum amount of judicial interference . . . any other such rule could spawn endless applications to the courts and indefinite delay. . . ." (internal quotation marks omitted)).

In this case, the district court's decision falls on the wrong side of the line. The district court erred in relying on that provision to entertain Meadowbrook's premature challenge to the fairness of the proceedings and the partiality of the arbitrators. Those issues are properly raised in a motion to vacate under 9 U.S.C. § 10 following the conclusion of the proceedings and the issuance of a final arbitration award. *See Gulf Guar. Life Ins.* 304 F.3d at 490–91.

IV. CONCLUSION

For the foregoing reasons, we reverse the judgment of the district court, dissolve the injunction, and remand the case for dismissal without prejudice.

CASE PREVIEWS. In the JAMS cases you studied earlier in this chapter, both courts focused not just on non-disclosure but on timing.

Monster Energy Co. v. City Bevs., LLC

940 F.3d 1130 (9th Cir. 2019)

SMITH, Circuit Judge.

City Beverages, LLC, doing business as Olympic Eagle Distributing (Olympic Eagle), and Monster Energy Co. (Monster) signed an agreement providing exclusive distribution rights for Monster's products to Olympic Eagle for a fixed term in a specified territory. After Monster exercised its contractual right to terminate the agreement, the parties proceeded to arbitration to determine whether Olympic Eagle was entitled to protection under Washington law, and thus whether Monster had improperly terminated the agreement without good cause. From a list of several neutrals provided by JAMS, the arbitration organization specified in the agreement, the parties chose the Honorable John W. Kennedy, Jr. (Ret.) (the Arbitrator). At the outset of arbitration, the Arbitrator provided a series of disclosure statements. In the final arbitration award (the Award), the Arbitrator determined that Olympic Eagle did not qualify for protection under Washington law.

The parties filed cross-petitions in the district court, with Monster seeking to confirm the Award and Olympic Eagle moving to vacate it. The district court ultimately confirmed the Award.

We conclude, given the Arbitrator's failure to disclose his ownership interest in JAMS, coupled with the fact that JAMS has administered 97 arbitrations for Monster over the past five years, that vacatur of the Award is necessary on the ground of evident partiality. We therefore reverse the district court and vacate the Award. We also vacate the district court's award of post-arbitration fees to Monster for its petition to confirm the Award.

ANALYSIS

The district court held, and Monster continues to argue, that Olympic Eagle waived its evident partiality claim because it failed to timely object when it first learned of potential "repeat player" bias and the Arbitrator disclosed his economic interest in JAMS.

In *Fidelity Federal Bank, FSB v. Durga Ma Corp. (Fidelity)*, we joined several of our sister circuits that utilize a constructive knowledge standard when considering whether a party has waived an evident partiality claim. 386 F.3d 1306, 1313 (9th Cir. 2004). There, we held that the disgruntled party was on notice that the challenged arbitrator may have been non-neutral given the process the parties employed to pick their arbitration panel: each party picked one arbitrator and the arbitrators picked the third. *Id.* Moreover, the party had failed to request disclosures from the arbitrator or object to the lack of disclosures. *Id.* Given these facts, we concluded that the party had waived its partiality objection. *Id.*

Our post-*Fidelity* waiver cases involved less complicated factual scenarios than the case before us. *See Johnson v. Gruma Corp.,* 614 F.3d 1062, 1069 (9th Cir. 2010) (finding waiver where the party knew for at least "a year or two" of the prior professional relationship between the arbitrator and opposing counsel's spouse before the arbitrator ruled); *Metalmark Nw., LLC v. Stewart*, No. 06-35321, 2008 U.S. App. LEXIS 10339, 2008 WL 11442024, at *1 (9th Cir. May 6, 2008) (finding no waiver because the arbitrator failed to disclose conflicts and neither party had selected the arbitrator). Unlike these prior cases, the situation here is more akin to a partial disclosure—the Arbitrator disclosed his "economic interest" in JAMS prior to arbitration, but Olympic Eagle did not know it was an ownership interest. Although the district court correctly noted that an ownership interest is "merely a type of economic interest," the key issue is whether Olympic Eagle had constructive notice of the Arbitrator's potential non-neutrality.

We find that Olympic Eagle lacked the requisite constructive notice for waiver. To be sure, it knew that the Arbitrator had some sort of "economic interest" in JAMS. But the Arbitrator expressly likened his interest in JAMS to that of "each JAMS neutral," who has an interest in the "overall financial success of JAMS." The Arbitrator also disclosed his previous arbitration activities that directly involved Monster, in which he ruled against the company. In context, these disclosures implied only that the Arbitrator, like any other JAMS arbitrator or employee, had a general interest in JAMS's reputation and economic wellbeing, and that his sole financial interest was in the arbitrations that he himself conducted. Thus, even if the number of disputes that Monster sent to JAMS was publicly available, that information alone would not have revealed that this *specific* Arbitrator was potentially non-neutral based on the totality of JAMS's Monster-related business.

The crucial fact—the Arbitrator's ownership interest—was not unearthed through public sources, and it is not evident that Olympic Eagle could have discovered this information prior to arbitration. In fact, JAMS repeatedly stymied Olympic Eagle's efforts to obtain details about JAMS's ownership structure and the Arbitrator's interest post-arbitration. Accordingly, Olympic Eagle did not have constructive notice of the Arbitrator's ownership interest in JAMS—the key fact that triggered the specter of partiality.

Furthermore we have repeatedly emphasized an arbitrator's duty to investigate and disclose potential conflicts. *See, e.g.*, *New Regency*, 501 F.3d at 1110–11 (holding that the arbitrator's new employment triggered duty to investigate possible conflicts). The Arbitrator undoubtedly knew of his ownership interest in JAMS prior to arbitration yet failed to disclose it. To find waiver in this circumstance would "'put a premium on concealment' in a context where the Supreme Court has long required full disclosure." *Tenaska Energy, Inc. v. Ponderosa Pine Energy, LLC*, 437 S.W.3d 518, 528 (Tex. 2014) (quoting *Middlesex Mut. Ins. Co. v. Levine*, 675 F.2d 1197, 1204 (11th Cir. 1982)). Thus, we hold that Olympic Eagle did not have constructive notice of the Arbitrator's potential non-neutrality, and therefore did not waive its evident partiality claim.

Martin v. NTT Data, Inc.

No. 20-CV-0686, 2020 U.S. Dist. LEXIS 109490 (E.D. Pa. June 23, 2020)

JOYNER, Judge.

Petitioner has failed to explain why she waited for some two months after the November 5, 2019 disclosures were made and until after the award in favor of the Respondent was entered on January 6, 2020 to lodge her challenge to the Arbitrator. Under JAMS Arbitration Rule 27(b):

If any Party becomes aware of information that could be the basis of a challenge for cause to the continued service of the Arbitrator, such challenge must be made promptly, in writing to the Arbitrator or JAMS. Failure to do so shall constitute a waiver of any objection to continued service by the Arbitrator.

In addition, the Third Circuit has also made clear that in the arbitration context it frowns upon affording the losing party "a second bite at the apple." *Freeman*, 709 F.3d at 250. Indeed, it now adheres to the "constructive knowledge standard" such that a party will be held to have waived a later challenge where it knew or should have known of the facts indicating partiality. *Goldman, Sachs & Co. v. Athena Venture Partners, L.P.*, 803 F.3d 144, 149 (3d Cir. 2015). This standard thereby encourages the parties to conduct adequate due diligence prior to issuance of the award and promotes the arbitration goals of efficiency and finality while allowing a party to challenge an arbitration when it had no way of discovering the arbitrator's bias beforehand. *Id.* Here, while Petitioner may not have been able to discover the Arbitrator's interests before they were actually disclosed, her failure to offer any explanation whatsoever as to why she waited until *after* the award was entered in this case is glaring. In the absence of any evidence that she made any effort to question or to even mention Arbitrator Shelanski's non-disclosures and potential bias promptly after the November 5, 2019 mailing or at the closing arguments of the case, it appears that Petitioner was trying to "game the system by rolling the dice on whether to raise the challenge during the proceedings or wait until [losing] to seek vacatur on the issue." *Goldman*, 803 F.3d at 150. By so doing, Petitioner waived her objections. For these reasons, we therefore decline to set aside the award on the basis of waiver.

Notes and Questions

1. There should be little debate about the wisdom of the Sixth Circuit's central holding that review of arbitration awards "comes at the beginning or the end, but not in the middle" of an arbitration proceeding, and that "there are sound policy reasons . . . for generally withholding judicial review until the conclusion of an arbitration proceeding." The slippery slope that would otherwise result would run the risk of wholly undermining the FAA's statutory purpose in creating an alternative to the courts. There would instead be an explosion of "litigation about arbitration," none of it advancing the merits, all of it costing the client's money, and all of it further clogging up the court system. Should there, however, be a provision for exceptional cases, or will lawyers in their skill and wisdom argue that every one of their cases meets the exception?
2. Should review at an "interlocutory" level be more permissible when, as in *National Union*, there has been at least one arbitration award issued by the arguably tainted panel? That occurs when a case is bifurcated, as here. Why should the parties have had to proceed to yet another stage with a panel where one arbitrator was overtly and repeatedly excluded from deliberations and the parties were so brazen about *ex parte* contacts that lawyers billed for these contacts and then submitted them with their fee applications? Should the rule be that interlocutory appeal is disfavored, rather than prohibited, but can be permissible in exceptional cases where (a) the disclosure was incomplete and (b) the arbitrators are mid-way through a tainted and "partial" process? Return to the concept of "efficiency" in arbitration. Which path is more efficient: allowing a tainted arbitration to proceed so as to avoid interlocutory challenges, or stepping in immediately so that the parties don't have to go through what may be a charade and then commence the arbitration again?

Chapter 7
Discovery in Arbitration

Discovery in any dispute resolution format is much maligned, and for good reason. It creates abuses, intrusions, delays, and costs. It is often the single, longest-lasting phase of a case and, especially for that large majority of cases that do not go to trial or hearing, the most expensive part as well. It can just as frequently be the most contentious: it is not uncommon for there to be more motions about aspects of the discovery process than about the merits themselves.

But discovery can also be the most necessary portion of a case. It is, to start with, that rarest of legal terms that actually means what it says. In a constructive discovery process, the parties *learn*—they "discover"—facts that they did not know, would otherwise have been impossible to learn, and which are material to their case. Although discovery has come to be associated with the worst kind of abuses, this does not mean that it is always a bad thing or even that it need always be accompanied by the negatives which too often characterize it.

Arbitration offers the opportunity to steer the discovery ship down the middle. The parties can customize and agree to the discovery they want. This is a key part of "building your own courthouse" and can be an opportunity for lawyers to both save their clients substantial sums of money while also obtaining the information they need.

I. Two Myths

There are two myths about discovery in arbitration. The first is that there is none. The second, at the opposite extreme, is that there is a set type of rules for "discovery in arbitration." Neither is true.

We begin with an old-guard case holding that parties who agree to arbitrate abandon all hope of obtaining discovery unless they "apply to the district court."

Burton v. Bush

614 F.2d 389 (4th Cir. 1980)

RUSSELL, J.

William G. Burton, t/a William Burton Nurseries seeks review of an arbitration panel's award in favor of the appellees The Bush Organization. Burton sued The Bush Organization for failure to make payments as called for under the terms of their contract. The Bush Organization counterclaimed for damages based on the alleged breach of certain guarantees in the contract.

In January and February of 1974 the parties entered into two contracts which required Burton to install trees, shrubs, and sod at the appellee's job site. The relationship between the parties was strained by difficulties encountered during the course of performance. Finally in April of 1975 Bush notified Burton that he was replacing him on the contract work. A dispute arose over Burton's claim of payment for part performance and Bush's claim for breach of warranty. The parties agreed to submit their dispute to an arbitration panel, and on February 6, 1978 an award was rendered in favor of the appellees in the amount of $83,258.35.

The appellant challenged the arbitration award on two grounds. First, Burton contended that the award should be set aside due to unfair surprise and prejudice. When testimony before the arbitration panel concluded on September 8, 1977 all parties agreed that the proceedings would be continued to October 27th. On October 5th Burton's counsel requested a continuance until the latter part of November. Counsel argued that a continuance was necessary in light of the prejudice visited upon his client through the "surprise" testimony of opposition witnesses. This request was denied. Given the facts of this case, such an argument is unbelievable, and was so found by both the arbitration panel and the district court.

When the panel first convened more than two years had elapsed since The Bush Organization had given notice to Burton that his work was unsatisfactory. During this time period Burton was well aware of Bush's complaints. The gist of these complaints was that Burton's trees were dying and his grass would not grow. The obvious theory underlying Bush's claim was that these unfortunate results were caused by Burton's negligence. Since the final demise of the trees and the grass was not in issue, Burton knew or should have known that a proper defense required some showing of alternative causation. Thus, even though the applicable arbitration rules did not provide for pre-trial discovery, and the parties chose to forego any voluntary or gratuitous discovery, it cannot be said that Burton was somehow taken unawares.

An arbitration hearing is not a court of law. *Walden v. Local 71, International Brotherhood of Teamsters*, (4th Cir. 1972) 468 F.2d 196. When contracting parties stipulate that disputes will be submitted to arbitration, they relinquish the right to certain procedural niceties which are normally associated with a formal trial. *Great Scott Markets Inc. v. Local Union No. 337, International Brotherhood of Teamsters*, (E.D. Mich. 1973) 363 F. Supp. 1351; *Commercial Solvents Corporation v. Louisiana*

Liquid Fertilizer Co., (S.D.N.Y. 1957) 20 F.R.D. 359. One of these accoutrements is the right to pre-trial discovery. While an arbitration panel may subpoena documents or witnesses, *Commercial Metals Co. v. International Union Marine Corp.*, (S.D.N.Y. 1970) 318 F. Supp. 1334; the litigating parties have no comparable privilege. *Foremost Yarn Mills, Inc. v. Rose Mills, Inc.*, (E.D. Pa. 1960) 25 F.R.D. 9; 9 U.S.C. § 7; Fed. Rules Civ. Proc. Rule 81(a)(3), 28 U.S.C.; 74 Harv. L. Rev. 940, 943 (1961); 4 Moore's Fed. Practice § 26.54 (2d Ed. 1975).

Since Burton never applied to the district court for an order to compel discovery we need not consider those cases allowing discovery upon a showing of special need, *Bigge Crane and Rigging Co. v. Docutel Corp.*, (E.D.N.Y. 1973) 371 F. Supp. 240; *Ferro Union Corp. v. SS Ionic Coast*, (S.D. Tex. 1967) 43 F.R.D. 11; *International Association of Heat and Frost Insulators and Asbestos Workers, Local 66, AFL-CIO v. Leona Lee Corp.*, (5th Cir. 1970) 434 F.2d 192; *Penn Tanker Co. v. C. H. Z. Rolimpex, Warszawa*, (S.D.N.Y. 1961) 199 F. Supp. 716; or need we consider those cases allowing the district court to permit limited discovery as to the arbitrability of a particular dispute, *H. K. Porter Co. Inc. v. Local 37 United Steelworkers of America, AFL-CIO*, (4th Cir. 1968) 400 F.2d 691; *International Union of Electrical, Radio & Machine Workers, AFL-CIO v. Westinghouse Electric Corp.*, (S.D.N.Y. 1969) 48 F.R.D. 298. In passing, however, we note that the former cases would not have aided the appellant since there is a total absence of special need or hardship. The latter group of cases is equally unpersuasive, since there was no contention that the controversy in question was not the proper subject of arbitration.

While at least one commentator has referred to the limited discovery provisions during arbitration as a return to the "sporting theory of justice," Jones, *The Accretion of Federal Power in Labor Arbitration The Example of Arbitral Discovery*, 116 Penna. L. Rev. 830, 837 (1968); we believe that such limitations are in keeping with the policy underpinnings of arbitration speed, efficiency, and reduction of litigation expenses.

Burton's second contention that the arbitration award was contrary to the facts as established at the hearing is without merit.

We conclude that the arbitration award was correct and accordingly we affirm the judgment of the district court.

AFFIRMED.

Comment: The Myths Exploded

Is the Fourth Circuit's comment correct that parties who agree to arbitrate "relinquish the right to certain procedural niceties which are normally associated with a formal trial" and "[o]ne of these accoutrements is the right to pre-trial discovery"?

The answer is yes and no. Contrast the arbitration party to a litigation party. A party to court litigation comes to that dispute with a guaranteed set of discovery rights, and obligations. Nothing can be opted out of—that party *must* answer interrogatories, produce documents, and answer requests for admissions when asked. Similarly, that party has the right to propound all of those discovery requests on the opposing party. The rules are pre-set and baked in. The rules of civil procedure, in state and in federal court, contain extensive, mandatory discovery rules.

But the *Bush* court is wrong in suggesting that as a result, there is no discovery in arbitration. That is the first our exploded myths. The parties can agree to whatever discovery they want—and, as you will see in the next session, sometimes they may "agree" without even knowing. Discovery is not antithetical to arbitration. Only forced, guaranteed, definite discovery is antithetical to arbitration.

Which takes us to the second myth. Discovery in arbitration is customized, not the one-size-fits-all of civil procedure rules. If your opposing counsel, when you attend your first scheduling conference in an arbitration, tells you that he is entitled to a certain kind of discovery—a certain number of interrogatories, or depositions, or interrogatories or depositions at all—because "that's what happens in arbitration," you should look at him, smile, and tell him he is wrong. Discovery in arbitration is not an entitled right. It is a matter for negotiation and agreement. It is a matter, above all, of party autonomy.

We turn next to the means by which parties can exercise that autonomy.

II. Legal Bases of Discovery in Arbitration

Party autonomy on discovery in arbitration can play out in three different ways, separately or in combination.

A. The Arbitration Clause

Parties can address discovery directly in the contract's arbitration clause. The amount of that control can range in intensity and detail. Parties have the discretion to

- bar any discovery at all, *see* G. Born, International Commercial Arbitration in the United States, Commentary & Materials 83 (1994) ("It is widely recognized that one of the reasons that parties agree upon arbitration to resolve their disputes is to avoid the expense and delay of discovery");
- provide generally for discovery to be determined by the arbitrator's discretion;
- provide that some modes of discovery (for example, document production) are permitted while others (e.g., depositions) are not;
- limit the number of productions or depositions (*see also* scheduling conference discussion below); or

- at the other extreme from no discovery, provide for litigation-style discovery. An example would be parties choosing that their arbitration be "governed by the Federal Rules of Civil Procedure."

The advantage of addressing discovery in detail in the dispute resolution clause is that it leaves no doubt as to either consensus or mandate. The clause instructs the arbitrator how to decide what discovery is and is not allowed as the dispute proceeds. That can cut down substantially on discovery motion practice and its resulting costs.

This approach also comes with substantial disadvantages, the biggest one being ignorance. Dispute resolution clauses are typically crafted by transactional lawyers who are properly focused on the deal, not its dissolution, and who may have no idea at the time the deal closes what type of discovery will best suit any future dispute (or, more narrowly, their particular client's needs in that dispute). Overscheduling and over-layering a dispute resolution clause has the same risks and advantages as a prepackaged vacation tour: you know exactly where you are going and staying, with no surprises, but you lack the flexibility to take detours and side trips that look quite attractive once you are there.

B. Institutional Rules

Parties may not realize that by selecting certain kinds of institutional arbitration, they buy into discovery. Nowhere is the myth of "no discovery in arbitration" refuted more than in these clauses. Rather than bar discovery outright, *the arbitration rules for each of the leading U.S. arbitration institutions contain at least a presumption in favor of limited discovery.* There is an increasing trend in the United States toward amending the institutional rules so as to provide for more, not less, prehearing discovery. As you read these rules, consider the basic question of whether it is both possible, and advisable, to open the door a crack. By providing for some limited amount of discovery, do the institutional rules provide a "Goldilocks approach" of just enough material discovery without letting discovery costs become a runaway train, or are they the first step down to a slippery slope that will make arbitration just as expensive as litigation but without the protection of an appeal?

CPR, Rule 11. Disclosure (2019)

The Tribunal may require and facilitate such disclosure as it shall determine is appropriate in the circumstances, taking into account the needs of the parties and the desirability of making disclosure expeditious and cost-effective. The Tribunal may issue orders to protect the confidentiality of proprietary information, trade secrets and other sensitive information disclosed.

JAMS, Rule 17. Exchange of Information

(a) The Parties shall cooperate in good faith in the voluntary and informal exchange of all non-privileged documents and other information (including electronically stored information ("ESI")) relevant to the dispute or claim immediately after commencement of the Arbitration. They shall complete an initial exchange of all relevant, non-privileged documents, including, without limitation, copies of all documents in their possession or control on which they rely in support of their positions, and names of individuals whom they may call as witnesses at the Arbitration Hearing, within twenty-one (21) calendar days after all pleadings or notice of claims have been received. The Arbitrator may modify these obligations at the Preliminary Conference.

(b) Each Party may take one deposition of an opposing Party or of one individual under the control of the opposing Party. The Parties shall attempt to agree on the time, location and duration of the deposition. If the Parties do not agree, these issues shall be determined by the Arbitrator. The necessity of additional depositions shall be determined by the Arbitrator based upon the reasonable need for the requested information, the availability of other discovery options and the burdensomeness of the request on the opposing Parties and the witness.

(c) As they become aware of new documents or information, including experts who may be called upon to testify, all Parties continue to be obligated to provide relevant, non-privileged documents to supplement their identification of witnesses and experts and to honor any informal agreements or understandings between the Parties regarding documents or information to be exchanged. Documents that were not previously exchanged, or witnesses and experts that were not previously identified, may not be considered by the Arbitrator at the Hearing, unless agreed by the Parties or upon a showing of good cause.

(d) The Parties shall promptly notify JAMS when a dispute exists regarding discovery issues. A conference shall be arranged with the Arbitrator, either by telephone or in person, and the Arbitrator shall decide the dispute. With the written consent of all Parties, and in accordance with an agreed written procedure, the Arbitrator may appoint a special master to assist in resolving a discovery dispute.

AAA, Rule 22. Pre-Hearing Exchange and Production of Information

(a) *Authority of arbitrator.* The arbitrator shall manage any necessary exchange of information among the parties with a view to achieving an efficient and economical resolution of the dispute, while at the same time promoting equality of treatment and safeguarding each party's opportunity to fairly present its claims and defenses.

(b) *Documents.* The arbitrator may, on application of a party or on the arbitrator's own initiative:

i. require the parties to exchange documents in their possession or custody on which they intend to rely;

ii. require the parties to update their exchanges of the documents on which they intend to rely as such documents become known to them;

iii. require the parties, in response to reasonable document requests, to make available to the other party documents, in the responding party's possession or custody, not otherwise readily available to the party seeking the documents, reasonably believed by the party seeking the documents to exist and to be relevant and material to the outcome of disputed issues; and

iv. require the parties, when documents to be exchanged or produced are maintained in electronic form, to make such documents available in the form most convenient and economical for the party in possession of such documents, unless the arbitrator determines that there is good cause for requiring the documents to be produced in a different form. The parties should attempt to agree in advance upon, and the arbitrator may determine, reasonable search parameters to balance the need for production of electronically stored documents relevant and material to the outcome of disputed issues against the cost of locating and producing them.

Notes and Questions

1. *Self-Executing Discovery.* Return for a moment to a litigation standard for discovery. Rule 26(a) of the Federal Rules of Civil Procedure provides for what is known as "self-executing discovery," by which a party must provide information about its case *before it is asked.* The Federal Rules thus not only mandate discovery but require further that the discovery process begin with a party's own production of materials "that the disclosing party has in its possession, custody, or control and may use to support its claims or defenses." Fed. R. Civ. P. 26(a)(1) ("Initial Disclosure"). Should arbitration practice adopt the same self-executing rule? Some of the above institutional rules do go down that path. Should those rules, which nudge the parties toward self-executing discovery at the outset, provide for "opt-out" provisions by which a party which may not want self-executing disclosure can elect not to provide it at the beginning of the case? What if the other party agreed to institutional rules in order to obtain self-executing disclosures—do opt-out provisions destroy "consensus"? Finally, do provisions for self-executing discovery make discovery fights more or less likely to occur?

2. *How Mandatory Is Self-Executing Disclosure in the JAMS Rules?* JAMS Rule 17 states that the parties "shall" (mandatory wording) cooperate in the "voluntary" (discretionary wording) production of information. If a JAMS party resists providing discovery, what would be the sanction? What would be the arbitrator's power to compel?
3. *How Much Additional Discovery Should There Be in Arbitration After Self-Executing Disclosures?* The general thrust of the above institutional rules is to create a presumption in favor of permitting discovery—but you still have to ask. Is a standard requiring production of documents on which a party "intends to rely" a useful basis or starting point for ordering discovery? What if the producing party does not know on day 1 about a particular document that, by day 100 of the case, has assumed paramount importance? How long, and under which rules, does the duty to update these documents on which a party may "rely" continue? What if a party does not intend to rely but knows that her opponent may rely on the documents? What if a party lies? Is the solution to allow future requests? Or would that convert arbitration all the more into discovery-plagued litigation-style dispute resolution?

Problem

Respondent patented a technology which filtered water in ice machines, so that the resulting ice was of a greater purity than those in standard ice machines. Respondent licensed the manufacturing and distribution rights for the water purification technology to Claimant, a large kitchen appliance manufacturer. Respondent agreed further to sell Claimant water purification "kits" which could easily be incorporated into refrigerators. Claimant incorporated the design into the next generation of its refrigerators so that the fresh water option on the front of the refrigerator could now be marketed as special "filtered" water. This provided a ready and efficient market for Respondent's technology. The parties' contract was called a "license and supply agreement," which contained an arbitration clause calling for arbitration under AAA rules. The arbitration clause does not otherwise address discovery or its limits.

Claimant was initially satisfied with the product's performance and featured the new "water purification" heavily in its marketing materials for its next year of refrigerators. In the middle of Claimant's advertising campaign, however, Respondent was sold to a new owner, who decided that the margins on the license and supply agreement were too small and elected to stop supplying Claimant. Claimant claimed breach of the license and supply agreement and brought an AAA arbitration. The parties' scheduling order allows for each party to serve a single request for document production upon the other party. Claimant served Respondent with requests for document production that centered on Respondent's alleged economic reasons for stopping supply.

Six months later, as the arbitration progressed, Claimant learned that a number of refrigerators using the new system, and that had been sold by Claimant to its customers, had developed cracks that resulted in explosive leaking of jet water streams on the customers' premises. The customers complained to Claimant and demanded refunds and other damages. Claimant suspected that Respondent knew of this design flaw and that the cost of fixing it was one of the reasons Respondent had breached the contract. Claimant served a new set of discovery requests on Respondent that probed the product's design, engineering, and performance. Unfortunately for Claimant, by now the arbitration had progressed so far that Claimant had already exhausted all the discovery requests it had available under the scheduling order. Respondent refused to comply with the new requests, arguing that arbitration requires an end point.

As the arbitrator, how would you rule and why? Does it matter which institutional rules the parties have agreed to operate under? Do the self-executing obligations of any rules come into play in your decision?

Comment

Rules follow reality, and so the discovery rules in litigation have accommodated the fact that many communications are by email or other electronic means and are stored electronically. The odds are overwhelming that any law student graduating in the next decade who elects to enter litigation or arbitration practice will become highly familiar with these rules and with the processes for producing ESI. An entire body of law has grown around so-called ESI-discovery. *See* Fed. R. Civ. P. 34(b); Steven C. Bennett, *E-Discovery Issues: What Parties and Their Counsel Need to Know in Anticipation of and During Arbitration*, 64 AAA Disp. Resol. J. 20 (2009); John E. Bulman & R. Thomas Dunn, *Managing Exchange of Electronically Stored Information in Construction Arbitration*, 67 AAA Disp. Resol. J. 68 (2012). Certain institutional arbitration rules mimic the Federal Rules' embrace of ESI. *See, e.g.*, AAA Rule 22(b)(iv) (requiring agreement on electronic search parameters).

Notes and Questions

1. Do clients who agree to arbitration in their dispute resolution clauses necessarily anticipate that one day they are going to have to respond to discovery requests based on electronic search terms? Is subjecting clients to ESI consistent with arbitration being speedy and efficient in comparison to litigation in that it speeds up the information disclosure process, or inconsistent because it is yet another expensive imitation of litigation?
2. *The JAMS Rule and "Control."* The parties may, as discussed in greater detail in the next section, agree on or petition the arbitrator for addi-

tional modes of discovery beyond document production, but the JAMS rules take that one step further. Rule 17(b) eliminates any need to ask for at least the first deposition "of an opposing party or of one individual under the control of the opposing party." The arbitrator has the power to determine "the necessity of additional depositions." When would depositions in arbitration ever be "essential"? How is "control of the opposing party" to be determined?

3. *Changes to Institutional Rules.* When adopting institutional rules, parties should be aware that the rules can change. If the parties state that the "arbitration shall be governed by the Commercial Arbitration Rules of the American Arbitration Association," precisely *what* AAA rules do they mean? Some dispute resolution clauses contain the phrase "the rules of the American Arbitration Association in effect at the time of the notice of the dispute" or "the then-current rules of the American Arbitration Association." But parties can then be buying the proverbial pig in a poke, because what the rules provided in a 2013 contract may not be what they provide in a 2021 dispute. A best practice point here is to agree to the rules in effect at the time the parties enter into the dispute resolution clause. You know those. You don't know the future rules.

Class Exercise

Claimant is a leading manufacturer of baseball cards. The cards have a high resale value in the collector's market. Resale value is determined by the popularity of the player, the number of such cards in the market, and the quality of the card. One of the quality components is the regularity of the white border around the player's picture. Another is how square are the cuttings at each corner of the card. Claimant historically performed all manufacturing in-house, but with the explosion of the trading market it cannot keep up. Claimant's chief engineer leads a study and concludes that Respondent, a small machinery manufacturing company located in a different state, can construct a machine to fit Claimant's needs. After a one-year try-out program, Claimant switches all its card-cutting operations to Respondent's machines. The machines cannot handle this quantity of orders and repeatedly break down. As a result, cards are made with irregular borders that the market will reject.

Claimant fires its chief engineer, whose idea it was in the first place to contract with an outside machinery firm, and brings an arbitration against Respondent under the contract's dispute resolution clause, which calls for arbitration under JAMS Rules. The arbitration proceeds along and Respondent notices (demands) the deposition of Claimant's *former* chief engineer pursuant to the "one deposition" rule of JAMS Rule

17. Nobody else at Claimant knows useful information about the decision-making process or negotiations that led to the machine's purchase. By this time, the engineer has been gone for two years and, his non-compete restrictions having expired, he is working for Claimant's leading competitor. Claimant objects that the engineer is neither a party nor under the "control" of a party. You are the arbitrator. How do you rule in a manner that protects the interests of both parties?

C. Procedural Orders

The third source of discovery in arbitration is the procedural order that typically results from the scheduling conference examined in Chapter 7. Any agreements between the parties regarding discovery will, through the principles of party autonomy and consensus, result in an order codifying for case purposes the discovery path going forward. Any disagreements between the parties on the scope of discovery will be resolved by the arbitrator.

Discovery should be among these details. This is especially so because, by definition, by the time of the scheduling conference, the disagreements between the parties have ripened into a formal proceeding. The lawyers may not know as much as they *will* know about the case, but they know a lot more than, for example, anybody could have anticipated at the time the dispute resolution clause was drafted and executed at the contract's closing. By now, the lawyers have interviewed their clients, have more likely than not exchanged pointed letters with their adversaries, and have reviewed the relevant law that is likely to affect the dispute. This should sharpen the advocates' views of what discovery they might wish to seek—and, notably, to shield—as they approach the conference.

The three sources of discovery rules in arbitration—the arbitration clause itself, institutional rules that govern where the parties choose institutional arbitration, and the procedural order—need not be mutually exclusive. Parties can refer to discovery in their arbitration clause and still choose institutional arbitration, and then submit further to procedural orders. More often, where the parties do not refer to discovery at all but choose institutional arbitration, the procedural conference will be the forum where the discovery rules and schedule are set out. Because, as noted immediately above, understanding one's case is an evolutionary process as the matter goes forward, a good practitioner will take care to understand, prior to the conference, what is the proper interplay between clause, rules, and the conference.

The procedural conference will usually issue a scheduling order that sets out many of the details of the arbitration, including but not limited to discovery. The following is one such example (sanitized here to preserve the parties' anonymity, consistent with arbitrations being confidential). *See infra* at 567 (discussing confidentiality as the hallmark feature of arbitration).

International Centre for Dispute Resolution*

In the matter of the Arbitration between

Claimant,	:	
	:	Case No.
and	:	
Respondent	:	

FIRST PROCEDURAL ORDER

Preliminary hearing teleconferences were held on __________ commencing at approximatelyand on __________ commencing at approximately __________ before Arbitrator __________. Collectively appearing at the teleconferences were __________and __________—all Counsel for Claimant; __________, and __________—all Counsel for Respondent; and __________ (hereinafter, all counsel for the parties are collectively referred to as simply "Counsel" except where the context specifically indicates otherwise).

A. As a result of the teleconferences:

1. Neither the Arbitrator nor Counsel had any further disclosures for the other.
2. The following schedule, to which Counsel have mutually agreed, is now in effect (all deadlines are on the date indicated):
   (a) By __________—All discovery will close.
   (b) By __________—Each side will identify its experts to the other. Expert reports are to be exchanged.
   (c) By __________—Rebuttal expert reports are to be exchanged.
   (d) By __________—Counsel will exchange witness lists.
   (e) By __________—Counsel will exchange supplemental witness lists and exhibits.
   (f) By __________—Pre-hearing briefs are to be exchanged and filed with the Arbitrator.

* "ICDR" is the International Centre for Dispute Resolution, the global component of the American Arbitration Association which provides conflict-management services in more than 80 countries with a staff fluent in 14 languages.

3. The Evidentiary (Arbitration) Hearing will take place in __________ and start on __________ and continue on successive days through __________, if necessary.

   The parties will decide later what specific facility to use for the hearing based on seating capacity and/or other salient factors. This and all other hearing-related issues (e.g., obtaining a stenographic record, and the type of award requested—bald, partially reasoned, fully reasoned) will all be appropriately addressed by Counsel and the Arbitrator at a subsequent teleconference.

B. Further Aspects

4. Counsel will use the "direct exchange" program, as offered by the AAA and ICDR, under which Counsel may send all their submissions directly to the Arbitrator by e-mail (and/or by Courier where necessary for shipments of electronic media), provided the submitting Counsel copies both Counsel for the other side and the ICDR on each such submission then being sent.

5. The Panel adopts the attached PROCEDURAL CHECKLIST which will govern: submissions to the Panel, hearing exhibits, hearing testimony and transcripts. The Panel welcomes any suggestion which Counsel may have to any item set forth in the CHECKLIST in the interest of simplifying the proceeding or Counsels' efforts, or increasing the efficiency of the proceeding.

6. Several discovery disputes currently exist between Counsel, including, e.g., a limit on the number of depositions to be taken by each side; what categories of documents should be searched by each side, including whether and to what extent electronically stored information is to be included in any such search; and a schedule of document production. To quickly resolve these and other discovery disputes, the Arbitrator has suggested and Counsel has agreed to the following:

   (a) by __________, Counsel for each side will serve their document requests on the other;

   (b) later during the week of __________ and extending through April 1, 2013, Counsel will meet and confer, in light of their requests, in an effort to resolve their existing discovery disputes and, in view of the discovery cutoff, attempt to anticipate whatever future discovery disputes might otherwise arise and reach suitable agreements to avoid them; and

   (c) on __________ at __________ and through facilities provided by the ICDR, a teleconference will occur with Counsel and the Arbitrator to:

(i) address all these disputes, including the resolutions reached by Counsel; and

(ii) present to the Arbitrator for resolution all unresolved discovery disputes then remaining.

Further procedural and logistical aspects of the proceeding, including additional periodic status teleconferences and a pre-hearing teleconference, will also be discussed with the Arbitrator during the April 2nd teleconference.

7. Motions

In the event either party desires to file a motion during this proceeding, Counsel' for that party will first submit to the Arbitrator a brief letter memo (not to exceed approximately three pages):

(a) requesting permission to file the motion;

(b) explaining the nature of the requested motion;

(c) explaining why the motion is necessary, particularly addressing any beneficial effect the motion, if granted, will likely have on the proceeding; and

(d) explaining why the Arbitrator is more likely than not to grant the motion.

The non-requesting party will then have five working days, from the date on which the requesting party filed its supporting memo, to file its own letter memo, also not to exceed approximately three pages, providing its response. The pendency of any request to file a motion, absent a procedural ruling by the Arbitrator, will not stay any aspect of this proceeding or modify any existing due dates. Motions are only to be filed with the approval of the Arbitrator and in accordance with a briefing schedule established by the Arbitrator and the parties.

8. This arbitration shall be governed by the Commercial Arbitration Rules (amended and effective June 1, 2009) as referenced in __________ of the __________ signed by the parties and dated __________ 2008.

All provisions of this order shall remain in effect unless and until amended by a subsequent order of the Arbitrator.

SO ORDERED.

(ICDR case number:)

PROCEDURAL CHECKLIST

The following is a procedural checklist, which will supplement the First Procedural Order and govern the proceedings in the above referenced arbitration.

I. Submissions to the Arbitrator

A. Form

1. The Arbitrator is to receive submissions preferably just in electronic form. This drastically reduces the amount of paper which the Arbitrator needs to store and handle, and also reduces various costs and clerical effort otherwise incurred by Counsel.

Electronic form is to be in either MS Word or searchable Adobe pdf form. MS PowerPoint is also acceptable, where appropriate. Each submission shall be sent to the Arbitrator by: (a) e-mail, with each of the various documents being a separate email attachment, and (b) as protection against any loss in receiving the e-mail message(s) or in receiving corrupted attachment data, and, where practical, recorded on a CD (or DVD), USB flash drive or other media with the media sent to the Arbitrator by overnight courier (such as Federal Express).

The Arbitrator's in-house MS Exchange e-mail server is currently set to a 100 Mb outgoing and incoming cumulative e-mail size limit (meaning a single e-mail message and all attachments to it should be no larger than 100 Mb). Should any Counsel desire to send larger e-mails to the Arbitrator, then that Counsel should notify the Arbitrator accordingly before doing so, or simply spread the attachments over multiple e-mail messages, each of which is less than 100 Mb in total size.

Submissions that are too large or cumbersome to be sent by e-mail attachment can simply be sent on any convenient storage media. The media is to be sent to the Arbitrator using courier, such as Federal Express. If, for any reason, the Arbitrator finds an electronic submission to be unreadable by virtue of being in a format which the Arbitrator cannot view, the Arbitrator will simply request a replacement version from Counsel who submitted it and in a format useable by the Arbitrator or alternatively request that Counsel to provide either a copy of a free (no-charge) installation file for the appropriate viewer application (for execution on a Windows-based workstation running MS Vista/Windows 7 64-bit business edition) or a URL pointing to that file on the Internet. Alternatively, any such submission to the Arbitrator can be made through a download website maintained by that Counsel along with providing suitable instructions to the Arbitrator to access and download the submission (using Microsoft Internet Explorer version 9 or higher, or Mozilla Firefox version 19.0.2 or higher).

a. Each document or pleading shall be stored in its own separate electronic file, with each file carrying a self-descriptive file name. Do not put multiple documents in a common pdf or other file, as doing so complicates fast access to each individual document. Do not label a file merely as "Claimant Exhibit 1" or the like as doing so conveys no useful information and requires the Arbitrator to use a cross-reference list, which, in turn, frustrates rapid access to any particular document. Rather, label the file as "Claimant Exhibit 1—xxxx" where xxx is a self-descriptive name, such as "letter 3/10/09 John Smith to Jane Doe" or the like. Providing file names in this (or a similar) fashion greatly simplifies and expedites the Arbitrator's task in finding necessary documents amongst all those submitted, and particularly in the hierarchical archival data structure which the Arbitrator constructs, in real-time, to consolidate all documents he receives during the entire proceeding.

b. Contrary to the security practices in place at some law firms, Counsel should not submit any pdf document to the Arbitrator that contains text which originated in MS Word or another common word processor but has then been embedded into or converted to a graphical object prior to the associated document file itself having been converted into a pdf file. Should the Arbitrator need to copy text from any such pdf document that contains such graphical objects, the Arbitrator would need to print out the relevant page(s) of the document, and then scan and process the scanned result through optical character recognition software (such as Nuance OmniPage Professional version 17 or the like). Doing so invariably yields formatting and other errors that are time-consuming to correct and are thus best avoided.

Rather, each such textual document, where practical, should be in a form from which the Arbitrator can readily copy text, as needed, from that document into another document which the Arbitrator is then preparing. In that regard, if a document has been created by Counsel in MS Word but, for security reasons (such as, e.g., to remove metadata and other hidden content) is to be submitted in a pdf document, the Word document is to be directly converted into pdf form using the pdf converter furnished with MS Word (such as in MS Office 2010) or a functionally equivalent pdf converter (such as Nuance Professional PDF Converter 6) such that text in the resulting pdf document is editable/searchable and thus can be readily selected and copied, as such and not as a graphical object, into another application through the Windows clipboard.

c. Counsel shall organize their submissions, where applicable, to facilitate easy and quick access by the Arbitrator.

2. In each submission, Counsel shall provide a complete copy, to the Arbitrator, of each authority on which that Counsel relies. These need only be provided in electronic form, with each authority in a separate file with a self-descriptive

file name. The resulting files can be provided directly to the Arbitrator by any convenient modality, such as, e.g., by e-mail attachment, through a download website maintained by that Counsel, or recorded on a CD (or DVD). These authorities should be provided in a format (preferably either editable pdf or MS Word) from which the Arbitrator can readily select and copy text.

B. Hearing Exhibits (hard-copy form)

Counsel may provide these exhibits at or before the hearing in hard-copy form. If a hard-copy version is being provided to the Arbitrator, all the following considerations apply. If these exhibits are being provided solely in electronic form only, then only those considerations below which are pertinent to electronic documents apply.

1. General considerations
   a. Claimant and Respondent are to use different colored exhibit binders.
   b. Each document shall be separately tabbed with pages numbered consecutively (and without reference to Bates numbers) using any of the following approaches:
      i. Page numbering for the entire submission shall start at "1" and continue sequentially throughout all the exhibits in that submission; or
      ii. Each individual document shall be numbered, starting at "1" for its first page, provided that number also carries the exhibit number, for example, CL 1-1 for the first page of Claimant's Exhibit 1, CL 3-5 for the 5th page of Claimant's Exhibit 3, and so forth. The same numbering scheme is to be used for both party submissions and joint submissions; or
      iii. Any other simple numbering scheme that provides rapid and consistent access to documents; can rapidly permit pages and documents, which the Arbitrator has removed from the binders, to be easily re-inserted, in their proper order, back into their respective binders with minimal error; and can permit Counsel for either side to readily add exhibits as necessary while maintaining their basic numbering scheme. For example, such a scheme could reserve exhibit numbers 1–500 for the Claimant, and 501–1000 for the Respondent even though the number of exhibits initially contemplated by each side is considerably less than 500.
      iv. For ease and consistency across all exhibits and before any submissions are made to the Arbitrator, Counsel for both sides shall agree on one common page numbering scheme to use

with all submissions of exhibits to the Arbitrator and then use that scheme accordingly.

c. Each binder shall:

i. Have a table of contents cross-referenced to tabbed sections. Entries in the electronic version of the table of contents can be hyperlinked to individual sections, if Counsel so chooses.

ii. Use strong loose leafs for all binders such that any page can be readily removed and inserted. Hence, do not use Velobind (plastic pins) or spiral binding or any other permanent type of binding.

iii. Only provide the Arbitrator with relevant documents and, to the extent reasonably possible, only those that will be directly relied upon at hearing. The parties should resist the urge to include documents that are cumulative, duplicative or of limited probative value. The Arbitrator will carefully and very deliberately review and consider all documents presented to it. Generally speaking, the fewer documents the Arbitrator gets, the better.

2. Exhibits and Authorities

a. Exhibits need not be separately offered into evidence. At the start of the hearing, the Arbitrator will admit all exhibits, which are not the subject of any objections and that are to be introduced by the parties during the hearing, into evidence without any formal offer of admission for each individual exhibit.

b. All submitted exhibits will be deemed to be authentic unless either party indicates to the Arbitrator, before or at the start of the hearing, that it intends to object to the authenticity of any particular document when the other party introduces it into the hearing.

3. Joint Exhibits and Binders

a. The parties will submit a joint exhibit binder to the Arbitrator. Counsel shall collaborate to fullest extent in formulating the joint binder and making it as comprehensive as possible, thus eliminating unnecessary duplication that might otherwise arise across the exhibit binders for each of the parties.

b. The joint binder shall have its own unique set of exhibit numbers, for example, Joint-1, J Exhibit-1, JX-1, or the like; or a unique range of exhibit numbers, e.g. Exhibits 1000–1500.

4. Party Exhibits and Binders

a. Pre-hearing brief: If practical, the electronic version of the pre-hearing brief may include hyperlinks to all authorities referred to therein, if Counsel so chooses.

b. To the extent practical, the parties will provide each witness testifying on direct examination with a loose leaf binder of exhibits to be referenced during that witness' testimony. Copies of the binder will also be provided to the Arbitrator and opposing counsel. The exhibits should preferably be organized in the specific order (e.g., starting with the Claimant's Trial Exhibits followed by the Respondent's Trial Exhibits) through which the witness will discuss them during direct, cross, re-direct and re-cross. The pages of each individual exhibit shall be numbered, as requested by the Arbitrator, with the exhibit number and page number, beginning with page 1, to facilitate easy handling of those pages.

e. After the hearing and if the Arbitrator so desires, the parties will provide the Arbitrator with binders containing all of the exhibits used during the hearing, organized in numerical order—as such exhibits may be considerably fewer in number than all the exhibits initially admitted into evidence. Alternatively, if the Arbitrator so desires, this submission may be solely made electronically on a CD (or DVD) with each exhibit stored in its own separate file carrying a self-descriptive file name, rather than in hard-copy form.

f. Post-hearing brief: Exhibits shall be organized in order of presentation at closing argument. Here too and if practical, the electronic version of the post-hearing brief may include hyperlinks to all authorities referred to therein.

II. Testimony and Transcripts

a. To the extent that the parties make use of "real time" or "live" transcription, the parties will provide the Arbitrator, if he so requests, with hookups and technical assistance for such transcription, as well as the associated display software if necessary.

b. At the end of each hearing day or as soon as practical thereafter, the Court Reporter shall provide the Arbitrator with an electronic draft version of that day's testimony. At the beginning of each hearing day or as soon as practical thereafter, the Court Reporter shall provide the Arbitrator with an electronic final version of the previous day's testimony. As soon as practical after the conclusion of the entire hearing, the Court Reporter shall provide the Arbitrator with a complete electronic transcript of the entire hearing.

If practical, each of these transcripts should be in e-transcript or similar searchable form, with an index, and be provided to the Arbitrator either through an e-mail attachment or on a suitable storage media, such as a separate CD, DVD or on a USB flash drive. There is no need to provide the Arbitrator with a hard-copy version of any transcript.

c. The Arbitrator may make his own digitized audio recording of each hearing day and any prior teleconference with Counsel. That recording will either be as an unprotected WMA (Windows Media Audio) or MPEG-3 file. While that recording is for the Arbitrator's own use in supplementing his own notes of the event, nevertheless the Arbitrator will gladly provide, on request, each Counsel with a copy of any such recording in the format in which that recording was made.

PREVIEW: Two experienced arbitrators, both of whom try to strike a balance between the need for discovery and its potential abuses, rely heavily on party feedback and on the procedural conference, as shown in the following articles. As you read the following, consider how you would approach a scheduling conference with them if you believed that you needed either more discovery than they may have been prepared to give, or less.

John Wilkinson, *Arbitration Discovery: Getting It Right*

21 Disp. Resol. Mag. 4 (2014–2015)

When I started practicing as an arbitrator, the scope of discovery in arbitration was not an issue. Arbitrated cases were relatively small, and arbitrating parties typically were content with a swift dose of rough justice without any discovery at all. More recently, however, the size of cases has increased dramatically, to the point where arbitrations involving millions of dollars are almost commonplace.

As the amounts at stake in these cases have increased, there has been an effort to include in arbitration many of the expensive, time-consuming elements of cases litigated in court such as interrogatories, broadly worded document requests, extensive depositions, dispositive motions, and even appeals. This is understandable, since a multi-million-dollar corporate dispute clearly requires more intense preparation than has historically been available in arbitration. The problem, however, is that: (i) arbitration must still be significantly faster and more cost-effective than litigation since otherwise, arbitration will lose much of its value; and (ii) contrary to this core principle, a few arbitrators have taken expanded arbitration discovery to an extreme and have opened the floodgates by permitting oppressive, expensive, and unnecessary discovery. While these instances are relatively rare, they get more than their share of publicity. Such publicity is misleading, though, because statistics furnished by the largest arbitration providers indicate that the average time from commencement of a domestic commercial arbitration to issuance of a final award ranges from 7 to 7.3 months. By contrast, the median length of time in 2011 from the filing of a civil case in district court to the disposition of appeal by the U.S. Circuit Courts of Appeal was 30.8 months—and in some of the busier courts, considerably longer.

Statistics aside, criticism of the time and cost of commercial arbitration persists, with the result that many constructive, remedial measures have been introduced. The American Arbitration Association and other arbitration providers, for example, have adopted rules aimed at maintaining the speed and cost-effectiveness of arbitration while at the same time allowing for sufficiently broad discovery to permit a fair result in a complex case. After months of exhaustive study, the New York State Bar Association issued *Guidelines for the Arbitrator's Conduct of the Pre-Hearing Phase of Domestic, Commercial Arbitrations* (*NY Guidelines*). And subsequent to the *NY Guidelines*, the College of Commercial Arbitrators released its *Protocols for Expeditious, Cost-Effective Commercial Arbitration*, which address arbitration discovery issues from the varying perspectives of business users, in-house counsel, arbitration providers, outside counsel, and arbitrators.

The purpose of this brief article is to present in summary form some of the more important practices that help achieve limited, cost-effective, and sufficiently comprehensive discovery in arbitration.

First Preliminary Conference

Shortly after appointment of the arbitrator in a commercial dispute, the arbitrator typically convenes a conference with the parties for the purpose of planning the entire case. This conference is the single most important event in an arbitration; it is the engine that makes the process run and can be the foundation for a limited, cost-effective discovery program. Following the conference, the arbitrator typically drafts and circulates a procedural order that sets forth dates for everything that needs to be done between the conference and the hearing on the merits and establishes the dates for the actual hearing. Equally as important, the procedural order will, in most cases, set forth rules and guidelines for the cost-effective conduct of discovery.

The Occasional Problem of Comprehensive Discovery

Occasionally, both sides come to the first preliminary conference in agreement that there will be comprehensive discovery in accordance with the Federal Rules of Civil Procedure. If the parties persist with this approach, there is little the arbitrator can do, since he or she has no power other than what is conferred by agreement of the parties. In these situations, I recommend that the arbitrator make a concerted effort to dissuade the parties from following the Federal Rules—an effort I have found to be successful in a surprising number of instances. Outside counsel, for example, often want all-encompassing discovery; if the arbitrator is able to include in-house counsel (who pay the bills) in the arbitration planning process, the approach to discovery often can be significantly reduced from what outside counsel initially proposed.

First Procedural Order

Assuming both sides are receptive to limiting arbitration discovery in a reasonable way, a number of measures can be included in the first procedural order to help accomplish this. Some of the more important ones are discussed below.

Scope of Document Requests

The scope of document discovery should always be discussed at the first preliminary conference. In many cases, the parties are able to devise their own reasonable standard for inclusion in the procedural order. In other cases, the parties might adopt the limited document discovery suggested in the *NY Guidelines* or in the International Centre for Dispute Resolution *Guidelines for Arbitrators Concerning Exchanges of Information* (*ICDR Guidelines*). (See an excerpt from the *ICDR Guidelines* [below].)

ICDR Guidelines on the Scope of Document Requests

The tribunal may, upon application, require one party to make available to another party documents in the party's possession, not otherwise available to the party seeking the documents, that are reasonably believed to exist and to be relevant and material to the outcome of the case. Requests for documents shall contain a description of specific documents or classes of documents, along with an explanation of their relevance and materiality to the outcome of the case.

When the parties adopt a reasonable standard for document production at the start of an arbitration, the arbitrator is well on the way to achieving the goal of an expeditious, cost-effective, and fair proceeding.

eDiscovery

By far the most expensive and time-consuming aspect of discovery in both arbitration and litigation arises from the recent growth of electronically stored information, or ESI. The delay and increased cost arising from ESI is attributable to the following, among other things:

1. Unlike paper files, ESI is typically located in a wide variety of storage media such as company servers, clouds, personal computers, smartphones, iPads and other tablets, and social media.
2. ESI can be stored in many different formats, some of which may not be readable by humans.
3. To locate and present ESI in forms readable by human beings, many different information technology mechanisms are often required.
4. ESI is often widely disseminated, which means electronic documents may have many custodians. This can lead to expensive, time-consuming redundancies if all or most potential sources of electronic documents are searched.

5. Most electronically stored documents are accompanied by metadata, which tell the history of the document. When significant amounts of metadata are included in the eDiscovery process, discovery's time and cost increase dramatically.

While it is unrealistic to expect arbitrators to be experts in the enormously complex technology of eDiscovery, they should at least familiarize themselves generally with the kinds of technological questions that might arise. Having done that, they should ask the parties to look carefully at eDiscovery issues that might potentially be in dispute and to be prepared to discuss them (perhaps including a technological expert) at the first preliminary conference.

When discussing eDiscovery at the first preliminary conference, the goals of the arbitrator should include the following:

- Limit the custodians of data whose hard drives must be searched.
- Restrict the scope of eDiscovery to matters that are directly relevant and material to the outcome of the case.
- Narrow the number of storage devices to be searched.
- Define a reasonable time period to be covered by the search.
- Reduce to the extent possible the number of search terms to be used when scanning the ESI for relevant data.

The procedural order following the first preliminary conference should encourage the parties to finalize limits on eDiscovery along the above lines. In addition, the *NY Guidelines* suggest that the order contain language such as the following with respect to other aspects of eDiscovery.

New York Guidelines eDiscovery Recommendations

There shall be production of electronic documents only from sources used in the ordinary course of business. Absent a showing of compelling need, no such documents are required to be produced from back-up servers, tapes or other media.

Absent a showing of compelling need, the production of electronic documents shall normally be made on the basis of generally available technology in a searchable format which is usable by the party receiving the e-documents and convenient and economical for the producing party. Absent a showing of compelling need, the parties need not produce metadata with the exception of header fields for email correspondence.

When the costs and burdens of e-discovery are disproportionate to the nature and gravity of the dispute or to the relevance of the materials requested, the arbitrator shall either deny such requests or order disclosure on condition that the requesting party advance the reasonable cost of production to the other side, subject to further allocation of costs in the final award.

Discovery Disputes

If there are no ground rules at the outset concerning presentation and resolution of discovery disputes, an arbitration can grind to a halt as the participants attempt to deal with voluminous discovery motions accompanied by lengthy briefs, affidavits, and hours of oral argument. To avoid such a result, the first preliminary conference should include discussion of possible disputes over discovery, and the first procedural order should contain guidelines such as the following:

- In cases involving a three-arbitrator panel, any discovery disputes should be decided by one of the three. This should be done with agreement of the parties and with the understanding that the deciding arbitrator can consult with the other panel members if an issue appears particularly important. This approach avoids the time and expense of having three arbitrators plod through and come to agreement on every objection to every document request. And if there is to be argument, the single-arbitrator approach avoids the scheduling delays that can typically occur with three busy arbitrators.
- Objections to document requests should be exchanged on a date certain, after which the parties should be required to engage promptly in a good-faith "meet and confer" to resolve any objections.
- If all objections are not resolved at the meet and confer, on a specified date shortly after that gathering, the parties should submit four- or five-page letter briefs succinctly explaining their discovery differences and why they think their respective positions are correct.
- Following receipt of the letter briefs, the tribunal should render a prompt decision on the basis of the letters or quickly convene a telephonic conference for the purpose of addressing the discovery issues. Only in extraordinary circumstances should the tribunal take more than two weeks from the time of receipt of the letter briefs to decide the issues presented.
- Following resolution of the discovery issues, the parties should promptly produce documents responsive to requests as to which objections were overruled. This production should be on an expedited basis, generally not later than two or three weeks following the tribunal's decision, and
- In no event should resolution of discovery objections delay compliance with document requests as to which there was no objection.

Depositions

Traditionally, depositions have not been a part of arbitration, and that is one of the distinctions drawn as to why arbitration is so much more cost-effective and efficient than litigation. But as the use of arbitration has mushroomed and as general counsel have put increasingly complex matters into arbitration, we have seen increased use of depositions in arbitration. If kept in control, this is not a bad development. Absent depositions, cross-examination at arbitration hearings can slog aimlessly through one fruitless area after another as the questioner gropes for even a tidbit of helpful information. Thus the arbitration can sometimes resemble a discovery deposition, and when it does, the testimony can go on for much too long on issues that are largely unimportant.

While depositions no doubt have a place in complex, commercial arbitrations, they must never approach the scope of deposition discovery in court. In light of this, the procedural order following the first preliminary conference in a commercial arbitration must place meaningful limits on any depositions. For example, each side might be allocated 10, 15, or 20 hours of depositions to be taken over a four- or five-week period. Or each side might be allowed a few two-hour depositions—again, over a limited period. Either way, speaking objections should not be permitted because the lawyer defending the deposition could use up most of the allotted deposition time with objections.

Final Analysis

Arbitrators and parties must strike a delicate balance in commercial arbitrations, especially in complex cases, working to ensure that the discovery will allow the case to be resolved more quickly and less expensively than it would be in litigation while at the same time providing sufficient discovery to allow for a truly fair resolution.

Achieving such a balance is no doubt challenging, but as participants have become increasingly knowledgeable and focused on the need to attain this goal, effective and efficient arbitration discovery has more and more become a reality that parties have a right to expect.

Janice L. Sperow, *Discovery in Arbitration: Agreement, Plans, and Fairness: One arbitrator's view of how you can structure the discovery process*

ABA (Apr. 10, 2019)

https://www.americanbar.org/groups/litigation/committees/alternative-dispute-resolution/practice/2019/discovery-in-arbitration-agreement-plans-and-fairness/

Discovery in arbitration, like the arbitration process itself, starts with the parties' agreement. The basic arbitration concept stems from contractual parties who have anticipated potential problems and designated arbitration as their chosen dispute resolution process. As a result, I, like most arbitrators, look first to the parties' contract for guidance. If the parties have specified the types and quantity of discovery permissible in the arbitration clause, then the contract controls. As the arbitrator, my job at that point is to fairly and objectively enforce the parties' agreement, not to superimpose what I think best or what one side now wishes they had included in the contract.

But what if the contract is silent? Perhaps, as is often the case, the parties identified binding arbitration, the applicable forum, and the governing rules, but neglected to mention discovery. If the contract is silent on the issue, then I still focus on party agreement. Have the parties met and conferred and orally agreed upon the discovery parameters they would like to follow in the arbitration? If so, then again, my job as the arbitrator is to fairly and objectively enforce the parties' discovery agreement. If not, perhaps with my nudging, they wish to create a discovery plan now. Instead of an "order," I give the parties time to meet and confer and craft a sensible, cost-effective discovery plan.

The Forum's Rules

We also look to the governing arbitration rules. If the arbitration clause provides for a specific forum's rules, then we will follow the rules' guidance, if any. Many arbitral fora have a list of presumptively discoverable documents, depending on the type of arbitration case. For example, the American Arbitration Association (AAA) maintains its "Initial Discovery Protocols for Employment Arbitration Cases" which lists both required production and recommended parameters. Similarly, the Financial Industry Regulatory Authority (FINRA) has a "Discovery Guide" which sets out a list of presumptively producible documents for mutual exchange between the parties in all of its consumer cases. Typically, the arbitrator and/or the parties can modify these guidelines but the chosen forum's rules is an excellent starting point and resource. Indeed, in some fora, the discovery rules are mandatory and must be incorporated into the case's discovery plan, unless the arbitration contract provides otherwise.

Crafting a Sensible Cost-Effective Discovery Plan

Often, however, the parties have contractually agreed to arbitration but have not discussed—much less agreed upon—their discovery preferences and now are so acrimonious that they cannot agree upon hearing dates—let alone discovery parameters. Now what? Well, it is time to roll up our sleeves at the case management conference and craft one together. I start by asking each side what they believe they need to prove their case. Each side is also invited to comment on the other side's "wish list." We then hash out a plan together.

Documentary Discovery

Fishing expeditions and burdensome requests are quickly shutdown, but legitimate documentary needs are always granted. An early exchange of the key documents in the case often leads to settlement or the removal of some issues from the dispute. We set date parameters so the documents to be produced do not span irrelevant timeframes but instead are tightly narrowed to the dispute. I usually start with a three-year presumption for relevant documents, but the case particulars may dictate a shorter or longer timeframe.

We also discuss the need for and craft, as appropriate, a confidentiality agreement and protective order. We discuss the early production, organization, and labeling of the document production. No one wants or gets to produce a disorganized data dump! Fair and reasonable document production only will be allowed.

We specifically address electronic documents and data, the burden of IT production, the need for metadata, if any, and email chains. I will limit the number of custodians whose hard drives must be searched to the most relevant players and witnesses. The parties and I will also work out an agreed-upon, limited number of search terms for e-discovery. Absent a showing of compelling need, I usually do not permit metadata production except for email information fields.

Deposition Discovery

Traditionally, depositions have not been part of the arbitration process. However, as arbitration cases increase in number, some parties and counsel have imported deposition discovery into the arbitration process. Accordingly, we will discuss the need, if any, for depositions at the initial case management conference.

I start with a presumption against depositions as they are one of the costliest discovery tools but always grant them if the parties agree to them or a party has demonstrated a need for them. Fairness is the key. Each side will get the same discovery access. If one side needs a single day deposition, then the other side will get one as well, if it wants it. We also discuss creative ways to breakdown deposition time. Perhaps, each side gets 4 hours of deposition time to spend however they wish as long as multiple witnesses can be scheduled in a single session to lower the costs of multiple court reporter and counsel appearances.

I also invite the parties to stipulate to undisputed background facts, qualifications, authentication, and other "basic" facts to limit the need for or time of deposition discovery. Declarations can also sometimes substitute for a deposition, particularly those of custodians and most knowledgeable persons.

Expert Discovery

If the case merits, we discuss expert discovery. Typically, an expert report exchange is sufficient, but occasionally expert depositions are desirable and/or necessary. We will set time and subject matter limits on the deposition. If experts are out of town, we can agree upon depositions by videoconference, Skype, or other means to cut down costs.

No Formal Discovery Requests

There is no need for formal discovery requests—no interrogatories, no document requests, no deposition notices, no requests for admissions—none of the costly paperwork generated in classic courtroom litigation. Instead, either the parties have already or we will agree upon a discovery plan together in our first case management conference with deadlines, due dates, response times, and specific content. No one needs to file an objection because the parties have already voiced, and I have already ruled upon, any objections during the conference. The case management order then captures the agreed-upon discovery plan in both a substantive, narrative format and as part of a larger case calendar.

A typical case calendar in an expedited case might look like this:

Due date	Time	Activity
9/24/18	5 pm	LD to submit list of requested essential documents
9/25/18	5 pm	LD to submit objections to requested essential documents
9/28/18	5 pm	LD for respondent to file dispositive motion showing
10/3/18	5 pm	LD to amend claim, specify claim, file answer, or file counterclaim
10/5/18	5 pm	LD to produce discovery documents
10/16/18	9 am	Second Case Management Conference Call
10/26/18	5 pm	LD to designate and identify experts
11/5/18	5 pm	LD to complete all depositions
11/5/18	5 pm	LD to request hearing postponement
11/6/18	9 am	LD to exchange exhibit lists
11/6/18	9 am	LD to exchange witness lists
11/6/18	9 am	Proposed stipulations due to opposing party
11/6/18	9 am	LD to produce exhibits
11/6/18	TBA	Parties must meet and confer in preparation for the final pre-hearing conference call
11/9/18	5 pm	LD to email objections to exhibits with challenged documents to Arbitrator
11/12/18	5 pm	Parties simultaneously exchange pre-hearing briefs and serve on Arbitrator
11/13/18	9 am	Parties submit stipulations
11/13/18	9 am	Final Case Management Call and pre-hearing conference
11/17/18	5 pm	LD to respond to any specified or amended pleading
11/19/18	9 to 5	Hearing
11/19/18	9 am	Draft award due
11/19/18	9 am	Attorneys' fees and costs requests due
11/19/18	9 am	Joint Exhibits due

11/19/18	9 am	Each parties' separate exhibits, if any, due
11/20/18	9 to 5	Hearing
11/21/18	9 to 5	Hearing
11/26/18	9 am	Objections, if any, to attorneys' fees and costs requests due
11/26/18	9 to 5	Hearing
11/27/18	9 to 5	Hearing

No Motion Practice

Abolishing discovery motion practice is another important cost-saving arbitration tool. Instead of formal motion practice, I permit the parties, after exhausting meet and confer obligations, to email a summary of their discovery dispute in a paragraph. The other side presents their position, and then I either email a ruling or call for a short discovery conference call if I need further input from the parties before ruling. Either way, no one files any motions to compel, motions to quash, or other costly paper practice. Instead, the dispute is resolved typically within 24 hours.

Fairness Governs

Ultimately, fairness governs the discovery process in arbitration. As the arbitrator, I am bound by the parties' agreement, the applicable arbitration rules, the jurisdiction's law, and the needs of the case and the parties. Fairness, neutrality, and cost-effectiveness guide all arbitration discovery decision-making.

As you work through the interplay of clause, rules, and conference, consider the following problem, and how it might be affected by different wording in any of the three bases we have studied in this chapter.

Problem

Buyer agrees to purchase Seller's fruit at a stated price and quantity. Buyer in turn sells to organic grocery stores which understandably insist on pesticide-free fruit. The parties' contract accordingly provides that Seller use no pesticides. The contract also contains an arbitration clause that both provides for arbitration pursuant to AAA rules unless otherwise excepted, and then, in the exceptions, prohibits any discovery including document production.

Buyer's customers complain of a taste of pesticides and terminate their dealings with Buyer. Buyer in turn refuses to pay for the last lot of fruit it ordered from Seller and announces it will not make any future orders either. Seller brings an arbitration for breach of contract. At the organizational conference held early by the arbitrator with the parties, Buyer argues that it needs document production to prove that Seller ordered pesticides. Seller objects, citing the discovery prohibition in the arbitration clause. The arbitrator, citing his power under AAA Rule 22, orders limited discovery of all Seller's "contracts, purchase orders, or other communications with any seller, manufacturer, delivery agent, or other purveyor of pesticides." The documents confirm that Seller used pesticides, and Buyer wins the arbitration. Does the arbitrator's disregard of the arbitration clause's prohibition jeopardize confirmation of the award? *See* FAA Section 10 and *infra* Chapter 13.

III. The Growing Importance of e-Discovery

Given that discovery is generally alive, well, and robust in arbitration, any discussion of contemporary arbitration discovery must include e-discovery. How much should e-discovery's insinuation into what is now the standard discovery protocol in court litigation be incorporated into arbitration? Does the more limited role of discovery in arbitration affect your answer? The following is one arbitrator's view:

Richard Posell, *E-Discovery in Arbitration*

MEDIATE.COM (May 2010)
https://www.mediate.com/articles/posellR1.cfm

The business world has undergone a digital transformation, so it is probably not surprising to learn that 90% of all business information is electronically stored. Recent changes in Federal and State statutory schemes, the evolution of case material and the expansion of continuing education programs on the subject of E-discovery reflect this growing reality. Overlooked in the proliferation of commentary on retaining, finding, processing and producing electronically stored information ("ESI") is the question of how to deal with such discovery in an arbitration setting.

Why are the problems and issues different in court and arbitration? To begin with, despite the pressure in some quarters to mirror litigation, most arbitrators are sensitive to the need to keep arbitration faster and cheaper than court. One important method of doing that is to suppress discovery, a material cause of runaway costs in litigation. While California law has always encouraged full discovery, and Federal Law only ameliorates it in certain specific ways (e.g. the number of interrogatories permitted), the rules of most arbitration tribunals either ignore specific references to discovery or permit very limited discovery (for example, JAMS Rule 17 (b) permits one deposition of an opposing party). Instead, the published arbitration rules generally combine a required voluntary exchange of documents and discretionary discovery to ensure that the parties have what they need to try their case.

While the Federal and State statutory framework for discovery has been modified to address electronic discovery (see, Fed. Rule of Civil Proc. 26 and Cal. Code Civ. Proc. Secs. 2031.010 et seq.), arbitration rules either give a token nod to the existence of ESI (see, JAMS Rule 17 [a]) or ignore it altogether. This leaves the entire issue in the hands of the parties and the Arbitrator. The task in arbitration is to balance the realistic discovery needs of the parties with a rational cost-suppression regime. To achieve that balance, this article proposes a three part approach to ESI discovery.

PRELIMINARY CONFERENCE:

If an arbitration involving ESI is to proceed efficiently, the parties and the Arbitrator need to decide as early as possible how ESI is going to be used. Issues of retention, collection, processing and production of ESI are likely to arise and become intractable unless they are attended to early. The first meaningful opportunity to raise these issues is the preliminary conference—usually telephonic and among the attorneys and arbitrator—which can create focus and set the agenda for E-discovery issues downstream. Although the attorneys may be only vaguely familiar with their clients' ESI systems at this stage they should be prepared to raise and discuss the following:

1. **Preservation:** What is the client's normal retention protocol and has the client (including the Claimant) been informed of the need to preserve all relevant documents for the duration of the case? If this cannot or will not be done, the parties need to discuss whether an order will be necessary.
2. **Scope of Discovery:** Even without an understanding of their adversary's ESI systems, the parties should be able to articulate, at least generally, what documents or data they believe they are going to need to prosecute or defend the case. Is the Claimant simply seeking a few emails, or does the case involve a compendium of communications, agreements, drafts, spreadsheets, or research documents? Even if the scope of discovery changes, this information will give all sides the ability to start a dialogue with their client, and to think about ways to limit discovery costs.
3. **Preliminary production issues.** Is the exchange of information, including ESI likely to be simple and cooperative or is it more likely that there will be complexity and disagreement? Do counsel know enough about their clients' systems and data storage to make commitments about some or all of the requested information? Are counsel sufficiently versed in the relevant technological issues to gather the necessary information, or will additional expertise be needed to address these issues?
4. **Deadlines.** It is common to set discovery deadlines and hearing dates at the preliminary conference, but in more complex matters, it may take a number of scheduling conferences to arrive at firm dates. Counsel should use the first preliminary conference to gain an understanding of some realistic discovery and hearing dates, or to commit to reschedule a conference for the purpose of determining such dates after meeting and conferring as discussed below.

If more can be accomplished at the preliminary conference, it should be. It is this arbitrator's experience, however, that the attorneys often lack a detailed understanding of their clients' ESI systems and the technical problems inherent the requested discovery at this early stage of the proceeding.

MEET AND CONFER:

If the Arbitrator concludes that the parties will need to do more work on E-discovery, he or she should order a meet and confer, tailored to fit the circumstances. In discussing the meet and confer, the Arbitrator and parties should approach it as a discovery crossroads. One possible outcome of the meet and confer is that the parties will resolve their discovery issues without assistance and arrive at the hearing, exhibits in hand. But if that result isn't likely or does not occur, some or all of the following approaches may be selected voluntarily or ordered by the Arbitrator:

1. **IT experts:** If it is apparent that resolution of some or all of the discovery issues will require technical expertise not possessed or likely to be possessed by the attorneys, each side may have to bring to the meeting an IT expert familiar with the respective client's systems. While this may be an added financial burden at the outset, it may save multiples of the added cost in attorney time, and avoid costly mistakes.
2. **E-Discovery experts:** As those who have been through the e-discovery wars can attest, minefields abound. Creating search protocols that are efficient without being over or under-inclusive; that protect client proprietary information, applications and programs; that produce data in a useable form without damage to the underlying applications; and that provide evidentiary reliability, may require outside experts who do this for a living. If the Arbitrator concludes that such an expert is necessary, he or she may strongly urge the parties to add such a person to the roster of attendees. In some cases, the need to hire such an expert is obvious and justified by the value of the dispute. If the parties resist, in appropriate cases, the Arbitrator may hire his own expert and allocate the costs appropriately.
3. **Report.** Unless the parties think further intervention is unnecessary, the Arbitrator should require the parties to submit a joint report of the meet and confer to the Arbitrator briefly describing their areas of disagreement and proposed solutions.
4. **Specificity of issues:** If the discovery issues are sufficiently clear at the preliminary conference, the Arbitrator should order the parties to discuss and attempt to resolve isolated unresolved issues at the meet and confer. These might involve retention of data, the treatment [of] privileged information, the reduction or shifting of costs, the terms of a protective order and the format or formats in which data is produced (e.g. native form, .pdf, .tif, .xcel, or other format).

HEARING:

After a well-organized meet and confer, the discovery issues that remain, if any, are likely to be specific, limited and difficult. At this point, the Arbitrator may conduct a hearing designed to resolve (and not postpone) those issues. The primary focus of this hearing is to make a cost-benefit analysis with less deference to the concept of full discovery, than to the concepts of economy and usefulness. Again, IT and E-discovery experts may be required to attend. While a complete list of solutions is not possible here, the Arbitrator could do some of the following to resolve the dispute:

1. **Mediate agreements for costs controls:** Sometimes, the parties just need a push to do things which will save everyone money. Such agreements could be: (a) to produce all documents without advance screening for privilege, permitting later retrieval without waiver; (b) to settle on a sampling test protocol which all parties agree is reasonable to determine the validity of the scope of collection methods; (c) to defer, stage, or drop certain searches which are less likely to produce valuable information; (d) substitute cheaper methods of discovering the same information, such as using hard copies instead of electronic versions, extrapolating the information from existing documents, or seeking the information from a third, less costly, source.
2. **Cost adjustment or allocation:** Most discovery disputes involve an issue of cost. It is common for parties to complain that the discovery requested is simply too expensive. As we have seen, there are a number of ways to address this problem, but if all else fails, where one party insists on a burdensome search, the Arbitrator may condition the discovery in question on the proponent's willingness to pay for it. Another solution is to include discovery costs in arbitration costs to be allocated at the end of the proceeding.
3. **Decisions:** In many cases, the Arbitrator may simply end up as a discovery judge, deciding on such things as the production format or formats, what information is privileged, and what data must or need not be produced.

The combination of people, processes and technology tends to lead to error and expense. The developers of ESI were not lawyers or judges, and most systems are designed to promote the businesses which install them, not to resolve legal disputes. As a result, the discovery of ESI is often costly, and in some cases, prohibitively so. With the important caveat, that only so much can be done to reduce cost and burden, arbitration's flexibility, timeliness and concern for economy make it a better forum than court in which to balance realistic discovery needs, usefulness, and costs to end up with a fair result.

IV. Fairness and Efficiency

The question of the proper role of discovery in arbitration takes us back to two issues that predominated in Chapters 3 and 4 of this book: fairness and efficiency.

On fairness, what if the situation we are considering is not the negotiated commercial contract in which each party can exercise "autonomy" but instead is a one-sided business-to-consumer contract that the business will not change? Here, again, we come to whether an arbitration contract formed by adhesion is subject to ordinary contract rules. If a consumer is relegated to but a single lawsuit—if he is that fanatic who will sue for $30.22—then is he entitled to ask a discovery question about how many thousands of millions of other consumers were also allegedly overcharged? Is the business entitled to cut off such a discovery request by putting into the arbitration clause a prohibition on asking about any other contracts besides this one? Or, on the flip side, should there be a presumption, especially in consumer cases, of at least a bare minimum of guaranteed discovery? For an argument strongly supporting a "yes" to this question, see E. Brunet, *Questioning the Quality of Alternate Dispute Resolution*, 62 TUL. L. REV. 1 (1987).

The courts have recognized that full-blown discovery akin to what the federal rules require is inconsistent with the "speedy, inexpensive, and informal" virtues that arbitration is supposed to offer. *See National Broadcasting v. Bear Stearns & Co. Inc.*,165 F.3d 184, 190–91 (2d Cir. 1999); *Yasuda Fire & Marine Ins. Co. v. Continental Casualty Co.*, 840 F. Supp. 578, 579 n.4 (N.D. Ill. 1993); *Commercial Solvents Corp. v. Louisiana Liquid Fertilizer Co.*, 20 F.R.D. 359, 361 (S.D.N.Y. 1957).

That said, there remains a sharp, and as modern arbitral practice shows, a growing, difference between the absence of an automatic right to discovery and the absence of any discovery at all. *See, e.g., AT&T Corp. v. Tyco Telcoms (U.S.) Inc.*, 255 F. Supp. 2d 294, 303 (S.D.N.Y. 2003) ("*Although arbitrators must have before them enough evidence to make an informed decision*, they need not compromise the speed and efficacy that are the goals of arbitration by allowing the parties to present every piece of relevant evidence." (emphasis added) (citation omitted)); *Roberts v. A.G. Edwards & Sons, Inc.*, Misc. Case No. B-06-17, 2007 U.S. Dist. LEXIS 11853, at *22 (S.D. Tex. Feb. 21, 2007) (collecting cases) ("*Although arbitrators may not deny discovery of documents which are central to a dispute*, they may conduct only such discovery as they find necessary and can refuse discovery of evidence of uncertain relevance related to non-merits issues." (emphasis added) (citations omitted)). Into this gap, the skilled practitioner can step and mold that process to her client's best advantage.

What if the parties do not pick institutional rules or otherwise provide for discovery? Can the parties complain that they are being denied the opportunity to make their case? Section 10(a)(3) of the Federal Arbitration Act allows a court to *deny* confirmation of an arbitrator's award where the arbitrator "refused to hear evidence pertinent and material to the controversy." *See infra* at 516. Is denying a party the opportunity to *take* and *obtain* discovery the same as refusing to hear that evidence? *See Finkelstein v. UBS Global Asset Mgmt. (US)*, No. 11 CV 00356 (GBD), 2011 U.S. Dist. LEXIS 89800, at *31–36 (S.D.N.Y. Aug. 9, 2011) (arbitration panel's denial of petitioner's request for *additional* discovery did not constitute a refusal to hear evidence pertinent and material to the controversy within the meaning of section 10(a)(3), where the court found that the "scope of inquiry [already] afforded Petitioner was certainly sufficient to enable the arbitration panel to make an informed decision, and to provide Petitioner a fair and reasonable opportunity to be heard").

On efficiency, the question is even simpler: is one way to make arbitration *really* efficient to cut out discovery all together? Or does efficiency mean something more than lower costs, and if arbitration is really going to cut to the chase and get to the inherent nature of the dispute, then at least some discovery is not merely acceptable but preferred? The AAA's rules on discovery speculate openly on this tradeoff, stating that the rules should be administered "with a view to achieving an efficient and economic resolution of the dispute, while at the same time promoting equality of treatment and safeguarding each party's opportunity to fairly present its claims and defenses." AAA, *Commercial Arbitration Rules and Mediation Procedures*, ADR.org (Oct. 1, 2013), https://www.adr.org/sites/default/files/CommercialRules_Web.pdf.

Chapter 8

Third-Party Evidence

The law on evidence from third parties in arbitration merits a completely separate chapter—primarily because that law is a mess. Unlike the general arbitration/discovery rules covered in the preceding chapter, in which the parties can achieve consensus on the procedures and scope of discovery from their respective files, discovery from third parties depends on external law beyond party consensus—and that law is in chaos. Its confused and divided state is the result of ambiguity in the Federal Arbitration Act, divisions among the courts, and at bottom, a fundamental difference of opinion about what "efficiency" in arbitration should mean when we get to third parties. Should there be an efficient means of reaching third-party testimony so that the arbitrator can consider all evidence about the case? Or does "efficiency" mean that enough is enough and discovery should only mean *party* discovery?

Third-party evidence, and in particular pre-hearing discovery from third parties, is a topic that returns us to the tension explored at the beginning of this book between the public and private nature of arbitration. Arbitration is intended primarily to be an outsourced private dispute resolution mechanism free and clear of the courts, but for third-party discovery to be effective, arbitration must frequently return to the court system.

The source of arbitrator authority over evidence from third parties is neither mandate nor consensus, since, by definition, third parties are not parties to the arbitration agreement and so have not given their consensus to be discovery targets. Instead, any authority that an arbitrator has to order third-party discovery comes from Section 7 of the Federal Arbitration Act, which allows the arbitrator to "summon in writing any person to attend before them or any of them as a witness and in a proper case to bring with him or them any book, record, document, or paper which may be deemed material as evidence in the case." If the person thus "summoned" does not attend, then "upon petition the United States district court for the district in which such arbitrators, or a majority of them, are sitting may compel the attendance of such person or persons before said arbitrator or arbitrators, or punish said person or persons for contempt."

This language has led to confusion and inconsistent judicial results by circuit. Plainly, Section 7 gives the arbitrator the authority to compel the giving of evidence by third parties. Just as plainly, that authority extends at a minimum to the hearing in the case, since the arbitrators will be present at the hearing and the statute commands attendance of the witness "before them [the arbitrators]." And, again plainly, the statute requires not just oral testimony, but also document production: "any book, record, document, or paper which may be deemed material as evidence in the case."

But the certainty ends there. The ability to compel the giving of evidence by third parties does not necessarily mean that the arbitrators have authority to order *pre*-hearing discovery. This has led to confusion on three separate issues: when, where, and by whom.

When? Courts are split on the precise stage in an arbitration when a third-party witness may be compelled to give testimony, and in particular, whether third parties can be compelled to be part of the discovery process as opposed to (just) the hearing process.

Where? It is not entirely clear, even after (and perhaps because of) recent amendments to the Federal Rules of Civil Procedure about third-party subpoenas, whether the power to compel testimony in an arbitration rests with the court where the witness sits or where the arbitration will take place. The increased use of virtual hearings and depositions adds further uncertainty to this subject.

The "when" and "where" questions combine because, as you will see below, lawyers who attempt a workaround and schedule a mini-hearing in advance of the final hearing, just so they can obtain the testimony of the witness (or at least documents from her), have to be careful to schedule this hearing within 100 miles of the issuing court for reasons of personal jurisdiction. The result can be serious constraint on third-party evidence in arbitration, with arbitration lawyers singing the old Marvin Gaye song, "Can I Get a Witness?"

The law emerging from these three questions is fluid and essential for a practitioner to know. Central to these questions lies the never-ending debate as to the importance of "efficiency" in arbitration. Efficiency is always laudable but may pale in comparison to a party's critical need for documents and witnesses in order to win a case. Moreover, parties who agree to arbitration, perhaps because of its "efficiency," might not realize that in so doing, they may forego access to critical proof. This is not necessarily a wrong choice—but it should be an informed one—and this chapter will allow you to assist your clients in making that informed decision.

I. "When" Question: When Can Third Parties Be Compelled to Give Evidence in Arbitration?

At first blush, Congress would appear to have done an admirable job in stepping in to ensure that however private arbitration may be, there will be times when judicial compulsion is needed to ensure an adequate evidentiary record. Section 7 of the FAA, as seen above, speaks directly to evidence, both oral and written, from third parties. A party to an arbitration can call witnesses to the hearing and require those witnesses to show up with documents. But what about any stage of a case other than the final hearing? On that, Section 7 is silent.

That is a significant statutory gap, especially given the manner in which complex dispute resolution has developed. It has been estimated that over 95% of federal lawsuits settle. *See, e.g.*, Theodore Eisenberg & Charlotte Lanvers, *What Is the Settlement Rate and Why Should We Care?* 6 J. Empirical Legal Stud. 111 (2009). Thus, deferring third-party discovery until the final stage of the case—the arbitration hearing—can often be the same as not getting any third-party discovery at all, since most cases do not progress to a final hearing. For all the criticisms of discovery—and they are many and justified—there is no question that discovery helps lawyers and their clients evaluate their case. Discovery brings knowledge, and third-party discovery frequently brings the most credible knowledge and evidence because it frequently (not always) comes from a party without a grudge or a stake in the outcome. Third parties may tell you what neither your client nor your opponent will. That is critical to the lawyer's evaluation of her case.

One could therefore argue that a statute recognizing the vital importance of third-party *evidence* to arbitration would be of little to no utility if its use is confined only to the very last stage of the case. One could just as easily, and perhaps with more textual support, argue that if Congress had wanted to expand the burdens that a private dispute resolution process imposes on strangers to the dispute, it would have done so.

The following exercise shows that need for certainty. Unfortunately, as you will see in the cases following the problem, the federal circuit courts react to this in strikingly different ways. Perhaps nowhere in arbitration are the courts so divided as on the question of how far they will let Section 7 go *before* a hearing. The Supreme Court has now allowed that circuit split on this important issue to continue for a generation despite granting review on countless other arbitration issues, as reflected elsewhere in this text.

Class Problem

Steven Johnson was a highly compensated professional at an international accounting firm, CPAInt. As his career developed, he moved increasingly into his firm's management structure and away from client service. He was a particular champion of CPAInt's expansion across the United States. At his urging, CPAInt opened offices in a number of western states, including Colorado.

A year before moving into management, Johnson led a CPAInt team that executed a complex structure on behalf of his client Mining Co in which Mining Co received a hefty down payment from Smelting Co, the buyer of Mining Co's leading copper mine, and would thereupon receive 10% each year of net profits (a so-called "earn-out structure"). That contract had an arbitration clause. There is now a dispute between Mining Co (Seller) and Smelting Co (Buyer) as to the measurement of those profits in year 2, and the parties are in arbitration. Johnson was the primary negotiator of the earn-out structure on behalf of his client Mining Co and, as such, his testimony is critical. Unfortunately, the new management of CPAInt decided that the firm's westward expansion was a huge, timewasting distraction, and it terminated Johnson, a move made all the easier by allegations of workplace harassment brought by a former assistant. Your firm has been hired by Mining Co. in the arbitration. Johnson's testimony is critical to a contract interpretation issue.

How can you get Johnson's testimony? When can you get it? What if the other side resists? What if Johnson resists? Can you ask the arbitrator to issue a subpoena? Will the subpoena be effective if it applies prior to the ultimate hearing in the case? Will the subpoena be effective if Johnson lives in a different district than the one in which the arbitration is taking place? Would it help matters if you just asked for his documents and not also for his testimony?

None of these questions would be subject to debate in federal court. However, each are questions in arbitration. In federal court, you would simply issue a Rule 45 subpoena and depose Johnson in a district where the court has jurisdiction over him. It might cost your client a plane ticket, but you would have the testimony of this key witness at the pre-trial stage, and it would factor into all subsequent decisions you make about the case. In arbitration, however, you may never get this testimony until the eleventh hour—if at all.

We begin with an opinion from then-Third Circuit Judge Alito.

Hay Grp., Inc. v. E.B.S. Acquisition Corp

360 F.3d 404 (3d Cir. 2004)

ALITO, Circuit Judge.

PriceWaterhouseCoopers ("PwC") and E.B.S., non-parties to an arbitration, seek to avoid compliance with an arbitration panel's subpoena requiring them to turn over documents prior to the panel's hearing. The District Court enforced the subpoena. We reverse.

I.

Hay Group ("Hay") is a management consulting firm. David A. Hoffrichter left Hay's employment and joined PwC in September 1999. In early 2002, PwC sold the division employing Hoffrichter to E.B.S.

Hoffrichter's separation agreement from Hay contained a clause that forbade him from soliciting any of Hay's employees or clients for one year. The agreement further provided for arbitration to resolve any dispute arising under the agreement. In February 2000, Hay commenced such an arbitration proceeding in Philadelphia, Pennsylvania, against Hoffrichter, claiming that he had violated the non-solicitation clause.

In an attempt to obtain information for the arbitration, Hay served subpoenas for documents on E.B.S. at its Pittsburgh office and on PwC at its Philadelphia office. Hay sought to have the documents produced prior to the panel's arbitration hearing.

PwC and E.B.S. objected to these subpoenas, but the arbitration panel disagreed. When PwC and E.B.S. still refused to comply with the subpoenas, Hay asked the United States District Court for the Eastern District of Pennsylvania to enforce the subpoenas. PwC and E.B.S. again objected, claiming, among other things, that the Federal Arbitration Act ("FAA") did not authorize the panel to issue subpoenas to non-parties for pre-hearing document production and that the Federal Rules of Civil Procedure prohibited the District Court from enforcing a subpoena on a non-party for documents outside the Court's territorial jurisdiction.

In November 2002, the District Court issued a decision enforcing the subpoenas and ordering the parties to resolve any remaining differences. In doing so, the District Court accepted the view of the Eighth Circuit and several district courts that the FAA authorizes arbitration panels to issue subpoenas on non-parties for pre-hearing document production. The District Court also held that even under the view of the Fourth Circuit, which permits such production only when there is a "special need," the panel's subpoenas would be valid. In addition, the District Court held that it had the power to enforce subpoenas on non-parties for document production even if the documents were located outside the territory within which the court's subpoenas could be served.

PwC and E.B.S. then filed the present appeal. The District Court denied their motion to stay its order pending appeal, but our Court granted their emergency motion for a stay.

II.

A.

On appeal, PwC and E.B.S. first argue that, under Section 7 of the FAA, 9 U.S.C. § 7, a non-party witness may be compelled to bring documents to an arbitration proceeding but may not simply be subpoenaed to produce documents. We agree.

An arbitrator's authority over parties that are not contractually bound by the arbitration agreement is strictly limited to that granted by the Federal Arbitration Act. Accordingly, we must look to the FAA to determine whether an arbitrator may issue a subpoena requiring pre-hearing document production by a person or entity that is not bound by the arbitration agreement (hereinafter a "non-party").

In interpreting a statute, we must, of course, begin with the text. Section 7 of the FAA provides as follows:

> The arbitrators selected either as prescribed in this title or otherwise, or a majority of them, may summon in writing any person to attend before them or any of them as a witness and in a proper case to bring with him or them any book, record, document or paper which may be deemed material as evidence in the case. The fees for such attendance shall be the same as the fees of witnesses before masters of the United States courts. Said summons shall issue in the name of the arbitrator or arbitrators, or a majority of them, and shall be directed to the said person and shall be served in the same

> manner as subpoenas to appear and testify before the court; if any person or persons so summoned to testify shall refuse or neglect to obey said summons, upon petition to the United States district court for the district in which such arbitrators, or a majority of them, are sitting may compel the attendance of such person or persons before said arbitrator or arbitrators, or punish said person or persons for contempt in the same manner as provided by law for securing the attendance of witnesses or their punishment for neglect or refusal to attend in the courts of the United States.

9 U.S.C. §7.

This language speaks unambiguously to the issue before us. The only power conferred on arbitrators with respect to the production of documents by a non-party is the power to summon a non-party "to attend before them or any of them as a witness and in a proper case *to bring with him or them* any book, record, document or paper which may be deemed material as evidence in the case." 9 U.S.C. §7 (emphasis added). The power to require a non-party "to bring" items "with him" clearly applies only to situations in which the non-party accompanies the items to the arbitration proceeding, not to situations in which the items are simply sent or brought by a courier. In addition, the use of the word "and" makes it clear that a non-party may be compelled "to bring" items "with him" only when the non-party is summoned "to attend before [the arbitrator] as a witness." Thus, Section 7's language unambiguously restricts an arbitrator's subpoena power to situations in which the non-party has been called to appear in the physical presence of the arbitrator and to hand over the documents at that time.

Some courts have argued that the language of Section 7 implies the power to issue pre-hearing subpoenas. *See Security Life Ins. Co. of Am. v. Duncanson & Holt, Inc. (In re Sec. Life Ins. Co. of Am.)*, 228 F.3d 865, 870–71 (8th Cir. 2000) ("We thus hold that implicit in an arbitration panel's power to subpoena relevant documents for production at a hearing is the power to order the production of relevant documents for review by a party prior to the hearing."); *Meadows Indemnity Co., Ltd. v. Nutmeg Insurance Co.*, 157 F.R.D. 42, 45 (M.D. Tenn. 1994) ("The power of the panel to compel production of documents from third-parties for the purposes of a hearing implicitly authorizes the lesser power to compel such documents for arbitration purposes prior to a hearing.").

We disagree with this power-by-implication analysis. By conferring the power to compel a non-party witness to bring items to an arbitration proceeding while saying nothing about the power simply to compel the production of items without summoning the custodian to testify, the FAA implicitly withholds the latter power. If the FAA had been meant to confer the latter, broader power, we believe that the drafters would have said so, and they would have then had no need to spell out the more limited power to compel a non-party witness to bring items with him to an arbitration proceeding.

Since the text of Section 7 of the FAA is straightforward, we must see if the result is absurd. *See United States ex rel. Mistick PBT*, 186 F.3d at 395. We conclude that it is not. Indeed, we believe that a reasonable argument can be made that a literal reading of Section 7 actually furthers arbitration's goal of "resolving disputes in a timely and cost efficient manner." *Painewebber Inc. v. Hofmann*, 984 F.2d 1372, 1380 (3d Cir. 1993). First, as noted above, until 1991 the Federal Rules of Civil Procedure themselves did not permit a federal court to compel pre-hearing document production by non-parties. That the federal courts were left for decades to operate with this limitation of their subpoena power strongly suggests that the result produced by interpreting Section 7 of the FAA as embodying a similar limitation is not absurd. Second, it is not absurd to read the FAA as circumscribing an arbitration panel's power to affect those who did not agree to its jurisdiction. The requirement that document production be made at an actual hearing may, in the long run, discourage the issuance of large-scale subpoenas upon non-parties. This is so because parties that consider obtaining such a subpoena will be forced to consider whether the documents are important enough to justify the time, money, and effort that the subpoenaing parties will be required to expend if an actual appearance before an arbitrator is needed. Under a system of pre-hearing document production, by contrast, there is less incentive to limit the scope of discovery and more incentive to engage in fishing expeditions that undermine some of the advantages of the supposedly shorter and cheaper system of arbitration. *See COMSAT Corp. v. NSF*, 190 F.3d at 269, 276 (4th Cir. 1999) ("The rationale for constraining an arbitrator's subpoena power is clear. Parties to a private arbitration agreement forego certain procedural rights attendant to formal litigation in return for a more efficient and cost-effective resolution of their dispute. A hallmark of arbitration—and a necessary precursor to its efficient operation—is a limited discovery process."). Thus, contrary to Hay's claim, heeding the clear language of Section 7 does not lead to absurd or even unreasonable results.

Of course, one may well think that it would be preferable on policy grounds for arbitrators to be able to require non-parties to produce documents without also subpoenaing them to appear in person before the panel. But if it is desirable for arbitrators to possess that power, the way to give it to them is by amending Section 7 of the FAA, just as Rule 45 of the Federal Rules of Civil Procedure was amended in 1991 to confer such a power on district courts.

The Fourth Circuit has interpreted Section 7 in a way that is largely consistent with our reading. In *COMSAT Corp. v. Natl. Science Foundation, supra*, the court held that the plain meaning of Section 7 did not empower an arbitrator to issue pre-hearing discovery subpoenas to nonparties:

> Nowhere does the FAA grant an arbitrator the authority to order non-parties to appear at depositions, or the authority to demand that non-parties provide the litigating parties with documents during pre-hearing discovery. By its own terms, the FAA's subpoena authority is defined as the power of

> the arbitration panel to compel non-parties to appear 'before them;' that is, to compel testimony by non-parties at the arbitration hearing.

190 F.3d at 275.

In dicta, however, the *COMSAT* court suggested that an arbitration panel might be able to subpoena a non-party for pre-hearing discovery "under unusual circumstances" and "upon a showing of special need or hardship." *Id.* at 276. While we agree with COMSAT's holding, we cannot agree with this dicta because there is simply no textual basis for allowing any "special need" exception. Again, while such a power might be desirable, we have no authority to confer it.

We have carefully considered but must respectfully disagree with the Eighth Circuit's holding in *Security Life* that Section 7 authorizes arbitrators to issue pre-hearing document-production subpoenas on non-parties. In *Security Life*, the Eighth Circuit reasoned that the "the interest in efficiency is furthered by permitting a party to review and digest relevant documentary evidence prior to the arbitration hearing." *Security Life*, 228 F.3d at 870. In our view, however, this policy argument cannot supersede the statutory text.

Even if we were to look outside the statutory text to make our decision, any argument in favor of ignoring the literal meaning of the FAA in the name of efficiency seems to cut against Supreme Court precedent regarding the role of efficiency considerations in interpreting the Act. Although efficiency is certainly an objective of parties who favor arbitration over litigation, efficiency is not the principal goal of the FAA. Rather, the central purpose of the FAA is to give effect to private agreements. *See Dean Witter Reynolds, Inc. v. Byrd*, 470 U.S. 213, 218–19, 84 L. Ed. 2d 158, 105 S. Ct. 1238 (1985) ("*Byrd*") ("The legislative history of the Act establishes that the purpose behind its passage was to ensure judicial enforcement of privately made agreements to arbitrate. We therefore reject the suggestion that the overriding goal of the Arbitration Act was to promote the expeditious resolution of claims.").

* * *

In sum, we hold that the FAA did not authorize the panel to issue a pre-hearing discovery subpoena to PwC and E.B.S. We further reject any "special needs exception" to this rule. If Hay wants to access the documents, the panel must subpoena PwC and E.B.S. to appear before it and bring the documents with them. [E]fficiency considerations clearly cannot override the terms of Section 7. Interpreting Section 7 as we do shifts the balance of power slightly from the party that seeks the documents to the non-party that is subpoenaed. Under our interpretation, the party seeking the documents cannot simply obtain a subpoena requiring the documents to be shipped from one warehouse to another; instead, the party will be forced to appear at a proceeding during which the documents are produced. This slight redistribution of bargaining power is unlikely to have any substantial effect on the efficiency of arbitration. Moreover, as we noted in the previous section, the rule we adopt in this case may in fact facilitate efficiency by reducing overall discovery in arbitration. In any event, if patent inefficiency, such as that resulting from the bifurcated proceedings at issue in *Byrd*, is insufficient to overcome a textual command, an ambiguous efficiency effect certainly cannot do so.

CHERTOFF, J., concurring.

I join Judge Alito's opinion in full. But I appreciate the reason that a number of courts have been motivated to read a pre-hearing discovery power into the arbitration rules. I write separately to observe that our opinion does not leave arbitrators powerless to require advance production of documents when necessary to allow fair and efficient proceedings.

Under section 7 of the Federal Arbitration Act, arbitrators have the power to compel a third-party witness to appear with documents before a single arbitrator, who can then adjourn the proceedings. This gives the arbitration panel the effective ability to require delivery of documents from a third-party in advance, notwithstanding the limitations of section 7 of the FAA. In many instances, of course, the inconvenience of making such a personal appearance may well prompt the witness to deliver the documents and waive presence. *See* David M. Heilbron, "The Arbitration Clause, the Preliminary Conference, and the Big Case", 45 Arb. J. 38, 43–44 (1990).

To be sure, this procedure requires the arbitrators to decide that they are prepared to suffer some inconvenience of their own in order to mandate what is, in reality, an advance production of documents. But that is not necessarily a bad thing, since it will induce the arbitrators and parties to weigh whether advance production is really needed. And the availability of this procedure within the existing statutory language should satisfy the desire that there be some mechanism "to compel pre-arbitration discovery upon a showing of special need or hardship." *COMSAT Corp. v. Nat''l Sci. Found.*, 190 F.3d 269, 276 (4th Cir.1999).

CASE PREVIEW. As recognized by Justice Alito in *Hay Group*, the Eighth Circuit sits on the opposite end of the third-party discovery spectrum.

Sec. Life Ins. Co. of Am. v. Duncanson & Holt

228 F.3d 865 (8th Cir. 2000)

HEANEY, Circuit Judge.

Transamerica Occidental Life Insurance Company (Transamerica) appeals the district court's order concerning the enforcement of a subpoena issued by an arbitration panel pursuant to §7 of the Federal Arbitration Act (FAA), 9 U.S.C. §§1–16 (2000). We affirm in part and dismiss in part.

I. BACKGROUND

Security Life Insurance Company (Security) is a small Minnesota insurance company that underwrites health and life insurance in 41 states. In July 1992, Security launched a new group health insurance product. Because it lacked sufficient resources to sell the product without reinsurance, Security entered into a reinsurance contract (or "Treaty") with a group of seven major insurers, among them Transamerica.

The reinsurance contract was managed by Duncanson & Holt (D&H), and provided that the reinsurers would assume 85% of the risk of Security's policies in exchange for 85% of the premiums. The reinsurers also agreed to assume 85% of all loss adjustment expenses, including legal fees incurred in the investigation or defense of all claims. This obligation included "extra-contractual" items such as "punitive, exemplary, compensatory, or consequential damages." The reinsurers also agreed to assume 85% of liability for "alleged or actual bad faith or negligence" in handling health insurance claims, provided Security counseled with and obtained the concurrence of D&H "with respect to the actions giving rise to the extra contractual obligation."

Security later lost a $14 million judgment in a Georgia state court (hereinafter, the *Clark* litigation). D&H and the reinsurers refused to acknowledge liability for their share of the *Clark* judgment and related liabilities. They also refused to pay their share of expenses related to four similar cases. According to D&H and the reinsurers, Security failed to honor the "counsel and concur" portion of the reinsurance contract. Security asserts that it abided by this requirement.

The reinsurance contract contained the following provision regarding arbitration of disputes:

> If any dispute shall arise between [Security] and [the reinsurers] with reference to the interpretation of this Contract or their rights with respect to any transaction involved, whether such dispute arises before or after termination of this Contract, such dispute, upon written request of either party, shall be submitted to three arbitrators, one to be chosen by each party, and the third by the two so chosen. If either party refuses or neglects to appoint an arbitrator within thirty (30) days after the receipt of written notice from the other party requesting it to do so, the requesting party may appoint two arbitrators. If the two arbitrators fail to agree in the selection of a third arbitrator within thirty (30) days of their appointment, each of them shall name two, or whom the other shall decline one and the decision shall be made by drawing lots.

Security demanded arbitration on its alleged failure to counsel and concur, and addressed its request to D&H, including its designation of an arbitrator. D&H designated a second arbitrator within the 30-day period. The two arbitrators selected a third. Transamerica took the position that it was not a party to the arbitration, insisting that the counsel-and-concur dispute was not arbitrable, and that in any event it was entitled to arbitrate the dispute in a separate proceeding against it alone.

In April 1999, Security petitioned the arbitration panel for a subpoena duces tecum, which it issued to Transamerica at its offices in Los Angeles. The subpoena required Transamerica to produce documents and to provide the testimony of a certain employee.

Transamerica, however, refused to respond to the subpoena, contending that it was not a party to the arbitration, and the arbitration panel thus had no authority under the Federal Arbitration Act (FAA) to issue the subpoena. In May 1999, Security petitioned the district court for the District of Minnesota to compel Transamerica to comply with the subpoena, or alternatively to compel Transamerica to participate in the arbitration proceedings. The district court referred the matter to a magistrate.

The magistrate noted that section 7 of the FAA (9 U.S.C. §7) provides that the district court for the district in which the arbitrator sits may compel attendance or punish for contempt in the same manner provided by law for securing the attendance of witnesses in federal court. 9 U.S.C. §7. The court noted Transamerica's argument that the court's power to enforce a subpoena under §7 was limited by Federal Rule of Civil Procedure 45(b)(2). Under Rule 45(b)(2), a subpoena "may be served at any place within the district of the court by which it is issued, or at any place without the district that is within 100 miles of the place of the deposition, hearing, trial, production, or inspection specified in the subpoena." Transamerica's Los Angeles office was far outside the 100-mile reach of the federal court in Minnesota, where the arbitration was to take place.

The magistrate resolved the issue by referring to *Amgen Inc. v. Kidney Center of Del. County, Ltd.*, 879 F. Supp. 878 (N.D. Ill. 1995). Faced with a similar conundrum, the *Amgen* court reasoned that the federal policy in favor of arbitration required that the subpoena power of an arbitrator under the FAA be enforced. Accordingly, the *Amgen* court concluded that under Rule 45(a)(3)(B), the petitioner's attorney, as an officer of the court, could be directed to issue and sign the subpoena on behalf of the court for the district in which the deposition or production was compelled by the subpoena. *Id.* at 882–83. The magistrate therefore directed Security's attorney to issue a subpoena to Transamerica. Transamerica appealed to the district court, which found the magistrate's order neither clearly erroneous nor contrary to law. Transamerica appeals to this court.

In the instant appeal, Transamerica argues (1) §7 of the FAA does not authorize prehearing deposition subpoenas; (2) the arbitration panel lacked authority to issue a subpoena to be served in California; (3) the Minnesota court lacked authority to instruct Security's attorney to issue a subpoena of the California court; (4) Security failed to show the materiality of the information it sought from Transamerica, and thus the district court should have refused to compel compliance with the subpoena; (5) the district court's order is an impermissible advisory opinion; and (6) the subpoena issued by the arbitration panel was never properly served because Security failed to tender a witness fee.

In response, Security argues (1) Transamerica is a party to the underlying arbitration and can therefore be compelled to provide discovery; (2) the district court properly devised a procedure that allowed it to enforce the subpoena; (3) the district court's order was not an improper advisory opinion; (4) even if Transamerica is not a party to the underlying arbitration it could be compelled to provide discovery anyway; and (5) the relevancy of Security's discovery is a matter entrusted to the arbitration panel, and in any event the discovery sought is relevant. We affirm in part and dismiss in part.

II. DISCUSSION

First, we address Transamerica's contention that the arbitration panel's subpoena was not authorized by the FAA. Section 7 explicitly grants arbitrators authority to "summon in writing any person to attend before them or any of them as a witness and in a proper case to bring with him or them any book, record, document, or paper which may be deemed material as evidence in the case." It does not, however, explicitly authorize the arbitration panel to require the production of documents for inspection by a party.

Although the efficient resolution of disputes through arbitration necessarily entails a limited discovery process, we believe this interest in efficiency is furthered by permitting a party to review and digest relevant documentary evidence prior to the arbitration hearing. We thus hold that implicit in an arbitration panel's power to subpoena relevant documents for production at a hearing is the power to order the production of relevant documents for review by a party prior to the hearing.

We believe the panel's exercise of this implicit power was proper whether or not Transamerica is ultimately determined to be a party to the arbitration. While the parties hotly dispute Transamerica's right to a separate arbitration proceeding, we conclude it is unnecessary for us to resolve the issue. Transamerica is not a mere bystander pulled into this matter arbitrarily, but is a party to the contract that is the root of the dispute, and is therefore integrally related to the underlying arbitration, if not an actual party. *Cf. Meadows Indem. Co. v. Nutmeg Ins. Co.*, 157 F.R.D. 42, 45 (M.D. Tenn. 1994) (holding arbitration panel may order non-party's production of documents prior to hearing where non-party was nevertheless "intricately related to the parties involved in the arbitration and are not mere third-parties who have been pulled into this matter arbitrarily").

Transamerica further contends that §7 required the district court to make an independent assessment of the materiality of the information sought by Security before acting to compel compliance with the panel's subpoena. According to Transamerica, this requirement is contained in the language of §7 itself, because the statute directs a district court to compel compliance with a panel's subpoena "in a proper case." We disagree. The language quoted by Transamerica refers only to a panel's power to require a witness subpoenaed under §7 to bring along documents. Transamerica's attempt to transform this language into a requirement that the district court second-guess the panel's judgment is thus misleading at best. Although there is some support for imposing such a requirement on the district court, *see Oceanic Transport Corp. v. Alcoa Steamship Co.*, 129 F. Supp. 160, 161 (S.D.N.Y. 1954), we believe it is antithetical to the well-recognized federal policy favoring arbitration, and compromises the panel's presumed expertise in the matter at hand. We therefore decline to saddle the courts of this circuit with such a burden.

CASE PREVIEW. Some circuits have opted for a middle ground between outright prohibiting and outright permitting third party discovery. These circuits require some arbitrator involvement in the process rather than leaving discovery entirely to the parties.

Stolt-Nielsen Transp. Grp., Inc. v. Celanese AG

430 F.3d 567 (2d Cir. 2005)

KRAVITZ, District Judge.

Stolt-Nielsen SA, Stolt-Nielsen Transportation Group, Ltd., Stolt-Nielsen Transportation Group, BV, and Stolt-Nielsen Transportation Group, Inc. (collectively, "Stolt") appeal from an order of the United States District Court for the Southern District of New York (Jed. S. Rakoff, District Judge) granting a motion to enforce four subpoenas served on Stolt's custodians of records and denying Stolt's request to quash a subpoena served on its former counsel. The subpoenas were issued by an arbitration panel presiding over an arbitral proceeding to which neither Stolt nor its former counsel is a party. Section 7 of the Federal Arbitration Act (FAA) provides that arbitrators "may summon in writing any person to attend before them as a witness and in a proper case to bring with him or them any book, record, document, or paper which may be deemed material as evidence in the case." 9 U.S.C. §7. We have previously stated that "open questions remain as to whether §7 may be invoked as authority for compelling pre-hearing depositions and pre-hearing document discovery, especially where such evidence is sought from non-parties." *Nat'l Broadcasting Co., Inc. v. Bear Stearns & Co.*, 165 F.3d 184, 188 (2d Cir. 1999). In this appeal, Stolt asks us to resolve the question left open in *Bear Stearns* and hold that Section 7 does not authorize arbitrators to issue subpoenas to compel pre-hearing depositions and document discovery from non-parties.

We decline to decide whether Section 7 authorizes arbitrators to issue subpoenas to non-parties to compel pre-hearing discovery, because there is no occasion to do so in this case. Contrary to Stolt's claim, the subpoenas in question did not compel pre-hearing depositions or document testimony and documents to the arbitration panel itself at a hearing held in connection with the arbitrators' consideration of the dispute before them. The plain language of Section 7 authorizes granting the motion to compel or in denying the motion to quash.

BACKGROUND

The present case arises out of a dispute over alleged anti-competitive behavior in the business of shipping and transporting chemicals by specialized shipping vessels known as parcel tankers. Celanese AG, Celanese Ltd., and Millenium Petrochemicals, Inc. (collectively, "Claimants") develop, produce, and sell chemical products. Between 1990 and 2002, Claimants entered into numerous contracts for the shipment of chemical products by Stolt and by two other groups of companies known in this case as "Odfjell" and "JO Tankers." In 2003 and 2004, certain of the Odfjell and JO Tankers groups of companies (as well as certain individuals) pled guilty to a criminal conspiracy to rig bids and fix prices in the parcel tanker market in violation of the Sherman Act, 15 U.S.C. §1. Stolt admitted participation in the conspiracy but was granted conditional amnesty from prosecution under the Sherman Act in connection with its parcel tanker operations.

Pursuant to an arbitration clause contained in the parties' shipping contracts, Claimants instituted arbitration proceedings against Odfjell and JO Tankers for price-fixing, bid-rigging, and other wrongful behavior. Stolt is not a party to Claimants' arbitration with JO Tankers and Odfjell. Claimants' arbitration with Odfjell and JO Tankers is to be conducted in New York under the rules of the Society of Maritime Arbitrators, which provide that the powers and duties of the arbitrators will be governed by the Society's rules and the Federal Arbitration Act, 9 U.S.C. §1 *et seq.* The arbitration panel consists of three arbitrators. The parties appointed two arbitrators, who in turn chose the Honorable John J. Gibbons, former Chief Judge of the United States Court of Appeals for the Third Circuit, as chairman of the panel.

In April 2004, the arbitration panel, at Claimants' request, issued a subpoena ad testificandum and subpoena duces tecum directing non-party Hendrikus van Westenbrugge, a former executive of JO Tankers then incarcerated at a federal correctional facility in New Jersey, to appear for a pre-hearing deposition before Claimants and to produce at that time various documents sought by Claimants. After Mr. van Westenbrugge failed to comply with the subpoena, Claimants moved the District Court to compel compliance with the arbitration panel's subpoena. The District Court declined. After considering the language of Section 7 and case law interpreting that provision, the court held that Section 7 grants arbitrators the power to compel non-parties to provide testimony and documents before the arbitrators themselves, but it does not authorize arbitrators "to compel a *pre-hearing* deposition of or *pre-hearing* document production from a non-party." *Odfjell ASA v. Celanese AG*, 328 F. Supp. 2d 505, 507 (S.D.N.Y.2004) (emphasis in original).

In August 2004, the arbitration panel issued five more subpoenas, four of them directed to Stolt custodians of records and one to Stolt's former general counsel, Paul O'Brien. The subpoenas directed the recipients to "appear and testify in an arbitration proceeding" and to bring certain documents with them. Stolt moved the District Court to quash the subpoena directed to Mr. O'Brien (the "O'Brien subpoena"), and after Stolt indicated its intention not to comply with the custodians of records' subpoenas (the "Stolt subpoenas"), Claimants moved the District Court to compel compliance with the Stolt subpoenas.

On December 7, 2004, the District Court issued an order granting Claimants' motion to compel compliance with the Stolt subpoenas and denying Stolt's motion to quash the O'Brien subpoena. Having been apprised of the court's order, the arbitration panel informed Stolt that the subpoenas would be returnable on December 21, 2004. Stolt then appealed the December 7 order to this Court, and after the arbitration panel rejected Stolt's request for a continuance, Stolt asked the District Court to stay the arbitration hearing pending this appeal.

On December 18, 2004, the District Court denied Stolt's motion for a stay pending appeal and provided the parties with a written explanation for its December 7 order. *Odfjell ASA v. Celanese AG*, 348 F. Supp. 2d 283 (S.D.N.Y. 2004). The District Court rejected Stolt's argument that the subpoenas were "thinly disguised attempt[s] to obtain the pre-hearing discovery" that the court had previously prohibited. *Id.* at 286. The District Court explained that in contrast to the van Westenbrugge subpoenas, "the instant subpoenas call for the non-party to appear before the arbitrators themselves." *Id.* According to the court, "[t]his difference is dispositive" because Section 7 authorizes arbitrators to summon witnesses to testify "before them" and to bring documents, and that "is precisely what the instant subpoenas require." *Id.* at 287. Finally, the court rejected Stolt's argument that the subpoenas were unenforceable on grounds of inadmissibility and privilege, concluding that the arbitration panel was the proper venue to raise such arguments in the first instance. *Id.* at 287–88.

On December 21, 2004, a panel of this Court denied Stolt's motion for an emergency stay pending the present appeal. That same day, Mr. O'Brien and Stolt's custodians of records appeared before the arbitration panel in accordance with the subpoenas. Stolt's custodians of records brought with them more than 300 boxes of documents in response to the subpoenas. Due to the logistical difficulties in having the witnesses authenticate 300 boxes of documents, the parties agreed to continue compliance with the Stolt subpoenas, pending Claimants' review of the documents Stolt had produced.

Mr. O'Brien, however, did testify before the arbitration panel and also provided documents to the panel, in accordance with the subpoena. Stolt's counsel asserted attorney-client privilege at several points during the hearing in objection to questions asked of Mr. O'Brien. Based on Stolt's assertion of privilege, Mr. O'Brien refused to answer thirty-two questions that the panel directed him to answer; Stolt also objected to Mr. O'Brien's production of several documents. After the hearing was adjourned,

Claimants moved the District Court to compel Mr. O'Brien to answer the thirty-two questions and to produce the requested documents. *Id.* The District Court denied the motion, ruling that Stolt first should be allowed to produce evidence establishing the validity of its claim of attorney-client privilege. The court remanded the matter to the arbitration panel for further proceedings consistent with its opinion.

DISCUSSION

Section 7 provides in relevant part that "[t]he arbitrators . . . or a majority of them, may summon in writing any person to attend before them or any of them as a witness and in a proper case to bring with him or them any book, record, document, or paper which may be deemed material as evidence in the case." 9 U.S.C. § 7. The subpoenas at issue in this appeal directed Mr. O'Brien and the Stolt custodians to appear and testify, and also provide documents, at a hearing convened before the arbitration panel. No party to this appeal contests the materiality of the evidence sought by the subpoenas. Therefore, as the District Court rightly recognized, in issuing the O'Brien and Stolt subpoenas, the arbitration panel invoked precisely the authority that Section 7 unambiguously grants them.

Stolt does not dispute the power of arbitrators to subpoena non-parties for testimony and documents at what Stolt calls a "trial-like arbitration hearing on the merits." What fuels Stolt's objection, and what Stolt devotes its entire brief to arguing, is that Section 7 does not empower arbitrators to summon non-parties for the purpose of compelling testimonial and documentary discovery in advance of a "merits hearing," and that the subpoenas in question were "a thinly disguised effort to obtain pre-hearing discovery." Evidencing this subterfuge, according to Stolt, is a letter from Claimants to the arbitration panel explaining the need-in light of the District Court's ruling on the van Westenbrugge subpoena-to convene a hearing so that non-party evidence and documents could be obtained. Stolt also makes much of the fact that the subpoena was returnable on December 21, 2004, during the period that the arbitration panel had scheduled for fact depositions and months in advance of October 17, 2005, the date set by the panel for commencement of the "Arbitration hearing on the merits." In sum, Stolt alleges that Claimants and the arbitration panel have conspired to "circumvent Section 7's limitations through the contrivance of conducting its discovery in the presence of the arbitrators."

Like the District Court, we are not persuaded that the December 21 hearing was the ruse Stolt claims it to be. Therefore, we have no occasion to rule on the authority of arbitrators to order non-parties to participate in discovery. Any rule there may be against compelling non-parties to participate in discovery cannot apply to situations, as presented here, in which the non-party is "summon[ed] in writing ... to attend before [the arbitrators] or any of them as a witness and . . . to bring with him . . . [documents] which may be deemed material as evidence in the case." 9 U.S.C. § 7.

Several factors convince us that the subpoenas were well within the authority provided arbitrators under Section 7, although we hasten to add that we do not suggest that all of these factors need be present in every case in order to justify arbitration subpoenas under Section 7. First, the custodians and Mr. O'Brien were not ordered to appear for depositions. Depositions usually take place outside the presence of the decision maker, and they are designed to allow parties to prepare for the eventual presentation of evidence or examination of witnesses before the decision maker at trial or a hearing. *See* Black's Law Dictionary 451 (7th ed. 1999) (defining "deposition" as "[a] witness's out-of-court testimony that is reduced to writing ... for later use in court or for discovery purposes" (emphasis added)). Here, by contrast, the custodians and Mr. O'Brien were directed to appear at a hearing before the arbitrators, and all three arbitrators were present at that hearing. *See Hay Group, Inc. v. E.B.S. Acquisition Corp.*, 360 F.3d 404, 407 (3d Cir. 2004) (noting that while Section 7 does not permit a subpoena to compel production from a non-party in absence of a hearing, it does permit subpoenas in which "the non-party has been called to appear in the physical presence of the arbitrator and to hand over the documents at that time").

Second, the arbitrators heard testimony directly from Mr. O'Brien, and unlike a deposition, the panel ruled at the hearing on evidentiary issues such as admissibility and privilege and reserved on other evidentiary issues. Indeed, the hearing transcript reveals that the hearing was primarily devoted to resolving evidentiary issues, especially the issue of whether and to what extent attorney-client privilege foreclosed Mr. O'Brien's testimony. While the custodians were not required to testify, that was the result of a consensual agreement between Stolt and Claimants and not a function of the arbitration subpoena or the hearing process itself.

Third, the testimony provided at the hearing became part of the arbitration record, to be used by the arbitrators in their determination of the dispute before them. Finally, we note that if Judge Rakoff had been of the view that the arbitrators and Claimants were attempting by artifice to undermine his prior order forbidding the use of Section 7 to take discovery of non-parties, there is every reason to believe he would have so found. But, in fact, he concluded based upon the record before him and the representations of the parties that the December 21 hearing was convened by the arbitrators in good faith and that it complied with Section 7, as well as the spirit and terms of his prior ruling. Section 7 does not deny arbitrators the power to summon witnesses to a hearing under such circumstances.

Contrary to Stolt's assertions, the mere fact that the session before the arbitration panel on December 21 was preliminary to later hearings that the panel intended to hold does not transform the December 21 hearing into a discovery device. As Judge Rakoff rightly recognized, "Nothing in the language of the FAA limits the point in time in the arbitration process when [the subpoena] power can be invoked or says that the arbitrators may only invoke this power under section 7 at the time of the trial-like final hearing." *Odfjell ASA*, 348 F. Supp. 2d at 287. To the contrary, the language of Section 7 is broad, limited only by the requirement that the witness be summoned to appear "before [the arbitrators] or any of them" and that any evidence requested be material to the case. *See* 9 U.S.C. § 7.

According to Stolt, that "Section 7 speaks of a 'witness' providing 'evidence'" suggests that the provision applies only to a merits hearing akin to a full-blown trial. Yet, often witnesses are called and evidence is adduced in contexts other than trials. For instance, courts hear evidence and testimony at preliminary hearings on issues such as the admissibility of evidence or on a motion for interim relief.

So, too, arbitrators may need to hear testimony or receive evidence on preliminary issues-such as whether an arbitration clause is enforceable or whether a claim is barred by relevant statutes of limitations-in advance of an ultimate hearing on the substantive merits of the underlying claims in the arbitration. Arbitrators may also need to hold a preliminary hearing to decide whether to preserve the status quo, as well as to decide issues of privilege, authenticity, and admissibility. In any case, we doubt that arbitrators are prohibited from making use of their powers under Section 7 to hear testimony and gather evidence as to the merits of a dispute so long as they do so by summoning witnesses and evidence before them.

Just as a subpoena can issue under Rule 45 of the Federal Rules of Procedure to compel witnesses "to attend and give testimony" and "produce . . . books, documents, or tangible things" at a "trial or hearing," Section 7 authorizes arbitrators to subpoena witnesses "to attend before them . . . and . . . bring with him or them any [relevant] book, record, document, or paper ... *in the same manner as subpoenas to appear and testify before the court.*" 9 U.S.C. §7 (emphasis added). Moreover, as the District Court correctly observed, Section 7's reference to hearings "before [the arbitrators] or any of them " suggests that the provision authorizes the use of subpoenas at preliminary proceedings even in front of a single arbitrator, before the full panel "hears the more central issues." *Odfjell*, 348 F. Supp. 2d at 287. Thus, there is nothing in the language of Section 7 that requires, or even suggests, the limitation that Stolt advances.

Furthermore, the present case demonstrates the usefulness of employing subpoenas at a preliminary hearing before the arbitration panel. Because Stolt's interests and those of Mr. O'Brien were not aligned, Mr. O'Brien did not object to appearing before the arbitrators. In view of Stolt's assertion of privilege, however, issues remained as to which questions Mr. O'Brien would be permitted to answer, even if he were willing to provide answers. Rather than be forced to deal with thorny issues of privilege at the "final" hearing, the arbitrators were instead able to subpoena Mr. O'Brien for a preliminary session in which those issues could be resolved. Similarly, even though the parties dispensed with the testimony of the Stolt custodians, the hearing could also have usefully resolved issues of foundation and admissibility regarding the Stolt documents in advance of a final hearing.

Stolt objects that if non-party witnesses may be summoned to hearings other than the final "merits hearing," witnesses will face the burdensome prospect of being recalled to testify at multiple sessions. In that regard, however, it is worth noting that Claimants assured the District Court before it decided to enforce the subpoenas that

Claimants would not recall Stolt's custodians of records for multiple hearings. *Id.* at 287 n. 2. Nor should we lightly assume that arbitrators will subpoena third-party witnesses gratuitously, since the arbitrators themselves must attend any hearing at which such subpoenas are returnable. *See Hay Group, Inc. v. E.B.S. Acquisition Corp.*, 360 F.3d 404, 414 (3d Cir. 2004) (Chertoff, J., concurring) (noting that Section 7's "procedure requires the arbitrators to decide that they are prepared to suffer some inconvenience of their own" when they subpoena third-party witnesses). Arbitrators issuing subpoenas and district courts asked to enforce them can, and should, take steps to minimize the burden on non-party witnesses. Indeed, that is precisely what happened here.

Finally, there is an artificiality about Stolt's argument that further confirms the wisdom of rejecting it. Arbitration hearings, even "trial-like merits hearings," are often continued, frequently with many months elapsing between hearing sessions. If the arbitrators had summoned Mr. O'Brien or the Stolt custodians for the first day of the scheduled hearings on the merits on October 17, 2005, heard their testimony, and then adjourned for ten months, before reconvening, even Stolt would concede that Section 7 would authorize the subpoenas. Yet, according to Stolt, the ten-month gap here between the December 21, 2004, hearing and the beginning of the "merits" hearing somehow rendered the subpoenas invalid. Nothing in the language of Section 7 or common sense dictates such a result. Here, as noted above, all three arbitrators participated in a hearing in which they received testimony and documents, took evidence, and considered matters of admissibility and privilege, resolving many of them. Preliminary or not, what occurred on December 21, 2004, was the sort of hearing to which Section 7 authorizes arbitrators to summon non-party witnesses.

CONCLUSION

In sum, we again leave to another day the question whether Section 7 authorizes arbitrators to issue discovery-type subpoenas to those who are not parties to the arbitration. We decide only that Section 7 unambiguously authorizes arbitrators to summon non-party witnesses to give testimony and provide material evidence before an arbitration panel, and that is precisely what occurred in this case. Accordingly, the O'Brien and Stolt subpoenas were authorized by Section 7, and the District Court's judgment is affirmed.

Note

You have just read three different approaches to handling pre-hearing third-party evidence in arbitration. At one extreme, the Alito majority opinion for the Third Circuit in *Hay* bars any evidence whatsoever, written or oral, prior to the actual hearing on the merits. At the other, the Eighth Circuit in *Security Life* treats arbitration as little different from litigation and thus would permit liberal pre-trial discovery from third parties. In the middle, Judge Chertoff's concurring opinion in *Hay*, adopted by the Second Circuit in the *Stolt-Nielsen* case immediately above, would commence a "hearing" for purposes of taking third-party testimony and receiving third-party documents, and require at least one arbitrator to attend. That hearing could take place before the full hearing on the merits.

PRACTICE POINTER. Almost 20 years after *Hay*, this circuit split remains. *Be conscious of where the third-party battle is being fought.* To recap, the circuit split is as follows:

Expansive Pre-Hearing Discovery

- **Sixth Circuit**, *Television and Radio Artists v. WJGK-TV*, 164 F.3d 1004 (6th Cir. 1999)
- **Eighth Circuit** (*Security Life, supra*)

Pre-Hearing Discovery "Middle Ground"

- **Second Circuit** (*Stolt-Nielsen SA, supra*) ("mini-hearing" with at least one arbitrator present)
- **Fourth Circuit**, *COMSAT Corp. v. Natl. Science Found.*, 190 F.3d 269, 275 (4th Cir. 1999) (presumption against third-party discovery absent "unusual circumstances" or "showing of special need or hardship")

No Pre-Hearing Discovery

- **Third Circuit** (*Hay, supra*)
- **Ninth Circuit**, *CVS Health Corp. v. Vivdus LLC*, 878 F.3d 703, 708 (9th Cir. 2017)

Not surprisingly, this tension has led to a multitude of commentary, at both the practitioner and scholarly levels. *See, e.g.*, Heather L. Heindel, *Third-Party Discovery in Arbitration? Do Not Count on It*, ABA (Oct. 8, 2018), https://www.americanbar.org/groups/construction_industry/publications/under_construction/2018/fall/discovery-in-arbitration/; Peter Jacobus, *Third Party Subpoenas in Arbitration: The Growing Circuit Court Split*, KILPATRICK TOWNSEND (Mar. 20, 2019), https://www.kilpatricktownsend.com/Insights/Perspectives/2019/3/Third-Party-Discovery-Subpoenas-in-Arbitration-The-Growing-Circuit-Court-Split; Alan Scott

Rau, *Evidence and Discovery in American Arbitration: The Problem of "Third Parties"*, 19 AM. REV. INT'L ARB. 1 (2008).

Notes and Questions

1. *"Workarounds."* The combination of this circuit split and the ongoing need of lawyers to obtain third-party testimony for their cases has led to a number of "workarounds" which have met with mixed degrees of success in the courts. In *Westlake Vinyls v. Cooke*, No. 3:18-MC-00018-DJH-LLK, 2018 U.S. Dist. LEXIS 221033 (W.D. Ky. Aug. 20, 2018), one party attempted the "Chertoff" compromise of a mini-hearing with just one arbitrator present, but with that presence by telephone. The court seemed to indicate that the mini-hearing was acceptable in theory but not (for some reason) without the physical presence of the arbitrator. In so ruling, the court acknowledged that this impacted arbitration's goal of offering a "convenient" forum for dispute resolution, a goal that we earlier saw trotted out repeatedly in the SCOTUS cases on class action bans but which carries less force in this area:

   > The Court is mindful that requiring the arbitrator(s) to be physically present during a preliminary hearing in Massachusetts while conducting a merits hearing in Kentucky would be inconvenient . . . but that does not warrant ignoring the limits of the FAA. . . . Due to lack of physical presence of at least one arbitrator at the hearing described by the subpoena, the Court lacks authority to enforce it pursuant to FAA, Section 7.

2. *Is This "Efficient"?* In *Hay*, then-Judge Alito stated that he was unmoved by arguments of efficiency, because "efficiency is not the principal goal of the FAA. Rather, the central purpose of the FAA is to give effect to private agreements." But the Eighth Circuit, coming out on the other end of the pre-hearing discovery "spectrum," stated, "Although the efficient resolution of disputes through arbitration necessarily entails a limited discovery process, we believe this interest in efficiency is furthered by permitting a party to review and digest relevant documentary evidence prior to the arbitration hearing." If we assume efficiency is the goal of arbitration, then is it more or less efficient to have pre-hearing discovery from third parties?

3. *Documents.* In a complex case with a substantial number of documents, lawyers usually spend significant time on their deposition outlines in order to work in appropriate questions about the documents. Sometimes a lawyer may look to a third party merely for explanation of a document; sometimes the document is considered vital and the lawyer may wish for an admission or an accusatory statement about it from the

third party. Sometimes documents that appear important are explained away by a witness as not being very important at all. Depositions are useful for resolving these questions and sorting through the record, so that the trial (hearing) is focused, persuasive, and without unnecessary surprise. The Sixth Circuit's "third way," set out in *American Federation of Television & Radio Artists v. WJBK-TV*,, 164 F.3d 1004 (6th Cir. 1999), in which Section 7 may be used to require advance production of documents but not of witnesses, helps eliminate the surprise problem described above but does not allow the "sorting" process that a deposition then brings to the documents. Is it nevertheless an appropriate balance between the need for third-party testimony and the need to minimize disruption to third parties who never submitted to arbitration? How would you change it?

4. *Virtual Hearings*. Is summoning a third party to attend a virtual hearing acceptable under Section 7? This question has particular relevance and importance in the wake of the sharp rise in virtual proceedings during the COVID 19 crisis. In *Managed Care Advisory Grp. v. CIGNA Healthcare*, 939 F.3d 1145 (11th Cir. 2019), the Eleventh Circuit first lined up with the Second, Third, Fourth, and Ninth Circuits when it stated that "the plain language of [Section 7] is unambiguous in requiring witnesses to appear before an arbitrator and bring any documents with them, thus prohibiting pre-hearing discovery from non-parties." 939 F.3d at 1159. From there, the court turned to the particular subpoena at issue and found that even though counsel had attempted a workaround in the form of a "hearing" that was before the ultimate hearing—the middle ground in the chart above—the particular workaround was unacceptable since the witness was only asked to attend virtually.

> The non-parties will not be in the physical presence of the arbitrator. Instead, the arbitrator will be located in Miami while the non-parties are in their respective states, and the hearing will take place via video conference. We hold that the district judge abused his discretion. . . . Looking to dictionaries from the time of Section 7's enactment makes clear that a court order compelling the "attendance" of a witness "before" the arbitrator meant compelling the witness to be in the physical presence of the arbitrator. In 1925, "attendance" meant the "act of attending" and "attend" meant "be present at". . . .. Accordingly, we interpret the plain meaning of Section 7 as requiring the physical presence of the arbitrator as opposed to a video conference or teleconference.

939 F.3d at 1160, 1161. Was the court correct to focus on century-old definitions of attendance? Should virtual hearings be a solution for the problems addressed here? Or do they simply create a new battleground, new costs, and less efficiency?

II. Where Should a Section 7 Subpoena Be Enforced?

The circuit split on pre-hearing discovery is further exacerbated by uncertainty as to whether a third-party subpoena from an arbitrator should be enforced by the court in which the arbitrator sits or instead by the court where the witness sits. Here again, as we will see in the following cases, there is sharp divergence in approach.

A. The Changes to the Federal Rules Regarding Third-Party Subpoenas in Litigation

To best understand the open "where" questions surrounding arbitration subpoenas, we need to start with how this issue is handled in court. The rules changed with the 2013 amendments to Rule 45 of the Federal Rules of Civil Procedure. Rule 45 addresses subpoenas which demand evidence located in a jurisdiction other than that where the dispute is pending. Prior to the amendments, a subpoena had to issue from the district in which the witness (or documentary evidence) was located and could only be served within the jurisdiction of the issuing court. Following the amendments, a subpoena must "issue from the court where the action is pending," *see* Rule 45(a)(2), and can now be served nationwide ("at any place within the United States"), *see* Rule 45(b)(2). For third-party witnesses, the witness can only be compelled to attend a hearing, deposition, or trial within 100 miles of where the witness resides. *See* Rule 45(c)(1).

These changes shifted the locus of the subpoena from witness location to action location. But since, by definition in these circumstances, the witness is located somewhere *other* than where the action is being heard, that set up a problem regarding the battlefield: where should a witness challenging a Rule 45 subpoena bring a motion to quash that subpoena? The amended rule states that "if the court finds exceptional circumstances" (or the nonparty-target of the subpoena consents), the local district court can transfer a dispute to the issuing court. *See* Rule 45(f). If a subpoena-related motion is transferred to the issuing court, the new rule permits an attorney for a nonparty who is admitted in the local district court to file papers and appear in the issuing court. *See id.* The committee notes also encourage the issuing court to permit telephonic appearances to minimize the burden of transfer on nonparties. The result has been a lack of clarity and uniformity as to where—issuing court or witness court—disputes over the subpoena should be heard. *See, e.g., Amended Rule of Civil Procedure 45: One Year Later*, THOMPSON REUTERS PRACTICAL LAW (Jan. 20, 2105), https://content.next.westlaw.com/Document/Ib5cbf671a09d11e498db8b09b4f043e0/View/FullText.html?contextData=(sc.Default)&transitionType=Default&firstPage=true&bhcp=1 ("Courts have found exceptional circumstances that warrant transferring a subpoena-related motion to the issuing court where the transfer would promote judicial economy and avoid inconsistent rulings. . . . [and a]void disrupting management of the underlying litigation because the court presiding over the underlying litigation has already ruled on issues relating to the subpoena-related motion") (internal citations omitted).

Should arbitration follow a similar path? The usual process is for a party to the arbitration to obtain a subpoena from the arbitrator and then, per Section 7 of the FAA, seek to have that subpoena enforced in court. But which court? What if the arbitration is pending in a district that permits pre-hearing discovery, but the witness is in a district that does not? And what if the witness then does not cooperate? Would the court in the district in which the arbitration is located have jurisdiction in contempt proceedings against the witness?

Problem

Blast is the maker of an energy drink that is more popular in Europe than it is in the United States. The new owners of Blast, based in Madrid, want to gain a foothold in the U.S. market. They hire a new U.S. licensee and distributor called Splash, based in Nashville, which true to its name specializes in flashy, showy marketing techniques. The parties conclude a licensing agreement under which Splash has rights to use the Blast trademark in the U.S. market. The licensing agreement provides for arbitration in New York under New York law. For a short period, things go well. Splash signs up A-List celebrities to film provocative ads which score high on social media. Sales increase but costs due to the marketing campaign are even higher, and so the business operates at a loss for the first two years after the signing of the licensing agreement. By year three, relations between the parties have cratered: Blast believes that Splash is spending way too much on supermodel ads, while Splash despairs as to whether Blast will ever understand the U.S. market. Finally, Splash begins to take matters into its own hands. Believing that the product itself needs improvement, Splash suggests entirely new flavors and designs. When Blast rejects these ideas as undermining the entire trademark and product, Splash secretly contracts with a food laboratory sitting in Cleveland, Ohio, called RevEng, to "reverse engineer" the Blast formula and come up with new flavors based on this formula. Such reverse engineering and product design is directly contrary to the express terms of the parties' licensing agreement.

Blast hears rumors that Splash is shopping the product around within the industry and to food labs but has no direct proof. It sends a formal letter to Splash asking Splash to disclose these activities, if they have taken place. Splash denies the accusations entirely—and falsely.

Six months later, relations have deteriorated to the point that Blast withholds any brand support to Splash, and Splash withholds remittance of royalties to Blast. The parties initiate arbitration before the AAA in New York City pursuant to their arbitration agreement. As part of its claim against Splash, Blast charges that Splash violated the reverse engineering provisions of their licensing agreement. Splash again denies any wrongdoing but, in a slip, produces in discovery an email between a Splash employee and RevEng, the Ohio-based reverse engineering lab.

Blast senses blood and wants to take discovery from the Ohio lab. The case is sitting within the Second Circuit, which bars pre-hearing discovery, but the lab is sitting in the Sixth Circuit, which permits it.

Pursuant to new Rule 45, Blast requests that the arbitrator issue a subpoena for documents and a corporate deposition. Blast then serves the subpoena on RevEng in Ohio. Challenging the subpoena in Ohio, RevEng notes that its testimony would not be permitted under the Second Circuit precedent in *Stolt-Nielsen SA*. Splash enthusiastically agrees and notes that allowing the subpoena would be "futile" since the testimony would never come in.

How would you rule, and which court should decide?

Alliance Healthcare Servs. v. Argonaut Private Equity, LLC

804 F. Supp. 2d 808 (N.D. Ill. 2011)

KENNELLY, District Judge:

Argonaut Private Equity, LLC (Argonaut) and Medical Outsourcing Services, Inc. (MOS) have moved to enforce subpoenas an arbitration panel issued in connection with an arbitration being conducted in Chicago. The subpoenas are directed to the accounting firm Grant Thornton, LP (GT) and Marc Chiang, who works for GT. The subpoenas call for oral testimony and production of records before a member of the arbitration panel at a hearing in San Francisco, California. GT and Chiang (collectively "GT") object, arguing that the subpoenas are beyond the arbitrators' authority and that, in any event, this Court cannot enforce them. For the reasons stated below, the Court denies the motion to enforce the subpoenas.

Facts

Alliance Healthcare Services, Inc. (Alliance) entered into an agreement with Argonaut and MOS to purchase Medical Outsourcing Services, LLP. The agreement contained a provision requiring arbitration of disputes.

Alliance hired GT to assist in conducting due diligence for the purchase. GT is headquartered in Chicago. Chiang, GT's director for transaction advisory services, oversaw the due diligence. Chiang lives and works in the San Francisco area.

In June 2010, Alliance demanded arbitration, alleging fraud and breach of warranty on the part of Argonaut and MOS. The arbitration is being conducted in Chicago. In late April 2011, Argonaut and MOS obtained from the arbitrators two subpoenas directing GT and Chiang to produce documents and give testimony in San Francisco at a preliminary hearing before one of the three arbitrators. The hearing is not the final merits hearing for the arbitration. Argonaut and MOS say they chose San Francisco for the convenience of GT and Chiang.

GT and Chiang declined to comply with the subpoenas. *Id.* at 6. Argonaut and MOS have moved this Court for an order enforcing the subpoenas. GT and Chiang oppose the motion.

Discussion

1. Validity of the arbitration subpoena

GT argues that the subpoena amounts to a request for pre-hearing arbitration discovery and thus is not enforceable in court. The Sixth and Eighth Circuits have held that the power to compel pre-hearing discovery from a third party is implicit in the power of an arbitrator to compel production of documents from a third party for a hearing. *See In re Sec. Life Ins. Co. of Am.*, 228 F.3d 865, 870–71 (8th Cir. 2000); *Am. Fed'n of Television and Radio Artists, AFL-CIO v. WJBK-TV (New World Communications of Detroit, Inc.*), 164 F.3d 1004, 1009 (6th Cir. 1999). The Second and Third Circuits have ruled to the contrary. *Life Receivables Trust v. Syndicate 102 at Lloyd's of London*, 549 F.3d 210, 212 (2d Cir. 2008); *Hay Group., Inc. v. E.B.S. Acquisition Corp.*, 360 F.3d 404, 408–09 (3d Cir. 2004). The Fourth Circuit has read section 7 of the FAA in more or less the same way as the Third, though it has suggested that an arbitration panel may subpoena a non-party for prehearing discovery upon a showing of a "special need." *See COMSAT Corp. v. Nat'l. Sci. Found.*, 190 F.3d 269, 275–76 (4th Cir. 1999). There is no Seventh Circuit authority directly on point.

All of these decisions aside, the Court agrees with the Second Circuit that "[a]ny rule there may be against compelling non-parties to participate in discovery cannot apply to situations ... in which the non-party is 'summon[ed] in writing ... to attend before [the arbitrators] or any of them as a witness and ... to bring with him ... [documents] which may be deemed material as evidence in the case.'" *Stolt-Nielsen SA v. Celanese AG*, 430 F.3d 567, 577–78 (2d Cir. 2005) (quoting 9 U.S.C. § 7); *see also, Hay Group*, 360 F.3d at 407 (noting that although FAA section 7 does not authorize enforcement of an arbitration subpoena directed to a non-party in absence of a hearing, it permits a subpoena in which "the non-party has been called to appear in the physical presence of the arbitrator and to hand over the documents at that time"). The Court also agrees that permitting an arbitrator to hold a preliminary hearing that is not a hearing on the merits "does not transform [the preliminary hearing] into a [prohibited] discovery device." *Stolt-Nielsen SA*, 430 F.3d at 578.

This conclusion is, in the Court's view, compelled by the plain language of the FAA. Section 7 unambiguously authorizes an arbitrator to summon any party witnesses before an arbitration panel, *or before any member of the panel*, to give testimony and provide material evidence. 9 U.S.C. § 7. As the Second Circuit concluded in *Stolt*, "[n]othing in the language of the FAA limits the point in time in the arbitration process when [the subpoena] power can be invoked or says that the arbitrators may only invoke this power under Section 7 at the time of the final hearing." *Id.* at 578 (internal quotation marks and citation omitted). FAA section 7's reference to hearings "'before [the arbitrators] or any of them' suggests that the provision authorizes the use of subpoenas at preliminary proceedings even in front of a single arbitrator, before the full panel hears the more central issues." *Id.* at 579 (quoting 9 U.S.C. § 7).

In this case, as in *Stolt*, Argonaut and MOS asked the arbitration panel to issue a subpoena for GT and its representative Mr. Chiang to produce evidence and give oral testimony before one of the arbitrators. Though the entire panel was present at the hearing in *Stolt*, FAA section 7 expressly allows subpoenas before just one of the arbitrators. Because the statute, by its terms, authorizes court enforcement of a subpoena in these circumstances, GT's characterization of the subpoena as involving discovery is beside the point.

2. Enforcement of the arbitration subpoena

Under FAA section 7, a federal court's authority to enforce an arbitrator's subpoena is coextensive with the court's authority to enforce one of its own subpoenas. *See* 9 U.S.C. § 7. Service and enforcement of subpoenas in federal court is governed by Federal Rule of Civil Procedure 45. *See Dynegy Midstream Servs., LP v. Trammochem*, 451 F.3d 89, 94 (2d Cir. 2006).

Argonaut and MOS sought enforcement of the subpoenas in this district even though they call for production of documents and attendance at a hearing in San Francisco. They did so presumably because FAA section 7 confers authority to enforce a subpoena only upon "the United States district court for the district in which [the] arbitrators, or a majority of them, are sitting." 9 U.S.C. § 7. Because the arbitration proceeding is being conducted in Chicago, only a court in this district may enforce a subpoena issued by the arbitrators.

Two provisions of Federal Rule of Civil Procedure 45 make it clear, however, that the Court lacks the authority to enforce the arbitrators' subpoena directing GT and Chiang to attend a hearing and produce documents in San Francisco. First, a subpoena summoning a person to attend a hearing or trial must be issued "from the court for the district where the hearing or trial is to be held." Fed. R. Civ. P. 45(a)(2)(A). Second, a subpoena may be served only within the district of the issuing court, or if outside that district, at a place within 100 miles of the hearing. Fed. R. Civ. P. 45(b)(2).

The subpoenas at issue here satisfy neither of these requirements. First, they were issued from this district, even though the hearing is to be held in San Francisco, which is within the Northern District of California. Second, the subpoenas were served in San Francisco, which is well outside the territorial scope of this Court's subpoena authority.

In support of their request for enforcement of the subpoenas, Argonaut and MOS rely on a decision issued by the undersigned judge's respected colleague, Judge Robert Gettleman. In *Amgen Inc. v. Kidney Ctr. of Delaware County, Ltd.*, 879 F. Supp. 878

(N.D. Ill. 1995), the parties were involved in arbitration proceedings taking place in Chicago. The arbitrator issued a subpoena for a non-party to produce evidence and a representative to testify at a deposition in the Eastern District of Pennsylvania, where the non-party was located. When the non-party refused to comply, a party sought enforcement of the subpoena in that district. A judge in that district ruled that the FAA required the enforcement proceeding to be bought in the Northern District of Illinois and transferred the proceeding there. Following transfer, the non-party argued that under FAA section 7, the Northern District of Illinois was the only court in which the enforcement action could take place, because the arbitration proceeding was being held here. The non-party argued, however, that because a subpoena must, under Fed. R. Civ. P. 45(a)(2), be issued from the district in which the proceeding is to take place (in *Amgen*, the Eastern District of Pennsylvania), a court in the Northern District of Illinois could not compel the non-party to attend a deposition in Pennsylvania.

Judge Gettleman rejected the non-party's argument that the law in effect contained a gap precluding court enforcement of the arbitration subpoena. He stated that Congress had declared a national policy favoring arbitration. *Id.* at 882 (citing *Perry v. Thomas*, 482 U.S. 483 (1987)). He further noted that arbitration proceedings commonly involve parties in more than one district or state. Judge Gettleman concluded that "[to] find that the wording of the FAA precludes issuance and enforcement of an arbitrator's subpoena of [a non-party] outside the district where he sits . . . would likely lead to rejection of arbitration clauses altogether," contrary to Congress' intent. *Id.*

Accordingly, Judge Gettleman read the FAA and Rule 45 in a way that plugged the gap. He concluded that the party that wished to issue the subpoena could do so under the district court case number assigned in connection with the subpoena enforcement proceeding and could then serve and enforce the subpoena in the Eastern District of Pennsylvania pursuant to Federal Rule of Civil Procedure 45(a)(3)(B). *Id.* at 883. Judge Gettleman relied in part on the fact that the parties to the arbitration had expressly agreed to arbitrate their dispute according to the provisions of the Federal Rules of Civil Procedure. *Id.*

In *Dynegy*, the Second Circuit disagreed with the analysis the court had used in *Amgen*. *Dynegy*, 451 F.3d at 96. Faced with a predicament similar to that in *Amgen*, the court in *Dynegy* concluded that a district court in New York, which was being asked to enforce an arbitration subpoena to a non-party located in Texas, lacked personal jurisdiction over the non-party and thus could not compel it to produce documents in the District Court in Texas. *Id.* at 95–96. The court concluded that the text of the FAA did not support the decision in *Amgen*.

The Second Circuit agreed with *Amgen* that the FAA contains a gap precluding court enforcement of out-of-district subpoenas. It concluded, however, that there was no basis "to come up with an alternate method to close a gap that may reflect an intentional choice on the part of Congress, which could well have desired to limit the issuance and enforcement of arbitration subpoenas in order to protect non-parties from having to participate in an arbitration to a greater extent than they would if the dispute had been filed in a court of law." *Id.* at 96. The court agreed that "the FAA expresses a strong federal policy in favor of arbitration" but noted that "the purpose of the FAA was to make arbitration agreements as enforceable as other contracts, but not more so." *Id.* (internal quotation marks and citation omitted). *See also Gotham Holdings, LP v. Health Grades, Inc.*, 580 F.3d 664, 665 (7th Cir. 2009) (stating, in response to an argument that there is a national policy favoring arbitration, that "[t]here is no such policy . . . the federal policy is simply to ensure the enforceability, according to their terms, of private agreements to arbitrate . . .") (internal quotation marks and citations omitted).

This Court agrees with the Second Circuit's decision in *Dynegy* and respectfully disagrees with Judge Gettleman's decision in *Amgen.* The express terms of FAA section 7 limit this Court's arbitration subpoena enforcement authority to the authority it has under existing law. That authority is limited to the power conferred by Rule 45; there is no other rule or statutory provision that applies in this case. Rule 45, in turn, precludes issuance of a subpoena from this district to attend a hearing in the Northern District of California. This, combined with the fact that FAA section 7 permits only a court in the district where the arbitration is being conducted to enforce an arbitration subpoena, no doubt creates an enforcement gap. But it is up to Congress, not a court, to fill such gaps.

For these reasons, the Court denies the motions to enforce the subpoenas in their current form. This does not leave Argonaut and MOS entirely without a solution, albeit a partial one. Grant Thornton LLP, as previously noted, is headquartered in Chicago. If a court has jurisdiction over a person or entity—as it does with respect to GT—Rule 45 permits the court to require that person or entity produce records pursuant to a subpoena even if they are not physically located in the District in which Rule 45 permits the subpoena to be served. *Hay Group*, 360 F.3d at 412 (citing Fed. R. Civ. P. 45, 1991 advisory committee notes). *See also* 9 J. Moore, *Moore's Federal Practice* 45.03 (3d ed. 2000) ("The subpoena should issue from the Court where the production of documents is to occur, regardless of where the documents are located."); 9A C. Wright, A. Miller, M. Kane & R. Marcus, *Federal Practice and Procedure* § 2456 at 31 (1995 & 2011 Supp.) ("Even records kept beyond the territorial jurisdiction of the district court issuing the subpoena may be covered if they are controlled by someone subject to the court's jurisdiction."). This will not permit the parties to obtain Chiang's testimony, given his place of residence, but it will at least permit them to obtain GT's records regarding the due diligence.

Notes and Questions

Service vs. Jurisdiction: The 100-Mile Rule Lives. The Amendments to Rule 45 made life easier for lawyers by allowing for nationwide service of process, as noted above. But the amendment did not erase territorial limits on *jurisdiction*. The court where the witness is summoned to testify must still have jurisdiction over that witness.

In litigation, this is usually not a problem: the subpoena can now issue from a court where the witness is located.

In arbitration, however, where, as you have seen, many circuits do not permit prehearing discovery and so the third-party witness must be summoned to a "hearing," matters become more difficult. If the hearing is not within the 100 miles permitted by the rules, taking the witness' testimony may not be possible. A 2020 decision from the Southern District of Florida, a court bound by the Eleventh Circuit's pro-*Hay* view, ruled as follows:

In re Managed Care Litig.

Nos. 00-01334-MD, 1334, 2020 U.S. Dist.
LEXIS 117788 (S.D. Fla. July 6, 2020)

O'SULLIVAN, Chief United States Magistrate Judge.

III. The Arbitral Summonses Violate Rule 45's Geographical Limitation

MCAG argues that the subject arbitral summonses are enforceable because they eliminate what the Eleventh Circuit held problematic in *Managed Care*. The subject arbitral summonses require the out-of-state non-party recipients to provide in person testimony and produce documents at a final arbitration hearing before the arbitrator in Miami, Florida.

MCAG argues that in *Managed Care* the Eleventh Circuit determined that the out-of-state non-parties can be forced to appear as witnesses far from the 100 mile limit in Rule 45. The undersigned disagrees. The *Managed Care* decision is devoid of any ruling that authorizes the arbitrator to require the out-of-state non-party witnesses to come to Miami, Florida to testify at the final hearing. *Id. at 1156–61.* MCAG argues that in *Managed Care*, the Eleventh Circuit held that *Section 7* of the FAA does not incorporate Rule 45(c)'s geographic provisions. MCAG's Reply at 3-4 (DE# 6663, 5/4/20). MCAG contends that "[i]f courts held the Arbitral Compliance Clause implicitly incorporates Rules 45(c) and (d), then arbitrators would be unable to hear from non-parties living outside the forum at all." MCAG's Reply at 4. MCAG maintains that "[t]he Eleventh Circuit's opinion would make little sense if requiring the Recipients to appear in Miami in the arbitrator's physical presence would violate the Arbitral Compliance Clause, which the Eleventh Circuit expressly interpreted as being consistent with its ruling." *Id.* at 5 (citing *Managed Care*, 939 F.3d at 1158).

CIGNA, the Epiq recipients and the Millennium recipients argue that the Eleventh Circuit did not address the 100-mile geographical limitations of *Rule 45* because the initial arbitral summonses required compliance via video conference within 100 miles of the out-of-state non-party recipients' respective place of business or residence. CIGNA, the Epiq recipients and the Millennium recipients argue that the subject arbitral summonses violate the geographical limitations of Rule 45 of the Federal Rules of Civil Procedure. *See* CIGNA's Motion at 1 (DE# 6659, 4/20/20); *see also* Epiq recipients' Response at 2-3, 13 (DE# 6660, 4/20/20) and Millennium recipients' Opposition at 7-8. The undersigned agrees.

Although the Eleventh Circuit expressly found that Rule 45(d) is incorporated in Section 7 of the FAA, the Eleventh Circuit did not address the geographical limitations because the first set of arbitral summonses did not require the out-of-state non-parties to appear in Miami, Florida. The Epiq recipients argue that the Eleventh Circuit "only ruled on the issues necessary to reach a decision as to the matter before it—i.e., the Initial Summonses; [the Eleventh Circuit] did not issue an advisory opinion to guide MCAG's future actions." Millennium recipients' Opposition at 7 (citing *Gagliardi v. TJCV Land Trust*, 889 F.3d 728 (11th Cir. 2018) ("We are not in the business of issuing advisory opinions that do not 'affect the rights of litigants in the case before' us or that merely opine on 'what the law would be upon a hypothetical state of facts.'" (quoting *Chafin v. Chafin*, 568 U.S. 165, 172 (2013)). The undersigned agrees.

Although the Eleventh Circuit held that the arbitral summonses can be served nationwide, it did not hold that the arbitrator can compel attendance nationwide. *Managed Care*, 939 F.3d at 1157. The Eleventh Circuit did not address the 100 mile geographical limit under Rule 45(c) because the summonses directed the out-of-state non-parties to appear via video conference where they reside, not in Miami, Florida where the arbitration is pending and the arbitrator is located.

The Epiq recipients argue that MCAG acknowledged that the 100-mile rule applies when it issued its first arbitral summonses. Epiq recipients' Response at 13 (citing Cunningham Declaration Exhibit 1 at 14 of MCAG's Initial Motion to Enforce (DE# 6493) (citing *Rule 45* and explaining that "each summons compelled attendance . . . within one hundred miles of each *third party* witness' place of business or residence"); *see also id.* Ex. 5 (Transcript of December 16, 2016 Hearing) at 49-50) ("[The Arbitrator] has determined that the proper way to do that . . . is through having them appear in their districts via videoconference . . . That complies with the hundred mile rule. They will be one hundred miles of [sic] where they reside.")).

Pursuant to Rule 45, an arbitral summons can only command a non-party to attend a final hearing within 100 miles of where the non-party resides, is employed or regularly transacts business. *See, e.g., Me. Cmty. Health Options v. Walgreen Co.*, No. 18-mc-0009, 2018 U.S. Dist. LEXIS 214029, 2018 WL 6696042, at *2-3 (W.D. Wisc. Dec. 20, 2018) (applying Rule 45 territorial limits to an arbitral subpoena and stating that it can only require attendance within 100 miles of where the witness resides. . . .); *Ping-Kuo Lin v. Horan Capital Mgmt. LLC*, No. 14-CIV-5202, 2014 U.S. Dist. LEXIS

114631, 2014 WL 3974585 at *1 (S.D.N.Y. August 13, 2014) (holding that an arbitrator may not summons a witness outside of the 100 mile limit allowed by the Federal Rules); *see also Legion Ins. Co. v. John Hancock Mutual Life Ins. Co.*, 33 Fed. App'x 26 (3d Cir. 2002) ("In light of the territorial limits imposed by Rule 45 upon the service of subpoenas, we conclude that the District Court did not commit error in denying John Hancock's motion to enforce the arbitration subpoena against SCIS, which, as a non-party located in Florida, lies beyond the scope of the court's subpoena enforcement powers."). Because the second set of arbitral summonses require the Epiq recipients and the Millennium recipients, who are non-parties that reside thousands of miles away from Miami, Florida, to provide testimony and provide documents in Miami, Florida, the arbitral summonses violate the geographical limits of Rules 45(c) and 45(d) and should not be enforced.

MCAG has not cited a case that holds that the geographical limit of Rules 45(c) and 45(d) do not apply to arbitral summonses. Because the second set of arbitral summonses seek to require the out-of-state non-party witnesses to come to Miami, Florida to produce documents and provide testimony at the final hearing far beyond the geographical limitation of Rule 45(c), the undersigned finds that the second set of arbitral summonses violate Rule 45 and are unenforceable.

Notes and Questions

1. *The Dichotomy. Managed Care* shows that it remains substantially difficult to obtain third-party evidence in arbitration. The arbitration advocate faces two hurdles that the litigation advocate does not: the sharp, circuit-by-circuit limitations on pretrial discovery and the requirement that a witness not testify beyond 100 miles from the courthouse issuing the subpoena.
2. *Governing Law.* Assume the arbitration is taking place in Philadelphia (Third Circuit), but the witness lives in Cincinnati (Sixth Circuit). Claimant sends a subpoena to the witness in Ohio for a pre-hearing deposition. Will the deposition be permitted under Sixth Circuit precedent or barred under Third Circuit precedent?
3. *State Law Amendments.* Certain states have eliminated the tension here by simply authorizing arbitrators to allow third-party discovery. *See, e.g.*, Cal. Code Civ. Proc. Sec. 1282.6 (empowering arbitrators to issue subpoenas requiring testimony and production of documents); K.S.A. Sec. 5-407 (same); N.J. Stat. Sec. 2A:23B-17(f) ("All laws compelling a person under subpoena . . . apply to an arbitration proceeding as if the

controversy were the subject of a civil action in this State."). The Uniform Arbitration Act takes a similar approach:

> In order to make the proceedings fair, expeditious, and cost effective, an arbitrator may permit a deposition of any witness to be taken for use as evidence at the hearing, including a witness who cannot be subpoenaed for or is unable to attend a hearing. The arbitrator shall determine the conditions upon which the deposition is taken.

Can parties operating under the Federal Arbitration Act include these provisions in their dispute resolution clause? This would provide the arbitrators with a mandate, but what would be the objections under the principles of consensus and of party autonomy? Would amendments to the FAA be appropriate? What would you propose, and in so doing, how would you account for the distinct interests of parties and non-parties, convenience, the need for prompt resolution, and the differences between documents and oral testimony?

4. Why are there so many U.S. Supreme Court cases on arbitrability and class actions, while the Supreme Court, plainly very interested in arbitration, has let the circuit splits examined in this chapter remain on issues of practice and practicality?

Class Problem

Refer to the ice-making machine problem in Chapter 7. What if Respondent wanted to demonstrate that the complaints of exploding ice machines at the premises of Claimant's customers were, in fact, due more to improper installation procedures and thus the fault of Claimant's instructions or to Claimant's customers being sloppy in their employ of these instructions? Assume the case were pending in Massachusetts, governed therefore by First Circuit law, and that (as of December 2020) the First Circuit has not yet come to a view on the central issue discussed in this chapter. What means might you employ as counsel for Respondent to obtain the customers' documents and, perhaps, oral testimony in advance of the hearing? Meanwhile, if you are counsel for Claimant, you were already nervous about these customers, given the explosions, and so you want to block them from being deposed in order to shield them from your supplier dispute and prevent their further inconvenience. What can you do to block customer discovery?

III. Closing Note—An "Immodest Proposal"

Benjamin Eichel & Matthew H. Adler, *When, Where, and Whether: The Confusing Law of Third-Party Evidence*

37 ALTERNATIVES TO THE HIGH COST OF LITIG. 4 (2019)

An Immodest Proposal

The FAA's third-party discovery provision needs to be amended. Arbitration right now is not working to achieve the full exposition of the facts necessary in complex cases requiring third-party evidence. That is a fact. Whether that is worth it—whether the intent of arbitration is an incomplete record—is a question worth pondering.

But given that most institutional arbitration rules now swing sharply in favor of more discovery, including electronic discovery, that seems a difficult proposition to maintain. AAA Commercial Arbitration Rules and Mediation Procedures (effective Oct. 1, 2013) (R.-23 empowers the arbitrator to enforce its rules relating to "imposing reasonable search parameters for electronic and other documents)"; JAMS Comprehensive Arbitration Rules & Procedures, (effective July 1, 2014) (R-17: "The Parties shall cooperate in good faith in the voluntary and informal exchange of all non-privileged documents and other information (including electronically stored information ('ESI')) relevant to the dispute or claim immediately after commencement of the Arbitration."); *but see* CPR Institute Administered Arbitration Rules (effective March 1, 2019) (Rule 11—Discovery: "The Tribunal may require and facilitate such discovery as it shall determine is appropriate in the circumstances, taking into account the needs of the parties and the desirability of making discovery expeditious and cost-effective. The Tribunal may issue orders to protect the confidentiality of proprietary information, trade secrets and other sensitive information disclosed in discovery.").

The solution, which should *not* be controversial, is to amend the FAA. It should provide for (a) the right to take third-party document and deposition discovery and (b) the means to enforce any arbitral subpoena. The following changes to Section 7 reflected in the italicized words below would achieve both of these goals:

"*Upon a showing of good cause*, the arbitrators selected either as prescribed in this title or otherwise, or a majority of them, may summon in writing any person to attend before them *at a hearing or for a pre-hearing deposition outside the presence of any arbitrators* or any of them as a witness and *to order any witness* in a proper case to bring with him or them any book, record, document, or paper which may be deemed material as evidence in the case. The fees for such attendance shall be the same as the fees of witnesses before masters of the United States courts. Said summons shall issue in the name of the arbitrator or arbitrators, or a majority of them, and shall be signed by the arbitrators, or a majority of them, and shall be directed to the said person and shall be served in the same manner as subpoenas to appear and testify before the court. If any person or persons so summoned to testify shall refuse or neglect to obey said summons, upon petition the United States district court for the district in which such arbitrators, or a majority of them, are sitting may compel the attendance of *the witness and/or evidence resides shall have jurisdiction to hear any petition to compel* such person or persons *to comply with the subpoena and* before said arbitrator or arbitrators, or punish said person or persons for contempt in the same manner provided by law for securing the attendance of witnesses or their punishment for neglect or refusal to attend in the courts of the United States."

Chapter 9

Third Parties and Arbitration

"What is 'never'?" At first glance, this would seem to be the right Jeopardy response to the "answer" of "when can third parties be held to an arbitration agreement?" By definition, that "agreement" is not one between the third party and any party to the arbitration agreement. Since, as we have studied repeatedly, arbitration is a matter of consent and there can be no arbitration without party agreement, this would seem to conclude the matter. It would be reasonable to state that without a consensus between the parties to the arbitration, there cannot be an arbitration at all.

Yet that is not the law. It is a fallacy to say that third parties cannot be held to arbitration agreements, just as it is a fallacy to say that third parties can never be held to contracts. Students of contract law are familiar with principles such as agency, third-party beneficiary, and assignment, which make third parties able to enforce and be obligated by contracts they never signed. Since, as we have studied, arbitration is a creature of contract, it follows that arbitration agreements are subject to the same third-party contract rules as any other contracts. None of these principles is in the Federal Arbitration Act, but courts at every level in the United States have carved out with exacting care the bases on which a third party can be made a party to an arbitration and, separately, can enforce an arbitration clause against a signatory.

The question of third parties in arbitration arises frequently in the courts and invokes several topics we have seen earlier in this book.

The first topic is consent. Should the third party's own consent matter? Can third party arbitration be involuntary? Should there be any difference in outcomes between cases in which a third party to an arbitration agreement is dragged into that arbitration by a party (under the contract principles we will review here) and cases in which a third party voluntarily invokes those principles to join the arbitration?

The second is the oft-stated judicial preference for arbitration. We have studied how, despite the repeated mantra that arbitration should be treated like any other contract, the Supreme Court is extremely sensitive to any outcomes that are somehow deemed to be hostile to arbitration and do not put it on an "equal footing" to other agreements. As examples, we saw in Chapter 4 that the Court did not apply the principle of "effective vindication" (*Italian Colors*) or the contract maxim of *contra proferentem* (*Lamps Plus*) to an arbitration agreement.

The third is efficiency. From *Concepcion* forward, we have seen courts rule that a goal of arbitration is efficiency, especially as compared to the presumably less-efficient forum of our courts. Hold that thought and then ponder a complex commercial dispute with multiple parties and contractual relationships, some of which have arbitration clauses and some of which do not. If party A is suing both B and C but only has an arbitration clause with B, is it more efficient to drag C into the arbitration as well, so that all of the disputes can be heard in one forum? Is it fair? Must C consent? And what if C does want to join in but either A or B, the parties with contractual privity as to their arbitration clause, does not want to let C into their arbitration?

This chapter allows you to review those themes of consent, judicial preference, and efficiency against a new factual background. The foremost point to keep in mind is the application of state common law contract principles in solving the puzzle. That point is made clear in the following SCOTUS case.

Arthur Andersen LLP v. Carlisle

556 U.S. 624, 129 S. Ct. 1896 (2009)

JUSTICE SCALIA delivered the opinion of the Court.

Section 3 of the Federal Arbitration Act (FAA) entitles litigants in federal court to a stay of any action that is "referable to arbitration under an agreement in writing." 9 U.S.C. § 3. Section 16(a)(1)(A), in turn, allows an appeal from "an order . . . refusing a stay of any action under section 3." We address in this case whether appellate courts have jurisdiction under § 16(a) to review denials of stays requested by litigants who were not parties to the relevant arbitration agreement, and whether § 3 can ever mandate a stay in such circumstances.

I.

Respondents Wayne Carlisle, James Bushman, and Gary Strassel set out to minimize their taxes from the 1999 sale of their construction-equipment company. Arthur Andersen LLP, a firm that had long served as their company's accountant, auditor, and tax adviser, introduced them to Bricolage Capital, LLC, which in turn referred them for legal advice to Curtis, Mallet-Prevost, Colt & Mosle, LLP. According to respondents, these advisers recommended a "leveraged option strategy" tax shelter designed to create illusory losses through foreign-currency-exchange options. As a part of the scheme, respondents invested in various stock warrants through newly created limited liability companies (LLCs), which are also respondents in this case. The respondent LLCs entered into investment-management agreements with Bricolage, specifying that "[a]ny controversy arising out of or relating to this Agreement or the breach thereof, shall be settled by arbitration conducted in New York, New York in accordance with the Commercial Arbitration Rules of the American Arbitration Association."

As with all that seems too good to be true, a controversy did indeed arise. The warrants respondents purchased turned out to be almost entirely worthless, and the Internal Revenue Service (IRS) determined in August 2000 that the "leveraged option strategy" scheme was an illegal tax shelter. The IRS initially offered conditional amnesty to taxpayers who had used such arrangements, but petitioners failed to inform respondents of that option. Respondents ultimately entered into a settlement program in which they paid the IRS all taxes, penalties, and interest owed.

Respondents filed this diversity suit in the Eastern District of Kentucky against Bricolage, Arthur Andersen and others (all except Bricolage and its employees hereinafter referred to as petitioners), alleging fraud, civil conspiracy, malpractice, breach of fiduciary duty, and negligence. Petitioners moved to stay the action, invoking § 3 of the FAA and arguing that the principles of equitable estoppel demanded that respondents arbitrate their claims under their investment agreements with Bricolage. The District Court denied the motions.

III.

We consider the Sixth Circuit's underlying determination that those who are not parties to a written arbitration agreement are categorically ineligible for relief.

Section 2—the FAA's substantive mandate—makes written arbitration agreements "valid, irrevocable, and enforceable, save upon such grounds as exist at law or in equity for the revocation of a contract." That provision creates substantive federal law regarding the enforceability of arbitration agreements, requiring courts "to place such agreements upon the same footing as other contracts." *Volt Information Sciences, Inc. v. Board of Trustees of Leland Stanford Junior Univ.*, 489 U.S. 468, 478 (1989) (internal quotation marks omitted). Section 3, in turn, allows litigants already in federal court to invoke agreements made enforceable by § 2. That provision requires the court, "on application of one of the parties," to stay the action if it involves an "issue referable to arbitration under an agreement in writing." 9 U.S.C. § 3.

Neither provision purports to alter background principles of state contract law regarding the scope of agreements (including the question of who is bound by them). Indeed § 2 explicitly retains an external body of law governing revocation (such grounds "as exist at law or in equity"). And we think § 3 adds no substantive restriction to § 2's enforceability mandate. "[S]tate law," therefore, is applicable to determine which contracts are binding under § 2 and enforceable under § 3 "*if* that law arose to govern issues concerning the validity, revocability, and enforceability of contracts generally." *Perry v. Thomas*, 482 U.S. 483, 493, n. 9 (1987). *See also First Options of Chicago, Inc. v. Kaplan*, 514 U.S. 938, 944 (1995). Because "traditional principles" of state law allow a contract to be enforced by or against nonparties to the contract through "assumption, piercing the corporate veil, alter ego, incorporation by reference, third-party beneficiary theories, waiver and estoppel," 21 R. Lord, *Williston on Contracts* § 57:19, p 183 (4th ed. 2001), the Sixth Circuit's holding that nonparties to a contract are categorically barred from § 3 relief was error.

Respondents argue that, as a matter of federal law, claims to arbitration by nonparties are not "referable to arbitration *under* an agreement in writing," 9 U.S.C.

§3 (emphasis added), because they "seek to bind a signatory to an arbitral obligation *beyond* that signatory's strictly contractual obligation to arbitrate." Perhaps that would be true if §3 mandated stays only for disputes between parties to a written arbitration agreement. But that is not what the statute says. It says that stays are required if the claims are "referable to arbitration under an agreement in writing." If a written arbitration provision is made enforceable against (or for the benefit of) a third party under state contract law, the statute's terms are fulfilled.

Respondents' final fallback consists of reliance upon dicta in our opinions, such as the statement that "arbitration. . . . is a way to resolve those disputes—but only those disputes—that the parties have agreed to submit to arbitration," *First Options, supra,* at 943, and the statement that "[i]t goes without saying that a contract cannot bind a nonparty," *EEOC v. Waffle House, Inc.*, 534 U.S. 279, 294 (2002). The former statement pertained to *issues* parties agreed to arbitrate, and the latter referred to an entity (the Equal Employment Opportunity Commission) which obviously had no third-party obligations under the contract in question. Neither these nor any of our other cases have presented for decision the question whether arbitration agreements that are otherwise enforceable by (or against) third parties trigger protection under the FAA.

Respondents may be correct in saying that courts' application of equitable estoppel to impose an arbitration agreement upon strangers to the contract has been "somewhat loose." But we need not decide here whether the relevant state contract law recognizes equitable estoppel as a ground for enforcing contracts against third parties, what standard it would apply, and whether petitioners would be entitled to relief under it. These questions have not been briefed before us and can be addressed on remand. It suffices to say that no federal law bars the State from allowing petitioners to enforce the arbitration agreement against respondents and that §3 would require a stay in this case if it did.

We hold that the Sixth Circuit had jurisdiction to review the denial of petitioners' requests for a §3 stay and that a litigant who was not a party to the relevant arbitration agreement may invoke §3 if the relevant state contract law allows him to enforce the agreement. The judgment of the Court of Appeals for the Sixth Circuit is reversed, and the case is remanded for further proceedings consistent with this opinion.

It is so ordered.

Notes and Questions

1. *Voluntary vs. Involuntary.* Did it—and should it—have mattered that in *Carlisle*, the third party wanted to join the arbitration, as opposed to being dragged in as a non-party?

2. *Contract Rules Rule.* Given the opportunity in *Carlisle* to carve out arbitration agreements from other third-party contracts, the Supreme Court declined the invitation. "If a written arbitration provision is made enforceable against (or for the benefit of) a third party under state contract law, the statute's terms are fulfilled." The Supreme Court could just as easily have found that because of arbitration's foundation upon consensus, a per se rule exists by which arbitration agreements can never be imposed on (or used by) third parties. In the battle between consensus and state contract principles, the latter prevailed.
3. *The Consent of the Parties to the Arbitration Agreement Is Not Controlling.* The contract rules for binding third parties still have to apply. The Colorado Supreme Court made that clear in the following case.

N.A. Rugby Union LLC v. United States Rugby Football Union

442 P.3d 859 (Colo. 2019)

JUSTICE GABRIEL delivered the Opinion of the Court.

In this original proceeding pursuant to C.A.R. 21, we must determine whether a nonsignatory to an arbitration agreement can be required to arbitrate under that agreement by virtue of the fact that it is a purported agent of a signatory to the agreement. Specifically, we are asked to decide whether the district court erred when it entered an order requiring petitioner Rugby International Marketing ("RIM"), which is a defendant below and a nonsignatory to a Professional Rugby Sanction Agreement (the "Sanction Agreement"), to arbitrate pursuant to an arbitration provision in that Agreement that covered the parties and their agents. The court found that because RIM was an agent for United States of America Rugby Football Union ("USAR"), a signatory of the Sanction Agreement, RIM fell "squarely within the broad language of the arbitration provision."

We issued a rule to show cause and now make the rule absolute. Although we have not yet opined on the issue, the weight of authority nationally establishes that, subject to a number of recognized exceptions, only parties to an agreement containing an arbitration provision can compel or be subject to arbitration. Here, because RIM was not a party to the Sanction Agreement and because respondents N.A. Rugby Union LLC d/b/a Professional Rugby Organization ("PRO Rugby") and Douglas Schoninger, who are the plaintiffs below, have not established that any of the recognized exceptions apply, we conclude that the district court erred in determining that RIM is subject to arbitration under the Sanction Agreement.

Facts and Procedural History

Schoninger, a New York financier, was interested in launching a professional rugby league in the United States. Toward that end, he formed PRO Rugby and approached USAR, which was the national governing body for rugby in the United States.

Ultimately, PRO Rugby and USAR entered into the Sanction Agreement, which authorized PRO Rugby to establish a professional rugby league in the United States.

As pertinent here, section 2.1 of the Sanction Agreement provided:

> g. N.A. Rugby Union LLC agrees to appoint Rugby International Marketing as its exclusive Player Representation agency through which it will contract with all Players and Coaching staff on a to be agreed fee basis (it being understood that such agency shall be the subject of an agency agreement and shall not be effective until such agency agreement has been executed by N.A. Rugby Union LLC and Rugby International Marketing).
>
> h. N.A. Rugby Union LLC agrees to appoint Rugby International Marketing as a non-exclusive agency to present the commercial rights of the Competition to potential sponsors on a to be agreed fee basis (it being understood that such agency shall be the subject of an agency agreement and shall not be effective until such agency agreement has been executed by N.A. Rugby Union LLC and Rugby International Marketing).

Notably, it appears undisputed that as of the date of this Agreement, RIM did not yet exist (it was not established until two months later).

The Sanction Agreement also contained an arbitration provision that stated, in part:

> [T]he parties agree that any claim or dispute between them or against any agent, employee, successor, or assign of the other, whether related to this Agreement or otherwise, and any claim or dispute related to this agreement or the relationship or duties contemplated under this Agreement, including the validity of this arbitration clause, shall be resolved by binding arbitration by the American Arbitration Association under the Commercial Arbitration Rules then in effect.

RIM was not a party to the Sanction Agreement. Moreover, notwithstanding the fact that the Agreement states that PRO Rugby agreed to appoint RIM as its agent for player representation and commercial rights, no such agreement was ever executed.

After allegedly investing six million dollars of his personal funds, Schoninger folded the league after its first season. He and PRO Rugby then filed suit in Boulder County District Court, naming nine different defendants, including USAR and RIM, and alleging that the defendants had engaged in a concerted effort to force PRO Rugby out of business.

In their complaint, plaintiffs asserted an array of tort and contract claims, the latter arising out of alleged breaches of the Sanction Agreement.

RIM subsequently moved to dismiss plaintiffs' breach of contract claims against it based on the undisputed fact that it was not a party to the contract. Plaintiffs responded that the above-quoted provisions of the Sanction Agreement demonstrated that USAR had assigned to RIM the obligations under that Agreement to act as PRO Rugby's exclusive player representation agency and to be the nonexclusive agency to present the commercial rights of the competition to potential sponsors. Based on this alleged assignment, plaintiffs contended that RIM was bound by the Agreement.

The district court disagreed with plaintiffs' assertion, noting that (1) a party to a contract cannot delegate duties to a nonparty without the nonparty's consent; (2) plaintiffs had conceded that RIM did not affirmatively agree to any promises in the Sanction Agreement; and (3) plaintiffs cited no evidence of any other agreement by RIM to assume any of the Sanction Agreement's obligations. The court thus dismissed plaintiffs' contract claims against RIM.

After further pretrial proceedings resulted in orders compelling arbitration as to certain defendants and dismissing for lack of personal jurisdiction the claims against certain other defendants, RIM became the sole remaining defendant in the lawsuit. Plaintiffs then moved to stay the proceedings against RIM to allow plaintiffs to arbitrate their claims against it. In support of this motion, plaintiffs argued that the plain language of the Sanction Agreement's arbitration provision, which bound the parties and agents of the other, bound RIM because it was allegedly USAR's agent. Plaintiffs further contended that, in any event, any dispute as to whether the claims at issue were arbitrable was to be decided by the arbitrator. RIM opposed the motion to stay, arguing that it was not a party to the Sanction Agreement and that it had never manifested an agreement to be bound by that Agreement's terms, including the arbitration provision. In light of this position, RIM did not directly respond to plaintiffs' assertion that RIM was bound by the arbitration provision because it was USAR's agent.

Notwithstanding its prior order dismissing the contract claims against RIM on the ground that RIM was not a party to the Sanction Agreement, the district court granted plaintiffs' motion to stay the case pending arbitration. In support of this ruling, the court did not rely on any claim that RIM was a party to the Sanction Agreement or that it had a prospective agency agreement with PRO Rugby. Instead, the court focused on the purported agency relationship between RIM and USAR. Specifically, the court found that the arbitration provision is phrased broadly and plainly subjects agents of both PRO Rugby and USAR to resolution by arbitration of any disputes brought by the other that are related to the Sanction Agreement. The court further found that USAR's control of and delegation of obligations to RIM (notwithstanding the court's prior finding that USAR had *not* delegated any obligations to RIM) established that RIM was USAR's agent "and thus squarely within the broad language of the arbitration provision." The court therefore ordered a "full stay of this case pending the completion of arbitration."

RIM then filed the present C.A.R. 21 petition, and we issued a rule to show cause.

Standard of Review and Applicable Law

It is well-settled that "arbitration is a matter of contract and a party cannot be required to submit to arbitration any dispute which he has not agreed so to submit." *United Steelworkers of Am. v. Warrior & Gulf Navigation Co.*, 363 U.S. 574, 582, 80 S. Ct. 1347, 4 L. Ed. 2d 1409 (1960); *accord Lane*, 145 P.3d at 679; *see also Smith v. Multi-Fin. Sec. Corp.*, 171 P.3d 1267, 1272 (Colo. App. 2007) ("Generally, when the requirement to arbitrate is created by an agreement, it can be invoked only by a signatory of the agreement, and only against another signatory.").

Although we do not appear to have spoken on the issue, other courts, including divisions of our court of appeals, have recognized certain exceptions to this general rule. For example, courts have observed that ordinary principles of contract and agency law may apply to bind a nonsignatory to an arbitration agreement. *See, e.g., Covington v. Aban Offshore Ltd.*, 650 F.3d 556, 558 (5th Cir. 2011); *Smith*, 171 P.3d at 1272. Specifically, these courts have recognized the following theories for binding a nonsignatory to an arbitration agreement: (1) incorporation of an arbitration provision by reference in another agreement; (2) assumption of the arbitration obligation by the nonsignatory; (3) agency; (4) veil-piercing/alter ego; (5) estoppel; (6) successor-in-interest; and (7) third-party beneficiary. *See Bridas S.A.P.I.C. v. Gov't of Turkm.*, 345 F.3d 347, 356 (5th Cir. 2003); *Thomson-CSF, S.A. v. Am. Arbitration Ass'n*, 64 F.3d 773, 776 (2d Cir. 1995); *Smith*, 171 P.3d at 1272.

We agree that the foregoing general rule and the above-described exceptions to it comport with settled principles of contract and agency law, and we now adopt that rule and those exceptions. Having done so, we turn to the merits of RIM's contentions.

Application

RIM contends that neither general contract principles nor any of the above-described exceptions apply to require it to arbitrate here.

Plaintiffs respond that under the plain language of the Sanction Agreement, RIM is bound by the arbitration clause and that, in any event, the Agreement delegated all issues of arbitrability to the arbitrator. Based on this, plaintiffs contend that we should discharge our order to show cause without reaching the above-described exceptions. Plaintiffs argue in the alternative, however, that should we reach the exceptions, then RIM is still bound by the arbitration provision of the Sanction Agreement because it was a third-party beneficiary of that Agreement, it was USAR's agent, and it is bound under a theory of equitable estoppel because it is seeking to enforce the rights and benefits that it received under the Agreement.

Plaintiffs first contend that the Sanction Agreement clearly and unambiguously required arbitration of any claim or dispute between PRO Rugby and USAR or against "any agent, employee, successor, or assign of the other, whether related to [the Sanction] Agreement or otherwise." Plaintiffs further contend that because RIM is USAR's agent, it is bound by the arbitration provision's above-quoted plain language. Plaintiffs never explain, however, how a party to a contract can bind a nonparty to the terms of that contract without establishing legal or equitable grounds for doing so (e.g., assumption by the nonsignatory of obligations under the agreement, applicable agency principles, veil-piercing, equitable estoppel, or the nonsignatory's status as a successor-in-interest to a party to the contract or as a third-party beneficiary of the contract).

The cases that we cited in *Allen*, 71 P.3d at 379–80, in support of the proposition that a nonparty may fall within the scope of an agreement if the parties so intend confirm this point. For example, *Jefferson County School District No. R-1 v. Shorey*, 826 P.2d 830, 843 (Colo. 1992), concerned whether an employee who was a third-party beneficiary to a collective bargaining agreement had standing to sue for benefits under that agreement (we said she did but concluded that her claim should be stayed pending exhaustion of the grievance process established by the collective bargaining agreement). *Parker v. Center for Creative Leadership*, 15 P.3d 297, 298 (Colo. App. 2000), concerned whether a third-party beneficiary who was seeking to enforce a contract was bound by the arbitration provision of that same contract (the division said he was). And both *Everett v. Dickinson & Co.*, 929 P.2d 10, 12 (Colo. App. 1996), and *Eychner v. Van Vleet*, 870 P.2d 486, 489 (Colo. App. 1993), concerned whether a *nonsignatory* to an arbitration agreement could compel a *signatory* to arbitrate, a scenario not at issue here. Notably, in *Everett*, the nonsignatory sought to enforce the arbitration provision at issue based on the very types of contract principles set forth above. *See Everett*, 929 P.2d at 12-13 (concluding that the nonsignatory could not enforce an arbitration provision to which it was not a party because it was not a third-party beneficiary of that agreement).

In short, neither *Allen* nor the cases on which it relied support the proposition that a nonsignatory like RIM can be compelled to arbitrate merely because the signatories to an arbitration agreement, without more, intended to bind the nonsignatory. Rather, the signatory must establish one of the recognized legal or equitable bases to compel the nonsignatory to arbitrate.

For similar reasons, we reject plaintiffs' contention that we should uphold the district court's order requiring RIM to arbitrate because, even if there were a dispute as to whether plaintiffs' claims against RIM are arbitrable, under the Sanction Agreement, issues of arbitrability are to be decided by the arbitrator. Although plaintiffs contend that when contracting parties empower an arbitrator to determine issues of arbitrability, this constitutes "clear and unmistakable evidence of intent to delegate those issues to the arbitrator," *Ahluwalia v. QFA Royalties, LLC*, 226 P.3d 1093, 1098 (Colo. App. 2009), plaintiffs again do not explain how the contracting parties' intent can bind a nonparty to a contract, absent a legal or equitable basis for doing so.

Conclusion

We conclude that the district court erred in determining that RIM is required to arbitrate the claims against it. We therefore make the rule to show cause absolute.

Notes and Questions

You have just seen that there is no per se rule stating that only signatories to an arbitration agreement can/must arbitrate. Courts have had to consider a variety of situations in which third parties collide with arbitration. Consider the following four scenarios:

1. *Signatory Sues Non-Signatory in Court. Non-Signatory Moves to Compel Arbitration.* Robotics, a California start-up, pioneers a hospital robotics technology that administers patient drug intake through robotics, eliminating human error. Robotics has no sales force and so licenses the product to Noved Co., an East Coast sales organization. Under the licensing agreement, Noved is the licensed agent for hospital sales and pays Robotics a royalty on each sale. The licensing agreement has an arbitration clause. Noved proves incompetent, particularly in describing to potential customers the product's capabilities. In an attempt to remedy this flaw, Robotics sends one of its senior officers, John Pargas, to Noved. Pargas is named Chief Operating Officer (COO) of Noved, but this does not help, as sales remain non-existent. Ultimately, Robotics terminates the contract. Instead of bringing an arbitration under the licensing agreement's dispute resolution clause, Noved sues Mr. Pargas in the Eastern District of New York, where Noved is headquartered and does business. Noved's Complaint alleges that by allowing the licensing agreement to be terminated, Mr. Pargas breached the separate fiduciary duty he owed Noved as its COO. Mr. Pargas moves to stay the federal court complaint and argues that any and all claims against him personally should be arbitrated, since they all arise from the fundamental contract relationship between Robotics and Noved and that agreement requires that disputes be arbitrated. Noved claims that its suit is against a third-party individual and not the company that agreed to arbitrate, and further, that it is raising tort (breach of fiduciary duty) claims, not contract claims, so its suit should be in a separate forum (court) from the arbitration.

   Should Noved's breach of fiduciary duty suit be heard in court or in arbitration?

2. *Signatory Brings Arbitration Against Non-Signatory. Non-Signatory Wants Court.* Blaze Ltd., a well-known developer of distinctive office buildings in major cities, contracts with Crane Company for the primary construction services on Blaze's latest building, a 100-story brass and zinc colossus that will blink "Blaze" 24 hours a day across the Las Vegas desert. The Blaze-Crane contract has an arbitration clause.

   Crane sub-contracts out the lighting portion of the construction to Brilliant Designs, Ltd. The Crane-Brilliant Designs sub-contract does not contain an arbitration clause, calling instead for any and all disputes to be resolved in the United States District Court for the Central District of California.

When the building is completed and the lights turned on, Blaze's President is furious, claiming that the lighting of "BLAZE" is too low in brilliance as it does not, as Blaze had contracted with Crane, outshine all of the other lights on the Vegas Strip. Blaze brings an arbitration against Crane under the arbitration clause in the Blaze-Crane primary contract. Blaze's statement of claim in the arbitration includes a separate third-party claim against Brilliant Designs, claiming that Blaze was the intended beneficiary of the Crane-Brilliant Designs contract. Brilliant Designs objects to the arbitration and demands that any claims by Blaze must be heard in court.

Should Blaze's claims against Brilliant Designs be heard in arbitration or court?

3. *Non-Signatory Brings Arbitration Against Signatory. Signatory Wants Court.* Burgers Inc., a well-known fast-food franchise, operates an affiliate called Burger Dollars Ltd., which acts as a loan facility for franchisees. Only Burgers franchisees are eligible for loans from Burger Dollars. Franchisees often take out these loans as an advance in order to make required capital improvements in their local Burgers stores. They then repay the loans through a low-interest payment that is tacked on to their franchise fee repayments to Burgers each month. The franchise agreement and the loan agreement are in separate contracts. The franchise agreement with Burgers has an arbitration clause. The loan agreement with Burger Dollars does not.

   Mike Smedley is a Burgers franchisee in Cleveland. After a successful first year in business, Mr. Smedley fails to make his required franchise fee payments and fails to repay his loans in year 2. At the end of year 2 and after proper notice that passes without cure under the Burgers contract's dispute resolution provisions, Burgers terminates Smedley's franchise and Burger Dollars calls Smedley into default on the loan. The Burgers-Smedley dispute goes to arbitration. Burger Dollars seeks to join the arbitration to seek the unpaid loan amounts. Smedley's lawyers advise him that he can more readily slow down Burger Dollars' claim in court. Smedley opposes the attempt of Burger Dollars to join arbitration and demands that Burger Dollars sue him in court.

   Should the *Burger Dollars v. Smedley* dispute be heard in court or arbitration?

4. *Non-Signatory Sues Signatory in Court. Signatory Wants Arbitration.* Benefits Co. contracts with Susan Johnson to invest and manage Ms.

Johnson's financial portfolio. The parties' contract contains an arbitration clause. Ms. Johnson dies. The administrator of her estate is her husband, Samuel Johnson, but the chief beneficiary is her beloved niece, Zoe. It turns out that Benefits has performed so poorly that instead of there being the $10 million in assets that Zoe expects, the account is not only drained but the estate actually owes the federal government back taxes. Mr. Johnson, as administrator, raises appropriate claims of fraud and malpractice in arbitration under the Johnson-Benefits investment contract's arbitration clause. Zoe, meanwhile, brings a suit against Benefits in federal court, claiming that as the intended third-party beneficiary of the estate management services, she has standing and has been damaged. Benefits Co. moves to bring her into the arbitration.

Can Zoe be brought into the arbitration?

As illustrated by these hypotheticals, there are situations that provide the basis for compelling third parties to arbitrate (or by which they can compel signatories to arbitrate with them). All told, there are six theories that can be used to compel a non-party into an arbitration, which are widely recognized in U.S. courts: (a) incorporation by reference; (b) assumption; (c) agency; (d) veil-piercing/alter ego; (e) estoppel; and (f) third-party beneficiary. The following cases illustrate these theories in practice.

PRACTICE POINTERS

1. The following are common law, state contract decisions, and they are not universal or uniform among our state and federal courts. Accordingly, it is critical that you research which theory or theories for bringing in a third party may be available in the jurisdiction whose law governs your dispute. What follows below is but a representational sample.
2. It might be possible to resolve all these situations by consent. In any one of the above scenarios and in any one of the cases that follow, one or more of the parties objected to the extension of the arbitration clause to the third party. But, since arbitration is, as always, a creature of consent, the parties could just as easily agree, even once a dispute has arisen, to craft a post-dispute arbitration clause that brings in all the parties, whether or not they were a party to the original arbitration clause. In practice, it may often be a good first step to seek that consensus rather than leave the outcome to the courts as in these cases.

I. Incorporation by Reference

Incorporation by reference is used to compel a party to arbitrate where the arbitration agreement is incorporated in a separate contract other than the one in which the opposing party bases the arbitration. There is no question in these cases that the party whose presence is demanded in the arbitration *did* agree to arbitration in some other agreement—but should the twain meet? When should consent to arbitrate a dispute under one agreement be held as consent to arbitrate a dispute under a second?

Spinks v. Krystal Co.

No. 6:07-2619-HMH, 2007 U.S. Dist. LEXIS 94571 (D.S.C. Dec. 20, 2007)

HERLONG, Jr. District Judge.

This matter is before the court on the Defendant's motion to compel arbitration pursuant to 9 U.S.C. § 2 of the Federal Arbitration Act ("FAA") and stay the action. For the reasons set forth below, the court grants the Defendant's motion.

I. FACTUAL AND PROCEDURAL BACKGROUND

The case arises from two franchise agreements between Spinks Investments, Inc. ("Spinks Investments") and the Defendant to operate two Krystal restaurants, one in Liberty and one in Greenville, South Carolina. The Liberty franchise agreement was executed on May 11, 2004. The same day, the Plaintiffs executed a guaranty agreement for the Liberty franchise agreement. The Greenville franchise agreement was executed on June 22, 2004. Likewise, the same day, the Plaintiffs executed a guaranty agreement for the Greenville franchise agreement. According to the Defendant, Spinks Investments abandoned the Liberty restaurant on March 18, 2007, and abandoned the Greenville restaurant on April 1, 2007. The Defendant sent a demand for arbitration to Spinks Investments dated June 8, 2007, seeking to recover damages as a result of Spinks Investments' abandonment of the two franchises. The Defendant named the Plaintiffs as respondents in the demand for arbitration.

The franchise agreements contain an arbitration provision. Paragraph 24.A.(4) of the franchise agreements provides in pertinent part that

> [e]xcept as specifically otherwise provided in Paragraph 24.A.(4) regarding Krystal's right to seek preliminary and/or or [sic] permanent injunctive relief in a court of law, any and all disputes and controversies between Krystal and Franchisee and any claim by either party that cannot be amicably settled shall be determined exclusively by arbitration conducted in Hamilton County, Tennessee in accordance with the Uniform Arbitration Act, Tennessee Code Annotated § 29-5-301 et seq. . . .

The guaranty agreements were attached to the franchise agreements and made exhibits thereto. The guaranty agreements provide that each guarantor "agrees to be personally bound by . . . each and every provision in the Franchise Agreement."

On March 18, 2007, Spinks Investments allegedly closed and abandoned the Liberty restaurant. Spinks Investments allegedly closed and abandoned the Greenville restaurant. The Defendant alleges that it notified Spinks Investments that they were in default of the Franchise Agreements on March 19, 2007, and April 2, 2007, respectively. On June 8, 2007, the Defendant alleges that it forwarded notice to Spinks Investments and the Plaintiffs notifying them of the Defendant's intent to proceed with a demand for arbitration with the American Arbitration Association. (*Id.*) On June 25, 2007, the Plaintiffs filed suit in the Court of Common Pleas of Greenville County, South Carolina seeking a declaration that (1) the two alleged guaranty agreements are unenforceable and void; (2) the Spinkses are not obligated to Krystal for any damages it alleges it has suffered as a result of any actions or omissions by Spinks Investments; and (3) regardless of whether the alleged guaranty agreements are otherwise enforceable, the Spinkses are not subject to arbitration of any dispute arising under the alleged guaranty agreements or the franchise agreements to which Krystal alleges they pertain.

A. Arbitration Clause

The Plaintiffs argue that they did not agree to submit any claims to arbitration because the guaranty agreements do not contain an arbitration clause, and further, the guaranty agreements do not specifically incorporate the arbitration provision contained in the franchise agreements. In deciding whether a party agreed to arbitrate a particular dispute, "the court should apply ordinary state-law principles that govern the formation of contracts." *Johnson v. Circuit City Stores*, 148 F.3d 373, 377 (4th Cir. 1998) (internal quotation marks omitted). The guaranty agreements provide that they are "governed by and construed in accordance with the laws of the State of Tennessee."

Under Tennessee law, generally, "arbitration clauses are not binding on third parties who are not parties to the contract." *Cocke County Bd. of Highway Comm'rs v. Newport Utilities Board*, 690 S.W.2d 231, 237 (Tenn.1985). However, "nonsignatories may be bound to an arbitration agreement under ordinary contract and agency principles." *Javitch v. First Union Sec., Inc.*, 315 F.3d 619, 629 (6th Cir. 2003). "Five theories for binding nonsignatories to arbitration agreements have been recognized: (1) incorporation by reference, (2) assumption, (3) agency, (4) veil-piercing/alter ego, and (5) estoppel." *Id.* "[A] subcontract with a guarantor or surety may incorporate a duty to arbitrate by reference to an arbitration clause in a general contract." *Gingiss Int'l, Inc. v. Bormet*, 58 F.3d 328, 331 (7th Cir. 1995).

In *Gingiss*, the court found that the franchise agreement was incorporated by reference into the guaranty agreement, which stated that the guarantors "agreed to be bound by all obligations of" the franchisee "under the franchise agreement as if each was the franchisee." *Id.* at 330. Further, the court found that the guaranty "expressly incorporated the arbitration clause." *Id.* at 331–32. In addition, in *Maxum Foundations, Inc. v. Salus Corp.*, the United States Court of Appeals for the Fourth Circuit found that an arbitration clause in a general contract was incorporated by reference in a subcontract, which stated that "[t]o the extent applicable to, or arising in connection with, the Work, the Subcontractor shall be bound by, and expressly assumes for the benefit of the Contractor, all obligations and liabilities which the Contract Documents impose upon the Contractor." 779 F.2d 974, 979 (4th Cir. 1985). Notably, the subcontract did not specifically incorporate the arbitration provision in the general contract. *Id.; see also* Philip L. Bruner and Patrick J. O'Connor, Jr., *Bruner and O'Connor on Construction Law,* 6 Bruner & O'Connor Construction Law § 20:32 (West 2007) ("As a general rule broad general incorporation language is sufficient to capture an arbitration provision, particularly when the federal policy favoring arbitration is factored into the equation."). In *Exchange Mut. Ins. Co. v. Haskell Co.,* 742 F.2d 274, 276 (6th Cir. 1984), the Sixth Circuit found that an arbitration provision in a subcontract was incorporated in a performance bond. The court found that the performance bond specifically referred to and incorporated the subcontract. The subcontract provides that the same obligations and responsibilities apply in the subcontract as apply in the general contract. And, finally, the general contract provides that there is a duty to arbitrate. Thus, the performance bond incorporates by reference the subcontract, the subcontract incorporates by reference the general contract and hence the duty to arbitrate. *Id.* Again, the arbitration provision was not specifically incorporated in the performance bond.

The Plaintiffs rely on *Morrie & Shirlee Mages Foundation v. Thrifty Corp.,* to support their argument that the arbitration provision must be explicitly incorporated in the guaranty agreements. 916 F.2d 402 (7th Cir. 1990), *overruled on other grounds by, IDS Life Ins. Co. v. SunAmerica, Inc.,* 103 F.3d 524 (7th Cir. 1996). The Seventh Circuit noted that "[t]he Guaranty does not contain an arbitration clause and does not incorporate the arbitration provision of the Agreement between the Mages and [a subsidiary of Thrifty]. . . ." *Id.* at 406 n. 1. However, the court finds that *Thrifty* is not persuasive in light of the fact that the court did not indicate whether the guaranty incorporated the terms of the main agreement generally. In the instant action, the guaranty agreements signed by the Plaintiffs state that they were entered into "in consideration of, and as an inducement to, the execution of" the franchise agreements.

Further, the guaranty agreements state that the Plaintiffs "agree[ ] to be personally bound by . . . each and every provision in the [Franchise] Agreement, both monetary obligations and obligations to take or refrain from taking specific actions or to engage or refrain from engaging in specific activities, including without limitation the provisions of Paragraphs 9 and 12." Based on the plain language of the guaranty agreements and the case law discussed above, the arbitration provisions in the franchise agreements were incorporated into the guaranty agreements. Therefore, the Plaintiffs are obligated to arbitrate Krystal's claims pursuant to the arbitration clause in the franchise agreements. The Plaintiffs argue that "even if the Court finds that the alleged guaranty agreements incorporate an arbitration clause, Plaintiffs did not personally sign the alleged guaranty agreements and, therefore, may not be compelled to arbitrate."

However, this issue concerns the enforceability of the contract generally. As noted above, "federal courts may not address the validity or enforceability of the contract as a whole." *Ticknor,* 265 F.3d at 937 (citing *Prima Paint,* 388 U.S. at 401). Therefore, this issue must be decided in the arbitration. However, to the extent the Plaintiffs' argument affects the enforceability of the arbitration clause, the court finds that the guaranty agreements bind the Plaintiffs in their individual capacities.

Based on the foregoing, the guaranty agreements bind the Plaintiffs in their individual capacity.

ORDERED that Defendant's motion to compel arbitration is granted.

Notes and Questions

The *Spinks* court looked to state law contract principles on two points: first, whether the contract without the arbitration clause incorporated the contract with the arbitration clause, and second, whether state law principles of guaranty law extended here to arbitration. In both cases, the court found the answer to be yes.

II. Assumption

A non-party may also be bound to an arbitration agreement if its subsequent conduct indicates that it is assuming the obligation to arbitrate. The term "assumption" is often intertwined with the phrase "intent to be bound" under this theory.

Gvozdenovic v. United Air Lines, Inc.

933 F.2d 1100 (2d Cir. 1991)

MINER, Circuit Judge.

Plaintiffs-appellants appeal from a judgment entered on August 29, 1990 in the United States District Court for the Southern District of New York (Griesa, J.), dismissing a class action suit brought against defendants-appellees United Airlines, Inc. ("United") and the Association of Flight Attendants ("AFA"). In the complaint, appellants sought to vacate an arbitral award and sought damages, based on alleged breach of the statutory duty of fair representation, enforcement of compulsory union membership, improper dues assessment and breach of contract by appellees.

Appellants are 1202 former flight attendants of Pan American World Airways, Inc. ("Pan Am"), who began working for United after United purchased Pan Am's Pacific Division, in which they had been employed. On appeal, they contend that the district court improperly dismissed their petition for vacatur of the arbitration award because they were not parties to the agreement providing for the arbitration and because certain conduct of the AFA during the arbitration violated its duty to represent all its members fairly. Appellants also argue that the district court improperly dismissed on statute of limitations grounds their claims that the AFA ran an illegal "closed shop" and unlawfully raised their union dues, and that United improperly had given financial assistance to incumbent United employees to engage in the arbitration.

We hold that, because appellants participated voluntarily and actively in the arbitration process, they are bound by its outcome and the district court therefore properly dismissed their petition to vacate the award. Accordingly, we affirm the judgment of the district court.

BACKGROUND

On April 22, 1985, United entered into an agreement with Pan Am under which it would acquire the routes and related assets of Pan Am's Pacific Division. As part of the acquisition agreement, United promised to hire at least 1202 of the Pan Am Pacific Division flight attendants and, "subject to agreement . . . with the collective bargaining representatives of Buyer's employees, . . . [to] give [the incoming flight attendants] full recognition to all periods of service with" Pan Am.

On August 1, 1985, United and the AFA, the collective bargaining representative for United employees, began negotiations over a new collective bargaining agreement. An important issue to be resolved in the negotiations was the method of determining the seniority status of the 1202 incoming flight attendants in relation to that of United's pre-acquisition flight attendants. On December 6, 1985, representatives of United and the AFA entered into a Letter of Agreement setting out the terms and conditions of employment for the incoming flight attendants. The Letter of Agreement, ultimately incorporated into the collective bargaining agreement, was ratified by the AFA's members on March 14, 1986. The Letter of Agreement provided that the new employees would become AFA members on the date they commenced work with United and that the issue of their seniority status would be determined through arbitration in which the incoming flight attendants and the incumbent United flight attendants would be the only participants. The arbitration was to be financed largely by United. The Letter of Agreement also provided that "the arbitrator shall determine the appropriate method of integration, based upon equitable and contractual considerations. In making this or any other determination, the arbitrator shall . . . not reduce the seniority accrued by any United flight attendant."

On three successive dates, December 6, 1985, January 8 and 24, 1986, Pan Am Pacific Division flight attendants were notified in conditional offers of employment sent to them by United that their seniority rights were to be determined through this process. Pan Am's Pacific Division employees were guaranteed continued employment under their collective bargaining agreement with Pan Am and were under no compulsion to transfer to United. On February11, 1986, the 1202 Pan Am flight attendants who had accepted United's offer of employment became flight attendants for United.

On March 7, 1986, United deposited $132,700 into each of the bank accounts it had opened for the 1202 incoming flight attendants and the incumbent United employees to cover their costs of arbitration. Both sides drew on their respective accounts for this purpose. The Independent Union of Flight Attendants ("IUFA"), which had represented the incoming flight attendants during their employment at Pan Am, selected a committee of five to represent the former Pan Am attendants in the arbitration. Similarly, the United Master Executive Council ("UMEC"), the AFA's representative body at United, created a five-member committee to represent the incumbent United flight attendants. Each committee chose legal counsel, who in turn selected Arthur Stark to act as arbitrator.

The first arbitration hearing was held on June 27, 1986. The incumbent flight attendants argued that the seniority of the 1202 incoming flight attendants should be based on their date of hire by United, while the incoming flight attendants contended that they should receive full credit for their entire term of employment with Pan Am. In an interim decision issued on September 8, 1986, Arbitrator Stark decided that the new flight attendants would be integrated into the United seniority list. After additional hearings, he established in a final decision issued on September 26, 1987 an integration formula entitling them to partial credit for their service at Pan Am. Specifically, under Stark's formula, the first 1500 most senior employees on the integrated seniority list would be the first 1500 on the existing United list; thereafter, one Pan Am transferring flight attendant would be inserted on the list of United flight attendants on the basis of a ratio of 1:7.47. United revised the seniority list accordingly.

Judge Griesa determined that the agreement was not void and that plaintiffs were bound by it because of their willing participation in the arbitration, and that the no-reduction provision did not prejudice the placement of the 1202 incoming flight attendants on United's seniority list. Judge Griesa then dismissed all claims relating to the duty of fair representation.

In an Opinion dated August 17, 1990, Judge Griesa dismissed the remaining claims of unlawful imposition of union membership and illegal financing, finding that they were barred by a six-month statute of limitations. In the opinion, Judge Griesa also formally confirmed the class status of the action.

DISCUSSION

I. Validity of Arbitration Award

Appellants contend that the Letter of Agreement, in which United and the AFA agreed to submit the seniority issue to arbitration, is void because it was entered into before their employment with United effectively began. Because they were neither formal employees of United nor members of AFA at the time of the Letter of Agreement, appellants argue, they could not be parties to any arbitration agreement and are not bound by the arbitral outcome.

Although a party is bound by an arbitral award only where it has agreed to arbitrate, an agreement may be implied from the party's conduct. *See Teamsters Local Union No. 764 v. J.H. Merritt & Co.*, 770 F.2d 40, 42 (3d Cir. 1985); *cf. Kamakazi Music Corp. v. Robbins Music Corp.*, 684 F.2d 228, 231 (2d Cir. 1982) ("it is hornbook law that parties by their conduct may agree to send issues outside an arbitration clause to arbitration."). Here, appellants' conduct manifested a clear intent to arbitrate the dispute. The record demonstrates their active and voluntary participation in the arbitration; for example, through the IUFA, they chose a committee to represent them in the arbitration, and, on their behalf, the committee withdrew funds from the bank account set up to cover its expenses, chose counsel to represent the transferring flight attendants in the arbitration and argued vigorously that they should receive full credit for their time of employment with Pan Am. Also, there is no evidence that, at any point before or during the arbitration, appellants objected to the process, refused to arbitrate or made any attempt to seek judicial relief.

CONCLUSION

We affirm the judgment of the district court dismissing appellants' complaint in its entirety.

III. Agency

While parties can be held to arbitration agreements on the basis of agency law, courts will parse those relationships carefully. Just as they apply state contract law to arbitration agreements generally, courts apply the common law of agency to determine when and in what circumstances non-signatory agents or their principals can be held to arbitrate.

In the first case below, an arbitration clause was held to cover the principal's agent. In the second case, which cites and distinguishes the first case, the court determined that the arbitration clause did not cover the principal's agent. What differences do you see?

Grand Wireless, Inc. v. Verizon Wireless, Inc.

748 F.3d 1 (1st Cir. 2014)

RIPPLE, Circuit Judge.

Grand Wireless, Inc. ("Grand") brought this action in Massachusetts state court against Verizon Wireless, Inc. ("Verizon") and Verizon employee Erin McCahill. It alleged a violation of the federal Racketeer Influenced and Corrupt Organizations Act ("RICO") against Ms. McCahill, as well as several state law claims against both Ms. McCahill and Verizon. The defendants removed the case to the United States District Court for the District of Massachusetts and moved for an order compelling arbitration of Grand's claims. Grand opposed the motion. It contended that the arbitration clause should be interpreted narrowly and that, because Ms. McCahill was not a signatory to the contract containing the arbitration clause, the claim against her could not be arbitrated in this case. Adopting Grand's memorandum in opposition to the motion, the district court denied the defendants' motion to compel and also denied their subsequent request for reconsideration.

The defendants timely appealed. They submit that Grand's claims were within the scope of the parties' arbitration agreement and that arbitration of the claims against Ms. McCahill is not barred despite her status as a non-signatory of the arbitration agreement. We agree and therefore reverse the judgment of the district court and remand the case for further proceedings.

I. BACKGROUND

A. Facts

In September 2002, Grand and Verizon entered into an Exclusive Authorized Agency Agreement for Commercial Mobile Radio Service ("Agreement"). The Agreement authorized Grand to act as a Verizon sales agent within a defined geographic area. The Agreement governed the business relationship between Grand and Verizon. It required Grand to provide services exclusively for Verizon by offering customers Verizon services, such as sales, installation, warranty service and equipment maintenance. The Agreement also addressed the relationship between Grand, Verizon and subscribers who purchased products and services through Grand. On this point, the Agreement provided that subscriber lists were "the exclusive confidential property of Verizon Wireless." The Agreement provided for an initial term of five years; at that point, the Agreement would continue on a month-to-month basis, terminable by either party on thirty days' written notice to the other.

The Agreement contained a provision entitled, "DISPUTE RESOLUTION AND ARBITRATION." It stated, in pertinent part:

> Except to the extent explicitly provided below, ANY CONTROVERSY OR CLAIM ARISING OUT OF OR RELATING TO THIS AGREEMENT, OR ANY PRIOR OR FUTURE AGREEMENT BETWEEN THE PARTIES, SHALL BE SETTLED BY ARBITRATION ADMINISTERED BY THE AMERICAN ARBITRATION ASSOCIATION ("AAA") IN ACCORDANCE WITH THE WIRELESS INDUSTRY ASSOCIATION ("WIA") RULES OF THE AAA, AS MODIFIED BELOW, AND JUDGMENT ON THE AWARD RENDERED BY THE ARBITRATORS MAY BE ENTERED IN ANY COURT HAVING JURISDICTION.

The subsequent paragraphs explicitly stated that the disputes not covered included several intellectual property issues, as well as "[s]eeking to compel arbitration"; "[s]eeking to confirm or challenge any arbitral award"; seeking judicial relief for breaches of sections 3.3 and 7 of the Agreement; and seeking emergency injunctive relief pending the appointment of arbitrators. Provisions followed addressing the procedural aspects of commencing and conducting arbitration.

There is no dispute that, under the Agreement, Grand operated retail locations for Verizon products and services beginning in 2002 until the five-year term expired in September 2007. The parties then continued their relationship on a month-to-month basis until July 19, 2011, when Verizon notified Grand of its intent to terminate the relationship. Verizon submits that at Grand's request, Verizon extended the termination date to October 31, 2011, in order to "g[i]ve Grand additional time to attempt to sell certain of its stores to another Verizon Wireless agent."

In October 2011, according to Grand's complaint:

[Verizon] mailed an oversized (6″ by 11″) color postcard, featuring the picture of an attractive young woman, to the customers of eight remaining Grand Wireless stores, proclaiming that these Grand Wireless stores had "CLOSED." The mailing provided the customers with the address of the nearest competing Verizon Wireless store.

Grand further alleged that Ms. McCahill had "authorized the mailing and knew when the mailing went out that it was false." Grand stated that it was, at the time of the mailing, in negotiations with another wireless provider, T-Mobile, to become an authorized T-Mobile agent. Further, Grand alleged that Ms. McCahill knew that the mailing "would deal a body blow to Grand Wireless' ability [to] continue in business as a T[-]Mobile outlet" and that the mailing "was a deliberate attempt to eliminate Grand Wireless as a competitor to nearby Verizon stores." Grand alleged that its T-Mobile venture failed and that it has since ceased operations.

II. DISCUSSION

We have jurisdiction to review an order denying a motion under the Federal Arbitration Act to compel arbitration. *See* 9 U.S.C. § 16(a)(1)(C). Our review of such a denial is de novo because whether a matter is arbitrable is a matter of contract interpretation, and contract interpretation is a matter of law. *Combined Energies v. CCI, Inc.*, 514 F.3d 168, 171 (1st Cir. 2008). To compel arbitration, the defendants "must demonstrate that a valid agreement to arbitrate exists, that the[y are] entitled to invoke the arbitration clause, that the other party is bound by that clause, and that the claim asserted comes within the clause's scope." *Soto-Fonalledas v. Ritz-Carlton San Juan Hotel Spa & Casino*, 640 F.3d 471, 474 (1st Cir. 2011) (internal quotation marks omitted).

The parties do not dispute the validity of the Agreement's arbitration clause. Instead, they dispute: (1) whether Grand's claims are within the scope of the arbitration clause; and (2) whether Ms. McCahill is entitled to invoke the arbitration clause. We address each contention in turn.

B. Ms. McCahill's Ability to Invoke the Arbitration Clause

The allegations against Ms. McCahill arise out of actions that she allegedly took as part of her employment by Verizon. She therefore wants to avail herself of the arbitration clause in the Agreement signed by her employer, Verizon. The district court, by adopting Grand's memorandum, must be understood to have ruled that the claims against Ms. McCahill are not covered by the arbitration clause because she was not a party to the Agreement and because the arbitration clause does not call specifically for arbitrating disputes with individual employees. Verizon and Ms. McCahill now challenge this determination. They take the view that, because Ms. McCahill was acting as an agent of Verizon and the claims against her "relate solely to her performance as an employee," she is entitled to invoke the arbitration clause.

In order to compel arbitration of the claims against her, Ms. McCahill must establish that she is "entitled to invoke the arbitration clause." *Soto-Fonalledas*, 640 F.3d at 474 (internal quotation marks omitted). "[T]he FAA does not require parties to arbitrate when they have not agreed to do so." *Volt Info. Scis.*, 489 U.S. at 478. "[N]or does it prevent parties who do agree to arbitrate from excluding certain claims from the scope of their arbitration agreement." *Id.* We recognize that, of course, as a general proposition, a contract cannot bind a non-party. We also recognize, however, that "there are exceptions allowing non-signatories to compel arbitration" and that "[a] non-signatory may be bound by or acquire rights under an arbitration agreement under ordinary state-law principles of agency or contract." *Restoration Pres. Masonry, Inc. v. Grove Eur. Ltd.*, 325 F.3d 54, 62 n.2 (1st Cir. 2003).

Grand's complaint makes clear that Ms. McCahill's alleged actions were taken in her capacity as Verizon's agent or employee. She allegedly mailed (or directed to have mailed) postcards to the company's customers while she was employed for the company and in furtherance of company business. These allegations form the sole basis of liability against Verizon and against Ms. McCahill. Grand, in naming Ms. McCahill in its complaint, identified her as "Director of Indirect Communication, Erin McCahill." It further suggested that it was suing Ms. McCahill in her capacity as a Verizon agent when it stated that its claims were against Ms. McCahill "and all other [Verizon] executives who aided and abetted her in issuing the mailed announcements."

Grand puts forward but *one* argument as to why Ms. McCahill cannot invoke the arbitration clause: that the mention of employees in certain parts of the Agreement, combined with the lack of mention of employees in the arbitration clause, makes clear that the parties never agreed that claims against employees—even those sued for actions taken within the scope of their employment—could avail themselves of the arbitration agreement.

We have examined the Agreement from stem to stern, both with respect to its wording and with respect to its structure. We see no basis for Grand's assertion. In the contract, the parties do refer to employees in other contexts, such as ensuring that employees of Grand are not considered the employees of Verizon. Given the nature of the relationship established by the contract between the two companies, it is not at all surprising that this consideration would be the focus of special attention in the text of the agreement. The remaining references are likewise in areas where specific reference to employees would be expected. We fail to see how such references and the absence of an explicit reference to employees in the arbitration clause in any way evince an intent on the part of the parties to bar employees, acting in the scope of their employment, from the protection of the arbitration clause adopted by their employer.

Verizon and Grand certainly wished to have their disputes settled by arbitration. Since Verizon could operate only through the actions of its employees, it would have made little sense to have agreed to arbitrate if the employees could be sued separately without regard to the arbitration clause. Notably, contrary to Grand's assertion, the arbitration clause is written in broad language to encompass "any controversy or claim arising out of or relating to" the Agreement. Moreover, the parties entered into this agreement knowing that the legal landscape recognized the right of employees to seek the protection of their employers' arbitration clauses.

Indeed, a number of our sister circuits have addressed this issue, and all have held that an agent is entitled to the protection of her principal's arbitration clause when the claims against her are based on her conduct as an agent. When the non-signatory party is an employee of the signatory corporation *and* the underlying action in the dispute was undertaken in the course of the employee's employment, these circuits have fashioned, uniformly, a federal rule designed to protect the federal policy favoring arbitration. That rule, founded on general state law principles of agency, is that when "a principal is bound under the terms of a valid arbitration clause, its agents, employees, and representatives are also covered under the terms of such agreements." *Pritzker v. Merrill Lynch, Pierce, Fenner & Smith, Inc.*, 7 F.3d 1110, 1121 (3d Cir. 1993).

Such a rule is necessary, our sister circuits have reasoned, because a corporate entity or other business can only operate through its employees and an arbitration agreement would be a meaningless arrangement if its terms did not extend to them. *See id.* at 1122. Any other rule, in the view of these courts, would permit the party bringing the complaint to avoid the practical consequences of having signed an agreement to arbitrate; naming the other party's officers, directors or employees as defendants along with the corporation would absolve the party of all obligations to arbitrate. *See, e.g., Arnold v. Arnold Corp.-Printed Commc'ns for Bus.*, 920 F.2d 1269, 1281 (6th Cir. 1990). Indeed, long before the signing of the contract in this case, our circuit, although not elaborating the rule or the reasons for it, had expressed its approval of the rule. *Hilti, Inc. v. Oldach*, 392 F.2d 368, 369 n.2 (1st Cir. 1968) ("If arbitration defenses could be foreclosed simply by adding as a defendant a person not a party to an arbitration agreement, the utility of such agreements would be seriously compromised."). Notably, the highest court of New York State, the state whose law generally governs this contract in the absence of any federal preemption, has taken the view that the need to respect the basic policy of the FAA—the protection of the agreement to arbitrate—requires the use of the federal rule articulated by these circuits. *See Hirschfeld Prods., Inc. v. Mirvish*, 88 N.Y.2d 1054, 673 N.E.2d 1232, 1233, 651 N.Y.S.2d 5 (N.Y. 1996).

The Supreme Court's decision in *Arthur Andersen LLP v. Carlisle*, 556 U.S. 624, 129 S. Ct. 1896, 173 L. Ed. 2d 832 (2009), calls into some question the propriety of relying on a rule based on federal law in this situation. In that case, Carlisle and his associates had consulted with the accounting firm Arthur Andersen LLP about minimizing their tax liability. *Id.* at 626. On the basis of that consultation, Carlisle entered into management contracts with Bricolage Capital, LLC. *Id.* These management contracts contained arbitration clauses. *Id.* After the Internal Revenue Service determined that the tax strategy was illegal, Carlisle and his associates filed a diversity action against Arthur Andersen, Bricolage and others. *Id.* at 626–27. Claiming that equitable estoppel required Carlisle and his associates to arbitrate these claims under the agreements with Bricolage, Arthur Andersen sought a stay of the diversity action pending arbitration. *Id.* at 627. In the course of its decision, the Supreme Court wrote:

> Because "traditional principles" of *state* law allow a contract to be enforced by or against nonparties to the contract through "assumption, piercing the corporate veil, alter ego, incorporation by reference, third-party beneficiary theories, waiver and estoppel," the Sixth Circuit's holding that nonparties to a contract are categorically barred from § 3 relief was error. *Id.* at 631 (emphasis added) (quoting 21 Richard A. Lord, Williston on Contracts § 57:19, at 183 (4th ed. 2001)).

Carlisle holds that, at least as a general principle, state law governs the inquiry as to whether a non-party to an arbitration agreement can assert the protection of the agreement. *See id.* at 630–32; *Lawson v. Life of the S. Ins. Co.*, 648 F.3d 1166, 1170–71 (11th Cir. 2011). *Carlisle* leaves unclear, however, whether the Court intended to disturb the uniform body of precedent in the courts of appeals, which we just have examined, holding that a uniform federal rule is required with respect to the amenability of *employees* acting within the scope of their employment to the arbitration clauses in their employers' contracts. As we have noted earlier, the cases requiring that the employees of a company be bound by the arbitration agreements of their employers are based on the specific rationale that such a rule is necessary to protect the federal policy embodied in the FAA of favoring arbitration. Without it, according to the rationale of those cases, a party could frustrate an arbitration clause by simply naming employees as party defendants along with the signatory company in a judicial action. Nothing in *Carlisle* specifically disapproves the fashioning of federal law to avoid this specific abuse. Notably, at one point in *Carlisle*, the Court seemingly limited the scope of its holding; it wrote:

> We have said many times that federal law requires that "questions of arbitrability . . . be addressed with a healthy regard for the federal policy favoring arbitration." Whatever the meaning of this vague prescription, it cannot

> possibly require the disregard of state law *permitting* arbitration by or against nonparties to the written arbitration agreement.

556 U.S. at 630 n.5 (quoting *Moses H. Cone Mem'l Hosp. v. Mercury Constr. Corp.*, 460 U.S. 1, 24–25, 103 S. Ct. 927, 74 L. Ed. 2d 765 (1983)). Moreover, as we have just noted, in *Carlisle*, the Court specifically noted that the state law in that case permitted arbitration and was therefore compatible with and, indeed, supportive of the federal policy embodied in the FAA. *See id.*

We need not decide definitively whether *Carlisle* has abrogated this specific line of federal cases. Even if the Supreme Court's decision in *Carlisle* does signal the abrogation of the principle that, as a matter of *federal* law, the employees of a signatory of an arbitration agreement are protected by the agreement, Grand has not suggested any principle of New York law that impedes the interpretation of the agreement to protect the employee under the contract. It relies solely on the text of the contract—a text that does not support the illogical and impractical vision that an employee who acts solely within the scope of her employment is not protected by her employer's arbitration clause.

Conclusion

The district court incorrectly denied the motion by Verizon and Ms. McCahill to compel Grand to arbitrate its claims against them. Accordingly, we reverse and remand to the district court for further proceedings consistent with this opinion.

REVERSED AND REMANDED.

Ouadani v. TF Final Mile LLC

876 F.3d 31 (1st Cir. 2017)

LYNCH, Circuit Judge.

Djamel Ouadani worked as a delivery driver from March to August 2016, delivering products for Dynamex Operations East, LLC ("Dynamex"), now known as TF Final Mile LLC. As a condition of his employment, Ouadani was required to associate with a vendor affiliated with Dynamex, named Selwyn and Birtha Shipping LLC ("SBS"). Ouadani received his compensation from SBS, which had a written contract with Dynamex. Ouadani did not have a written contract either with Dynamex or with SBS.

In August 2016, Ouadani complained to Dynamex that he lacked the independence of a contractor, and that he should be paid as an employee if Dynamex continued to exert the same degree of control over his work. He was terminated shortly after he complained.

After his termination, Ouadani brought various wage-and-hour claims against Dynamex in federal district court, styling his action as a putative class action on his behalf and on behalf of others similarly situated. Dynamex responded by filing a motion to compel arbitration, pointing to an agreement between Dynamex and SBS that contained a mandatory arbitration clause.

The district court denied Dynamex's motion, reasoning that Ouadani had never signed the agreement containing the arbitration clause and had no idea that the agreement even existed. *Ouadani v. Dynamex Operations E., LLC*, No. 16-12036, 2017 U.S. Dist. LEXIS 71275, 2017 WL 1948522, at *3–5 (D. Mass. May 10, 2017). On appeal, Dynamex argues that Ouadani should nonetheless be compelled to arbitrate under federal common law principles of contract and agency. Because these arguments are without merit, we affirm.

I. Background

A. Facts

In early 2016, Ouadani applied to Dynamex for a job as a delivery driver, transporting products ordered through Google Express. After contacting Dynamex, Ouadani was invited to a meeting at the Dynamex offices in Wilmington, Massachusetts. At the meeting, Dynamex employees interviewed Ouadani and asked him to complete a number of forms, including one indicating his available days and hours. Dynamex also gave Ouadani a Dynamex shirt, albeit one that he had to pay for; took his photograph for a Dynamex identification badge; told him that he needed to pass a drug test; and provided him with information about the services the company provided for Google Express. Dynamex told Ouadani that he would be paid eighteen dollars per hour, or seventy-two dollars for a four-hour shift.

During the meeting at the Dynamex offices in Wilmington, Dynamex also gave Ouadani the names and telephone numbers of three Dynamex-affiliated vendors and told Ouadani that he would have to "associate" with one of them. For aught that appears, the term "associate" was never defined. Ouadani decided to associate with SBS. SBS was owned and managed by another Dynamex delivery driver, Edward Alwis, whom Ouadani had never met. Neither SBS nor Dynamex classified Ouadani as an employee.

Unbeknownst to Ouadani, Dynamex and SBS had entered into an "Independent Contractor Agreement for Transportation Services" (the "Agreement") in January 2016, pursuant to which SBS agreed to perform delivery services "brokered or subcontracted by Dynamex" (the "Contracted Services"). SBS was permitted to hire employees or subcontractors to perform some or all of the Contracted Services. The Agreement included the following arbitration provision:

> In the event of a dispute between the parties, the parties agree to resolve the dispute as described in this Section (hereafter "the Arbitration Provision"). This Arbitration Provision is governed by the Federal Arbitration Act, 9 U.S.C. § 1, et seq., and applies to any dispute brought by either [SBS] or Dynamex arising out of or related to this Agreement, [SBS's] relationship with Dynamex (including termination of the relationship), or the service

> arrangement contemplated by this Agreement, including cargo claims and payment disputes, but excluding all claims that may be adjudicated in small claims court. The provisions of this Arbitration Provision shall remain in force after the parties' contractual relationship ends. BY AGREEING TO ARBITRATE ALL SUCH DISPUTES, THE PARTIES TO THIS AGREEMENT AGREE THAT ALL SUCH DISPUTES WILL BE RESOLVED THROUGH BINDING ARBITRATION BEORE AN ARBITRATOR AND NOT BY WAY OF A COURT OR JURY TRIAL.

In a subsection entitled "Claims Covered By Arbitration Provision," the Agreement stated that "[u]nless carved out below, claims involving the following disputes shall be subject to arbitration under this Arbitration Provision regardless of whether brought by Contractor, Dynamex or any agent acting on behalf of either. . . ." The arbitration provision expressly extended to "disputes regarding any city, county, state or federal wage-hour law."

The Agreement also contained a provision that required SBS's subcontractors to "satisfy and comply with all the terms of th[e] Agreement" and required SBS to provide Dynamex with a written agreement from any subcontractor that SBS utilized attesting that the subcontractor had agreed to comply with the terms of the Agreement. SBS did not have Ouadani execute such a written agreement.

After passing his drug test, shadowing another delivery driver for a couple of days, receiving his Dynamex identification badge, and obtaining a cell phone and scanner set up with Google Express's software, Ouadani began working as a delivery driver for Dynamex. Dynamex required Ouadani to wear a Dynamex-issued shirt, which was marked by a large Dynamex logo, and his Dynamex identification badge when he delivered products for Dynamex. Ouadani used a Dynamex-issued e-mail address to receive communications and directions from Dynamex managers. Dynamex provided Ouadani with his assigned shifts for each week, and gave Ouadani specific instructions about his delivery schedules, including delivery locations, the order of deliveries, and delivery timeframes.

For each four-hour shift worked by Ouadani, Dynamex paid SBS seventy-two dollars, from which Dynamex subtracted, as to Ouadani, amounts related to insurance, use of cell phones and scanners, technology charges, failure to work assigned shifts, late log-ins, and damaged or stolen products. In addition to these amounts, SBS deducted, as to Ouadani, 17.5 percent of the net payment it received from Dynamex to pay for workers' compensation, other insurance, and payroll expenses. SBS then provided the remaining funds to Ouadani. To perform his duties, Ouadani used his own car and paid for his own gas without reimbursement. Ouadani calculates that, after mileage costs and the various deductions by Dynamex and SBS, his net pay for a four-hour shift ranged from $1.35 to $8.10 per hour.

In August 2016, Ouadani complained to Dynamex that he was not given the independence of a contractor, and that he would need to be paid as an employee if

Dynamex continued to exercise the same degree of control over his work. Shortly after receiving Ouadani's complaint, Dynamex permanently removed him from the driver schedule, thereby effecting the termination of his employment.

B. District Court Proceedings

On October 11, 2016, Ouadani filed a putative class action complaint against Dynamex, asserting that Dynamex misclassified him and other delivery drivers as independent contractors in violation of state and federal wage-and-hour laws. The complaint also alleged that the misclassification had unjustly enriched Dynamex, and that Dynamex had improperly retaliated against Ouadani in violation of Mass. Gen. L. ch. 149, § 148A. Ouadani sought to recover unpaid wages, reimbursement of improper deductions and unpaid travel expenses, and damages resulting from Dynamex's retaliation.

On February 9, 2017, Dynamex filed a motion to compel arbitration pursuant to the Federal Arbitration Act ("FAA"), 9 U.S.C. §§ 1–16. Ouadani opposed the motion. On May 10, 2017, the court entered a memorandum and order denying Dynamex's motion. Dynamex timely appealed the order.

II. Analysis

We review de novo a district court's interpretation of an arbitration agreement and its decision regarding whether or not to compel arbitration. *S. Bay Bos. Mgmt. v. Unite Here, Local 26*, 587 F.3d 35, 42 (1st Cir. 2009).

The FAA provides that written arbitration agreements concerning transactions in interstate commerce "shall be valid, irrevocable, and enforceable, save upon such grounds as exist at law or in equity for the revocation of any contract." 9 U.S.C. § 2; *see also Circuit City Stores, Inc. v. Adams*, 532 U.S. 105, 111–12 (2001). The FAA embodies a "liberal federal policy favoring arbitration." *Moses H. Cone Mem'l Hosp. v. Mercury Constr. Corp.*, 460 U.S. 1, 24 (1983). That policy requires "ambiguities as to the scope of the arbitration clause itself [to be] resolved in favor of arbitration." *Volt Info. Scis., Inc. v. Bd. of Trs. of Leland Stanford Junior Univ.*, 489 U.S. 468, 476 (1989).

On the other hand, a "basic precept" underlying the FAA is that "arbitration is a matter of consent, not coercion." *Stolt-Nielsen S.A. v. AnimalFeeds Int'l Corp.*, 559 U.S. 662, 681 (2010) (quoting *Volt Info. Scis.*, 489 U.S. at 479). As such, "a party cannot be required to submit to arbitration any dispute which he has not agreed so to submit." *AT&T Techs., Inc. v. Commc'ns Workers of Am.*, 475 U.S. 643, 648 (1986) (quoting *United Steelworkers of Am. v. Warrior & Gulf Navigation Co.*, 363 U.S. 574, 582 (1960)). It is undisputed that Ouadani never signed the Agreement containing the arbitration clause at issue, or even knew about it. A party that seeks to compel arbitration "must show [1] that a valid agreement to arbitrate exists, [2] that the movant is entitled to invoke the arbitration clause, [3] that the other party is bound by that clause, and [4] that the claim asserted comes within the clause's scope." *InterGen N.V. v. Grina*, 344 F.3d 134, 142 (1st Cir. 2003).

The pertinent question on appeal concerns the third prong: is Ouadani, a nonsignatory to the Agreement, bound to arbitrate his claims against Dynamex? To answer that question, we look to federal common law, which incorporates "general principles of contract and agency law." *Id.* at 144. Examples of such principles include incorporation by reference, assumption, agency, alter ego, estoppel, and third-party beneficiary. *See id.* at 146–50, *Thomson-CSF, S.A. v. Am. Arbitration Ass'n*, 64 F.3d 773, 776 (2d Cir. 1995). The theories asserted by Dynamex on appeal include (1) that Ouadani is bound to arbitrate inasmuch as he is an "agent" of SBS, (2) that Ouadani should be equitably estopped from refusing to arbitrate, and (3) that Ouadani is bound by the arbitration clause because he is a third-party beneficiary of the Agreement.

A. Agency

Dynamex asserts that Ouadani should be bound to arbitrate because he is an "agent" of SBS. We disagree. Dynamex notes that the arbitration clause in the Agreement reaches disputes "brought by [SBS], Dynamex *or any agent acting on behalf of either.*" (emphasis added). But Ouadani is not, in this context, bringing his wage-and-hour claims as an "agent acting on behalf" of SBS. To the contrary, Ouadani is bringing his claims against Dynamex on his own behalf and purportedly on behalf of other similarly situated drivers. The alleged agency relationship between Ouadani and SBS is irrelevant to the "legal obligation in dispute." *See InterGen*, 344 F.3d at 148 (refusing to compel arbitration against a parent corporation which was not a signatory to an arbitration agreement, even though its subsidiary was a signatory and acted as the parent's agent in certain other contexts, because there was no evidence that the subsidiary acted as the parent's agent when it committed the specific acts that were the subject of the dispute).

Cases from other circuits which have found an agent to be subject to a principal's arbitration agreement are distinguishable. Those cases held that nonsignatory defendants who are agents of a signatory corporation may compel arbitration against signatory plaintiffs. *See Grand Wireless, Inc. v. Verizon Wireless, Inc.*, 748 F.3d 1, 10–11 (1st Cir. 2014) (holding that a nonsignatory employee of a signatory corporation may compel arbitration against signatory plaintiffs); *Pritzker v. Merrill Lynch, Pierce, Fenner & Smith, Inc.*, 7 F.3d 1110, 1121- 22 (3d Cir. 1993) (holding that a nonsignatory employee and a nonsignatory corporate sister of a signatory corporation may compel arbitration against signatory plaintiffs); *Arnold v. Arnold Corp.-Printed Commc'ns For Bus.*, 920 F.2d 1269, 1281–82 (6th Cir. 1990) (holding that nonsignatory officers and directors of a signatory corporation are entitled to compel arbitration against signatory plaintiffs); *Letizia v. Prudential Bache Sec., Inc.*, 802 F.2d 1185, 1187–88 (9th Cir. 1986) (holding that nonsignatory employees of a signatory broker are entitled to compel arbitration against signatory plaintiffs). These holdings were predicated on (1) the fact that the claims of the signatory plaintiffs arose from the nonsignatory agents' conduct on behalf of the signatory principals, and (2) the signatory principals' intent to protect their agents by means of the arbitration provisions. *See*

Grand Wireless, 748 F.3d at 10–11; *Pritzker*, 7 F.3d at 1122; *Arnold*, 920 F.2d at 1282; *Letizia*, 802 F.2d at 1188. These rationales are inapposite here because Ouadani is a nonsignatory *plaintiff* who is trying to *avoid* arbitration, not a nonsignatory *defendant* seeking to *compel* it.

Comment

Should the reach of the arbitration clause depend on whether the alleged agent *wants* arbitration or not? On whether the alleged agent is plaintiff or defendant? In *Grand Wireless*, the agent was one of the two defendants, with her principal, and wanted to be joined in the defense of the case, in arbitration, with her principal. In *Ouadani*, the agent wanted to freelance and sue in court the party with whom its principal had an arbitration agreement. Did you find the distinction from *First Wireless* compelling? Was the agent's suit sufficiently distinct from the principal-agent relationship?

IV. Veil-Piercing/Alter Ego

Under the veil-piercing/alter ego theory, the corporate relationship between a parent and its subsidiary is sufficiently close as to justify piercing the corporate veil and holding one corporation legally accountable for the actions of the other. In such situations, a corporation that is a non-party to an arbitration agreement can be compelled to arbitration.

Keystone Shipping Co. v. Textport Oil Co.

782 F. Supp. 28 (S.D.N.Y. 1992)

EDELSTEIN, District Judge:

Background

Petitioner Chas. Kurz & Co., Inc. ("Kurz") owns the United States flag tanker Valley Forge (the "vessel"), which it operates through an affiliated company, petitioner Keystone Shipping Corporation ("Keystone"). In April 1991, respondent Texport Oil Company ("Texport") chartered the vessel to carry gasoline blending stocks from a United States Gulf port to an east coast port. The contract, which was signed by Kurz and Texport, but not by Keystone, provided that "any and all disputes and differences of whatever nature arising out of this Charter shall be put to arbitration" in New York. The parties agree that at all times Keystone acted as agent for its disclosed principal Kurz.

After delivery of the cargo, a dispute arose among petitioners, respondent and GATX Terminals Corporation, which stored the cargo, concerning the cargo's condition. Texport sued the vessel *in rem,* GATX, Kurz and Keystone in Texas state court. With the consent of the parties, the case was removed to the Southern District of Texas. The case was then transferred to the District of New Jersey.

On July 2, 1991, Kurz and Keystone served a demand for arbitration on Texport. While Texport agreed to arbitrate its dispute with Kurz, it refused to arbitrate its conflict with Keystone. Texport reasoned that because Keystone did not sign the contract that contains the arbitration clause, Keystone had no right to compel arbitration. Keystone and Kurz have petitioned this Court for an order directing Texport to arbitrate its action with Keystone. Keystone also seeks a stay of its litigation with Texport pending arbitration.

Discussion

Section 4 of the Federal Arbitration Act (the "Act") provides that:

> A party aggrieved by the alleged failure, neglect or refusal of another to arbitrate under a written agreement may petition any United States District Court... for an order directing that such arbitration proceed in the manner provided for in such agreement. 9 U.S.C. § 4.

The Second Circuit has held that "in an appropriate situation, the corporate veil may be pierced and a party may be held bound to arbitrate as the signatory's alter ego." *Interocean Ship Co. v. National Shipping and Trading Corp.,* 523 F.2d 527, 537 (2d Cir. 1975), *cert. denied,* 423 U.S. 1054, 46 L. Ed. 2d 643, 96 S. Ct. 785 (1976); *see McAllister Bros., Inc. v. A & S Transp. Co.,* 621 F.2d 519 (2d Cir. 1980) (non-signatory bound to arbitration agreement because contract expressly provided that companies affiliated with signatory are contractually bound); *Wren Distrib., Inc. v. Phone-Mate, Inc.,* 600 F. Supp. 1576, 1579 (E.D.N.Y. 1985). Nevertheless, "corporate relationship alone does not provide a basis for allowing" a non-signatory to enforce the arbitration clause. *Fried, Krupp, GmbH v. Solidarity Carriers, Inc.,* 674 F. Supp. 1022, 1027 (S.D.N.Y.), *aff'd without opinion,* 838 F.2d 1202 (2d Cir. 1987). The corporate bond necessary is one where "the parent corporation so dominates and controls the affairs of its subsidiary that the subsidiary cannot be said to have any independent existence or will of its own." *Coastal States Trading, Inc. v. Zenith Navigation, S.A.,* 446 F. Supp. 330, 336–37 (S.D.N.Y. 1977). Moreover, "absent findings of fraud or bad faith, a corporation ... is entitled to a presumption of separateness from a sister corporation ... even if both are controlled by the same individuals." *American Renaissance Lines, Inc. v. Saxis S.S. Co.,* 502 F.2d 674, 677 (2d Cir. 1974). Keystone has not alleged that it enjoys the type of relationship with Kurz that justifies piercing the corporate veil. Keystone alleges only that the companies are affiliated. A lone allegation of mere affiliation, however, does not suggest, let alone prove, that Kurz controls Keystone or that they are essentially one entity. Accordingly, this Court cannot pierce the corporate veil and permit Keystone, a non-signatory, to enforce the arbitration agreement between Kurz and Texport.

V. Third-Party Beneficiary

A non-signatory third-party beneficiary under an agreement containing an arbitration provision may compel arbitration against signatories of the arbitration agreements, and a third-party beneficiary of an arbitration may similarly be compelled to arbitrate. Here again, state contract law rules apply, and the courts will look to whether the contract containing the arbitration clause must reflect an intent to confer a direct benefit on the third party.

Flexi Van Leasing, Inc. v. Through Transp. Mut. Ins. Ass'n

108 F. App'x 35 (3d Cir. 2004)

POLLAK, District Judge.

Flexi-Van Leasing, Inc. ("Flexi-Van"), a lessor of chassis and related shipping equipment, appeals from the District Court's order dismissing Flexi-Van's lawsuit against Through Transport Mutual Insurance Association, Ltd. ("the Association") and Thomas Miller (Americas) Inc. ("Thomas Miller") and compelling the parties to submit their insurance coverage dispute to arbitration. We have jurisdiction pursuant to 28 U.S.C. § 1291, and we affirm.

I.

Because the parties are familiar with the facts, we recite only those necessary to aid in understanding our decision. Flexi-Van, a Delaware corporation with its principal place of business in New Jersey, leases intermodal chassis and generator sets to container shipping lines. Intermodal chassis are specialized trailers used to transport cargo containers over American roadways; generator sets attach to the underside of intermodal chassis and provide power to refrigerated containers being transported by road. From 1995 to 1997, Flexi-Van executed eleven leases for chassis and generator sets to Cho Yang Shipping Co., Ltd. ("Cho Yang"), a Korean corporation with its United States headquarters in New Jersey and, at the time, one of the world's largest container shipping lines. Each lease contained a provision requiring Cho Yang to obtain and maintain "'All Risk' Physical Damage insurance" equal to the replacement value of the equipment leased.

In accordance with its obligations under the leases, Cho Yang obtained an insurance policy from the Association, a Bermudan mutual indemnity insurance association managed in London. The policy provided coverage for the total loss, including constructive loss, of the equipment. A clause in the policy provides that "if any difference or dispute shall arise between you (or any other person) and the Association arising out of or in connection with any insurance provided by the Association . . . , it shall be referred to arbitration in London." Joint Appendix ("J.A.") at 158 (Policy § G4, P 2.1). The policy also directs that the arbitration proceedings shall be subject to English law, and that no other legal proceedings upon such a dispute may be maintained until the dispute has been referred to arbitration and the award has become final. *See* J.A. at 158 (Policy § G4, PP 2.2, 2.3). "You" is defined by the policy as "an Assured and any Co Assured and Joint Assured under the Assured's insurance." J.A. at 163 (Policy § G5). The policy designates Cho Yang as a "Co-Assured" and its subsidiary, Cho Yang America, Inc., as an "Assured." Flexi-Van is not named in the policy as an insured party of any type.

Cho Yang began to experience financial difficulties in late 2000, and failed to make the timely payment of rental fees and maintenance and repair charges to Flexi-Van under the leases. By letter dated April 16, 2001, Flexi-Van notified Cho Yang that it was in default of the leases and demanded the immediate return of the equipment. Flexi-Van then conducted recovery operations at terminals, truck depots, storage facilities, and rail yards across the United States, but was unable to recover all of its equipment.

Flexi-Van filed a breach of contract action against Cho Yang in the United States District Court for the District of New Jersey on May 4, 2001, seeking the return of the equipment and damages. In July 2001, Cho Yang filed for liquidation in the Republic of Korea, but never filed for bankruptcy in the United States. Flexi-Van ultimately obtained a default judgment against Cho Yang on January 4, 2002, in the amount of $12,287,970.32. According to Flexi-Van, approximately $1 million of the default judgment represented the value of equipment that had been lost, stolen, or damaged beyond repair while on lease to Cho Yang. Flexi-Van soon learned that Cho Yang's liabilities vastly exceeded its assets, and that Flexi-Van would not receive any further payments from Cho Yang to satisfy the default judgment.

Meanwhile, on August 29, 2001, Flexi-Van had submitted a claim to the Association under the policy for the value of the lost chassis and generator sets. In a letter dated October 2, 2001, Thomas Miller, the Association's general correspondent for its members in the Americas, formally denied the claim on behalf of the Association. The letter asserted that Flexi-Van had no right to assert a direct claim, because it was "not an insured or loss payee" under the policy. J.A. at 184.

On May 13, 2002, Flexi-Van filed suit against the Association and Thomas Miller (collectively, "appellees") in the Union County, New Jersey, Superior Court. The appellees removed the action to the United States District Court for the District of New Jersey under 9 U.S.C. § 205, a provision of the Federal Arbitration Act implementing the Convention on the Recognition and Enforcement of Foreign Arbitral Awards, June 10, 1958, 3 U.S.T. 2517 ("Convention"), *reprinted as note following* 9 U.S.C. § 201. In federal court, the appellees moved to compel arbitration and dismiss, arguing that the policy required Flexi-Van to arbitrate its claim in London. Flexi-Van then amended its complaint to allege that its claim was governed by New Jersey's direct action statute, N.J.S.A. § 17:28-2.

The District Court initially denied, without an opinion, the appellees' motion to compel arbitration and dismiss. Upon the appellees' motion for reconsideration, the District Court reversed itself and granted the motion on July 31, 2003, ordering the parties to submit to arbitration and dismissing the action with prejudice. Ruling from the bench, the District Court found that (1) New Jersey's direct action statute did not supersede the policy's arbitration clause; (2) Flexi-Van was a third-party beneficiary of the policy and thus bound by its arbitration clause; and (3) the Association was not an "unauthorized insurer" subject to restrictions under New Jersey law on its ability to litigate this matter. Flexi-Van appealed.

II.

Flexi-Van argues that the District Court erred by compelling Flexi-Van to submit to arbitration without first making a finding that Flexi-Van was bound by the policy's arbitration clause. Generally speaking, a party cannot be required to participate in arbitration, rather than adjudication, of a dispute unless it has agreed to submit that dispute, or disputes of like nature, to the arbitral process. *See United Steelworkers of America v. Warrior & Gulf Navigation Co.*, 363 U.S. 574, 582, 4 L. Ed. 2d 1409, 80 S. Ct. 1347 (1960). Flexi-Van was not a signatory to the insurance policy, nor was it listed in the policy as an "Assured," a "Joint Assured," or a "Co-Assured."

However, we have recognized that non-signatories to an arbitration agreement may be bound by that agreement through the application of "traditional principles of contract and agency law." *E.I. DuPont de Nemours & Co. v. Rhone Poulenc Fiber & Resin Intermediates, S.A.S.*, 269 F.3d 187, 194–95 (3d Cir. 2001). One such traditional principle, applicable in the arbitration context, is the principle that a third-party beneficiary is bound by the terms of a contract where its claim arises out of that contract. *Id.* at 195; *see also Jansen v. Salomon Smith Barney, Inc.*, 342 N.J. Super. 254, 776 A.2d 816, 820 (N.J. Super. Ct. App. Div. 2001) ("Nonsignatories of a contract . . . may . . . be subject to arbitration if the nonparty is an agent of a party or a third party beneficiary to the contract") (internal quotations omitted).

In *Sandvik AB v. Advent International Corp.*, 220 F.3d 99 (3d Cir. 2000), this court held that a party could not be required to submit to arbitration before the district court determined that the party was bound to a valid arbitration agreement. *Id.* at 107. Flexi-Van argues that, under *Sandvik*, the District Court should not have ordered Flexi-Van to submit to arbitration, because it never determined that Flexi-Van was a loss payee, joint insured, co-insured, or third-party beneficiary under the policy. The record suggests otherwise. Ruling from the bench, the District Court stated that Flexi-Van "stands in the shoes of Cho Yang, or [is] a third-party beneficiary of the insurance policy taken by Cho Yang. That insurance [policy] calls for arbitration in the United Kingdom." J. A. at 29. The District Court thus made the requisite finding that Flexi-Van, as either a subrogee of Cho Yang or a third-party beneficiary of the policy, was bound by the policy's arbitration clause.

III.

For the foregoing reasons, we will affirm the District Court's order granting the appellees' motion to compel arbitration and motion to dismiss.

* * *

N.A. Rugby Union LLC v. United States Rugby Football Union

442 P.3d 859 (Colo. 2019)

JUSTICE GABRIEL delivered the Opinion of the Court.

The "'critical fact' that determines whether a nonsignatory is a third-party beneficiary is whether the underlying agreement 'manifest[s] an intent to confer *specific legal rights* upon [the nonsignatory].'" *Ouadani v. TF Final Mile LLC*, 876 F.3d 31, 39 (1st Cir. 2017) (quoting *InterGen N.V. v. Grina*, 344 F.3d 134, 147 (1st Cir. 2003)). Nonsignatories who are intended third-party beneficiaries of an agreement containing an arbitration clause are bound by that agreement. *See id.*; *see also Everett*, 929 P.2d at 12 ("A third-party beneficiary may enforce a contract only if the parties to that contract intended to confer a benefit on the third party when contracting; it is not enough that some benefit incidental to the performance of the contract may accrue to the third party.").

Here, the Sanction Agreement did not confer—and could not have conferred—specific legal rights on RIM because at the time that Agreement was signed, RIM did not exist. Moreover, to the extent that the Sanction Agreement envisioned a future conferral of rights or benefits on RIM, those rights or benefits would have been bestowed by way of a separate agreement between RIM and PRO Rugby, not by way of the Sanction Agreement. Accordingly, the record does not support plaintiffs' assertion that RIM was a third-party beneficiary of the Sanction Agreement and therefore is bound by that Agreement's arbitration provision.

VI. Estoppel

Among the more frequently used means for bringing in third parties is estoppel. When can a party who has allegedly—and we stress the "allegedly" here, because that is a test the courts use—benefited from a contract that contains an arbitration agreement be forced to arbitrate pursuant to that agreement? Keep in mind again the critical role here of contract law principles. Estoppel means that having taken one position, you cannot then take a different one, especially where the other party relies on your first position. In the age of click-through agreements and online services, estoppel has particular vibrancy. Have you ever borrowed a friend's password to order something off "their" website?

A.D. v. Credit One Bank, N.A.

885 F.3d 1054 (7th Cir. 2018)

RIPPLE, Circuit Judge. A.D., by and through her mother, Judith Serrano, brought this putative class action under the Telephone Consumer Protection Act.

She seeks compensation for telephone calls placed by Credit One Bank, N.A. ("Credit One") to her telephone number in an effort to collect a debt that she did not owe. After discovery, Credit One moved to compel arbitration and to defeat A.D.'s motion for class certification based on a cardholder agreement between Credit One and Ms. Serrano. The district court granted Credit One's motion to compel arbitration but certified for interlocutory appeal the question whether A.D. is bound by the cardholder agreement. We granted A.D.'s request for permission to appeal. *See* 28 U.S.C. § 1292(b). We now reverse the district court's grant of Credit One's motion to compel arbitration and remand for further proceedings consistent with this opinion. A.D. is not bound by the terms of the cardholder agreement to arbitrate with Credit One, and she has not directly benefited from the cardholder agreement such that equitable principles convince us to apply the arbitration clause against her.

I. BACKGROUND

A.

In 1991, Congress amended the Communications Act of 1934 to address "the advent of automated devices that dial up to 1,000 phone numbers an hour and play prerecorded sales pitches." *Moser v. FCC*, 46 F.3d 970, 972 (9th Cir. 1995). The amending statute, the Telephone Consumer Protection Act ("TCPA"), makes it unlawful to use an "automatic telephone dialing system or an artificial or prerecorded voice" to call a cell phone without "the prior express consent of the called party." 47 U.S.C. § 227(b)(1)(A). An individual who provides her cell phone number to a creditor through a credit application "reasonably evidences prior express consent . . . to be contacted at that number regarding the debt." *Rules & Regulations Implementing the Tel. Consumer Prot. Act of 1991*, 23 FCC Rcd. 559, 564 (FCC 2008).

The TCPA provides a private right of action for individuals to claim that their rights under the TCPA have been violated. *See* 47 U.S.C. § 227(b)(3). Successful plaintiffs may recover the greater of the amount of (1) actual damages or (2) $500 for each violation, meaning each phone call. *Id.*

Ms. Serrano opened a credit card account with Credit One in 2003. In 2010, she used A.D.'s cell phone to access her Credit One account by calling Credit One and providing her account number and the last four digits of her social security number. Using caller ID capture software, Credit One attached A.D.'s cell phone number to Ms. Serrano's account.

Ms. Serrano later fell behind on her credit card payments, and Credit One began calling the telephone numbers previously stored with her account in an attempt to collect the debt. In her complaint, A.D. alleges that, in the course of this collection process, Credit One repeatedly called her about her mother's debt. Specifically, A.D. alleges that she received a good number of calls from Credit One in October and November 2014.

Upon opening her account with Credit One, Ms. Serrano had signed a standard cardholder agreement. This agreement included, among other terms, an arbitration clause and class action waiver, which stated:

> **Agreement to Arbitrate:**
>
> You and we agree that either you or we may, without the other's consent, require that any controversy or dispute between you and us (all of which are called "Claims"), be submitted to mandatory, binding arbitration. This arbitration provision is made pursuant to a transaction involving interstate commerce, and shall be governed by, and enforceable under, the Federal Arbitration Act (the "FAA"), 9 U.S.C. § 1 et seq., and (to the extent State law is applicable), the State law governing this Agreement.
>
> Claims subject to arbitration include not only Claims made directly by you, but also Claims made by anyone connected with you or claiming through you, such as a co-applicant or authorized user of your account, your agent, representative or heirs, or a trustee in bankruptcy.
>
> If you or we require arbitration of a particular Claim, neither you, we, nor any other person may pursue the Claim in any litigation, whether as a class action, private attorney general action, other representative action or otherwise.

When A.D. first filed this action, Credit One was not aware that it had a cardholder agreement with her mother. A.D. did not state in her complaint that her mother was the probable target of Credit One's phone calls (although she was listed as A.D.'s guardian *ad litem* in the complaint). After eighteen months of discovery, and after reviewing its own records, Credit One finally realized that its caller ID capture system had added A.D.'s phone number to its database when Ms. Serrano used A.D.'s phone to access her account. At that point, Credit One sought to compel arbitration with A.D. based on the arbitration clause in Ms. Serrano's cardholder agreement.

The only evidence that A.D. ever used Ms. Serrano's Credit One credit card was Ms. Serrano's deposition testimony that, on at least one occasion, Ms. Serrano had preordered smoothie drinks for her daughter and herself from a stand in the local mall and had sent A.D. to pick them up. She had instructed A.D. to pay for the smoothies with her Credit One card. This transaction occurred in 2014, when A.D. was fourteen years old.

The district court ruled with Credit One that A.D. was bound by the cardholder agreement's arbitration clause. In its view, even though A.D. had not signed the cardholder agreement, she must be considered an "Authorized User" under its terms. Therefore, continued the court, she is bound by the arbitration clause under the "direct benefits estoppel" theory. Under this theory, explained the court, a person should not receive a benefit under a contract while, at the same time, repudiating a disadvantage under the contract. The court then reasoned that the cardholder agreement had allowed A.D., when picking up the drinks ordered by her mother, to represent to the store that Credit One would pay for the purchase. She therefore had benefited from the cardholder agreement between her mother and Credit One. Having accepted a benefit under the contract, the district court concluded, she must accept the burden of the arbitration clause.

Because it concluded that the arbitration clause in the cardholder agreement was applicable, the court stayed the case pending the outcome of arbitration. A.D. filed a motion to reconsider, or, in the alternative, to certify the arbitration question for interlocutory appeal under 28 U.S.C. § 1292(b). The district court denied the motion to reconsider but granted the motion to certify the ruling for interlocutory appeal. In certifying the question for interlocutory appeal, the court noted that "[t]here is a substantial ground for difference of opinion because the contours of the arbitration-by-estoppel doctrine in the Seventh Circuit are unclear." We later granted a petition for certification.

II. DISCUSSION

We review a district court's ruling on a motion to compel arbitration de novo. *Scheurer v. Fromm Family Foods LLC*, 863 F.3d 748, 751 (7th Cir. 2017). Any findings of fact underlying that decision are reviewed for clear error. *Id.* As we noted in *Scheurer*, "arbitrability may depend on equitable doctrines such as waiver and estoppel, which may require a court to resolve issues such as prejudice and reliance." *Id.* at 752 n.2. We review a district court's decision to apply an equitable doctrine for an abuse of discretion, and "nothing about arbitration would seem to call for a different approach." *Id.*

The general rule is that non-signatories are not bound to arbitration agreements. *See Zurich*, 417 F.3d at 687. We will enforce an arbitration agreement against a non-signatory if the party seeking to compel arbitration can show that an exception to this general rule applies. *Id.*

The direct benefits estoppel doctrine applied by the district court is one such exception. *See id.* To determine whether an exception applies to make "a contract, including an arbitration agreement, . . . enforceable by or against a non-party," we look to "traditional principles of state law." *Scheurer*, 863 F.3d at 752 (quoting *Arthur Andersen LLP v. Carlisle*, 556 U.S. 624, 631, 129 S. Ct. 1896, 173 L. Ed. 2d 832 (2009)); *see also Warciak v. Subway Rests., Inc.*, 880 F.3d 870, 872 (7th Cir. 2018). Here, the cardholder agreement specifies that Nevada law applies to disputes arising under the contract, and the parties have not suggested that any other law is applicable.

From these observations, the analytical framework that we must follow in our resolution of this matter becomes evident. We first must determine whether A.D. is bound by the arbitration clause. If she is not, we must determine whether Nevada law nevertheless would bind her under the direct benefits estoppel theory.

B.

We first examine whether, under ordinary principles of contract law, A.D. is bound by the arbitration clause.

Credit One submits that A.D. is bound by the cardholder agreement as an Authorized User. The cardholder agreement provides a mechanism for cardholders to designate other individuals as Authorized Users of their accounts:

> **3. AUTHORIZED USER:** At your request, we may, at our discretion, issue an additional card in the name of an Authorized User with your credit card account number. If you allow someone to use your Account, that person will be an Authorized User. By designating an Authorized User who is at least fifteen years of age, you understand that: 1) you will be solely responsible for the use of your Account and each card issued on your Account including all charges and transactions made by the Authorized User and any fees resulting from their actions to the extent of the credit limit established for the Account; 2) the Authorized User will have access to certain account information including balance, available credit and payment information; 3) we reserve the right to terminate the Card Account privileges of an Authorized User by closing your Account and issuing you a new account number; 4) the Account may appear on the credit report of the Authorized User. . . . ; 5) the Authorized User can make payments, report the card lost or stolen and remove him or herself from the Account; 6) you can request the removal of the Authorized User from your Account via mail or telephone.
>
> **Authorized User Annual Participation Fee:** An Authorized User Annual Participation Fee of $19.00 will be imposed for issuing a card in the Authorized User's name. This Fee will be assessed annually in the month the Authorized User was added to the account.

Notably, by its terms, the arbitration clause specifically applies to claims "made by anyone connected with" the account holder, "such as a co-applicant or authorized user" of the account.

The district court held that because Ms. Serrano told A.D. to use the credit card to pick up the smoothies, Ms. Serrano had made her an authorized user of the account. The court seemingly relied on the language from the cardholder agreement that "[i]f you allow someone to use your Account, that person will be an Authorized User."

In our view, the district court's analysis is difficult to square with the overall language of the cardholder agreement.

The cardholder agreement sets forth a *specific* procedure that an account holder must follow to add an authorized user to her account. This provision makes it clear that an individual does not become an Authorized User simply by *using* the credit card to complete the cardholder's transaction. Rather, the term clearly foresees an Authorized User as playing a far more durable role in the account.

In order to designate a person as an Authorized User, an account holder must notify Credit One that she wishes to add an Authorized User to the account, so that Credit One can issue a card in the Authorized User's name. The Authorized User has many of the same rights under the cardholder agreement as the account holder and can use the card to complete her own transactions, not just those of the account holder. The durability of the arrangement is also made clear by the nineteen-dollar fee imposed on the account holder for adding an Authorized User. Furthermore, and most importantly for A.D.'s case, the Authorized User must be at least fifteen years old.

It is undisputed that neither Ms. Serrano nor Credit One followed any step of this process. Ms. Serrano did not request that Credit One add A.D. as an Authorized User. Credit One did not send A.D. a card with her name on it (and in fact, Credit One was unaware of A.D.'s relationship to Ms. Serrano until eighteen months after A.D. filed this action). A.D. did not have any rights under the cardholder agreement that the contract gives to true Authorized Users. Credit One never assessed Ms. Serrano the nineteen-dollar annual fee for adding an Authorized User. Indeed, A.D. was fourteen years old at the time of the smoothie transaction and, therefore, not even eligible to become an Authorized User under the cardholder agreement.

Although this analysis seems straightforward, we turn to examine two possible arguments to the contrary. First, the arbitration clause of the cardholder agreement does not capitalize "authorized user." This style might suggest that a different meaning should be attributed to the term in the arbitration clause from the one prescribed for the rest of the contract. Secondly, Credit One submits that the Authorized User clause creates more than one category of Authorized User: those who are Authorized Users because the account holder "allow[s] [them] to use [the] Account," and those who are "at least fifteen years of age" and subject to all of the rights and responsibilities identified in the Authorized User provision.

Neither the contract language read as a whole nor the governing law supports these arguments. Even if we were to accept, for the sake of argument, that the contract creates multiple categories of Authorized Users (or "authorized users," as the arbitration clause reads), and even if someone can become one kind of authorized user just by using the credit card, Credit One's position cannot surmount two major stumbling blocks. First, as we have noted earlier, it is a fundamental principle of arbitration law that "a party cannot be required to submit to arbitration any dispute which he has not agreed so to submit." *United Steelworkers of Am. v. Warrior & Gulf Navigation Co.*, 363 U.S. 574, 582 (1960). A.D. simply did not consent to arbitrate with Credit One. More fundamentally, A.D. did not have legal capacity to enter into a contractual relationship with Credit One. A.D. was a minor at the time of the smoothie transaction. Under applicable state law, minors lack capacity to enter into contracts and can disaffirm their obligations under contracts formed before they reach the age of eighteen. Moreover, A.D. certainly engaged in an act of dis-affirmation by filing this lawsuit and asserting her status as a minor. Assuming, for the sake of argument, that A.D. formed *any* kind of contractual relationship with Credit One before she reached the age of majority, she has disaffirmed any obligation under that contractual relationship that she might have had.

Credit One also argues that A.D. has waived any argument that she does not qualify as an Authorized User under the terms of the agreement or that, as a minor, she has a right to disaffirm the contract. It is true that, at the district court level, A.D. did not make any specific arguments about the scope of the authorized user provision of the cardholder agreement.

Estoppel is an equitable doctrine that prevents a non-signatory "from refusing to comply with an arbitration clause 'when it receives a "direct benefit" from a contract containing an arbitration clause.'" *Id.* at 661 (quoting *Int'l Paper Co. v. Schwabedissen Maschinen & Anlagen GMBH*, 206 F.3d 411, 418 (4th Cir. 2000)). Credit One maintains that A.D. *directly* benefited under the cardholder agreement because Ms. Serrano asked her to make purchases with the card. According to Credit One, "A.D. obtained the same type of contractual benefit as Serrano," which is the ability to use the credit card to make purchases. But any "benefit" that A.D. received with respect to the credit card was limited to following her mother's directions to pick up the smoothies that her mother had ordered previously. This limited direction derived from the mother-daughter relationship.

Conclusion

For the reasons set forth in the foregoing opinion, we reverse the judgment of the district court and remand for further proceedings. A.D. may recover the costs of this appeal.

Nicosia v. Amazon.com, Inc.

384 F. Supp. 3d 254 (E.D.N.Y. 2019)

MEMORANDUM AND ORDER

GLASSER, Senior United States District Judge:

On January 30, 2013 and April 19, 2013, Plaintiff Dean Nicosia went on Amazon.com and placed orders of 1 Day Diet, a product marketed as a weight-loss supplement, which contained the harmful compound sibutramine. The account from which these purchases were made was held in his wife's name and was previously enrolled in a program called "Amazon Mom." As described below, to enroll in Amazon Mom, a user must accept the "Amazon Prime Terms and Conditions," which incorporate an arbitration provision. Plaintiff subsequently brought a putative class action against Defendant Amazon.com, Inc. ("Amazon"), asserting that Amazon's sales of 1 Day Diet violated the Consumer Product Safety Act, 15 U.S.C. § 2051, et seq., and state law.

After Amazon moved to compel arbitration, the matter was referred to the Hon. Lois Bloom for a Report and Recommendation ("R&R"), which advised that the motion be granted.

The Court adopts the R&R's conclusion that arbitration be granted, finding that it is supported by its careful analysis of the facts and the law which is manifest, and not impugned by Plaintiff's objections to it, which are denied.

BACKGROUND

I. Factual Background

1. *The Nicosias' Amazon.com Account*

Plaintiff Dean Nicosia ("Plaintiff") resides with his wife, Annemarie Nicosia ("Annemarie"), and his family in North Carolina. Before March 2012, he and his family lived in New York.

"Amazon.com" is an online retail website and marketplace through which consumers may purchase hundreds of millions of products. In order to make a purchase on Amazon.com, a customer must create an Amazon account or use an existing account. It is not possible to check out as a "guest" on Amazon.com.

On June 9, 2008, an Amazon account was created in the name of "Annemarie Nicosia" (the "Account"). At all relevant times, the Account was used by both Plaintiff and Annemarie, although Plaintiff relied on Annemarie to manage it.

2. *The Amazon Conditions of Use*

It is undisputed that, at the time the Account was created, Amazon's Conditions of Use ("Conditions of Use" or "COU") did not contain an arbitration provision. On August 19, 2011, the following arbitration clause was added to the COU:

> **Any dispute or claim relating in any way to your visit to Amazon.com or to products or services sold or distributed by Amazon or through Amazon.com will be resolved by binding arbitration, rather than in court,** except that you may assert claims in small claims court if you qualify.

The arbitration provision was also accompanied by a class action waiver, which provides that "**any dispute resolution proceedings will be conducted only on an individual basis and not in a class, consolidated or representative action.**" Finally, the COU contains a choice-of-law clause specifying that "the Federal Arbitration Act, applicable federal law, and the laws of the state of Washington . . . will govern these Conditions of Use and any dispute of any sort that might arise between you and Amazon."

3. *Amazon Prime and Amazon Mom*

Amazon Prime ("Amazon Prime" or "Prime") is a bundle of services, including free two-day shipping, discounted one-day shipping, and access to movies and television shows, offered to Amazon accountholders for an annual membership fee.

Amazon Mom ("Amazon Mom" or "Mom") was a free membership program launched by Amazon in September 2011 which offered limited, promotional Prime benefits. By signing up for Mom, an accountholder could receive discounts on diapers and baby products, as well as three months of free two-day shipping. By purchasing products on Mom, the accountholder could extend their free two-day shipping benefits to up to one year.

Amazon Mom was explicitly promoted as a kind of free trial for Prime. In the promotional FAQ, the free shipping benefits were expressly referred to as "Amazon Prime benefits." Extending these benefits by making qualifying purchases on Mom gave the accountholder "more free months of Prime." (*Id.*). The Amazon Mom sign-up page contained text reading: "**After your free period, you'll be charged $79 for a year of Amazon Prime and Amazon Mom benefits. . . .**" Bolded language near the sign-up button read: "**Amazon Prime membership continues until cancelled. If you do not wish to continue for $79/year, select 'Do not renew' from Your Account before your annual renewal date.**" Annemarie testified that, before this lawsuit was brought, she believed in her mind that Prime and Mom were the same program. Amazon's Associate General Counsel for Marketing, too, viewed Mom as an "an addition" to Prime, whose "underlying program is a Prime program."

4. *September 30, 2011: The Account enrolls in Amazon Mom*

Annemarie testified that, while she was pregnant with her second son, she heard about Amazon Mom from a friend, Albert Dennis ("Dennis"), who told her that the program offered diapers at a "good price." Annemarie gave Dennis her password, and Dennis told her that he was signing her up for Mom "to get diapers and formula if [she] needed it." On September 30, 2011, Dennis enrolled Annemarie in Mom with her "permission":

> "Q: And your friend Al Dennis told you, 'There's this Amazon.com Mom program where you can get a discount on diapers,' right?
>
> "A: Yes, sir.
>
> "Q: And that sounded pretty good to you?
>
> "A: Yes, sir.
>
> "Q: So your friend Al Dennis signed you up for that?
>
> "A: Yes, sir.
>
> "Q: And that was okay with you?
>
> "A: Yes, sir."

As of September 30, 2011, in order to sign up for Amazon Mom, a customer would be required to complete a two-step process. First, the customer would enter certain information about themselves and click a button that says "Continue." Directly above the "Continue" button was a line that read: "By clicking the **Continue** button, you acknowledge that you agree to the Amazon Mom Terms and Conditions." The underlined term was a hyperlink to the Amazon Mom Terms and Conditions ("Mom T&C"), which contained the following language:

> Welcome to the terms and conditions ("Terms") for Amazon Mom, which govern the Amazon Mom membership. Please note that your use of the Amazon.com website and the Amazon Mom membership are also governed by our Conditions of Use, . . . Amazon Prime Terms and Conditions, as well as all other applicable terms, conditions, limitations and requirements on the Amazon.com Web Site.

The Mom T&C further provide: "Once your free shipping benefits have expired, you may continue to receive Amazon Prime shipping benefits by enrolling in Amazon Prime for an annual membership fee of $79."

Second, the customer was taken to a page where they must input their payment and billing information and click a button that says, "Sign up for Amazon Mom." Directly below this button was text that read: "By signing up, you acknowledge that you have read and agree to the Amazon Prime Terms and Conditions. . . ." The underlined term was a link to the Amazon Prime Terms and Conditions ("Prime T&C"), which contained the following language:

> Welcome to the terms and conditions ("Terms") for Amazon Prime. These Terms are between you and Amazon Services LLC and/or its affiliates ("Amazon.com" or "Us") and govern our respective rights and obligations. The Terms, together with applicable terms and conditions related to any promotional offers provided to you for use with Prime, constitute the entire agreement between you and Amazon.com related to the Prime membership. Please note that your use of the Amazon.com website and Prime membership are also governed by our Conditions of Use and Privacy Notice, as well as all other applicable terms, conditions, limitations, and requirements on the Amazon.com website, all of which (as changed over time) are incorporated into these Terms. If you sign up for a Prime membership, you accept these terms, conditions, limitations and requirements.

The underlined "Conditions of Use" text was a hyperlink to the then-current version of the COU, which contained the arbitration clause reproduced above.

5. *October 11, 2012: Annemarie signs up for a paid subscription of Prime*

In September or October 2012, Annemarie's membership in Amazon Mom expired. On October 11, 2012, she signed up for a paid subscription for Prime using her Account. Plaintiff became aware that the Account was enrolled in Prime some time in 2012.

6. *January and April 2013: Plaintiff purchases 1 Day Diet*

1 Day Diet was a product promoted and sold for weight loss. On January 30, 2013 and April 19, 2013, Plaintiff made two purchases of 1 Day Diet, using Annemarie's

Account. In order to execute each purchase, Plaintiff would have been required to click through a checkout page which contained a button that said, "Place your order," and text which read, "By placing your order, you agree to Amazon.com's privacy notice and conditions of use", with the underlined "conditions of use" text hyperlinked to the COU.

In November 2013, the U.S. Food and Drug Administration ("FDA") issued a press release stating that "laboratory analysis confirmed that '1 Day Diet' contains sibutramine," a "controlled substance that was removed from the market in October 2010 for safety reasons." The FDA has advised consumers using 1 Day Diet to "stop using this product immediately and throw it away." Plaintiff testified that, in January 2014, after having a conversation with friends about 1 Day Diet, he performed a Google search of the product and came upon the November 2013 FDA press release. Nevertheless, he did not contact Amazon to request a return or refund.

DISCUSSION

I. Substantive Legal Principles

3. *Hybridwrap agreements*

While "new commerce on the Internet . . . has not fundamentally changed the principles of contract," *Register.com, Inc. v. Verio, Inc.*, 356 F.3d 393, 403 (2d Cir. 2004), it has exposed courts to novel applications of those principles. Many online agreements merely present the user with a hyperlink to their terms and conditions, rather than displaying the terms themselves. "Where an offeree does not have actual notice of certain contract terms, he is nevertheless bound by such terms if he is on inquiry notice of them and assents to them through conduct that a reasonable person would understand to constitute assent." *Starke v. SquareTrade, Inc.*, 913 F.3d 279, 289 (2d Cir. 2019). A website user is deemed to be on inquiry notice of contract terms so long as the "design and content" of the webpage renders "existence" of those terms "reasonably conspicuous." *Nicosia*, 834 F.3d at 233.

Some websites—such as Amazon—prompt the user to manifest their assent to particular terms by engaging in some dual-purpose action, such as creating an account, *see, e.g.*, *Meyer v. Uber Technologies, Inc.*, 868 F.3d 66, 70–71, 81–82 (2d Cir. 2017); *Berkson v. Gogo LLC*, 97 F. Supp. 3d 359, 372–373, 374–375 (E.D.N.Y. 2015), executing a purchase order, *see, e.g.*, *Nicosia*, 834 F.3d at 227, 241–242, or downloading an application, *see, e.g.*, *Specht v. Netscape Communications Corp.*, 306 F.3d 17 (2d Cir. 2002). In determining whether these "hybridwrap" terms should be enforced, the focal point of the inquiry is whether "a reasonably prudent offeree would know that the [terms and conditions] governed," such that their performance of the action (such as creating the account or executing the purchase) "manifested implied assent to the additional terms." *Nicosia*, 834 F.3d at 236. Courts will give effect to hybridwrap terms where the button required to perform the action manifesting assent (*e.g.*, signing up for an account or executing a purchase) is located directly next to a hyperlink to the terms and a notice informing the user that, by clicking the button, the user is agreeing to those terms. *See, e.g.*, *May v. Expedia, Inc.*, No. 16-CV-1211 (RP) (ML), 2018 U.S. Dist. LEXIS 167118, 2018 WL 4343445, at *3 (W.D. Tex. Jul. 19, 2018), *report and recommendation adopted*, 2018 U.S. Dist. LEXIS 167121, 2018 WL 4343427 (W.D. Tex. Aug. 27, 2018). The more the hybridwrap design diverges from this basic layout—such as by placing the notice further away from the action button, cluttering the screen with potentially distracting content, or omitting the language explicitly saying that by performing the action the user agrees to be bound by the terms—the less likely courts are to find that inquiry notice has been provided. *See, e.g.*, *Nicosia*, 834 F.3d at 236–237 (holding that Amazon's checkout page was not sufficient as a matter of law to place a user on inquiry notice of the COU, because the notice and accompanying hyperlink was "not directly adjacent to the 'Place your order' button so as to indicate that a user should construe clicking as acceptance," and the page was spatially cluttered with unrelated options and promotions which rendered the notice not "conspicuous in light of the whole webpage"); *Lee v. Intelius Inc.*, 737 F.3d 1254, 1261–62 (9th Cir. 2013) (declining to enforce hybridwrap terms, where the website did not explicitly say that the user was agreeing to the terms and conditions); *Wilson v. Huuuge, Inc.*, 351 F. Supp. 3d 1308, 1314–15 (W.D. Wash. 2018) (notification merely stated "Read our Terms of Use," rather than explicitly indicating that downloading the application meant agreeing to the terms of use, and the notice was not located near the download button), *appeal filed*, No. 18-36017 (9th Cir.).

II. Plaintiff's Evidentiary Objections

1. *Amazon Prime sign-up flow*

Amazon did not produce a copy of the Prime sign-up flow that a customer would have seen on October 11, 2012, claiming that it "does not have a depiction" of these webpages. Instead, Amazon provided several "current and historical examples" of the Prime sign-up screens. But the record shows that none of these screens could have been the ones viewed by Annemarie when she re-enrolled in Prime in 2012. Nor does the record even contain a statement that these Prime sign-in screenshots are *similar* to the one Annemarie would have seen. As such, the Court finds that the Prime sign-up screens produced by Amazon lack relevance. Therefore, the Court cannot consider them in adjudicating this motion.

2. *Amazon Mom sign-up flow*

Plaintiff objects that the Mom sign-up flow produced by Amazon bears a 2012 copyright notice, and therefore could not have been the exact screen that Dennis viewed when the Account enrolled in Mom on September 30, 2011. But Ressmeyer's declaration establishes that the same sign-up flow "was in place on September 30, 2011." Therefore, Plaintiff's objections to the Mom sign-up images are denied.

3. *Ressmeyer's description of the Prime sign-up process*

Other than the Prime sign-up images, which the Court disregards as irrelevant, *see* Discussion II.1, *supra*, the only other evidence pertaining to the 2012 Prime sign-up process is Ressmeyer's description of the process in her declaration.

However, reliance on these statements would contravene the best evidence rule, codified in Federal Rule of Evidence 1002, which provides that "[a]n original writing is required in order to prove its content unless these rules or a federal statute provide otherwise." *See Rui Chen v. Premier Financial Alliance, Inc.*, No. 18-CV-3771 (YGR), 2019 U.S. Dist. LEXIS 10280, 2019 WL 280944, at *1 n. 3 (N.D. Cal. Jan. 22, 2019) (finding that declaration of defendant's attorney describing online arbitration agreement was precluded by the best evidence rule). Although an exception to the best evidence rule provides that "[a]n original is not required and other evidence of the content of a writing, recording, or photograph is admissible if . . . all the originals are lost or destroyed, and not by the proponent acting in bad faith," Fed. Evid. 1004, Amazon has not provided even the faintest excuse for its failure to produce the 2012 Prime sign-up flow. *See Bobcar Media, LLC v. Aardvark Event Logistics, Inc.*, 354 F. Supp. 3d 375, 382 (S.D.N.Y. 2018) (where "nothing in the declaration[] [or] deposition testimony . . . addresses what happened to the original [document], . . . the 'factual predicates' for invoking the Rule 1004 exception are not satisfied").

Even if Ressmeyer's description of the Prime sign-up process were not precluded by the best evidence rule, it would not be sufficient to establish, *as a matter of law*, that Annemarie entered into a binding arbitration agreement when she signed up for Prime. *See Rui Chen*, 2019 U.S. Dist. LEXIS 10280, 2019 WL 280944, at *3 ("Defendants have not offered evidence explaining the design and content of the webpage. . . . [T]he Court cannot determine other factors that might contribute to determining plaintiffs' notice of the terms, such as the size of the font or other aspects of the appearance and presentation of the terms online"). The declaration is certainly probative as to how the Prime sign-up screen would have appeared in 2012, but it is not conclusive. At most, it raises a question of fact as to the appearance of the Prime sign-up screen in 2012. *See id.* Under the FAA, such questions must be submitted to trial. *See* 9 U.S.C. § 4; *Nicosia*, 834 F.3d at 229; *Bensadoun*, 316 F.3d at 175. Because the Court finds that arbitration can be compelled on other grounds, it need not give further consideration to the 2012 Prime sign-up process or Ressmeyer's descriptions thereof.

IV. Plaintiff is Equitably Estopped from Avoiding Arbitration

The preceding analysis shows that Annemarie entered into a binding arbitration agreement by signing up for Amazon Mom and that the agreement covered purchases of products, whether Prime-eligible or not, made after Annemarie re-enrolled in Prime in 2012. Thus, if it were Annemarie herself who purchased 1 Day Diet, she would be bound to arbitrate this dispute. The question at the heart of Amazon's "derivative rights" argument is whether the Amazon Mom Arbitration Agreement can be circumvented when it is a third party (*i.e.*, the Plaintiff), rather than Annemarie herself, who makes purchases on the Account.

To ask this question is to answer it. Password-sharing is a "ubiquitous, useful, and generally harmless" activity that "millions of people" engage in, *United States v. Nosal*, 844 F.3d 1024, 1048 (9th Cir. 2016) (Reinhardt, J., dissenting), but it cannot be used as a back door to undermine the contractual landscape governing internet commerce. Plaintiff protests that "Amazon anthropomorphizes [the] Prime account" and that it is "individuals . . . not inanimate objects," who "consent to arbitration." But the entire purpose of an "account" on a platform like Amazon is to assume virtual personhood—to enter into contracts and, crucially, to *remain bound* by the contracts to which it has previously, and with due authority, agreed. If the validity of these contract terms waxed and waned depending on the identity of the human user behind the screen, it would impose a cloud of uncertainty over any contract formed over the internet. Any individual could avoid the terms of a website by simply logging on to a friend's or relative's account instead of creating their own. Common sense dictates that this could not possibly be the rule; and where common sense goes, the law must follow.

Although Plaintiff himself did not enter into the arbitration agreement described above, "a nonsignatory party may be bound to an arbitration agreement if so dictated by the 'ordinary principles of the relevant contract principles of contract and agency. *See Arthur Andersen v. Carlisle*, 556 U.S. 624, 630 (2009) (the FAA does not "purport[] to alter background principles of state contract law regarding the scope of agreements (including the question of who is bound by them)").

Several district courts have considered facts analogous to this case and have held that a third-party user of an account is bound by the terms governing the account. *See Roberts v. eBay*, No. 14-CV-4904 (HMH) (MGB), 2017 WL 9289378, at *8 n. 6 (D.S.C. Jul. 29, 2017); *Burcham v. Expedia, Inc.*, No. 07-CV-1963 (CDP), 2009 U.S. Dist. LEXIS 17104, 2009 WL 586513, at *4 (E.D. Mo. Mar. 6, 2009); *Motise v. America Online, Inc.*, No. 04-CV-1494, 2005 U.S. Dist. LEXIS 36991, 2005 WL 1667658, at *2 (E.D. Va. Jun. 24, 2005) (*Motise II*); *Motise v. America Online, Inc.*, 346 F. Supp. 2d 563, 565–566 (S.D.N.Y. 2004) (*Motise I*). In *Motise I*, the case upon which all of the others rely, the Court held that the plaintiff, who used his stepfather's AOL account, was bound by a forum-selection provision appearing in the account's member agreement. *See* 346 F. Supp. 3d at 566. The court reasoned that the plaintiff was a "sub-licensee" of his stepfather and "could not, therefore, have greater rights" than his stepfather. *Id.*; *see also Metropocs Wireless, Inc. v. Virgin Mobile USA, L.P.*, No. 08-CV-1658 (SAF), 2009 U.S. Dist. LEXIS 88527, 2009 WL 3075205, at *22 (N.D. Tex. Sept. 25, 2009) (observing that the situation in *Motise I* was "analogous to an assignment [of the license] because the user [stood] in the shoes of the account holder to assume his place in the contract with the service provider"). The court further held that "[a]ny other conclusion would permit individuals to avoid the Defendant's Terms of Service simply by having third parties create accounts and then using them as the Plaintiff did." *Motise I*, 346 F. Supp. 2d at 566. The Court agrees with the result of *Motise I*, but it finds that the doctrine of equitable estoppel rather than the licensee-sublicensee metaphor employed by that court, more accurately captures the legal principles at work.

2. *Direct benefits estoppel*

In the arbitration context, most courts have applied a modified test for equitable estoppel, known as the "direct benefits test," pursuant to which a nonsignatory may be compelled to arbitrate where it "'knowingly accepts the benefits' of an agreement with an arbitration clause." *MAG Portfolio Consult, GMBH v. Merlin Biomed Group LLC*, 268 F.3d 58, 61 (2d Cir. 2001) (quoting *Deloitte Noraudit A/S v. Deloitte Haskins & Sells*, 9 F.3d 1060, 1064 (2d Cir. 1993)); *see also Mundi v. Union Sec. Life Ins. Co.*, 555 F.3d 1042, 1046 (9th Cir. 2009) ("[A] nonsignatory may be held to an arbitration clause 'where the nonsignatory "knowingly exploits the agreement containing the arbitration clause despite having never signed the agreement"'") (quoting *Comer v. Micor, Inc.*, 436 F.3d 1098, 1101 (9th Cir. 2006)); *Payne v. Amazon.com, Inc.*, No. 17-CV-2313 (PMD), 2018 U.S. Dist. LEXIS 135020, 2018 WL 4489275, at *6-*7 (D.S.C. Jul. 25, 2018) (applying Washington law); *Townsend v. Quadrant Corp.*, 173 Wash. 2d 451, 461, 268 P.3d 917 (Wash. 2012); 21 Williston on Contracts § 57:19 (4th ed.); 1 Alt. Disp. Resol. § 8:8 (4th ed.). The direct benefits test "closely approaches the paradigm for [traditional] equitable estoppel," although it is not a "perfect overlap." Kingsley, 820 F. Supp. 2d at 1024.

Consider the facts in *Bridge v. Credit One Financial*, 14-CV-1512 (LDG) (NJK), 2016 U.S. Dist. LEXIS 44626, 2016 WL 1298712 (D. Nev. Mar. 31, 2016), a case which in all relevant respects resembles this one. The plaintiff's mother held an account at the defendant bank, Credit One. *See* 2016 U.S. Dist. LEXIS 44626, [WL] at *1. In order to establish this account, she was required to sign a "cardholder agreement," which included an arbitration provision. *See* 2016 U.S. Dist. LEXIS 44626, [WL] at *1–2. She underwent surgery and was hospitalized, and the plaintiff, concerned about her finances in the event that she should pass away, called Credit One's toll-free automated information system in order to inquire about her account. *See* 2016 U.S. Dist. LEXIS 44626, [WL] at *1. The automated system prompted the plaintiff to enter "your sixteen digit card number" and "the last four digits of your social security number," to which the plaintiff entered his mother's card number and social security number digits. *Id.* Upon successful authentication of the account and social security information, the plaintiff's was able to access the information he sought, but his phone number became linked to his mother's account. *See id.* After his mother's account became delinquent, calls were made to recover the debt, including to the plaintiff's phone number. *See id.* The plaintiff sued under the Telephone Consumer Protection Act, and the bank moved to compel arbitration. Although the plaintiff himself did not sign the arbitration agreement, the court held that he "benefitted from the agreement by calling Credit One, inputting his mother's validation information, and gaining access to his mother's financial information." 2016 U.S. Dist. LEXIS 44626, [WL] at *3. The court found that plaintiff's claims were so related to the underlying cardholder agreement that he could be estopped from avoiding the arbitration provision. *See id.*

Although the court in *Bridge* analyzed Credit One's motion to compel under the direct benefits test rather than traditional equitable estoppel, it is easy to see how the same result could have been reached under the latter theory. When the plaintiff provided his mother's personal information to Credit One's automated information system, he implicitly represented that he was the true accountholder. Credit One justifiably relied on that representation when it subsequently provided the information plaintiff sought.

This case is essentially no different from *Bridge*. When Plaintiff accessed the Annemarie Account and used it to place purchases of 1 Day Diet, he, like the plaintiff in *Bridge*, implicitly represented that he was the true accountholder. Like the plaintiff in *Bridge*, he directly benefited from the making of that representation, in that it allowed him to step into the shoes of his wife and enjoy the same contractual rights she enjoyed, *viz.*, the right to place an order on Amazon.com. Because plaintiff knowingly accepted the benefit of Annemarie's contractual relationship with Amazon, he must also be held to the arbitration clause that governs that relationship.

For these reasons, under either a traditional theory of equitable estoppel or direct benefits estoppel, Plaintiff is bound by the Amazon Mom Arbitration Agreement.

Ouadani v. TF Final Mile LLC

876 F.3d 31 (1st Cir. 2017)

LYNCH, Circuit Judge.

Equitable Estoppel

Equitable estoppel "precludes a party from enjoying rights and benefits under a contract while at the same time avoiding its burdens and obligations." *InterGen*, 344 F.3d at 145. Federal courts generally "have been willing to estop a *signatory* from avoiding arbitration with a nonsignatory when the issues the nonsignatory is seeking to resolve in arbitration are intertwined with the agreement that the estopped party has signed." *Id.* (quoting *Thomson-CSF*, 64 F.3d at 779). But courts have been reluctant to estop a nonsignatory attempting to avoid arbitration. Id. at 145- 46. In the latter scenario, "estoppel has been limited to 'cases [that] involve non-signatories who, during the life of the contract, have embraced the contract despite their non-signatory status but then, during litigation, attempt to repudiate the arbitration clause in the contract.'" *Id.* at 146 (quoting *E.I. DuPont de Nemours & Co. v. Rhone Poulenc Fiber & Resin Intermediates, S.A.S.*, 269 F.3d 187, 200 (3d Cir. 2001)).

Dynamex claims that Ouadani knowingly sought and obtained benefits from the Agreement because he performed the "Contracted Services" pursuant to the Agreement for compensation. It also argues that the Agreement would be "useless" without drivers like Ouadani to perform the contemplated services. These arguments are unpersuasive because the benefits of the arbitration clause of the Agreement accrue to the contracting signatories—Dynamex and SBS—not to Ouadani. Ouadani can hardly be said to have "embraced" the Agreement when he was unaware of its existence.

Dynamex presses another, similar argument: Ouadani "knowingly exploit[ed]" the Agreement by asserting claims that can only be determined by reference to the Agreement. In particular, Dynamex argues that Ouadani's claims "are premised on his position that he performed the 'Contracted Services'" on behalf of SBS, and that "such a relationship could only exist through the Agreement" because Ouadani acknowledges that "he associated with [SBS] and was paid directly by [SBS]."

To support this argument, Dynamex cites two distinguishable California cases concerning an arbitration clause involving SuperShuttle International ("SuperShuttle"), a provider of door-to-door airport shuttling services. Dynamex first cites *Kairy v. Supershuttle International Inc.*, No. 08-CV-02993, 2012 U.S. Dist. LEXIS 134945, 2012 WL 4343220 (N.D. Cal. Sept. 20, 2012), a case in which former SuperShuttle franchisees who drove for SuperShuttle, as well as nonsignatory secondary drivers who drove for SuperShuttle pursuant to a relationship with the franchisees, brought wage-and-hour claims against SuperShuttle. 2012 U.S. Dist. LEXIS 134945, [WL] at *1, *9. There, the district court compelled arbitration against the secondary drivers, even though they were not signatories to the relevant franchise agreements, because they "knowingly exploited the rights and privileges granted under the [franchise] agreements" by "participat[ing] actively and for compensation in the rights and duties described in the [franchise agreements]." 2012 U.S. Dist. LEXIS 134945, [WL] at *9. Notably, the secondary drivers' federal and state labor law claims required the drivers to "specifically perform[] under the [franchise agreements]." *Id.*

Dynamex also cites *Supershuttle International, Inc. v. Aysov*, Nos. CIV 535204-08, 2015 WL 10388413 (Cal. Super. Dec. 23, 2015). In that case, a California state trial court compelled arbitration against nonsignatory SuperShuttle drivers because they were found to have received financial benefits from the franchise agreement, which provided the only basis for their assertion of state labor law claims against SuperShuttle. *Id.* at *2.

These cases are distinguishable. Unlike the secondary SuperShuttle drivers, Ouadani did not "knowingly exploit[]" or "participate actively and for compensation," *Kairy*, 2012 U.S. Dist. LEXIS 134945, 2012 WL 4343220, at *9, in the rights described in the Agreement—he did not even know that the Agreement existed. And the Agreement does not provide the only basis for Ouadani's claims, which stem from his arrangement with Dynamex.

With these contractual concepts in mind, return to the four scenarios in this chapter.

Notes and Questions

1. Is there a federalism issue here? One court has criticized the applicability of this viewpoint to third-party questions: "Federal policy favoring arbitration does not apply in a situation like this when a court is determining whether an agreement to arbitrate exists. Rather, it applies when a court is determining whether the dispute in question falls within the scope of the arbitration agreement already found to exist." *California Fina Group, Inc. v. Herrin*, 379 F.3d 311, 316 n.6 (9th Cir. 2004). *See generally* Bruce E. Meyerson, *But I Didn't Sign an Arbitration Agreement!*, BRUCEMEYERSON.COM, http://www.brucemeyerson.com/articles/documents/ArbitrationandNonsignatories.pdf.
2. *Third Parties and Severability*. In keeping with our "for every *what* question there is a *who* question," who should decide the question of whether an arbitration clause reaches a third party? In the severability rules reviewed in Chapter 3, we learned that questions about the contract are for the arbitrator, but questions about the arbitration clause itself are generally reserved for the court. Is that delineation still appropriate where the arbitration clause is being reviewed but along traditional contract law principles and not arbitration principles? *See Bridas v. Turkmenistan*, 345 F 3d 347, 353 (5th Cir. 2003); *see also Perez v. Welch*, 960 F.2d 534, 537 (5th Cir 1992).
3. Is the answer to the above question determinable, like all arbitrability questions, by use of an allocation/*First Options* provision? Could this be resolved simply by providing in a contract that "any question as to the applicability of this arbitration provision to third parties shall be determined by the arbitrator and not the courts"? Might parties be reluctant to draft such provisions to avoid potentially indicating that they were contemplating bringing others in under their arbitration tent? Would the inclusion of such a provision be credible and competent evidence that they were cognizant of this concern and thus be evidence of party intent? Or would they simply be viewed as being prudent?

PRACTICE POINTERS

1. *Drafting*. Now that you know the reach of arbitration can be expanded by the courts or arbitrators to include nonparties, how would you approach the drafting of an arbitration clause differently? Is it possible to exclude third parties, or will contract rules simply outweigh party consent?

2. *Scheduling.* If you think that the claims are going to, or should, involve a third party, how might you handle the first conference with the arbitrator?
3. *Consensus.* Keep in mind that the rules of party consensus still apply even in this unorthodox situation, and so there is the possibility that you can resolve the question presented in (2) above by negotiation and consensus.

Chapter 10

Injunctions

We have seen that a fundamental advantage of arbitration is the ability to "build your own courthouse." Instead of buying whatever car one finds on the lot, parties can customize the color, the seats, and the sound system: they can pick the number of arbitrators, the way in which arbitration handles discovery, and the myriad of other details we reviewed in Chapter 1. Then, once the arbitration panel is chosen and empowered, the parties can further particularize their arbitration, working at the scheduling conference with the arbitrator to set briefing schedules, discovery parameters, the type of award to be rendered, and a further host of other specifics. By sharp contrast, very little of this control is available to litigants in court.

But what if, while this entire process is being negotiated and then finally formalized, the very reason for the case risks rotting away? While all of that "building your own courthouse" activity is going on, the real world continues to march forward, and some of that marching forward can run the risk of extinguishing a party's existence.

Injunctions exist for precisely that circumstance. An injunction freezes the status quo of a case pending its ultimate determination on the merits. As you likely saw in your civil procedure course, injunctions are necessary to protect parties who cannot wait for a case to meander its way to a conclusion. If injunctions are sometimes a necessary part of the litigation process because courts can move too slowly, are they not an even *more* necessary feature of arbitration, which, since the "courthouse" must be "built,", moves more slowly in the beginning compared to litigation? Here we come to another inherent conflict in arbitration. The interplay we have seen so far between courts and arbitration has been limited to procedural issues. Courts intrude, as the cases show, on issues such as arbitrability, third-party discovery, and arbitrator partiality. They intrude further, as we will see in Unit III of this book, at the enforcement stage. One area where courts generally do *not* intrude is upon the merits of the dispute itself. This makes perfect sense since the parties agreed to send their merits dispute to arbitration.

Therein lies the conflict. Injunctions generally take place in court. Arbitrations take place outside of court. Why should a party who has expressly bargained away her right to sue in court, and been given in return a promise not to be sued in court, suddenly find herself a defendant in, of all places, a court—and on an injunction of all things? Injunctions are the comets of litigation: they are a short, concentrated burst of frenetic activity. They can be expensive, emotional, and detailed. Where arbitration takes a great deal of time to get going (by the time an arbitrator is selected, schedules are set, and other preliminary matters attended to), injunctions happen (when granted) virtually upon demand. Where arbitration rests on party consensus on matters such as briefing, discovery, and other stops on the dispute resolution road, court injunctions take their cues on these issues from the rules of civil procedure and from express precedent on the requirements for a successful injunction. Injunctions are, in short, everything that arbitration is not.

Which is precisely why some disputes with arbitration clauses wind up in injunctions anyway. There are times when arbitration is not equipped to deal with particular disputes between the parties. Where a party can demonstrate the classic injunction standards of likelihood of success, the balance of harms favoring its remedy, and especially an irreparable injury without prompt action, the presence of an arbitration clause generally will not bar immediate equitable relief in court. Injunctions remain, as they should, difficult to obtain, just as they are in any civil case. An arbitration clause should impose further judicial wariness, but as seen below, arbitration clauses do not act as a complete block on an injunction motion.

This chapter will address the evolution of the law of injunctions in arbitration. We will see how, originally, courts were hostile to any form of judicial intervention in the middle of the arbitration, and then see how courts became comfortable with acting where the arbitration would otherwise be futile—a so-called "hollow formality" —unless immediate court action were taken to freeze the status quo while still allowing the final decision on the merits to be made by the arbitrator. From there, we will turn to the modern arbitration clause, which usually embraces the possibility of injunctions in an arbitration and may provide that such interim relief be confined to specific areas of the parties' dispute or contract. We will examine particular problems and drafting points that such clauses raise. Finally, we will conclude with a study of injunctions in the arbitration itself, particularly when permitted by the arbitration's governing institutional rules.

I. Early Judicial Hostility to Court-Imposed Injunctions in an Arbitration

Injunctions are not contrary to the express language of the Federal Arbitration Act. In commanding that cases with arbitration clauses be stayed, the FAA focuses on a particular phase of litigation. Focus on the italics:

> If any suit or proceeding be brought in any of the courts of the United States upon any issue referable to arbitration under an agreement in writing for such arbitration, the court in which such suit is pending, upon being satisfied that the issue involved in such suit or proceeding is referable to arbitra-

> tion under such an agreement, shall on application of one of the parties *stay the trial of the action* until such arbitration has been had in accordance with the terms of the agreement, providing the applicant for the stay is not in default in proceeding with such arbitration.

9 U.S.C § 3 (emphasis added). Does the FAA's commandment to stay *trials* mean that *pre*-trial court proceedings fall outside of the mandatory stay and that injunctions can therefore proceed unimpeded?

CASE PREVIEW. In the case you are about to read, *Merrill Lynch, Pierce, Fenner & Smith, Inc. v. Hovey*, 726 F.2d 1286 (8th Cir. 1984), the United States Court of Appeals for the Eighth Circuit, relying on the *Moses Cone* line of cases, held that an arbitration clause precluded an injunction. Is this always the case? Can an injunction actually preserve the controversy for a later final resolution in arbitration? Consider, as you go forward, whether the hard and fast rule established here is correct.

Merrill Lynch, Pierce, Fenner & Smith, Inc. v. Hovey

726 F.2d 1286 (8th Cir. 1984)

LAY, Chief Judge.

Merrill Lynch, Pierce, Fenner & Smith, Inc. sought injunctive relief against five former employees to prevent their use of Merrill Lynch's records and their solicitation of Merrill Lynch clients. The employees counterclaimed seeking to compel arbitration under the Federal Arbitration Act, 9 U.S.C. §§ 1–4 (1982). The district court granted injunctive relief and refused to submit the dispute to arbitration. The employees have appealed.

As former account executives with Merrill Lynch, Ivan Hovey, Mary Wichmann, Bruce Markey, and Richard Kadry each signed employment agreements. The agreement provides, *inter alia*, that certain records "shall remain the property of Merrill Lynch at all times during my employment with Merrill Lynch and after termination of my employment . . . with Merrill Lynch" and prohibits former account executives from removing or retaining copies thereof; and it purports to prohibit these employees from "soliciting" clients of Merrill Lynch for one year after the termination of employment. The employees subsequently resigned from Merrill Lynch and joined E.F. Hutton, a competitor. The employees admit that they have retained some limited information entrusted to them by clients whom they had serviced while at Merrill Lynch. Moreover, the employees admit that they have solicited these customers while at E.F. Hutton. On appeal, we are not addressing whether this constitutes a breach of the employment agreement nor do we address the validity of the clauses that purport to prohibit this conduct. The issue presented on appeal is whether the dispute is subject to arbitration or whether Merrill Lynch may properly proceed in the federal district court.

II. Preliminary Injunction

In addition to determining that the controversy was nonarbitrable, the district court granted a preliminary injunction. We consistently have held that the grant of preliminary relief is within the district court's discretion. *Dataphase Systems, Inc. v. C L Systems, Inc.*, 640 F.2d 109, 114 (8th Cir. 1981); *Planned Parenthood of Minnesota, Inc. v. Citizens for Community Action*, 558 F.2d 861, 866 (8th Cir. 1977). In light of our determination that the controversy is arbitrable, however, we find that the issuance of injunctive relief abrogates the intent of the Federal Arbitration Act and consequently was an abuse of discretion. *Cf. Merrill Lynch, Pierce, Fenner & Smith, Inc. v. Scott*, No. 83-1480 (10th Cir. May 12, 1983) (summary order staying the injunction pending arbitration).

Merrill Lynch urges this court to continue the preliminary injunction during the arbitration procedures. Merrill Lynch asserts that the continuance of the injunction is necessary to avoid irreparable harm and to assure the viability of an adequate remedy at law. The cases cited by Merrill Lynch support the contention that injunctions can be granted to preserve the status quo. However, in view of our determination that the Federal Arbitration Act applies, we decline to pass on these contentions. The parties have not alleged that the contract provides for or contemplates injunctive relief along the lines granted. Accordingly, the Act directs the court to stay the judicial action. 9 U.S.C. § 3.

The congressional intent revealed in the Arbitration Act is to facilitate quick, expeditious arbitration. In *Moses H. Cone Memorial Hospital v. Mercury Construction Corp.*, 460 U.S. 1, 103 S. Ct. 927, 74 L. Ed. 2d 765 (1983), the district court had stayed ruling on a party's motion to compel arbitration because a similar action was proceeding in state court. Reversing, the Supreme Court held:

> This refusal to proceed was plainly erroneous in view of Congress's clear intent, in the Arbitration Act, to move the parties to an arbitrable dispute out of court and into arbitration as quickly and easily as possible. . . . [The Federal Arbitration Act calls] for an expeditious and summary hearing, with only restricted inquiry into factual issues. . . . The [district court's] stay thus frustrated the statutory policy of rapid and unobstructed enforcement of arbitration agreements.

Moses H. Cone, 103 S. Ct. at 940–41 (footnote omitted). Here, the judicial inquiry requisite to determine the propriety of injunctive relief necessarily would inject the court into the merits of issues more appropriately left to the arbitrator. *See Prima Paint Corp. v. Flood & Conklin Manufacturing Co.*, 388 U.S. 395, 18 L. Ed. 2d 1270, 87 S. Ct. 1801 (1967) (issue of fraud in inducement of contract was for arbitrator); *see also Buffalo Forge Co. v. United Steelworkers of America, AFL-CIO*, 428 U.S. 397, 412, 49 L.

Ed. 2d 1022, 96 S. Ct. 3141 (1976). In *Buffalo Forge*, the Court refused to enjoin a strike pending arbitration of the validity of the strike. The Court recognized that sanctioning judicial intervention at this preliminary stage would eviscerate the intent of arbitration agreements. *Id. at 412.*

We find this compelling authority to hold that, where the Arbitration Act is applicable and no qualifying contractual language has been alleged, the district court errs in granting injunctive relief. In doing so, we sustain not only "the plain meaning of the statute but also the unmistakably clear congressional purpose that the arbitration procedure, when selected by the parties to a contract, be speedy and not subject to delay and obstruction in the courts." *Prima Paint Corp.*, 388 U.S. at 404.

For the reasons stated above, we reverse and remand to the district court for proceedings consistent with the determinations here.

Comment

The Eighth Circuit's holding in *Hovey* is an outlier. Other courts hold that an injunction is an appropriate form of relief where the court was asked to act not to decide the merits, but simply to preserve the status quo—for example, where a party was likely to be insolvent by the time of the final arbitration award.

Performance Unlimited v. Questar Publishers

52 F.3d 1373 (6th Cir. 1995)

MILBURN, Circuit Judge.

This is a case of first impression in this circuit involving the question of whether a district court can issue a preliminary injunction under *§ 3 of the Federal Arbitration Act,* 9 U.S.C. § 3 (1982), when the parties to this action have agreed that arbitration "shall be the sole and exclusive remedy for resolving any disputes between the parties arising out of or involving [the] Agreement" sued upon. Plaintiff Performance Unlimited, Inc. ("Performance") appeals the district court's order denying its motion for a preliminary injunction, filed pursuant to 28 U.S.C. §§ 1332(a)(1), 2201, and 2202, which would have required defendant Questar Publishers, Inc. ("Questar") to pay royalties to Performance while their contract dispute was resolved in arbitration. On appeal, the issues are (1) whether the district court erred in finding that it was precluded from issuing a preliminary injunction because of the mandatory arbitration provision in the parties' licensing agreement and (2) whether the district court erred in finding that Performance did not satisfy the four factors considered in its decision to grant or deny a preliminary injunction. For the reasons that follow, we reverse and remand.

This is an action for breach of contract, for a declaration of the parties' contractual rights, and for a preliminary injunction arising from the nonpayment of royalties pursuant to a licensing agreement between Performance and Questar. The royalties which are at the core of the parties' dispute stem from the publication of *The Beginner's Bible*, a compilation of children's bible stories.

Don Wise, the president of Performance, developed the idea of publishing a series of children's bible stories, illustrated with drawings that would appeal to small children and aimed toward beginning readers. This concept was developed into a series of bible story books which were written by Karyn Henley and were sold under the name *Dovetales*. James R. Leininger invested in Performance in order to develop and promote the *Dovetales* books.

Eventually, however, Wise and Leininger agreed to separate their activities. As a result, Leininger received ownership of the copyrights and trademarks in the *Dovetales* product. Leininger licensed the rights to publish the *Dovetales* stories to Performance. In turn, Wise entered into a license agreement, a sublicense, with Questar to publish a book containing all of the original *Dovetales* stories along with some additional stories written by Karyn Henley, titled *The Beginner's Bible*. The license agreement between Performance and Questar is dated June 22, 1989, and is the subject of this action.

Pursuant to the license agreement, Questar published and began to sell *The Beginner's Bible*. Further, the license agreement obligated Questar to make semiannual royalty payments to Performance based upon the sales of *The Beginner's Bible*. Que- star regularly made the royalty payments to Performance until July of 1994. However, in a letter, dated July 28, 1994, Questar informed Performance that Performance had breached the license agreement. Furthermore, Questar refused to pay the accrued royalties to Performance, indicating in its letter that it wished to initiate a "mediation/arbitration process pursuant to paragraph 11 of the [license] agreement." J.A. 20. Instead, on July 29, 1994, Questar opened an account, the "Beginner's Bible Royalty Escrow Account," at the United States National Bank of Oregon in Sisters, Oregon, and deposited $184,484.94, the accrued royalties, into that account. J.A. 65.

The license agreement between Questar and Performance includes a provision for resolution of disputes. Paragraph 11 of the agreement provides in relevant part:

> The Licensor [Performance] and the Publisher [Questar] agree that God, In His Word, forbids Christians to bring lawsuits against other Christians in secular courts of law . . . and that God desires Christians to be reconciled to one another when disputes of any nature arise between them. . . .
>
> In their resolution of any disputes that may arise under this Agreement, each party agrees that the provisions for mediation and arbitration set forth below shall be the sole and exclusive remedy for resolving any disputes between the parties arising out of or involving this Agreement.

> It is further agreed that the Licensor and the Publisher hereby waive whatever right they might otherwise have to maintain a lawsuit-against the other in a secular court of law, on any disputes arising out of or involving this Agreement.
>
> In the event of such a dispute, the Licensor and the Publisher agree to take the following steps, in the order indicated, until such a dispute is resolved:
>
> (1) the Licensor and the Publisher shall meet together, pray together, and purpose to be reconciled....
>
> (2) The Licensor and the Publisher shall invite other witnesses, who may have knowledge of the actual facts of the dispute or whose knowledge would be helpful in resolving the dispute, to meet together with both parties, to pray together, and to purpose to be reconciled....
>
> (3) Both the Licensor and the Publisher shall each appoint one person as a Mediator; these two persons chosen shall then appoint a third Mediator. The three Mediators shall together determine the process of mediation, to which the Licensor and the Publisher agree to comply, and shall be free to act as Arbitrators, to whose authority the Licensor and the Publisher agree to submit. The three Mediators shall also determine to what degree the Licensor and the Publisher shall be liable for all costs related to the mediation process.

On August 10, 1994, Performance filed a complaint in district court, asserting a claim of breach of contract based upon Questar's refusal to pay accrued royalties due and owing to Performance pursuant to the licensing agreement between the parties and seeking a declaration of the parties' rights under the agreement. At the same time that it filed its complaint, Performance filed a motion for a preliminary injunction, seeking to enjoin Questar from refusing to pay the royalties due and owing to Performance under the license agreement and directing that Questar pay the royalties to Performance as provided in the agreement. Questar filed a brief in opposition to the motion for a preliminary injunction on August 24, 1994.

Pursuant to the agreement of the parties, the motion for a preliminary injunction was submitted to the district court based upon the documentary evidence in the record. Oral argument on the motion was held before the district court on August 25, 1994; however, the parties presented no testimonial evidence to the district court at that time.

On September 2, 1992, the district court denied Performance's motion for a preliminary injunction. Specifically, in denying Performance's motion, the district court found that it need not address the issue of whether Performance was likely to succeed on the merits of its claim that Questar breached the license agreement, "because the agreement has a mandatory arbitration provision." J.A. 26. The district court further concluded that it should not involve itself in the merits of a dispute when the parties, in their agreement, have clearly provided that arbitration is the sole and exclusive means to remedy disputes.

In summary, the Court does not feel that Performance is likely to succeed on the merits given the mandatory arbitration provision in the agreement.

Furthermore, the district court stated that while it realized that the royalties [provided for in the licensing agreement] are necessary for the operation of Performance's business, ... because Performance has come to the Court with "unclean hands," the Court concludes it should not grant Performance's request for equitable relief even though Performance's business might suffer irreparable harm.

Performance argues that the district court erred in finding that it could not issue injunctive relief because of the mandatory mediation/arbitration provision in the agreement between the parties. Performance asserts that the district court's refusal to grant injunctive relief because of the mandatory arbitration provision is contrary to the rule adopted by the majority of the United States Circuit Courts of Appeals. Performance further asserts that injunctive relief is appropriate in this case to preserve the status quo pending the arbitration of the parties' dispute, because absent injunctive relief Performance will suffer irreparable harm; namely, the collapse of its business, which will render the process of arbitration a hollow and meaningless formality.

In its opinion, the district court acknowledged that this issue was one of first impression in the Sixth Circuit. The district court further acknowledged that a number of other Circuits have held that district courts may issue injunctive relief under appropriate circumstances pending arbitration. Nevertheless, the district court rejected that approach, concluding instead "that it should not involve itself in the merits of a dispute when the parties, in their agreement, have clearly provided that arbitration is the sole and exclusive means to remedy disputes." J.A. 27-18.

We begin our analysis by noting that this court stated long ago

> that the object and purpose of a preliminary injunction is to preserve the existing state of things until the rights of the parties can be fairly and fully investigated and determined.... The legal discretion of the judge or court in acting upon applications for provisional injunctions is largely controlled by the consideration that the injury to the moving party, arising from a refusal of the writ, is certain and great, while the damage to the party complained of, by the issuance of the injunction, is slight or inconsiderable.

American Fed'n of Musicians v. Stein, 213 F.2d 679, 682 (6th Cir.) (quoting *Blount v. Societe Anonyme du Filtre Chamberland Systeme Pasteur*, 53 F. 98, 101 (6th Cir. 1892)), *cert. denied*, 348 U.S. 873 (1954).

The issue of "whether the Arbitration Act deprives the district court of subject matter jurisdiction to enter preliminary injunctive relief is an issue of law subject to plenary review." *Ortho Pharmaceutical Corp. v. Amgen, Inc.*, 882 F.2d 806, 812 n.6 (3d Cir. 1989).

"The Federal Arbitration Act, 9 U.S.C. §§ 1–14 (1976), makes enforceable an agreement to arbitrate." "Federal law applies to enforcement of a duty to arbitrate, whenever interstate commerce is involved" as is the situation in this case. "Thus, the principle issue on appeal is whether § 3 of the Federal Arbitration Act, 9 U.S.C. § 3 (1982), absolutely precludes a district court from granting one party a preliminary injunction to preserve the status quo pending the arbitration of the parties' dispute." *Merrill Lynch, Pierce, Fenner & Smith, Inc. v. Bradley*, 756 F.2d 1048, 1050 (4th Cir. 1985).

The starting point for this inquiry is 9 U.S.C. § 3. Although we have not had occasion to interpret the meaning of § 3, a number of other Circuits have done so. In *Bradley*, the Fourth Circuit stated:

> Section 3 does not contain a clear command abrogating the equitable power of district courts to enter preliminary injunctions to preserve the status quo pending arbitration. Instead, § 3 states only that the court shall stay the "trial of the action"; it does not mention preliminary injunctions or other pre-trial proceedings. Certainly Congress knows how to draft a statute which addresses all actions within the judicial power. Furthermore, nothing in the statute's legislative history suggests that the word "trial" should be given a meaning other than its common and ordinary usage: the ultimate resolution of the dispute on the merits. See Senate Rep. No. 536, 68th Cong. 1st Sess. (1924); H.R. Rep. No. 96, 68th Congress., 1st Sess. (1924).

Bradley, 756 F.2d at 1052 (footnote omitted).

Based upon its analysis of § 3, the Fourth Circuit held that where a dispute is subject to mandatory arbitration under the Federal Arbitration Act, a district court has the discretion to grant a preliminary injunction to preserve the status quo pending the arbitration of the parties' dispute if the enjoined conduct would render that process a "hollow formality." The arbitration process would be a hollow formality where "the arbitral award when rendered could not return the parties substantially to the status quo ante." *Id.* at 1053–54.

Subsequently, in *Teradyne, Inc. v. Mostek Corp.*, 797 F.2d 43 (1st Cir. 1986), the First Circuit thoroughly analyzed the three Supreme Court decisions relied on by the Eighth Circuit in *Hovey* and rejected the position taken by the Eighth Circuit. In *Teradyne*, the First Circuit stated that as a result of its review of the three Supreme Court decisions relied on in *Hovey*, it saw "nothing in the Supreme Court's reasoning to indicate that the Court would be opposed to the issuance of an order designed to preserve the meaningfulness of an arbitration agreement." *Id.* at 50. The First Circuit further stated that it saw "no incompatibility between the Court's language and the availability of preliminary injunctive relief to preserve the meaningfulness of the arbitration process. The risk that the arbitrator will be unduly influenced by the court's prior ruling is offset by the necessity of preserving the status quo." *Id.*

Consequently, the First Circuit held:

> Having thus outlined our disagreement with both the reasoning and approach of the Eighth Circuit, we are persuaded that the approach taken by the Second, Fourth and Seventh Circuits should be followed. We hold, therefore, that a district court can grant injunctive relief in an arbitrable dispute pending arbitration, provided the prerequisites for injunctive relief are satisfied. We believe this approach reinforces rather than detracts from the policy of the Arbitration Act, which was most recently described by the Supreme Court in *Dean Witter Reynolds v. Byrd*, 470 U.S. 213, 105 S. Ct. 1238, 84 L. Ed. 2d 158 (1985): "passage of the Act was motivated first and foremost by a Congressional desire to enforce [arbitration] agreements into which parties had entered." 470 U.S. at ___, 105 S. Ct. at 1242. We believe that the congressional desire to enforce arbitration agreements would frequently be frustrated if the courts were precluded from issuing preliminary injunctive relief to preserve the status quo pending arbitration and, ipso facto, the meaningfulness of the arbitration process. Accordingly, we hold that it was not error for the district court to issue the preliminary injunction before ruling on the arbitrability of this dispute. 797 F.2d at 51 (footnote omitted).

After a thorough review of the relevant case law, we adopt the reasoning of the First, Second, Third, Fourth, Seventh, and arguably the Ninth, Circuits and hold that in a dispute subject to mandatory arbitration under the Federal Arbitration Act, a district court has subject matter jurisdiction under § 3 of the Act to grant preliminary injunctive relief provided that the party seeking the relief satisfies the four criteria which are prerequisites to the grant of such relief. We further conclude that a grant of preliminary injunctive relief pending arbitration is particularly appropriate and furthers the Congressional purpose behind the Federal Arbitration Act, where the withholding of injunctive relief would render the process of arbitration meaningless or a hollow formality because an arbitral award, at the time it was rendered, "'could not return the parties substantially to the status quo ante.'" *Bradley*, 756 F.2d at 1053 (quoting *Lever Bros. Co. v. International Chemical Workers Union, Local 217*, 554 F.2d 115, 123 (4th Cir. 1976).

Accordingly, we hold that the district court erred as a matter of law when it found that it could not enter preliminary injunctive relief in this case because the dispute between the parties was the subject of mandatory arbitration.

For the reasons stated, the district court's judgment denying Performance's motion for a preliminary injunction is REVERSED and the case is REMANDED to the district court for the issuance of a preliminary injunction consistent with this opinion.

II. Arbitration Clauses and Injunctions

We have studied repeatedly that consensus is the backbone of arbitration—but does it matter at all here? In neither of the two above cases, *Hovey* or *Performance*, did the court consider an arbitration clause that dealt with injunctions. One court denied an injunction, the other granted one, but both times without reference to what should always be the determining factor in assessing party intent: the agreement to arbitrate.

The modern trend is to deal up front with the subject of injunctions directly in the arbitration agreement. Most modern arbitration clauses therefore contain language along the following lines:

> *Injunctive Relief*: Notwithstanding the foregoing, each party shall be permitted to institute proceedings in a federal or state court of competent jurisdiction to seek temporary or preliminary injunctive relief to maintain the status quo in any dispute arising out of relating to this Agreement pending the resolution of that dispute through Arbitration.

This is called an injunction "carve-out" in an arbitration clause. The parties may further limit the carve-out and allow an injunction in only certain situations, such as a violation of a contractual agreement to protect trade secrets.

CASE PREVIEW. Three years after *Performance*, the Second Circuit had before it an arbitration clause where the parties had expressly consented to an injunction in particular circumstances. With consensus thus resolved, and a conceptual war between arbitration and litigation thus averted, the task for the court is the same as in any other injunction case: are the standards for an injunction met? When this happens, the courts will consider the classic elements of likelihood of success, irreparable injury, balancing of harms, and (in some jurisdictions) whether public policy favors an injunction.

American Express Fin. Advisors v. Thorley

147 F.3d 229 (2d Cir. 1998)

CALABRESI, Circuit Judge:

Must a district court, faced with a request for a preliminary injunction in a case whose underlying merits will ultimately be settled in arbitration, consider the merits of the injunction, or may it leave the question of temporary relief, like the ultimate resolution of the case, to the arbitrator? Plaintiff American Express, having begun arbitration proceedings against five of the defendants before us, sought a preliminary injunction pending the outcome of the arbitration. The district court declined to consider the petition on its merits and held that, in the circumstances of this case, the proper forum for plaintiff's request was arbitration. *American Express Fin. Advisors Inc. v. Thorley*, 971 F. Supp. 780 (W.D.N.Y. 1997). When American Express later renewed its motion and added the final defendant, the district court in a consolidated action once again denied the motion. We vacate the district court's order and remand for a consideration of the merits of the preliminary injunction.

Defendants are six financial planners who formerly practiced their trade as independent contractors affiliated with American Express. Under the terms of their contracts, the defendants agreed that in the event that they left American Express, they would not disclose confidential information that they had learned in the course of their work with American Express and they would refrain for a period of one year from soliciting customers whom they had served while with American Express. Between May and July of 1997, all six defendants left American Express. American Express alleges that since that time the defendants have been soliciting their former clients in violation of their contractual obligations. The contracts between American Express and each of the defendants expressly state that all disputes arising under those agreements are to be settled by arbitration before the National Association of Securities Dealers (NASD).

The contracts also specify, however, that American Express "is entitled to an injunction from a court of competent jurisdiction" to prevent continuing violations while arbitration is pending. On July 25, 1997, concurrently with its filing of a Statement of Claim before the NASD arbitrators, American Express filed a complaint against five of the defendants in the federal court for the Western District of New York. The complaint sought a preliminary injunction to prevent the defendants from continuing to solicit or transact business with clients whom they had served before leaving American Express.

Chief Judge Larimer, however, declined to issue a temporary injunction. He recognized that, as this Court held in *Roso-Lino Beverage Distribs., Inc. v. Coca Cola Bottling Co.*, 749 F.2d 124, 125 (2d Cir. 1984) (per curiam), the pendency of arbitration proceedings does not usually constitute a basis on which a district court can decline to consider the merits of a preliminary injunction. But he concluded that this case should be treated as an exception to the *Roso-Lino* rule because American Express could just as quickly obtain the same temporary equitable relief from the arbitrator as from a court. Chief Judge Larimer reasoned that a judicial proceeding would be a waste of time, thereby defeating a major purpose of arbitration. Noting the proarbitration policy of the Federal Arbitration Act, 9 U.S.C. §1 et seq. ("FAA"), which seeks to avoid costly litigation by resolving disputes in arbitration, he referred the question of temporary relief to the arbitrator. *See American Express*, 971 F. Supp. at 781–82. While Chief Judge Larimer commented on the merits, he made no formal decision as to them. American Express subsequently renewed its motion against the five original defendants and added an additional defendant. For the same reasons as before, the district court again denied the injunction.

The *Roso-Lino* rule, that courts should consider the merits of a requested preliminary injunction even where the validity of the underlying claims will be determined in arbitration, does not admit of the exception that the district court made in this case. As we explained in *Blumenthal v. Merrill Lynch, Pierce, Fenner & Smith, Inc.*, 910 F.2d 1049 (2d Cir. 1990), the expectation of speedy arbitration does not absolve the district court of its responsibility to decide requests for preliminary injunctions on their merits. *See id.* at 1052–54. Nor is this duty affected by the pro-arbitration policy manifested in the FAA. *Id.* at 1052, 1054.

In *Blumenthal,* we identified two reasons why such an exception should not be created. First, it would lead parties seeking injunctions to show that arbitral relief would be slow in coming, and such a showing would complicate the preliminary relief process. *See id.* at 1054. Since this process is supposed to be relatively streamlined, adding layers of procedure to it is generally unwise. This is especially so when the layers involve factors, like the possibility of delay, that are frequently speculative. *See id.* Second, temporary injunctions often foster rather than contradict the policy favoring arbitration. In many instances, it is by freezing the status quo that the meaningfulness of arbitration is best protected. *See id.* at 1053–54. For if events proceed unenjoined, the subject matter of arbitration may be irretrievably altered before an arbitral decision can be reached. *See id.*

In the present case, the contracts at issue explicitly state that the plaintiff is entitled to seek a temporary injunction in a court of competent jurisdiction while waiting for arbitration to occur. Accordingly, the matter is even clearer than it was in *Blumenthal.* To be sure, parties cannot by private agreement confer powers on the federal courts that those courts are barred from accepting. *See, e.g., CFTC v. Schor,* 478 U.S. 833, 850–51, 106 S. Ct. 3245, 92 L. Ed. 2d 675 (1986) (parties cannot, by consent, remedy defects in Article III jurisdiction). But where, as here, courts do have the authority to consider the merits of requested injunctions, a contractual provision stating that plaintiffs may seek such relief in a court of competent jurisdiction amply reaffirms what the law already directs.

In this case, then, the contractual language entitling American Express to seek a preliminary injunction in a court of competent jurisdiction locates the contracts squarely within the *Roso-Lino* line of cases. *See American Express Fin. Advisors, Inc. v. Makarewicz,* 122 F.3d 936, 940 (11th Cir. 1997) (construing, under Florida law, the same contract as validly permitting American Express to seek temporary judicial injunction pending arbitration), *cert. denied,* 140 L. Ed. 2d 469, 118 S. Ct. 1303 (1998); *Koob v. IDS Fin. Servs. Inc,* 213 A.D.2d 26, 31, 629 N.Y.S.2d 426 (N.Y. App. Div. 1995) (same, applying Minnesota law).

CONCLUSION

We therefore VACATE the order of the district court and REMAND for a decision on the merits of plaintiff's motion for a preliminary injunction pending arbitration—a decision that remains within the sound discretion of the district court.

PRACTICE POINTER. *Thorley* featured consensus in favor of an injunction where appropriate, so the result was to some degree easy—but what about the reverse: can parties outright prohibit any court from ever acting? Instead of conferring power to a court, can they be so adamant in their arbitration agreement as to insist that no matter the circumstances, no court can ever take action, interim or otherwise? Most authority suggests that an anti-injunction bar in an arbitration clause would *not* be enforceable. "To be sure, parties cannot by private agreement confer powers on the federal courts that those courts are barred from accepting. But where, as here, courts do have the authority to consider the merits of requested injunctions, a contractual provision stating that plaintiffs may seek such relief in a court of competent jurisdiction amply reaffirms what the law already directs." *American Express v. Thorley*, 147 F.3d 229 (2d Cir 1998).

III. Drafting and the Modern Approach to Injunction Carve-Out Clauses

So far, we have seen three different approaches to injunctions and arbitration:

1. The court denies injunctive relief on the view that a court injunction is inconsistent with arbitration (*Hovey*).
2. The court allows injunctive relief even without an injunction carve-out in the arbitration clause (*Performance*).
3. The parties provide for an injunctive carve-out in their arbitration clause, thus consenting to court intervention under certain prescribed circumstances (*Thorley*).

Within the third option, there are a number of drafting choices. The parties may elect to preserve the option of an arbitration for any emergency situation that would otherwise render the arbitration a "hollow formality." Or they may confine the arbitration option to alleged violations of only particular sections of their agreement.

Problem

You represent Lens Guys, a contact lens company which currently has a market share of 26%, with stores across the country. Lens Guys has noticed that a small company in the southwest called See Clearly, Ltd., has been picking up more and more business, apparently on the basis of a much more comfortable type of lens that See Cleary offers its customers. That lens was invented by Dr. Mary Baydo, who is also the 100% owner of See Clearly. Lens Guys wants to buy See Clearly before it becomes a direct threat—if you can't beat them, then acquire and own them. Obviously, a key part of the purchase would be Lens Guys having access to the See Clearly technology on the new type of lens.

Your law firm draws up a purchase agreement by which Lens Guys acquires the stock and all intellectual property rights of See Clearly. Section 8 of the purchase agreement is what is known as a "non-competition agreement," and provides that for a period of three years, Dr. Baydo cannot work for any contact lens business nor can she open any contact lens business of her own. Section 9 is what is known as a "confidentiality clause" and provides that none of the sellers may disclose any confidential information or trade secrets of their (former) business.

Your client, the owner of Lens Guys, was involved in complicated litigation several years ago and has vowed never to set foot in court again if he can help it. He has also, however, told you that See Clearly had a lot of other suitors, and he is worried that Dr. Baydo may get lured away despite having pocketed your client's millions in the sale. His express words to you were, "I don't want to be in court, but I sure didn't just pay $10 million in order to set Mary up with a new business!"

With those concerns in mind, how might you draft the arbitration clause? Would you have an injunction carve-out? Would you limit the carve-out to specific subject areas of the contract? Which areas? What are the advantages and disadvantages of that kind of limitation?

* * *

What happens when, instead of limiting a court's injunctive power to particular subject matters (such as trade secrets) or even to "emergencies" (like a trade secret or patent violation that can put your client out of business), the parties are broader and allow a court to impose "equitable relief"? The following article explores that problem.

A. Going Overboard on "Equitable" Relief

Benjamin J. Eichel & Matthew H. Adler, *Injunction Carve-Outs in Arbitration: Emergency Only, or All Equity Claims?*

36 ALTERNATIVES TO THE HIGH COST OF LITIG. 1 (Jan. 2018)

Arbitration may end sooner and more efficiently than litigation, but it is slower to begin. A courthouse is just sitting there waiting for a complaint to be filed. An arbitrator, by contrast, has to be appointed, and it can take time for the process to get going. And when a case does not present issues that must be resolved immediately, that may not be a problem.

But where a case has emergency features—the dissemination of trade secrets, the raiding of a party's customers, the destruction of its facilities—arbitration can be particularly ill-suited. Parties who need relief *now* cannot tolerate being imprisoned in the cage of a drawn-out arbitrator-selection process.

For precisely this reason, the common law has long recognized an exception to the general rule in favor of enforcing the exclusive nature of arbitration clauses. Even when parties state that "any and all issues under this contract shall be resolved by arbitration," courts have found that a party can seek injunctive relief to prevent irreparable injury, so long as the court is not deciding the core issue committed by the parties to arbitration. *Merrill Lynch, Pierce, Fenner & Smith Inc. v. Bradley*, 756 F.2d 1048, 1053 (4th Cir. 1985) ("where a dispute is subject to mandatory arbitration under the Federal Arbitration Act, a district court has the discretion to grant a preliminary injunction to preserve the status quo pending the arbitration of the parties' dispute if the enjoined conduct would render that process a 'hollow formality.'"); *Alliance Consulting Inc. v. Warrior Energy Res. LLC*, No. 5:2017-cv-03541, 2017 BL 283376 (S.D. W. Va. Aug. 14, 2017) (addressing a preliminary injunction when the dispute resolution clause did not specifically provide a court with jurisdiction to hear such a dispute).

For that same reason, parties electing arbitration frequently insert into their clauses a provision allowing for temporary and emergent equitable relief, which makes clear to the court that arbitration is not the exclusive remedy in these situations. Such a provision may read "provided that, nothing in this clause shall bar a party from seeking injunctive relief in emergent circumstances, including but not limited to the dissemination of its intellectual property."

But what happens when parties intending to preserve their right to seek emergency relief in court instead safeguard their right to seek all equitable relief? All emergency relief is, to be sure, equitable—but not all equitable relief is emergent. Consider the following clause:

> Any controversy or claim arising out of or relating to this Agreement or the breach, termination, or validity thereof, except for temporary, preliminary, or permanent injunctive relief *or any other form of equitable relief*, shall be settled by binding arbitration. (Emphasis added.)

A strict textual reading of this arbitration clause reveals an inherent tension: on the one hand, the clause gives the arbitrator the power to hear "any controversy or claim arising out of or relating to this Agreement."

Yet, at the same time, the clause pulls away from the arbitrator the power to hear claims for "temporary, preliminary, or permanent injunctive relief or any other form of equitable relief." What did the parties intend? Should *all* non-emergent merits issues be arbitrated? Or just non-equitable issues?

This tension is exacerbated by the leading doctrinal underpinnings of arbitration law—namely, that (1) arbitration agreements are a creature of contract and should be enforced as written, (2) enforcing arbitration agreements promotes efficiency, and (3) contracts should generally be interpreted so as to promote arbitration.

This puts courts in a bind. Presented with a non-emergent equitable claim stemming from an agreement with an equitable carve-out like the provision above, a court may adopt a strictly textual approach and bar the arbitrator from considering the equitable claims.

This may especially be the case where a party either has second thoughts about arbitrating, or simply wants to slow down the case. The arbitration's defendant—that is, the respondent—can file a motion before the arbitrator attempting to strip the tribunal from jurisdiction over the equitable claims.

If that party is a plaintiff ("claimant"), it can simply tack on a specific performance claim, which sounds in equity, to its core breach of contract claims. And presto! At least some of the claims are now in court. The "mandatory" arbitration clause is no longer exclusive, and instead has been defeated by a court interpreting literally the above equitable carve-out, notwithstanding the principles of efficiency and promoting arbitration.

This cannot be right. The exception should not swallow the rule. Parties should not be saddled with piecemeal procedures. Parties should be permitted to make emergent exceptions to their mandatory arbitration clauses, but that is *all* they should be permitted to do once they commit to arbitration.

Literal enforcement here is bad policy. Courts should be encouraged to favor the Federal Arbitration Act's pro-arbitration policy, not to mention the mandate of Rule 1 of the Federal Rules of Civil Procedure that courts should seek "to secure the just, speedy, and inexpensive determination of every action and proceeding."

It is a daunting thing to tell a commercial court not to follow clear contract language crafted by sophisticated parties. That flies in the face of basic contract law.

This article nevertheless takes the position that in this situation, that is precisely what courts should do. Courts should only enforce the equitable carve-outs to confer jurisdiction when there is an actual emergency requiring a quick decision or when a decision is otherwise necessary to preserve or in aid of the ultimate arbitration.

Any other result violates public policy, the Federal Arbitration Act, and can result in ridiculous and unintended outcomes in practice. The tension must be resolved in favor of efficiency and promoting arbitration.

The Carve-Out Problem

Let's consider how these arbitration principles apply in the following hypothetical. Assume that Company A manufactures washing machines, but has no sales force. It enters into an exclusive five-year distribution agreement with Company B. Things go well in year 1, but in year 2, Company B sees greener pastures, stops selling Company A's machines and instead signs an exclusive distribution agreement with better-selling washing machine Company C. Company A is not only without a distributor, but its sales slow to a standstill and it is without valuable inventory that remains sitting in Company B's warehouse.

Company A decides to take action against Company B for both legal damages—alleged sales that would have occurred had Company B not breached exclusivity—and for an equitable order that Company B return all of the Company A inventory in Company B's warehouse. The parties' distribution agreement contains the same arbitration provision that appears in the introduction to this article:

> Any controversy or claim arising out of or relating to this Agreement or the breach, termination, or validity thereof, except for temporary, preliminary, or permanent injunctive relief *or any other form of equitable relief*, shall be settled by binding arbitration. (Emphasis added.)

Look at the problem created by the emphasized language: under a strict and literal interpretation of those words, Company A must arbitrate its claim for money damages against Company B, but its equitable claim for return of its inventory ("or any other form of equitable relief") is not arbitrable and therefore must be resolved in court. The strict reading deprives the arbitration panel of jurisdiction over the equitable claim.

This can lead to inconsistent results, since *both* the court *and* the arbitrator will be required to address the central question of the case: whether Company B breached the distribution agreement. The client is now paying not just for two procedures but, given the potential inconsistency, two procedures which may not resolve the dispute if their results are in opposition.

Unfortunately, this is the result under much of the existing caselaw. This should change.

Supporting Arbitration

Carve-outs should be interpreted in favor of arbitration.

While many courts have concluded that they are obligated to enforce the literal terms of an arbitration agreement regardless of the consequences of that decision, other courts have acknowledged this inherent tension.

In doing so, some courts, in particular the District Court for the Southern District of New York, have reached the conclusion advocated in this article, that equitable carve-outs to arbitration clauses should only be enforced to carve out temporary and emergent equitable relief.

"[W]here a contract has both a broad arbitration clause and a clause permitting the parties to seek injunctive relief before a court, courts in this District have construed the latter clauses as permitting the parties to seek '*injunctive relief . . . in aid of arbitration, rather than . . . transforming arbitrable claims into nonarbitrable ones depending on the form of relief prayed.*'" *Baldwin Tech. Co. v. Printers' Serv., Inc.*, No. 15 Civ. 07152 (GBD), 2016 BL 22555, at * 3, n. 4 (S.D.N.Y. Jan. 27, 2016) (quoting *Remy Amerique Inc. v. Touzet Distribution, S.A.R.L.*, 816 F. Supp. 213, 218 (S.D.N.Y. 1993)) (emphasis added).

In *WMT Investors v. Visionwall Corp.*, the parties' License Agreement contained an arbitration clause that provided that "any dispute or controversy arising under, out of, in connection with or in relation to this Agreement shall be resolved by final and binding arbitration . . ." and also contained a provision that "in the event of a breach or threatened breach . . . [the party] shall have the right to equitable relief, including but not limited to the issuance of a temporary or permanent injunction or restraining order, by any court of competent jurisdiction." 2010 U.S. Dist. LEXIS 65869 *4, (S.D.N.Y. June 28, 2010).

WMT filed a complaint in New York's Southern District seeking declaratory and injunctive relief, and Visionwall moved to compel arbitration. The court found that the gateway question of arbitrability should be decided by the arbitrator but that even assuming that the question of arbitrability was before the court, it would likely find that WMT's claims should be arbitrated.

In so finding, the court explained that "if there is a reading of the various agreements that permits the arbitration clause to govern, the court will choose it." *Id.* (citations omitted). The court also pointed to case law in which parties were prohibited from attempting to circumvent a broad arbitration clause by disguising their claims as seeking equitable relief. *Id.* at *10.

The court reasoned that the agreement is susceptible of the interpretation that the equitable relief provision relates to preserving the status quo between the parties pending the outcome of the arbitration. Id. The court found that its conclusion was "buttressed by Plaintiff 's . . . assertion that an arbitrator should determine the validity and enforceability of the License Agreement." *Id.* at *11. The court ultimately compelled arbitration. *Id.*

Two recent decisions also reached the same conclusions that the equitable carve-outs are only to be interpreted to aid in arbitration and not to remove a case or claims from the proper jurisdiction of the arbitrator. In *Davis v. SEVA Beauty LLC*, the arbitration agreement was broad, and carved out many claims from arbitration: "any action for declaratory or equitable relief, including, without limitation, seeking preliminary or permanent injunctive relief, specific performance, [or] other relief in the nature of equity to enjoin any harm or threat of harm to such party's tangible or intangible property, brought at any time, including, without limitation, prior to or during the pendency of any arbitration proceedings initiated hereunder." No. C17-547 TSZ, 2017 BL 322579, at *3–4 (W.D. Wash. Sept. 13, 2017).

The court held that even though the plaintiffs brought equitable claims seeking rescission, those claims belonged in arbitration because they were not brought "in aid of arbitration." *Id.* at *4. "A party may not, however, circumvent the arbitration clause by simply seeking equitable remedies for claims that are squarely within the scope of matters to be arbitrated. This interpretation brings the arbitration provision and the exception at issue into harmony with each other and the federal policy favoring arbitration." *Id.*

Similarly, in *Info. Sys. Audit & Control Ass'n v. TeleComm. Sys. Inc.*, the court interpreted a facially broad carve-out to only except from arbitration claims for "temporary equitable relief once a dispute has been submitted to arbitration" or "as authorizing courts to enforce arbitral awards once arbitration is complete." No. 17 C 2066, 2017 BL 216900, at *5–6 (N.D. Ill. June 23, 2017).

The court also explained that interpreting the clause in any broader way "would permit a party to obtain from a court essentially the same relief as that otherwise reserved for the arbitrator."

DXP Enters., *Davis* and *Info. Sys.* get to the right result, but have to work too hard to get there.

Those courts feel compelled to state that they are "interpreting" the arbitration clause in such a way as to permit the arbitrator to hear the equitable claims. They should not have to so strain. They could, and should, have focused on (1) the lack of any emergency or (2) that the equitable claims were not brought somehow in aid of the arbitration. As a result, they should have held that the parties have to arbitrate all of their claims.

> *Where parties have a mandatory arbitration clause and a non-emergent situation, cases should not be split, irrespective of whether the case presents a non-emergent equitable claim.*

The most that courts should be permitted to do in cases with a mandatory arbitration provision is enter an injunction that freezes the status quo ante in order to prevent irreparable injury until such time as the merits are determined by the arbitrator.

A party that agreed to arbitrate its disputes should not be able to circumvent that very agreement by artfully pleading its claims to include equitable relief. Any other result compromises arbitration, increases party expense, and overburdens the court system—all in favor of enforcing a contract term contrary to public policy.

PRACTICE POINTER. In light of this issue, is there any reason to use equitable relief rather than emergency relief in drafting your clause?

B. How Far Can a Court Go? Mandatory vs. Permissive Injunctions

There is a distinction in injunction law between so-called "negative" injunctions and so-called "mandatory" injunctions. In a negative injunction, a party is ordered to cease particular activity. In a mandatory injunction, a party is ordered to *take* particular action, not merely to refrain from it. There is a general presumption, well beyond the arbitration field and extending generally into civil procedure, that mandatory injunctions are disfavored except in the most unusual circumstances. *Stanley v. Univ. of S. Cal.*, 13 F.3d 1313, 1320 (9th Cir. 1994); *O Centro Espirita Beneficente Uniao do Vegetal v. Ashcroft*, 389 F.3d 973, 1011 (10th Cir. 2004); *Tiffany v. Forbes Custom Boats, Inc.*, No. 91-3001,1992 U.S. App. LEXIS 6268, *20 (4th Cir. Apr. 6, 1992); *Tom Doherty Assocs. v. Saban Entm't, Inc.*, 60 F.3d 27, 34 (2d Cir. 1995). Should there be any different presumption in arbitration?

Consider the following client situation:

Practical Exercise

Guitar Co. designs and manufactures custom made electric guitars. It has cultivated a reputation as the elite electric guitar of the moment, with prices and a waiting list to match. Guitar Co.'s particular mystique is in the quality of its "pick up" components, which amplify the sound made by strumming the strings. The components are made from a copper alloy using copper from a particular mine in Montana (hence the name of the leading priced Guitar Co. model, the Butte5000). Guitar Co. has a long-term, ten-year contract with Montana Mines, which produces the copper and then manufactures the alloy. The contract calls for binding arbitration in Helena, Montana. The contract also contains a carve-out for injunctions.

In year 3 of the contract, Montana Mines informs Guitar Co. that it has received a better offer for its copper and alloys from a rival guitar manufacturer and accordingly is terminating the contract with Guitar Co. Montana Mines knows that it will be sued by Guitar Co. for breach of contract, but the new offer is so good that it will cover any monetary damages awarded to Guitar Co.

Without the alloy, Guitar Co. might as well be just another guitar company. Its products will have no cachet and will not be desired by the market. It could buy substitute alloys, but the resulting instruments could not be sold as Butte5000s or any of the other elite product names used by rock stars, and aspiring rock stars, everywhere. Moreover, the "cover" price will actually be less, not more, than the Montana Mines copper alloy, and so a traditional UCC-based contract remedy affording it the difference between the contract price and the market price would be ineffective.

Guitar Co. sends a demand for arbitration, alleging breach of contract, and seeking as damages the value of its entire business. On the same day that it files the arbitration demand, it also brings suit in the United States District Court for the District of Montana, seeking an injunction that could compel the delivery to Guitar Co. of the copper and alloys called for by the parties' contract. The complaint and accompanying motion for a TRO and preliminary injunction note the absence of any *force majeure* or other conditions that would otherwise bar Montana Mines from honoring the contract.

Can Guitar Company obtain an injunction? Assume Montana Mines argues that this circumvents the arbitration clause. What arguments would you use on behalf of Montana Mines to keep this in arbitration rather than in court?

PRACTICE POINTERS

1. *Start the Arbitration!* If you assess that your client needs an injunction notwithstanding that you are facing a very strong arbitration clause, then look that beast in the eye. Your opponent will likely argue that you are "ignoring" the arbitration clause and undermining the "strong federal policy in favor of arbitration" that we studied earlier in this book. The best way to undermine this attack is to act in a manner in which you too embrace the arbitration. Commence the arbitration, if at all possible, just as you bring the injunction motion in court. Attach the statement of claim (or other early arbitration document) from the arbitration to your motion seeking injunction. Time may be short and you may not be able to prepare a full arbitration proceeding at the same time you are moving in court, but at a minimum follow the contractual prerequisites for at least commencing an arbitration—which may be no more than sending a demand letter or notice of arbitration claim. This is a concrete demonstration to the court that your client is still seeking an ultimate determination on the merits in arbitration, as the parties agreed. It also makes the distinction, seen above, in Section 3's application of a stay to a "trial" of the action rather than to preliminary motions. By starting the action, you emphasize that your client is not evading the Section 3 stay.

2. *Don't Go Overboard!* Only seek an injunction on that part of the claim where the status quo needs to be frozen. The requested injunctive relief should be narrowly focused. Example:

> Buyer of a complex computer platform system gave progress payments to Seller of the system in order to wholly revamp Buyer's customer inventory and accounting. The contract has an arbitration clause. Seller is on site at Buyer to study the inventory systems. In the process, Seller becomes aware of confidential information. Buyer believes that Seller is not keeping the information sufficiently confidential and that one of Seller's employees may be leaking it to competitors. Buyer should seek an injunction against leaks of confidential information and to impose controls on access—but should *not* seek court relief on the entire contract price. Pick your spots.

C. Injunction Orders by the Arbitrator

Up to this point in the chapter, we have reviewed situations in which judicial intervention in the arbitration process was necessary in order to prevent an alleged "hollow formality." The inherent thinking of this policy is that by the time an arbitration is set up—the appointment of arbitrators, the organizational conference, and other steps—the house would effectively have burned down. By contrast, the courthouse filled with judges is just sitting there waiting.

But what if the arbitration process itself was speedier? What if it were set up to order injunctions just as courts do—either because the arbitration has already commenced or because there is an emergency arbitrator appointed and standing by? Modern institutional arbitration rules increasingly permit the arbitrator to impose injunctive relief (or, in the parlance of international arbitration, "interim measures of protection"). Parties who elect institutional arbitration should be aware that in so doing, they are introducing a potential additional arbitration phase directly into their arbitration, even if their arbitration clause is otherwise silent on the point.

This raises three potential problems, as we will see. First, if the parties' arbitration agreement still provides for court injunctions in an emergency, where must the party go for its injunction: to court or to arbitration? Second, who decides—court or arbitrator—this question? Third, how far should an emergency injunction arbitrator be permitted to take the decision on the merits at the injunction stage?

> **American Arbitration Association Injunction Rules**
>
> R-37(a) The arbitrator may take whatever interim measures he or she deems necessary, including injunctive relief and measures for the protection or conservation of property and disposition of perishable goods.
>
> R-38 (b) A party in need of emergency relief prior to the constitution of the panel shall notify the AAA and all other parties in writing of the nature of the relief sought and the reasons why such relief is required on an emergency basis. The application shall also set forth the reasons why the party is entitled to such relief. Such notice may be given by facsimile or e-mail or other reliable means, but must include a statement certifying that all other parties have been notified or an explanation of the steps taken in good faith to notify other parties.
>
> R-38 (d) The emergency arbitrator shall as soon as possible, but in any event within two business days of appointment, establish a schedule for consideration of the application for emergency relief. Such a schedule shall provide a reasonable opportunity to all parties to be heard, but may provide for proceeding by telephone or video conference or on written submissions as alternatives to a formal hearing. The emergency arbitrator shall have the authority vested in the tribunal under Rule 7, including the authority to rule on her/his own jurisdiction, and shall resolve any disputes over the applicability of this Rule 38.
>
> R-38 (e) If after consideration the emergency arbitrator is satisfied that the party seeking the emergency relief has shown that immediate and irreparable loss or damage shall result in the absence of emergency relief, and that such party is entitled to such relief, the emergency arbitrator may enter an interim order or award granting the relief and stating the reason therefore.

JAMS Injunction Rule

JAMS Rule 24(e) Interim Measures. The Arbitrator may grant whatever interim measures are deemed necessary, including injunctive relief and measures for the protection or conservation of property and disposition of disposable goods. Such interim measures may take the form of an interim or Partial Final Award, and the Arbitrator may require security for the costs of such measures. Any recourse by a Party to a court for interim or provisional relief shall not be deemed incompatible with the agreement to arbitrate or a waiver of the right to arbitrate.

ICDR Injunction Rule

ICDR Article 24.1 At the request of any party, the arbitral tribunal may order or award any interim or conservatory measures it deems necessary, including injunctive relief and measures for the protection or conservation of property.

D. Is There a Conflict Between Arbitrator Injunctions and Court Injunctions?

Do the parties have two options or just one? If the parties agree to an injunctive carve-out AND agree to institutional rules that permit arbitrators to issue preliminary injunctions, can they still go to court? Or are they relegated to arbitration and arbitration only, no matter how dire the alleged emergency?

The next three cases apply modern injunction/arbitration precedent in the context of particular arbitration clauses. Do you agree with the strategies the lawyers pursuing an injunction followed? Would you have sought the injunction in court or in the arbitration? What would you argue *against* the injunction remedy in these cases, and where would you have been better situated to make this argument?

Toyo Tire Holdings of Ams., Inc. v. Cont'l Tire N. Am., Inc.

609 F.3d 975 (9th Cir. 2010)

GWIN, District Judge:

Appellant Toyo Tire Holdings of Americas, Inc. ("Toyo") appeals the district court's denial of its motion to enjoin Appellees Continental Tire North America, Inc. ("Continental") and Yokohama Corporation of America ("Yokohama") from dissolving the parties' joint venture and from distributing the partnership assets until an arbitration panel can consider Toyo's claims. In denying Toyo's motion for a preliminary injunction, the district court reasoned that our holding in *Simula, Inc. v. Autoliv, Inc.*, 175 F.3d 716 (9th Cir. 1999), precluded granting injunctive relief when the parties have agreed to arbitrate and the arbitration panel has the power to issue injunctive relief. Because we believe that the district court incorrectly concluded that *Simula* controls in the present circumstances, we reverse and remand for the district court to consider the merits of Toyo's request for a preliminary injunction.

I

Toyo, Continental, and Yokohama all manufacture and distribute tires. In 1988, Continental's predecessor General Tire, Inc., Toyo, and Yokohama formed a general partnership, Appellee GTY Tire Co. ("GTY"). GTY manufactures truck and bus radial tires ("TBR tires") for each of the partners to distribute.

The 1998 Partnership Agreement contains an arbitration clause that says in pertinent part: "Failing . . . amicable resolution all disputes arising in connection with this Partnership Agreement or any other Basic Document shall be finally settled by arbitration. . . . All arbitration shall be conducted . . . in accordance with the Rules of Conciliation and Arbitration of the International Chamber of Commerce by three arbitrators appointed in accordance with such Rules." As hereafter described, those International Chamber of Commerce Rules allow judicially imposed interim relief, including injunctive relief.

On December 22, 2009, Continental and Yokohama sent Toyo a letter saying they would dissolve the partnership at the end of 2009. In the letter, Continental and Yokohama said that Toyo had agreed to a collaboration agreement with Bridgestone Corporation, a competitor. Continental and Yokohama said Toyo's relationship with Bridgestone gave them the right to dissolve the joint venture under the Partnership Agreement and a 1990 Amendment thereto. Continental and Yokohama indicated that, pursuant to the Partnership Agreement, they could acquire Toyo's 2010 share of TBR tires and could enforce a non-competition clause that would prohibit Toyo from selling non-GTY TBR tires in North America for five years.

At Toyo's request, Continental and Yokohama agreed to a January 8, 2010, meeting of the general partners and temporarily suspended the notice of dissolution. At the meeting, Continental and Yokohama said they intended to dissolve the partnership, effective January 13, 2010, and that they planned to take Toyo's entire allocation of GTY tires. On January 9, 2010, Toyo wrote to Continental and Yokohama, stating that it believed it had a right to purchase TBR tries from GTY for the current and two following fiscal years, even if the partnership was dissolved. Neither Continental nor Yokohama responded.

On January 11, 2010, Toyo requested arbitration with the International Chamber of Commerce ("ICC") International Court of Arbitration. Within its Request for Arbitration, Toyo requested interim injunctive relief.

On the same day, Toyo sued Continental, Yokohama, and GTY. With its Complaint, Toyo brings claims for breach of contract, breach of fiduciary duty, breach of the duty of loyalty, breach of the covenant of good faith and fair dealing, violation of California's fair business practices law, tortious interference with business relations, and slander.

On January 14, 2010, Toyo asked the district court for a preliminary injunction to prevent the Appellees from: (1) terminating Toyo's status as a partner in GTY, (2) disrupting GTY's supply of TBR tires to Toyo, and (3) making false, disparaging, inflammatory, or other defamatory statements to Toyo's customers or other third parties regarding Toyo's assets, the partnership, or Toyo's ability to supply tires. Toyo also moved for a temporary restraining order.

On January 25, 2010, the district court heard argument and orally denied Toyo's motion for a preliminary injunction. At that hearing, the district court gave clear indication that injunctive relief should be given unless *Simula* foreclosed such relief. The district court concluded that our opinion in *Simula* created a "blanket judgment" that a district court may not grant a preliminary injunction when the parties have agreed to arbitrate and the arbitrator has the power to grant interim injunctive relief. Finding that *Simula* controlled this case, the district court denied Toyo's motion.

Toyo now appeals that denial. We have jurisdiction under 28 U.S.C. § 1292(a)(1) and we reverse.

IV

In *PMS Distributing Co. v. Huber & Suhner, A.G.*, we recognized that "the congressional desire to enforce arbitration agreements would frequently be frustrated if the courts were precluded from issuing preliminary injunctive relief to preserve the status quo pending arbitration and, ipso facto, the meaningfulness of the arbitration process." 863 F.2d 639, 641–42 (9th Cir. 1988) (quoting *Teradyne, Inc. v. Mostek Corp.*, 797 F.2d 43, 51 (1st Cir. 1986)). We thus held in PMS that a district court has authority to issue equitable relief in aid of arbitration. *Id.* at 642.

The importance of the courts' ability to issue interim injunctive relief is even more apparent now than when we decided *PMS* twenty-two years ago. We assume that parties ordinarily choose to arbitrate, inter alia, to lower costs and increase efficiency and speed. *See Stolt-Nielsen S.A. v. AnimalFeeds Int'l Corp.*, 130 S. Ct. 1758, 1775 (2010). However, arbitration's promised speed and efficiency frequently do not materialize in practice. *See* Bruce M. Selya, Arbitration Unbound?: The Legacy of McMahon, 62 Brook. L. Rev. 1433, 1446–47 (1996) (describing arbitration process as becoming "increasingly litigious," resulting in shrinking margins of savings in time and cost between arbitration and litigation).

Moreover, one party to the arbitration often has an incentive to delay arbitration proceedings to its own advantage. *See, e.g., Int'l Union of Petroleum & Indus. Workers v. W. Indus. Maint., Inc.*, 707 F.2d 425, 428 (9th Cir. 1983) (upholding award of attorney's fees against party who refused to abide by arbitrator's award to deter "frivolous dilatory tactics [which] not only den[y] the individual prompt redress, [but also] threaten[] the goal of industrial peace"); *Engalla v. Permanente Med. Group, Inc.*, 15 Cal. 4th 951, 969, 64 Cal. Rptr. 2d 843, 938 P.2d 903 (Cal. 1997) (finding evidence that defendant insurance company delayed appointment of neutral arbitrator until after plaintiff's death, resulting in merger of surviving spouse's loss of consortium and malpractice claims and reducing defendant's potential liability).

Thus, the very rules that the parties agreed would govern their arbitration proceedings allow a party to request the relief that Appellant Toyo seeks in this case. And the same rules allow a party to seek interim or conservatory relief before the file is transmitted to the Arbitral Tribunal, "and in appropriate circumstances even thereafter."

Accordingly, we conclude that a district court may issue interim injunctive relief on arbitrable claims if interim relief is necessary to preserve the status quo and the meaningfulness of the arbitration process-provided, of course, that the requirements for granting injunctive relief are otherwise satisfied. This holding is consistent with our rulings in *PMS* and *Simula*, as well as the holdings of a majority of our sister circuits.

We therefore hold that the district court erred by finding as a matter of law that it lacked the power to grant injunctive relief in this case.

REVERSED and REMANDED.

Smart Techs v. Rapt Touch Ir. Ltd

197 F. Supp. 3d 1204 (N.D. Cal. 2016)

CHHABRIA, United States District Judge.

ORDER DENYING APPLICATION FOR TEMPORARY RESTRAINING ORDER; ORDER TO SHOW CAUSE WHY CASE SHOULD NOT BE DISMISSED

SMART's application for a temporary restraining order is denied. A federal court's issuance of emergency relief is a matter of discretion, and an injunction is "an extraordinary remedy that may only be awarded upon a clear showing that the plaintiff is entitled to such relief." *Winter v. NRDC, Inc.*., 555 U.S. 7, 22, 129 S. Ct. 365, 172 L. Ed. 2d 249 (2008); *see id.* at 24; *Standard Innovation Corp. v. Lelo (Shanghai) Trading Co.*, No. 15-cv-04858-BLF, 2015 U.S. Dist. LEXIS 151212, 2015 WL 6828317, at *1 (N.D. Cal. Nov. 6, 2015). SMART has not shown an urgent need for a federal court to exercise its discretion to award interim relief.

The contract underlying this dispute contains an arbitration provision that the parties agree applies here. It's true that, notwithstanding the arbitration provision, the contract allows the parties to seek emergency relief from a court in certain limited circumstances. But as SMART's lawyer admitted at the hearing on the TRO application, the arbitration rules allow SMART to request emergency relief from an arbitrator as well. Under those rules, an emergency arbitrator would be assigned within a day, and a schedule would be set for considering the application for relief within a handful of days. The rules also allow for procedures (such as giving notice to the opposing party by email, and the use of video conferencing instead of in-person hearings) that are not necessarily available in court.

With the parties having agreed that their underlying dispute should be arbitrated, SMART has offered no explanation for why a federal court (rather than an arbitrator) should adjudicate the request for emergency relief. Indeed, the only justification SMART's lawyer gave at the hearing for asking a federal court rather than an arbitrator to dive into this dispute at the preliminary stage was his belief that a federal court would be more likely to issue a TRO *automatically*. Even if that were true (and it certainly shouldn't be), it would not be a good reason for a federal court to get involved in a dispute whose merits both parties agree should be arbitrated.

Accordingly, the Court declines to exercise its discretion to issue preliminary relief.

A & C Disc. Pharm., L.L.C. v. Caremark, L.L.C.

Civil Action, No. 3:16-CV-0264-D, 2016 U.S. Dist. LEXIS 82888 (N.D. Tex. June 27, 2016)

FITZWATER, United States District Judge.

The instant motion to compel arbitration presents the question whether the court or the arbitrator should decide whether plaintiff's request for preliminary injunctive relief is arbitrable. Concluding that the arbitrator, not the court, should decide this issue, the court grants the motion to compel, stays this case, and directs that it be administratively closed for statistical purposes.

I

This is a removed action in which plaintiff A & C Discount Pharmacy LLC d/b/a Medcore Pharmacy ("A&C") sues defendants CaremarkPCS, LLC and Caremark, LLC (collectively, "Caremark") for injunctive relief and declaratory relief. Caremark, a pharmacy benefits manager that administers the pharmacy benefits of its health plan clients, maintains networks of retail pharmacies at which health plan members can fill their prescriptions. When a patient fills a prescription at a retail pharmacy in the Caremark network, Caremark reimburses the pharmacy and then seeks repayment from its health plan client. A&C is a retail pharmacy that is in Caremark's network. Among other things, A&C dispenses to its patients compounded medications, which are drugs that are prepared from individual ingredients by the dispensing pharmacy. Compounded medications are unlike most prescription medications that come in the form of a tablet, capsule, or other delivery mechanism that is finalized by the drug manufacturer and approved by the U.S. Food and Drug Administration (the "FDA"). A&C, like many compounding pharmacies, charges prices for its compounded medications that greatly exceed those for FDA-approved prescription medications.

A&C's participation in Caremark's network is governed by a written contract between A&C and Caremark. In January 2015 A&C entered into a Provider Agreement with Caremark. The Provider Agreement expressly incorporates the Caremark Provider Manual, which is issued and routinely updated by Caremark through an agreed-upon amendment process. The parties agree that the 2016 Caremark Provider Manual ("Provider Manual") governs their contractual relationship for purposes of this case. The parties' relationship is also governed by an Addendum to the Caremark Provider Agreement ("Addendum") that A&C signed in March 2015.

In June 2015 A&C began submitting claims for complex compound pharmaceuticals to Caremark, which Caremark contends is a breach of the Addendum. The Addendum provides that "Provider agrees, unless otherwise expressly authorized by Caremark in writing, that Provider is not permitted under the Provider Agreement to dispense complex compounds and shall not submit claims for complex compounds," and it further provides:

> Provider agrees that dispensing complex compounds are outside the scope of Provider's permitted Pharmacy Services and submission of claims to Caremark for complex compounds is therefore a breach of the Provider Agreement, subject to all available remedies Caremark may have under the Provider Agreement (which includes the Provider Manual) including but not limited to recoupment of the claims and termination of the Provider Agreement.

Caremark notified A&C of this breach by letters dated June 9 and August 17, 2015. It instructed A&C to immediately cease and desist submitting complex compound claims, acknowledge in writing that it would abide by the restriction against complex compound claims, and reverse the claims identified in the letters. A&C continued, however, to submit complex compound claims after these notifications.

On October 7, 2015 Caremark sent A&C a written Notice of Termination, informing A&C that, due to its failure to follow submission guidelines, it would be terminated from the Caremark network on January 5, 2016. At A&C's request, Caremark later agreed not to terminate A&C from its network until January 29, 2016.

One day before the extended termination date, A&C filed this suit in Texas state court, seeking a temporary restraining order ("TRO") and temporary and permanent injunctive relief. The state court granted an ex parte TRO that restrained Caremark from terminating A&C's participation in its network. The state court scheduled a temporary injunction hearing, but before the hearing was held, Caremark removed the case to this court. Judge Godbey, to whom the case was initially assigned, extended the TRO for 14 days. After the case was reassigned to the undersigned's docket, A&C filed a first amended complaint, application for TRO, and application for preliminary and permanent injunctive relief. The court, finding that the state court TRO should not have been entered in the first place, permitted the

TRO to expire, as scheduled, on February 25, 2016, and it denied as moot Caremark's motion to dissolve the TRO. A&C's requests for preliminary and permanent injunctive relief remain pending.

Caremark now moves to compel arbitration, contending that the Provider Manual's arbitration clause ("Arbitration Agreement") requires that all disputes between the parties be arbitrated, and that preliminary injunctive relief can only be sought in arbitration:

> Any and all disputes between Provider and Caremark . . ., including but not limited to, disputes in connection with, arising out of, or relating in any way to, the Provider Agreement or to Provider's participation in one or more Caremark networks or exclusion from any Caremark networks, will be exclusively settled by arbitration. This arbitration provision applies to any dispute arising from events that occurred before, on or after the effective date of this Provider Manual. Unless otherwise agreed to in writing by the parties, the arbitration shall be administered by the American Arbitration Association ("AAA") pursuant to the then applicable AAA Commercial Arbitration Rules and Mediation Procedures (available from the AAA).

A&C opposes the motion. It maintains that, although the parties' dispute is arbitrable, the American Arbitration Association Commercial Arbitration Rules and Mediation Procedures ("AAA Rules"), which are incorporated into the Arbitration Agreement, permit it to seek preliminary injunctive relief in court.

IV

The court now turns to A&C's application for preliminary injunctive relief. The sole issue is who—as between the court and the arbitrator—should decide A&C's request for preliminary injunctive relief when the court has determined that all of A&C's claims must be sent to arbitration.

A

The Arbitration Agreement provides, in pertinent part, that "[t]he above notwithstanding, nothing in this provision shall prevent either party from utilizing the AAA's procedures for emergency relief to seek preliminary injunctive relief to halt or prevent a breach of this Provider Agreement." The parties agree that the AAA Rules govern A&C's request for preliminary injunctive relief, but they disagree about which specific AAA Rule governs, as well as about the interpretation of the applicable AAA Rules. A&C maintains that Rule 37(c), which addresses interim measures, and Rule 38(h), which addresses emergency measures of protection, permit it to submit a request for injunctive relief to a court. A&C further maintains that the majority of federal circuit courts have held that a district court can issue injunctive relief to preserve the status quo pending arbitration, and that the Fifth Circuit, in *Janvey v. Alguire*, 647 F.3d 585 (5th Cir. 2011), held that a district court can issue injunctive relief to protect the status quo pending resolution of a motion to compel arbitration.

Caremark maintains that the Arbitration Agreement, by stating that the parties may "utiliz[e] the AAA's procedures for emergency relief to seek preliminary injunctive relief," clearly refers to Rule 38 and its procedures for obtaining "emergency relief." And it posits that A&C's situation is directly addressed by Rule 38(b). Caremark also asserts that, under Rule 38(a), Rule 38 is mandatory because the Arbitration Agreement does not contain any provision that would invalidate Rule 38, and that A&C has not identified any other agreement that would in any way alter Rule 38. Caremark also posits that the AAA Rules relied on by A&C do not authorize a party to seek preliminary injunctive relief from a court and do not provide "procedures" for doing so. Rather, Caremark argues that Rules 37(c) and 38(h) preserve the jurisdiction of the arbitrator by stating that no request to a judicial tribunal will be deemed "a waiver of the right to arbitrate."

Alternatively, Caremark maintains that the AAA Rules explicitly reserve to the arbitrator, not the court, the power to decide the correct interpretation of the AAA Rules and the appropriate jurisdiction of the arbitrator. Caremark relies on Rule 7(a), which provides: "The arbitrator shall have the power to rule on his or her own jurisdiction," and Rule 8, which provides: "The arbitrator shall interpret and apply these rules insofar as they relate to the arbitrator's powers and duties[.]"

B

The court declines to rule on A&C's application for preliminary injunctive relief. The case relied on by A&C, *Janvey*, 647 F.3d 585, is inapposite. In *Janvey* the Fifth Circuit held that a district court can rule on a motion for preliminary injunction to preserve the status quo while a motion to compel arbitration is pending. *Id.* at 595. It did not address the present situation—where the court has already decided that the case is arbitrable. The *Janvey* panel acknowledged the circuit split concerning whether "'the [FAA] require[s] that a federal court immediately divest itself of any power to act to maintain the status quo once it decides that the case before it is arbitrable.'" *Id.* at 594 (emphasis in original) (quoting *RGI, Inc. v. Tucker & Assocs., Inc.*, 858 F.2d 227, 228–29 (5th Cir. 1988) (acknowledging, but not entering, the circuit split)). But *Janvey* did not enter the circuit split. *See id.* at 595 n.7 ("[W]e reserve for another day the issues of whether a district court divests itself of the discretion to maintain the status quo once it decides the case before it is arbitrable and, if not, what the limits of that discretion may be.").

The court in *Grasso Enterprises, LLC v. CVS Health Corp.*, 143 F. Supp. 3d 530 (W.D. Tex. 2015), addressed a situation similar to the present case. The *Grasso* court first determined that the parties had agreed to arbitrate their dispute. In doing so, it held that the arbitration clause in the Provider Manual, which was incorporated into the Provider Agreement, constituted an agreement to arbitrate. *Id.* at 537–40. And it concluded that the parties' dispute fell within the scope of that agreement because the parties, by incorporating the AAA Rules into the arbitration clause, agreed to arbitrate arbitrability.

The *Grasso* court also concluded that no legal constraints rendered the dispute nonarbitrable. *Id.* at 542. The *Grasso* court then turned to the plaintiff's motion for preliminary injunction, and it considered whether the following clause in the arbitration agreement allowed the parties to seek injunctive relief outside of arbitration: "The above notwithstanding, nothing in this provision shall prevent either party from seeking preliminary injunctive relief to halt or prevent a breach of this Provider Agreement in any state or federal court of law." *Id* at 543. As an initial matter, the court explained that "there is no case that would require this Court to issue a ruling on the preliminary injunction motion even though it has ordered the case proceed in arbitration." *Id.* The Grasso court declined to rule on the preliminary injunction motion, reasoning that "'the judicial inquiry requisite to determine the propriety of injunctive relief necessarily would inject the court into the merits of issues more appropriately left to the arbitrator.'" *Id.* (quoting *Merrill Lynch, Pierce, Fenner & Smith, Inc. v. Hovey*, 726 F.2d 1286, 1292 (8th Cir. 1984)). It also reasoned that, because the parties, by incorporating the AAA Rules into their arbitration agreement, had agreed to arbitrate arbitrability, "an arbitrator, not this Court, [must] decide whether the issue that underlies the claim for preliminary injunctive relief is within the scope of the arbitration agreement or is covered by the exception." *Id.* (citing *Crawford*, 748 F.3d at 262; *Petrofac*, 687 F.3d at 675).

The court in *RX Pros, Inc. v. CVS Health Corp.*, 2016 U.S. Dist. LEXIS 8983, 2016 WL 316867 (W.D. La. Jan. 26, 2016), also addressed a similar issue. In *RX Pros* the parties agreed that the arbitration agreement governed their underlying dispute, and the only issues before the court were whether the state court had authority to enter the TRO in the first place, and if not, whether the court had authority to dissolve the TRO before compelling arbitration. 2016 U.S. Dist. LEXIS 8983, [WL] at *2. And the court addressed a provision in an arbitration clause identical to the one at issue in the present case: "The above notwithstanding, nothing in this provision shall prevent either party from utilizing the AAA's procedures for emergency relief to seek preliminary injunctive relief to halt or prevent a breach of this Provider Agreement." 2016 U.S. Dist. LEXIS 8983, [WL] at *2 n.2. The *RX Pros* court held that the state court improperly granted the TRO, and it dissolved the state court TRO. 2016 U.S. Dist. LEXIS 8983, [WL] at *3–4. In doing so, the court explained:

> Under the clear language of the 2016 Provider Manual, this question was for the arbitrator to decide. *See Crawford*, 748 F.3d at 262–63. In *Crawford*, the court held that express incorporation of the rules of the arbitration service constitutes clear and unmistakable evidence that the parties have agreed to arbitrate arbitrability. *Id.* Then, the court noted that the arbitration clause in the 2014 Provider Manual incorporated the rules of the AAA. According to the Fifth Circuit, incorporation of those rules constituted "clear and unmistakable" evidence that the parties agreed to arbitrate arbitrability. *Id.*

> The 2016 Provider Manual contains the same express incorporation of the rules of the arbitration service that the Fifth Circuit held constitutes "clear and unmistakable evidence" that the parties agreed to arbitrate arbitrability. Therefore, when faced with the Petition for a TRO, the state court should have referred the matter to arbitration. *See Grasso*, 143 F. Supp. 3d 530, 2015 WL 6550548 at *12 (construing 2014 Provider Manual and finding that arbitrator should determine whether exception allowing party to file for injunctive relief in federal or state court applied).

143 F. Supp. 3d 530, *Id.* at *3.

In the present case, the court need not enter the circuit split and decide whether it can consider a request for preliminary injunctive relief after it has decided that the case is arbitrable. This is so because both parties agree that the AAA Rules are incorporated into the Arbitration Agreement, and the express incorporation of the AAA Rules into the Arbitration Agreement "constitutes clear and unmistakable evidence that the parties agreed to arbitrate arbitrability." *Crawford*, 748 F.3d at 262–63 (citing *Petrofac*, 687 F.3d at 675). As in *Grasso* and *RX Pros*, because the parties agreed to arbitrate arbitrability, the arbitrator, not the court, should rule on who has the primary power to decide whether A&C's request for preliminary injunctive relief is arbitrable. *Cf. Petrofac*, 687 F.3d at 675 (citing *First Options of Chi., Inc. v. Kaplan*, 514 U.S. 938, 943, 115 S. Ct. 1920, 131 L. Ed. 2d 985 (1995)) ("'Just as the arbitrability of the merits of a dispute depends upon whether the parties agreed to arbitrate that dispute, so the question who has the primary power to decide arbitrability turns upon what the parties agreed about that matter.'") (internal quotations omitted) (emphasis in original).

Accordingly, the court declines to rule on A&C's request for preliminary injunctive relief.

For the reasons explained, Caremark's motion to compel arbitration is granted. The court stays this case and directs that it be administratively closed for statistical purposes.

SO ORDERED.

E. How Far Should the "Emergency Arbitrator" Go?

Emergency injunctions are not once but twice removed from the ultimate merits determination. They exist, by definition, in situations where a double emergency is being alleged: that the situation demands an injunction and that there is no time to follow the standard institutional injunction procedures. Pressed into service in these circumstances, how far should an emergency injunction arbitrator go?

The AAA rule on emergency arbitrators, and the limits of that emergency arbitrator's power to award injunctive relief, was put to vivid test in a 2013 dispute between technology giants Yahoo and Microsoft. Was the arbitrator's award within the confines of the emergency powers rule?

Yahoo! Inc. v. Microsoft Corp.

983 F. Supp. 2d 310 (S.D.N.Y. 2013)

PATTERSON, JR., U.S.D.J.

On October 15, 2013, Petitioner Yahoo! Inc. ("Petitioner" or "Yahoo") moved this Court, sitting in Part One, to vacate an arbitration award of equitable relief. (*See* Pet'r's Mem. of Law in Supp. of Pet. to Vacate Arbitration Award ("Pet'r's Mem.)). On October 16, 2013, Respondent Microsoft Corporation ("Respondent" or "Microsoft") opposed the motion to vacate and cross-petitioned for a confirmation of the arbitration award. Yahoo filed a reply on October 17, 2013 in further support of its motion to vacate and objecting to Microsoft's cross-petition, to which Microsoft replied solely on the issue of the cross-petition to confirm the arbitration award. On October 18, 2013, Yahoo filed a sur-reply in response to the legal authority cited by Microsoft in its reply.

The arbitration award (the "Award") that is the subject of the instant dispute was issued on October 14, 2013 by an Emergency Arbitrator appointed by the American Arbitration Association ("AAA"). The Emergency Arbitrator issued the Award under the legal authority granted to him by the arbitration provision of an agreement between Microsoft and Yahoo in 2009, the 2009 Search and Advertising Services and Sales Agreement (the "Agreement"). In that Award, the Arbitrator denied Microsoft's request for specific performance, but granted its request for injunctive relief.

For the reasons discussed below, Yahoo's motion to vacate the arbitration award is DENIED. Further, given the interest in enforcement of the equitable award made by the Arbitrator, and for the additional reasons discussed below, Microsoft's crosspetition to confirm the arbitration award is GRANTED.

I. BACKGROUND

A. The Search Alliance and the Agreement to Transition

Microsoft runs the internet search engine Bing, where search ads are provided by Microsoft's Bing Ads system. Yahoo runs its own search engine and system for providing search ads, called Panama. In the 2009 Agreement, Microsoft and Yahoo agreed to merge their search capabilities internationally to better compete with their main market competitor, Google. The Agreement provides that Yahoo would migrate its search and search ad services from Panama to Bing Ads. To begin this transition, the global market was divided into sixteen individual geographic markets.

The process of transitioning from Panama to Bing Ads in a given geographic market is broken down into phases, the most important of which are the "Demand" phase and the "Ramp" phase. During the first phase of transition, the Demand phase, the orders of all current Yahoo advertisers are set up in the Bing Ads system, by copying information from Yahoo's Panama system. During this phase, advertisers' orders are generally duplicated and present in both systems. The Ramp phase follows the Demand phase. During the Ramp phase, search traffic is shifted from Yahoo's system to the Bing Ads system. The shift of search traffic to Bing Ads "ramps up" over time. Thus, at "10% Ramp," 10% of users' searches are answered by the Bing Ads system; at "100% Ramp," the search traffic has been entirely moved over to Bing Ads. In fourteen out of the sixteen of its geographic markets, Yahoo has completed the transition of its advertising business to Bing Ads. The remaining two markets, Taiwan and Hong Kong, are the subject of the instant dispute.

B. Transitioning the Taiwan and Hong Kong Markets

Microsoft and Yahoo originally agreed for the migration of the Taiwan and Hong Kong markets to be completed by 2011. However, technical problems leading up to the transition led to several delays by mutual agreement. In February 2013, Microsoft and Yahoo agreed to a final plan to transition the Taiwan and Hong Kong markets by the end of October 2013.

By mid-September 2013, the Ramp phase of the transition was ready to begin. Leaders of the transition efforts from both parties agreed that the quality criteria had been met, indicating that the transition was ready to proceed. However, on Friday, September 20, 2013, Yahoo informed Microsoft that it was not proceeding with the transition at that time, and noted that it "hope[d] to proceed with the migration of [Taiwan] and [Hong Kong] in early 2014." Yahoo gave as its reason "concerns about Microsoft's level of commitment to the Bing Ads platform" in light of Microsoft CEO Steve Ballmer's announcement that he planned to step down sometime before August 2014. That same day, Microsoft informed Yahoo that it considered "Yahoo's conduct concerning search migrations [] a breach of the parties' Search and Advertising Services and Sales Agreement."

C. The Emergency Arbitration

On September 26, 2013, Microsoft initiated "an emergency arbitration." It did so pursuant to § 17.4.2 and § 17.5 of the Agreement, which collectively provide for emergency arbitration in some circumstances. The AAA-appointed Emergency Arbitrator directed the proceeding, which involved extensive briefing and testimony.

On October 14, 2013, the Arbitrator issued a decision finding "that by imposing its pause and refusing to proceed with the scheduled Taiwan and Hong Kong migrations, Yahoo is in breach of the Agreement." The Arbitrator also concluded, inter alia, that "based on [his] evaluation of the testimony and affidavits submitted," it is "critical that the Ramp phase follow the Demand phase that has been successfully completed because advertiser orders and preferences change over time." Therefore, he found that the "urgency of the transition establishes the emergency required by the Emergency Rules." He further concluded that the testimony and affidavits demonstrated that the Yahoo's breach of the Agreement "establishe[d] irreparable harm to Microsoft."

The Arbitrator rejected Microsoft's request for specific performance and issued an injunction that "restores the parties to the activities they were ready to proceed with before the pause." The Arbitrator ordered that Yahoo is "restrained and enjoined from continuing any pause in transitioning" and is "commanded to use all efforts" to complete the Taiwan transition by October 28, 2013 and the Hong Kong transition by November 11, 2013. Finally, although the Arbitrator awarded an injunction rather than specific performance, he noted that "[a]n injunction can achieve the same goal as specific performance, namely to get the Taiwan and Hong Kong migrations completed."

II. VACATUR OF THE ARBITRATION AWARD

Yahoo argues that the Arbitrator exceeded his authority and manifestly disregarded the law, and therefore this Court should vacate the award under 9 U.S.C. § 10(a)(4). The Second Circuit has "consistently accorded the narrowest of readings to [§ 10(a)(4)] in order to facilitate the purpose underlying arbitration: to provide parties with efficient dispute resolution, thereby obviating the need for protracted litigation." *ReliaStar*, 564 F.3d at 85. Given the narrow interpretation of § 10(a)(4) by the Second Circuit and for the reasons discussed below, Yahoo's petition to vacate is denied.

1. The Arbitrator Did Not Exceed His Authority by Issuing a Final Award

Yahoo first alleges that the Award must be vacated because the Emergency Arbitrator awarded Microsoft "final permanent relief" even though the parties' Agreement—and the AAA Optional Rules for Emergency Measures of Protection (the "Emergency Measures") expressly incorporated therein—only permit an Emergency Arbitrator to award "interim relief." Yahoo characterizes "interim relief" as "relief necessary to preserve the status quo until the matter can be fully and fairly decided by a three-Arbitrator panel of industry experts following discovery." Yahoo alleges that the Emergency Arbitrator's award was final because migration in the Taiwan and Hong Kong markets, which is required by the injunction, is irreversible.

Yahoo's argument fails, however, because there is a more than colorable basis for finding that the Arbitrator was authorized to grant the relief that was awarded. The 2009 Agreement between Yahoo and Microsoft adopts the Emergency Measures "with respect to any claim for interim, injunctive, or other emergency relief." Yahoo argues that this section indicates that an Emergency Arbitrator may only enter "an interim award" for emergency relief "prior to the constitution of a panel." But the Agreement itself, in the same provision that adopts the Emergency Measures, states that "[t]he parties agree that the arbitrator is authorized to compel and award interim injunctive or emergency relief... and the arbitrator[s] may compel and award specific performance (in addition to any other remedies and including in connection with claims for interim, injunctive or emergency relief)." The Agreement further states, in the same provision providing for emergency arbitration, that "[a]ny nonmonetary relief will be tailored to preserve, to the greatest extent possible, the scope of Services provided under this Agreement and the parties' intent with respect to such Services."

The language in the Agreement suggests that Yahoo and Microsoft empowered an Emergency Arbitrator to grant non-monetary relief necessary to restore the status quo. During arbitration, the Emergency Arbitrator addressed Yahoo's argument that the preliminary injunction Microsoft was seeking was inappropriate because of its finality, but nevertheless found that injunctive relief was needed to restore the status quo, stating that "the injunction imposed hereby merely restores the parties to the activities they were ready to proceed with before [Yahoo's unilateral pause]." Because restoration of the status quo may appropriately require one party to perform contractual obligations, the Arbitrator had a colorable basis for concluding that an injunction requiring Yahoo to continue to perform was necessary. *See Tom Doherty Assocs., v. Saban Entm't, Inc.*, 60 F.3d 27, 34 (2d Cir. 1995) ("Confusion in breach of contract cases as to whether an injunction is mandatory or prohibitory may stem from the meaning of 'status quo.' A plaintiff's view of the status quo is the situation that would prevail if its version of the contract were performed.").

The Second Circuit has held that "[a]s long as the Arbitrator is even arguably construing or applying the contract and acting within the scope of this authority," the district court must uphold the Arbitrator's award. *ReliaStar*, 564 F.3d at 86 (internal quotation and citation omitted). Here, the record makes clear that the Emergency Arbitrator reached his decision out of effort to construe and apply the 2009 Agreement. Accordingly, the Arbitrator acted within his authority in granting an injunction as to the migration to Bing, even though the equitable relief that was granted is, in essence, final.

2. The Arbitrator Did Not Exceed His Authority by Finding an Emergency and Irreparable Harm.

Yahoo also argues that there were no facts on the record demonstrating an emergency, and therefore the Emergency Arbitrator did not have jurisdiction to award any relief. Yahoo argues that the parties' regular course of conduct—which Yahoo alleges has included numerous delays as operational or business issues arose—makes clear that the latest delay was no emergency. Further, under the Emergency Measures, the Emergency Arbitrator is required to find "that the party seeking the emergency relief has shown that immediate and irreparable loss or damage will result in the absence of emergency relief" before granting relief. Yahoo argues that this standard was not met because mere fear or speculation cannot constitute irreparable harm, *see JSG Trading Corp. V. Tray- Wrap, Inc.*, 917 F.2d 75, 80 (2d Cir. 1990), and Yahoo alleges that during the hearing, Microsoft did not offer any non-speculative evidence.

These arguments lack merit, however, because the Arbitrator made factual findings of both emergency and immediate irreparable harm based on the evidence that had been presented in arbitration. "[A]n arbitration award may not be vacated because of disagreement with the Arbitrator's evaluation of the evidence." *Data & Development*, 513 F. App'x at 118. Moreover, the record shows that the Arbitrator reached his factual determinations based on significant evidence showing that it was critical that the Ramp phase immediately follow the Demand phase, including affidavits, dozens of exhibits, and the testimony of ten witnesses. Accordingly, deference to the Arbitrator's determinations is appropriate.

Notes and Questions

1. There were two sources of the emergency arbitrator's mandate to issue equitable relief. The first was the arbitration clause's adoption of Rule 38 of the AAA Rules (the emergency arbitrator section). The second, as the court noted, was "the Agreement itself," which contained additional language affording the arbitrator the power to order "interim, injunctive, or emergency relief" and to "preserve . . . the scope of services provided." Would the emergency rules have been enough, or did the arbitrator's award require the clause's additional language as well?
2. After reviewing this case, what advice would you give a client as to limitations (if any) on an arbitrator's power? How, for example, would you define in the agreement (and explain to your client) what is meant by "interim" and "emergency"? Should drafters place a time limit or expiration date on the interim relief afforded by the emergency process?
3. As the court's decision makes clear, the record was extensive. For example: "Both Yahoo and Microsoft filed lengthy briefs, and each submitted affidavits from witnesses." There were "two days of hearings" with testimony featuring the "presentation and cross-examination of ten witnesses, including the CEOs of both Microsoft and Yahoo." What should be the collateral estoppel effect of that testimony going forward in a full arbitration before the three-arbitrator panel selected by the parties and authorized by the contract?
4. The arbitrator's award did not, by any measure, "freeze" the status quo. As the Second Circuit noted, the word "mandatory" (in the context of mandatory injunctions) can take on a shifting meaning based on where one defines status quo, but leaving those legal terms aside, the indisputable fact is that the emergency arbitrator ordered that action be taken going forward. He expressly ordered that Yahoo complete the Taiwan and Hong Kong transitions by specific dates. Yahoo's appeal was understandably based on a view that this was something other than, indeed greater and more lasting than, mere "interim" relief. In rejecting that challenge, the federal district court looked less to injunction law than to arbitration law, finding that the ruling survived the very limited scrutiny we will study in Unit III.

5. Return to this case after you review the standards in Unit III for vacatur of arbitration awards. Should this award have withstood FAA Section 10 scrutiny?
6. Who would rule on challenges to the jurisdiction of the emergency arbitrator? *See* AAA Rule 38. Who should?

F. Injunctions Limited to Specific Areas

The conflicts examined above can at least be limited by restricting the mandate of the courts and the arbitrator to issue injunctions. "Restrict" does not mean "prohibit." Parties may recognize in advance which situation or situations in their relationship may one day require prompt judicial relief, while others can take a more leisurely time to resolve. They can draft their clause to allow injunctive relief to be entered on some issues, and *only* on those issues.

Class Exercise

Fboard is a third-generation family business. It sells packaging and packaging materials. Fboard's packaging uses a patented fiberboard component and an application process that has been a vigorously guarded trade secret over the years. Integrated, Ltd., believes that Fboard's business will fit well into the full spectrum of packaging services that Integrated offers its customers. The parties conclude an executed purchase agreement. Section 3 sets the purchase price in three components: $12 million paid up front, $2 million on the first anniversary of the closing, and an adjustable earn-out figure between zero and $3 million based on the first six quarters' earnings post-closing.

Section 5 of the purchase agreement reflects Integrated's concern that it does not end up competing against Fboard the day after buying the business, and so the parties agree to a three-year non-compete provision, during which no member of the management team of Fboard can work in any business related to packaging or to fiberboard construction. Each of the four members of the Fboard management team also executes an individual joinder to the purchase agreement expressly consenting to the non-compete.

Section 11 of the purchase agreement contains an arbitration clause stating: "Any and all disputes concerning, arising under, or relating to this agreement shall be resolved by binding arbitration under the Commercial Arbitration Rules of the American Arbitration Association by a sole arbitrator sitting in Seattle, Washington."

Section 12 of the Purchase Agreement provides:

> *Injunctive Relief*: Notwithstanding the foregoing, each party shall be permitted to institute proceedings in a federal or state court of competent jurisdiction to seek temporary or preliminary injunctive relief to enforce Section 5

> of this Agreement in any dispute relating to this Agreement pending the resolution of that dispute through Arbitration.

Thirteen months after the transaction closes, with Integrated having made both the $12 million initial payment and the $2 million first-anniversary payment, Integrated learns that two of the former members of the Fboard management committee have started a new company called "Gboard," which uses the former Fboard technology and pitches its product to former Fboard customers. Integrated's worst fears have come to realization: it paid $14 million so far, only to find itself competing with the very business it bought. Furious, it institutes (a) an arbitration seeking a declaration that since Fboard is in breach of the non-compete, Integrated is relieved from the remaining earn-out payments; and (b) an action in court seeking immediate enforcement of the Section 5 obligations, including an order barring any former Fboard member who signed the joinder from working for Gboard.

Gboard and the individual defendants move to stay the arbitration, claiming that the mandatory arbitration clause bars the action.

1. What section of the FAA should Gboard move on to stay the arbitration?
2. Can the injunction action survive the mandatory arbitration clause?
3. What if the injunction request also included a demand for an immediate declaratory judgment from the court that the defendants had breached the agreement and so Integrated was relieved from future payment obligations?
4. What if Integrated only moved for an injunction and did not also simultaneously file an arbitration demand? Does a party to an arbitration clause that contains an injunction carve-out still have to institute an arbitration in order to employ the carve-out?
5. What if Section 12 of the contract had not carved-out Section 5 (non-compete) actions for injunctions and instead had provided simply that "notwithstanding the foregoing, each party shall be permitted to institute proceedings in a federal or state court of competent jurisdiction to seek temporary or preliminary injunctive relief as appropriate"? Would that affect Integrated's remedy in court?

Each of these are points that drafters should consider in crafting the dispute resolution clause in a contract. Injunction provisions are particularly relevant and useful in situations like the above that involve the risk of imminent irreparable harm by the disclosure of confidential information. Injunction provisions are also critical where there is a timing element to a party's performance that will simply have lapsed or otherwise be effectively mooted if the parties must wait for an injunction to gear up.

IV. Wrapping Up: The Drafting

You have just studied how, within the context of a non-court system, the parties can find themselves in court. You have seen court-ordered injunctions, arbitrator injunctions, and even specially quick arbitrator injunctions.

What would you do with this knowledge when drafting an arbitration clause? Should injunctions be made harder or easier to obtain than in some of the cases you have reviewed above? Should injunction power be more centered on the arbitrators rather than the courts? What language might you use when next drafting such clauses? Or is it your view that the balance is perfectly struck?

Chapter 11

Consolidation and Waiver

So far we have studied disputes about arbitrability: whether there exists a dispute that is subject to arbitration, and the statute and case law that guide courts in making this decision. But arbitration disputes do not stop at the border of arbitrability. Courts and arbitrators sometimes have to struggle with battles that arise notwithstanding the existence of a clear and unambiguous arbitration clause. This chapter explores two of those issues: consolidation and waiver.

It bears repeating that in both cases, there is no question that the parties agreed to arbitrate. It further bears emphasizing further that in both cases, there is not even a question as to whether the arbitration clause covers a dispute in question. So, as you go forward in your study of this chapter, assume again that arbitrability is not the issue. These are both "post-arbitrability" questions.

In the case of consolidation, the question looks at which arbitration clause governs a collection of related disputes and whether such disputes, with a common nexus of factual and legal questions, should be arbitrated together or separately. In waiver, the question is whether a party has acted so contrary to its agreement to arbitrate that, no matter how plainly that clause applies to the dispute, that party has waived its right to arbitration.

Both issues emphasize another theme of this book: the importance of contract law to arbitration. Both issues also raise the "who decides" question you reviewed earlier in this course.

I. Consolidation

Commercial transactions frequently involve multiple agreements and/or multiple parties. Consider, for example, the sale of a business. The parties may enter multiple agreements: one that covers the sale itself (as between buyer and seller), one for its financing (as between buyer and lender), and one that addresses the parties' confidentiality expectations regarding the terms of the deal (as between buyer and the individuals sellers, executing the agreement as natural persons). Or consider a complex construction project, with multiple parties all working on components of the same overall plan. Or parties who have worked with one another for years, in which they are doing business on different contracts at different times, such as an ongoing series of purchase orders for a service or product.

In each of these examples, a dispute under one contract can lead to a chain reaction of disputes under other contracts, just as a dispute between two parties could result in disputes with additional parties. But what happens when the varying underlying contracts have different dispute resolution procedures? In the above sale of business example, what if the agreement between buyer and seller calls for resolution in court, but the companion confidentiality agreement has an arbitration clause, and then fights break out all over? These disputes generally must be heard separately, as befits the separate dispute resolution clauses (arbitration, or otherwise) under which they arise. Recall none other than *Moses Cone's* assertion that if one of the consequences of upholding arbitration clauses in complex disputes is "piecemeal litigation," so be it: "The relevant federal law *requires* piecemeal resolution when necessary to give effect to an arbitration agreement."

Now let's vary the hypothetical. Still a sale of business, still multiple contracts between multiple and different parties, and still with different dispute resolution clauses—but this time each contract calls for arbitration as the method of dispute resolution, *but with separate arbitration clauses, each providing for arbitration in a different location or before a different arbitral institution.*

In that situation, there may be common issues of law and/or fact that are more efficiently resolved by merging the arbitrations into a single proceeding, despite the multiple contracts or parties. Where multiple disputes are heard in a single arbitration, this is called "**consolidation**."

This chapter considers whether disputes can, and should, be consolidated. Depending on the circumstances, the parties may be enthusiastic about the option of consolidation, especially if it promises to save time and money. At the same time, one or more parties may want separate proceedings, perhaps because it fits their litigation strategy to spend (and force their opponent to spend) *more* time and money. Or, parties may simply disagree that the factual or legal issues are all that common, and believe that the cases must be heard separately.

Consolidation therefore brings into conflict two competing values of arbitration: consensus and efficiency. As seen below, without consensus there can frequently be no consolidation, yet the absence of consolidation can create multiple, and thus inefficient, proceedings.

Parties in litigation face no such trade-off. There, consolidation is the rule if the court determines that this is the best way to proceed (and has jurisdiction over the various defendants). Rule 42 of the Federal Rules of Civil Procedure instructs judges to consolidate, either in whole or in appropriate part(s), cases with "a common question of law or fact." By contrast, nothing in arbitration law speaks with the same certitude. The Federal Arbitration Act is silent on consolidation. Courts presented with the question have held consistently that the decision on whether to consolidate is left expressly to the arbitrators and is not appropriate for the court to resolve. Some familiar topics from previous chapters, including what qualifies as a "gateway" issue, come into direct play here.

Absent consensus by the parties, or a ruling by an arbitrator, sharply similar arbitrations will proceed separately. As you read, consider whether the Federal Arbitration Act should be amended to include a feature such as Federal Rule of Civil Procedure Rule 42 on consolidation. What would be the criteria for deciding whether to consolidate—and which of the various involved arbitrators, or which judge(s), should make the decision?

A. Consolidation Scenarios

There are numerous ways in which lawyers in an arbitration can quickly find themselves in situations where at least one of them craves consolidation. The following are four common scenarios:

1. *A v. B, B v. A—one transaction, different contracts.* Sometimes a single business objective and "deal" may result in multiple contracts, and sometimes, those multiple contracts may have inconsistent dispute resolution clauses.

   Example: Valley Drug Co. develops novel hip replacement devices. Because it concentrates on research and development, it has never developed an effective sales force. For its products to make money, it relies on third-party sales organizations. One such organization is Distribute, Inc. In the course of their discussions, Distribute tells Valley that Distribute does not like commission agreements, and that its usual practice is to take title (ownership) of the goods it is selling and then pay a royalty to the original owner. Valley agrees to that structure. As a result, the parties ultimately conclude two different contracts: the Manufacturing Agreement and the Royalty Agreement. By the terms of the Manufacturing Agreement, Valley sells the product to Distribute at a discount from fair market value. By the terms of the Royalty Agreement, Distribute pays Valley a stated price on each unit that Distribute sells to its own clients (doctors and patients). Both contracts call for AAA arbitration, but since neither party wanted to arbitrate anywhere but on its home turf, they compromised: the Manufacturing Agreement calls for arbitration in New York, but the Royalty Agreement calls for arbitration in Santa Fe. When Distribute's projected sales fall far short of the parties' expectations, Distribute blames the quality of the products and brings an action under the Manufacturing Agreement for breach of the quality control provisions of that contract. Valley, incensed that Distribute is withholding royalties, brings a separate arbitration under the Royalty Agreement.

   How many arbitrations should there be? If two, why? If one, where?

2. *A v. B, A v. C, A v. D, etc.—different parties, similar contracts.* Sometimes a single party may have a similar contract with many different parties—for example, non-exclusive licensing agreements with a collection of licensees. In the ultimate form, this could, of course, lead to class actions, but on a smaller scale, it may be easier to resolve a common contract question in one setting.

   Example: Property Co. owns commercial office buildings and leases them out to businesses. In the wake of the 2020 pandemic and shutdown, several tenants in a building at a prime K Street location in Washington, D.C., invoke the force majeure clauses of their lease and demand rent forgiveness. Property Co. disputes that force majeure applies here to reduce rent. Each tenant's lease has an identical arbitration provision calling for AAA arbitration in Washington, D.C. The facts will not greatly differ from arbitration to arbitration: pandemic, tenant, shutdown, no rent, same contract clause. The tenants learn about the arbitrations and propose that they be consolidated to save money. Property Co. is just fine with the tenants spending more money on the arbitration and insists that the cases each proceed separately.

   How many arbitrations should there be? Why?

3. *A v. B, A v. B, A v. B, etc.—same parties, different contracts.* Sometimes the parties may have concluded different contracts for different transactions, but the issues may still be the same.

   Example: Fruit Co. contracts with Waysafe, a leading grocery store chain, to deliver grapes. The following year, Fruit Co. contracts with Waysafe to deliver oranges. In year 3, Fruit Co. contracts with Waysafe to deliver plums. Each contract has an identical arbitration clause. In year 4, the grapes, oranges, and plums delivered to Waysafe all show up with insect infestation. When Waysafe protests, Fruit Co. blames Waysafe, stating that in order to comply with Waysafe's strict supplier requirements, it used the brand of pesticide required by Waysafe of its fruit suppliers in the parties' terms and conditions. Waysafe rejects that claim and argues that Fruit Co. applied the pesticide incorrectly. As a result, Waysafe brings three separate arbitrations against Fruit Co., one for each of the three contracts (and kinds of fruit).

4. *A v. B, B v. C, B. vs. D—different parties, related contracts.* Consider situations in which one party's ability to deliver its own performance depends in whole or part on a third party's performance. One party, "B" here, has contracts with two other parties.

   Example: Franklin J. Hedgefund is constructing a palatial estate on the shores of Bar Harbor, Maine. He has engaged Robert General to perform all construction-related activities. The Hedgefund-General contract has an arbitration clause. Mr. General has in turn engaged several sub-contractors to perform various phases of the work, including installing air conditioning, flooring, landscaping, and roofing. Each of those sub-contracts has an arbitration clause. After the first rainy Maine spring, Hedgefund's palace is flooded. Hedgefund brings an arbitration against General. General, in turn, brings arbitrations against Flooring Co. and Drainage Co.

Should the arbitrations be consolidated? Which ones? Which arbitrator should run the case? How should the parties account for differences in the respective arbitration clauses within a single overall fact pattern?

B. Consolidation: A Battle Between Efficiency and Consensus?

In each of the above examples, the arbitrations could easily and readily be consolidated if the parties agreed. It is that simple. The parties could jointly decide to pick a single arbitrator (or single panel of arbitrators) and then have all claims between them heard in that single forum. They will have to agree on the themes you have so far studied in this book: the scope of the arbitration and issues to be decided; the location; and the rules that will govern. Once they form that consensus, there is no question as to arbitrability, and no question as to the arbitrator's jurisdiction over the parties to issue a final award resolving the dispute. In this way, consolidation cases are no different from those of any of the other cases you have so far studied here.

This chapter exists because parties do not always so agree. One party may want consolidation, or perhaps consolidation of a particular kind, and the other party resists consolidation or wants it somewhere and somehow else.

This makes it difficult to consolidate cases and, in the process, throws the parties into a battle between competing arbitration themes. We have reviewed how a central value of arbitration, especially in the modern arbitration law following *Concepcion*, is efficiency. *See Concepcion*, 563 U.S. at 344 ("The point of affording parties discretion in designing arbitration processes is to allow for efficient, streamlined procedures tailored to the type of dispute."). We have seen multiple commentators exclaim the benefits of efficiency. *See, e.g.*, Mark Beckett, Hall Street Associates v. Mattel, Inc.: *Beyond Agnosticism: The Policy Justifications for the Supreme Court's Decision in* Hall Street Associates, 17 Am. Rev. Int'l Arb. 525 (2006). And so, if efficiency alone were the determining factor, then each of the examples above would be consolidated into a single arbitration proceeding. One city. One arbitrator (or panel). One scheduling order. One award. This, again, would be precisely the result in federal court (jurisdiction permitting) under Federal Rule 42's "common question of law or fact" standard.

But we are not in federal court. Arbitration requires consensus. This is not circular. It is not chicken and egg. Here, there is a strict order of primacy, and consensus comes first. "Efficiency" affects the kind of arbitration one may have, but "consensus" affects whether there is an arbitration at all. If parties are not going to buy a car in the first place, they never get to the point of discussing its color.

Source of Law. Given the conflict between consensus and efficiency, on what legal basis should consolidation be decided? To what source of law should the court (or arbitrator) look in resolving the question of "one or many"? The FAA is silent, as noted above. Silent too, in all the cases and examples in this chapter, is the parties' dispute resolution clause—otherwise the answer would be right there. Given silence in both the statute and the contract, what is the legal source of the consolidation answer? The following court struggled with several streams.

Specialty Bakeries v. RobHal, Inc.

Civil Action No. 97-1057, 1997 U.S. Dist. LEXIS 9095 (E.D. Pa. June 24, 1997)

BATTLE, III, District Judge.

Plaintiff Specialty Bakeries, Inc. ("Specialty Bakeries") instituted this diversity action on February 12, 1997 to compel its bagel store franchisees, defendants RobHal, Inc. and HalRob, Inc. ("HalRob"), to arbitrate a dispute under a franchise agreement. Pursuant to the Federal Arbitration Act, 9 U.S.C. §§ 1–14, the court ordered arbitration on March 26, 1997 and then on April 15, 1997 enjoined HalRob from proceeding with an action in the New Jersey Superior Court which violated the parties' agreement to arbitrate.

Presently before the court is the motion of HalRob to consolidate two arbitration proceedings currently before the American Arbitration Association ("AAA"). Defendants also ask this court to stay one of the arbitrations pending a decision from the Court of Appeals for the Third Circuit on their appeal from this court's April 15, 1997 order.

The first of the two arbitrations was filed by plaintiff Specialty Bakeries on March 7, 1997. It seeks to recoup attorney's fees which it has expended in this court and the New Jersey state court on the ground that HalRob improperly resorted to a lawsuit instead of arbitration as their franchise agreement requires. Because Specialty Bakeries seeks under $50,000, it is on an expedited arbitration track under AAA rules. This arbitration will most likely be heard before the second arbitration.

The second arbitration, filed by HalRob, was not instituted until April 8, 1997, a delay of almost two weeks after this court's order dated March 26, 1997 compelling such arbitration. In this proceeding HalRob alleges that Specialty Bakeries breached the non-competition provision in their franchise agreement. Since HalRob seeks damages in excess of $50,000, this arbitration is not on an expedited track under AAA rules.

On May 1, 1997, HalRob requested that AAA consolidate these two arbitrations, or in the alternative, stay the arbitration initiated by Specialty Bakeries pending a decision by the Court of Appeals on HalRob's appeal. Specialty Bakeries advised the AAA that it opposed any consolidation or stay. As a result, AAA informed counsel that it would neither consolidate nor stay the arbitration. In a letter dated June 4, 1997, AAA explained that "absent the agreement of all parties, applicable contractual provisions authorizing joint arbitrations, or a court order, the Association cannot consolidate the parties' disputes/claims."

The parties' franchise agreement requires arbitration of disputes by the AAA and specifically incorporates the Commercial Rules of the AAA.

The FAA makes no provision for consolidation. Likewise, neither the franchise agreement itself nor the Commercial Rules of the AAA, adopted by the parties in their franchise agreement, specifically provides for consolidation. Instead, HalRob relies on the Federal Rules of Civil Procedure for the authority to do so. Rule 81(a)(3) of the Federal Rules of Civil Procedure states that "in proceedings under Title 9, U.S.C., relating to arbitration [FAA] . . . these rules apply only to the extent that matters of procedure are not provided for in those statutes." Depending upon the scope and application of this rule, we may have the power to consolidate actions pursuant to Rule 42(a) which allows consolidation when there is a "common question of law or fact."

HalRob directs this court to the case of *Compania Espanola de Petroleos v. Nereus Shipping*, 527 F.2d 966, 974–75 (2d Cir. 1975), which held that a federal court has the power to order consolidation pursuant to these Federal Rules. This case was effectively overruled, however, by *Government of the United Kingdom of Great Britain v. Boeing*, 998 F.2d 68 (2d Cir. 1993). In Boeing, the Second Circuit held that Supreme Court cases subsequent to *Nereus*, had "undermined our previous conclusion" in that case and therefore, "to the extent our decision in Nereus is based on the Federal Rules of Civil Procedure and the 'liberal purposes' of the [FAA], we hold that it is no longer good law." *Id.* at 71, 74.

Current authorities conclude that Rule 81(a)(3), and through it all the Federal Rules, apply only to judicial proceedings, and not to proceedings before an arbitrator. See 14 James Wm. Moore et al., Moore's Federal Practice P 81.05 (3d ed. 1997); 4 Charles Alan Wright & Arthur R. Miller, Federal Practice and Procedure § 1015 (2d ed. 1987). Wright and Miller observes that "the federal rules do not govern the procedure in the hearings before the arbitrators, which, by agreement of the parties, normally is regulated by the American Arbitration Association's Commercial Arbitration Rules." Several federal courts have held that absent the parties' agreement to the contrary, the Federal Rules cannot be used to order consolidation of arbitrations. *Boeing*, 998 F.2d at 73–74; *Weyerhaeuser Co. v. Western Seas Shipping Co.*, 743 F.2d 635, 637 (9th Cir.), *cert. denied*, 469 U.S. 1061, 83 L. Ed. 2d 431, 105 S. Ct. 544 (1984); *In re Arbitration Between Coastal Shipping Ltd. and S. Petroleum Tankers Ltd.*, 812 F. Supp. 396, 403 (S.D.N.Y. 1993); *PaineWebber, Inc. v. Fowler*, 791 F. Supp. 821, 825–26 (D. Kan. 1992). We agree. Rule 81(a)(3) cannot be invoked in conjunction with Rule 42(a) to consolidate matters before an arbitrator.

HalRob next contends that we have the power under New Jersey law to consolidate the two arbitrations. It relies on the fact that paragraph 27 of the franchise agreement between the parties provides that it shall be construed according to the laws of that state. Thus, HalRob maintains that by applying New Jersey law we would simply be enforcing the terms of the franchise agreement.

Specialty Bakeries and HalRob, as noted, have incorporated New Jersey law into their franchise agreement. According to one state intermediate appellate court case, cited by HalRob, New Jersey "courts find no difficulty in consolidating arbitration proceedings where all parties are signatory to arbitration." *See, e.g., Manchester Township Bd. of Educ. v. Thomas P. Carney, Inc.*, 199 N.J. Super. 266, 489 A.2d 682, 689 (N.J. Super. Ct. App. Div. 1985). *Manchester* involved a dispute over a defective building. *Id.* at 683–84. The plaintiff board of education asked the court to consolidate its arbitration against the contractor with a court action it brought against the architect of the building. *Id.* at 688. The New Jersey court, however, declined to order consolidation because "a contractual right to arbitrate cannot be abridged in favor of consolidation with judicial proceedings." *Id.* at 689.

The New Jersey Arbitration Act, N.J. Stat. Ann. §§ 2A:24-3 (West 1997) *et seq.*, it should be noted, does not mention consolidation. Rather, it mirrors the FAA and provides that a court may "direct that arbitration proceed in the manner provided for in the agreement." *Id.* § 2A:24-3.

We need not decide whether New Jersey law allows a court to order consolidation or whether our venture into this arena is contrary to the Court of Appeals' admonition in *Great Western*. Even if we have the power to order consolidation, we would not do so here. In our view the two arbitrations are discrete. The decision in one will not affect the decision of the other. The issue in the first arbitration is whether HalRob breached the franchise agreement to arbitrate the parties' dispute and therefore whether HalRob owes attorney's fees and costs to Specialty Bakeries. This determination has no effect upon the issue in the second arbitration, that is, whether or not Specialty Bakeries has breached the non-competition portion of the franchise agreement and owes damages to HalRob. Moreover, under the AAA rules, HalRob had the opportunity in March, 1997 to file a counterclaim against Specialty Bakeries in the first arbitration. For tactical reasons it refused to do so. If HalRob had timely filed a counterclaim, the two arbitration issues would have been decided together. However, the door is now closed. HalRob in essence is asking this court to order what it had a chance at one point to achieve on its own. We see no reason to extricate HalRob from a situation of its own choosing now that it sees no advantage for itself in its earlier decision. To do so would be detrimental to Specialty Bakeries. To grant HalRob the relief it seeks would simply cause further delay in this already much delayed matter. The motion for consolidation will be denied.

Notes and Questions

Count the sources of law the court examined in *Specialty Bakeries.* The parties' contract. The FAA. Institutional rules (in this case, the AAA rules). The Federal Rules of Civil Procedure. The New Jersey arbitration act. New Jersey common law. Was it appropriate to look at each of these sources? Ultimately, which controlled? Which should have? How does the result here square with the principle you have studied that arbitration is a matter of contract, and that contract rules are, in turn, generally rules of state common law?

C. Consolidation and Arbitrability: Who Decides?

If parties cannot agree on whether or not to consolidate their dispute, then who decides? Should the question be put to the courts or to the arbitrator(s)? And, if to the arbitrators, in circumstances where there are multiple arbitrations pending, then to which one? Why?

You will recognize here some familiar concepts from earlier in this book. In Chapter 3, we saw the Supreme Court introduce the delineating factor of a "gateway issue" in its 2003 opinion in *Green Tree Fin. Corp. v. Bazzle*:

> In certain limited circumstances, courts assume that the parties intended courts, not arbitrators, to decide a particular arbitration-related matter (in the absence of "clear and unmistakable" evidence to the contrary). These limited instances typically involve matters of a kind that "contracting parties would likely have expected a court" to decide. They include *certain gateway matters*, such as whether the parties have a valid arbitration agreement at all or whether a concededly binding arbitration clause applies to a certain type of controversy.

Having identified the gateway concept as basically one of arbitrability—i.e., whether the parties, in fact, agreed to arbitrate their dispute—the Court then struggled with whether a particular issue raised an arbitrability question. We saw numerous cases where the Court (and thus the lower courts) grappled with whether the decision to hear an arbitration as a class action was one of arbitrability (a gateway issue) or one of process. Unless delegated (recall *First Options* and delegation clauses), arbitrability is for the courts to decide. But the issue of how an arbitration is conducted is distinctly not a gateway issue and thus, under *Greentree*, for the arbitrator to decide.

Where does consolidation fall? Is it a gateway issue or one of process? Is there any question in the consolidation cases that the parties agreed to arbitrate?

Certain Underwriters at Lloyd's London v. Westchester Fire Ins. Co.

489 F.3d 580 (3d Cir. 2007)

SLOVITER, Circuit Judge.

At issue in this appeal is whether an arbitrator or a court should decide whether coverage disputes under essentially identical insurance contracts should be arbitrated separately on a contract-by-contract basis or collectively in a consolidated arbitration. The District Court held that the issue of consolidation should be decided by an arbitrator. We believe that decision comports with the direction provided by two Supreme Court decisions and will affirm.

I.

The underlying dispute in this matter regards the payment of asbestos claims under reinsurance coverage that Westchester Fire Insurance Company ("Westchester Fire") purchased from certain Lloyd's of London reinsurers (the "Underwriters"). The parties disagree as to how to characterize the coverage at issue. Westchester Fire argues that we are dealing with two reinsurance programs: one being the Comprehensive Catastrophe Treaty, which was made up of six essentially identical contracts covering different time periods in effect from 1972–1985 inclusive, and the other, the Special Contingency Treaty, made up of two essentially identical contracts in effect from 1974–1982 inclusive.

By way of brief introduction to the industry terminology, "[t]here are two types of reinsurance contract: treaty and facultative." *North River Ins. Co. v. CIGNA Reinsurance Co.*, 52 F.3d 1194, 1199 (3d Cir. 1995). Unlike facultative reinsurance, which "entails the ceding of a particular risk or policy[,]" a reinsurance treaty involves an agreement by a reinsurer "to accept an entire block of business from the reinsured.... Because a treaty reinsurer accepts an entire block of business, it does not assess the individual risks being reinsured; rather, it evaluates the overall risk pool." *Id.*

On May 13, 2005, Westchester Fire sent two arbitration demand letters to the Underwriters, each based upon one of the two treaties. Westchester Fire captioned one demand as referencing the "Comprehensive Catastrophe Excess of Loss—All Layers" treaty, effective "7/1/72–6/30/85 Inclusive," and the other as referencing the "Special Casualty Contingency Excess of Loss" treaty, effective "7/1/74–6/30/82." Each letter stated that Westchester Fire "hereby demands and initiates arbitration under the above captioned Treaty.... [Underwriters] are requested and required in accordance with pertinent treaty provisions to name their arbitrator."

In response to each demand, the Underwriters filed a Verified Petition to Compel Arbitration and Stay Arbitration in the District of New Jersey. Their petition in response to the Comprehensive Catastrophe arbitration demand argued that the Comprehensive Catastrophe Treaty consists of at least six separate contracts, each with its own arbitration clause, and that "[n]one of the agreements provide for the consolidation of arbitration proceedings, let alone consolidation with proceedings under other contracts." They asked that the demand be stayed. Likewise, the petition in response to the Special Casualty Contingency arbitration demand argued that the demand should be stayed, as it was an effort to consolidate a dispute arising under at least two separate reinsurance contracts, each having its own arbitration clause.

The Underwriters' petitions also requested that the court order eight arbitrations in conjunction with the eight contracts the Underwriters had identified—i.e., six separate arbitrations in response to Westchester Fire's demand under the Comprehensive Catastrophe program and two separate arbitrations under the Special Contingency program. The Underwriters asked as well that Westchester Fire "produce all reinsurance agreements within the scope of its arbitration demand[,]" as there may exist "other agreements not presently known to petitioners[,]" and sought a declaration that "Westchester may not consolidate proceedings without the consent of all parties to the agreements[.]"

As the basis for its request for arbitration, Westchester Fire argues that the Underwriters have imposed onerous documentation and claim procedures before payment of asbestos claims that they had reinsured, and that these requirements differ from the parties' prior course of dealing. It complains that the Underwriters have subjected it to repetitive audits and requests for information, and have not paid the billings that Westchester Fire submitted. It seeks an award enforcing the payment requirement and confirming that it is under no obligation to meet the extra-contractual documentation or claim procedures that the Underwriters have asserted.

In response to each Underwriters' petition, Westchester Fire cross-moved to compel arbitration. In regard to the Special Contingency petition, Westchester Fire argued that, "[a]lthough the contract wording for the Reinsurance Program varied in certain respects over the years, the contract wording for the Reinsurance Program provides that the contract between the parties is continuous, even though it changes in certain respects over time. Disputes under the Reinsurance Program are to be resolved by arbitration in Morristown, New Jersey." Westchester Fire responded similarly to the Underwriters' Comprehensive Catastrophe petition, arguing that, while "[t]he Reinsurance Program consisted of several layers over the years[,]" the agreement between the parties was continuous and, similarly, called for arbitration in Morristown, New Jersey.

Following consolidation of the two actions, the District Court observed that it was "not presented with the question of whether a valid arbitration agreement exists[,]" but, rather, the question of whether the parties had contractually agreed to "separate arbitrations under the various contractual layers to the reinsurance program or [to] a single consolidated arbitration" with respect to each petition. This, the District Court concluded, was an issue "for the arbitrators not the courts to decide." It issued an order denying the Underwriters' petitions and granting Westchester Fire's cross-motions to compel arbitration. The order directed the Underwriters to appoint a single arbitrator in response to each of Westchester Fire's arbitration demands, and "proceed promptly with Westchester Fire Insurance Company to identify a single umpire in response" to each arbitration demand. The order also instructed that the "relief granted herein shall not, in any matter, preclude" the Underwriters from applying to the arbitration panel "for the same or similar relief sought in this proceeding nor in any way limit [the] Panel's authority to grant such relief."

The Underwriters (the reinsurers) argue that the District Court had no authority to order the parties to submit to an arbitral determination of the question of whether future arbitrations on the underlying merits issue would occur in consolidated or contract-by-contract fashion. The Underwriters argue that the arbitration clause in each agreement calls for an arbitration of all issues pertaining to that specific reinsurance contract, which they believe requires an "individually-convened" arbitration. Therefore, they continue, forcing all parties into a unified threshold proceeding in connection with each demand is beyond the scope of what the parties agreed to arbitrate. The issue of consolidated arbitration, they insist, should be presented to individual arbitration panels convened in accordance with each contract.

In contrast to the Underwriters, Westchester Fire argues that the question of whether the contracts should be arbitrated collectively or individually is itself a determination that must be made by an arbitrator. In the alternative, Westchester Fire argues that, were we to decide that it is the District Court that must make the consolidation decision, New Jersey law "authorizes court-ordered consolidation of multiple arbitrations under multiple contracts[.]" In light of our determination, we need not reach this issue.

Howsam and *Green Tree* together explain why no "question of arbitrability," as the Supreme Court has recently—and narrowly—defined that phrase, has been raised here. Under section 4 of the FAA, federal courts, "upon being satisfied that the making of the agreement for arbitration or the failure to comply therewith is not in issue," are authorized to "make an order summarily directing the parties to proceed to arbitration in accordance with the terms thereof." 9 U.S.C. § 4; *see also* 9 U.S.C. § 206 ("A court having jurisdiction under this chapter may direct that arbitration be held in accordance with the agreement. . . ."). This, the District Court has done.

As in *Green Tree*, the question here is "not whether the parties wanted a judge or an arbitrator to decide *whether they agreed to arbitrate a matter*," but rather "what *kind of arbitration proceeding* the parties agreed to." 539 U.S. at 452 (emphasis in original). In this case, the parties agree that they agreed to arbitrate the matter—the question is merely whether they agreed to individualized or consolidated proceedings as a matter of procedure. Therefore, "any doubt" here about the "scope of arbitrable issues should be resolved in favor of arbitration." *Id.* at 445 (internal quotation marks and citation omitted).

In *Employers Ins. Co. of Wausau v. Century Indemnity Co.*, 443 F.3d 573 (7th Cir. 2006), the Court of Appeals for the Seventh Circuit refused to accept a reinsurer's argument that "no mention of consolidation" in the agreements at issue between the parties necessarily meant that the reinsurer, Wausau, was "entitled to two separate arbitrations for the two reinsurance agreements it has with [the insured insurance company,] Century." *Id.* at 581, 574. The court stated that the "question of whether an arbitration agreement forbids consolidated arbitration is a procedural one, which the arbitrator should resolve." *Id.* at 577.

On the question of how the parties were then to proceed with the mechanics of the arbitration, the *Wausau* court acknowledged that the district court had crafted an order that required "Wausau to appoint one arbitrator and proceed to one arbitration, covering both Agreements." *Id.* at 581. It then considered the reinsurer's argument that the act of "ordering it to arbitrate both Agreements in one arbitration would conflict with the terms of the arbitration clauses, for example by not allowing 'each party to appoint its arbitrator.'" *Id.* at 581–82. The Court of Appeals soundly rejected any suggestion that the district court's order was in error. Citing both *Howsam* and *Green Tree*, the court stated,

> We should not and will not consider this argument. The question before us is whether the parties' Agreements specify *who* is to decide whether consolidated arbitration is allowed—the court or the arbitrator. We have determined that the Agreements do not specify and that questions regarding consolidation are presumptively for the arbitrator. Wausau is free to argue at the arbitration that separate arbitrations for the First Excess Agreement and Second Excess Agreement are required under the contracts' terms. If the arbitration panel agrees, it can require the parties to proceed as it deems appropriate. *Id.* at 582 (emphasis in original).

In light of the above authority, the parties' agreement to arbitrate their disputes, contractual silence as to the consolidation issue, and the longstanding federal policy favoring arbitration, we see no reason why this procedural issue should not be resolved in arbitration. Accordingly, we will affirm the District Court's order.

Comment

In the *Lloyd's* case you just read, there was a single body of arbitrators. The issue was whether that same panel should hear different arbitral disputes as one matter or several and, more immediately—in keeping with this text's concentration on the "who" question—whether that consolidation decision was to be made by the court or the arbitrator. Would the answer have changed if there were multiple panels rather than a single panel?

The question of a single panel's authority to consolidate multiple matters before it is explored further in the following case, which, as you will see, cites back to *Lloyd's*.

Champion Chrysler v. Dimension Serv. Corp.

118 N.E.3d 490 (Ohio Ct. App. 2018)

HORTON, J.

Defendant-appellant, Dimension Service Corporation ("Dimension"), appeals from a judgment of the Franklin County Court of Common Pleas that granted the plaintiffs-appellees' motion to confirm a final arbitration award and overruled Dimension's motion to vacate the final arbitration award. For the following reasons, we affirm the judgment.

FACTUAL AND PROCEDURAL HISTORY

Dimension administers vehicle service contracts to automobile purchasers. Each of the appellees, Champion Chrysler, Plymouth Jeep and Ed Parker, Bert Ogden Dealer Group, Ferguson Dealer Group, Allen Tillery Chevrolet and Great Lakes Insurance Agency, Inc., entered into a Profit Share Agreement ("PSA") with Dimension. All of the appellees, except Great Lakes Insurance Agency, Inc., were car dealers and offered consumers a Dimension vehicle service contract at the point of sale. On July 28, 2014, appellees and Darryl Hickman (collectively "claimants") served a joint arbitration demand on Dimension pursuant to the mandatory arbitration provisions in the PSAs, arguing that Dimension failed to make payments in violation of its obligation to do so under the PSAs. Claimants filed a single demand for consolidated arbitration because they were each pursuing claims for additional profit share payments pursuant to identical PSAs. The arbitration demand nominated Kirk Borchardt to serve as the claimants' selected arbitrator. Dimension nominated Frank A. Ray as its selected arbitrator. The final arbitrator, Richard Neville was selected. On January 12, 2015, Dimension objected to the consolidated arbitration.

After briefing, on March 16, 2015, the arbitration panel held that the claims of the six claimants would be consolidated for discovery and motion practice purposes. The panel examined the PSAs finding the same language in each granted the panel broad authority. The consolidation decision set forth that, "[t]he Panel, having been granted this broad authority, finds that this is a proper case for consolidated discovery and motion practice based in part on the principle that arbitration is intended to be an efficient, timely, and cost-effective alternative to litigation." The decision set forth that consolidation for discovery and motion practice purposes would "not prevent separate, individual evidentiary presentations as to defenses or claims," and Dimension was free to petition the arbitration panel to request a separate hearing for any individual claimant and the panel would consider the request.

ASSIGNMENTS OF ERROR

Dimension filed a timely notice of appeal and asserts the following assignments of error:

[I.] By holding that the arbitration panel had authority to consolidate six separate bilateral arbitration claim[s], the Trial Court erred in its legal conclusion and ruled in conflict with the U.S. Supreme Court ruling in *Stolt-Nielsen v. AnimalFeeds International*, by failing to recognize that parties must expressly consent to authorize consolidation of separate claims.

[II.] The Trial Court erred in finding that the arbitration panel did not exceed its authority under R.C. 2711.10(D), while failing to consider the language of the arbitration agreements, which did not grant the panel authority to consider the request to consolidate or authority to order consolidation.

[III.] The Trial Court erred in finding that the arbitration panel had authority to consider consolidation regarding Appellees' six separate claims against the Appellant Dimension, because R.C. 2712.52 specifically provides that a petition, along with proof of unanimous consent to consolidation, must be filed with the courts to consolidate separate arbitration claims.

[IV.] The Trial Court Erred in finding that the arbitration panel had authority to consolidate any two of the appellees' six separate claims against Dimension because the consolidation question is a threshold arbitrability question that was reserved for the Courts, as expressed in *Shakoor v. VXI Glob. Solutions, 2015-Ohio-2587, V 48, 35 N.E.3d 539 (7th Dist.)* and *Stolt-Nielsen*.

ANALYSIS

Dimension argues that the arbitrators exceeded their authority by consolidating the actions because the PSAs did not grant the panel authority to consider the request to consolidate or authority to order consolidation. The Federal Arbitration Act provides that an arbitration panel only has the rights and duties that are provided under the contract. *Reyna Capital Corp. v. McKinney Romeo Motors, Inc.*, 2d Dist. No. 24538, 2011-Ohio-6806, ¶ 37.

The arbitration provision in the PSAs provides:

> The arbitrators need not observe judicial formality or strict rules of evidence, and they shall make their award from a standpoint of practical business practices and equity rather than strict law.

(PSA at ¶ 13.)

The panel observed, based on this broad authority, that these cases were proper for consolidated discovery and motion practice as an efficient, timely, and cost-effective alternative to litigation. Since the contracts were identical and the defenses were likely identical, the panel found consolidation permissible by the contract language and efficient. (Mar. 16, 2015 Decision.) The arbitrators did not violate any provision in the agreements by consolidation. Rather, the language gives the arbitrators broad powers.

Dimension argues that R.C. 2712.52 requires a petition to the court and unanimous consent of the parties for consolidation of arbitration. R.C. 2712.52 provides, as follows:

> (A) If the parties to two or more arbitration agreements have agreed, in their respective arbitration agreements or otherwise, to consolidate the arbitrations arising out of those arbitration agreements, the court of common pleas, on application by one party with the consent of all the other parties to those arbitration agreements, may do one or more of the following:
>
> (1) Order the arbitrations to be consolidated on terms the court considers just and necessary;
>
> (2) If all the parties cannot agree on an arbitral tribunal for the consolidated arbitration, appoint an arbitral tribunal in accordance with section 2712.20 of the Revised Code;
>
> (3) If all the parties cannot agree on any other matter necessary to conduct the consolidated arbitration, make any other order it considers necessary.
>
> (B) Nothing in this section shall be construed to prevent the parties to two or more arbitrations from agreeing to consolidate those arbitrations and taking any steps that are necessary to effect that consolidation.

Dimension argues that consolidation is a threshold question of arbitrability for the courts to determine. Dimension cites *West v. Household Life Ins. Co.*, 170 Ohio App. 3d 463, (10th Dist.), for the proposition that "identifying the allowable parties to an arbitration is a fundamental question of arbitrability, which may only be decided by the courts, and not an issue of procedural arbitrability." However, again Dimension misconstrues the case law. In *West*, an insurer sought a motion to stay proceedings and compel arbitration. The insurer was not a party to the arbitration rider and the subject matter of the litigation was outside the scope of the arbitrable issues. *West* is distinguishable from the case at hand because its facts involved a motion to stay litigation already pending in the court, a party who was not a party to the arbitration rider and an issue that was not within the scope of the arbitrable issues. Thus, this court determined that the trial court needed to determine whether the parties before the court were the same parties named in the agreement to arbitrate and whether they agreed to arbitrate the dispute in question before the trial court orders arbitration. The holding was not that consolidation is a threshold question of arbitrability for the courts.

Federal Circuit Courts of Appeal have consistently held that the matter of consolidation is not a threshold question of arbitrability for a court to decide, but, rather, is a matter of procedure for the arbitrator. *See Certain Underwriters at Lloyd's London v. Westchester Fire Ins. Co.*, 489 F.3d 580, 587 (3d Cir. 2007) ("In this case, the parties agree that they agreed to arbitrate the matter—the question is merely whether they agreed to individualized or consolidated proceedings as a matter of procedure.") ("[I]n the face of contractual silence, arbitral resolution of procedural issues is presumed[.]"); *Emps. Ins. Co. of Wausau v. Century Indemnity Co.*, 443 F.3d 573, 577 (7th Cir. 2006), citing *Dockser v. Schwartzberg*, 433 F.3d 421, 427 (4th Cir. 2006) ("[T]he question of whether an arbitration agreement forbids consolidated arbitration is a procedural one, which the arbitrator should resolve."); *Shaw's Supermarkets, Inc. v. UFCW*, 321 F.3d 251, 254 (1st Cir. 2003) ("The issue before us is who should make the determination as to whether to consolidate the three grievances into a single arbitration: the arbitrator or a federal court. Since each of the three grievances is itself concededly arbitrable, we think the answer is clear.... This is a procedural matter for the arbitrator."); *Blimpie Int'l Inc. v. Blimpie of the Keys*, 371 F. Supp. 2d 469, 473–74 (S.D.N.Y. 2005) ("Whether an arbitration proceeding should be consolidated with one or more other arbitration proceedings is a question properly addressed by the arbitrator."). We find that the trial court did not err in finding that the arbitration panel did not exceed its authority in finding that the cases were proper for consolidated discovery and motion practice.

Notes and Questions

1. *Does Efficiency Matter?* There is no question that, even though efficiency is not expressly mentioned in the FAA, it has become a modern-day battle cry in those cases that insulate arbitration agreements from attack. As noted, we saw this repeatedly in the class action cases reviewed earlier in this book, in which the Supreme Court held that one reason arbitration was incompatible with class action procedures was that it would make arbitration less "efficient." *See* Justice Scalia's opinion in *Concepcion* ("Requiring the availability of classwide arbitration interferes with fundamental attributes of arbitration and thus creates a scheme inconsistent with the FAA.... The point of affording parties discretion in designing arbitration processes is to allow for efficient, streamlined procedures tailored to the type of dispute ... [and] the switch from bilateral to class arbitration sacrifices the principal advantage of arbitration—its informality—and makes the process slower, more costly, and more likely to generate procedural morass than final judgment.") and Justice Gorsuch's opinion in *Epic Systems* ("In the Court's judgment, the virtues Congress originally saw in arbitration, its speed and simplicity and inexpensiveness, would be shorn away and arbitration would wind up

looking like the litigation it was meant to displace.").

Critics of the efficiency argument contend that it is not so much a core value of arbitration as it is a convenient excuse for mowing down class actions in arbitration. The consolidation cases may prove their point: if it is more efficient to consolidate cases, then why not simply consolidate them? For example, in *Champion*, the arbitrators consolidated only for discovery purposes, rather than consolidating the cases all the way through the merits hearings. Did this make a difference? Should it have? Should there be more authority to consolidate (and less judicial review of that decision) when the scope of consolidation is narrower? Or is a gateway a gateway and so the discretion should be the same no matter the scope of consolidation?

The FAA could even be amended to address consolidation. *Champion* shows the effect of such a statute. In that case, there was a statute that would actually have prescribed the result and allowed the court to consolidate—but, as the court found, that statute applied only to international cases. This returns us to the question of FAA amendments. If the FAA were amended to allow judges to consolidate, would that lead to greater efficiency (since there would be less of the procedural skirmishing you have just read about) or less efficiency, because parties would run to court more often to seek this relief? And what would this do to the gateway concept?

2. *Gateways and Consolidation*. As used in consolidation, is gateway circular? The parties got to the stage of fighting about consolidation precisely because there is more than one arbitration going on, or that could go on. So sending this back to arbitration is sending this to . . . what? The question is easy when, as in both of the preceding cases, there is a single panel. The issue is procedural and for the arbitrators. But . . .

3. . . . *What Happens When There Is More Than One Arbitration Panel in Cases That Should Be Arbitrated?* It is one thing to say that the arbitrator(s) rather than the court should decide consolidation. It is quite another to then say *what arbitrator* decides. The court in *Employers Insurance Company of Wausau v. Hartford*, No. 2:18-cv-07240-CAS-AGR, 2018 U.S. Dist. LEXIS 205345, at *9, 2018 WL 6330425 (C.D. Cal. Dec. 3, 2018), identified this problem:

> Hartford is correct that the issue of whether it can consolidate its disputes with Wausau into a single arbitration is a question for the arbitrators, not this Court, to decide. Contrary to Hartford's suggestion, however, this determination does not resolve the matter in its favor. The parties remain at an impasse due to Hartford's insistence on a consolidated arbitration. Despite both

> parties appointing arbitrators, Hartford refuses to go forward with the umpire selection pursuant to the terms of the arbitration clause in Treaty 2718. Consequently, no umpire has been selected to form the requisite three-arbitrator panel. There is no one to whom the Court can refer the consolidation dispute for arbitration. As one district court explained, "[i]t would be nonsensical to package the parties' dispute and send it off addressed to 'arbitrator' when, in fact, there is no arbitrator to receive it." *Employers Ins. Co. of Wausau v. Century Indem. Co.*, No. 05 C 263 S, 2005 U.S. Dist. LEXIS 37147, 2005 WL 2100977, at *2 (W.D. Wis. July 19, 2005), *aff'd*, 443 F.3d 573 (7th Cir. 2006). Pursuant to § 4 of the FAA, this Court has the power to compel the parties to proceed to arbitration in accordance with the terms of their agreements. 9 U.S.C. § 4.

But the *Wausau* court had an easy out because within all the parties' various agreements was one which, at least according to the court, had a particular procedure that could and should resolve this issue:

> The Court finds that the operative arbitration agreement in this case is the arbitration clause found in Treaty 2718. The parties do not dispute that Treaty 2718 is a valid agreement and that the consolidation dispute falls within its terms. Treaty 2718 provides an unambiguous procedure for the creation of its own arbitration panel to resolve this and any other disputes that might later arise. Wausau and Hartford have agreed that "any dispute arising out of this contract" shall be submitted to three-arbitrator panel arbitration in Los Angeles, California. Treaty 2718 requires that each party shall appoint an arbitrator and that the two arbitrators shall choose an umpire before instituting the hearing. Once Wigmore and Pigatore appoint an umpire, the proceedings can begin, and the empaneled arbitrators can consider Hartford's request to consolidate.

Fair enough—but what if the parties lack such a clear provision on consolidation? One arbitrator must put himself out of business, standing aside to let the other arbitrator handle the consolidated cases. Is that likely?

It would seem that the answer is: no consolidation. If a court will not resolve the issue, and if the issue is left for the arbitrator(s), and if the arbitrator(s) then themselves do not reach a collaborative, joint result, then the parties are left back where they started: with separate arbitrations. Consensus—or here, more precisely, the lack of consensus—wins out over efficiency.

D. Institutional Arbitration and Consolidation

Party consensus can also address consolidation by reference to institutional arbitration clauses—to a point. The AAA Commercial Arbitration Rules are silent on consolidation, other than suggesting in its Prehearing Checklist that the parties should discuss this issue with the arbitrator at the prehearing/organizational conference.

The JAMS rules on consolidation are more robust:

> **JAMS, Rule 6(e)**
>
> Unless the Parties' Agreement or applicable law provides otherwise, JAMS, if it determines that the Arbitrations so filed have common issues of fact or law, may consolidate Arbitrations in the following instances:
>
> (i) If a Party files more than one Arbitration with JAMS, JAMS may consolidate the Arbitrations into a single Arbitration.
>
> (ii) Where a Demand or Demands for Arbitration is or are submitted naming Parties already involved in another Arbitration or Arbitrations pending under these Rules, JAMS may decide that the new case or cases shall be consolidated into one or more of the pending proceedings and referred to one of the Arbitrators or panels of Arbitrators already appointed.
>
> (iii) Where a Demand or Demands for Arbitration is or are submitted naming Parties that are not identical to the Parties in the existing Arbitration or Arbitrations, JAMS may decide that the new case or cases shall be consolidated into one or more of the pending proceedings and referred to one of the Arbitrators or panels of Arbitrators already appointed.
>
> When rendering its decision, JAMS will take into account all circumstances, including the links between the cases and the progress already made in the existing Arbitrations.
>
> Unless applicable law provides otherwise, where JAMS decides to consolidate a proceeding into a pending Arbitration, the Parties to the consolidated case or cases will be deemed to have waived their right to designate an Arbitrator as well as any contractual provision with respect to the site of the Arbitration.

The obvious limitation on the scope of the JAMS rules is that all the actions to be consolidated must call for JAMS arbitration. Return on this basis to the four scenarios at the beginning of this chapter. Would these situations be solved if they were all in JAMS? What if one was JAMS and the other AAA?

The AAA's international arm, the International Center for Dispute Resolution (ICDR) recently promulgated a more detailed rule on consolidation. Where there are two ICDR arbitrations, the ICDR will—at the request of just one party—appoint a special "consolidation arbitrator" to rule on consolidation:

IDCR, Article 8. Consolidation

1. At the request of a party, the Administrator may appoint a consolidation arbitrator, who will have the power to consolidate two or more arbitrations pending under these Rules, or these and other arbitration rules administered by the AAA or ICDR, into a single arbitration where:
   a. the parties have expressly agreed to consolidation; or
   b. all of the claims and counterclaims in the arbitrations are made under the same arbitration agreement; or
   c. the claims, counterclaims, or setoffs in the arbitrations are made under more than one arbitration agreement; the arbitrations involve the same parties; the disputes in the arbitrations arise in connection with the same legal relationship; and the consolidation arbitrator finds the arbitration agreements to be compatible.
2. A consolidation arbitrator shall be appointed as follows:
   a. The Administrator shall notify the parties in writing of its intention to appoint a consolidation arbitrator and invite the parties to agree upon a procedure for the appointment of a consolidation arbitrator.
   b. If the parties have not within 15 days of such notice agreed upon a procedure for appointment of a consolidation arbitrator, the Administrator shall appoint the consolidation arbitrator.
   c. Absent the agreement of all the parties, the consolidation arbitrator shall not be an arbitrator who is appointed to any pending arbitration subject to potential consolidation under this Article.
   d. The provisions of Articles 13–15 of these Rules shall apply to the appointment of the consolidation arbitrator.
3. In deciding whether to consolidate, the consolidation arbitrator shall consult the parties and may consult the arbitral tribunal(s) and may take into account all relevant circumstances, including:
   a. applicable law
   b. whether one or more arbitrators have been appointed in more than one of the arbitrations and, if so, whether the same or different persons have been appointed;
   c. the progress already made in the arbitrations;

d. whether the arbitrations raise common issues of law and/or facts; and

e. whether the consolidation of the arbitrations would serve the interests of justice and efficiency.

4. The consolidation arbitrator may order that any or all arbitrations subject to potential consolidation be stayed pending a ruling on a request for consolidation.

5. When arbitrations are consolidated, they shall be consolidated into the arbitration that commenced first, unless otherwise agreed by all parties or the consolidation arbitrator finds otherwise.

6. Where the consolidation arbitrator decides to consolidate an arbitration with one or more other arbitrators, each party in those arbitrations shall be deemed to have waived its right to appoint an arbitrator. The consolidation arbitrator may revoke the appointment of any arbitrator and may select one of the previously-appointed tribunals to serve in the consolidated proceeding. The Administrator shall, as necessary, complete the appointment of the tribunal in the consolidated proceeding. Absent the agreement of all parties, the consolidation arbitrator shall not be appointed in the consolidated proceeding.

7. The decision as to consolidation, which need not include a statement of reasons, shall be rendered within 15 days of the date for final submissions on consolidation.

E. Consolidation and the Arbitration Clause

PRACTICE POINTER. We end with a *practice pointer.* Here, as in most other procedural issues, the parties can go a long way toward avoiding the cost of resolving this issue by exercising foresight in their arbitration clauses. Particularly where they know that they are concluding multiple contracts in connection with the transaction, they should contemplate how they want the transactions resolved—singly or together. They can approach this in a number of different ways:

a. expressly authorizing consolidation in a single proceeding of any and all disputes related to [defined transaction];

b. expressly authorizing consolidation in a single proceeding of any and all disputes brought under two or more of the following contracts [named contracts]; or

c. expressly authorizing consolidation in theory, but leaving it up to the arbitrator to decide whether consolidation as to a particular dispute is appropriate.

Any such provisions should also identify the particular arbitrator charged with this duty. One approach would be to vest this power in the arbitrator in the first-filed case. Another would be to vest the duty in the particular arbitrator as to a particular contract. Such an approach would resolve the mandate questions that might otherwise arise.

For the practitioner,

a. think at the beginning of the transaction, when you are asked to draft an arbitration clause, whether you are doing so for a standalone contract or a contract that is one of many.

b. If you are drafting an arbitration clause for parties who already have done business with one another, consider whether you want to bring in disputes about the prior contracts into the dispute resolution provision you presently are drafting.

c. In multi-party situations with multiple contracts, consider whether you want to vest one panel with jurisdiction to hear all disputes or, as in the *Wausau* case, with jurisdiction to determine jurisdiction.

II. Waiver

Since arbitration is a creature of contract law, it is subject to the same defenses as any contract claim under Section 2 of the FAA (the "saving clause")—including waiver. As you may recall from your contracts course, a party can waive a contractual right by acting in a manner inconsistent with that right. *See, e.g.*, 13 Williston on Contracts 39:15 (2020). A party who seeks to resist arbitration can in certain circumstances defend against the motion to compel arbitration by arguing waiver.

The waiver defense arises in arbitration when the party resisting a motion to compel arbitration argues that the party seeking arbitration has acted inconsistently with the arbitration clause, such as by pursuing pursues remedies other than arbitration. If a party first either sues, or defends, in court, and only later seeks arbitration, has that party lost the right to arbitrate its dispute? What if the party only dipped a toe in the court waters—how deep must the party's court involvement be before arbitration is waived? Does participation in an injunction or attachment proceeding in court waive a later right to arbitrate? Does seeking documents in a discovery fight constitute waiver? See also *Lobster 207, LLC v. Pettegrow*, 1:19-CV-00552-LEW, 2020 WL 2839287 (D. Me. June 1, 2020).

What about mixed cases: what if a party moves to dismiss some, but not all, counts in a complaint and moves to compel those counts to arbitration? And what if that moving party's choice was based on a legitimate assessment of arbitrability, such that the complaint presented certain claims that invoke the parties' agreement to arbitrate but certain others that did not? Is arbitration of certain counts "waived" when other counts must proceed in court? How much splitting of the causes of action—as between the arbitrable and non-arbitrable counts—should a court permit?

Finally, does waiver require prejudice to the other party? If the party seeking arbitration simply changes its mind, but the other party has not otherwise relied on the initial non-arbitration steps, should a court find waiver? Or should, as is frequently the case, arbitration be joined with issues of estoppel, and before a court must find waiver it must first find that the other party has relied (on the non-arbitration conduct) to its detriment? *See* Restatement (Second) of Contracts Section 84 at comment b ("'Waiver' is often inexactly defined as 'the voluntary relinquishment of a known right.' When the waiver is reinforced by reliance, enforcement is often said to rest on 'estoppel.'").

As you review the following cases, keep in mind above all else the "liberal federal policy in favor of arbitration" from *Moses Cone* (itself a case where a party argued waiver). Does that policy put a judicial foot on the scale against waiver? How much should traditional contract law doctrines—waiver, consideration, maxims of construction like contra proferentum (recall *Lamps Plus*)—be changed by the subject of the contract being arbitration?

CASE PREVIEW. In the first of the two cases below, the party resisting arbitration simply went too far down the litigation road. In the second, the Court found that even though the party seeking arbitration had otherwise waived its right to arbitrate, the party resisting arbitration had not been prejudiced. Should prejudice be part of the test? And most of all, how far is too far?

Solo v. United Parcel Service Company

947 F.3d 968 (6th Cir. 2020)

STRANCH, Circuit Judge.

Plaintiffs Joe Solo and BleachTech LLC sued Defendant United Parcel Service Co. (UPS) in July 2014 alleging that it had systematically overcharged customers for insurance on their shipments. The first time this case was appealed, we held that the contract governing the shipments was "at least ambiguous" as to the contested charge, *Solo v. UPS Co.*, 819 F.3d 788, 796 (6th Cir. 2016), and reversed the order granting UPS's motion to dismiss. After remand and several months of discovery, UPS moved to compel arbitration, citing an arbitration provision contained in a contract effective after the contested shipments occurred. For the reasons explained below, we AFFIRM the district court's denial of the motion to compel arbitration.

I. BACKGROUND

Both Solo and BleachTech purchased liability insurance for valuable packages shipped through UPS before December 30, 2013. The price of that insurance, called "declared value coverage," was set by the contract governing the shipments, the UPS Tariff/Terms and Conditions of Service (the Original UPS Terms).

According to Solo and BleachTech, [the] language plainly states that there is no additional charge for the first $100 of coverage whether or not a shipper purchases additional declared value coverage. But when Solo and BleachTech shipped their packages, they were charged $0.85 for each hundred-dollar increment, including the first.

Solo and BleachTech sued UPS on behalf of a proposed class of similarly situated UPS customers. UPS moved to dismiss the suit in its entirety because all the claims "require a misinterpretation" of the Terms. UPS argued that the controlling phrase was "total value declared" and that "total" value necessarily includes the first $100.

The final paragraph of that motion stated that UPS "reserves its right to move to compel arbitration and does not by this motion in any way waive this contractual right." UPS referenced an arbitration clause found in the amended contract that became effective December 30, 2013 (the Amended UPS Terms)—after the shipments at issue in this suit were mailed, though BleachTech shipped packages with UPS under the amended terms post-December 30, 2013. The Amended UPS Terms, unlike the Original UPS Terms in use at the time of the shipments, provide that "any controversy or claim, whether at law or equity, arising out of or related to the provision of services by UPS, regardless of the date of accrual of such dispute, shall be resolved in its entirety by individual (not class-wide nor collective) binding arbitration." UPS's motion to dismiss stated that because the Complaint alleges shipments only prior to the effective date of the Amended UPS Terms, "UPS does not have sufficient information at this time to know whether its arbitration clause could apply in this action."

The district court granted the motion to dismiss, agreeing with UPS that the first $100 of declared value is part of the total value declared under the plain meaning of that term, and accordingly, an $0.85 charge applies to that declared value under the contract. Solo and BleachTech appealed. We reversed, relying on the complaint's allegations that UPS routinely credits customers who complain about the overcharge and so "itself acknowledges the validity of Solo's reading of the contractual provision." *Solo*, 819 F.3d at 795–96. We held that the provision was "at least ambiguous," *id.* at 796, and remanded for further proceedings.

On remand, UPS filed its answer, raising the obligation to arbitrate as its first affirmative defense, and sought limited discovery focused on arbitration. The district court appears to have rejected the proposed limitation, and after six months of full discovery, UPS moved to compel arbitration. The district court denied the motion on the basis that UPS "waived its right to arbitrate by taking actions inconsistent with reliance on the arbitration provision and delaying its assertion of the need to arbitrate, to the actual prejudice of Plaintiffs." UPS appeals.

II. ANALYSIS

This case, now in its fifth year of litigation, makes its second appearance in this court.

B. Waiver

Even if the scope of the arbitration agreement in the Amended UPS Terms were ambiguous, the district court properly concluded that UPS waived its right to arbitrate.

As discussed above, the FAA's "liberal federal policy favoring arbitration agreements," *Hergenreder*, 656 F.3d at 416 (quoting *Javitch*, 315 F.3d at 624), encourages "efficient and speedy dispute resolution," *Dean Witter Reynolds*, 470 U.S. at 221. Because a valid arbitration provision avoids court process, courts resolve arbitration disputes with dispatch, including via interlocutory appeals such as this one. But the benefits of "efficient and speedy" arbitration are lost if a party seeks arbitration only after insisting upon court process. Thus, although "we will not lightly infer a party's waiver of its right to arbitration," we may find waiver if a party (1) "tak[es] actions that are completely inconsistent with any reliance on an arbitration agreement; and (2) 'delay[s] its assertion to such an extent that the opposing party incurs actual prejudice.'" *Hurley v. Deutsche Bank Tr. Co. Ams.*, 610 F.3d 334, 338 (6th Cir. 2010) (quoting *O.J. Distrib., Inc. v. Hornell Brewing Co.*, 340 F.3d 345, 356 (6th Cir. 2003)).

We begin with the first prong—action that is inconsistent with reliance on arbitration—and UPS's motion to dismiss. "Not every motion to dismiss is inconsistent with the right to arbitration." *Hooper v. Advance Am., Cash Advance Ctrs. of Mo., Inc.*, 589 F.3d 917, 922 (8th Cir. 2009) (collecting cases). For example, the Eighth Circuit has held that a motion to dismiss raising "jurisdictional and quasi-jurisdictional grounds" but seeking "no action with respect to the merits of the case" is not inconsistent with later seeking arbitration. *Dumont v. Sask. Gov't Ins.*, 258 F.3d 880, 886–87 (8th Cir. 2001). Similarly, where a complaint asserts a mix of arbitrable and nonarbitrable claims, "the portions of the motion [to dismiss] addressed to nonarbitrable claims do not constitute a waiver." *Sweater Bee by Banff, Ltd. v. Manhattan Indus.*, 754 F.2d 457, 463 (2d Cir. 1985). On the other hand, a motion to dismiss that seeks "a decision on the merits" and "an immediate and total victory in the parties' dispute" is entirely inconsistent with later requesting that those same merits questions be resolved in arbitration. *Hooper*, 589 F.3d at 922. A party may not use a motion to dismiss "to see how the case [is] going in federal district court," *id.* (quoting *Cabinetree of Wis., Inc. v. Kraftmaid Cabinetry, Inc.*, 50 F.3d 388, 391 (7th Cir. 1995)), while holding arbitration in reserve for "a second chance in another forum," *Hurley*, 610 F.3d at 339 (quoting *Rush v. Oppenheimer & Co.*, 779 F.2d 885, 890 (2d Cir. 1985)).

UPS's motion to dismiss was thoroughly enmeshed in the merits. It sought dismissal of all claims on the basis that Solo and BleachTech misinterpreted contractual language. By asking the court to decide the meaning of the key contractual language, UPS sought "immediate and total victory." UPS had good reason to think this strategy was sound. The same district court had just accepted UPS's contractual argument in a virtually identical case, and it then did so here.

Only after we reversed that favorable ruling did UPS change course, filing an answer invoking arbitration and seeking to rely on the arbitration agreement to limit discovery to arbitration-related issues. Had that been UPS's course of conduct from the outset of the litigation, it likely would not have waived its right to arbitrate. *See Johnson Assocs. Corp. v. HL Operating Corp.*, 680 F.3d 713, 718 (6th Cir. 2012) (approving the practice of raising arbitration in the answer). But by that time, UPS had already spent two years vigorously litigating the merits of the claims in the district court and on appeal. By waiting to "attempt to enforce [its] arbitration rights until after the [appellate] court entered an unfavorable decision" on its merits arguments, *Hurley*, 610 F.3d at 339, UPS's actions were inconsistent with reliance on an arbitration agreement.

UPS responds by highlighting the statement in its first motion to dismiss that UPS "reserves its right to move to compel arbitration and does not by this motion in any way waive this contractual right." But "[a] statement by a party that it has a right to arbitration in pleadings or motions is not enough to defeat a claim of waiver." *Martin v. Yasuda*, 829 F.3d 1118, 1125 (9th Cir. 2016). UPS also argues that, in some circumstances, a clearly annunciated, well-supported reservation that is otherwise consistent with a party's litigating position might forestall a finding of waiver. But UPS did not adopt an internally consistent position. Rather, it simultaneously asked the district court to resolve the merits of all claims in its favor and reserved the right to submit those same claims to an arbitrator. "A party cannot keep its right to demand arbitration in reserve indefinitely while it pursues a decision on the merits before the district court." *MC Asset Recovery LLC v. Castex Energy, Inc. (In re Mirant Corp.)*, 613 F.3d 584, 591 (5th Cir. 2010).

UPS was aware of the basis of Solo's claim from the moment the complaint was filed. UPS knew or should have known all the information necessary to advance these arguments before it filed its motion to dismiss. Its continued pursuit of legal victory based on the merits is inconsistent with reliance on an arbitration agreement.

We turn next to the prejudice prong. We have previously found prejudice where, "in addition to an eight-month delay and expenses involved with numerous scheduling motions and court-supervised settlement discussions, plaintiffs also engaged in discovery." *Johnson Assocs.*, 680 F.3d at 720; *see also Hurley*, 610 F.3d at 340 (finding prejudice based on two years of active litigation, including extensive discovery and filing of multiple summary judgment motions). In contrast, we have not found prejudice based on actions such as refusal to arbitrate "substantively weak" claims before the commencement of litigation, where arbitration was sought in the "second substantive submission in the litigation." *Shy v. Navistar Int'l Corp.*, 781 F.3d 820, 829–30 (6th Cir. 2015) (noting that the first litigation submission was opposing a motion to intervene that did not address the validity of the parties' claim). Here, the arbitration motion was filed over two years into the suit, after the plaintiffs incurred the expenses of defending against a merits-based motion to dismiss, appealing that decision, and then engaging in many months of discovery. Even if we accepted UPS's argument that some of the discovery-related expenses were due to the plaintiffs' refusal to limit discovery, UPS received the necessary admissions about shipments pursuant to the Amended UPS Terms in June 2016. UPS then allowed another five months of discovery to pass before moving to invoke its right to arbitration. All together, these circumstances amount to actual prejudice.

III. CONCLUSION

For the foregoing reasons, we AFFIRM the decision of the district court and REMAND for further proceedings consistent with this opinion.

Creative Solutions Group v. Pentzer Corp.

252 F.3d 28 (1st Cir. 2001)

SCHWARZER, Senior District Judge.

This case presents the question of whether the disputes between the parties are subject to arbitration under their agreement and, to the extent they are, if arbitration has been waived.

The case arises out of an agreement ("the Agreement") by which plaintiffs Creative Solutions Group (through its predecessor, Heritage Fund II Investment Corporation—"Heritage") purchased the capital stock of five companies known as Creative Solutions Group, Inc. from defendant Pentzer Corporation ("Pentzer"). Pentzer and Heritage entered into the Agreement on March 31, 1999, the closing date for the transaction. The stipulated purchase price, based on December 31, 1998, financial statements, was subject to post-closing adjustments made pursuant to procedures delineated in the Agreement. To that end, the Agreement required Pentzer to deliver to Heritage certain financial information called the Purchase Price Financials, which reflected the position of the companies as of March 31, 1999. Heritage had the right under the Agreement to review related work papers of Deloitte & Touche, Pentzer's auditors. The Agreement provided that "in the event that [Heritage or its accountants] dispute any portion of [Pentzer's] calculation of any of the Purchase Price Financials," notice shall be given to Pentzer and, if the dispute is not resolved, it shall be submitted to arbitration. The Agreement further provided for adjustment of the purchase price to the extent the March 31, 1999, book value or net worth of the five companies being purchased differed from the book value or net worth as of December 31, 1998.

Following the closing, Pentzer delivered the Purchase Price Financials to Heritage on August 5, 1999, and advised that as a result of the Deloitte & Touche audit, Heritage was entitled to an adjustment of the purchase price in addition to the adjustment agreed on at the closing. Heritage then requested access to the Deloitte & Touche work papers pursuant to the terms of the Agreement, but the parties were unable to arrive at mutually satisfactory terms for access and Heritage never received the papers.

Plaintiffs filed this action on April 7, 2000, stating causes of action for breach of certain representations and warranties in the Agreement, breach of the implied covenant of good faith and fair dealing, fraud, negligent misrepresentation, and violation of Massachusetts General Laws Chapter 93A (1997) ("Regulation of Business Practices for Consumers Protection"). In support of these causes of action, plaintiffs alleged three breaches of the Agreement by Pentzer: (1) overstatement of the companies' 1998 earnings before interest, taxes, depreciation and amortization (the EBITDA claim); (2) overstatement of the companies' net worth as of March 31, 1999 (the NWO claim); and (3) failure of two companies to comply with OSHA (29 U.S.C. §§ 651–678) standards. The last claim is not an issue in this appeal.

Pentzer waived formal service of the complaint and at the end of the sixty-day period obtained an extension to plead to July 6, 2000, when it moved to dismiss four of the six counts of the complaint. Plaintiffs served partial initial disclosures on July 25, 2000. Because damage computations were not included, Pentzer made a request for them. On August 11, 2000, plaintiffs served document requests on Pentzer. On September 7, 2000, Pentzer invoked the dispute resolution procedure under the Agreement, including a demand for arbitration. Plaintiffs did not respond and Pentzer, on September 11, 2000, moved to compel arbitration.

On November 13, 2000, the district court ruled on the motion. It held that plaintiffs' claims were not based on mistakes of accounting in the Purchase Price Financials, but on the overall course of the negotiations leading up to the Agreement. Accordingly, the dispute was not one over the calculation of any of the Purchase Price Financials subject to the arbitration clause, but over Pentzer's representations and warranties concerning the financial strength of the companies. Because the court concluded "that the majority of the plaintiffs' claims relate not to the Purchase Price Financials," it denied the motion.

Pentzer moved for reconsideration. On January 5, 2001, the court reaffirmed its prior order. The court specifically addressed the NWO claim, which expressly concerns calculation of the final purchase price derived from the Purchase Price Financials. While the court found this claim to be governed by the arbitration agreement, it held that Pentzer had waived its right to arbitrate. It found that plaintiffs had been prejudiced by Pentzer and Deloitte & Touche's failure to turn over accounting records and work papers, forcing plaintiffs to seek to compel production, investigate the suspected fraud, and commence the litigation, incurring legal expenses along the way. Pentzer had also caused plaintiffs to incur legal expense by making discovery requests and refusing to return settlement documents to plaintiffs. Given the narrow scope of this arbitration agreement, the court found that it would be inefficient to require plaintiffs to arbitrate the NWO claim while simultaneously or subsequently litigating the far more substantial EBITDA and OSHA claims. The court denied the motion and denied a stay pending appeal.

II. WAS ARBITRATION WAIVED?

In considering whether a party has waived its arbitration right, courts are consistently mindful of the strong federal policy favoring arbitration. The Supreme Court has stated that any doubt concerning arbitrability "should be resolved in favor of arbitration, whether the problem at hand is the construction of the contract language itself or an allegation of waiver, delay, or a like defense to arbitrability." *Moses H. Cone Mem'l Hosp. v. Mercury Constr. Corp.*, 460 U.S. 1, 25 (1983). Waiver is not to be lightly inferred, and mere delay in seeking [arbitration] without some resultant prejudice to a party cannot carry the day." (citations omitted).

"We have repeatedly held that a party may, by engaging in litigation, implicitly waive its contractual right to arbitrate." *Navieros Inter-Americanos v. M/V VASILIA EXPRESS*, 120 F.3d 304, 316 (1st Cir. 1997). But in order for plaintiffs to prevail on "their claim of waiver, they must show prejudice." *Menorah Ins. Co., Ltd. v. INX Reinsurance Corp.*, 72 F.3d 218, 221 (1st Cir. 1995) (quoting *Sevinor v. Merrill Lynch, Pierce, Fenner & Smith, Inc.*, 807 F.2d 16, 18 (1st Cir. 1986)). This Circuit has laid down a set of factors to guide the determination of whether a waiver has occurred:

> In determining whether a party to an arbitration agreement, usually a defendant, has waived its arbitration right, federal courts typically have looked to whether the party has actually participated in the lawsuit or has taken other action inconsistent with his right,. . .whether the litigation machinery has been substantially invoked and the parties were well into preparation of a lawsuit by the time an intention to arbitrate was communicated by the defendant to the plaintiff,. . . whether there has been a long delay in seeking the stay or whether the enforcement of arbitration was brought up when trial was near at hand . . .
>
> Other relevant factors are whether the defendants have invoked the jurisdiction of the court by filing a counterclaim without asking for a stay of the proceedings, . . . whether important intervening steps (e.g., taking advantage of judicial discovery procedures not available in arbitration . . .) had taken place, . . . and whether the other party was affected, misled, or prejudiced by the delay. . . .

Jones Motor Co., Inc. v. Chauffeurs, Teamsters, and Helpers Local Union No. 633, 671 F.2d 38, 44 (1st Cir. 1982) (quoting *Reid Burton Constr. Inc. v. Carpenters Dist. Council*, 614 F.2d 698, 702 (10th Cir. 1980)).

Pentzer filed its motion to compel arbitration on September 11, 2000, two months after it was required to plead to the complaint (and five months after plaintiffs filed the action). In pleading to the complaint, Pentzer moved to dismiss, an appropriate responsive pleading. It initiated no formal discovery; in response to plaintiffs' voluntary initial disclosure, it requested (but apparently did not receive) the damage calculations omitted from the disclosure. *See* Fed. R. Civ. P. 26(a)(1)(C). No other activity had occurred in the lawsuit other than plaintiffs' filing of a request for production. It could hardly be said that "the litigation machinery had been substantially invoked and the parties were well into preparation of a lawsuit by the time an intention to arbitrate was communicated," *Jones Motor Co., Inc.*, 671 F.2d at 44, or that Pentzer had taken other steps inconsistent with its right to arbitration.

In its January 5, 2001, order, the district court found, however, that plaintiffs had shown prejudice. It relied principally on the failure of Deloitte & Touche to turn over on plaintiffs' request the accounting records and work papers as required by Article 1.6 of the Agreement. "Instead of a timely arbitration," the court found, plaintiffs were forced to incur legal expense to compel production of the records and work papers and commence this litigation. While it appears that Deloitte—and, by extension, Pentzer—did not comply with their obligation under the Agreement, there is no basis whatever for inferring that as a result plaintiffs were forced into litigation instead of going to arbitration. Plaintiffs have never made such an argument, and the district court itself appropriately rejected the argument that the failure to turn over these documents was sufficient to support a finding of waiver, their production not being a condition precedent to the arbitration agreement. There does not appear to be any logical connection between the failure to produce these documents and Pentzer's right to arbitration. Moreover, the legal expense to compel their production would have been incurred in any event because plaintiffs presumably would need them to support their NWO claim regardless of whether this claim is arbitrated or litigated. Prejudice is relevant to waiver when it is the product of a defendant's failure to timely invoke the arbitration procedure. If there was prejudice here, it was not because of a failure timely to request arbitration. *Cf. Navieros Inter-Americanos*, 120 F.3d at 316.

Similarly unpersuasive is the district court's finding waiver because of the legal expense incurred by plaintiffs in responding to Pentzer's discovery request and litigating Pentzer's refusal to return settlement documents. As noted above, Pentzer did not invoke formal discovery and only requested plaintiffs to complete the initial disclosure they had voluntarily initiated by providing damage calculations. As for the failure to return the settlement documents, plaintiffs have offered no argument in this court that the legal expense of compelling their return resulted in prejudice supporting a finding of waiver and we are unable to discern any basis for one.

CONCLUSION

For the reasons stated, we AFFIRM the district court's order insofar as it found the EBITDA claim not to be arbitrable and VACATE the order insofar as it denied the motion to compel arbitration of plaintiffs' NWO claim and we REMAND for further proceedings consistent with this opinion. We leave it to the district court's discretion whether to stay the litigation pending arbitration of the NWO claim but we assume the court will defer entry of judgment until all claims have been resolved.

It is so ordered.

Example

The Weir family has long operated a vineyard in Marin County, California. The Weir Vineyard does business at two levels: it sells grapes on the wholesale market to other growers, and it operates a tasting room which charges a flat fee for admission and pours glasses for tourists. The family has been doing so for three generations. After a series of wildfires, Donna and Mickey Weir, the second-generation owners who now own the business in whole and employ their son Warren, decide to sell off the wholesaling business and just operate the tasting room. The family finds a buyer, NRPS Enterprises, which has long wanted a foothold in the wine business but has never owned or run anything wine-related before. Knowing what it doesn't know, NRPS wants Warren Weir to join the new NRPS venture and use his expertise to help launch it.

The parties conclude three main agreements: an asset purchase agreement by which NRPS buys the wholesaling operation from Donna and Mickey Weir; a non-competition agreement in which Warren, Donna, and Mickey agree not to sell wines on the wholesale market; and an employment agreement by which Warren Weir becomes CEO of the newly created NRPS Wines label. The asset purchase agreement has a dispute resolution provision calling for any dispute thereunder to be resolved in state or federal district court in Marin County, California. The non-competition agreement has no dispute resolution provision at all. The Employment Agreement has an arbitration clause calling for any disputes "under, relating to or concerning this Agreement" to be resolved by "arbitration under the then-current rules of the American Arbitration Association" in which "the arbitration shall take place in San Francisco, California."

Things go badly. The new label struggles for a foothold. NRPS loses money at an alarming rate. Warren and his family continue to operate the tasting room, which does fine. NRPS suddenly fires Warren, alleging that he is doing a poor job and, more seriously, that he and his family members are surreptitiously selling wine on the wholesale market, in breach of their various agreements. NRPS brings suit in the Northern District of California alleging breach of each of the three contracts (asset purchase, non-competition, and employment) and for fraud and unjust enrichment.

Assume that California has a statute which requires employers to furnish employees their personnel files on demand. After demanding his records so that he can fight his firing and having NRPS refusing to supply them, Warren files a state action under California law demanding his file from NRPS. Separately, Warren joins with his parents in a motion to dismiss the fraud counts with respect to the non-competition agreement and asset purchase agreement. Warren files a separate motion seeking to compel arbitration of the employment agreement counts since that contract has an arbitration clause. In its response to Warren's motion to compel arbitration, NRPS argues that Warren waived his right to arbitrate by (a) bringing suit to seek his employment records under California law and (b) joining with his parents in their motion to dismiss the fraud claims on the other two contracts.

Has Warren waived his right to arbitrate? Why or why not? What facts would have to change for you to change your answer?

Chapter 12

The Arbitration: Before, During, and After the Hearing

I. Overview

Assume you have gotten through the preliminaries covered in this book so far, and so you have overcome any objections to arbitrability. Ahead of you lies the dispute itself—not "litigation about litigation," not procedural arguments divorced from the merits, but instead a need to schedule, read into documents, interview witnesses, think about your demonstrative exhibits and your presentation of witness testimony, resolve any discovery disputes by motion or otherwise, prepare cross-examinations and opening and closing statements—and then win the case. How is this different than a court trial? What should you be conscious of before and during the hearing that a skilled arbitration lawyer would know, but that even an experienced trial lawyer, new to arbitration, might not?

There are few reported cases on this because, as we have seen, arbitration is confidential. As a result, this book contains few decisions actually written by arbitrators (outside of the international "investment arbitration" field reviewed in Chapter 16 *infra*, since those are public proceedings against a government).

As we walk into an arbitration in this chapter, let's begin by reviewing the similarities and differences between arbitration and trial. The similarities abound because both are formal processes designed to resolve a dispute through a formal adversary proceeding. The goal of both processes is a decision on the merits of a dispute between two or more parties. Both a trial and an arbitration hearing put on evidence in what is designed to be a fair and reasonable manner so that the decision maker (a judge or jury in a trial, the arbitrator(s) in arbitration) can render a reasoned judgment/award.

But while the goal is the same, the means toward that goal vary profoundly. You studied in the earlier sections of this book how the process leading to the hearing differs in many respects from the pretrial process in litigation. Those differences continue during the hearing. They begin with what are basic *physical* differences. In an arbitration, one genuinely does "build your own courthouse." The construction of the setting itself, in which the parties generally sit around a conference table rather than before a judicial bench, can be up to the parties. This chart summarizes the differences in setting:

Trial in U.S. state or federal court	Arbitration
Location: state or federal courthouse	Location: great variety; everything from an arbitral institution's hearing room, to a law firm's office, to a hotel conference room
Personnel beyond parties and their counsel: the courtroom may have a judge, clerk(s), stenographer, jury, and audience (typically open to public)	Personnel beyond parties and their counsel: usually only the arbitrator(s) and possibly an administrative assistant/ Tribunal Secretary and a stenographer (if agreed by the parties). Not open to the public—the process and the result are confidential.
Rules of Evidence: followed	Rules of Evidence: may be followed, but not required
Discovery: conducted per Federal Rules of Civil Procedure (or state rules), as of right	Discovery: increasingly common, but not automatic and not as of right. Provided by institutional rules and/or as matter of arbitrator discretion or party agreement.
Demonstratives: permitted but must follow evidentiary rules, and judges/courtrooms may have particular rules that must be followed	Demonstratives: typically permitted but advisable to reach agreement with other side and liaise with arbitrator(s)
Appeals of interlocutory issues: generally not permitted but depends on issue and applicable rule	Appeals of interlocutory issues: rarely permitted but depends on institutional rules (if any) and parties' agreements
Dispositive motions: standard practice and provided by rule	Dispositive motions: depends on institutional rules and discretion of arbitrator. Not as common as in court.

To put to use these beginning concepts and others that will emerge in the arbitration let's use a hypothetical complex commercial dispute. We will call it the "BatPow" arbitration.

II. *BatPow v. GyScope*: A Hypothetical Complex Arbitration

A. Facts

The President of the United States is concerned about reports of China's plans to penetrate the U.S. smartphone industry. Reports circulate of Chinese government-funded efforts to make longer-lasting, more receptive phones that will move consumers away from iPhones and toward what the Government of China hopes will become known as "cPhones." Beyond the risk of economic loss that this presents to American companies, elements of the U.S. national security community are concerned about the risk that the phones may be implanted with surveillance mechanisms that make spying by the Government of China easier. A political surge develops to "do something to protect our cellphone industry."

The Administration decides that the best way to meet this oncoming challenge is to call together the leading U.S. smartphone technology firms, including those U.S. firms which make smartphone components, with an aim toward creating a new phone with better, sleeker, longer-lasting features that will dominate the market: the AmeriPhone. The White House invites 10 leading smartphone technology companies to a summit to discuss this idea. Among the attendees are GyScope, which makes the internal gyroscope built into a smartphone that allows it to work whichever way the phone is oriented in one's hand, and BatPow, a leading innovator of smartphone batteries. BatPow recently announced that it was developing a battery with a 20-year life but had a series of cash shortages of late and has missed both revenue projections and payroll, resulting in the loss of some of its leading scientists and engineers to high-paying offers from other tech firms in the Silicon Valley.

The summit is a huge PR success. Many speeches are given about the importance of the project, how it can create jobs, ensure U.S. superiority in a critical market, and protect national security. Government officials promise support.

Six of the attendees, including GyScope and BatPow, ultimately agree to work together in group now named "the Consortium." They each sign the "Consortium Agreement," which provides that they will work together on the design of a new smartphone and share all intellectual property developed during this common enterprise. They agree further that any design "jointly developed as a result of Consortium work" is collectively owned by each of the Consortium members. The goal is to incentivize each member to freely contribute its intellectual property and its work effort, since they stand the prospect of getting a share of valuable intellectual property back in return. Meanwhile, the administration pushes a bill through Congress, the Smartphone Security Act, which provides each Consortium member with a generous financial grant, including both cash payments and tax credits, as well as antitrust immunity.

The material sections of the Consortium Agreement are:

1. A "common ownership clause," providing that the ownership of any new designs jointly developed as part of the Consortium will be split on 1/6 basis equally among Consortium members. "Ownership" includes all intellectual property rights including, but not limited to, patent ownership.
2. A five-year term unless terminated earlier by agreement of all parties. Any party can withdraw on 30 days' notice, but its efforts devoted through that date remain Consortium property.
3. An "already existing clause" ("AEC"), which recognizes that each Consortium Member, already a leading technology company in its own right, came into the project with its own intellectual property, and therefore any already existing intellectual property ("AEIP") does NOT belong to the Consortium. Only jointly developed IP becomes "common" property to the Consortium as described in the common ownership clause in section (1) above. The AEC recognizes as well that each member will continue to carry on its own business during the period of the Consortium—nobody expects the members to drop everything else and work 24/7 on the Consortium's project.
4. A dispute resolution clause as follows:

    > **Any and all disputes under this contract, including any disputes concerning the scope and interpretation of this clause, shall be resolved by binding arbitration in Washington, D.C. The Arbitrator shall have the power to decide all issues related to the arbitration, including but not limited to all issues relating to arbitrability and jurisdiction of the Arbitrator. The arbitration award may be enforced in any court of competent jurisdiction. Notwithstanding the binding nature of this clause, any party may apply in court for injunctive relief in order to preserve the status quo in the event of allegations of immediate and irreparable injury.**

The Consortium is launched with great fanfare. The President announces that this will be "the greatest advancement in the history of technology" and notes that no such project was launched under his predecessor. He promises very high government funding of Consortium projects.

In actuality, however, the Consortium has a troubled history. The members never come to trust one another, and Administration funding is held up when voices on the left decry "corporate socialism" and voices on the right point out that historically, many of the Silicon Valley funding recipients had been active opponents of the administration and huge donors to his political opponents. The funding goes through, but the project is launched with bitterness and suspicion, and rumor has it that some members are holding back as a result of this climate.

The members meet monthly for two years, and exchange drawings and plans, but ultimately develop only one Consortium patent, for a new non-glare front panel on a smartphone.

Among the new designs circulated within the Consortium during these two years is one submitted by GyScope, which presents a new and improved version of its stabilizing gyroscope for the planned AmeriPhone. That gyroscope design is unrelated to the front-panel glare patent developed jointly by Consortium members. No Consortium member collaborated with GyScope on this new design, and it never results in a final product or a patent during the Consortium's term.

BatPow also circulates a new design for battery power that will extend existing life by five years. Like the GyScope design, this design does not find its way into the glare patent. This does not result in a new product or a patent during the Consortium's term.

By year 3, the President is tweeting about the "awful, corrupt Big Tech Silicon Valley scum" who form the Consortium. On December 31 of year 3, the Consortium officially dissolves.

In year 4, GyScope, flush with new investment capital and following a successful merger with other smartphone players, issues an entirely new smartphone on the market called the gPhone. It quickly becomes a leading seller.

BatPow looks at the gPhone and concludes that this new smartphone makes use of the new gyroscope design that GyScope had submitted to the Consortium. BatPow sends a "cease and desist" letter to GyScope demanding a 1/6 portion of ownership of the new gPhone under the Consortium Agreement's common ownership clause, alleging that since the new gPhone uses intellectual property developed during the Consortium period, the resulting product is Consortium property. GyScope rejects this demand. GyScope claims that the gyroscope found in the new, post-Consortium gPhone was preexisting property under the Consortium Agreement's AEC.

BatPow sends a demand for arbitration under the Consortium Agreement, declaring GyScope to be in material breach of the Consortium Agreement and seeking as a remedy ownership rights and a distribution of its share of profits from gPhone sales. The letter also reserves the right to seek injunctive relief to freeze all sales of the gPhone going forward, pending resolution of this dispute.

Problem

Freeze Frame. This is the stage of a dispute where the arbitration lawyer frequently first learns the parties and the facts. Up until this point, the Consortium contract was likely negotiated by lawyers for your client who had entirely different skill sets, including intellectual property, transactional, and in this case perhaps antitrust law. Now there is a dispute. The demand letter crosses your desk for the first time. *What will you look at?*

Look first at the dispute resolution clause. Is it clear? Is jurisdiction a slam dunk? Are there challenges to be made? What about process: where is the arbitration? Under what rules? What are the timing requirements?

This is also the time to educate your client about the differences between arbitration and litigation, particularly in the relative slowness of arbitration proceedings to commence.

If you represent the Claimant (BatPow), you have an aggrieved client who more likely than not will want you to push the arbitration forward as quickly as possible. The client may be thinking about court procedures, having watched TV shows and movies about trials over the years, and may not appreciate that it takes time to get an arbitration up and running—so you need to start building that courthouse, *now.* If you represent the Respondent (GyScope), you need to focus on the time you have to respond to the demand letter and then on how to involve yourself in the arbitrator selection process, such as it may exist. Again, *start with the dispute resolution clause.* Recall everything we have studied here to date regarding arbitration being a matter of contract—the dispute resolution clause is now your contract.

B. Injunction

Shortly after sending the demand letter, BatPow moves in the United States District Court for the District of Columbia for an injunction commanding GyScope to immediately cease and desist from manufacturing the gPhone or, in the alternative, to deposit all proceeds from the gPhone into a "constructive trust": a court-supervised account preserved for access by BatPow should BatPow succeed in the arbitration.

GyScope objects that the court does not have jurisdiction to hear any arbitrable disputes. BatPow responds by pointing to the injunction carve-out in the arbitration clause:

> **Notwithstanding the binding nature of this clause, any party may apply in court for injunctive relief in order to preserve the status quo in the event of allegations of immediate and irreparable injury.**

The court notes that the arbitration clause allows a carve-out for status quo court injunctions and so rejects GyScope's argument that the arbitrator is perfectly capable of awarding injunctive relief and there is no need for court proceedings. But, having assumed jurisdiction of the injunction under the carve-out, the court denies it on the merits, finding that any injury that BatPow may be able to demonstrate will be compensable on monetary grounds, making immediate emergency equitable relief unnecessary. The arbitration therefore goes forward as the only proceeding between the parties.

C. Arbitrator Selection

1. In a case with an *ad hoc* dispute resolution clause like this (meaning that there is no provision in the arbitration clause that addresses the selection of the arbitrator), the parties have a choice. They can, as with all things in arbitration, attempt to reach consensus and simply agree on one or more arbitrators. They can exchange names and see if they can agree, within a given time, on a single arbitrator; they can see if they can agree on a panel of three arbitrators; or they can each nominate a party-appointed arbitrator and leave the task of selecting the Chair of the arbitration panel (or "Tribunal") to the two "party-selected" arbitrators. Failing agreement, the parties would have to proceed with appointment of an arbitrator by the court, under Section 5 of the FAA (*see* note 3 below). In a case unlike this hypothetical dispute, where the dispute resolution clause is institutional, the parties would follow the selection processes outlined in Chapter 5. *See, e.g.*, JAMS Rule 3, AAA Rule 5, and *supra* pages 202–203.

2. Does the technical nature of this case, in which the finder of fact will likely have to determine inventorship, affect your view as to arbitrator qualifications? Will you want a patent lawyer? Trademark lawyer? Someone with particularized knowledge? Or will you concentrate instead on an arbitrator with experience, calculating that you can "teach" the arbitrator the case since you prefer that the arbitrator not have preexisting, contrary thoughts or conclusions in her head?

3. What if the parties to an ad hoc arbitration clause are not able to agree on anything? In the early days of a dispute, emotions are high and trust is low, and the submission of a potential arbitrator's name to opposing counsel can be the kiss of death for that nominee, no matter how qualified or appropriate for the dispute. What happens then? Recall Section 5 of the Federal Arbitration Act:

> If in the agreement provision be made for a method of naming or appointing an arbitrator or arbitrators or an umpire, such method shall be followed; but if no method be provided therein, or if a method be provided and any party thereto shall fail to avail himself of such method, or if for any other reason there shall be a lapse in the naming of an arbitrator or arbitrators or umpire, or in filling a vacancy, then upon the application of either party to the controversy *the court shall designate and appoint an arbitrator* or arbitrators or umpire, as the case may require, who shall act under the said agree-

> ment with the same force and effect as if he or they had been specifically named therein; and unless otherwise provided in the agreement the arbitration shall be by a single arbitrator.

For purposes of this hypothetical, assume that the parties could not reach any agreement. BatPow applies for an order to the Chief Judge of the United States District Court for the District of Columbia since that is the place of the arbitration under the Consortium Agreement's dispute resolution clause. The Chief Judge, Howell, J., appoints Lowell George, a well-known Washington, D.C., patent law litigator, as the arbitrator.

D. The Scheduling Conference

Now we are truly into the "build your own courthouse" phase of the case. As a first step, the arbitrator will set a scheduling conference, which is the initial organizational meeting and the first formal proceeding in any arbitration after the arbitrator is appointed. This is the time to set up the arbitration's timetable. You will have far more leeway than if you were in court, where the parties would have to deal with formalized rules of procedure and a judge with a busy docket that she has to manage and move. And in this particular hypothetical, you have an increased degree of flexibility because, at least for now as you headinto the scheduling conference, there are no timetables set by any institutional rules. Instead, as noted in the arbitration selection discussion above, the arbitration is ad hoc.

Put yourself in the position of either the lead attorney for BatPow (Claimant) or GyScope (Respondent). At this very early stage of the case, you likely have not yet interviewed a lot of witnesses or read a lot of documents. You have a basic overview of the facts of the case, and you have talked to a few people at the client's offices, and maybe the general counsel's office, but your deep dive into the facts—and deep it will be—lies ahead of you. With the limited knowledge you presently have, and the biased and incomplete views often given by clients early in the case, you need to make some decisions before the scheduling conference:

- What schedule do you propose? Long or short?
- Do you want pre-hearing motion practice?
- What discovery do you want?
- Will any of the discovery you want/need include third-party discovery? Based on jurisdiction and the discussion in Chapter 8, do you think you will be able to obtain/oppose it?
- What discovery do you *not* want?
- The information in the case involves current business, and so may be seen as highly confidential. How should it be protected?

- Will you need expert testimony? On inventorship? On damages models?
- Is this a case that could see a useful summary judgment or other pretrial motion, to narrow the issues? Or will it be too factually complex with no "knockout" issues of law?
- Do you want the case bifurcated (separated into distinct liability and damages phases)? In a bifurcated case, by definition, you never get to damages unless the claimant wins at the liability stage. Bifurcation has the advantage of potential cost savings, but the disadvantage is that it usually stretches out a case longer.
- Might you want to adopt institutional rules now that it looks like you have a complicated arbitration ahead?
- What form of award do you prefer? Full-blown like a court judgment, with thorough findings of fact and conclusions of law? Or the opposite extreme, with one or two lines stating who wins and the amount? Or, the modern trend, a "reasoned award," which contains the reasons and basis for the award without a full-blown exposition of the facts? Here again, there are advantages and disadvantages; a longer award lets the parties know more about what happened in the process that they paid for. But it is also more expensive as it takes longer for the arbitrator to write, and with more detail, there is more for a party to try to challenge at the confirmation process (which we will study in Chapter 13).
- What other issues do you want to raise on behalf of your client?

It is critical to identify these issues in advance, discuss them with your client, come to the scheduling conference prepared to identify them, and, as with any negotiation, have identified with your client acceptable positions to fall back upon. It may even be a good idea (the author is known to do this) to arrive at the scheduling conference with a schedule drafted out, for the arbitrator's consideration—this way you have at least taken control of the drafting.

Once you have those details down, you are ready for the scheduling conference. Remember what we studied at the beginning of this book about consensus: at the scheduling conference, that consensus—the degree of agreement you can achieve with your opponent—translates quite literally into "mandate," i.e., the powers of the arbitrator to decide this dispute and the rules that will govern her as she goes about that decision. In the absence of consensus on specific issues, the arbitrator will reach her own decision.

The following is a hypothetical result.

E. Procedural Order No. 1

The parties meet with Arbitrator George and agree on some issues, disagree on others, and have him resolve the disputed ones. Among other things, they decide that an arbitration this complex and expected to be this long and involved should proceed according to the Commercial Arbitration Rules of the American Arbitration Association.

The arbitrator issues the following order, entitled "Procedural Order No. 1." Orders regarding process in arbitration are usually designated as "Procedural Order" and then numbered—it is not uncommon for a long, complex arbitration to have multiple procedural orders. Further, on the subject of terminology, arbitrators (or a single arbitrator) may refer to themselves as "the Arbitration Tribunal" or, for short, "the Tribunal." We follow that form here:

AMERICAN ARBITRATION ASSOCIATION

BatPow, Ltd., Claimant, vs. GyScope Corporation, Respondent.	Docket 2021: 1958LF

PROCEDURAL ORDER NO. 1

1. AAA Arbitration. Notwithstanding the ad hoc nature of the parties' pre-dispute dispute resolution clause, the parties agree to proceed under the Commercial Arbitration Rules of the American Arbitration Association in effect as of the date of this Procedural Order, *provided that*, in the event of any conflict between the Rules and this Procedural Order No. 1, the terms of this Order (and any future Procedural Orders) govern.

2. Protective Order. The Tribunal is mindful that the evidence in this arbitration will include highly confidential and proprietary information. Proprietary information must still be produced if relevant, and proprietary information once produced must be safeguarded strictly by the recipient. The Tribunal intends to enforce both elements of this directive. On day 3, Respondent will draft and send to claimant for review a proposed Protective Order. On day 7, the parties shall submit either an agreed Protective Order, or letters from each party (not to exceed three (3) pages), to the Tribunal detailing the parties' differences as to the Protective Order. The Protective Order shall be entered on day 10.

3. Discovery.

   a. Written discovery is limited to one (1) Request for Production of Documents by each party. Further requests shall be by application to the Arbitrator identifying specific need.

b. Document Requests will be served on day 3. Responses, with documents and a privilege log, are due on day 40.

c. In the event of any dispute over the scope of document production pursuant to Paragraph 3(b) of this Procedural Order, the parties are directed to meet and confer in good faith by day 47. In the event that the parties' meet and confer efforts do not resolve the dispute, then the party claiming inadequate production may serve a motion to compel production by day 68. The party opposing the motion to compel may serve a response by day 78. The moving party may serve a response by day 80. The Tribunal will rule on the motion to compel by day 90.

d. In the event that the process in Paragraph 3(c) of this Procedural Order results in an Order to produce further documents, all such documents will be produced by day 100.

e. There shall be no depositions unless otherwise ordered by the Tribunal for good cause and upon request.

4. Bifurcation. This Arbitration shall be bifurcated between a liability and a damages (quantum) phase. This Procedural Order is directed only to the liability phase. In the event that Claimant prevails as to liability, the Tribunal shall issue further directions as to the quantum schedule. The parties are advised that the Tribunal anticipates a brisk schedule for any quantum phase. The parties agree not to file any actions to confirm or to vacate any Order in this Arbitration until the Arbitration is concluded, which will be either by an Award for Respondent finding no liability, or at the conclusion of the quantum stage.

5. Experts. Each party is entitled to designate one (1) expert in the liability phase of the matter. Claimant's expert report is due on day 130. Respondent's expert report is due on day 160. There shall be no rebuttal reports. There shall be no expert depositions. Any procedural directions as to experts at the quantum stage will await that stage per Paragraph 4 immediately above.

6. Dispositive Motions.

a. The parties may, at their option, file motions for summary judgment by day 200.

b. Opposition Briefs are due on Day 220.

c. Reply Briefs are due on Day 230.

d. The summary judgment motions may include witness statements (affidavits) and documents, provided that any such documents referenced in a witness statement/affidavit have been produced pursuant to Paragraph 3 of this Procedural Order.

e. The Tribunal shall rule on the summary judgment motion(s) by day 250. Paragraphs 7, 8 and 9 of this Procedural Order are subject to any dispositive motion rulings made under this Section.

7. Pre-Hearing Procedures.

a. Briefs. Prehearing Briefs will be served simultaneously on day 280. Documents cited in the Prehearing Briefs are subject to the same restrictions as in 6(d) of this Procedural order.

b. Hearing Witnesses and Documents.

(1) Between days 260 and Day 270, the parties are directed to exchange witness lists.

(2) Between days 260 and 270, the parties are also directed to exchange a list of documents they intend to rely upon at the hearing. The parties are encouraged to prepare a Joint Appendix of documents with a common exhibit number (e.g., JX-1), but may also serve supplementary and individual schedules of documents. The Tribunal will issue further procedural directions at the appropriate time regarding hard copy vs. electronic copies of documents.

(3) Final witness lists, and all documents (individual and joint) must be provided to the Tribunal by day 275. Any witness not on the final list will not be permitted to testify at the hearing. Any documents not on the list shall not be admitted into evidence at the hearing. The Tribunal reserves the right to make exceptions to this direction for good cause and in the interests of justice.

8 Hearing. A five (5) day hearing will begin on day 300.

9. Post-hearing submissions. Any post-hearing submissions including briefs are to be at the discretion of the Arbitrator.

10. Award. The Tribunal shall issue a Reasoned Award within 30 days of the hearing.

Dated: February 21, 202x

For the Tribunal

____

Lowell George, Chair

Freeze Frame. This order attempts to balance the parties' competing goals. Claimant wants a brisk schedule; Respondent wants bifurcation. Claimant wants prompt document production so it can determine the origin of the offending product; Respondent wants to protect confidential information. Both parties want expert evidence given the technical nature of the case and the need to present arguments about origin of the product to the arbitrator.

1. Do you think this is a balanced order? Are issues that could be dealt with up front left out? Does the order favor one party or the other?
2. Recall that the arbitration clause contains what we have studied to be an "injunction carve-out": "*Notwithstanding the binding nature of this clause, either party may apply in court for injunctive relief in order to preserve the status quo in the event of allegations of immediate and irreparable injury.*" Recall as well from this chapter that BatPow moved for an injunction before a court and lost on the merits. Now that an arbitrator is in place, and since the AAA rules permit an arbitrator to hear actions seeking "conservatory measures," *see* AAA R. 37(a) (allowing that arbitrator to take "whatever interim measures he or she deems necessary, including injunctive relief"), can BatPow seek injunctive relief again? Is there jurisdictional power in the arbitrator to hear such an application? Does the first decision, by the court, have issue preclusion or claim preclusion effects on another bite at the apple? What would happen to the schedule established by Procedural Order No. 1 if BatPow initiated this effort? Should BatPow have established a schedule for this in the procedural order?

F. Pre-Hearing Discovery

As a result of the parties' election (as memorialized in Procedural Order No. 1) to proceed under AAA Rules, the parties are now subject to enhanced pre-hearing discovery obligations. In addition to those obligations imposed by Paragraphs 2 and 3 of Procedural Order No. 1, the parties must adhere to AAA Commercial Arbitration Rule 22. The AAA's Rule 22 on discovery states:

Pre-Hearing Exchange and Production of Information

a. Documents. The arbitrator may, on application of a party or on the arbitrator's own initiative:

   .... require the parties to exchange documents in their possession or custody on which they intend to rely;

i) require the parties to update their exchanges of the documents on which they intend to rely as such documents become known to them;

ii) require the parties, in response to reasonable document requests, to make available to the other party documents, in the responding party's possession or custody, not otherwise readily available to the party seeking the documents, reasonably believed by the party seeking the documents to exist and to be relevant and material to the outcome of disputed issues; and

iii) require the parties, when documents to be exchanged or produced are maintained in electronic form, to make such documents available in the form most convenient and economical for the party in possession of such documents, unless the arbitrator determines that there is good cause for requiring the documents to be produced in a different form. The parties should attempt to agree in advance upon, and the arbitrator may determine, reasonable search parameters to balance the need for production of electronically stored documents relevant and material to the outcome of disputed issues against the cost of locating and producing them.

As a result, the parties exchange prehearing document requests and then, pursuant to those requests, produce documents to one another.

BatPow's theory of the case is that the gPhone uses work developed during the Consortium period and so was "jointly developed" under the Consortium Agreement. BatPow will have to prove that the invention was not developed independently by GyScope either before, during, or after the Consortium period. BatPow therefore seeks information on all of GyScope's development work on cell phone gyroscopes in the three years prior to the Consortium's reorganization. BatPow also seeks the personal PC and notes of a particular GyScope engineer, Dr. Portia Raitt. During a Consortium program, held during year 2 for federal agencies which were funding the Consortium, Dr. Raitt appeared at a panel discussion and presented a PowerPoint on progress that the Consortium members had made on the gyroscope. BatPow contends that this is material evidence of development work during, not before, the Consortium.

GyScope seeks information on BatPow's business failures in its repeated but unsuccessful efforts in the years before the Consortium's establishment to obtain funding for its novel battery technology. GyScope argues that BatPow was hanging on by a sliver and is now using the Consortium to grab a share of money and projects that it could never have achieved on its own. GyScope also intends to show that BatPow was "worthless" in the Consortium and "never contributed a thing."

BatPow refuses to produce anything responsive to these requests. It argues that its case in this arbitration does not depend upon its own contribution but rather on whether GyScope invented something as part of, and during, the Consortium process. BatPow argues that the common ownership clause in the Consortium Agreement does not require that each party have contributed to an invention and looks solely to what any one party contributed, how, why, and especially when. BatPow argues that GyScope is trying to distract from its own theft of common property and tear down BatPow in the eyes of the arbitrator for no good or relevant reason.

GyScope argues that the documents must be produced because it would be inequitable for BatPow to have title to an invention when it effectively sat on its hands. GyScope argues further that in federal court, lack of relevance is not a valid basis for refusing to produce documents but is instead that documents must be produced if they are "reasonably calculated to lead to the discovery of admissible evidence."

Unlike BatPow, GyScope does produce documents. But, in comparing its own email records during the Consortium period with the documents produced by GyScope, BatPow notices that GyScope has produced substantially fewer emails than BatPow knows exists. For example, GyScope produces only 70% of the emails that the parties exchanged (again, as BatPow knows from its own records) in year 2 of the Consortium project. This prompts BatPow to do a more considered examination of GyScope's document production, and it ultimately concludes that GyScope has failed to produce substantial documentation. BatPow petitions the arbitrator to order GyScope to make Dr. Raitt's PC hard drives available for forensic examination by an outside computer expert, who can go into files and see what might be on hard drives but was not produced in either paper or electronic form, and, further, what was deleted from the hard drives. GyScope at first refuses but then, when the arbitrator grants the motion anyway, informs the arbitrator that compliance with this ruling is not possible as Dr. Raitt recently lost the hard drives accidentally, having left them at the Dulles Airport security line and been unable to locate and find them ever since.

BatPow states that it does not believe this tale to be true and files a motion for an "adverse inference," meaning that the arbitrator should make advance findings of fact about the contents of Dr. Raitt's files and that those findings should be in BatPow's favor.

Freeze Frame. How would you rule on these motions? Would your views be guided by any particular arbitration principles? Why? Is the arbitration now becoming too much like a complicated federal court matter, or are these precisely the procedures the parties bargained for? Should relevance matter? Should hiding documents matter? Is adverse inference an appropriate arbitration concept?

---

1. Third-Party Discovery

BatPow argues that testimony and documents from the other four Consortium members will show that GyScope was working with them during the Consortium period on an improved gyroscope for the planned AmeriPhone design. BatPow was not present for all of these meetings and so wants to see what the record of other participants might show. Since none of the other Consortium members joined BatPow as a claimant in this arbitration, these discovery requests to the other members are "third-party discovery," studied in Chapter 8. The arbitrator signs the subpoenas.

Three of the four subpoena recipients are in Silicon Valley, California. The fourth is in St. Paul, Minnesota. All four of the subpoena recipients contest the subpoena on the grounds that under applicable circuit court authority, they do not have to produce any information before a hearing.

Freeze Frame. What law will govern these disputes? Did the arbitrator have jurisdiction over these witnesses?

Three of them are successful in this challenge, owing to the circuit court split we discussed in Chapter 8. One of them, CThru, which makes the glass panels for smartphones and is located in the Eighth Circuit, realizes that the governing law in its jurisdiction will require it to appear for a deposition. It cuts a deal with BatPow counsel wherein it produces documents voluntarily in exchange for not having to show up at a deposition.

---

2. *Depositions*

Recall that the scheduling order, in Paragraph 3(e), left open the issue of depositions. Now, with legal fees climbing, the parties agree to each take one deposition, totaling seven hours (the same limit as in the Federal Rules of Civil Procedure). They agree further that the depositions may be conducted pursuant to Fed. R. Civ. P. 30(b)(6), in which the party taking the deposition submits a list of particular subject areas on which it wants to conduct inquiry (e.g., the negotiation of the Consortium Agreement, GyScope's development of the gPhone's gyroscope, etc.), and the party to be deposed must produce a witness "knowledgeable" on each subject. Parties may have more than one witness where, as here, there is more than one subject, so long as the total time does not exceed the aforementioned seven hours. Two BatPow witnesses and three GyScope witnesses appear and testify.

3. *Dispositive Motions*

In BatPow's mind, the deposition testimony and records produced by GyScope leave little doubt that GyScope developed the gPhone's gyroscope during the Consortium period and with Consortium resources.

GyScope, meanwhile, elicits testimony in depositions, and otherwise identifies documents, showing that BatPow is desperate for survival and held meetings with the goal of developing "survival strategies," including aggressive litigation postures. GyScope also believes it has established that virtually everything BatPow did during the Consortium project was worthless and that the other Consortium members had mocked BatPow reps behind their backs, calling them "the Low Energy Bars."

On this pre-hearing record, both parties elect to file motions for summary judgment on all liability counts, as they had provided for in section 6 of their scheduling order. They are guided here procedurally as well by AAA Rule 33:

> **Rule 33. Dispositive Motions**
>
> The arbitrator may allow the filing of and make rulings upon a dispositive motion only if the arbitrator determines that the moving party has shown that the motion is likely to succeed and dispose of or narrow the issues in the case.

Under this rule, such a motion may not be filed unless and until the arbitrator grants permission. As a result, the parties both prepare detailed five-page letters, which purport to merely request "permission" but in actuality set out their reasons for wanting to file actual motions for summary judgment. Three days after receiving the other party's letter of "request," each also files a detailed three-page letter explaining why the other party's request is baseless and no motion should be allowed from that party (while also drawing a sharp contrast to their own desired motion).

The arbitrator now has sixteen pages of single-spaced letters arguing about whether motions should be filed. It is seven weeks before the hearing.

G. Procedural Order No. 2

On receiving these various discovery and summary judgment motions, the arbitrator issues Procedural Order No. 2.

AMERICAN ARBITRATION ASSOCIATION

BatPow, Ltd., Claimant, vs. GyScope Corporation, Respondent.	Docket 2021: 1958LF

PROCEDURAL ORDER NO. 2

1. Adverse Inference Motion. BatPow's motion for findings of adverse inference as a result of GyScope and Dr. Raitt's alleged loss of computer hard drives is neither granted nor denied at this time. The motion is reserved until further findings at the liability hearing (see below). At the hearing, the Arbitrator will consider closely the

admissible evidence on the disputed issues of GyScope's development efforts and will not hesitate to make adverse inference findings if the admissible evidence so suggests. At this juncture, the Arbitrator notes his concern that GyScope's alleged loss of the relevant hard drives would appear to be an excuse of convenience that is otherwise unsupported by credible evidence. The Arbitrator therefore awards BatPow 75% of its costs of the adverse inference motion, not to exceed $50,000 (fifty thousand dollars). The parties are instructed to submit their relevant billing records as part of the arbitration record, redacted appropriately for privilege reasons, and the Arbitrator will incorporate this costs award into the Final Award.

2. Summary Judgment Motions. The Arbitrator has considered the parties' respective letters requesting leave to file motions for summary judgment on liability, together with the party responses thereto, and hereby *denies* all requests to move for summary judgment. The Arbitrator is confident that any dispositive law and/or facts can be efficiently presented at the hearing itself.

3. The dates for the liability hearing, and all other procedures to follow from dispositive motions, as set out in Procedural Order No. 1, are extended by sixty (60) days.

4. A Partial Final Award on Liability shall be rendered by the Arbitrator no later than sixty (60) days after the close of evidence in the liability phase. The date of the closing of evidence shall be determined by further order, as the Arbitrator has not yet rendered a decision (and will not until the hearing ends) as to the need for post-hearing briefs.

   a. In the event that the Partial Final Award on Liability determines that Claimant has failed to sustain its burden of proof as to breach of the Consortium Agreement, then this arbitration will have terminated, subject to any post-Award submissions on costs.
   b. In the event that the Partial Final Award on liability determines that Claimant has met its burden of proof as to breach, then, as contemplated by Procedural Order No. 1, this Arbitration shall proceed to a quantum (damages) phase. The quantum phase shall be held over a three-day period beginning October 15, 202x. The parties are directed to clear their schedules and calendars for that phase. Any petitions for an exception to this rule shall be met with extreme disfavor.

5. The parties may petition for any change to this Order upon due cause shown.

Dated: March 22, 202x

Lowell George, Arbitrator

H. The Liability Hearing

As a result of Procedural Order No. 2, the parties proceed to arbitrate the issue of liability only. The hearing is held in a conference room at the Madison Hotel in Washington, D.C. Due to the confidentiality of the arbitration and the particular sensitivity of some of the related business dealings (including the ongoing development of the gPhone), GyScope requests that a security guard be posted at the door. BatPow contests the need for this cost. The Arbitrator rejects the request.

On day 1, after each party offers opening statements, BatPow's case opens with testimony from BatPow's president about what his company expected to receive as a result of its participation in the Consortium. He is followed by his chief marketing officer, a combat veteran. Both speak to their love of country, their concern about potential inroads by the Government of China into U.S. high tech, and their pride in being part of such a patriotic and valuable enterprise.

On cross-examination, GyScope's lawyers spend time with BatPow's financial reports in the three years immediately preceding the Consortium. The lawyers put up on the screen in the hearing room BatPow's board meeting minutes showing increased desperation for funding, especially after three different approaches to investment banks and to Silicon Valley "angels" fell on deaf ears. Finally, GyScope's lawyers show emails between BatPow's CEO and CFO discussing the prospect of bankruptcy "if we cannot get credit for a good product coming out of the Consortium." One of the minute entries states, "Commence interviews for aggressive arbitration lawyers."

BatPow's lawyers move to strike this testimony on grounds of prejudice and relevance. GyScope argues that BatPow "opened the door" by waving the flag and talking about its good intentions and pure motive.

The arbitrator grants the motion to strike, finding that breach of contract is not a motive cause of action and that the only relevant fact is whether the gyroscope was developed as a result of the Consortium, not why BatPow brought the action.

Freeze Frame. If you represented BatPow and believed your client had a bona fide claim on the substantive issue in the case—whether GyScope took advantage of Consortium work in order to then develop its own product—would you let your client open itself to this attack by setting a theme of its own patriotism and goodwill? When is this type of color and optics important, and when is it risky? Trial lawyers, in and out of arbitration, face this choice all the time. We want to humanize our witnesses but often their resulting faces are all TOO human.

On day 2, BatPow calls a witness who speaks to all the work that BatPow alleges it performed on the Consortium. Detailed minutes of lab work are produced. On cross-examination, the BatPow witness is forced to admit that BatPow made no contribution to the gyroscope invention. BatPow's lawyer objects to the lack of relevance. Arbitrator George overrules the objection.

On day 3, BatPow calls "as if on cross-examination" —that is, as a hostile witness, so that BatPow can ask leading questions—Dr. Raitt, the chief GyScope scientist. Dr. Raitt is confronted with a statement she made to U.S. Department of Commerce and U.S. Department of Defense officials in attendance at a briefing conference in year 2 to see where the government's money was going, in which she stated that the Consortium project was "well on its way to developing a new gyroscope" and "you will see that the taxpayers' money has been well spent." On rehabilitative examination by her own lawyers, GyScope's counsel asks Dr. Raitt to explain the context of this PowerPoint. She states that at this point in time, she was demoralized at how little progress had been made within the Consortium project and so was "throwing them a bone," using in fact already existing work at GyScope under the Consortium Agreement as a cover for what she actually had felt was the complete failure of the Consortium to date. When asked why, she responded, "I wanted to keep funding going."

Freeze Frame. What else could GyScope have done here? They knew this attack was coming. Could they have done more on the substantive defense side? Or was this a case of "get ready for the attack and hope you live through it"? All cases have bad facts. This was likely the worst fact for GyScope. It is important to identify bad facts early, identify inconsistencies, and be forthright with the client and the arbitrators.

On day 4, GyScope presents testimony from its young scientific team in which they show that they had been working on an improved product for many years before the Consortium began. The work was brilliant and original and exactly the type of subject covered by the already existing work clause in the Consortium Agreement.

Freeze Frame. You saw above how BatPow punctured GyScope's story about the PowerPoints. This was GyScope's turn to tell its story. Every case has a story, and every arbitrator is human. A good lawyer determines how to convey the human elements of the case. Complex cases are not only no exception, but actually will often lean even more on this human element so that the facts can be understood better and laid out against this background. Here, GyScope went with the struggling, inspired young scientist story to kick start the case. That doesn't replace the need for further facts, but it does supply the background.

Day 5 is "expert day." BatPow's expert testifies that the gyroscope now present in the GyScope gPhone is a direct result of the technology discussed by Dr. Raitt in her now-infamous PowerPoint. Accordingly, the expert concludes, the gPhone uses a design "jointly developed as a result of Consortium work" under the Consortium Agreement. The expert testifies further that the differences between the gPhone gyroscope and the gyroscope worked on during the Consortium period are indistinguishable and immaterial.

After lunch, GyScope's expert takes the stand and could not disagree more. The expert, Dr. Paul de Varrere, references the testimony earlier from the young GyScope scientific team. From there, he points to the AEC in the Consortium Agreement and draws a straight line—literally, on one of his demonstrative exhibits—between that work and the final gyroscope now in the gPhone, and states that this was never touched by work performed by the Consortium.

Confronted on cross with Dr. Raitt's PowerPoint and asked to explain, the expert—not a native English speaker—begins murmuring in French, starts coughing, and then asks to be excused. He does not return after the lunch break.

GyScope, concerned about its expert's performance, as well as how the oral testimony has come in, asks for the opportunity to file a post-hearing brief pursuant to section 9 of Procedural Order No. 1, which leaves post-hearing briefing to the arbitrator's "discretion." BatPow, satisfied with where the record stands at this point, declines to join in this request. The arbitrator denies leave to file post-hearing briefs, commenting, "This is arbitration, it is supposed to be efficient, and these proceedings have got to come to an end at some point. You can't keep arguing for the last word."

The liability hearing then closes.

Freeze Frame. How would you rule on liability?

I. Partial Final Award on Liability

On June 15, the arbitrator issues a partial final award on liability. The award is, as agreed to by the parties, a "reasoned award." It states the material facts and reasons for the award but does not contain detailed findings of fact and conclusions of law.

AMERICAN ARBITRATION ASSOCIATION

BatPow, Ltd., Claimant, vs. GyScope Corporation, Respondent.	Docket 2021: 1958LF

PARTIAL FINAL AWARD ON LIABILITY

The Arbitrator finds that:

a. The Consortium Agreement was a valid contract.

b. The Consortium Agreement provided for arbitration and the parties here have submitted to arbitration jurisdiction. The parties then agreed subsequently to the proceeding taking place under AAA Commercial Arbitration Rules.

c. BatPow performed its part of the Consortium Agreement by joining the project and attending meetings. BatPow did not have to develop any products of its own in order to be entitled to Consortium Property per article 1 of the Consortium Agreement.

d. The gyroscope was not Already Existing Work under article 3 of the Consortium Agreement. Although it is clear that such work had in fact begun pre-Consortium by GyScope, the Arbitrator finds that Dr. Raitt's PowerPoint has great weight and that GyScope made the conscious decision to donate that work to the Consortium and continue work on it under Consortium auspices. GyScope cannot have it both ways. Accordingly, the gScope was jointly developed during the Consortium Period and any further work and improvements to it are Consortium property under section 1 (Common Ownership Clause).

e. GyScope breached the Consortium Agreement by failing to offer BatPow an ownership percentage of the gPhone. This breach was material.

f. The arbitration will therefore proceed to the quantum (damages) phase.

Dated: June 15, 202x

____

Lowell George, Arbitrator

J. Confirmation and Vacatur Proceedings Under FAA Section 10

GyScope argues that the liability award is a final judgment as to liability, and it proceeds to move for vacatur of the award pursuant to Section 10 of the Federal Arbitration Act before the United States District Court for District of the District of Columbia. *See infra* Chapter 13. GyScope argues that

a. the Arbitrator's evidentiary rulings and especially the refusal to hear evidence on BatPow's financial condition and motivation for bringing the suit are grounds for vacatur under Section 10(a)(3) of the Federal Arbitration Act since these rulings were a "refus[al] to hear evidence pertinent and material to the controversy";

b. these rulings suggested that the Arbitrator was partial to BatPow, thereby constituting a violation of Section 10(a)(2) ("evident partiality or corruption in the Arbitrator");

c. these rulings also suggested that the Award was "procured by fraud, corruption or other means" pursuant to section 10(a)(1); and, finally,

d. the Partial Final Award on Liability contained repeated manifest errors of the law and misread the Consortium Agreement, including misapplication of the Already Existing Clause.

BatPow argues that the court does not have jurisdiction to consider the vacatur motion since the parties agreed to proceed under the Procedural Orders of the Arbitration and Section 4 of Procedural Order No. 1 states that there shall be no challenge in court until the arbitration is definitively concluded: "The parties agree not to file any actions to confirm or to vacate any Order in this Arbitration until the Arbitration is concluded, which will be either by an Award for Respondent finding no liability, or at the conclusion of the quantum stage." BatPow moves in the alternative, if this argument is denied, for confirmation of the award under FAA Section 9.

BatPow also moves in arbitration for its costs and fees for the court battle, arguing that GyScope's vacatur motion amounts to contempt of Paragraph 4 of Procedural Order No. 1. GyScope, in the words of BatPow, "hedged its bets, directly contrary to the letter and spirit of the Procedural Order No. 1 and in a manner directly contrary to the intended speed and efficiency of the arbitration process." BatPow also asks Arbitrator George to order GyScope to withdraw its vacatur motion.

The arbitrator issues a ruling stating that he has no jurisdiction to preclude vacatur rights conferred by statute. The arbitrator states further, however, that by virtue of the partial final award on liability, he continues to have jurisdiction over the case, and therefore the deadlines in Procedural Order No. 1 remain in effect. GyScope moves for reconsideration on the grounds that the parties should not be subject to double tracking of their case, moving forward on damages in the arbitration while simultaneously litigating the vacatur proceedings in court, and that this can hardly be "efficient" under classic arbitration letter and spirit. BatPow opposes the reconsideration motion on the grounds that any double-tracking is wholly of GyScope's own making in moving for vacatur in piecemeal fashion rather than waiting for a final award. The arbitrator denies reconsideration.

The United States District Court denies GyScope's motion for vacatur on the basis that "arbitration is a matter of contract," the parties agreed to proceed under Arbitrator George's jurisdiction, and that accordingly, Paragraph 4 of Procedural Order No. 1 cuts off any vacatur rights at this stage. Oddly, however, the court grants BatPow's cross-motion for confirmation of the partial final award on liability.

Comment

Come back to this section of the BatPow hypo after review of Chapter 13 (Enforcement) and see if you agree with the court's rulings on vacatur and confirmation.

K. Procedural Order No. 3

Following conclusion of the court proceedings, the Arbitrator issues the following Procedural Order No. 3.

AMERICAN ARBITRATION ASSOCIATION

BatPow, Ltd., Claimant, vs. GyScope Corporation, Respondent.	Docket 2021: 1958LF

PROCEDURAL ORDER NO. 3

1. This Procedural Order is directed toward the bifurcated quantum (damages) stage of this proceeding, pursuant to section 4 of Procedural Order No. 1 and the Partial Final Award on Liability.

2. The parties are directed to meet and confer and submit an agreed schedule regarding the times for: expert reports on damages, rebuttal reports, submission of exhibits and hearing demonstratives, prehearing briefs, and other open matters as either party sees fit.

3. Failing agreement, the parties are to notify the Arbitrator, who will set dates that will not otherwise be changed absent an extreme showing of good cause. This Arbitration must proceed forward with dispatch.

4. There shall be a conference call with counsel and the Arbitrator no later than the 10th day prior to the quantum hearing. Counsel for Claimant is directed to establish procedures for the call.

____

Lowell George, Arbitrator

Following receipt of Procedural Order No. 3, the parties agree on all dates.

L. The Quantum (Damages) Phase

After these rulings, the parties proceed to the damages phase.

1. *Expert Reports*

Each party files an expert witness report. BatPow files a report from FutureVision Diagnostics ("FVD"), an econometrics valuation firm that specializes in constructing future-based damages models. FVD's report is authored by Dr. William Payne, who has a PhD in Economics from MIT and an undergraduate degree in economics from Claremont McKenna College. Dr. Payne's disclosure statement in his expert report notes that he has testified in thirty prior disputes, 10 of which were arbitrations, and that three court cases went to a full hearing and award/decision. On one occasion, in 2012, his testimony was stricken on *Daubert* grounds, meaning that the court found that Dr. Payne's expert opinion was not supported by commonly accepted knowledge in the field.

Dr. Payne's report takes two independent, alternative approaches to the damages sought by BatPow. In Part I, "Actual Profits Earned/Extended," Dr. Payne looks at the profits earned by GyScope to date in the launch of the gPhone. He extends those profits out by five (5) years, which in Dr. Payne's opinion is the expected life of a tech product. Dr. Payne then reduces that to a present value effective as of the date of the report and arrives at a figure of $33,786,519. This is the "Actual Profits Earned/Extended Model."

In Part II of his report, Dr. Payne states affirmatively that he is ignoring the actual data—that is, GyScope's actual profits—and is instead constructing his own values for these numbers based on his projection of how much more successful the gPhone would have been if it had been rolled out in the patriotic fervor around the "AmeriPhone" when the Consortium was first proposed. Dr. Payne opines that in this environment, more people would have switched from their iPhones and Androids to a phone "that any patriotic American would have wanted. It would have been a national coming together." Dr. Payne calls this a "Consortium AmeriPhone Model." Dr. Payne finds that this model would have lasted seven, not five, years due to the patriotic enthusiasm for it, and would have had less defections to other or pre-existing products like the iPhone. He finds as well that keeping the Consortium together would have resulted in continuous improvements and so there would have been an AmeriPhone 2, with another seven years of product life. On this basis, he calculates a profit share of 10 times his first model, for a total of over $330,000,000 (three hundred thirty million dollars).

GyScope retains PracticalMetrics Ltd., an equally well-known econometrics firm, as its expert damages consultants. GyScope submits a report from that firm authored by Richard Haywood. Mr. Haywood's disclosure statement shows that he has an undergraduate degree in economics, with honors, from George Washington University in 1980, has no graduate degrees, and spent the majority of his career in big accounting firms on the audit side, before leaving accounting in 2014 to pursue a full time career in consulting and expert witness assignments. He has since testified in eight proceedings, none of which ultimately went to trial. His testimony has never been stricken or formally challenged. He has never testified for a plaintiff or claimant but rather has always provided testimony on the defense side, that is, for the party arguing against (or for a smaller amount of) damages.

Mr. Haywood's expert report rejects entirely the Consortium AmeriPhone Model as "wildly speculative" since "there is no evidence that more people would have purchased the AmeriPhone, which was never developed and might have had other flaws." Mr. Haywood instead proceeds on the same assumptions as Dr. Payne's "actual profits earned/extended model," but takes issue with several inputs as to costs, discount rate, and other projections. As a result, Mr. Haywood's "actual profits extended model" in his expert report is $24,831,486, considerably less than the $33-plus million in BatPow's model.

2. *Expert Depositions*

GyScope moves to take the deposition of BatPow's expert. The Arbitrator finds that no such agreement was made by the parties in the scheduling conference and that under the successive procedural orders he has the discretion to decide this issue. He issues a brief opinion during a phone conference, stating again that the arbitration has gone on for long enough, and further stating that if the parties have any questions for the other side's expert, "that's why we have hearings." On this basis, he denies the motion for expert depositions.

3. *The Motion to Strike Claimant's Expert*

GyScope then files a motion to strike BatPow's expert report on the grounds that GyScope has found, through an Internet search, early marketing materials by FutureVision Diagnostics, BatPow's expert, that state "you dream your castle in the sky, and we'll build it." The materials were only available for one year. GyScope argues that "this type of marketing shows that BatPow's expert will say anything for a price no matter how delusional or fantastic." BatPow opposes the motion on the grounds that this was a long time ago, has nothing to do with Dr. Payne's actual report, and that in any event Dr. Payne's disclosure statement shows that he is far more qualified than is Mr. Hayward, who does not have an advanced degree, does not have sufficient experience as an econometric forecaster, and has never testified at a live hearing. The arbitrator denies the motion to strike.

Freeze Frame. The parties here did not elect to use the Federal Rules of Evidence. Would that choice have made a difference in the arbitrator's ruling? What are the advantages and disadvantages of electing through party consensus to use these rules? How might that choice have affected the rulings here? Is it possible to elect to use the rules during a hearing even if the arbitration clause does not contemplate or otherwise provide for their use?

---

4. The Damages Hearing

Direct examination at the damages hearing is brief, as is customary of experts who have issued a formal expert report. Counsel for BatPow introduces Dr. Payne and has him affirm his expert report and disclosure statement. Dr. Payne then briefly affirms and describes the highlights of his expert report, noting the two models and two different numbers. BatPow's counsel then asks Dr. Payne for his view of Mr. Hayward's rebuttal expert report. Dr. Payne states that he has great respect for Mr. Hayward who, "despite not having a PhD, does his best to master complex topics and occasionally gets that right," but that here he has "missed every fundamental involved in an accurate projection" in an effort to "drive the numbers down to levels nobody familiar with this industry and with basic econometric concepts would have seriously attempted." Dr. Payne proceeds to criticize the assumptions made by Mr. Hayward's alternative model in considerable detail. When BatPow's counsel objects that none of this was in Dr. Payne's report, GyScope's counsel responds, "Of course it wasn't. This is rebuttal to your rebuttal. And you declined our request to take depositions." The arbitrator overrules the objection.

GyScope's counsel cross-examines Dr. Payne by attempting to show that his projections do not match up with overall growth rates forecasted for the smartphone industry. He succeeds in casting doubt on the aggressive "Consortium model." He does not attack in great detail the more conservative, "actual profits earned/extended model," given Dr. Payne's rebuttal testimony.

Similarly, on direct, Mr. Hayward reserves most of his fire for the more aggressive Consortium model. He does not concentrate on the "actual profits earned/extended" model.

The parties call no other witnesses at the damages phase beyond their experts. The hearing lasts for two and a half days of testimony. The arbitrator asks if the parties desire to make closing arguments. Both parties waive closing in favor of post-hearing briefs, which the arbitrator agrees to consider. The post-hearing briefs are due 10 days after the hearing.

Both parties submit briefs that repeat the highlights of the witness testimony from their respective experts. BatPow, however, goes further and notes that "GyScope has essentially accepted the Actual Profits Extended model submitted by Claimant."

M. The Partial Final Award on Damages

Thirty days after receiving the parties' post-hearing briefs on damages, the arbitrator issues a Partial Final Award on Damages. The award is quite brief. In Part I, the arbitrator finds that the "Consortium AmeriPhone Model" is overly aggressive and makes several assumptions not supported by the record. In Part II, the arbitrator makes findings similar to the arguments made by the claimant following the experts' respective reports and live hearing testimony. The arbitrator finds as a result that GyScope failed to adequately rebut the claimant's "Actual Profits Earned/Extended" model and therefore finds for Claimant in the amount of $33,786,519.

The parties made no provision for costs, but pursuant to AAA Rules, the arbitrator has authority to award costs. The arbitrator therefore asks for post-hearing submissions on costs and fees. The parties each submit fee petitions with sharply redacted time descriptions for privilege purposes. The arbitrator awards the claimant an additional $875,000 for costs and fees in a final award.

> ***Freeze Frame.*** As you can see, the opportunity to build your own courthouse extends to the laying of the very last brick. The parties here decided long ago to request a "reasoned award," rather than a detailed finding-of-fact-and-conclusion-of-law laden, court-like opinion. After your study of enforcement, vacatur, and confirmation in Unit III, return to this decision and ask yourself if this always makes the most sense. Generally, if you lose, you want a more extensive record to take up on a Section 10 vacatur challenge. If you win, then it's precisely the opposite and very likely that the less, the better. Is it worth trying to game the result in advance, predict where you might fall, and press for something different? Even if that costs the parties substantially more arbitrator time and thus money?

The matter concludes. GyScope does not challenge the award in court. BatPow moves for confirmation of the award. The Court grants the motion and GyScope pays BatPow the amount awarded by the arbitrator.

UNIT III
Enforcing the Arbitration

Chapter 13

Enforcing and Appealing Arbitration Awards

Let's end at the beginning, and go back to the wheel with which we opened this book:

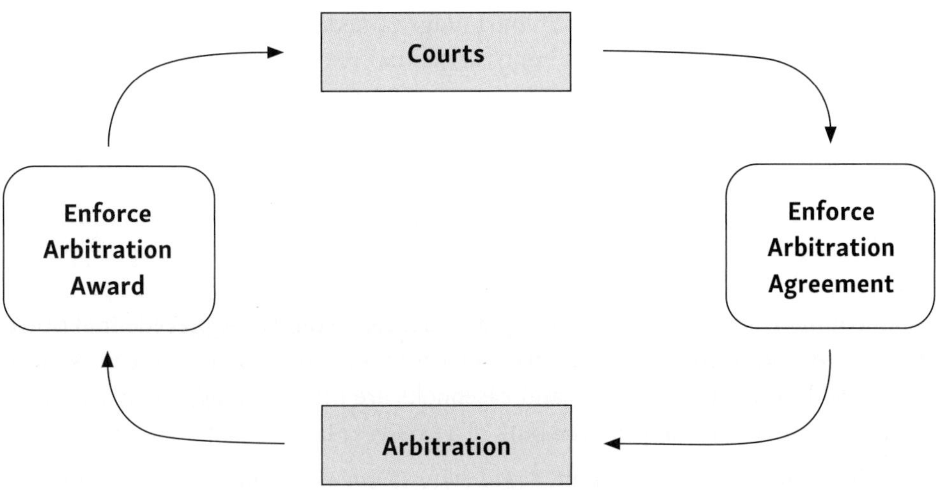

We are now on the 9-to-12 o'clock part of that wheel, where the long dance between courts and arbitration comes to a close. We have studied the judicial presumption in favor of enforcing arbitration agreements. We have seen the severability doctrine confine challenges to arbitration, and judicial deference to an arbitrator's decision about procedural matters other than gateway issues. We have seen courts enforce delegation clauses that allow arbitrators to decide arbitrability. What about when all the procedure, all the arbitrator selection, all the possible injunctions and discovery and the other preliminaries are completed, the hearing has taken place, and all that remains is the actual decision of the arbitrator? At that point, after the arbitration award is rendered, what role is left for the courts? How great is the deference at the *end* of the process? In starker terms, how wrong can an arbitrator be without a court overturning his award?

You will see a return in this chapter to the doctrine of "presumption." Just as courts are instructed to presume a finding in favor of an arbitration *agreement* in the 12-to-3 o'clock portion of the wheel, so are courts instructed to presume the validity of an arbitration *award* in the 9-to-12 portion of the wheel. The party who challenges an arbitration award has the same uphill climb as the party challenging an arbitration agreement. The law is clear that arbitration awards are presumptively valid, subject to very narrow statutory exceptions. The courts have instructed that these inquiries start with a foot already on the scale.

I. The Differences Between Review of Court Decisions and Arbitral Awards

We start with a contrast. Consider the standard of review in court. Trial-level judges are not permitted to get the law "wrong." Legal error by a lower court judge is subject to plenary review. There is no high bar to climb to establish this review, and no presumption that the lower court judge necessarily was correct. The review is de novo, without deference. By contrast, factual review by the appellate court is very deferential and dependent upon the jurisdiction of the lower court. The factual review standard is "arbitrary and capacious" in administrative law, "substantial evidence" for a jury trial, and "clearly erroneous" for a bench trial.

Consider as well the architectural structure of our court system. There is an inherent presumption in this structure that trial level judges *will* get it wrong. Appellate courts exist for this very reason. The law is difficult and capable of misinterpretation. In our common law system, errors in a particular case would have precedential ripple effects if not corrected. Every trial-level judge writes her opinion with the possibility of reversal lurking. Our libraries and casebooks are filled with appellate decisions, and those cases often comprise the bulk of a first-year law student's readings.

Arbitration is entirely different. *Legal error is not sufficient grounds to refuse to enforce an arbitration award.* The bar is quite a bit higher. That bar was set by Congress, and it has been interpreted by the courts to impose significant hurdles on any party seeking judicial review of an arbitration award. There are, to be sure, grounds for not enforcing an arbitration award, and we will examine them in the succeeding pages—but the takeaway is that these are far more procedural than substantive. An arbitrator can get the law wrong and still have his award enforced.

While this is now accepted practice, it does not necessarily have to be this way. The common mantra of those favoring this approach is that if arbitration were subject to extensive judicial review, then the very essence of arbitration would evaporate, with arbitration becoming just a preliminary step in the court process rather than a complete alternative to judicial resolution. A successful party in arbitration would still have to pass at least two levels of judicial scrutiny (at the trial- and then appellate-level courts). Who would want to consent to such an elongated and costly a process?

There is much to be said for this view, and it prevails today. But it goes too far to say that a more penetrating review by the courts would "destroy" arbitration. The factual and legal development of the case, including the extensive and expensive pretrial process, would still take place outside of the court system, thus relieving the courts of substantial management and other burdens. Review of arbitration decisions would, admittedly, put some of this docket stress back on the courts at the review stage, but likely not nearly as much as if the court had had to manage the case from day 1. Courts would be relieved of that burden, but could still sit as reviewers of the legal correctness and validity of the arbitration award.

This is not, however, our system of arbitration review. Instead, the scope of review is far narrower. As you review these cases, and now that you are familiar with the history, goals and nature of arbitration, consider these policy issues as well. Is review that is limited to process and ignores merits sufficient? If not, what element of merits review would you introduce?

II. The Mechanics of Arbitration Enforcement

Enforcement means "once is enough." The goal of any "enforcement" regime is to protect the winning party from having to win twice on the merits. The concept exists throughout the law. It is a reason for the deference to facts (as distinct from law) on court review, and the reason for the full faith and credit clause in the U.S. Constitution: judgments from sister states are given full faith and credit so that a party who wins in Pennsylvania but has to execute against assets in Wyoming does not have to go to Wyoming court and put his case on all over again.

Enforcement also means "getting paid." A judgment is merely a piece of paper. Courts don't sit on piles of money. Successful plaintiffs are not like winners at a casino, where one turns in chips for cash on the way out the door. Some, maybe most, unsuccessful defendants pay on demand when they lose their case or appeal, but for those who do not, winning a court case is just a further step along the dispute resolution road. A judgment is merely a court order that allows a plaintiff to go find assets and turn them into money. This may involve seizures, attachments, sheriff's sales, and other collection devices, all done under color of law once a judgment issues.

"Once is enough" and "getting paid" can potentially collide where the assets are in a different forum than the place where the court judgment, or arbitration award, was rendered. The enforcing court has to decide whether it will simply rubber stamp the judgment/award and allow the plaintiff to execute on the assets in the enforcing court's jurisdiction, or whether the plaintiff has to prove its case all over again. In the Pennsylvania-Wyoming example above, should and will the Wyoming court examine the Pennsylvania judgment? A successful and efficient enforcement regime minimizes the need to retry the case (the "once is enough" part) so that the winning party can efficiently conclude the case (the "getting paid" part). The inherent challenge is for the enforcing court to be fair: something more than a rubber stamp but less than a de novo forum.

Arbitration awards start one step behind in this process. A party may execute upon a court judgment as soon as that judgment is rendered. That court judgment, unless appealed, can be taken to a sheriff and used as a basis to seize bank accounts, garnish income streams, or replevin property. An arbitration award, as of the moment it is rendered, does not have that same power. Rather, an arbitration award must first be blessed by a court—or, in the words of the FAA, "confirmed" —in order to then have the full force of law.

How exactly does the winning party in arbitration confirm the award so that it can then be enforced in court? The Federal Arbitration Act lays out the enforcement regime in Sections 9 through 12 of the Act. Section 9 provides:

> If the parties in their agreement have agreed that a judgment of the court shall be entered upon the award made pursuant to the arbitration, and shall specify the court, then at any time within one year after the award is made any party to the arbitration may apply to the court so specified for an order confirming the award, and thereupon the court must grant such an order unless the award is vacated, modified, or corrected as prescribed in sections 10 and 11 of this title. If no court is specified in the agreement of the parties, then such application may be made to the United States court in and for the district within which such award was made. Notice of the application shall be served upon the adverse party. . . .

Two practice points leap out from section 9. One is in the drafting. The other is in the timing.

1. Drafting: *put confirmation language in the arbitration clause*. The parties can either specify the particular court to which a confirmation application must be made (note the words of the statute: "*and shall specify the court*"), or, as is more usual, can extend this to any court. The typical enforcement language in a modern arbitration clause provides that "[t]he award may be confirmed in any court of competent jurisdiction."
2. Timing: *act within a year*. Arbitration awards spoil and go bad after one year. Section 9 requires that successful parties seek confirmation "within one year after the award is made."

If the losing party elects not to contest the arbitrator's award, then the confirmation process is short and sweet: the winning party files a Section 9 petition to confirm, the district court enters the order, and the confirmed award then has the force of any other federal court judgment. *See, e.g., PaySafe Partners LP v. Merch. Payment Grp. LLC*, Case No. 19 Civ. 495 (LGS), 2019 U.S. Dist. LEXIS 75885 (S.D.N.Y. May 6, 2019) (court order confirming an uncontested award issued by an arbitrator).

If the successful party moves for confirmation within one year, before the proper court, and the losing party does not contest confirmation, then this is frequently a quick and streamlined process. Unopposed motions for confirmation of an arbitration award should result in a judicially confirmed award shortly after the successful party makes its Section 9 motion. With this court judgment in hand, the successful party may then proceed to execute on any assets needed to satisfy the award. The arbitration award now has the force of law.

But what if the losing party in the arbitration now takes that battle to court at the confirmation process? This brings Section 10 of the Federal Arbitration Act into play.

III. The Grounds for Vacating an Arbitration Award

Congress was express in Section 10 of the FAA about the precise grounds for contesting the judicial confirmation of an arbitration award. The challenging party files what the statute terms a "motion to vacate the award." The grounds for vacating an arbitration award are:

1. where the award was procured by corruption, fraud, or undue means;
2. where there was evident partiality or corruption in the arbitrators, or either of them;
3. where the arbitrators were guilty of misconduct in refusing to postpone the hearing, upon sufficient cause shown, or in refusing to hear evidence pertinent and material to the controversy; or of any other misbehavior by which the rights of any party have been prejudiced; or
4. where the arbitrators exceeded their powers, or so imperfectly executed them that a mutual, final, and definite award upon the subject matter submitted was not made.

Notice what is *not* in the above law. There is no language in the statute that provides that "an error of law" is a basis for seeking vacatur, or legal error or anything remotely of the sort. Two of the bases for vacating the award are entirely behavioral and have nothing to do with the merits of the ruling (fraud and partiality). Another is procedural (refusing to postpone hearings or hear evidence). The fourth, as we will see, ties to the arbitrator's mandate rather than to legal error.

The absence of appellate review for legal error is one of the fundamental differences between arbitration and litigation. At a basic, fundamental, statutory level, arbitration is designed to be "one and done." The Supreme Court has made clear that any merits review is highly limited. The one exception—the breadth of the "manifest disregard" theory—is considered in the next chapter and remains unfortunately confused.

Consider the Supreme Court's observation in *First Options*, 514 U.S. 938 (1995), which we first studied in our examination of delegation clauses:

> Where the party has agreed to arbitrate, he or she, in effect, has relinquished much of that right's practical value. The party still can ask a court to review the arbitrator's decision, but the court will set that decision aside only in very unusual circumstances.

Do the "unusual circumstances" referenced in *First Options* include where the arbitrator is flat-out wrong? The Supreme Court expanded on this question in the 2013 term. As you review the following decision, recall that in the very same 2013 term, the author, Justice Kagan, wrote a spirited anti-arbitration dissent in the *Italian Colors* case. *See* Chapter 4. There, she took on the majority's decision to uphold a class action ban even though that effectively ended the case by preventing retention of an antitrust expert:

> So if the arbitration clause is enforceable, Amex has insulated itself from antitrust liability—even if it has in fact violated the law. The monopolist gets to use its monopoly power to insist on a contract effectively depriving its victims of all legal recourse.
>
> And here is the nutshell version of today's opinion, admirably flaunted rather than camouflaged: Too darn bad.

It is thus all the more striking that it fell to Justice Kagan that same year to stake out just how far arbitrators are allowed to go.

Oxford Health Plans LLC v. Sutter

569 U.S. 564, 133 S. Ct. 2064 (2013)

JUSTICE KAGAN delivered the opinion of the Court.

Class arbitration is a matter of consent: An arbitrator may employ class procedures only if the parties have authorized them. *See Stolt-Nielsen S. A. v. AnimalFeeds Int'l Corp.*, 559 U.S. 662, 684 (2010). In this case, an arbitrator found that the parties' contract provided for class arbitration. The question presented is whether in doing so he "exceeded [his] powers" under §10(a)(4) of the Federal Arbitration Act (FAA or Act), 9 U.S.C. §1 *et seq.* We conclude that the arbitrator's decision survives the limited judicial review §10(a)(4) allows.

I

Respondent John Sutter, a pediatrician, entered into a contract with petitioner Oxford Health Plans, a health insurance company. Sutter agreed to provide medical care to members of Oxford's network, and Oxford agreed to pay for those services at prescribed rates. Several years later, Sutter filed suit against Oxford in New Jersey Superior Court on behalf of himself and a proposed class of other New Jersey physicians under contract with Oxford. The complaint alleged that Oxford had failed to make full and prompt payment to the doctors, in violation of their agreements and various state laws.

Oxford moved to compel arbitration of Sutter's claims, relying on the following clause in their contract:

> No civil action concerning any dispute arising under this Agreement shall be instituted before any court, and all such disputes shall be submitted to final and binding arbitration in New Jersey, pursuant to the rules of the American Arbitration Association with one arbitrator.

The state court granted Oxford's motion, thus referring the suit to arbitration.

The parties agreed that the arbitrator should decide whether their contract authorized class arbitration, and he determined that it did. Noting that the question turned on "construction of the parties' agreement," the arbitrator focused on the text of the arbitration clause quoted above. He reasoned that the clause sent to arbitration "the same universal class of disputes" that it barred the parties from bringing "as civil actions" in court: The "intent of the clause" was "to vest in the arbitration process everything that is prohibited from the court process." And a class action, the arbitrator continued, "is plainly one of the possible forms of civil action that could be brought in a court" absent the agreement. Accordingly, he concluded that "on its face, the arbitration clause . . . expresses the parties' intent that class arbitration can be maintained."

Oxford filed a motion in federal court to vacate the arbitrator's decision on the ground that he had "exceeded [his] powers" under §10(a)(4) of the FAA. The District Court denied the motion, and the Court of Appeals for the Third Circuit affirmed.

While the arbitration proceeded, this Court held in *Stolt-Nielsen* that "a party may not be compelled under the FAA to submit to class arbitration unless there is a contractual basis for concluding that the party *agreed* to do so." 559 U.S., at 684. The parties in *Stolt-Nielsen* had stipulated that they had never reached an agreement on class arbitration. Relying on §10(a)(4), we vacated the arbitrators' decision approving class proceedings because, in the absence of such an agreement, the arbitrators had "simply . . . imposed [their] own view of sound policy." *Id.*, at 672.

Oxford immediately asked the arbitrator to reconsider his decision on class arbitration in light of *Stolt-Nielsen*. The arbitrator issued a new opinion holding that *Stolt-Nielsen* had no effect on the case because this agreement authorized class arbitration. Unlike in *Stolt-Nielsen*, the arbitrator explained, the parties here disputed the meaning of their contract; he had therefore been required "to construe the arbitration clause in the ordinary way to glean the parties' intent." And in performing that task, the arbitrator continued, he had "found that the arbitration clause unambiguously evinced an intention to allow class arbitration." The arbitrator concluded by reconfirming his reasons for so construing the clause.

Oxford then returned to federal court, renewing its effort to vacate the arbitrator's decision under §10(a)(4). Once again, the District Court denied the motion, and the Third Circuit affirmed. The Court of Appeals first underscored the limited scope of judicial review that §10(a)(4) allows: So long as an arbitrator "makes a good faith attempt" to interpret a contract, "even serious errors of law or fact will not subject his award to vacatur." 675 F.3d 215, 220 (2012). Oxford could not prevail under that standard, the court held, because the arbitrator had "endeavored to give effect to the parties' intent" and "articulate[d] a contractual basis for his decision." *Id.*, at 223–224. Oxford's objections to the ruling were "simply dressed-up arguments that the arbitrator interpreted its agreement erroneously." *Id.*, at 224.

We granted certiorari to address a circuit split on whether §10(a)(4) allows a court to vacate an arbitral award in similar circumstances. Holding that it does not, we affirm the Court of Appeals.

II

Under the FAA, courts may vacate an arbitrator's decision "only in very unusual circumstances." *First Options of Chicago, Inc. v. Kaplan*, 514 U.S. 938, 942 (1995). That limited judicial review, we have explained, "maintain[s] arbitration's essential virtue of resolving disputes straightaway." *Hall Street Associates, L. L. C. v. Mattel, Inc.*, 552 U.S. 576, 588 (2008). If parties could take "full-bore legal and evidentiary appeals," arbitration would become "merely a prelude to a more cumbersome and time-consuming judicial review process." *Ibid.*

Here, Oxford invokes §10(a)(4) of the Act, which authorizes a federal court to set aside an arbitral award "where the arbitrator[] exceeded [his] powers." A party seeking relief under that provision bears a heavy burden. "It is not enough . . . to show that the [arbitrator] committed an error—or even a serious error." *Stolt-Nielsen*, 559 U.S., at 671. Because the parties "bargained for the arbitrator's construction of their agreement," an arbitral decision "even arguably construing or applying the contract" must stand, regardless of a court's view of its (de)merits. Only if "the arbitrator act[s] outside the scope of his contractually delegated authority"—issuing an award that "simply reflect[s] [his] own notions of [economic] justice" rather than "draw[ing] its essence from the contract"—may a court overturn his determination. So the sole question for us is whether the arbitrator (even arguably) interpreted the parties' contract, not whether he got its meaning right or wrong.

And we have already all but answered that question just by summarizing the arbitrator's decisions. They are, through and through, interpretations of the parties' agreement. The arbitrator's first ruling recited the "question of construction" the parties had submitted to him: "whether [their] Agreement allows for class action arbitration."

To resolve that matter, the arbitrator focused on the arbitration clause's text, analyzing (whether correctly or not makes no difference) the scope of both what it barred from court and what it sent to arbitration. The arbitrator concluded, based on that textual exegesis, that the clause "on its face . . . expresses the parties' intent that class action arbitration can be maintained." When Oxford requested reconsideration in light of *Stolt-Nielsen*, the arbitrator explained that his prior decision was "concerned solely with the parties' intent as evidenced by the words of the arbitration clause itself." He then ran through his textual analysis again, and reiterated his conclusion: "[T]he text of the clause itself authorizes" class arbitration. Twice, then, the arbitrator did what the parties had asked: He considered their contract and decided whether it reflected an agreement to permit class proceedings. That suffices to show that the arbitrator did not "exceed[ ] [his] powers." §10(a)(4).

The arbitrator did construe the contract (focusing, per usual, on its language), and did find an agreement to permit class arbitration. So to overturn his decision, we would have to rely on a finding that he misapprehended the parties' intent. But §10(a)(4) bars that course: It permits courts to vacate an arbitral decision only when the arbitrator strayed from his delegated task of interpreting a contract, not when he performed that task poorly. *Stolt-Nielsen* and this case thus fall on opposite sides of the line that §10(a)(4) draws to delimit judicial review of arbitral decisions.

Nothing we say in this opinion should be taken to reflect any agreement with the arbitrator's contract interpretation, or any quarrel with Oxford's contrary reading. All we say is that convincing a court of an arbitrator's error—even his grave error— is not enough. So long as the arbitrator was "arguably construing" the contract—which this one was—a court may not correct his mistakes under §10(a)(4). The potential for those mistakes is the price of agreeing to arbitration. As we have held before, we hold again: "It is the arbitrator's construction [of the contract] which was bargained for; and so far as the arbitrator's decision concerns construction of the contract, the courts have no business overruling him because their interpretation of the contract is different from his." *Enterprise Wheel*, 363 U.S., at 599. The arbitrator's construction holds, however good, bad, or ugly.

Comment: The Deferential Standard

The "good, bad and ugly" point made by Justice Kagan reveals the extremely deferential standard of judicial review of arbitration awards. "The role of a district court in reviewing an arbitration award is 'narrowly limited' and 'arbitration panel determinations are generally accorded great deference under the [FAA].'" *Envtl. Chem. Corp. v. Coastal Envtl. Grp., Inc.*, 2018 U.S. Dist. LEXIS 157246, at *14 (2d Cir. Sept. 14, 2018) (quoting *Kolel Beth Yechiel Mechil of Tartikov, Inc. v. YLL Irrevocable Tr.*, 729 F.3d 99, 103 (2d Cir. 2013)) (internal citations and quotation marks omitted)."Consequently, the burden of proof necessary to avoid confirmation of an arbitration award is very high, and a district court will enforce the award as long as there is a barely colorable justification for the outcome reached." *Id.* (internal citations and quotation marks omitted).

Courts will almost always stretch to enforce these awards. *See Floridians for Solar Choice v. PCI Consultants, Inc.*, 314 F. Supp. 3d. 1346, 1359 (2018) (the FAA "imposes a heavy presumption in favor of confirming arbitration awards; therefore, a court's confirmation of an arbitration award is usually routine or summary . . . The provision for judicial confirmation carries 'no hint of flexibility' because '[o]n application for an order confirming the arbitration award, the court must grant the order unless the award is vacated, modified, or corrected as prescribed in sections 10 and 11 of this title.'") (citing *Cat Charter, LLC v. Schurtenberger*, 646 F.3d 836, 842 (11th Cir. 2011)).

How are these broad terms of deference to arbitration awards applied in the four specific statutory subsections in Section 10(a)? We examine each subsection in turn.

A. "Procured by Fraud, Corruption, or Other Means" (Section 10(a)(1))

Does "fraud" mean lying to the arbitration panel? How does one make that showing after the fact—is it possible to take discovery after an award? Does "corruption" mean that of the party or the arbitrator? And what is the border between vehemently disagreeing with your opponent's argument versus believing it to be "fraudulent"?

Consider the different approaches to the fraud accusation in the next two cases.

Floridians for Solar Choice v. PCI Consultants, Inc.

314 F. Supp. 3d 1346 (S.D. Fla. 2018)

BLOOM, United States District Judge.

THIS CAUSE is before the Court upon three motions: Defendants PCI Consultants, Inc. and Angelo Paparella's Motion to Vacate Arbitral Award, filed on October 18, 2017; Plaintiff Floridians for Solar Choice, Inc.'s ("FSC") and Claimant in Arbitration Southern Alliance for Clean Energy, Inc.'s ("SACE," together with FSC, "Solar") Motion to Confirm Arbitration Award, with Supporting Memorandum of Law, ("Motion to Confirm"), filed on November 1, 2017; and a separately filed motion entitled "Defendant PCI's Supplemental Memorandum in Support of the Motion to Vacate", filed on November 21, 2017. The Court has reviewed the motions, the filings in support and opposition, the record, and is otherwise fully advised. For the reasons stated below, the Motion to Confirm is granted and the Motion to Vacate and Supplemental Motion to Vacate (together, the "Motions to Vacate"), are denied.

I. PROCEDURAL BACKGROUND

Plaintiff FSC initially filed its Complaint on December 23, 2015 against Defendants PCI Consultants, Inc. ("PCI"), and PCI's principal, Angelo Paparella ("Paparella"). FSC amended its complaint on January 13, 2016 ("Amended Complaint"). In the Amended Complaint, FSC alleged causes of action for breach of contract, fraud in the inducement, conversion, and unjust enrichment against PCI, and fraud in the inducement and conversion against Paparella. Simultaneous to filing its Complaint, FSC filed a Motion to Compel Arbitration, arguing that the claims asserted relate to contracts under which Defendants agreed to arbitrate. Defendants opposed the motion. The Court granted the motion to compel on January 22, 2016 and administratively closed the case.

On October 13, 2017, Defendants filed their Motion to Reopen Case, advising the Court that the parties had participated in an arbitration administered by the American Arbitration Association ("AAA") in April 2017. Defendants further advised the Court that the "sole arbitrator issued a non-final award on July 20, 2017 and on October 10, 2017, the arbitrator, retired Broward Circuit Court Judge Jeffrey Streitfeld ("Arbitrator"), issued a 'Final Award' adopting the non-final award." In the Motion to Reopen, Defendants stated that they planned to move to vacate the award. The Court granted the Motion to Reopen.

Now before the Court are the Motions to Vacate, as well as Plaintiff's Motion to Confirm.

In their Motions, Defendants make five arguments in favor of vacatur. First, Defendants argue that the award must be vacated because Solar employed "fraud and/or undue means" to procure an arbitration award in its favor. Second, Defendants argue that the Arbitrator lacked jurisdiction to enter an award exceeding one million dollars. Third, Defendants argue that the Arbitrator had "irrefutable bias" against Defendants. Fourth, Defendants claim that the Arbitrator failed to hear evidence related to Solar's "surprise damages claim." Lastly, Defendants argue that the AAA Rules barred entry of the October 10, 2017 final award ("October Final Award") in favor of Solar because the July 20, 2017 award ("July Award") was a "final award" that terminated the Arbitrator's jurisdiction. In response, Solar argues that the Arbitrator's award is supported by the record evidence and that Defendants have failed to meet their burden on their claim of fraud or undue means under *Bonar v. Dean Witter Reynolds Inc.*, 835 F.2d 1378 (11th Cir. 1988), and on their claim of arbitrator bias under *Gianelli Money Purchase Plan & Tr. v. ADM Inv'r Servs., Inc.*, 146 F.3d 1309 (11th Cir. 1988).

II. FACTUAL BACKGROUND

This case stems from a failed initiative to qualify a solar energy constitutional amendment for the 2016 election in Florida. Based on the Court's grant of the motion to compel arbitration, FSC filed a Demand for Arbitration with the AAA against Defendants PCI and Paparella seeking damages of $500,000-$1,000,000, plus punitive damages, attorneys' fees, interest, and arbitration costs. Defendants subsequently filed a separate Statement of Claim with AAA seeking $212,479.67, plus punitive damages, attorneys' fees, interest, and arbitration costs against FSC, as well as two of FSC's officers, Stephen Smith ("Smith") and George Cavaros, and Southern Alliance for Clean Energy Action Fund, Inc. ("SACEAF"). The two matters were consolidated, and during the pendency of the arbitration, Defendants added SACE as a respondent. SACE counterclaimed against PCI and Paparella.

The Arbitrator held a three-day hearing on April 25, 26, and 28, 2017 during which the parties presented witness testimony and numerous exhibits. On July 20, 2017, the Arbitrator issued the July Award in favor of Solar ("July Award"). The following facts were found by the Arbitrator or elicited through uncontroverted testimony, unless otherwise noted:

FSC is a not-for-profit corporation formed for the purpose of qualifying a solar energy amendment in Florida's general election in 2016. PCI is a "national leader in obtaining signed petitions for ballot initiatives." In order to be included on the ballot, Florida law required FSC to seek prior approval by the Supreme Court of Florida of the amendment's language and nearly 700,000 signed voter petitions. The parties entered into several contracts through which PCI agreed to obtain a fixed amount of signed petitions for the solar energy initiative based on a price per signature. The Arbitrator highlighted three provisions of the contracts that he found of particular importance:

1. PCI was to be paid per signature, with all signature collection expenses to be the responsibility of PCI;
2. Amendments to the contracts must be made in writing and signed by the parties;
3. Until the final invoice was paid in full, the signed petitions remained the property of PCI.

The Arbitrator found that the first two contracts between the parties—which included amendments agreed to through an exchange of emails—were fully performed: PCI collected the required number of signatures and FSC paid PCI for those signatures on a per-signature basis. Under the third contract dated June 5, 2015, PCI agreed to collect 5,000 signatures per week at a cost of $2.65 per signature.

In late summer while the parties were still waiting for approval from the Supreme Court of Florida, a competing constitutional amendment sponsored by the utility companies was introduced. In response, the Arbitrator found that the parties amended the June 5, 2015 agreement through a series of email exchanges to increase PCI's signature collection rate to 15,000 signatures per week.

During the fall, after the Supreme Court approved the amendment language, PCI informed FSC that the price per signature agreed to in the June 5, 2015 contract was increasing from $2.65 to $4.00, and then again to $5.25, and that FSC would be responsible for substantial additional expenses related to the travel, housing, and per diem expenses for independent contractors hired to collect signed petitioners ("Petitioner Expenses"). Defendants memorialized this demand for a price increase in a spreadsheet ("October Spreadsheet").

For approximately one month, between October 22, 2015 and November 18, 2015, PCI submitted invoices—which FSC paid without objection—that included both the per signature charge of $5.25, plus the additional Petitioner Expenses contained in the October Spreadsheet. During this time, Plaintiff also engaged SACE to help educate voters regarding the competing solar energy petitions and defray some of the rising costs. According to the testimony during the hearing, the parties agreed that FSC and SACE would split the $5.25 price per petition, with FSC paying $2.25 for the signatures and SACE paying $3.00 for voter education. In furtherance of that agreement, on October 27, 2015 SACE signed a separate contract with PCI under which PCI agreed to "use its network of independent contractors to educate Florida citizens about the benefits of solar electric power" and SACE would pay $3.00 for each "educational impression."

On November 18, 2015, Defendants sent a new expense spreadsheet to Solar, once again increasing the required Petitioner Expenses ("November Spreadsheet"). In the email containing the spreadsheet, Paparella told FSC's principal, Steven Smith, "don't have a heart attack." The following day, Solar informed Defendants that it could not fund the initiative at the levels proposed in the November Spreadsheet and terminated the ballot initiative. At the time of termination, Solar had paid all costs and Petitioner Expenses as reflected in the October Spreadsheet, including $5.25 per petition for 217,000 petitions in PCI's custody, plus $130,000 in Petitioner Expenses for those petitions. Solar had not paid any additional Petitioner Expenses as reflected in the November Spreadsheet. After termination, PCI demanded that Solar pay $212,479 in Petitioner Expenses per the November Spreadsheet in order to receive the 217,000 signed petitions it had already paid for. According to the Arbitrator's findings, after Solar refused, the dispute took on "a nasty tone," leading to this litigation.

Meanwhile, throughout 2015, Defendants had another client that was simultaneously seeking to qualify a constitutional amendment in Florida for medical marijuana. Paparella testified that he had worked on several medical marijuana initiatives in the past, had a personal relationship with the individuals running the medical marijuana campaign in Florida, and considered medical marijuana an issue that he "was passionate about." PCI charged the medical marijuana campaign a fixed per-petition price of $2.25. Because both the medical marijuana campaign and the solar campaign needed petitioners on the ground to gather signatures, and petitioners typically carry more than one petition, there were at least some discussions between the principals of Solar, PCI, and the medical marijuana campaign regarding sharing the Petitioner Expenses. The parties and non-party witnesses presented conflicting testimony regarding the content, timing, and agreements reached during these discussions. Paparella testified that Solar understood that the expenses in the October 2015 spreadsheet only reflected half the Petition Expenses Solar would be required to pay. He further testified that Solar orally agreed to pay all the expenses incurred by both campaigns—that is, double the expenses listed in the October 2015 spreadsheet—with the understanding that the medical marijuana campaign would pay what it could towards the Petitioner Expenses on an ad hoc basis. Paparella testified that Smith understood that Solar would "subsidize" the medical marijuana campaign.

Smith testified that he never understood the October 2015 spreadsheet to represent half of the Petitioner Expenses and never agreed to pay the medical marijuana campaign's expenses or subsidize that campaign. Smith further testified that when the expenses dispute arose, he tried to resolve the issue with Paparella amicably. For example, he stated in an email: "Please help me understand why we should be responsible for $374,479 in expenses."

The Arbitrator found Paparella's testimony not credible. Accordingly, the Arbitrator concluded that there was no oral agreement for Solar to cover either medical marijuana's expenses or expenses that were double those listed in the October spreadsheet. Specifically, the Arbitrator found: "It is clear to me that PCI has sued the Solar parties for money owed to it by its medical marijuana client." Because there was no agreement to pay the additional Petitioner Expenses in the November Spreadsheet, the Arbitrator found that Defendants breached the contract when they retained the 217,000 paid-for petitions. Thus, Solar was entitled to judgment on its breach of contract claim in the total amount paid for the retained petitions per the June 5, 2015 contract as modified by the October Spreadsheet, totaling $1,271,250. The Arbitrator further awarded interest from the date of initial filing and unspecified reasonable attorneys' fees and costs which the parties stipulated would be "reserved for post-trial resolution by the Arbitrator."

The Arbitrator subsequently received briefing on attorneys' fees, issued the October Final Award, and issued the Corrected Final Award on November 1, 2017. In the October Final Award, the arbitrator awarded to Solar, in addition to the $1,271,250 contained in the July Award, prejudgment interest of $230,218.34, costs of $18,277, and attorneys' fees of $340,000. The November Final Award corrected a typographical error in the October Final Award.

III. MOTION TO VACATE

A. LEGAL STANDARD

A motion to vacate is not a mechanism to appeal or otherwise challenge the merits of a dispute conclusively determined in arbitration. Indeed, Congress carefully circumscribed the narrow and exclusive grounds for vacatur to prevent arbitration from becoming "merely a prelude to a more cumbersome and time-consuming judicial review process." *Oxford Health Plans LLC v. Sutter*, 569 U.S. 564, 568–69 (2013) (quoting *Hall St. Assocs., LLC v. Mattel, Inc.*, 552 U.S. 576, 588 (2008)). Thus, on a motion to vacate an arbitration award under 9 U.S.C. § 10(a), a district court "may revisit neither the legal merits of the award nor the factual determinations upon which it relies." *Wiand v. Schneiderman*, 778 F.3d 917, 926 (11th Cir. 2015) (finding the "entire argument for vacatur is based on the weight of the evidence presented, and that is simply beyond this court's—or the district court's—power to review"); *Aviles v. Charles Schwab & Co.*, 435 F. App'x 824, 829 n.7 (11th Cir. 2011) (per curiam) ("[A]n incorrect legal conclusion by an arbitrator [is] no ground for setting aside an arbitration ruling."). Indeed, "as long as the arbitrator is even arguably construing or applying the contract and acting within the scope of his authority, that a court is convinced he committed serious error does not suffice to overturn his decision." *United Paperworkers Int'l Union, AFL-CIO v. Misco, Inc.*, 484 U.S. 29, 38 (1987) (citation omitted).

B. ANALYSIS

1. Fraud and Undue Means

Under Section 10(a)(1), a district court may vacate an award based on corruption, fraud, or undue means. To vacate an arbitration award based on fraud, the movant must fulfill a three-part test articulated by the Eleventh Circuit in *Bonar v. Dean Witter Reynolds, Inc.*, 835 F.2d 1378 (11th Cir. 1988). In particular, *Bonar* requires: 1) that "the movant establish fraud by clear and convincing evidence;" 2) that "the fraud must not have been discoverable upon the exercise of due diligence prior to or during the arbitration;" and 3) that "the fraud materially related to an issue in the arbitration." *Id.* at 1383. To vacate based on undue means, a party must demonstrate intentional misconduct that "measures equal in gravity to bribery, corruption, or physical threat to an arbitrator." *Liberty Sec. Corp. v. Fetcho*, 114 F. Supp. 2d 1319, 1321 (S.D. Fla. 2000).

In the Motions, Defendants argue that the Court should vacate the Award based on Solar's alleged fraud on the Arbitrator by repeatedly representing that it sought damages of only $487,588.50 during the hearing—the total paid by FSC for the 217,000 petitions at $2.25 per petition, exclusive of expenses and the $3.00 per petition paid by SACE—and then in post-hearing briefing arguing that it sought damages for the full contract price.

Defendants fail to meet their burden to demonstrate by clear and convincing evidence that Solar defrauded or used undue means to influence the Arbitrator. Defendants' challenge—cloaked in the nomenclature of fraud—amounts to no more than vehement disagreement with the Arbitrator's findings on the breach of contract claim. A change in damages theory, while vexing to Defendants, does not amount to clear and convincing evidence of fraud or undue means. *Cf. Bonar v. Dean Witter Reynolds, Inc.*, 835 F.2d 1378 (11th Cir. 1988) (finding fraud where expert testified to false credentials). Moreover, even if the Court considered Solar's change in damages theory sufficient to demonstrate fraud or undue means, "vacatur is precluded"—as here—"where the arbitrators had before them all material information relating to the alleged undue means." *Liberty*, 114 F. Supp. 2d at 1322.

Defendants cite to authority from Florida's state courts support of their argument for fraud. However, not only are these cases inapposite because they fail to apply Section 10(a)(1) under the FAA; they also lend no support to Defendants' argument because no case holds that a change in damages theory in post-trial briefing supports a theory of fraud. *See Boca Burger, Inc. v. Forum*, 912 So. 2d 561, 565 (Fla. 2005); *Addison v. Brown*, 413 So. 2d 1240, 1240 (Fla. 5th DCA 1982), *aff'd sub nom. Lubin v. Dist. Court of Appeal Fifth Dist.*, 428 So. 2d 663 (Fla. 1983); *Hays v. Johnson*, 566 So.

2d 260 (Fla. 5th DCA 1990). Accordingly, Defendants have not met their burden on the first factor [of Section 10(a)].

Notes and Questions

Compare the fraud analysis in *Floridians for Social Choice* to that in the following case from the Southern District of New York. Who must be defrauded for Section 10(a)(4) to preclude enforcement? Is the "fraud" underpinning the cause of action that of the underlying party? Is the fraud on counsel in the course of the arbitration? On the arbitrator(s)?

Envtl. Chem. Corp. v. Coastal Envtl. Grp., Inc.

Case No. 18 Civ. 3082 (GHW) (GWG), 2018 U.S. Dist. LEXIS 157246 (S.D.N.Y. Sept. 14, 2018)

GORENSTEIN, United States Magistrate Judge.

Invoking section 10 of the Federal Arbitration Act, 9 U.S.C. §§ 1–16 ("FAA"), petitioner Environmental Chemical Corporation ("ECC") seeks to vacate an arbitration award entered in favor of respondent Coastal Environmental Group, Inc. ("Coastal"). Coastal cross-moves to confirm the award, arguing that ECC's grounds for vacatur are without merit. For the following reasons, the motion to vacate should be denied and the arbitration award should be confirmed.

I. BACKGROUND

This case arises out of debris collection and removal efforts on Fire Island, New York, following Hurricane Sandy in October 2012. In the spring of 2013, the United States Army Corps of Engineers (the "USACE") awarded ECC a "Task Order"—that is, a work authorization issued pursuant to a standing contract between the parties—to collect and remove storm debris generated by Hurricane Sandy in exchange for payment based upon a stated price per volume of debris removed. ECC in turn subcontracted with Coastal to perform the required debris collection and removal, leaving for itself the provision of administrative and site support services.

The work did not proceed as planned, however, and both ECC and Coastal incurred unexpected costs in completing the cleanup efforts. ECC maintained that these extra costs resulted from Coastal's mismanagement of the cleanup efforts, while Coastal attributed these costs to USACE's failure to prepare a certain cleanup site, bad weather, and an overestimate of the total debris to be removed. After the cleanup efforts were completed, ECC contended that its extra costs exceeded the payments it owed Coastal under the parties' contract, and accordingly, refused to make any additional payments to Coastal. On June 6, 2016, Coastal commenced arbitration against ECC, claiming that "it was not fully paid for its work at the project." On

January 9, 2018, the Arbitrator, Sayward Mazur, issued a decision granting Coastal an award of $2,083,588.88.

C. Arbitration & Post-Arbitration Submissions

On June 6, 2016, claiming "it was not fully paid for its work," Pet. ¶ 15, Coastal filed a demand for arbitration with the American Arbitration Association ("AAA") as provided in the CSA. The Arbitration Demand listed David Westermann, Jr., and his law firm, as Coastal's representatives.

Following issuance of the Partial Final Award, Coastal "submitted a request for counsel fees and costs." Attached to its request were two agreements indicating that, prior to the arbitration, "all of the proceeds of Coastal's agreement with ECC had been fully assigned to Signature Bank, and also indicating that Signature Bank would "take over all efforts to prosecute and collect all amounts due and owing with respect to the [Subcontract] and retain any net amounts recovered from ECC."

D. Procedural History

On April 6, 2018, ECC filed this petition to vacate the arbitration award. The petition made a number of challenges: (1) that the award was "procured by fraud and undue means," because Coastal concealed Signature Bank's role in the arbitration; (2) that "concealment of Signature Bank's role in the arbitration" impeded ECC's ability "to conduct a full and meaningful conflict review"; (3) that Coastal's "improper withholding of relevant evidence" prevented the arbitrator from "consider[ing] a number of issues pertinent to the dispute"; and (4) that the "arbitrator exceeded his authority" by making a finding on estoppel that "fail[ed] to draw its essence from the contract," and which "was never briefed by the parties and was never raised at any point during the hearings." On May 18, 2018, Coastal cross-moved to confirm the award.

II. GOVERNING LEGAL STANDARDS

Section 9 of the FAA provides that parties to an arbitration agreement may apply to a court "for an order confirming the award, and thereupon the court must grant such an order unless the award is vacated, modified, or corrected as prescribed in sections 10 and 11 of this title." 9 U.S.C. § 9. "The role of a district court in reviewing an arbitration award is 'narrowly limited' and 'arbitration panel determinations are generally accorded great deference under the [FAA].'" *Kolel Beth Yechiel Mechil of Tartikov, Inc. v. YLL Irrevocable Tr.*, 729 F.3d 99, 103 (2d Cir. 2013) (quoting *Tempo Shain Corp. v. Bertek, Inc.*, 120 F.3d 16, 19 (2d Cir. 1997)). "This deference promotes the twin goals of arbitration, namely settling disputes efficiently and avoiding long and expensive litigation. Consequently, the burden of proof necessary to avoid confirmation of an arbitration award is very high, and a district court will enforce the award as long as there is a barely colorable justification for the outcome reached." *Id.* at 103–04 (internal citations and quotation marks omitted).

"Normally, confirmation of an arbitration award is 'a summary proceeding that merely makes what is already a final arbitration award a judgment of the court. . . .'"

D.H. Blair & Co., Inc. v. Gottdiener, 462 F.3d 95, 110 (2d Cir. 2006) (quoting *Florasynth, Inc. v. Pickholz*, 750 F.2d 171, 176 (2d Cir. 1984)). A petition to confirm should be "treated as akin to a motion for summary judgment based on the movant's submissions." *Id.* at 109. The FAA provides that "[a]ny application to the court hereunder shall be made and heard in the manner provided by law for the making and hearing of motions." 9 U.S.C. § 6. Thus, "[u]nder the FAA, the petition itself should be treated as a motion to confirm the award." *In re Certain "Default" Motions*, 2015 U.S. Dist. LEXIS 27093, 2015 WL 968125, at *5 (E.D.N.Y. Feb. 27, 2015) (citing 9 U.S.C. § 6); see also *id.* ("[A] petition represents the procedural device that should be used to resolve these cases.") (footnote omitted). As a result, "a court may decide the merits of a petition to confirm or vacate an arbitration award based solely on the papers submitted by the parties in support of their motions." *Companion Prop. & Cas. Ins. Co. v. Allied Provident Ins., Inc.*, 2014 U.S. Dist. LEXIS 136473, 2014 WL 4804466, at *2 (S.D.N.Y. Sept. 26, 2014) (citations and internal quotation marks omitted).

III. DISCUSSION

1. Corruption, Fraud, or Undue Means—9 U.S.C. § 10(a)(1)

A party moving to vacate an arbitration award on grounds of "fraud or undue means" must "adequately plead that (1) respondent engaged in fraudulent activity; (2) even with the exercise of due diligence, petitioner could not have discovered the fraud prior the award issuing; and (3) the fraud materially related to an issue in the arbitration." *Odeon Capital Grp. LLC v. Ackerman*, 864 F.3d 191, 196 (2d Cir. 2017) (citing *Karppinen v. Karl Kiefer Mach. Co.*, 187 F.2d 32, 34–35 (2d Cir. 1951)); *accord Kolel Beth Yechiel Mechil of Tartikov, Inc. v. YLL Irrevocable Tr. (Kolel I)*, 878 F. Supp. 2d 459, 464 (S.D.N.Y. 2012), *aff'd*, 729 F.3d 99 (2d Cir. 2013). "In order to vacate an award on [this] ground, the Second Circuit has held that it must be 'abundantly clear' that the award was the product of fraud, corruption, or undue means." *Kolel I*, 878 F. Supp. 2d at 464 (quoting *Karppinen*, 187 F.2d at 34). Here, it is not "abundantly clear" that the award was the product of fraud inasmuch as ECC has not established either of the first two elements of the fraud test.

(a) Fraudulent Activity

"Fraud" is "[a] knowing misrepresentation or knowing concealment of a material fact made to induce another to act to his or her detriment." Black's Law Dictionary 775 (10th ed. 2014); *accord Connaughton v. Chipotle Mexican Grill, Inc.*, 29 N.Y.3d 137, 142, 53 N.Y.S.3d 598, 75 N.E.3d 1159 (2017) (fraud under New York law requires a plaintiff to show "a misrepresentation or a material omission of fact which was false and known to be false by defendant, made for the purpose of inducing the other party to rely upon it, justifiable reliance of the other party on the misrepresentation or material omission, and injury") (internal quotation marks omitted) (quoting *Lama Holding Co. v. Smith Barney, Inc.*, 88 N.Y.2d 413, 421, 668 N.E.2d 1370, 646 N.Y.S.2d 76 (1996)); *accord Fin. Guar. Ins. Co. v. Putnam Advisory Co., LLC*, 783 F.3d 395, 402 (2d Cir. 2015).

[The Court went on to find that there were no false disclosures or material omissions in this case because, *inter alia*, "Coastal apprised ECC's counsel prior to arbitration of Westermann's role as Signature Bank's counsel and Coastal's co-counsel in the case" and "ECC attorneys repeatedly referred in writing to Westermann's role as Signature Bank's counsel, as well as to Signature Bank's financial interest and involvement in the arbitration."]

(b) Due Diligence

Even if it could be said that there was a false disclosure or material omission, ECC's motion would still fail because the information it did receive would have allowed it to uncover the purported fraudulent activity if it had acted with reasonable diligence.

To vacate an arbitration award for fraud under section 10(a)(1), "the party relying on [section 10(a)(1)] must first show that he could not have discovered [the concealed evidence] during the arbitration, else he should have invoked it as a defense at that time." *Karppinen*, 187 F. 2d at 35; *accord Salzman v. KCD Fin., Inc.*, 2011 U.S. Dist. LEXIS 147170, 2011 WL 6778499, at *3–4 (S.D.N.Y. Dec. 21, 2011) (petitioner could not show "that had he exercised due diligence, he could not have discovered the alleged fraud prior to the award."); *Biotronik Mess-Und Therapiegeraete GmbH & Co. v. Medford Med. Instrument Co.*, 415 F. Supp. 133, 138 (D.N.J. 1976) ("Karppinen suggests that the focus under [§] 10(a) is upon whether the protesting party had an opportunity to discover and reveal the purported fraud at the arbitration hearing.").

Here, ECC knew (1) that Westermann represented Signature Bank; and (2) that the Bank was financially involved and interested in the litigation. It was thus obviously free to seek to obtain information through the arbitration discovery process about the precise nature of the relationship. Its failure to do so means that it did not act with the "due diligence" required by case law. *Odeon Capital Grp. LLC*, 864 F.3d at 196. We thus reject ECC's assertion that it acted reasonably by doing nothing to pursue this question. Accordingly, ECC has not shown that the award should be overturned on the basis of fraud and thus there is no reason to vacate the decision under section 10(a)(1) of the FAA.

Comment

In the first case above, the court found that changing a damages theory was not fraud. In the second, the court found that the party now claiming fraud could easily have discovered it rather than waiting to raise the issue later. When should an advocate play the "fraud card"? We will return to this question when we study waiver later in this chapter.

Class Problems

Should the fraud standard in Section 10(a)(1) require a showing of common law fraud with all of its elements (false statement or omission, materiality, causation, and damages) and should it be pleaded with particularity as required in most procedural (e.g., Fed. R. Civ. P. 9) rules? Put differently: did Congress use the Federal Rules standard when fashioning Section 10(a)(1) of the AAA?

Problem 1. During the arbitration, Claimant presents a damages model that projects her damages on a 10-year basis given the expected lifetime of a project. Her model is supported by an expert witness with a PhD in econometrics. The expert, Dr. Jones, is employed by a leading consulting firm that renders expert opinions in complex commercial disputes like this one. On rebuttal, Respondent's expert, Dr. Smith, who works for a rival leading consulting firm, testifies that the model is a "pie in the sky fantasy" and that "no expert worth her salt" would run such a model. The arbitration tribunal cites this rebuttal testimony in its final award, which gives Claimant just 10% of what she was seeking (and the exact amount that Respondent's alternative model conceded was owing). Three months later, another lawyer at the firm that represented Claimant is in a different arbitration, this time defending the respondent. Dr. Smith is now testifying for the claimant, and in true hired-gun fashion, testifies to the same "pie in the sky" future-based model that he so denigrated in the earlier arbitration. Did he commit a fraud on the first tribunal for purposes of Section 10(a)(1)?

Problem 2. Assume the same facts as above, in which Dr. Jones offers an alternative model, but in this case based on numbers from his client, Respondent, showing that the project in question was losing money. Assume, again, that the arbitrator renders an award that gives Claimant only 10% of her claim. Three months later, a former employee of Respondent joins Claimant's organization, bringing with him a disc drive that shows that the figures supplied to Dr. Smith were completely false and that the project is instead making a LOT of money. Was this fraud upon the arbitrator for purposes of Section 10(a)(1)?

B. Evident Partiality (Section 10(a)(2))

Recall our examination in Chapter 6 of arbitrator conflict of interest. The "evident partiality" standard grows directly out of this subject. An arbitrator with a conflict of interest is one who, arguably and perhaps likely, will not be impartial. There is a straight line between that issue and Section 10(a)(2), because the statute makes arbitrator bias one of the very few reasons to vacate an award.

Under Section 10(a)(2), "an arbitration award may be vacated due to the 'evident partiality' of an arbitrator only when either (1) an actual conflict exists, or (2) the arbitrator knows of, but fails to disclose, information which would lead a reasonable person to believe that a potential conflict exists." *World Bus. Paradise, Inc. v. Suntrust*

Bank, 403 F. App'x 468, 470 (11th Cir. 2010) (quoting *Univ. Commons-Urbana, Ltd. v. Universal Constructors, Inc.*, 304 F.3d 1331, 1339 (11th Cir. 2002)). If an actual conflict does not exist, the movant must show that the partiality is "direct, definite, and capable of demonstration rather than remote, uncertain, and speculative." *Univ. Commons*, 304 F.3d at 1339 (internal citations and quotations omitted.) "The burden of proving facts which would establish a reasonable impression of partiality rests squarely on the party challenging the award." *Middlesex Mut. Ins. Co. v. Levine*, 675 F.2d 1197, 1201 (11th Cir. 1982).

Section 10(a)(2) does not, however, articulate the standards for measuring partiality. Just as there is a grey area between arbitrators who have a conflict versus those who are merely experienced and connected throughout their profession and field, so is there a difference between an arbitrator who is partial versus one who has merely ruled in a way that disappoints one of the parties. It would be no standard at all if the claim of partiality could be flung at every arbitrator who issued an award against the complaining party.

Lack of disclosure can, as studied in Chapter 6, lead to a finding of bias—but not always. Overt relationships can also lead to a finding of bias. One-sided decisions, however, fare poorly as bases for bias claims.

ErgoBilt, Inc. v. Neutral Posture Ergonomics, Inc.

Civil Action No. 3:97-CV-2548-L, 2002 U.S. Dist. LEXIS 12459, 2002 WL 1489521 (N.D. Tex. July 9, 2002)

SAM, District Judge.

I. Factual and Procedural History

This case involves a dispute between two manufacturers of office and industrial ergonomic chairs. On October 16, 1997, Plaintiff ErgoBilt, Inc. ("ErgoBilt") filed suit in this court against Defendant Neutral Posture Ergonomics, Inc. ("NPE"), alleging false advertising under the Lanham Act, 15 U.S.C. § 1125. ErgoBilt is a publicly traded company, incorporated in Texas, and is the parent company of BodyBilt, Inc. ("BodyBilt"). On November 26, 1997, NPE filed counterclaims and cross-claims against both ErgoBilt and BodyBilt (collectively, "Plaintiffs"). By Memorandum Opinions and Orders dated August 10, 1998, the court dismissed ErgoBilt's original complaint and dismissed certain of NPE's counterclaims. On January 24, 1999, the parties filed their Agreed Joint Motion to Refer Claims to Arbitration, in which they requested that NPE's remaining counterclaims be submitted to arbitration before the American Arbitration Association ("AAA"). This court granted the parties' request on February 19, 1999.

The parties arbitrated their dispute before Arbitrator Alvin Zimmerman ("Arbitrator"). The arbitration took place between April 10–14, 2000, and again between December 18–20, 2000. The Arbitrator considered numerous claims and counterclaims of the parties. Plaintiffs asserted claims for breach of contract, violation of the Lanham Act, unfair competition, tortious interference with contractual relations, and false advertising. NPE asserted claims for breach of contract, trademark infringement, patent infringement, and tortious interference with contract. Both parties sought injunctive relief, damages, and attorney's fees.

The Arbitrator issued the Final Award of Arbitrator on May 2, 2001, and a corrected Final Award of Arbitrator on June 5, 2001 (the "award"). The award ordered Plaintiffs to pay to NPE (1) $300,000 in damages for trademark infringement; (2) $25,000 in damages relating for disparagement; (3) $1,357,742.39 in attorney's fees and costs; and (4) $65,195.61 to reimburse NPE for fees it paid to the AAA in connection with the arbitration, with postjudgment interest for these monetary awards set "at 10% accruing from the 20th day from the date of this award." Additionally, the Award permanently enjoined Plaintiffs from the use of NPE's trademark. On June 25, 2001, NPE moved to confirm the arbitration award, requesting that this court enter final judgment and a permanent injunction in accordance with the Arbitrator's determination. Plaintiffs move to vacate the award.

1. Evident Partiality

The court first addresses Plaintiffs' contention that the award should be vacated under 9 U.S.C. § 10(a)(2). Section 10(a)(2) authorizes a district court to vacate an arbitration award "where there was evident partiality or corruption in the arbitrators." A party urging vacatur on the ground of evident partiality bears an "onerous burden," and must produce specific facts to show that the alleged partiality is "direct, definite, and capable of demonstration rather than remote, uncertain, or speculative." *Mantle v. Upper Deck Co.,* 956 F. Supp. 719, 729 (N.D. Tex. 1997) (citation omitted). Plaintiffs contend the arbitrator maintained a "long standing personal and professional relationship" with counsel for Defendant, and that the arbitrator did not disclose this relationship until approximately sixteen months into the arbitration proceedings. Upon disclosure, however, the AAA issued a letter to the parties, stating that "any objections to the continued service of the arbitrator based on the above disclosure should be filed with this office, copying all other parties, on or before 1:00 P.M. November 13, 2000." Plaintiffs did not file an objection.

The court determines that Plaintiffs waived any § 10(a)(2) complaint by failing to object to the continued service of the arbitrator after the relationship had been disclosed. A party "cannot stand by during arbitration, withholding certain arguments, then, upon losing the arbitration, raise such arguments in federal court." *Gateway Techs.*, 64 F.3d at 998 (*quoting National Wrecking Co. v. International Bhd. of Teamsters, Local 731*, 990 F.2d 957, 960 (7th Cir. 1993); *Wellman v. Writers Guild of America, West, Inc.*, 146 F.3d 666, 673 (9th Cir. 1998) ("It is well settled that a party may not sit idly through an arbitration proceeding and then collaterally attack that procedure on grounds not raised before the arbitrators when the result turns out to be adverse."). Accordingly, the court denies Plaintiffs' Motion to Vacate on § 10(a)(2) evident partiality grounds.

CASE PREVIEW. Timing is a huge issue in arbitration award challenges under FAA Section 10. Partiality raises a particularly difficult timing problem. When is too early, and when is too late? *Ergo-Bilt* found that the challenge was too late. In the following case, the party was found to have instead challenged too *early*. So when would you make a challenge on these facts? How should the lawyer seeking vacatur balance timing versus extremity? If the neutral arbitrator is partial, do you complain early? If you don't complain early because there is no procedural path to do so, then how do you avoid the waiver cases above? Consider these questions as you read the next case.

Savers Prop. & Cas. Ins. Co. v. Nat'l Union Fire Ins. Co.

748 F.3d 708 (6th Cir. 2014)

COLE, Circuit Judge.

National Union Fire Insurance Company ("National Union") appeals the grant of a preliminary injunction that halted an ongoing arbitration proceeding with Savers Property and Casualty Insurance Company, et al. (collectively, "Meadowbrook"). Because arbitration's essential virtue is resolving disputes straightaway, judicial review of arbitral awards is extremely narrow and exceedingly deferential. In the absence of a final arbitration award, the district court should not have interjected itself into this private dispute. Accordingly, we reverse the judgment, dissolve the injunction, and remand for dismissal.

I. BACKGROUND

A. Factual Background

[*See* Chapter 6 for additional background.]

The panel ordered Meadowbrook to pay National Union $1,950,680.48 for damages that were "capable of immediate calculation," and, in an effort to mete out a final award, ordered Meadowbrook to provide supporting documentation with respect to other reinsurance programs and their retained risk. The panel also ordered Meadowbrook to reimburse National Union for its attorneys' fees and costs. The panel denied all other requests for relief, ordered Meadowbrook to pay the sum-certain damages within fourteen days, and retained jurisdiction only to "adjudicat[e] those items requiring additional submissions"—i.e., to calculate National Union's damages prior to issuing a final arbitration award.

The Interim Final Award was silent with respect to the ban on ex parte communications that had gone into effect on June 14. Nevertheless, National Union's attorney and Arbitrator Rosen resumed ex parte communications immediately following issuance of the award, which National Union maintains was permissible under the panel's scheduling orders and the customs and practices of the reinsurance industry.

National Union disclosed these very communications when it submitted its Bill of Costs to Meadowbrook and the panel. Meadowbrook, however, argues that the communications were prohibited by the scheduling orders.

B. Procedural Background

Despite acknowledging that courts are generally prohibited from reviewing arbitration proceedings until a final award has been issued, the district court determined it could review the matter by re-casting Meadowbrook's challenge as a breach of contract dispute regarding the rules under which the arbitration was to proceed. Accordingly, the court enjoined the panel from issuing any further orders without the court's approval.

C. The Instant Appeal

National Union timely appealed, arguing that under the Federal Arbitration Act ("FAA"), 9 U.S.C. § 1 *et seq.*, parties to an ongoing arbitration may not challenge the fairness of the proceedings or the partiality of the arbitrators until after the conclusion of the arbitration and the rendition of a final award.

III. ANALYSIS

B. Judicial Review was Improper Before Issuance of a Final Arbitration Award

Based upon the text, structure, and purpose of the FAA, which all foster a speedy and less formal method of dispute resolution, we conclude that the district court erred in entertaining this interlocutory challenge to an ongoing arbitration proceeding. Parties to an arbitration generally may not challenge the fairness of the proceedings or the partiality of the arbitrators until the conclusion of the arbitration and the rendition of a final award. Because Meadowbrook's arbitration was ongoing, and because the panel had not yet issued a final award, the district court erred by prematurely interjecting itself into this private dispute.

Meadowbrook's request that the district court intervene to halt this ongoing arbitration proceeding was plainly improper. By initiating this arbitration, Meadowbrook "thereby implicitly agreed to defer judicial review until after the conclusion of the . . . Arbitration." Accordingly, Meadowbrook's action was premature.

C. Interlocutory Judicial Review was Improper Under 9 U.S.C. § 2

The district court recognized the general prohibition on interlocutory review of arbitration proceedings but granted the injunction anyway under a strained reading of Meadowbrook's pleadings and 9 U.S.C. § 2. We address this portion of the district court's decision to resolve any ambiguity over the type of judicial review that 9 U.S.C. § 2 does and does not permit. In doing so, we conclude that the district court erred in relying on § 2 to permit interlocutory review of the arbitration proceedings. Section 2 of the FAA provides that a written arbitration agreement "shall be valid, irrevocable, and enforceable, save upon such grounds as exist at law or in equity for the revocation of any contract." 9 U.S.C. § 2; *see also* Mich. Comp. Laws § 600.5001(2) (repealed 2012) (same). This provision was intended to place arbitration agreements on the "same footing as other contracts" and thereby overcome judicial hostility to arbitration. H.R. Rep. No. 68-96, at 1–2 (1924). Accordingly, § 2 preserves "generally applicable contract defenses" to arbitration agreements, such as fraud or duress. *See AT&T Mobility*, 131 S. Ct. at 1748. By its limitation to grounds that justify "revocation of any contract," the text of § 2 simply provides that an arbitration agreement, like any other contract, is subject to rescission or invalidation if there is a defect in the underlying contract containing the agreement to arbitrate. *Corey v. NYSE*, 691 F.2d 1205, 1212 (6th Cir. 1982).

Nothing in the text or history of the FAA suggests that § 2 was intended to displace § 10's limitation on judicial review of non-final awards. Id. Challenging the fairness of an arbitration proceeding or the partiality of an arbitrator is different in kind than challenging the underlying contract that contained the agreement to arbitrate. *See Aviall, Inc. v. Ryder Sys., Inc.*, 110 F.3d 892, 895 (2d Cir. 1997) ("Although the FAA provides that a court can vacate an award where there was evident partiality or corruption in the arbitrators, it does not provide for pre-award removal of an arbitrator. Thus, an agreement to arbitrate before a particular arbitrator may not be disturbed, unless the agreement is subject to attack under general contract principles as exist at law or in equity.").

In this case, the district court's decision falls on the wrong side of the line. Meadowbrook fails to cite a single decision from this circuit or any other in which a court halted an ongoing arbitration proceeding under circumstances similar to those presented here.

IV. CONCLUSION

For the foregoing reasons, we reverse the judgment of the district court, dissolve the injunction, and remand the case for dismissal without prejudice. This is not to suggest that Meadowbrook is without remedy, or that the arbitrators' decision-making will forever be protected from judicial review. Meadowbrook is entitled to its day in court to challenge the fairness of the proceedings and the partiality of the arbitrators—just not until the panel has concluded its work and issued a final award.

CASE PREVIEW. Notwithstanding the timing concerns regarding too late (*Ergo-Bilt*) or too early (*Sayers*), sometimes the facts are too compelling, the partiality too evident, and the challenge granted. As you read the next case, consider if extremes of this fashion, involving familial relations, are the floor for "evident partiality." Further, note how the court refers back to the *Commonwealth Coatings* decision we studied in Chapter 6.

Morelite Constr. Corp. v. N.Y.C. Dist. Council Carpenters Ben. Funds

748 F.2d 79 (2d Cir. 1984)

KAUFMAN, Circuit Judge:

In deciding this appeal, we are once again called upon to address the elusive standards under which an arbitrator's award may be vacated pursuant to Section 10 of the United States Arbitration Act, 9 U.S.C. § 10 (1982). Specifically, the question before us is whether a father-son relationship between an arbitrator and an officer of one party to the arbitration rises to the level of "evident partiality" required by Section 10 for vacating an award. Notwithstanding our traditional reluctance to inquire into the merits of an arbitrator's award, or to require of an arbitrator the same demanding level of impartiality as that dictated for judges, we believe this relationship deprived the opposing party of the impartiality to which it has a right. Accordingly, we reverse the decision of the district court, and remand with instructions to vacate the award.

An inquiry into issues of fairness, bias, partiality and the like overflows with factual questions. Consequently, we set forth the concrete background of the instant dispute before turning to the legal issues.

FACTS

Appellant Morelite Construction Corp. ("Morelite"), a division of Morelite Electric Services, Inc., is a construction contractor. Appellees are The District Council of New York City and Vicinity of the United Brotherhood of Carpenters and Joiners of America (the "District Union") and the Trustees of the New York City District Council Carpenters Benefit Funds (the "Benefit Funds"). The instant appeal arises from Morelite's alleged non-payment of contributions to the Benefit Funds pursuant to a collective bargaining agreement between Morelite and the District Union.

In 1979 and 1980, Morelite was engaged to perform contracting services in connection with two construction projects in New York City. Morelite entered into job agreements with the District Union applicable to each site. The agreements expressly incorporated the construction industry's "Master Collective Bargaining Agreement" and provided for arbitration of disputes arising from the agreements.

In 1980, the Benefit Funds audited Morelite's financial records, and charged that the company was delinquent in contributions to the Funds in the amount of some $80,000. On October 8, 1980, the Benefit Funds served notice upon Morelite of their intention to arbitrate their claim for unpaid contributions. Later that month, Morelite commenced a proceeding in New York State Supreme Court seeking to stay arbitration. The Benefit Funds removed the action to the United States District Court for the Southern District of New York, and cross-petitioned to compel arbitration. By order dated May 6, 1981, Judge Cannella denied Morelite's petition, and granted the Benefit Funds' cross-petition on the condition that the District Union be joined as a party to the arbitration (which it subsequently was).

On March 11, 1982, Morelite moved in the District Court to disqualify Patrick M. Campbell, Jr. as the arbitrator, because his father was then a Vice-President of the United Brotherhood of Carpenters and Joiners of America, the international union of which the District Union was a local. Campbell, Sr. also served as the international union's supervisor and trustee of the District Union. Judge Cannella denied the motion, holding the court had no authority to entertain an attack on an arbitrator's partiality until after the rendition of an award, and ordered the arbitration to proceed forthwith.

Hearings were held before Patrick Campbell, Jr. during the months of April and May of 1982, and in June of 1983, he filed his opinion and award. Campbell found that Morelite was "delinquent in payment of fringe benefit monies due under its written agreements and is also obligated to pay liquidated damages and interest on its delinquency." In sum, the District Union was awarded $128,429.50 plus interest from the date of the award.

In September 1983, Morelite moved pursuant to 9 U.S.C. § 10 (1982) to set aside the arbitration award, again claiming that the position of Campbell's father—who, during the pendency of the arbitration, had been named General President of the international union—precluded Campbell from acting impartially. Judge Cannella, noting that he "remained troubled by the relationship," nevertheless denied the motion and granted the District Union's cross-petition to confirm the arbitrator's award. In March of 1984, final judgment was entered in favor of the Benefit Funds and the District Union, and Morelite timely filed a notice of appeal.

DISCUSSION

In 1925, Congress promulgated the United States Arbitration Act, 9 U.S.C. §§ 1–14, which set forth the delicate relationship between the role of private arbitration and the federal courts. Section 10 of the Act delineates the grounds upon which a court may vacate an arbitrator's award. Subsection (b) provides that such a basis exists "where there was evident partiality . . . in the arbitrator[]. . . ."

Exactly what constitutes "evident partiality" by an arbitrator is a troublesome question. The Supreme Court, in *Commonwealth Coatings Corp. v. Continental*

Casualty Co., 393 U.S. 145, 21 L. Ed. 2d 301, 89 S. Ct. 337 (1968), attempted to resolve the issue, but the result of that decision appears to be ongoing uncertainty. In that case, a supposedly neutral arbitrator was discovered to have an undisclosed business relationship with the successful party to the arbitration. The arbitrator had been paid approximately $12,000 by the party in consulting fees, and the relationship "went so far as to include the rendering of services on the very projects involved in [the arbitration]." *Id.* at 146.

Justice Black, writing for a plurality of four justices, appeared to impose upon arbitrators the same lofty ethical standards required of Article III judges. The Justice suggested, in fact, that "we should, if anything, be even more scrupulous to safeguard the impartiality of arbitrators than judges, since the former have completely free rein to decide the law as well as the facts and are not subject to appellate review." *Id.* at 149. Using language that has since been seized upon by unsuccessful parties to arbitration, Justice Black concluded by writing that arbitrators, like judges, must avoid even the "appearance of bias." *Id.* at 150.

Four justices, however, do not constitute a majority of the Supreme Court. Justice White, writing for himself and Justice Marshall, concurred in the result, but made clear the Court was not holding that arbitrators' and judges' ethical standards are coextensive. Justice White wrote:

> The Court does not decide today that arbitrators are to be held to the standards of judicial decorum of Article III judges, or indeed of any judges. It is often because they are men of affairs, not apart from that of the marketplace, that they are effective in their adjudicatory function.... This does not mean the judiciary must overlook outright chicanery in giving effect to their awards; that would be an abdication of our responsibility. But it does mean that arbitrators are not automatically disqualified by a business relationship with the parties before them if both parties are informed of the relationship in advance, or if they are unaware of the facts but the relationship is trivial. I see no reason automatically to disqualify the best informed and most capable potential arbitrators.

Accordingly, much of Justice Black's opinion must be read as dicta, and we are left in the dark as to whether an "appearance of bias" will suffice to meet the seemingly more stringent "evident partiality" standard of 9 U.S.C. § 10. Against this murky backdrop of Supreme Court precedent, we examine prior decisions in this circuit.

The closest we can come to the gleaning of guidance in this elusive sphere is the decision in *International Produce, Inc. v. A/S Rosshavet*, 638 F.2d 548 (2d Cir.), *cert. denied*, 451 U.S. 1017 (1981). We held there that the mere fact a neutral arbitrator was also a witness in another arbitration involving the same law firms representing the parties in the arbitration in question did not provide grounds for vacating the award on the basis of his "evident partiality." *Id.* at 551. In reaching this conclusion, Judge

Lumbard wrote, "the Supreme Court in *Commonwealth Coatings* did not expand the § 10 standard of 'evident partiality' to include 'appearance of bias.'" *Id.* In the following sentence, however, he acknowledged that even an "'appearance of bias' [in this case] seems to us, at best, to be speculation without substance." *Id.* (citation omitted). Accordingly, it appears that his statement to the effect that "evident partiality" requires a showing of more than a mere "appearance of bias" was unnecessary to the result in that case, and thus must be read as something less than an absolute and final determination of the matter. We are left, then, with little guidance concerning what standard is to be applied in construing the "evident partiality" language of the statute. It is to that question we now turn.

In attempting to delineate standards of impartiality on a relatively clean slate, we are struck by the competing interests inherent in the use of arbitration. On the one hand, parties agree to arbitrate precisely because they prefer a tribunal with expertise regarding the particular subject matter of their dispute. *See United Steelworkers of America v. Warrior & Gulf Navigation Co.*, 363 U.S. 574, 581–82 (1960); *International Produce, Inc. v. A/S Rosshavet*, 638 F.2d 548, 552 (2d Cir.), *cert. denied*, 451 U.S. 1017 (1981). Familiarity with a discipline often comes at the expense of complete impartiality. Some commercial fields are quite narrow, and a given expert may be expected to have formed strong views on certain topics, published articles in the field and so forth. Moreover, specific areas tend to breed tightly knit professional communities. Key members are known to one another, and in fact may work with, or for, one another, from time to time. As this Court has noted, "expertise in an industry is accompanied by exposure, in ways large and small, to those engaged in it. . . ." *Andros Compania Maritima, S.A. v. Marc Rich & Co.*, 579 F.2d 691, 701 (2d Cir. 1978).

It comes as no surprise, then, that the standards for disqualification of arbitrators have been held to be less stringent than those for federal judges. *See Merit Ins. Co. v. Leatherby Ins. Co.*, 714 F.2d 673 (7th Cir. 1983), *cert. denied*, 464 U.S. 1009 (1983). For to disqualify any arbitrator who had professional dealings with one of the parties (to say nothing of a social acquaintanceship) would make it impossible, in some circumstances, to find a qualified arbitrator at all. Mindful of the trade-off between expertise and impartiality, and cognizant of the voluntary nature of submitting to arbitration, we read Section 10(b) as requiring a showing of something more than the mere "appearance of bias" to vacate an arbitration award. To do otherwise would be to render this efficient means of dispute resolution ineffective in many commercial settings.

On the other hand, we must not abjure our responsibility to maintain the integrity of the federal courts' role in affirming or vacating awards.

We need not, and do not, attempt to set forth a list of familial or other relationships that will result in the *per se* vacation of an arbitration award, except to suggest that such a list would most likely be very short. We do not intend to hold arbitrators to all the standards of Canon 3. Neither do we intend that unsuccessful parties to arbitration may have awards set aside by seeking out and finding tenuous relationships between the arbitrator and the successful party. We hold only that the uncontested relationship here at issue is such that reasonable people would have to believe it provides strong evidence of partiality by the arbitrator.

Accordingly, we reverse the judgment of the district court and remand with instructions to vacate the award.

Notes and Questions

The court in the above case wrestled with the same issue as did the court in *Commowealth Coatings* and courts ever since: what is the difference between bias and apparent bias, and when does that which may only be "apparent" ripen into actual bias? What should be the test? Or is this so fact-dependent that a workable test is impossible? Does *Commonwealth Coatings* need updating and clarification?

C. Failure to Allow Evidence (Section 10(a)(3))

In the federal courts, a judge's decisions on admissibility of evidence can be the basis of a de novo legal challenge on appeal. In the following arbitration case, that same type of decision served as the basis for a motion to vacate under Section 10(a)(3) ("refusing to hear evidence"). What do you see as the differences? What should they be? Does it make sense to allow an arbitration to be overturned for evidentiary reasons but not for ultimate merits reasons? Will enforcement of a stringent "refusing to hear evidence" standard intimidate arbitrators into admitting virtually everything—and is that necessarily a bad thing?

White v. Valero Ref. New Orleans, LLC

Civil Action No. 11-1014 Section "I", 2013 U.S. Dist. LEXIS 86158, 2013 WL 3154731 (E.D. La. June 19, 2013)

AFRICK, District Judge.

Before the Court is a motion to vacate the arbitration award filed on behalf of plaintiff, Calvin White, and an opposition filed on behalf of defendant, Valero Services, Inc. For the following reasons, plaintiff's motion to vacate is DENIED.

BACKGROUND

The present case arises from an arbitration award which resolved an intentional infliction of emotional distress ("IIED") claim alleging harassment at plaintiff's prior workplace, a refining facility. Plaintiff, Calvin White, worked for defendant, Valero Services, Inc. ("Valero"), at the time defendant acquired ownership of the facility in 2003. Plaintiff, however, began working at the facility in March 1998 when it was owned by Trans America Refining Co. and Orion Refining Corporation, respectively.

In December 2009, plaintiff made numerous reports to another employee's supervisor about said employee's failure to perform required job duties. Plaintiff claims these reports were never investigated or addressed. In January 2010, plaintiff was suspended with compensation for four working days pending an investigation regarding a sexual harassment grievance asserted against him. After a complete investigation proved the allegations lacked merit, plaintiff was reinstated to his prior position. Plaintiff then began having chest pains, headaches, and severe mental distress which he maintains were attributable to the unfounded sexual harassment complaint and other workplace harassment.

Plaintiff asserts that while employed by defendant, he was subject to mistreatment by many employees and supervisors. Plaintiff's harassment complaints against the supervisors include: (1) shaking plaintiff's hand with gloves on, (2) deliberately ignoring plaintiff's concerns and/or questions, (3) purchasing meals for other employees but not plaintiff, (4) not extending invitations to plaintiff, (5) calling plaintiff derogatory names, (6) failing to investigate plaintiff's allegations of co-workers' misconduct, (7) reprimanding plaintiff for providing the human resources director with 20–25 complaints, and (8) not providing plaintiff the opportunity for a promotion when other employees, who had not been there as long, were given such opportunities.

Following Valero's purchase of the facility in 2003, all employees were required to execute "Valero's Mandatory Dispute Resolution Program" ("Dialogue"), which contained a binding arbitration provision. Pursuant to the Dialogue agreement, plaintiff's initial lawsuit, filed in the 29th Judicial District Court for the Parish of St. Charles, was remanded for arbitration which proceeding was governed by American Arbitration Association ("AAA") guidelines. Throughout the arbitration proceeding, several status conferences were held and discovery was permitted from February 2011 until July 23, 2012.

Defendant filed a motion for summary judgment on July 27, 2012, plaintiff filed his response on August 17, 2012, and defendant filed its reply on August 28, 2012. On October 30, 2012, plaintiff and defendant presented oral arguments on the merits of the summary judgment motion before the arbitrator. On November 15, 2012, the arbitrator rendered his award granting defendant's motion for summary judgment based on his findings that: (1) defendant lacked the requisite intent to cause plaintiff severe emotional distress, as the investigation report shows defendant made a good faith attempt to respond to plaintiff's complaints; and (2) plaintiff's exclusive foundation for challenging defendant's motion was based on mere allegations in his pleading which did not rise to the necessary level to refute such a motion.

After the arbitration award was issued, plaintiff filed a motion for a new trial and defendant timely filed an opposition. On January 9, 2013, the arbitrator denied plaintiff's motion, concluding that he was without jurisdiction to grant such a motion. On April 12, 2013, plaintiff filed a motion to vacate the arbitration award in this Court, alleging that the arbitrator: (1) displayed evident partiality, (2) refused to hear and consider evidence that was pertinent and material to the controversy, and (3) did not determine the award in accordance with the applicable law. Plaintiff's motion to vacate was brought pursuant to 9 U.S.C. § 10(a) (2006).

LAW & ANALYSIS

I. STANDARD OF REVIEW

A court's review of an arbitration award is "exceedingly deferential." *Brabham v. A.G. Edwards & Sons, Inc.*, 376 F.3d 377, 380 (5th Cir. 2004). Courts should only vacate an arbitration award "on very narrow grounds." *La. Health Serv. Indem. Co. v. Gambro A B*, 756 F. Supp. 2d 760, 763 (W.D. La. 2010) (citing *Brabham*, 376 F.3d at 380). The moving party bears the burden of proving a court should vacate the arbitration award, but a court must "resolve any doubts or uncertainties in favor of upholding the award." *Brabham*, 376 F.3d at 385 n.9 (citing *Action Indus., Inc. v. U.S. Fid. & Guar. Co.*, 358 F.3d 337, 343 (5th Cir. 2004)). Whenever possible, a court must yield to the arbitrator's decision. *La. Health Serv. Indem.*, 756 F. Supp. 2d at 763 (citing *Antwine v. Prudential Bache Sec., Inc.*, 899 F.2d 410, 413 (5th Cir. 1990)).

II. DISCUSSION

B. *9 U.S.C. § 10(a)(3)*

Plaintiff claims that the arbitrator refused to hear and consider evidence that was pertinent and material to the controversy or otherwise engaged in misbehavior or misconduct with respect to the investigation report. Specifically, plaintiff alleges the arbitrator improperly: (1) prohibited plaintiff from conducting depositions or questioning any individual who assisted in preparation of the investigation report, and (2) accepted information stated in the investigation report as accurate and valid at the summary judgment hearing, even though the report had not been, or should not have been, admitted into evidence.

The Fifth Circuit has ruled that an "evidentiary error" pursuant to § 10(a)(3) must be more than an error of law:

> The arbitrator is not bound to hear all of the evidence tendered by the parties; however, he must give each of the parties to the dispute an adequate opportunity to present its evidence and argument. An evidentiary error must be one that is not simply an error of law, but which so affects the rights of a party that it may be said that he was deprived of a fair hearing.

Householder, 354 F. App'x at 851 (quoting *Householder Group v. Caughran*, 576 F. Supp. 2d 796, 802 (E.D. Tex. 2008)) (internal citations omitted). Given this burden, plaintiff has not established that the arbitrator's actions deprived plaintiff of a fair hearing, even assuming plaintiff's allegations are true.

Plaintiff has not offered affidavits on behalf of the preparers of the report, whom he maintains he was not permitted to question or depose, that would demonstrate he was deprived of a fair hearing. *Householder*, 354 F. App'x at 851. Without affidavits or further comparable evidence, plaintiff has not demonstrated that the alleged prohibition on witness depositions and/or his inability to question witnesses deprived him of an impartial hearing.

Plaintiff also challenges the investigative report on the ground that it should not have been admitted into evidence. Plaintiff argues that "[b]efore evidence is relied upon for the ultimate findings in a case, it should be subjected to customary evidentiary standards of scrutiny." This argument fails as the Dialogue agreement vests the arbitrator with broad authority to determine "the relevance, materiality, and admissibility of evidence offered." *See Weinberg v. Silber*, 57 F. App'x 211 (5th Cir. 2003) (in considering evidence, as long as the arbitrator does not exceed his authority provided for in the arbitration agreement, vacatur of the award is not appropriate). *Compare Textile Workers Union v. Am. Thread Co.*, 291 F.2d 894, 898 (4th Cir. 1961) (vacatur of an arbitration award is appropriate when the arbitrator considered evidence expressly prohibited in the arbitration agreement). Furthermore, the agreement allows the arbitrator to "subpoena witnesses or documents at the request of a Party, or on the arbitrator's own initiative."

Even assuming admission of the report was a legal error, a finding the Court does not make, plaintiff has failed to establish how it deprived him of a fair hearing. "To constitute misconduct requiring vacation of an award, an error in the arbitrator's determination must be one that is not simply an error of law, but which so affects the rights of a party that it may be said that he was deprived of a fair hearing." *Laws v. Morgan Stanley Dean Witter*, 452 F.3d 398 (5th Cir. 2006) (internal quotation marks omitted) (quoting *El Dorado Sch. Dist. No. 15 v. Continental Cas. Co.*, 247 F.3d 843, 848 (8th Cir. 2001)). Plaintiff does not dispute the accuracy of the information in the investigation report or its conclusions. Considering all evidence presented to the arbitrator in light of his award, plaintiff's unwarranted argument challenging the award is not an adequate, independent ground for a vacatur. *Householder*, 354 F. App'x at 851; *see Moore v. Potter*, 275 F. App'x 405, 411 (5th Cir. 2008) (declining to vacate arbitration award based on circular arguments).

Notes and Questions

1. The party challenging the arbitration award in *White* complained that it was deprived of the opportunity to cross-examine the preparers of the report. The court denied this challenge because "Plaintiff has not offered affidavits on behalf of the preparers of the report, whom he maintains he was not permitted to question or depose, that would demonstrate he was deprived of a fair hearing." But how was the plaintiff supposed to obtain post-award affidavits from the very witnesses he could not examine while the case was going on?

2. The plaintiff in *White* challenged the arbitrator's discovery rulings, arguing that the arbitrator should have allowed the plaintiff to take depositions. We have studied that discovery is *not* an inherent arbitration right and must instead be agreed upon in some manner: in a scheduling order, in the adoption of institutional rules containing these rights, or in the arbitration clause itself. The *White* plaintiff went further and argued that the arbitrator should have denied admission of a particular report especially without allowing the plaintiff to question the basis of that report. In court, the preparer of a report, and especially an expert report, is routinely subject to examination. The *White* court's decision not to apply the same standards here, despite the reference to evidence in subsection 3, shows the limitations of the evidence tool for vacatur.
3. Does the evidence component of Section 10(a) mean that the arbitrator must make correct evidentiary rulings under the law? Is this a grafting onto the statute of the Federal Rules of Evidence? Or do courts rule that Congress was committed simply to a party's ability to put on its case and thus introduce material evidence into the record? How strict should evidentiary rules be in arbitration? Is your answer changed now that you have reviewed Section 10(a)(3)?
4. How important is causation in this test? Should a party appealing an arbitration award have to establish that but for the evidentiary ruling she would have won? Or is it appropriate enough that the issue simply be material, without imposition of a strict but for test? Are there policy reasons why the standard should be more stringent in arbitration? Or do these policy reasons flow at least equally the other way, where persons other than judges steeped in the evidentiary rules may be excluding evidence?
5. What if the arbitrator allows in evidence very late, and permits testimony by telephone?

Floridians for Solar Choice v. PCI Consultants, Inc.

314 F. Supp. 3d 1346 (S.D. Fla. 2018)

[*See* ppp. 497–500 for factual background.]

D. EVIDENTIARY RULINGS

"Arbitrators enjoy wide latitude in conducting an arbitration hearing, and they are not constrained by formal rules of procedure or evidence." *Rosensweig v. Morgan Stanley & Co.*, 494 F.3d 1328, 1333 (11th Cir. 2007) (citation and quotation marks omitted). An arbitrator is not required to accept all the evidence a party seeks to introduce in an arbitration proceeding so long as the parties receive a fundamentally fair hearing. *Scott v. Prudential Sec., Inc.*, 141 F.3d 1007, 1017 (11th Cir. 1998), overruled on other grounds by *Hall St. Assocs., LLC v. Mattel, Inc.*, 552 U.S. 576, 588 (2008). Thus, when a party challenges an evidentiary decision of the arbitration panel, a federal court may vacate the award only if the arbitrator's refusal to hear pertinent and material evidence prejudiced the rights of the parties to the arbitration proceedings. *Rosensweig*, 494 F.3d at 1333.

Here, Defendants argue that had they understood Solar planned to seek the contract price of $5.25 in damages, they would have elicited certain additional testimony demonstrating that (1) SACE had paid $3.00 per petition for the value of educating the public and that those services had been fully performed; (2) Solar and SACE's division of the $5.25 price per signature was an attempt to avoid tax and election regulations; (3) the petitions in question could have been used for the 2018 election.

The Court has carefully reviewed the transcripts from the hearing and notes that for each of the areas of inquiry, the Arbitrator either allowed some limited evidence or precluded introduction of that evidence based on an evidentiary ruling stated on the record. The Arbitrator had a reasonable basis to limit the evidence introduced at the hearing to the 2016 ballot initiative and the contracts and parties before the Arbitrator, and to exclude evidence related to SACE's tax reporting requirements as more prejudicial than probative. *Rosensweig*, 494 F.3d at 1334 (finding "the arbitrators committed no misconduct because they had several reasonable bases for limiting evidence . . ."). Defendants admit that vacatur is only appropriate based on an evidentiary ruling that so affects the rights of the party that they were deprived of a fair hearing. Defendants' complained of evidentiary rulings do not meet that standard.

Comment

There does appear, however, to be a sliding scale on which some evidentiary determinations by arbitrators go too far. Where a party can demonstrate that the excluded evidence was material, even the rigorous standards of section 10 may be satisfied.

Hoteles Condado Beach, La Concha & Convention Ctr. v. Union de Tronquistas Local 901

763 F.2d 34 (1st Cir. 1985)

WISDOM, Senior Circuit Judge.

The arbitrator is the judge of the admissibility and relevancy of evidence submitted in an arbitration proceeding. *See* M. Hill & A. Sinicropi, Evidence in Arbitration 22 (1980). The arbitrator is not bound to hear all of the evidence tendered by the parties; however, he must give each of the parties to the dispute an adequate opportunity to present its evidence and arguments. *National Post Office, Mailhandlers,*

Watchmen, Messengers and Group Leaders Division, Laborers International Union of North America v. United States Postal Service, 751 F.2d 834, 841 (6th Cir. 1985); *Totem Marine Tug & Barge, Inc. v. North American Towing, Inc.*, 607 F.2d 649, 651 (5th Cir. 1979); *Bell Aerospace Company Division of Textron, Inc. v. Local 516, International Union, United Automobile Workers of America*, 500 F.2d 921, 923 (2nd Cir. 1974). The arbitrator must then determine "the truth respecting material matters in controversy, as he believes it to be, based upon a full and fair consideration of the entire evidence and after he has accorded each witness and each piece of documentary evidence, the weight, if any, to which he honestly believes it to be entitled." F. Elkouri & E. Elkouri, How Arbitration Works 273–74 (3d ed. 1973). Absent exceptional circumstances, therefore, a reviewing court may not overturn an arbitration award based on the arbitrator's determination of the relevancy or persuasiveness of the evidence submitted by the parties.

Every failure of an arbitrator to receive relevant evidence does not constitute misconduct requiring vacatur of an arbitrator's award. *Newark Stereotypers' Union No. 18 v. Newark Morning Ledger Co.*, 397 F.2d 594, 599 (3rd Cir.), *cert. denied*, 393 U.S. 954, 89 S. Ct. 378, 21 L. Ed. 2d 365 (1968). A federal court may vacate an arbitrator's award only if the arbitrator's refusal to hear pertinent and material evidence prejudices the rights of the parties to the arbitration proceedings. 9 U.S.C. § 10(c). An arbitration award must not be set aside for the arbitrator's refusal to hear evidence that is cumulative, *e.g. National Post Office Mailhandlers*, 751 F.2d at 841, or irrelevant, *e.g. Grahams Service Inc. v. Teamsters Local 975*, 700 F.2d 420, 422–23 (8th Cir. 1982). Vacatur is appropriate only when the exclusion of relevant evidence "so affects the rights of a party that it may be said that he was deprived of a fair hearing." *Newark Stereotypers' Union*, 397 F.2d at 599; *see also National Post Office Mailhandlers*, 751 F.2d at 841.

In the case at bar, no live testimony was available. The arbitrator therefore accepted into evidence the trial transcript of criminal proceedings concerning the event that allegedly justified the Company's dismissal of its employee. After accepting the transcript into evidence, however, the arbitrator refused to give any weight to this evidence. It is undisputed that the arbitrator was not bound by the Superior Court of Puerto Rico's findings in the criminal proceedings against Otero; however, the arbitrator's refusal to ascribe any weight to the *testimony* given at the criminal proceedings effectively denied the Company an opportunity to present any evidence in the arbitration proceeding. The testimony was unquestionably relevant to a determination of whether Otero actually engaged in immoral conduct in violation of the Company's disciplinary regulations. Moreover, no other evidence was available to substantiate or to refute the Company's charges that Otero had violated the rules regarding employment. The evidence effectively excluded by the arbitrator was both "central and decisive" to the Company's position; therefore, the arbitrator's refusal to consider this evidence was, as the district court concluded, "so destructive of [the

Company's] right to present [its] case, that it warrants the setting aside of the arbitration award." *Hoteles Condado Beach*, 588 F. Supp. at 685.

D. "Exceeded Powers" (Section 10(a)(4))

Of the four statutory vacatur grounds in section 10 of the FAA, Section 10(a)(4) has provoked the most commentary and is the section most often used by the party seeking to challenge the award. This is not surprising, as it is the closest of the four grounds to intruding upon the substantive ruling of the arbitrator. As noted above, the first two grounds are essentially behavioral, and look to facts other than the contents of the award: whether there was fraud, corruption (a word used in both Section 10(a)(1) and 10(a)(2)), or "undue means." The third ground is an entirely procedural inquiry, focusing, as we have seen, on the fairness of the process and the arbitrator's approach to the evidence.

What, though, are we to make of a standard whereby an award is vacated "where the arbitrators exceeded their powers"? What "powers"? What is the source of that power? What is "exceeded"? Does an arbitrator exceed her powers if she is asked to decide a case and gets that decision wrong? Wouldn't that just import merits review right back into the statute? If the "exceeding powers" cannot be interpreted that broadly, what *are* the limits?

If Section 10(a)(4) is confined to jurisdiction, then a powers determination is simple: if the parties have a contract about apples, and that contract has an arbitration clause, and they later make an agreement to buy oranges, and that contract does not have an arbitration clause, then the arbitrator can decide only their apples dispute. If the arbitrator rendered an award about oranges as well (and without the parties otherwise consenting), then he would, plainly, exceed his powers.

But what if that same arbitrator, in deciding the apples contract dispute—which he plainly has the power to do in this example—rendered a terrible decision that completely botched the contract language? Did he exceed his powers? Or just make a mistake? How bad does the mistake have to be before Section 10(a)(4) applies? Did Congress provide any floor at all?

As early as 1960, the Supreme Court emphasized that on issues of contract construction, the arbitrator was owed special deference. "It is the arbitrator's construction which was bargained for; and so far as the arbitrator's decision concerns construction of the contract, the courts have no business overruling him because their interpretation of the contract is different than his." *United Steelworkers of Am. v. Enter. Wheel & Car Corp*, 363 U.S. 593 (1960).

The Supreme Court returned to this question directly in the *Oxford Health* decision excerpted at the beginning of this chapter. Justice Kagan emphasized that the arbitrator's reading of the contract survives challenge "however good, bad, or ugly." The question was not how the arbitrator interpreted the contract, but simply whether the arbitrator looked at it: "the sole question for us is whether the arbitrator (even arguably) interpreted the parties' contract, not whether he got its meaning right or wrong." (emphasis added).

That broad language would seem to—and should—cut off most merits-based attempts to overturn an arbitration award. Getting it wrong may mean reversal of a district court decision, but we are not in court. All that matters, then, is what courts call the "essence test" —whether the award draws its essence from the contract itself. The essence test is often used to uphold arbitration awards where the disappointed party urges that the arbitrator exceeded his powers by deciding the contract claim incorrectly. Some—but not, as we will see, all—courts condemn this as merely merits-based review:

Barclays Capital Inc. v. Platt

No. 15-21850-CIV-MARTINEZ-GOODMAN, 2018 U.S. Dist. LEXIS 216879 (S.D. Fla. Dec. 21, 2018)

MARTINEZ, United States District Judge.

B. The Arbitration Panel Did Not "Exceed their Powers"

Next, Movant argues that the arbitration panel "exceeded their powers" when forgiving the debt owed by Respondents pursuant to the promissory notes and seek vacatur of the award in part under 9 U.S.C. § 10(a)(4). In *White Springs Agricultural Chemicals, Inc. v. Glawson*, the movant there appealed the final arbitration award that granted the respondent's, Glawson Investment Corp.'s, attorneys' fees, expert fees, and prejudgment interest. 660 F.3d at 1278. When considering whether the panel's award of attorneys' fees "exceeded the powers of the arbitration panel," the *Glawson* court looked to the parties' arbitration clause to see if the arbitrator "stray[ed] from interpretation and application of the agreement and effectively dispenses[ed] his own brand of industrial justice," thereby possibly making his decision "unenforceable." *Id.* at 1281 (citing *Stolt-Nielsen S.A. v. AnimalFeeds Int'l Corp.*, 559 U.S. 662, 671 (2010)). The court determined that the arbitration clause in fact provided for a party's ability to seek attorneys' fees and held that the movant could not "overcome the 'high hurdle' necessary for vacating an arbitration award when there is a plain basis for the panel's award in the parties' agreement." *Id.*

Moreover, when addressing movant's arguments that the arbitration panel misinterpreted Florida law when awarding attorneys' fees, the court found that the Federal Arbitration Act did not "empower" them to review "allegations of legal error." *Id.* Similarly, the court also declined movant's arguments as to the legality of the award of expert fees and prejudgment interest, holding that it could not "review the panel's award for underlying legal error." *Id.* at 1282–83 ("Even though White Springs presents its argument in terms of the FAA, it asks us to do what we may not—look to the legal merits of the underlying award."). As a result, the court found no basis for vacating the arbitration award.

The Eleventh Circuit's decision in *Glawson* controls here, and is binding on this Court. Like in *Glawson*, Movant seeks to vacate an arbitration award because the arbitrators exceeded their powers in forgiving the debts owed by Respondents and that such forgiveness was contrary to law. Here, Respondents and Movant agreed to arbitrate their claims. After a three-day arbitration hearing, where the arbitration panel considered pleadings, heard testimony, and reviewed evidence, on February 18, 2015, the panel issued its award. Movant's basis for vacatur, while made pursuant 9 U.S.C. § 10(a)(4), asks this Court to do exactly what it is not permitted to do—"look to the legal merits of the underlying award." *Glawson*, 660 F.3d at 1283. Specifically, in arguing that the arbitration panel exceeded its powers in forgiving the debt owed by Respondents, Movant argues that there is no basis in the promissory notes, applicable rule or decision derived from the FAA, or any body of law that "authorizes the Notes to be 'forgiven.'" As this Court finds that the issues related to whether Respondents owed anything under the promissory notes was properly before the arbitration panel, this Court declines to review the legality of the panel's award.

Comment

Barclay's stressed that a merits disagreement is far different from the arbitrator exceeding his mandate. One cannot dress up a merits dispute in the clothes of a Section 10(a)(4) powers challenge. Did the court in the following case follow the same approach? Is the essence test the following court applied a sufficient protection against a powers abuse?

Soaring Wind Energy, LLC v. Catic United States, Inc.

333 F. Supp. 3d 642 (N.D. Tex. 2018)

KINKEADE, United States District Judge.

The party seeking vacatur of an arbitration award bears the burden of proof, and the reviewing court must decide any uncertainties or doubts in favor of sustaining the award. *Brabham*, 376 F.3d at 385. In reviewing an arbitration award, the court applies the "essence" test. *See Timegate Studios, Inc. v. Southpeak Interactive, L.L.C.*, 713 F.3d 797, 802 (5th Cir. 2013); *Executone Info. Sys., Inc. v. Davis*, 26 F.3d 1314, 1320 (5th Cir. 1994). The court must confirm an arbitration award "as long as the arbitrator's decision 'draws its essence' from the contract," in other words "the arbitrator's decision is rationally inferable from the letter or purpose of the underlying agreement." *Timegate Studios*, 713 F.3d at 802 (quoting *Executone*, 26 F.3d at 1320). "[T]he question is whether the arbitrator's award was so unfounded in reason and fact, so unconnected with the wording and purpose of the . . . agreement as to manifest an infidelity to the obligation of an arbitrator." *Executone*, 26 F.3d at 1325 (internal quotations omitted).

It is irrelevant whether the reviewing court disagrees with the arbitrator's interpretation of the contract. *Timegate Studios*, 713 F.3d at 802. The reviewing court considers only the arbitrators' resulting decision and "does not review the language used by, or the reasoning of, the arbitrators in determining whether their award draws its essence from the contract." *Executone*, 26 F.3d at 1325 (internal quotations omitted). "Because the parties have contracted to have disputes settled by an arbitrator chosen by them rather than by a judge, it is the arbitrator's view of the facts and of the meaning of the contract that they have agreed to accept. Courts thus do not sit to hear claims of factual or legal error by an arbitrator as an appellate court does in reviewing decisions of lower courts." *United Paperworkers Int'l Union v. Misco, Inc.*, 484 U.S. 29, 37–38 (1987). The arbitrators' powers and authority are "'dependent on the provisions under which the arbitrators were appointed.'" *Brook v. Peak Int'l, Ltd.*, 294 F.3d 668, 672 (5th Cir. 2002) (quoting *Szuts v. Dean Witter Reynolds, Inc.*, 931 F.2d 830, 831 (11th Cir. 1991)). "Whether an arbitrator has exceeded his powers is tied closely to the applicable standard of review"—that being whether the arbitrator's decision "draws its essence" from the underlying contract. *Timegate Studios*, 713 F.3d at 802. The court looks to "whether the arbitrator's award 'was so unfounded in reason and fact, so unconnected with the wording and purpose of the [contract] as to "manifest an infidelity to the obligation of an arbitrator."'" *Id.* (quoting *Brotherhood of R.R. Trainmen v. Cent. of Ga. Ry. Co.*, 415 F.2d 403, 412 (5th Cir. 1969)). "'[A]s long as [an honest] arbitrator is even arguably construing or applying the contract and acting within the scope of his authority,' the fact that 'a court is convinced he committed serious error does not suffice to overturn his decision.'" *E. Associated Coal Corp. v. United Mine Workers of Am.*, 531 U.S. 57, 62 (2000) (internal citations omitted). The reviewing court must resolve all doubts in favor of arbitration. *Executone*, 26 F.3d at 1320–21.

b) The Panel Did Not Exceed Their Power

The parties to an arbitration agreement may agree by contract to the arbitrator selection process. *Brook v. Peak Int'l., Ltd.*, 294 F.3d 668, 672 (5th Cir. 2002).

When the arbitration agreement provides for the appointment method of the arbitrators, the FAA specifically requires that the agreed method "shall be followed." 9 U.S.C. § 5; *see id.* at 672–73; *see also Volt Info. Scis., Inc. v. Bd. of Trs. of Leland Stanford Junior Univ.*, 489 U.S. 468, 479 (1989)(recognizing "the FAA's primary purpose [is] ensuring that private agreements to arbitrate are enforced according to their terms" because "[a]rbitration under the [FAA] is a matter of consent, not coercion, and parties are generally free to structure their arbitration agreements as they see fit.").

Claiming the arbitrators exceeded their powers, AVIC USA first contends the arbitrators were not selected in accordance with the Arbitration Provision because the Panel was "dominated by [TEG] appointees" and AVIC USA never agreed to a selection provision which would allow such a lop-sided panel in a dispute. Next, AVIC USA argues the Arbitration Provision requires a panel of three arbitrators in any scenario and asks the Court to "give effect to the plain and objectively reasonable meaning of the arbitrator selection provision for this dispute as understood by AVIC USA: one arbitrator per side plus a third arbitrator as a tie-breaker." Finally, AVIC USA contends the arbitration selection provision was misinterpreted because the Non-Signatories were not allowed to select arbitrators. As a result of these factors, AVIC USA alleges that the Court's refusal to vacate the award issued by this arbitration panel as it was composed will cause "an absurd and fundamentally unjust result."

AVIC USA attempts to characterize its arguments as being centered on an arbitration panel appointed in violation of the method provided for in the parties' arbitration agreement, therefore requiring vacatur. However, the record does not bear this out. The Arbitration Provision does indeed clearly provide for a method of selecting the arbitrators, but it is not the method alleged by AVIC USA. Presented with a similar, if not identical, argument in the *AVIC USA I* appeal, the Fifth Circuit so astutely noted:

> Simply put, when [AVIC USA's] position is reduced to its bare essentials, AVIC [USA] is asking us to rewrite their agreement's arbitration provision to require that every arbitration among these multiple parties comprise only two "sides." It is apparent from the plain wording of that provision, however, that the agreement contemplates the possibility of there being three or more "sides" among the several parties to the agreement. More to the point, AVIC's strained interpretation of the arbitration provision would mandate that there be precisely three arbitrators in any and every instance, no more and no fewer—one selected by one "side," a second selected by the other "side," and the third selected by the first two. The unambiguous wording of the arbitration provision eschews such a reading: The agreement expressly contemplates the possibility of (1) an even number of arbitrators (an impossibility under AVIC's proposed, three-only arbitrators interpretation) and (2) adding either one *or two* more arbitrators to achieve an odd number (also an impossibility under a three-only arbitrator situation). *AVIC Int'l USA*, 614 F. App'x at 219 (emphasis in the original). It is readily apparent to this Court that the Fifth Circuit's summary is true and applicable even now as AVIC USA takes the same position.

As SWE Members, AVIC USA and the Movants contracted in their Arbitration Provision for a specific appointment method of the arbitrators in the event of a dispute. The FAA specifically mandates that if an appointment process is agreed-to, the agreed method "shall be followed." 9 U.S.C. § 5; *see Brook*, 294 F.3d at 672–73; *see also Volt Info. Scis.*, 489 U.S. at 479 (recognizing "the FAA's primary purpose [is] ensuring that private agreements to arbitrate are enforced according to their terms" because "[a]rbitration under the [FAA] is a matter of consent, not coercion, and parties are generally free to structure their arbitration agreements as they see fit."). The method by which these arbitrators were selected was in accordance with the exact process agreed to by the parties in their Arbitration Agreement. AVIC USA has established nothing to the contrary. The Panel did not exceed their powers and the Court will not vacate the arbitration award on these grounds.

How far will the courts permit the arbitrator to stray from the "essence"?

Hoteles Condado Beach, La Concha & Convention Ctr. v. Union de Tronquistas Local 901

763 F.2d 34 (1st Cir. 1985)

WISDOM, Senior Circuit Judge.

In rendering his decision in this dispute, the arbitrator made reference to the disciplinary regulations under which Otero purportedly was dismissed. The Company asserted that Otero was dismissed for a violation of rule nine, prohibiting "conduct which offends the morals or any offense involving moral depravation during working hours or within company premises." The arbitrator, however, considered Otero to have been dismissed under rule ten, which provides for suspension or dismissal of an employee found guilty of "a felony offense or one that involves moral depravation." The arbitrator further concluded that footnote "a" to rule ten limited the rule's applicability to casino employees. The rule was, therefore, inapplicable to the present controversy and did not require the arbitrator to find that, because of Otero's criminal conviction, the Company was justified in dismissing him. The arbitrator further determined that rule nine, like rule ten, was confined to casino employees and inapplicable to Otero. Having previously determined that the evidence produced by the Company could be accorded no weight, the arbitrator found that the Company had failed to prove that Otero's dismissal was justified on any other ground.

The district court found that the arbitrator's analysis of the disciplinary rules manifested an infidelity to the plain and unambiguous terms of the contract between the parties. According to the clear language of the disciplinary rules, rule nine provided for suspension or dismissal for conduct offending the morals during working hours or on company grounds. It contained no requirement that the dismissed employee be convicted of criminal charges and was in no way confined to casino employees. Rule ten, as limited by footnote "a," provided for suspension or dismissal of an employee convicted of a felony offense involving moral depravation. The district court concluded that the arbitrator had improperly interpreted the text of footnote "a" as restricting the applicability of rules nine and ten to casino employees; moreover, the court found the arbitrator to have disregarded the plain language of the contract in applying footnote "a" to rule nine, which contained no reference to footnote "a." The court therefore found the arbitrator's determination that Otero's dismissal was not justified to be based on the arbitrator's misconstruction and alteration of the collective bargaining agreement. The arbitrator had, therefore, exceeded his authority as interpreter of the collective bargaining agreement in issuing his award. Accordingly, the court vacated the arbitration award.

Absent exceptional circumstances, an arbitrator's interpretation of the collective bargaining agreement is final and binding on the parties because it is this interpretation that is bargained for by the parties. The arbitrator has great latitude in construing ambiguous language in the contract, and a court must not vacate an arbitration award simply because the court disagrees with the arbitrator's construction of the contract. *E.g., Westinghouse Elevators*, 583 F.2d at 1186. The arbitrator is, however, "confined to the interpretation and application of the collective bargaining agreement, and although he may construe ambiguous contract language, he is without authority to disregard or modify plain and unambiguous provisions."

We agree with the district court that the arbitrator in the instant case ignored the clear language of the contract in determining that footnote "a" applied to rule nine and limited that rule's applicability to casino employees. We decline to review the arbitrator's interpretation of the ambiguous language of footnote "a" itself. The arbitrator acted within his authority in construing this language. Whatever its meaning, however, the footnote is clearly inapplicable to rule nine and can in no case, therefore, be construed as limiting the application of rule nine to casino employees. Accordingly, the arbitrator abused his discretion in failing to consider whether the Company was justified in dismissing Otero under rule nine of the disciplinary rules appended to the collective bargaining agreement. This failure, coupled with the arbitrator's refusal to give any weight to the evidence presented at the arbitration hearing, resulted in conduct so improper as to warrant judicial review and to mandate vacatur of the arbitration award.

CASE PREVIEW. What happens when the arbitrator's decision is not merely "interpretive" of the contract but instead is expressly contrary to the contract's language? Is that still an award that avoids vacatur because the "essence" is still the contract? Or have we hit the floor, and the arbitrator has exceeded his powers under Section 10(a)(4)? The next case explores that question.

Gherardi v. Citigroup Global Mkts., Inc.

Case No. 1:18-cv-20969-UU, 2018 U.S. Dist. LEXIS 236992 (S.D. Fla. July 26, 2018)

UNGARO, United States District Judge.

THIS CAUSE is before the Court upon Petitioner's Motion to Confirm Arbitration Award (the "Motion to Confirm"), and Respondent's Motion to Vacate Arbitration Award (the "Motion to Vacate").

The Court has reviewed the pertinent portions of the record and is otherwise fully advised in the premises. For the reasons discussed below, the Motion to Vacate is GRANTED IN PART and DENIED IN PART, and the Motion to Confirm is GRANTED IN PART and DENIED IN PART.

I. Factual Background

A. Christian Gherardi's Employment History

Petitioner Christian S. Gherardi ("Gherardi") is a citizen of Florida. Defendant Citigroup Global Markets Inc., ("Citi") is a New York Corporation and a Financial Industry Regulatory Authority ("FINRA") regulated broker-dealer. Gherardi joined Citi in 1996 and worked as a financial advisor until he was terminated on December 11, 2015. At the time of his termination, Gherardi was working in Citi's Miami, Florida office where he had worked for at least fifteen years.

When terminated, Gherardi's employment with Citi was governed by the 2015 Citi U.S. Employee Handbook (the "Handbook"). The Handbook contained an employment arbitration policy and an "employment at-will" clause. The employment arbitration policy required that any employment-related disputes were to be arbitrated under the auspices of FINRA. The arbitration policy also contained a non-retaliation provision stating that "[r]etaliation against employees who file a claim under this Policy, including claims regarding the validity of this Policy or any provision thereof, is expressly prohibited." The "employment at-will" clause stated that Gherardi's "employment with Citi [was] at-will, which means it [could] be terminated by [Gherardi] or Citi at any time, with or without notice . . . for no reason or for any reason. . . ." Gherardi also signed the Handbook's acknowledgement, in which he confirmed that he understood that he was an "at-will" employee.

II. The Panel Exceeded its Powers under § 10(a)(4)

Citi argues that by granting Gherardi's claim for wrongful termination, the Panel modified the plain "at-will" language in the employment arbitration policy, in excess of their authority under § 10(a)(2). In contrast, Gherardi reiterates arguments made in his statement of claim and post-hearing briefing, which suggested methods by which the Panel could have "arguably interpreted" the employment arbitration policy to reconcile the award for wrongful termination with the "at- will" language in the employment arbitration policy. For the reasons discussed below, the Court agrees with Citi.

5. The "At-Will" Language in the Dual Employment Agreement, Employee Handbook, and Arbitration Policy is Unambiguous on its Face

Citi argues that Gherardi's employment was governed by three documents: the dual employment agreement, the Handbook and the employment arbitration policy contained in the Handbook (collectively, the "Employment Documents"). Citi argues that these three documents unambiguously stated that Gherardi's employment was "at-will" and subject to termination with or without cause at any time, and were therefore not open to interpretation. *See, e.g.*, D.E. 13-2 at 17–18 ("your employment relationship is 'at-will' and this agreement shall be governed by and construed and enforced in accordance with the laws of the State of New York . . . ."); D.E. 17-3 at 9 ("Your employment with Citi is at-will, which means it can be terminated by you or Citi at any time, with or without notice . . . for no reason or for any reason not otherwise prohibited by law."). Moreover, Citi notes that Gherardi signed the Handbook's acknowledgement, which emphasizes:

> WITH THE EXCEPTION OF THE EMPLOYMENT ARBITRATION POLICY, I UNDERSTAND THAT NOTHING CONTAINED IN THIS HANDBOOK, NOR THE HANDBOOK ITSELF, IS CONSIDERED A CONTRACT OF EMPLOYMENT. IN ADDITION, NOTHING IN THIS HANDBOOK CONSTITUTES A GUARANTEE THAT MY EMPLOYMENT WILL CONTINUE FOR ANY SPECIFIED PERIOD OF TIME. I UNDERSTAND THAT MY EMPLOYMENT WITH CITI IS AT-WILL, WHICH MEANS IT CAN BE TERMINATED BY ME OR CITI AT ANYTIME, WITH OR WITHOUT NOTICE FOR NO REASON OR ANY REASON NOT OTHERWISE PROHIBITED BY LAW.

Citi further asserts that under the dual employment agreement, Gherardi's employment was governed by New York law and there is no cause of action for wrongful termination of an "at-will" employee under New York law. *Murphy v. Am. Home Prods. Corp.*, 58 N.Y.2d 293, 448 N.E.2d 86, 461 N.Y.S.2d 232 (N.Y. 1983) ("New York does not recognize common law claims for wrongful termination."). Thus, Citi concludes that the Employment Documents unambiguously state that Gherardi could be terminated "at-will" and the Panel exceeded its authority in granting an award for wrongful termination because under applicable law, there is no cause of action for wrongful termination of an "at-will" employee.

Gherardi raises two principle arguments in response. First, Gherardi argues that the employment arbitration policy is ambiguous and was therefore open to interpretation by the Panel. Specifically, Gherardi argues that the anti-retaliation provision contained within the employment arbitration policy can be read to provide an exception to the "at- will" language, permitting a cause of action for wrongful termination. Second, Gherardi argues that even if the Employment Documents unambiguously stated that Gherardi's employment was terminable at will, the Employment Documents could be interpreted to contain implied terms negating his at-will employment status.

a. The Effect of the Anti-Retaliation Provision

Contract language is susceptible to interpretation "when it is sufficiently ambiguous on its face . . . or [w]hen there are two plausible interpretations of an agreement." *Wiregrass Metal Trades Council AFL-CIO*, 837 F.3d at 1088 (alteration in original) (internal quotations and citations omitted). There are not two plausible interpretations of the employment arbitration policy and it is therefore not susceptible to interpretation. The employment arbitration policy unambiguously and repeatedly emphasizes that Gherardi can be terminated "at-will" and that nothing in the employment arbitration policy waives that right or affords Gherardi a cause of action for wrongful termination. Therefore, Gherardi's argument that the anti-retaliation provision can be read as an exception to the "at-will" language is unavailing. To be sure, the Court must defer to the Panel's interpretation of the employment arbitration policy, but deference is not warranted where the Panel's interpretation directly contradicts the plain language of the employment arbitration policy. To the extent the Panel relied on this argument in granting Gherardi's claim for wrongful termination they exceeded their authority under § 10(a)(4).

Gherardi argues alternatively that even if the Employment Documents unambiguously state that Gherardi's employment was terminable "at-will," the Employment Documents nonetheless are susceptible to interpretation because the Employment Documents could contain implied terms negating his "at-will" status. *Wiregrass Metal Trades Council AFL-CIO*, 837 F.3d at 1088 ("[E]ven if we were to conclude that [a contract] is not ambiguous on its face, we would not be required to overturn [an arbitration] award. . . . That is true because collective-bargaining agreements may include implied, as well as express, terms, and an arbitrator is empowered to discover [those] implied terms. . . .") (internal citations, internal quotations, and quotation marks omitted) (alteration in original); *Int'l Bhd. of Elec. Workers, Local Union No. 199 v. United Tel. Co. of Fla.*, 738 F.2d 1564, 1568 (11th Cir. 1984) (explaining that even if an arbitrator's award contradicts the plain language of an agreement, where the award "draws its essence" from the agreement it will not be vacated).

Gherardi argues that his statement of claim asserted wrongful termination in violation of the common law of securities arbitration, which provides that in employment agreements subject to mandatory arbitration clauses, such as Citi's employment arbitration policy, there is an implied "for-cause" termination requirement. In support of his argument, Gherardi cites *PaineWebber, Inc. v. Agron*, 49 F.3d 347, 352 (8th Cir. 1995), and *Shearson Hayden Stone, Inc. v. Liang*, 653 F.2d 310, 313 (7th Cir. 1981). In *PaineWebber*, the Eighth Circuit Court of Appeals held that submitting an employment dispute to arbitration "[n]ecessarily alters the employment relationship from at-will to something else—some standard of discernable cause is inherently required in this context where an arbitration panel is called on to interpret the employment relationship." *PaineWebber*, 49 F.3d at 352. Similarly, in *Shearson*, the Seventh Circuit Court of Appeals held that "[i]t has been held repeatedly that an agreement to arbitrate disputes about employee discharges implies a requirement that discharges be only for 'just cause.'" *Shearson*, 653 F.2d at 312. Gherardi also cites *Countrywide Sec. Corp. v. Varga*, 2009 WL 10674333 (C.D. Cal. Aug. 19, 2009), in which the court relied on *PaineWebber* to find that the arbitrator did not exceed his power in permitting a claim for wrongful discharge of an employee under California law, even though his employment contract expressly stated he was employed "at-will." As noted *supra*, Gherardi raised these arguments in his post-hearing briefing, thus, Gherardi concludes that the Panel agreed with his interpretation of *PaineWebber* and "arguably interpreted" the employment arbitration policy as containing an implied "for-cause" term.

The precedent Gherardi cites, permitting arbitrators to imply seemingly contradictory terms into unambiguous contracts, addressed the interpretation of collective bargaining agreements in the arbitration context. *See, e.g., Shearson*, 653 F.2d 310, 313. As the Supreme Court has made clear, unlike a private contract, a collective bargaining agreement:

> [I]s more than a contract; it is a generalized code to govern a myriad of cases which the draftsmen cannot wholly anticipate.... The collective agreement covers the whole employment relationship. It calls into being a new common law—the common law of a particular industry or of a particular plant.

United Steelworkers v. Warrior & Gulf Navigation Co., 363 U.S. 574, 578–79 (1960); *Loveless v. E. Air Lines, Inc.*, 681 F.2d 1272, 1280 (11th Cir. 1982) (explaining that when interpreting collective bargaining agreements "absent some express restriction upon the arbitrator's authority, the arbitrator is not limited to the bare words of the agreement and common law rules for the interpretation of private contracts") (emphasis added). The same considerations do not apply here in the case of private employment agreements between a financial advisor and a financial institution. This Court finds the Fourth Circuit's reasoning in *Raymond James* persuasive; where arbitrators imply a termination "for-cause" provision into a private employment agreement that expressly provides for termination "at-will," the arbitrators do more than commit a permissible error of law, they exceed their authority by ignoring the agreement's plain language. *Raymond James*, 596 F.3d at 194.

Notes and Questions

1. The arbitration panel in *Gherardi* based its ruling on the contract. The panel looked to the contract and found that it was wrongfully terminated. The court, as you have just read, criticized that ruling—but can there be any doubt that the arbitrators looked at the contract? Was the contract not, then, the essence of the award? Where does essence end and the invention of new terms begin? Is the problem with new terms entirely, as opposed to the construction of existing terms?
2. Does the standard of review become less deferential when the contract language that is allegedly ignored by the arbitrator is found not (only) in the contract's substantive provisions but in the arbitration clause itself? The court found that the "at-will" language was in three separate contractual places:

   > Citi argues that Gherardi's employment was governed by three documents: the dual employment agreement, the Handbook and the employment arbitration policy contained in the Handbook (collectively, the "Employment Documents"). Citi argues that these three documents unambiguously stated that Gherardi's employment was "at-will" and subject to termination with or without cause at any time, and were therefore not open to interpretation. *See e.g.*, D.E. 13-2 at 17–18 ("your employment relationship is 'at-will' and this agreement shall be governed by and construed and enforced in accordance with the laws of the State of New York. . . ."); D.E. 17-3 at 9 ("Your employment with Citi is at-will, which means it can be terminated by you or Citi at any time, with or without notice . . . for no reason or for any reason not otherwise prohibited by law."). Moreover, Citi notes that Gherardi signed the Handbook's acknowledgement.

   Return to our Russian dolls. The "at will" language was in both the first (the "dual employment agreement") and second ("employment arbitration policy") dolls. The arbitrator's award violated both, in the court's view. Should that matter? Is one worse than the other? What if there was a bar in the arbitration agreement against awarding attorney's fees, and the arbitrator ignored that provision—is that a Section 10(a)(4) violation? *See ErgoBilt, Inc. v. Neutral Posture Ergonomics*, Civil Action No. 3:97-CV-2548-L, 2002 U.S. Dist. LEXIS 12459 (N.D. Tex. July 9, 2002), *supra* p. 507 (vacating in part award of attorney's fees where attorney's fees clause stated that fees must be apportioned in relation to parties' relative success on claims, and arbitrator instead awarded fees to one party only).

3. Can the parties make legal error part of their contract? See the *Hall Street* discussion in Chapter 15, p. 576 .

4. Many cases agree with the statement in *Environmental Chemical* that "the arbitrator's rationale for an award need not be explained." *See Soaring Wind Energy, LLC v. Catic United States, Inc.*, 333 F. Supp. 3d 642, 651 (5th Cir, 2018); *Barzelatto v. Spire Sec., LLC*, Case No. 19 Civ. 6238 (CM), 2019 U.S. Dist. LEXIS 231274 at *8 (S.D.N.Y. Nov. 5, 2019). On that basis, is it safer to move away from the modern trend toward a "reasoned award" and instead ask the arbitrator for ruling and amount, and nothing more? Would that make for a safer appeal/vacatur process? But would it meet the parties' needs and expectations?

IV. Section 10(a) and the COVID-19 Crisis: Will Virtual Hearings Be Subject to Challenge?

In 2020, the COVID-19 crisis changed the way in which many legal proceedings were conducted. Virtual arbitrations that during the COVID-19 era were a necessity may become more common once public health returns, if enough persons find that they are fair, cheaper, and easier to organize than "live" hearings. But do live hearings have limitations? Will they lead to surreptitious witness coaching? To a lack of confrontation? As a result, will those changes lead to section 10(a)(3) challenges—and will those challenges find any traction?

Complex commercial arbitrations take place in a small room full of people—often there are three arbitrators, a court reporter, a video specialist, teams of lawyers and paralegals—and large stacks of binders. This is exactly the kind of experience most people want to avoid in a public health crisis. To the extent that arbitration hearing centers, and hotel and law firm conference rooms (where arbitrations also take place) are even built to provide for the mandated social distancing (many of them are not), you cannot sit six feet away from your witness. Or maybe you can, but not effectively.

As arbitration hearings move to virtual platforms, litigators are faced with logistical questions. Can you bring your full litigation team? How do you best present exhibits? How do you keep a witness from being coached by his phone? How, as any trial lawyer knows, do you gauge the look and feel of the room? How do you see when arbitrator 3 is whispering to arbitrator 1, and which seems to have the Chair's ear? That knowing grin, that nod, or that look of disdain?

Setting these practical concerns aside, do the preferences or objections of parties even matter? As we will explore more in this section, institutional rules often grant arbitrators discretion to require that a hearing be conducted over video. Challenges to arbitrator discretion in the context of witness testimony under Section 10 of the

FAA are unlikely to be successful. In light of the rules and cases below, does COVID-19 present a new basis for objections to wholly virtual hearings? Should parties have the right to object to virtual hearings per se, because of these concerns? And if the objections are denied, does that set up a new basis for FAA Article 10 challenges to confirmation of arbitration awards?

The two largest institutions—JAMS and AAA—provide for virtual pre-hearing and hearing procedures. JAMS and AAA have also granted discretion to arbitrators to conduct proceedings remotely has extended to hearings:

- **JAMS Rule 22.** The Arbitration Hearing: Section (g) of JAMS Rule 22 provides that "[the Arbitration] Hearing, or any portion thereof, may be conducted telephonically or videographically with the agreement of the Parties or at the discretion of the Arbitrator."
- **AAA Rule 32. Conduct of Proceedings:** Section (c) of AAA Rule 32 provides that "the arbitrator may [] allow for the presentation of evidence by alternative means including video conferencing, internet communication, telephonic conferences and means other than an in-person presentation", provided however, that "[s]uch alternative means [] afford a full opportunity for all parties to present any evidence that the arbitrator deems material and relevant to the resolution of the dispute and, when involving witnesses, provide an opportunity for cross-examination."

CASE PREVIEW. In the pre-COVID-19 era, when arbitrators employed their discretion to allow telephonic or virtual testimony, challenges have rarely been successful. In the next case, courts upheld arbitration awards granted after the arbitrators permitted remote testimony over the objection of one party.

Al-Haddad Commodities Corp. v. Toepfer Int'l Asia Pta, Ltd.

485 F. Supp. 2d 677 (E.D. Va. 2007)

This is an action to confirm an arbitration award pursuant to the United Nations Convention on the Recognition and Enforcement of Foreign Arbitral Awards, June 10, 1958 (the "New York Convention"), 21 U.S.T. 2517, T.I.A.S. No. 6997, implemented at 9 U.S.C. § 207 et seq., entered in favor of Petitioner Al-Haddad Commodities Corporation ("ACC" or "Petitioner") on December 15, 2006, in the amount of $2,006,570.10. For the reasons stated herein, Respondent Toepfer International Asia Pte., Ltd.'s ("Toepfer's" or "Respondent's") Motion in Opposition to Petition to

Confirm Arbitration Award and Cross-Petition to Vacate the Award is DENIED and ACC's Petition to Confirm Arbitration Award is GRANTED.

I. FACTUAL AND PROCEDURAL BACKGROUND

A. Factual Background

ACC is a commodities trader specializing in the supply of commodities to markets in the Middle East and Africa and operating under the laws of the state of Georgia. On October 27, 2005, ACC entered into a sales contract (the "Contract") with Toepfer. Under the Contract, ACC agreed to purchase, and Toepfer agreed to sell, a quantity of "US No. 2 Long Grain White Rice," to be shipped by bulk vessel to Umm Qasr, Iraq, by December 31, 2005, "at the latest." Toepfer tried to deliver the rice by at least two different vessels. Loading of the rice onto the first vessel began on January 9, 2006, but was interrupted on January 11, 2006, after the vessel owner refused to go to Iraq; a replacement vessel was found to be unsuitable for the shipment. The Contract sets forth the terms and conditions of the sale and shipment. The final paragraph of the Contract provides that "[a]ll other terms and conditions as per GAFTA [The Grain and Feed Trade Association] 122 and Arbitration as per U.S. Rice Millers Association Rules and Regulations."

A dispute arose between the parties regarding the parties' performance under the Contract. According to ACC, Toepfer failed to load the vessel and ship the rice to Iraq as required by the Contract. Toepfer contended that ACC was in breach of the Contract for failing to provide Toepfer with a deposit or bank guarantee against possible demurrage claims as prescribed in the Contract. ACC claimed that Toepfer waived the demurrage guarantee requirement.

On September 25, 2006, ACC sent a demand for arbitration to the U.S. Rice Millers' Association ("RMA"), headquartered in Arlington, Virginia. The Chairman of the Arbitration Committee for the RMA nominated a five-member Arbitral Panel ("Panel"), which, after a period of party-led discovery, held a hearing on the matter in the Houston, Texas, offices of American Rice Inc., on December 12, 2006. The dispute was to be governed by the RMA Arbitration Rules, which prescribe the procedures to be followed for arbitration of disputes and the issuance of an ultimate decision and award. On December 19, 2006, the Panel rendered a Final Award (the "Award"). It found that Toepfer breached its obligations under the Contract "by failing to nominate a suitable vessel and otherwise arrange for the loading and shipment of the rice to Umm Qasr." The Panel found that although ACC breached its obligation to provide a bank guarantee for demurrage claims, Toepfer, by its actions, waived that breach. The Panel ordered Toepfer to pay ACC $2,006,570.10 within seven days from the date of the Award.

B. Procedural History

ACC filed its Petition to Confirm Arbitration Award in this Court on January 8, 2007. The Petition asks the Court to enter an order confirming the Award and enforcing the judgment entered on it pursuant to 9 U.S.C. §§ 201–208. On January 31, 2007, Toepfer filed, subject to defect for lack of a certificate of service, an answer and cross-motion against ACC. Correcting the defect, Toepfer filed a motion entitled "Opposition to Petition to Confirm Arbitration Award and Cross-Petition to Vacate the Award" and accompanying memorandum on February 20, 2007, to which the Petitioner responded. This Court held a hearing on the parties' submissions on April 2, 2007.

II. DISCUSSION

Toepfer argues that the Award should be vacated because (1) the arbitrators were "guilty of misconduct" pursuant to § 10 in "refusing to postpone the hearing . . ., in refusing to hear evidence . . ., and other behavior" by which Respondent was "prejudiced."

1. Misconduct

Toepfer alleges that the arbitrators were "guilty of misconduct" under § 10(a)(3) because the Panel (1) failed to postpone the arbitration hearing despite Toepfer's request that it do so; (2) failed to consider the parties' submissions prior to the hearing; (3) permitted a witness to testify by telephone instead of by video link, as planned, and without a previously disclosed witness statement; and (4) limited the presentation of evidence and argument.

c. Telephone Testimony and Witness Statements

Another alleged example of misconduct was the Panel's acceptance of telephone testimony from Mr. Sahib Al-Haddad ("Mr. Al-Haddad"), a witness for ACC. Toepfer argues that it was prejudiced because (1) Mr. Al-Haddad was ACC's only witness; (2) Mr. Al-Haddad had not presented a witness statement to the Panel prior to the hearing; (3) Mr. Al-Haddad did not possess copies of the documents submitted to the Panel during the hearing, and therefore there was no fair opportunity to cross-examine him; and (4) there was "no fair opportunity for the Arbitration Panel to effectively weigh Mr. Sahib Al-Haddad's credibility based only [on] a telephone discussion."

On November 13, 2006, Ms. Bulow notified the Panel by email that Mr. Al-Haddad "will be attending[.]" On November 24, 2006, Ms. Bulow notified the Panel and opposing counsel that Mr. Al-Haddad would not attend the hearing because his doctor had "forbidden" him to travel to Houston for "health reasons." Ms. Bulow told the Panel that Mr. Al-Haddad would be available to testify "under oath on December 12 via video conferencing from Amman, Jordan," and "Mr. Basim Al-Haddad, who is President of Al-Haddad Commodities Corporation, will attend the hearing . . . ." Ms. Bulow did not elaborate on Mr. Al-Haddad's health problems. The Panel accepted Ms. Bulow's statement that Mr. Al-Haddad could not attend, and granted her request for a video conferencing link. The Panel director even suggested that Mr. Al-Haddad could testify by telephone instead. See Mem. in Supp., Bulow Aff, P 22 (The RMA director "often stated that if we encountered technical difficulties and could not use video, we could always have Mr. Al-Haddad testify by telephone."). On the day of the hearing, however, Toepfer learned that no arrangements for video conferencing had been made, and the Panel lacked the appropriate computer terminal for video conferencing provided via the Internet. Instead, the Panel permitted, over Toepfer's objection, Mr. Al-Haddad to testify by telephone.

The Panel's decision to permit Mr. Al-Haddad to testify via telephone may have been permissible under the RMA Arbitration Rules, but in the Court's view, it was an arbitrary deviation from the Panel's own order of November 17, 2006, in which it stated, "Any witness statement to be submitted by a party shall be submitted to the other party and the Panel within 14 days. If a witness statement is submitted from a witness employed by a party, that party should be prepared to produce the witness at the hearing." At this Court's hearing, counsel for ACC asserted that a "witness statement was not required" and suggested that because ACC did not submit a witness statement for Mr. Al-Haddad, it did not have to produce him at the hearing. This reasoning is absurd in light of the unambiguous language in the November 17, 2006, order requiring that witness statements be exchanged within fourteen days of the order, and that a party who intends to call an employee as a witness "should be prepared to produce the witness at the hearing." The Panel appears to have ignored its order when it overlooked Petitioner's failure to submit a witness statement for Mr. Al-Haddad and accepted, without any inquiry, Ms. Bulow's assertion that Mr. Al-Haddad was unable to attend for health reasons. The Court finds that the Panel's decision allowing Mr. Al-Haddad to testify by video, and not in person, was arbitrary in light of its November 17, 2007, order; however, the Court does not find that the consequences of that decision were prejudicial to Toepfer, which is a precondition to vacating an award pursuant to § 10(a)(3). Toepfer had notice well before the hearing that Mr. Al-Haddad would not appear in person. Most significantly, Toepfer had the opportunity, which it exercised, to extensively cross-examine Mr. Al-Haddad about the substance of the contract dispute, including the demurrage guarantee and ACC's access to lines of credit. While cross-examination in person or by video would have been preferable to cross-examination by telephone, the fact that telephonic testimony was ultimately used did not render the proceedings fundamentally unfair. Accordingly, the Court concludes that the Panel's decision to allow Mr. Al-Haddad to appear by telephone was not misconduct under § 10(a)(3). Moreover, there was no issue that Toepfer had failed to deliver in accordance with the Contract, but only whether they were excused by virtue of ACC's failure to obtain a demurrage guarantee.

The actions of the Panel as a whole may seem to be in disregard of its own rules and somewhat arbitrary. However, there was no showing that their actions prejudiced Toepfer's position. To Mr. O'Neil the Panel's hearing may well have appeared "painfully farcical" and a "complete sham from start to finish." Yet the Court's inquiry is limited to whether the arbitrator provided "a fundamentally fair hearing" that includes giving "each of the parties to the dispute an adequate opportunity to present its evidence and arguments." *Generica, Ltd. v. Pharmaceutical Basics, Inc.*, 125 F.3d 1123, 1130 (7th Cir. 1997) (quoting *Hoteles Condado Beach*, 763 F.2d at 39)). The evidentiary record compels the conclusion that Toepfer had a meaningful opportunity to cross-examine Mr. Al-Haddad, and that the Panel's orders, which may have negatively affected his cross-examination by Toepfer, do not constitute "misbehavior by which the rights of any party have been prejudiced." 9 U.S.C. § 10(a)(3).

III. CONCLUSION

Whether or not they regret it in hindsight, the parties selected the RMA in their contract as the forum for resolving any disputes arising from the contract. Finding no evidence that the actions of the Panel resulted in substantial prejudice to Toepfer, the Court "will not substitute [its] judgment" for the arbitrator's. *Upshur*, 933 F.2d at 231. Accordingly, Respondent's Motion to Vacate the Arbitration Award of December 15, 2006, is hereby DENIED and Petitioner's Petition to Confirm Arbitration Award is GRANTED.

Notes and Questions.

1. The arbitration panel in *Al-Haddad* was actually found to have committed an abuse of discretion and a violation of its own rules. In harshest terms, then, the panel violated consensus, since no party or parties ever gives an arbitrator the power to abuse its discretion. The court ultimately let this go due to the absence of prejudice. Should prejudice be the determining factor or should prejudice instead be presumed once there is a violation of the rules of the arbitration? If the former, what part of FAA section 10(a) supports a prejudice requirement?
2. In *Al-Haddad*, this witness was a third party. *See also Eaton Partners, LLC v. Azimuth Capital Mgmt. IV, Ltd.*, 18-cv-11112 2019 U.S. Dist. LEXIS 163771, at *12, 14 (S.D.N.Y. Sep. 24, 2019) ("Even if the Arbitrator had in fact refused to adjourn the hearing and only allowed [the third-party witness] to appear by video, this would not have constituted a deprivation of Azimuth's right to a fundamentally fair hearing."). Should it make a difference if the (non-attending) witness is a party witness versus a third-party witness?
3. If the arbitrators go virtual for one witness, should that then lead to a slippery slope for the rest of the hearing? Once you go virtual for one witness, is it therefore much easier to go virtual for all? The COVID-19 pandemic presents this issue going forward, as seen immediately below.
4. *Al-Haddad* was an institutional arbitration governed by that institution's procedural rules. What if the arbitration had been ad hoc? Assume that Company A and Company B agree to arbitrate disputes over their con-

tract, but not through a particular institution. Instead, the arbitration clause addresses various procedural aspects of the proceeding, such as discovery, motions, and hearings. The clause is silent as to remote or virtual proceedings. A dispute arises, and Company A brings a claim. Because of a pandemic, the selected arbitrator cannot convene an in-person hearing for several months. Company B wants to hold the hearing over video conference. Company A objects. Over that objection, the arbitrator convenes a virtual hearing and enters judgment against Company A. Will Company A have a better shot than in *Al-Haddad* at successfully arguing that the award should be vacated because there were no institutional rules granting the arbitrator discretion to hold the hearing virtually? Would it make a difference if Party B had been the party that objected? And what rules would govern if the arbitration is ad hoc? What standard would a court use?

V. Next Steps During—and Following?—the COVID Era

During the COVID era, institutions like JAMS and the AAA put forward guidance to help lawyers and parties prepare for hearings over video. This guidance consists of advice regarding videoconferencing platform technology, including how best to preserve security and how to best prepare for a video hearing. Below are the AAA's recommendations for "optimizing the virtual hearing experience."

1. Use a PC or laptop for the video portion of the hearing as monitor size will be important, particularly for hearings with many participants
2. The device/screen you are using to participate in the virtual hearing will not be available for other purposes, such as taking notes or viewing documents; arrange for alternate means of doing so
    a. Use of dual monitors (or even a single monitor with a laptop screen) is recommended, with the virtual hearing running on one screen
3. Use a good quality webcam if possible, and check lighting conditions. Backlighting is generally not desirable
4. Audio considerations
    a. Audio quality can be affected by a variety of factors and may take some experimentation to come up with the best way to connect, whether by phone, through your computer speakers/microphone, and with or without a headset; try to determine your best method prior to the scheduled event.
    b. If there are multiple participants in the same physical location, there

may be an echo if their microphones/phones are not muted (this is highly dependent on the equipment being used but is obvious when it occurs)

c. Find a quiet location
   - Minimize background noise
   - Mute yourself when you are not speaking
   - Avoid multi-tasking such as checking email

5. Consider steps that may be taken to establish a high-speed internet connection (e.g., if possible, a hard-wired internet connection is generally preferable to a wireless internet connection)

The AAA has also published a model language for virtual hearing orders. This language accounts for scenarios where the parties consent to the video conference and where the parties do not. In the latter scenario, the recommended language is as follows:

> The arbitrator/panel notes the [claimant's/respondent's/other parties'] objections to holding the hearing via [Platform Name]. The arbitrator/panel finds, however, that conducting the hearing via videoconference is a reasonable alternative to an in-person hearing in light of the COVID-19 pandemic, stay-at-home orders, and travel limitations. Videoconferencing technology will provide the parties a fair and reasonable opportunity to present their case and will allow the hearing to move forward on the dates previously scheduled instead of postponing the hearing to a future date.

The AAA provides for model language regarding the technical aspects of the hearing, the recording of the hearing, witnesses and exhibits, logistics, and the costs of video conferencing. Although JAMS has not changed any of its rules, it has provided technical advice for the use of video platforms (one of which is its own mediation platform called Endispute) and guidance on the security of virtual arbitration hearings.

These institutions unsurprisingly flaunt the benefits of virtual arbitrations, including the comfort of home, the low cost of travel, and the lack of disruption that results from having to attend an in person hearing. Arbitrators report that the virtual hearings permit more focused attention and efficiency.

One commentator had the following prediction about the competing considerations as arbitrators determine whether to hold a virtual hearing.

Neal Eiseman, *Can a Commercial Arbitrator Demand a Virtual Hearing?*

The National Law Journal, May 20, 2020

There are several factors an arbitrator may consider when confronted with the issue: Were any in-person evidentiary hearings previously held? Is it too early to determine whether the hearings should be moved online because the parties have not yet completed the activities set forth in the arbitrator's pre-hearing scheduling order? After considering who is making the request and who opposes it, and the reasons therefor, will any undue prejudice result by ruling one way versus the other? And, if so, after balancing the equities, what is the correct decision? What deference and weight should be given to the fact that the parties voluntarily selected an alternate dispute resolution process whose hallmarks are speed, efficiency and finality? Will denying the request, in effect, bring the arbitration to a halt? Is the arbitrator technically savvy enough to conduct the hearing online and, if not, will someone be present in real-time to address and resolve any technical issues that may arise? By analogy, how are the courts conducting their business at the time the arbitrator is asked to rule? Are they allowing online judicial proceedings and, if so, to what extent?

Perhaps the most important consideration is whether, by proceeding virtually, the arbitrator will be able to understand the testimony and exhibits, assess witnesses and decide the dispute fairly. Interestingly, one of the arguments often raised against having witnesses testify by video is that it hampers the arbitrator's ability to observe the witnesses up close to assess their credibility. Arguably, that argument disappears on online platforms that allow for facial close-ups. (Ironically, if social distancing required witnesses to wear masks to protect themselves from contracting COVID-19, having everyone together in the same room turns out to be a less effective way to assess credibility.)

All of the above assumes that arbitration clauses entered before COVID-19 are valid and enforceable in an environment that the parties did not contemplate when contracting for arbitration.

Lawyers involved in all forms of contracts are drafting force majeure clauses for their clients. Arbitration is a contract and should be no exception. There are two approaches lawyers might take: (1) build a virtual hearing protocol now, either in the arbitration clause itself or in reliance on institutional rules outlined above, or (2) more like force majeure, perhaps parties may contract to an arbitration commitment that evaporates if a live hearing is impossible either because of governmental orders, institutional policies, illness, or an unwillingness of the arbitrators or parties to appear in person for a hearing.

If parties take the latter approach, they should consider adding language to the arbitration clause that contemplates both pre-hearing, non-merits matters as well as merits hearings. The parties should consider virtual attendance of parties, third party witnesses, and experts, as well as delineating some protocol for entering exhibits. Perhaps this clause turns on the status of court operations in the chosen forum or other considerations outlined in the Eiseman article. Most importantly, in a post-pandemic reality, it is vitally important that parties give these issues consideration when agreeing to arbitration.

For more information, *see Virtual Arbitration Hearings, COVID-19, and Award Enforcement*, CROWELL MORING (April 29, 2020); Neal Eisman, *Can a Commercial Arbitrator Demand a Virtual Hearing?*, LAW.COM (May 20, 2020); Thomas Halket, *10 Important Elements of Arbitration Agreements*, PRIORI (January 25, 2017); Velislava Hristova and Malcom Robach, *Legal and Practical Aspects of Virtual Hearings During (and After?) the Pandemic: Takeaway from SCC Online Seminar Series*, Kluwer Arbitration Blog (May 16, 2020); *AAA-Model Order and Procedures for a Virtual Hearing via Videoconference*, AAA, go.adr.org; *Coronavirus Impact on Arbitration & OHO Hearings*, FINRA; *PODCAST: Virtual Mediation & Arbitration: The Benefits, Challenges and Attorney Reactions*, JAMS ADR BLOG (May 5, 2020).

Chapter 14

Special Issues in Arbitration Enforcement

Sections 9 and 10 of the FAA, which we have just reviewed, form the core of post-award arbitration practice. As we have seen, Section 9 is Congress's prescription for how to turn an arbitration award into an enforceable court judgment, and Section 10 is the opposite—it governs the specific grounds for vacating an arbitration award before it is enforceable.

With those basics mastered, the skilled and experienced arbitration practitioner is also likely to face a number of related procedural issues.

First, when can a party challenging an arbitration award use Section 11 rather than section 10, and change the award on the basis that it was merely a "mistake"? How close does this get to a prohibited challenge on the merit? Can you skirt that line?

Second, after the award, can the arbitrators take any action at all—for purposes of a Section 11 "mistake" petition, for enforcement of terms of the award, for monitoring continuing violations, or any other reason—or does the arbitration's life and arbitrator mandate end as of the moment the award is issued? This is the doctrine of *functus officio.*

Third, if a party is challenging an arbitration award in court, what happens to the confidentiality under which parties often agree (or think they are agreeing) to arbitrate? Arbitration is private, while the courts are public—so can one have a private challenge in a public forum, or does confidentiality get thrown overboard in enforcement proceedings?

I. Section 11—When Is a Mistake Just a Mistake?

Congress provided in Section 11 of the Federal Arbitration Act that a party may seek to "modif[y] or correct[]" an arbitration award in the case of error. In any of the following cases, the United States court in and for the district wherein the award was made may make an order *modifying or correcting* the award upon the application of any party to the arbitration—

(a) Where there was an evident material miscalculation of figures or an evident material mistake in the description of any person, thing, or property referred to in the award.

(b) Where the arbitrators have awarded upon a matter not submitted to them, unless it is a matter not affecting the merits of the decision upon the matter submitted.

(c) Where the award is imperfect in matter of form not affecting the merits of the controversy.

The order may *modify and correct* the award, so as to effect the intent thereof and promote justice between the parties.

Class Exercise

Consider again the *Batpow* hypothetical case in Chapter 12. Assume that Arbitrator George stated in his final award that he was adopting Claimant's "actual profits earned/extended" damages model. That model, per Claimant's expert report, stated damages of $33,786,519. The Final Award does not use this figure. Instead, after stating that he would adopt that model, Arbitrator George's final award is $44,786,519. Did he mean to award an extra $11 million on top of the expert's number, or did Arbitrator George simply mistype "44" where he meant to type "33"? Was this an "evident material miscalculation of figures" under Section 11(a)? How far should a reviewing court, on a Section 11 standard, be allowed to go?

A. Section 11 and the "Face of the Award" Test

The following case confronts head on the issue of whether the arbitrator's mistake should be examined on the face of the award, or if a reviewing court should go behind the award and look at whether the arbitrator considered correctly the building blocks that form the award (and particularly its numbers).

Mid Atl. Capital Corp. v. Bien

956 F.3d 1182 (10th Cir. 2020)

HOLMES, Circuit Judge.

A married couple, Ms. Beverly Bien and Mr. David Wellman, invested money with Mid Atlantic Capital Corporation ("Mid Atlantic"). Their investments performed poorly. Stung by the losses, Ms. Bien and Mr. Wellman initiated arbitration proceedings against Mid Atlantic. The arbitration panel awarded Ms. Bien and Mr. Wellman damages, attorney's fees, and arbitration costs. The panel also ordered Ms. Bien and Mr. Wellman to reassign their ownership interests in their investments to Mid Atlantic.

Mid Atlantic moved the federal district court to modify the arbitration award to correct "an evident material miscalculation of figures." 9 U.S.C. § 11(a). The district court denied the motion because the alleged error that Mid Atlantic sought to remedy did not appear on the face of the arbitration award. In the amended final judgment, in addition to ordering Mid Atlantic to pay Ms. Bien and Mr. Wellman certain damages, the court ordered that prejudgment interest would accrue on the damages portion of the award and that postjudgment interest would accrue at the federal rate specified in 28 U.S.C. § 1961. Lastly, the court ordered Ms. Bien and Mr. Wellman to reassign to Mid Atlantic their ownership interests in their investments, including any distributions that they had received since the arbitration award due to the investments.

Both parties appeal from the district court's order. Mid Atlantic specifically challenges the court's denial of its motion to modify the arbitration award. Ms. Bien and Mr. Wellman cross-appeal, challenging the court's rulings applying prejudgment interest to only the damages portion of the award and ordering them to reassign any distributions that they had received since the arbitration award due to their ownership interests in the investments. Exercising jurisdiction under 28 U.S.C. § 1291 and 9 U.S.C. § 16(a)(1)(D) and (a)(3), we affirm the district court's judgment in all respects.

I

Mid Atlantic is a brokerage firm registered with the Financial Industry Regulatory Authority ("FINRA"). Ms. Bien and Mr. Wellman opened several brokerage accounts with Mid Atlantic. Through those accounts, Ms. Bien and Mr. Wellman invested in two investment vehicles, Sonoma Ridge Partners and KBS REIT [i.e., real estate investment trusts] ("KBS"). Ms. Bien and Mr. Wellman's contracts with Mid Atlantic each included an identically worded arbitration clause. That clause obligated the parties to resolve all disputes through binding arbitration conducted according to FINRA rules.

A

After their investments in Sonoma Ridge Partners and KBS suffered heavy losses, Ms. Bien and Mr. Wellman initiated arbitration proceedings against Mid Atlantic. They alleged that Mid Atlantic had, among other things, sold them unreasonably risky investments. To remedy the resulting harm, Ms. Bien and Mr. Wellman sought damages, as well as attorney's fees, costs, and interest.

The arbitration panel held a hearing. At the hearing, Ms. Bien and Mr. Wellman's expert offered the panel two ways to calculate the losses at issue. The first option looked to Ms. Bien and Mr. Wellman's "net out-of-pocket" losses. The expert calculated Ms. Bien and Mr. Wellman's net out-of-pocket losses as $292,411. The second measure of damages looked to Ms. Bien and Mr. Wellman's "market-adjusted damages." The measure of those damages is "the difference between the actual return on these investments and what the return would have been if [Ms. Bien and Mr. Wellman's] money had been invested in a well-managed 'benchmark' account."

The expert calculated Ms. Bien and Mr. Wellman's market-adjusted damages as between $484,684 and $618,049. Mid Atlantic did not present any expert testimony on damages.

During the hearing's closing arguments, Ms. Bien and Mr. Wellman read into the record a written final prayer for relief. In it, they requested only market-adjusted damages. Indeed, they asserted that compensating them for their net out-of-pocket losses would be "inconsistent with the case law" and would not make them whole. And so Ms. Bien and Mr. Wellman prayed for market-adjusted damages. Together, they also requested $118,560 in attorney's fees, $26,812.82 in costs, interest on the damages at 8% per year, and punitive damages.

The arbitration panel ruled in substantial part in favor of Ms. Bien and Mr. Wellman. It ordered Mid Atlantic to pay them two forms of damages: (1) initial-investment-loss damages and (2) compensatory damages.

In addition, the arbitration panel ordered Mid Atlantic to pay interest at 8% per year on each form of damages. That interest would accrue from the date Ms. Bien and Mr. Wellman initiated arbitration proceedings until the damages were "paid in full." The award also called for Mid Atlantic to pay $118,560 in attorney's fees, $26,812.82 in costs, and all arbitration fees. The panel declined, however, to award any other remedies, such as punitive damages. And it did order Ms. Bien and Mr. Wellman to "reassign ownership of all Sonoma Ridge Partners and KBS REIT investments to [Mid Atlantic]."

B

Mid Atlantic moved the district court to modify the arbitration award. It argued, among other things, that the arbitration panel had given Ms. Bien and Mr. Wellman a double recovery. According to Mid Atlantic, the panel's $292,411 award in initial-investment-loss damages corresponded with Ms. Bien and Mr. Wellman's expert's testimony that their net out-of-pocket losses were $292,411. And the panel's $484,683 award in compensatory damages almost exactly matched the $484,684 in market-adjusted damages that the expert had at one point said Ms. Bien and Mr. Wellman incurred. Yet, that expert had presented net out-of-pocket damages and market-adjusted damages as *alternative* measures of their losses, and Ms. Bien and Mr. Wellman had asked for only market-adjusted damages in their final prayer for relief. Thus, by effectively awarding Ms. Bien and Mr. Wellman *both* net out-of-pocket damages and market-adjusted damages, the panel allegedly gave them a double recovery. To correct this purported double recovery, Mid Atlantic asked the district court to modify the arbitration award.

In response, Ms. Bien and Mr. Wellman moved the district court to confirm the award. As they saw it, the district court could modify the arbitration award to correct the alleged double recovery only if there was "an evident material miscalculation of figures" on the face of the award. And the alleged double recovery here appeared only when one delved into the arbitration record. Thus, they argued that the district court lacked authority to modify the award.

The district court sided with Ms. Bien and Mr. Wellman. Like Mid Atlantic, the court thought the arbitration award was "disturbing." It agreed that "what the panel called 'initial investment loss[es]'" and "compensatory damages" corresponded with what Ms. Bien and Mr. Wellman had called, respectively, "net out-of-pocket losses" and "market-adjusted damages." So the court found that by awarding "both net out-of-pocket losses . . . and market-adjusted damages," the panel effectively gave Ms. Bien and Mr. Wellman a double recovery. But the district court read 9 U.S.C. § 11(a) as authorizing it to correct "an evident material miscalculation of figures" only if the miscalculation appeared "on the face of the award." Because the alleged double counting at issue appeared only upon looking to the arbitration record, the district court concluded that it lacked authority to modify the award. For that reason, it denied Mid Atlantic's motion to modify and granted Ms. Bien and Mr. Wellman's motion to confirm the award.

C

Both parties filed timely appeals from the amended final judgment. Mid Atlantic's appeal presents one question for our review: Did the district court err by holding that it lacked authority to modify the arbitration award to correct an alleged evident material miscalculation of figures because that miscalculation does not appear on the face of the arbitration award?

III

We turn first to the question Mid Atlantic raises in its appeal. That question has two parts. First, does 9 U.S.C. § 11(a) permit courts to look beyond the face of the arbitration award when deciding whether to modify an award to correct an alleged evident material miscalculation of figures? And second, if not, does the face of the arbitration award here contain an evident material miscalculation of figures? As explained below, we answer each question in the negative.

A

Section 11(a) authorizes courts to modify an arbitration award if it contains "an evident material miscalculation of figures or an evident material mistake in the description of any person, thing, or property referred to in the award." 9 U.S.C. § 11(a). We are concerned with only the first half of § 11(a)—the "evident material miscalculation of figures" portion. The district court read that phrase as allowing it to correct only those miscalculations that appear on the face of the award. Mid Atlantic argues that the district court erred in interpreting the text of § 11(a) to embody such a face-of-the-award limitation.

Whether § 11(a) permits courts to go beyond the face of the arbitration award in looking for an evident material miscalculation of figures is a question of first impression in this circuit. We answer that question in the negative: that is, we conclude that § 11(a) embodies a face-of-the-award limitation. In reaching that conclusion, first and foremost, we draw inferences from the text and context of the FAA. Our independent reading of this text and context is reinforced by our recognition of the narrow and deferential standard of review applicable in the arbitration context. We close our analysis of this matter by recognizing, moreover, that the persuasive authority of our sister circuits has reached a similar conclusion.

We must interpret § 11(a) as written. *See, e.g., Henry Schein, Inc. v. Archer and White Sales, Inc.*, ___ U.S. ___, 139 S. Ct. 524, 529, 202 L. Ed. 2d 480 (2019). That endeavor entails giving words their plain meaning when "read in their context and with a view to their place in the overall statutory scheme." *Home Depot U.S.A., Inc. v. Jackson*, ___ U.S. ___, 139 S. Ct. 1743, 1748, 204 L. Ed. 2d 34 (2019) (quoting *Davis v. Michigan Dep't of Treasury*, 489 U.S. 803, 809, 109 S. Ct. 1500, 103 L. Ed. 2d 891 (1989)); *see* Antonin Scalia & Bryan A. Garner, READING LAW: THE INTERPRETATION OF LEGAL TEXTS 56–58 (2012) (discussing the "Supremacy-of-Text Principle"). Doing so, we conclude that § 11(a) embodies a face-of-the-award limitation.

Let's start with § 11(a)'s plain meaning. *See Jones v. Comm'r*, 560 F.3d 1196, 1200 (10th Cir. 2009). That section says, in relevant part, that a court may modify an award if it contains "an evident material miscalculation of figures." 9 U.S.C. § 11(a). In ordinarily English, a "miscalculation of figures" refers to mathematical, not legal, errors. *See Calculate*, NEW OXFORD AMERICAN DICTIONARY 242 (2d ed. 2005) ("Determine (the amount or number of something) mathematically."); *Figure, id.* at 626 (defining "figures" as "arithmetical calculations"). Likewise, "material" in this context takes its ordinary meaning of "important; essential; relevant." *Material, id.* at 1045. The word "evident," too, takes its ordinary meaning of "plain or obvious." *Evident, id.* at 585. The parties do not appear to dispute the ordinary meaning of these terms. Putting these definitions together, we read § 11(a) to allow courts to correct obvious, significant mathematical errors.

But even with these dictionary definitions, the meaning of § 11(a)—particularly the word "evident"—is not clear. Must a miscalculation be obvious on the face of the award or must it be obvious after one looks to the arbitration record? Devoid of context, the text arguably could support either possibility. Fealty to text, however, is more than blind adherence to dictionary definitions; we must consider context. And § 11(a)'s context supports reading the term "evident" as contemplating a face-of-the-award limitation.

Consider the FAA's purposes. Its "'principal purpose' ... is to 'ensur[e] that private arbitration agreements are enforced according to their terms.'" *AT&T Mobility LLC v. Concepcion*, 563 U.S. 333, 344, 131 S. Ct. 1740, 179 L. Ed. 2d 742 (2011) (alteration in original) (quoting *Volt Info. Scis., Inc. v. Bd. of Trs. of Leland Stanford Junior Univ.*, 489 U.S. 468, 478, 109 S. Ct. 1248, 103 L. Ed. 2d 488 (1989)). "This purpose is readily apparent from the FAA's text." *Id.* And it "reflects the overarching principle that arbitration is a matter of contract." *Am. Express Co. v. Italian Colors Rest.*, 570 U.S. 228, 233, 133 S. Ct. 2304, 186 L. Ed. 2d 417 (2013). Moreover, part of the parties' arbitration contract is their "bargain[] for the arbitrator's construction of their agreement." *Oxford Health Plans*, 569 U.S. at 569 (quoting *E. Associated Coal Corp. v. United Mine Workers*, 531 U.S. 57, 62, 121 S. Ct. 462, 148 L. Ed. 2d 354 (2000)). In striking that bargain, the parties "trade[] the procedures and opportunity for review of the courtroom for the simplicity, informality, and expedition of arbitration." *Gilmer v. Interstate/Johnson Lane Corp.*, 500 U.S. 20, 31, 111 S. Ct. 1647, 114 L. Ed. 2d 26 (1991) (quoting *Mitsubishi Motors Corp. v. Soler Chrysler-Plymouth, Inc.*, 473 U.S. 614, 628, 105 S. Ct. 3346, 87 L. Ed. 2d 444 (1985)).

Reading this statutory term "evident" as relating to a material miscalculation that appears on the face of the award furthers the FAA's purposes. A face-of-the-award limitation preserves the integrity of the parties' bargain. Specifically, it preserves the parties' deal for an arbitrator's, rather than a court's, resolution of their dispute. This bargain essentially negates the risk that a court may substitute its judgment (inadvertently or otherwise) for that of the arbitrator when it goes beyond the award's face in search of obvious, material mathematical errors. Further, a face-of-the-award approach also ensures that arbitration remains an efficient means to resolve disputes rather than "merely a prelude to a more cumbersome and time-consuming judicial review process." *Hall St.*, 552 U.S. at 588 (quoting *Kyocera Corp. v. Prudential-Bache Trade Servs., Inc.*, 341 F.3d 987, 998 (9th Cir. 2003)). Reading § 11(a) to allow courts to hunt through the arbitration record for "evident" miscalculations "opens the door to the full-bore legal and evidentiary appeals" that the parties would have contracted to avoid. Faced with one interpretation of § 11(a) that furthers the FAA's purposes and one that undermines them, we prefer the former.

This reading of § 11(a) draws additional support from the narrow and deferential standard of review applicable in the arbitration context. Recall that our "review of arbitral awards" is "*among the narrowest known to law.*" *Lovato*, 864 F.3d at 1083 (quoting *Brown*, 220 F.3d at 1182). We therefore do "not sit to hear claims of factual or legal error by an arbitrator." *Stolt-Nielsen*, 559 U.S. at 696 (Ginsburg, J., dissenting) (quoting *Misco*, 484 U.S. at 38); *accord Oxford Health Plans*, 569 U.S. at 569. Nor may we "disturb the arbitrators' judgment, even if convinced that 'serious error' infected the panel's award." *Stolt-Nielsen*, 559 U.S. at 696 (Ginsburg, J., dissenting) (quoting *Misco*, 484 U.S. at 38). "Once an arbitration award is entered, the finality of arbitration weighs heavily in its favor and cannot be upset except under exceptional circumstances." *Burlington*, 636 F.3d at 567 (quoting *Ormsbee*, 668 F.2d at 1146–47). While § 11(a) enumerates one such circumstance, it does *not* override the "extreme deference" we owe the arbitration award. *Lovato*, 864 F.3d at 1083 (emphasis omitted) (quoting *Brown*, 220 F.3d at 1182). Similarly, if we read § 11(a) to allow courts to hunt for errors lurking in the arbitration record—as Mid Atlantic does—we undercut such deference and open up arbitration awards to judicial second-guessing. We cannot countenance such a departure from our narrow and deferential review of arbitration awards.

Mid Atlantic's primary textual argument against the face-of-the-award limitation is unpersuasive. It argues that "[t]he only way to determine whether a miscalculation or mistake is 'material' is to analyze the [arbitration] record." And thus, as Mid Atlantic reasons, § 11(a) could not embody a face-of-the-award limitation because such a limitation would give the term "material" no effect.

We find this reasoning wholly unpersuasive. Take a hypothetical award that orders the defendant to pay $100,000 in punitive damages and $100,000 in compensatory damages but then adds these figures on the award's face for a total of $2,000,000. One need not dive into the arbitration record to say that the award includes a significant (i.e., material) mathematical error. It is untrue, then, that a face-of-the-award limitation renders null § 11(a)'s materiality requirement.

We are similarly unmoved by Mid Atlantic's related policy argument that a face-of-the-award limitation effectively produces arbitrary results. To illustrate these supposedly arbitrary results, Mid Atlantic offers the following hypothetical:

> [C]onsider a hypothetical award which grants postjudgment interest at the rate of 8%. Assume further that the award does not cite any source for the 8% rate of interest, but that the parties had in fact stipulated to the statute governing interest and that statute provides for a 4% rate of interest. In other words, assume the 8% interest rate is indisputably wrong but the "face of the award" does not contain information required to reach that conclusion. Under the District Court's interpretation, this error cannot be corrected.

According to Mid Atlantic, this hypothetical outcome is arbitrary. And Mid Atlantic reasons that it "advances zero compelling policy interests" to prevent courts from correcting this error concerning the interest rate, when—even under the face-of-the-award approach—courts would have been able to correct the error if the award had referenced explicitly the parties' stipulation concerning the 4% interest rate. Mid Atlantic concludes that the face-of-the-award approach thus "leaves the question of whether clear math errors can be corrected up to the random chance that arbitrators 'show their work.'"

Yet, contrary to Mid Atlantic's contentions, the FAA's purpose, history, and structure make it clear that this is precisely how Congress intended § 11(a) to function. And its operation is not arbitrary at all. Section 11 authorizes courts to review an arbitration award—not the arbitration record. Further, the face-of-the-award approach is congruent with Congress's purpose of providing "just the limited review needed to maintain arbitration's essential virtue of resolving disputes straightaway." *Hall St.*, 552 U.S. at 588. Irrespective of whether Mid Atlantic considers this purpose to be the stuff of compelling public policy, that is Congress's judgment, and we are obliged to defer to it.

What's more in dispelling Mid Atlantic's misguided notion that the statute functions in an arbitrary manner—under a face-of-the-award approach—it is important to keep in mind that "arbitration is a matter of contract." *Henry Schein*, 139 S. Ct. at 529. If Mid Atlantic wished to avoid the supposedly random chance that the arbitration panel would not show its work, it could have contracted for a fully explained award. *See Am. Express*, 570 U.S. at 233 (noting that parties can contract to specify the arbitrator and the rules for arbitration); *United Steelworkers v. Enter. Wheel & Car*

Corp., 363 U.S. 593, 598, 80 S. Ct. 1358, 4 L. Ed. 2d 1424 (1960) ("Arbitrators have no obligation to the court to give their reasons for an award."). But Mid Atlantic did not do so. In fact, the current contracts lead us to the opposite conclusion. Most obviously, Mid Atlantic's contracts with Ms. Bien and Mr. Wellman specify, "[t]he arbitrators do not have to explain the reason(s) for their award." We thus cannot (and would not attempt to) rewrite the parties' contracts just because Mid Atlantic is now dissatisfied with the fruits of its bargain. After all, "by agreeing to arbitrate," Mid Atlantic traded "procedures and opportunity for review of the courtroom for the simplicity, informality, and expedition of arbitration." *Gilmer*, 500 U.S. at 31 (quoting *Mitsubishi*, 473 U.S. at 628). Stated otherwise, that Mid Atlantic is displeased with the level of informality with which the arbitration panel resolved the dispute is not cause to undo the bargain it struck with Ms. Bien and Mr. Wellman. *Cf. Beumer Corp. v. ProEnergy Servs., LLC*, 899 F.3d 564, 566 (8th Cir. 2018) ("The parties bargained for the arbitrator's decision; if the arbitrator got it wrong, then that was part of the bargain.").

In sum, we conclude that § 11(a) allows courts to correct only those evident material miscalculations that appear on the face of the award. The provision's text compels that conclusion, when it is read in the context of the FAA's purposes, history, and structure. And this conclusion is bolstered by the narrow and deferential standard of review applicable in the arbitration context.

2

We recognize that Mid Atlantic marshals certain cases that purportedly bolster its position. Chief among them is *Eljer Manufacturing, Inc. v. Kowin Development Corp.*, 14 F.3d 1250 (7th Cir. 1994). The arbitration award there gave the defendant, Kowin, almost $15 million in damages. *See* 14 F.3d at 1253. The award divided these damages "into three separate" categories of (1) about $3 million, (2) around $8.4 million, and (3) $3.5 million. *Id.* The award itself did not clarify what these amounts represented or how the arbitrator calculated them. *Id.* But as it turned out, the three categories "duplicated precisely the amounts requested by Kowin in the damages section of its post-hearing brief." *Id.* By consulting that brief, the district court determined that the first category inadvertently included $1.25 million that Eljer had already paid Kowin, and that the third category included $2.5 million that the first category had already accounted for. To correct these errors, the district court granted Eljer's motion for modification under § 11. Kowin appealed this decision.

The Seventh Circuit in *Eljer* agreed with the district court that the "[t]he basis for each of the arbitrator's awards" was Kowin's brief. *Id.* at 1254. It rejected Kowin's contention that "the [district] court's reduction of the award rest[ed] on impermissible speculation as to what each of the arbitrator's three awards was attempting to redress," reasoning that "[i]t was hardly speculative for the district court to base its analysis on Kowin's own explanation of its damages." *Id.* The court observed that "Kowin confuses a narrow standard of review with a nonexistent standard of review." *Id.* With this information from beyond the face of the award, the Seventh

Circuit concluded that the award provided for double recoveries. And it reasoned that a "[d]ouble recovery constitutes a materially unjust miscalculation which may be modified under section 11." *Id.* Thus, the Seventh Circuit affirmed the district court's order modifying the award. *See id.* at 1257.

The face-of-the-award limitation that we adopt here is admittedly in some tension with the Seventh Circuit's decision in *Eljer.* But we do not find *Eljer*'s analysis persuasive, and, thus, it gives us no pause. *See, e.g., United States v. Krueger*, 809 F.3d 1109, 1116 n.9 (10th Cir. 2015) (declining to rely on "unpersuasive out-of-circuit cases"). For starters, *Eljer* did not expressly hold that § 11(a) permits district courts to go beyond the face of the arbitration award to find evident material mathematical miscalculations. And, notably, *Eljer* undertook no textual analysis of § 11(a); for instance, the word "evident" appears nowhere in the body of the opinion. *See Eljer*, 14 F.3d at 1253 n.4. This failing is particularly salient given the Supreme Court's repeated instruction to "interpret the [FAA] as written." *Henry Schein*, 139 S. Ct. at 529; *see also Hall St.*, 552 U.S. at 587–88. Therefore, we are not persuaded by *Eljer*'s analysis, and it does not lead us to question the face-of-the-award limitation we adopt here.

The other cases Mid Atlantic cites are similarly unpersuasive. Consider *Transnitro, Inc. v. M/V Wave*, 943 F.2d 471 (4th Cir. 1991). The arbitrator there awarded M/V damages accounting for, among other things, certain expenses that M/V had incurred and about $57,000 in interest that had accrued on a bond. After the award was issued, M/V discovered that it had failed to inform the arbitrator or Transnitro that it had already earned about $34,000 in interest on the bond. Likewise, M/V had not reported some $28,000 in expenses. In federal court, Transnitro moved to modify the award to subtract the unreported $34,000 from the $57,000 interest award. For its part, M/V asked to collect the $28,000 in unreported expenses. The district court agreed to subtract the $34,000 from the interest award because it would be "unfair to permit [M/V] to reap the benefit of [its own] failure." *Id.* at 474. But fairness did not likewise compel the court to allow M/V to collect the unreported expenses.

On appeal, M/V argued "that the district court had no power under 9 U.S.C. § 11 to modify" the award because the provision's "last sentence . . . [which speaks of modifications to awards "so as to . . . promote justice between the parties"] d[id] not create an independent basis for modification." *Id.* at 473–74. Rather, it contended that § 11 authorized "modification only if the provisions of one of subparagraphs (a), (b) or (c) [were] met." *Id.* The Fourth Circuit sidestepped that question. It reasoned instead that whatever the effect of the last sentence of § 11, "there were, within the meaning of subsection (a), material mistakes made in the arbitration proceeding as to interest on the bond and . . . as to other expenses." *Id.* True, the court noted, "[t]hose errors were apparently not the fault of the arbitrators." *Id.* However, that fact did "not also mean that where there is 'an evident material mistake' attributable to one or both parties to an arbitration, a district court lacks power under subsection (a) to do *equity and justice*," the court explained. *Id.* (emphasis added). The Fourth Circuit further reasoned that "the court below was right in reaching and correctly determining the interest issue. However, that court also should have reached and determined the additional expenses issue." *Id.* Therefore, the Fourth Circuit affirmed the interest modification and remanded for the district court to consider the expense issue further.

Mid Atlantic relies heavily on *Transnitro.* At bottom, Mid Atlantic reads *Transnitro* to stand for the proposition that when, "as here, there is a mathematical error in an award, the district court could have (and should have) looked at the materials in the arbitration record . . . to determine the fix for that mathematical error." Drilling down on it, however, *Transnitro* is less helpful than Mid Atlantic thinks. To begin, that case interpreted the language "evident material mistake" from the second half of § 11(a). *See Transnitro*, 943 F.2d at 474. And recall, we are concerned here with only the language from the first half of § 11(a), which authorizes courts to correct an "evident material miscalculation."

At the end of the day, what is important is what the *Transnitro* court did—and, especially, did *not* do—in reaching its holding, not the theory that motivated its actions. And, in addition to tacitly eschewing a textual analysis of § 11(a), the court in *Transnitro* did not consider the FAA's purposes, history, or structure in arriving at its holding. Yet, as explained above, it is these sources (combined with § 11(a)'s plain text) that ultimately led us to the conclusion that we reach here concerning the face-of-the-award limitation. Therefore, even if *Transnitro* were the only word from the Fourth Circuit on § 11(a), the fact that the court elided these key sources in reaching its holding would render it an unpersuasive touchstone for our own interpretation of that provision. In sum, contrary to Mid Atlantic's reading of the case, we do not find that *Transnitro* speaks persuasively—if at all—to the circumstances before us.

B

Having concluded that § 11(a) incorporates a face-of-the-award limitation, we now must determine whether the face of the arbitration award here contains an evident material miscalculation of figures. It is Mid Atlantic's burden to prove that such a miscalculation appears on the face of the award. Put simply, Mid Atlantic has not satisfied that burden.

Mid Atlantic's double-counting argument would not permit it to prevail. Most obviously, the alleged material miscalculation did not appear on the face of the award. Further, the award did not even state that the "initial investment loss" damages corresponded to what the expert had called net out-of-pocket losses. Nor did the award say that the "compensatory damages" were equivalent to the market-adjusted damages that the expert discussed. Critically, missing from the award was an explanation as to *how* the panel calculated the damages figures. In short, "there is no math issue" on the face of the award. And Mid Atlantic does not suggest otherwise, arguing instead that courts are free to look beyond the face of the award.

V

For the reasons stated above, we AFFIRM the amended final judgment in all respects.

Notes and Questions

1. *Is the Rigid Approach Too Arbitrary? Mid Atlantic* takes a rigid approach to correcting mistakes in arbitration awards under Section 11. Return to the court's hypothetical: "Take a hypothetical award that orders the defendant to pay $100,000 in punitive damages and $100,000 in compensatory damages but then adds these figures on the award's face for a total of $2,000,000." Presumably, even the *Mid Atlantic* court would correct that award and adjust it down to $200,000. The components of the correct amount of $200,000 are, presumably in the court's hypothetical, both stated in the award itself. But what if the award did not use actual numbers, just concepts, for the two components—for example, if the court stated that it was accepting the claimant's submitted figures in its post-hearing brief for, respectively, punitive and compensatory damages? Now the numbers are not on the face of the award. The reviewing court would have to go back to the claimant's post-hearing brief. Should that make a difference? For another example, return again to the *Batpow* hypothetical case and the question posed just before *Mid Atlantic.* We considered a scenario where, after stating that he was adopting the particular model advocated by one party, the arbitrator then stated a number precisely $11 million higher—to the penny—than the number in that expert report. The last six digits remain 786,519, but instead of writing $33 million to start, the arbitrator wrote $44 million. Typing error? Conscious decision? It would not be hard to show the discrepancy between award and report, and certainly the six-digit similarity bespeaks of error rather than consciousness. But under *Mid Atlantic*, unless the arbitrator wrote something along the lines of "I will now add four plus two and compute a total of five"—that is, unless the error can be seen on the *face* of the award rather than only by reference to collateral materials (such as the *Batpow* expert report), the award will be sustained. Should Section 11 have that limit?

2. *Mistakes and Reasoned Awards. Mid Atlantic* pointed out that the party claiming mistake and stuck with the face of the award had made its own bed: "[To] avoid the supposedly random chance that the arbitration panel would not show its work, it could have contracted for a fully explained award." The *Mid Atlantic* parties not only did not adopt that language, but then went further and stated expressly that "[t]he arbitrators do not have to explain the reason(s) for their award." Here again, as the court pointed out, arbitration is a matter of contract, and so Mid Atlantic was undone by its own language. This gives drafters a trade-off. Contemporary practice opts for a "reasoned award" which provides an

explanation of the arbitrator's findings. A reasoned award makes a Section 11 (and Section 10) challenge easier. Is the clarity of the award, so that your clients can understand the bases for the ruling, worth the increased enforcement challenge?

B. Section 11 and New Evidence

What if the correction to the arbitrator's award is not based on the arbitrator's alleged error but on new and highly relevant evidence emerging after the award. Is this a correction? A vacatur challenge? Or a call for a new arbitration? Consider that in the context of the following case.

Transnitro, Inc. v. M/V Wave

943 F.2d 471 (4th Cir. 1991)

KAUFMAN, Senior United States District Judge.

Springwave Marine Limited, owner of the vessel, M/V WAVE (owner), entered into a charter party with Transnitro, Inc. (charterer) pursuant to which the vessel loaded a cargo of prilled urea in Holland, for shipment to and unloading in Saginaw, Michigan. Because of difficulties in unloading at that Great Lakes port, the vessel proceeded to Norfolk, Virginia where it accomplished the cargo's discharge. Then, the charterer filed suit in rem against the vessel in the United States District Court for the Eastern District of Virginia, Norfolk Division, alleging breach of the charter party and attaching the vessel. The latter was released after the owner filed a Release Bond in the amount of $200,000.00. Following the filing by the owner of an answer to the charterer's complaint, the matter was referred to an arbitration panel by the Norfolk district court, and all further proceedings in that court were stayed pending arbitration pursuant to the terms of the charter party. The arbitrators awarded detention damages, attorney's fees and costs of the Release Bond to the owner, as well as $57,676.71 of interest on the amount of the bond at the annual rate of 9.5%. Thereafter, the charterer paid the detention damages, the attorney's fees and the cost of the Release Bond, but not the interest.

Following the announcement of the arbitration award, correspondence ensued among counsel for the parties, in the course of which counsel for the owner advised counsel for the charterer that counsel for the owner had not known, at the time of the arbitration, that the collateral for the Release Bond had been placed by the owner in an interest bearing account and had earned $34,000 of interest. However, during that correspondence, counsel for the owner also stated that the owner had incurred a number of expenses relating to the bond, including premiums and commissions, totaling $28,147.01, which had not been claimed by the owner during the arbitration proceeding. The owner suggested that the charterer receive credit for the $34,000.00

interest item and that the owner should get credit for the $28,147.01 of expenses. In that context, the owner would have received $5,852.99 less than it would have received under the arbitration award itself.

The arrangement suggested by the owner was not accepted by the charterer. Accordingly, after paying all parts of the arbitration award except the interest on the bond in the amount of $57,676.71, the charterer filed suit in the United States District Court for the Southern District of New York, seeking to modify and to correct the arbitration award as to the interest element. That court transferred the case to the United States District Court for the Eastern District of Virginia, at Norfolk, where it was consolidated with the original Norfolk case.

I.

9 U.S.C. §11, a part of the Federal Arbitration Act, which is applicable in this admiralty dispute, provides as follows:

> In either of the following cases the United States court in and for the district wherein the award was made may make an order modifying or correcting the award upon the application of any party to the arbitration—
>
> (a) Where there was an evident material miscalculation of figures or an evident material mistake in the description of any person, thing, or property referred to in the award.
>
> (b) Where the arbitrators have awarded upon a matter not submitted to them, unless it is a matter not affecting the merits of the decision upon the matter submitted.
>
> (c) Where the award is imperfect in matter of form not affecting the merits of the controversy.
>
> The order may modify and correct the award, so as to effect the intent thereof and promote justice between the parties.

Acting pursuant to that statutory provision, the Norfolk district court concluded that it had the power to modify and correct the award of the arbitration panel "so as to effect the intent thereof and promote justice between the parties." Concluding that it was totally unfair for the owner to collect interest in the amount of $57,676.71 without deduction for the $34,000.00 of interest which the owner had earned, the district court reduced the arbitration award as to the item of interest to $23,676.71. However, that court refused to permit the owner to recover, in whole or in part, for the additional expenses in the amount of $28,147.01, and did not resolve in any way the lack of agreement between the parties as to whether the owner did in fact incur such expenses, whether, on the merits, the owner is entitled to be reimbursed for those expenses by the charterer, and whether those expenses do in fact total the amount claimed, namely, $28,147.01. Seemingly, the owner was not given the opportunity in the court below to establish those expenses and that they totaled in that said amount.

The district court apparently took the position that the owner had had the opportunity to submit evidence concerning the extra expenses to the arbitration panel, had failed so to do, and was not entitled to any further opportunity in that regard. As to the interest amount, however, the district court proceeded on the basis that the owner had not informed the charterer of the previously earned interest and that it was unfair to permit the owner to reap the benefit of such failure.

II.

In the within appeal, the owner takes the position that the district court had no power under 9 U.S.C. § 11 to modify or correct the award of the arbitration panel. In so doing, the owner seemingly contends that the last sentence of 9 U.S.C. § 11 does not create an independent basis for modification by the district court, and that the district court is empowered to make such a modification only if the provisions of one of subparagraphs (a), (b) or (c) are met. In this instance, it is not necessary for this court to reach that question because there were, within the meaning of subsection (a), material mistakes made in the arbitration proceeding as to interest on the bond and, according to the owner, as to other expenses. True, those errors were made, in the first place, primarily by the owner in not presenting all of the relevant and material facts and, secondarily, perhaps, by the charterer, at least insofar as the charterer did not seek information from the owner concerning whether or not the collateral for the bond earned interest. Those errors were apparently not the fault of the arbitrators. If they had been, relief under 9 U.S.C. § 11(a) would have been available.

But that does not also mean that where there is "an evident material mistake" attributable to one or both parties to an arbitration, a district court lacks power under subsection (a) to do equity and justice. Thus, the court below was right in reaching and correctly determining the interest issue. However, that court should also have reached and determined the additional expenses issue. On a common sense basis, a district court can so proceed without requiring the parties to return to the arbitrators.

Accordingly, we affirm the district court's determination as to the interest item and remand the within cases to the district court for determination of the extra-expense issue in accordance with this opinion.

AFFIRMED IN PART AND REMANDED IN PART

Notes and Questions

1. How does *Transnitro* deal with the "face of the award" test that you reviewed in *Mid-Atlantic*? Did the Court even consider it, or look to documents submitted post-award?

2. *Mistake by Whom?* It does not appear that the arbitrator made a mistake. The award was based on evidence then before the arbitrator and did not misconstrue that evidence. Instead, the mistake developed later. As the court found:

   > True, those errors were made, in the first place, primarily by the owner in not presenting all of the relevant and material facts and, secondarily, perhaps, by the charterer, at least insofar as the charterer did not seek information from the owner concerning whether or not the collateral for the bond earned interest. Those errors were apparently not the fault of the arbitrators.

   Is that mistake, as the *Transnitro* court found? Or is it instead fraud by one party that is better dealt with not by Section 11 but by the fraud language in Section 10(a)(4)? Does this open the floodgates to post-award evidentiary submissions?

3. Should Section 11 be read expansively to "do equity" as *Transnitro* suggests? Do you read Section 11 to allow for an equitable as opposed to a rigid consideration of the award? How does this square with the view you have several times read that arbitration should be efficient? Is there a trade-off between efficiency and equity?

II. *Functus Officio* and Its Limits

Much of the uncertainty in the above cases could have been eliminated if the parties could have returned to the arbitrator(s) instead of having to fight out in court what the arbitrators "meant" to do.

Wouldn't it be easier to return to the arbitrator for a direct explanation? Yes, but the arbitration is over. And not just "over" in the colloquial sense, but rather, legally and definitively over. Just as the arbitration courthouse had to be built at the beginning of the arbitration, so does that courthouse vanish upon issuance of the award. The arbitrator did not exist, juridically, before the dispute and she does not exist after it. Since arbitration is a matter of contract, the arbitrator only exists for purposes of resolving a claim under that contract. Unlike a courthouse, which continues to occupy its location and juridically exist after a judgment, an arbitrator is held to vanish. The issuance of the arbitrator's award terminates her existence.

The Latin term for this vanishing is *functus officio*. So let us return again to *Batpow*: if the arbitrator is *functus officio*, can a party faced with an apparent math error contact the arbitration tribunal to ask for reconsideration and correction? Or must counsel instead pursue Section 11 remedies—mindful, given *Mid Atlantic*, that these remedies might fail if the error is not absolutely obvious on the face of the award?

The following case considers the borders of *functus officio* and when the rule might—and should be—relaxed.

Gen. RE Life Corp. v. Lincoln Nat'l Life Ins. Co.

909 F.3d 544 (2d Cir. 2018)

POOLER, Circuit Judge:

General Re Life Insurance Corporation appeals from the March 31, 2017 ruling and order of the United States District Court for the District of Connecticut (Bolden, J.) denying its petition to confirm an arbitration award and granting the cross-petition of Lincoln National Life Insurance Company to affirm the award issued after the arbitral panel clarified the original award. General Re argues that the doctrine of functus officio—which limited the power of arbitrators to alter an award once the arbitrators have decided the issue—barred the arbitral panel here from clarifying how the parties were to calculate the amount of the award. Today we recognize an exception to functus officio: where an arbitration award is ambiguous, we hold that the arbitrators retain their authority to clarify that award. We agree with the district court that the arbitrators correctly exercised their authority in handing down the clarification at issue here.

DISCUSSION

A district court's authority to vacate an award "is strictly limited in order to facilitate the purpose underlying arbitration: to provide parties with efficient dispute resolution, thereby obviating the need for protracted litigation." *T.Co. Metals*, 592 F.3d at 342 (internal quotation marks omitted). The party moving to vacate an award "bears the heavy burden of showing that the award falls within a very narrow set of circumstances delineated by statute and case law." *Wallace v. Buttar*, 378 F.3d 182, 189 (2d Cir. 2004) (internal quotation marks omitted).

General Re argues that the arbitration panel exceeded its powers in issuing the Clarification because after issuing the Final Award, the arbitral panel was functus officio. "The functus officio doctrine dictates that, once arbitrators have fully exercised their authority to adjudicate the issues submitted to them, their authority over those questions is ended, and the arbitrators have no further authority, absent agreement by the parties, to redetermine those issues." *T.Co. Metals*, 592 F.3d at 342 (internal quotation marks and brackets omitted). "The traditional rationale underlying this rule is that it is necessary to prevent reexamination of an issue by a nonjudicial officer potentially subject to outside communication and unilateral influence." *LLT Int'l Inc. v. MCI Telecomms. Corp.*, 69 F. Supp. 2d 510, 515 (S.D.N.Y. 1999) (internal quotation marks omitted).

We join the Third, Fifth, Sixth, Seventh, and Ninth Circuits in recognizing an exception to functus officio where an arbitral award "fails to address a contingency that later arises or when the award is susceptible to more than one interpretation." *Sterling China Co. v. Glass, Molders, Pottery, Plastics & Allied Workers Local No. 24*, 357 F.3d 546, 554 (6th Cir. 2004) (internal quotation marks omitted); *Brown v. Witco Corp.*, 340 F.3d 209, 219 (5th Cir. 2003) ("An arbitrator can . . . clarify or construe an arbitration award that seems complete but proves to be ambiguous in its scope and implementation."); *Glass, Molders, Pottery, Plastics & Allied Workers Int'l Union v. Excelsior Foundry Co.*, 56 F.3d 844, 847 (7th Cir. 1995) (same); *Colonial Penn. Ins. Co. v. Omaha Indem. Co.*, 943 F.2d 327, 334 (3d Cir. 1991) ("[W]hen the remedy awarded by the arbitrators is ambiguous, a remand for clarification of the intended meaning of an arbitration award is appropriate."); *McClatchy Newspapers v. Central Valley Typographical Union No. 46*, 686 F.2d 731, 734 n.1 (9th Cir. 1982) (same).

Adopting this exception to functus officio furthers the well-settled rule in this Circuit that when asked to confirm an ambiguous award, the district court should instead remand to the arbitrators for clarification. *See Hyle v. Doctor's Assocs., Inc.*, 198 F.3d 368, 370 (2d Cir. 1999) ("[A] district court can remand an award to the arbitrator for clarification where an award is ambiguous."); *N.Y. Bus Tours, Inc. v. Kheel*, 864 F.2d 9, 12 (2d Cir. 1988) ("When an arbitration award provides no clear instruction as to how a court asked to enforce the award should proceed, the court should remand to the arbitrator for guidance."). An arbitrator does not become functus officio when it issues a clarification of an ambiguous final award as long as three conditions are satisfied: (1) the final award is ambiguous; (2) the clarification merely clarifies the award rather than substantively modifying it; and (3) the clarification comports with the parties' intent as set forth in the agreement that gave rise to arbitration. This narrowly drawn rule ensures that in those circumstances where an arbitral body issues an ambiguous award and must issue a clarification, it will do so in keeping with the twin objectives of arbitration: "settling disputes efficiently and avoiding long and expensive litigation." *Willemijn Houdstermaatschappij, BV v. Standard Microsystems Corp.*, 103 F.3d 9, 12 (2d Cir. 1997).

General Re argues that none of the relevant conditions are satisfied here. The Final Award provided in relevant part that:

> All premium and claim transactions paid by one party to the other following the effective date of the recapture (*i.e.*, from April 1, 2014) shall be unwound.

General Re argues this language unambiguously provides that General Re return all monies for premiums paid by Lincoln after the April 1, 2014 date, and Lincoln return all monies paid for claims by General Re, and the relationship between the two ends.

We find no ground to disturb the arbitrators' conclusion that the Final Award was ambiguous as to the disposition of the Unearned Premiums. While perhaps not dispositive, the arbitrators' finding of ambiguity is due deference, as is the norm with arbitral awards. *See Porzig v. Dresdner, Kleinwort, Benson, N. Am. LLC*, 497 F.3d 133, 138 (2d Cir. 2007) ("This Court has repeatedly recognized the strong deference appropriately due arbitral awards and the arbitral process, and has limited its review of arbitration awards in obeisance to that process."). Here, each party offered a different interpretation of what the language at issue meant, and the arbitral panel said it meant something else altogether. Given that the language is susceptible to multiple meanings, it is ambiguous. *See, e.g., York Research Corp. v. Landgarten*, 927 F.2d 119, 123 (2d Cir. 1991) ("We are unable to determine whether the arbitrators intended the word 'expenses' to include attorneys' fees. For this reason, we remand that portion of the case to the district court with instructions to seek clarification from the arbitrators.").

Notes and Questions

1. Was this a math error? Was this obvious on the face of the award? Or was the arbitrator's decision simply unclear?
2. Can you reconcile *General Re* with *Mid Atlantic*?
3. Separately, how many times should parties be allowed to return to the arbitrators? Does this flexibility allow arbitrators to be less than exacting in their awards?

Verizon Pa. LLC v. Communications Workers of Am., Local 1300

No. 18-394, 2020 U.S. Dist. LEXIS 54595 (E.D. Pa. Mar. 30, 2020)

RUFE, J.

Plaintiff Verizon Pennsylvania LLC filed suit pursuant to Section 301 of the Labor Management Relations Act against Communications Workers of America, AFL-CIO, Local 13000 and District 2-13 ("Union" or "CWA") seeking to vacate the award issued by the majority of a tripartite arbitration board. Both Verizon and the Union now move for summary judgment. For the reasons that follow, both motions will be granted in part and denied in part, and the award will be vacated and remanded to the arbitration board for a new calculation of remedies.

I. BACKGROUND

Since 1943, Verizon and CWA have entered into successive Collective Bargaining Agreements ("CBA") that set forth the terms and conditions of employment for Verizon employees in Pennsylvania. The CBA that applies to this matter was in effect from 2003–2008. Section 17.01 of the CBA provides that "[t]he Company will maintain its established policies as to the assignment of work in connection with the installation and maintenance of communications facilities owned, maintained and operated by the Company." The CBA also includes a grievance and arbitration procedure to resolve disputes between the parties.

In late 2006, Verizon began offering "FiOS TV." To receive FiOS TV, a customer must have a set top box connected to their television. How the set top boxes reached customers' homes and who installed them is at the heart of this case. Initially, either Verizon Service Technicians—members of the Union—delivered and installed the set top boxes or customers picked up a set top box from a local service center and installed it themselves. In 2007, Verizon introduced a new option: delivery by a common carrier such as UPS with the customer then installing the box.

In 2008, the CWA filed a grievance contesting this new option, alleging that Verizon's change in the established work practice for the delivery and installation of set top boxes violated Section 17.01 of the CBA. The parties were unable to resolve the issue through the grievance process, and the dispute was submitted to a tripartite arbitration board. In the Merits Award, the Panel directed Verizon to cease and desist from delivering set top boxes to customers by anyone other than a member of the bargaining unit, referred the issue of remedies back to the parties, and retained jurisdiction in case the parties could not agree on a monetary remedy.

Verizon then filed suit seeking to vacate the award. Because the award was not complete, the Honorable Gerald J. Pappert granted the Union's motion to dismiss without prejudice. Verizon then ceased delivering set top boxes to Pennsylvania customers by common carrier. However, instead of returning delivery duties to Service Technicians, Verizon created a new position, titled Assistant Technician, to perform deliveries for customer self-installation. The Assistant Technicians were members of the bargaining unit.

The Union and Verizon were unable to reach an agreement on the monetary remedy. Therefore, following briefs and hearings on the matter, the Panel issued a Supplemental Award setting forth the remedy ("Remedy Award"). The Remedy Award directed Verizon to return the delivery, installation, and maintenance of set top boxes, except where a customer picks up the box, to the Service Technicians. The Remedy Award further issued a monetary remedy based on the number of set top box shipments and deliveries, other than those performed by customers, to be calculated at the non-overtime rate of two hours per delivery at the top step wage rate.

Verizon then filed this action seeking to vacate the Merits and Remedy Awards, asserting laches; manifest disregard of the CBA; arbitrator bias; invalid punitive damages; and the doctrine of *functus officio*. After the Union's motion to dismiss was denied, the Union answered the Complaint and asserted a counterclaim for confirmation of the Awards. Both parties have now filed motions for summary judgment.

E. *Functus* Officio

Functus officio (Latin for "a task performed") is a shorthand term for a common-law doctrine barring an arbitrator from revisiting the merits of an award once it has issued. The doctrine is motivated by a perception that arbitrators, lacking the institutional protection of judges, may be more susceptible to outside influences pressuring for a different outcome and also by the practical concern that the ad hoc nature of arbitral tribunals makes them less amenable to re-convening than a court. Although the doctrine was applied strictly at common law . . . the federal courts have been less strict in applying the [doctrine] in reviewing labor disputes.

There are three recognized exceptions to the doctrine:

(1) an arbitrator "can correct a mistake which is apparent on the face of [her] award";

(2) "where the award does not adjudicate an issue which has been submitted, then as to such issue the arbitrator has not exhausted [her] function and it remains open to [her] for subsequent determination"; and

(3) "[w]here the award, although seemingly complete, leaves doubt whether the submission has been fully executed, an ambiguity arises which the arbitrator is entitled to clarify."

Verizon argues that the Remedy Award improperly revisited the Merits Award with regard to: 1) "Customer Self-Installation"; 2) "Use of Bargaining Unit Employees to Deliver Set-Top Boxes"; 3) "Customer Deliveries Included in Monetary Award"; 4) "Time Included in Computing Monetary Award"; and 5) "Deliveries Subject to Monetary Award."

A conflict exists between the decisions: the Merits Award explicitly held that customer installation did not violate the CBA while the Remedy Award barred such installation unless the customer personally transported the set top box to her home. By its terms, the Merits Award permitted delivery by a Union technician with installation by the customer, while the Remedy Award foreclosed that option. Accordingly, the injunction barring any customer self-installation can only stand if one of the exceptions to *functus officio* applies.

Verizon argues that the doctrine of *functus officio* barred the requirement in the Remedy Award that only Service Technicians could perform deliveries while the Union argues that the Remedy Award merely clarified the Merits Award.

In this regard, the Merits Award was "subject to at least two interpretations." In Verizon's view, the violation of the CBA lay in its outsourcing of delivery to non-Union members, and the Merits Award therefore only required that it use any Union member to deliver the set top boxes. The Union advances the equally plausible interpretation that the Merits Award required Verizon to return delivery to the category of workers who had performed delivery prior to Verizon's violation of the CBA, the Service Technicians. The Merits Award explained that Service Technicians had always delivered set top boxes to customer homes. Because the position of Assistant Technician was created after the Merits Award was issued, there was no need for the Merits Award to explicitly state that only Service Technicians could deliver set top boxes. Therefore, the Panel was entitled to clarify this ambiguity in the Remedy Award.

The Merits Award is undoubtedly ambiguous, if not outright contradictory. While the injunction indicates that all delivery—whether or not the customer self-installed—was covered by the CBA, some of the reasoning and language in the decision limits violations of the CBA to delivery where a Service Technician performs the installation. In the Remedy Award, the Panel cleared up the ambiguity and unequivocally held that all deliveries were bargaining unit work and that the remedy was based on all deliveries. Considering the ambiguity in the Merits Award, the Panel's clarification in the Remedy Award that the Union would be compensated for all deliveries performed by common carriers was not improper.

IV. CONCLUSION

For the foregoing reasons, the arbitration award in this matter is confirmed in part and vacated in part. Specifically, the Merits Award is confirmed and the Remedy Award is vacated. This matter is remanded for calculation of a remedy consistent with this opinion and shall be arbitrated before the arbitration panel.

Notes and Questions

1. Was there an error in the arbitration award? Or just an ambiguity? Should Section 11 apply to interpretive disputes about precisely what the arbitrator meant? If so, does that open the floodgates to merits appeals disguised in the sheep's clothing of Section 11 motions? If not, then how are the parties supposed to interpret an ambiguous award?
2. *What If Nobody Is Home Anymore?* The *Verizon* court treated the arbitration panel like an appellate court would treat a district court, and "remanded" the case: "This matter is remanded for calculation of a remedy consistent with this opinion and shall be arbitrated before the arbitration panel." But an arbitration panel does not sit there like a district court. Arbitrators can be busy, scheduled people. What if Arbitrator Jones agreed to hear the case, arranged her schedule appropriately, wrote the award, and is now off in California on four weeks of witness and trial preparation on a case of her own? What if Arbitrator Smith has finally taken that long-awaited trip to Australia and New Zealand and is not reachable? The practice pointer here is that, when faced with an error, parties need to act promptly. It is good practice to check with the arbitrators as to their availability and their plans. This should be done delicately, of course, to avoid suggesting that an ambiguous or mistaken award is expected!

III. Confidentiality

Arbitration is private. In this respect it differs greatly from litigation. Absent extreme circumstances, anybody can wander into a courtroom and watch the proceedings. We have become accustomed in modern times to television cameras in courtrooms. Any judgment is publicized virtually immediately and is accessible at the clerk's office (in the old days) and online (today).

Not so with arbitration. The pleadings and document productions are confidential. The hearings are closed to all but parties, lawyers, and witnesses. The award is released only to the parties and not to the public. To take us back to Chapter 1 and the choice between arbitration and litigation as the parties' preferred mode of dispute resolution, this veil of privacy, indeed of secrecy, is often a reason a party may decide on arbitration. It keeps the dirty laundry private.

Or does it? All arbitrations may start off as private, but they may not all remain confidential. Think of the cases in this and the previous chapter. Consider the detail in which the reviewing court, on a Section 10 application to vacate, went into the detail of the awards. They remained anything but confidential.

How can and how should confidentiality be balanced with post-award proceedings under Sections 9, 10, and 11? Must the entire award be published? Is arbitration's purported confidentiality simply a fig leaf that lasts only as long as the court challenge to it? If that's the case, what's the point of confidentiality in the first place? Is an aggrieved party faced with a Hobson's choice of publishing and publicizing his loss, by virtue of a motion to vacate, or else suffering silently by not filing the vacatur so as to avoid publicizing the loss?

The party seeking Section 9 confirmation can simply refer to the award without attaching it to the confirmation motion. But the party seeking Section 10 vacatur, or section 11 correction, has no such option since that party must persuade the court that the award offends one or more of the vacatur bases in the statute. Will a court accept a motion party under seal, where the party seeking vacatur does not file publicly the award itself? But even so, how is the court's decision then supposed to deal with the sealed award?

This can result, in some cases, of a game of chicken: a party seeking vacatur may tell the other party that it is about to initiate a vacatur motion unless the parties otherwise privately settle their differences about the contested award. Is this a good or bad thing? Are there other ways to balance the parties' confidentiality rights with their section 10 rights?

CASE PREVIEW. In the following case, the parties thought that their proceedings might be confidential and thus barred from the public. They were wrong.

Century Indem. Co. v. AXA Belgium

2012 U.S. Dist. LEXIS 136472 (S.D.N.Y. Sept. 24, 2012)

FURMAN, United States District Judge:

On October 14, 2011, Petitioners Century Indemnity Company, ACE INA Insurance ("ACE INA"), ACE American Insurance Company, and ACE Property and Casualty Insurance Company (collectively, "Petitioners" or "ACE") commenced this action, petitioning the Court pursuant to the Convention on the Recognition and Enforcement of Foreign Arbitral Awards of June 10, 1958 (the "Convention"), 9 U.S.C. §§ 201–208, to confirm three arbitral awards (the "Awards") against Respondent AXA Belgium ("Respondent"). On December 5, 2011, Respondent cross-petitioned to vacate the Awards under the Convention and the Federal Arbitration Act ("FAA"), 9 U.S.C. §§ 1–16. (Docket No. 19). In addition to filing these petitions, the parties have filed three motions to seal documents in light of a confidentiality agreement covering the arbitration.

For the reasons stated below, the petition to confirm the arbitration awards is GRANTED, the cross-petition to vacate the arbitration awards is DENIED, and the motions to seal are DENIED.

III. THE MOTIONS TO SEAL

As noted, in addition to the cross-petitions to confirm and vacate the arbitral awards, the Court has before it three motions—two by AXA and one by Petitioners—for leave to file certain documents under seal. Specifically, AXA seeks to seal portions of its Answer/Cross-Pet.; its Memorandum and Reply Memorandum of Law; and certain exhibits to its Answer/Cross-Pet., including Award Two, the Panel's Final Award and the dissent therefrom, its Petition to Modify, Petitioners' Brief in Opposition to the Petition to Modify, and correspondence with the Panel concerning the events at issue in the present action. Petitioners wish to seal portions of their Answer; their Memorandum and Reply Memorandum of Law; and exhibits to their Reply Memorandum of Law, including the prior arbitral award, the parties' pre-hearing position statements and briefs, the transcript of the January 2011 hearing, the parties' proposed final awards, Award One, and e-mails concerning matters at issue in the arbitration.

The parties request leave to file these documents under seal pursuant to a confidentiality agreement they entered, which provides that certain "Arbitration Information"—including "all briefs, depositions, and hearing transcripts generated in the course of this arbitration" as well as any "final award and any interim decisions"—shall remain confidential. The agreement acknowledges that such Arbitration Information may be disclosed in connection with a judicial proceeding to confirm, modify, or vacate an arbitration award, but provides that "the parties agree, subject to court approval, that all submissions of Arbitration Information to a court shall be sealed."

The question presented is whether these requests to seal are consistent with the well-established common law right of access to "judicial documents." That right, which is "firmly rooted in our nation's history," is "'based on the need for federal courts, although independent—indeed, particularly because they are independent—to have a measure of accountability and for the public to have confidence in the administration of justice.'" *Lugosch v. Pyramid Co. of Onondaga*, 435 F.3d 110, 119 (2d Cir. 2006) (quoting *United States v. Amodeo*, 71 F.3d 1044, 1048 (2d Cir. 1995) ("*Amodeo II*")). The right applies, however, only to "judicial documents." *See id.* Thus, the first step in the necessary inquiry is to determine whether the documents at issue "are indeed 'judicial documents.'" *Id.* As the Second Circuit has made clear, "the mere filing of a paper or document with the court is insufficient to render that paper a judicial document subject to the right of public access." *Id.* (quoting *United States v. Amodeo*, 44 F.3d 141, 145 (2d Cir. 1995) ("*Amodeo I*")). Instead, "[i]n order to be designated a judicial document, 'the item filed must be relevant to the performance of the judicial function and useful in the judicial process.'" *Id.* (quoting *Amodeo I*, 44 F.3d at 145).

If the item at issue is a "judicial document," the court must then determine the weight of the presumption of access. *See id.* As the Second Circuit has explained:

> [T]he weight to be given the presumption of access must be governed by the role of the material at issue in the exercise of Article III judicial power and the resultant value of such information to those monitoring the federal courts. Generally, the information will fall somewhere on a continuum from matters that directly affect an adjudication to matters that come within a court's purview solely to insure their irrelevance.

Id. (quoting *Amodeo II*, 71 F.3d at 1049). In the final step of the analysis, "the court must 'balance competing considerations against [the presumption of access].' Such countervailing factors include but are not limited to 'the danger of impairing law enforcement or judicial efficiency' and 'the privacy interests of those resisting disclosure.'" *Id.* at 120 (quoting *Amodeo II*, 71 F.3d at 1050).

Applying this test here, the parties have not shown a sufficient basis to seal the relevant documents. First, the documents sought to be sealed, which include the arbitral awards under review and portions of the parties' pleadings here, are indisputably judicial documents to which the presumption of access attaches.

Second, although the "public interest in the relationship between an insurer and its reinsurers is relatively low," the weight to be given the presumption of access here is reasonably high, at least as to some of the documents at issue. At a minimum, as the discussion of the cross-petitions above makes clear, the pleadings and the arbitration decisions at issue directly affected the Court's adjudication of the case.

Finally, the parties have not identified sufficient countervailing factors to overcome the presumption in favor of access. Indeed, like the respondent in *Church Insurance Co.*, the parties here argue "merely that disclosure 'is inconsistent with, and would undermine the objectives of the parties' Confidentiality Agreement and the reinsurance arbitration process in general.'" *Church Ins. Co.*, 2010 U.S. Dist. LEXIS 109774, 2010 WL 3958791, at *3. As the Court held in *Church Insurance Co.*, however, the "'mere existence of a confidentiality agreement' . . . does not demonstrate that sealing is necessary."

At bottom, the confidentiality agreement at issue in this case may be binding on the parties, but it is not binding upon the Court. And while parties to an arbitration are generally "permitted to keep their private undertakings from the prying eyes of others," the "circumstance changes when a party seeks to enforce in federal court the fruits of their private agreement to arbitrate, *i.e.* the arbitration award." *Global I*, 2008 U.S. Dist. LEXIS 121632, 2008 WL 126976, at *1; *see also, e.g.*, *Global II*, 2008 U.S. Dist. LEXIS 32419, 2008 WL 1805459, at *2 ("In circumstances where an arbitration award is confirmed, the public in the usual case has a right to know what the Court has done.").

IV. CONCLUSION

For the reasons discussed above, Petitioners' petition to confirm the Awards is GRANTED, Respondent's cross-petition to vacate the Awards is DENIED, and the parties' motions to seal are all DENIED.

PRACTICE POINTER. Here again, the parties can, and should, build their own courthouse. In institutional arbitrations, the parties, together or separately, can apply for an order from the arbitrator that the proceedings *and all documents and materials produced in the disclosure stage* are confidential:

AAA, Commercial Arbitration Rule 23

Enforcement Powers of the Arbitrator. The arbitrator shall have the authority to issue any orders necessary to enforce the provisions of rules R-21 and R-22 and to otherwise achieve a fair, efficient and economical resolution of the case, including, without limitation: (a) conditioning any exchange or production of confidential documents and information, and the admission of confidential evidence at the hearing, on appropriate orders to preserve such confidentiality. . . .

Does this rule appropriately address the outcome the parties wanted to avoid in *Century Indemnity*? Likely yes, because the parties agreed to institutional rules, and those rules continue the arbitrator's mandate for enforcement purposes. Consider as well, though, whether there would remain functus officio problems in the continuation of that mandate, or again, legalities aside, whether the same arbitrators were soon available.

But what if the parties have not made that arrangement? The following case shows the dangers.

Contship Containerlines, Ltd. v. PPG Indus., Inc.

2003 U.S. Dist. LEXIS 6857 (S.D.N.Y. Apr. 23, 2003)

PITMAN, United States Magistrate Judge:

Defendant, PPG Industries, Inc. ("PPG"), moves in these two consolidated actions to compel the production of certain documents exchanged between the plaintiffs in an arbitration involving the same incident that gives rise to this litigation. For the reasons set forth below, the motion is granted.

This is an action for damages arising out of a fire that occurred aboard the Contship France in the fall of 1997. Conti Zweite Cristallo Schiffarhrts GMBH & Co. ("Conti Zweite") is the owner of the Contship France; Contship Containerlines, Ltd. ("Contship") was the charterer of the vessel at the time of the fire.

In September 1997, PPG loaded four containers of calcium hypochlorite on board the Contship France in Norfolk, Virginia. PPG had manufactured the calcium hypochlorite, packaged it in drums and loaded the drums into the containers at its plant in West Virginia. These containers were then loaded onto the ship and placed in the lower cargo hold number 3. On October 15, 1997, while the ship was docked in Papeete, Tahiti, there was an explosion and fire in the lower cargo hold number 3. After the fire was extinguished, the ship was removed to Singapore for repairs. Conti Zweite and Contship claim here that PPG's calcium hypochlorite caused and/or contributed to the explosion and fire.

Conti Zweite and Contship filed claims against each other concerning their respective losses in an arbitration proceeding in London, and it is the documents generated in the course of that arbitration that give rise to the present motion. In response to PPG's request for all documents that comprise the record in that arbitration, Conti Zeite and Contship have produced here the documentary evidence that was submitted in the arbitration. They have not produced (1) expert submissions; (2) correspondence with the panel of arbitrators; (3) briefs and other submissions to the panel and (4) hearing transcripts. Conti Zweite and Contship claim that the four categories of materials that have been withheld are protected by the confidentiality that attached to the London arbitration proceedings and the work product doctrine. Neither argument is convincing.

The origin of the alleged confidentiality cited by Conti Zweite and Contship is not entirely clear. Neither has cited any contractual provision between them giving rise to an obligation of confidentiality, nor do they cite a regulation of any arbitral body as the source of confidentiality. Rather, they claim that, under English law, an obligation of confidentiality is implied in law as part of their agreement to arbitrate. *Insurance Co. v. Lloyd's Syndicate,* [1995] Vol. 1 Lloyd's Rep. 272, 274–75 (Q.B.); *Hassneh Ins. Co. v. Mew,* [1993] 2 Lloyd's L. Rep. 243, 246–47 (Q.B.).

Even if I assume that plaintiffs' contention as to the state of English law is correct, it does not preclude the disclosure sought here. The identical argument was rejected in *Caringal v. Karteria Shipping, Ltd.*, 2001 U.S. Dist. LEXIS 1312, No. Civ. A. 99-3159, 2001 WL 874705 (E.D. La. 2001):

> The Court has considered *Hassneh* and its progeny, but finds nothing in this line of cases from Great Britain that undermines the principle that the Court may order disclosure when appropriate. Even if documents are confidential, a Court may order disclosure if (1) the documents are relevant and (2) "disclosure is necessary for disposing fairly of the cause or matter or for saving costs." *Hassneh,* 2 Lloyd's Rep. at 250. However, the *Hassneh* court did note that disclosure in the absence of a court order may place a party at considerable risk of being accused at a later date by other participants in the arbitration of improper disclosure. In light of this reality, the Court understands why Karteria has sought review of Magistrate Shushan's order prior to disclosing the relevant documents. However, the Court finds that Magistrate Shushan properly determined that the arbitration documents should be produced.

2001 U.S. Dist. LEXIS 1312, 2001 WL 874705 at *1. *See also United States v. Panhandle E. Corp.*, 118 F.R.D. 346, 349–51 (D. Del. 1988) (arbitration proceedings not confidential where there was no evidence that the parties had, in fact, agreed to hold the proceedings in confidence).

In this case, as in *Caringal,* the documents are undeniably relevant. They relate to the very incident that is in issue here. Their disclosure is also necessary for disposing of this matter fairly and inexpensively. The documents will add to the information available to the parties concerning the cause of the explosion and fire, effectively prevent plaintiffs from asserting positions here that are inconsistent with the positions taken in the arbitration and minimize the possibility of duplication of effort.

Accordingly, PPG's motion to compel disclosure is granted in all respects.

CLOSING PRACTICE POINTER ON ENFORCEMENT. While prior chapters have presented cases where courts vacated or modified arbitration awards, this is very much the exception rather than the rule. Arbitration is, more often than not, the "sudden-death" version of litigation. The parties bargain for arbitration precisely for this reason—and if they do not realize that fact, one of your jobs should be to make sure that they do. You can (and likely should) provide for a reasoned award, and if you see mistakes or fraud you should, obviously, call these to the arbitrator's attention as soon as possible. You and your client should not, however, be under any illusions that if you lose, this is just like appellate court and all you need do is show error. Arbitration may be more difficult to get going than a court case—the "build the courthouse" point we covered in Chapter 1—but it ends much more quickly. This is the bargain, and you and your clients should go into it with eyes appropriately wide open on that point.

Note. *AAA Arbitration Appeal.* In 2013, the American Arbitration Association promulgated new rules that allowed parties to opt-in to an appeal process that would take place entirely within the arbitration. The parties could, in their dispute resolution clause or in a separate written agreement at the beginning of their AAA arbitration, elect to commit the final award to a three-member arbitration panel. *Optional Appellate Arbitration Rules*, AAA, https://www.adr.org/sites/default/files/AAA-ICDR_Optional_Appellate_Arbitration_Rules.pdf.

The standards for appeal under this rule are less stringent than for an FAA Section 10 appeal. The most significant difference is that legal—and factual—error is a basis for appeal. Rule A-10 allows appeal for an "error of law that is material and prejudicial" and for "determinations of fact that are clearly erroneous."

The procedure is, as noted, entirely optional. Parties who commit to AAA arbitration are *not* then held to this process unless they separately opt in. So far, the response has been tepid.

Chapter Preview. *"Exceeding Powers" and Manifest Disregard.* We will examine in the next chapter whether there is an additional vacatur standard called "manifest disregard." There is, as you shortly will see, considerable debate within the circuit courts about whether or not this standard exists and, if so, whether it is simply an independent basis for review that stands out from the four enumerated grounds in Section 10(a) or whether it is simply, as some courts hold, a gloss on the "exceeding powers" standard in Section 10(a)(4).

Chapter 15

The Rise, Fall, and Uncertain Life of Manifest Disregard

When "building their own courthouse," the parties exercise a high degree of discretion. They can, as we have seen, decide on one arbitrator or three, on what rules will govern, on whether there should be discovery, on the form of the final award, and on a host of other features. They can, one supposes, mandate that at the hearing the arbitrators must all wear purple, or, perhaps less frivolously, that the arbitrators all be alumni of Cornell University.

It would therefore seem the most logical of preferences for parties who are attracted by arbitration's flexibility, but appalled by its tolerance for "wrong" awards, to customize their clause to control for bad results. One would think that the drafters could agree on an arbitration clause that provided for review of arbitration awards for legal error. This would be the height of party autonomy: parties who are content with the streamlined review provided for in Section 10 would proceed with arbitration on that basis, while parties who want a less deferential, more legal-based standard of review would add a "legal error" clause to their agreement. True, they would be exposing themselves to the likelihood of greater post-arbitration battles in the courts by essentially creating an appeal right—but they would have made this choice with eyes wide open.

They cannot do so. The United States Supreme Court, as we will see below, has prohibited parties from expanding the Section 10 bases for vacating an arbitration award. Party autonomy only goes so far.

Had the Court stopped there, the result would be perhaps surprising but still certain: Section 10 of the Federal Arbitration Act, no more and no less, governs appeals. Instead, at the same time, and in the same case in which the Court prohibited parties from supplementing the statutory grounds for review, the Court purposely left open the question of whether there existed an additional ground for vacatur based on an arbitrator's manifest disregard of the law. The Court in a single decision both confined and (potentially) expanded the grounds for challenging arbitration awards.

This has created substantial confusion on a critical question. Why would the Supreme Court leave open this of all questions when it has tackled so many other arbitration issues head on? It is not as if the question were obscure—far from it. Think of all the cases you have read about arbitration to this point in the book. Some are esoteric, some involve commonplace issues. But *every* case has a winner and a loser, and the loser's instinctive reaction is to examine what appellate paths remain open. Given an opportunity to clarify whether "manifest disregard" of the law is one of those paths, the Supreme Court has, in successive cases, inexplicably refused to shine that light. The result is that despite the explosion of arbitration cases at the Supreme Court and the lower courts in the post-*Prima Paint* era, there is considerable judicial uncertainty on one of the most basic questions to arise in any dispute: "Can I appeal?"

CASE PREVIEW. As you read *Hall Street,* consider that it has two very separate parts, each of them important and each distinct. Do you agree with none, one, or both?

Hall St. Assocs., L.L.C. v. Mattel, Inc.

552 U.S. 576 (2008)

JUSTICE SOUTER delivered the opinion of the Court:

The Federal Arbitration Act (FAA or Act), 9 U.S.C. §1 *et seq.*, provides for expedited judicial review to confirm, vacate, or modify arbitration awards. §§9–11 (2006 ed.) The question here is whether statutory grounds for prompt vacatur and modification may be supplemented by contract. We hold that the statutory grounds are exclusive.

This case began as a lease dispute between landlord, petitioner Hall Street Associates, L.L.C., and tenant, respondent Mattel, Inc. The property was used for many years as a manufacturing site, and the leases provided that the tenant would indemnify the landlord for any costs resulting from the failure of the tenant or its predecessor lessees to follow environmental laws while using the premises.

Tests of the property's well water in 1998 showed high levels of trichloroethylene (TCE), the apparent residue of manufacturing discharges by Mattel's predecessors between 1951 and 1980. After the Oregon Department of Environmental Quality (DEQ) discovered even more pollutants, Mattel stopped drawing from the well and, along with one of its predecessors, signed a consent order with the DEQ providing for cleanup of the site.

After Mattel gave notice of intent to terminate the lease in 2001, Hall Street filed this suit, contesting Mattel's right to vacate on the date it gave, and claiming that the lease obliged Mattel to indemnify Hall Street for costs of cleaning up the TCE, among other things. Following a bench trial before the United States District Court for the District of Oregon, Mattel won on the termination issue, and after an unsuccessful try at mediating the indemnification claim, the parties proposed to submit to arbitration. The District Court was amenable, and the parties drew up an arbitration agreement, which the court approved and entered as an order. One paragraph of the agreement provided that:

> [t]he United States District Court for the District of Oregon may enter judgment upon any award, either by confirming the award or by vacating, modifying or correcting the award. The Court shall vacate, modify or correct any award: (i) where the arbitrator's findings of facts are not supported by substantial evidence, or (ii) where the arbitrator's conclusions of law are erroneous.

Arbitration took place, and the arbitrator decided for Mattel. In particular, he held that no indemnification was due, because the lease obligation to follow all applicable federal, state, and local environmental laws did not require compliance with the testing requirements of the Oregon Drinking Water Quality Act (Oregon Act); that Act the arbitrator characterized as dealing with human health as distinct from environmental contamination.

Hall Street then filed a District Court Motion for Order Vacating, Modifying And/Or Correcting Arbitration Accord, on the ground that failing to treat the Oregon Act as an applicable environmental law under the terms of the lease was legal error. The District Court agreed, vacated the award, and remanded for further consideration by the arbitrator. The court expressly invoked the standard of review chosen by the parties in the arbitration agreement, which included review for legal error, and cited *LaPine Technology Corp. v. Kyocera Corp.*, 130 F.3d 884, 889 (CA 1997), for the proposition that the FAA leaves the parties "free . . . to draft a contract that sets rules for arbitration and dictates an alternative standard of review."

On remand, the arbitrator followed the District Court's ruling that the Oregon Act was an applicable environmental law and amended the decision to favor Hall Street. This time, each party sought modification, and again the District Court applied the parties' stipulated standard of review for legal error, correcting the arbitrator's calculation of interest but otherwise upholding the award. Each party then appealed to the Court of Appeals for the Ninth Circuit, where Mattel switched horses and contended that the Ninth Circuit's recent *en banc* action overruling *LaPine in Kyocera Corp. v. Prudential-Bache Trade Servs., Inc.*, 341 F.3d 987, 1000 (2003), left the arbitration agreement's provision for judicial review of legal error unenforceable. Hall Street countered that *Kyocera* (the later one) was distinguishable, and that the agreement's judicial review provision was not severable from the submission to arbitration.

The Ninth Circuit reversed in favor of Mattel in holding that, "[u]nder *Kyocera* the terms of the arbitration agreement controlling the mode of judicial review are unenforceable and severable." 113 Fed. Appx. 272, 272–273 (2004). The Circuit instructed the District Court on remand to "return to the application to confirm the original arbitration award (not the subsequent award revised after reversal), and . . . confirm that award, unless . . . the award should be vacated on the grounds allowable under 9 U.S.C. § 10, or modified or corrected under the grounds allowable under 9 U.S.C. § 11." *Id.* at 273.

After the District Court again held for Hall Street and the Ninth Circuit again reversed, we granted certiorari to decide whether the grounds for vacatur and modification provided by §§ 10 and 11 of the FAA are exclusive. 550 U.S. 968 (2007). We agree with the Ninth Circuit that they are, but vacate and remand for consideration of independent issues.

II

Congress enacted the FAA to replace judicial indisposition to arbitration with a "national policy favoring [it] and plac[ing] arbitration agreements on equal footing with all other contracts." *Buckeye Check Cashing, Inc. v. Cardegna,* 546 U.S. 440, 443 (2006). As for jurisdiction over controversies touching arbitration, the Act does nothing, being "something of an anomaly in the field of federal-court jurisdiction" in bestowing no federal jurisdiction but rather requiring an independent jurisdictional basis. *Moses H. Cone Memorial Hospital v. Mercury Constr. Corp.,* 460 U.S. 1, 25, n. 32 (1983); *see, e.g.,* 9 U.S.C. § 4 (providing for action by a federal district court "which, save for such [arbitration] agreement, would have jurisdiction under title 28"). But in cases falling within a court's jurisdiction, the Act makes contracts to arbitrate "valid, irrevocable, and enforceable," so long as their subject involves "commerce." § 2. And this is so whether an agreement has a broad reach or goes just to one dispute, and whether enforcement be sought in state court or federal. *See ibid.; Southland Corp. v. Keating,* 465 U.S. 1, 15–16 (1984).

The Act also supplies mechanisms for enforcing arbitration awards: a judicial decree confirming an award, an order vacating it, or an order modifying or correcting it. §§ 9–11. An application for any of these orders will get streamlined treatment as a motion, obviating the separate contract action that would usually be necessary to enforce or tinker with an arbitral award in court. § 6. Under the terms of § 9, a court "must" confirm an arbitration award "unless" it is vacated, modified, or corrected "as prescribed" in §§ 10 and 11. Section 10 lists grounds for vacating an award, while § 11 names those for modifying or correcting one.

The Courts of Appeals have split over the exclusiveness of these statutory grounds when parties take the FAA shortcut to confirm, vacate, or modify an award, with some saying the recitations are exclusive, and others regarding them as mere threshold provisions open to expansion by agreement. As mentioned already, when this litigation started, the Ninth Circuit was on the threshold side of the split, *see LaPine,* 130 F.3d at 889, from which it later departed *en banc* in favor of the exclusivity view, *see Kyocera,* 341 F.3d at 1000, which it followed in this case, *see* 113 Fed. Appx., at 273. We now hold that §§ 10 and 11 respectively provide the FAA's exclusive grounds for expedited vacatur and modification.

III

Hall Street makes two main efforts to show that the grounds set out for vacating or modifying an award are not exclusive, taking the position, first, that expandable judicial review authority has been accepted as the law since *Wilko v. Swan,* 346 U.S. 427 (1953). This, however, was not what *Wilko* decided, which was that § 14 of the Securities Act of 1933 voided any agreement to arbitrate claims of violations of that Act, *see id.*, at 437–438, a holding since overruled by *Rodriguez de Quijas v. Shearson/American Express, Inc.*, 490 U.S. 477, 484 (1989). Although it is true that the Court's discussion includes some language arguably favoring Hall Street's position, arguable is as far as it goes.

The *Wilko* Court was explaining that arbitration would undercut the Securities Act's buyer protections when it remarked (citing FAA § 10) that "[p]ower to vacate an [arbitration] award is limited," 346 U.S., at 436, and went on to say that "the interpretations of the law by the arbitrators in contrast to manifest disregard [of the law] are not subject, in the federal courts, to judicial review for error in interpretation," *id.*, at 436–4378. Hall Street reads this statement as recognizing "manifest disregard of the law" as a further ground for vacatur on top of those listed in § 10, and some Circuits have read it the same way. *See, e.g., McCarthy v. Citigroup Global Markets, Inc.*, 463 F.3d 87, 91 (CA 2006); *Hoeft v. MVL Group, Inc.*, 343 F.3d 57, 64 (CA 2003); *Prestige Ford v. Ford Dealer Computer Servs., Inc.*, 324 F.3d 391, 395–396 (CA 2003); *Scott v. Prudential Securities, Inc.*, 141 F.3d 1007, 1017 (CA 1998). Hall Street sees this supposed addition to § 10 as the camel's nose: if judges can add grounds to vacate (or modify), so can contracting parties.

But this is too much for *Wilko* to bear. Quite apart from its leap from a supposed judicial expansion by interpretation to a private expansion by contract, Hall Street overlooks the fact that the statement it relies on expressly rejects just what Hall Street asks for here, general review for an arbitrator's legal errors. Then there is the vagueness of *Wilko*'s phrasing. Maybe the term "manifest disregard" was meant to name a new ground for review, but maybe it merely referred to the § 10 grounds collectively, rather than adding to them. *See, e.g., Mitsubishi Motors Corp. v. Soler Chrysler-Plymouth, Inc.*, 473 U.S. 614, 656 (1985) (Stevens, J., dissenting) ("Arbitration awards are only reviewable for manifest disregard of the law, 9 U.S.C. §§ 10, 207"); *I/S Stavborg v. National Metal Converters, Inc.*, 500 F.2d 424, 431 (CA 1974). Or, as some courts have thought, "manifest disregard" may have been shorthand for § 10(a)(3) or § 10(a)(4), the paragraphs authorizing vacatur when the arbitrators were "guilty of misconduct" or "exceeded their powers." *See, e.g., Kyocera, supra,* at 997. We, when speaking as a Court, have merely taken the Wilko language as we found it, without embellishment, *see First Options of Chicago, Inc. v. Kaplan,* 514 U.S. 938, 942 (1995), and now that its meaning is implicated, we see no reason to accord it the significance that Hall Street urges.

Second, Hall Street says that the agreement to review for legal error ought to prevail simply because arbitration is a creature of contract, and the FAA is "motivated, first and foremost, by a congressional desire to enforce agreements into which parties ha[ve] entered." *Dean Witter Reynolds Inc. v. Byrd,* 470 U.S. 213, 220 (1985). But, again, we think the argument comes up short. Hall Street is certainly right that the FAA lets parties tailor some, even many, features of arbitration by contract, including the way arbitrators are chosen, what their qualifications should be, which issues are arbitrable, along with procedure and choice of substantive law. But to rest this case on the general policy of treating arbitration agreements as enforceable as such would be to beg the question, which is whether the FAA has textual features at odds with enforcing a contract to expand judicial review following the arbitration.

To that particular question we think the answer is yes, that the text compels a reading of the §§ 10 and 11 categories as exclusive. To begin with, even if we assumed §§ 10 and 11 could be supplemented to some extent, it would stretch basic interpretive principles to expand the stated grounds to the point of evidentiary and legal review generally. Sections 10 and 11, after all, address egregious departures from the parties' agreed-upon arbitration: "corruption," "fraud," "evident partiality," "misconduct," "misbehavior," "exceed[ing]. . . powers," "evident material miscalculation," "evident material mistake," "award[s] upon a matter not submitted;" the only ground with any softer focus is "imperfect[ions]," and a court may correct those only if they go to "[a] matter of form not affecting the merits." Given this emphasis on extreme arbitral conduct, the old rule of *ejusdem generis* has an implicit lesson to teach here. Under that rule, when a statute sets out a series of specific items ending with a general term, that general term is confined to covering subjects comparable to the specifics it follows. Since a general term included in the text is normally so limited, then surely a statute with no textual hook for expansion cannot authorize contracting parties to supplement review for specific instances of outrageous conduct with review for just any legal error. "Fraud" and a mistake of law are not cut from the same cloth.

That aside, expanding the detailed categories would rub too much against the grain of the § 9 language, where provision for judicial confirmation carries no hint of flexibility. On application for an order confirming the arbitration award, the court "must grant" the order "unless the award is vacated, modified, or corrected as prescribed in sections 10 and 11 of this title." There is nothing malleable about "must grant," which unequivocally tells courts to grant confirmation in all cases, except when one of the "prescribed" exceptions applies. This does not sound remotely like a provision meant to tell a court what to do just in case the parties say nothing else.

In fact, anyone who thinks Congress might have understood § 9 as a default provision should turn back to § 5 for an example of what Congress thought a default provision would look like:

> "[i]f in the agreement provision be made for a method of naming or appointing an arbitrator. . . such method shall be followed; but if no method be provided therein, or if a method be provided and any party thereto shall fail

> to avail himself of such method, . . . then upon the application of either party to the controversy the court shall designate and appoint an arbitrator. . . ."

"[I]f no method be provided" is a far cry from "must grant . . . unless" in § 9.

Instead of fighting the text, it makes more sense to see the three provisions, §§ 9–11, as substantiating a national policy favoring arbitration with just the limited review needed to maintain arbitration's essential virtue of resolving disputes straightaway. Any other reading opens the door to the full-bore legal and evidentiary appeals that can "rende[r] informal arbitration merely a prelude to a more cumbersome and time-consuming judicial review process," *Kyocera*, 341 F.3d at 998; *cf. Ethyl Corp. v. United Steelworkers of America*, 768 F.2d 180, 184 (CA 1985), and bring arbitration theory to grief in postarbitration process.

Nor is *Dean Witter*, to the contrary, as Hall Street claims it to be. *Dean Witter* held that state-law claims subject to an agreement to arbitrate could not be remitted to a district court considering a related, nonarbitrable federal claim; the state-law claims were to go to arbitration immediately. *Id.*, at 217. Despite the opinion's language "reject[ing] the suggestion that the overriding goal of the [FAA] was to promote the expeditious resolution of claims," *id.*, at 219, 105 S. Ct. 1238, 84 L. Ed. 2d 158, the holding mandated immediate enforcement of an arbitration agreement; the Court was merely trying to explain that the inefficiency and difficulty of conducting simultaneous arbitration and federal-court litigation was not a good enough reason to defer the arbitration, *see id.*, at 217.

When all these arguments based on prior legal authority are done with, Hall Street and Mattel remain at odds over what happens next. Hall Street and its amici say parties will flee from arbitration if expanded review is not open to them. One of amici foresees flight from the courts if it is. We do not know who, if anyone, is right, and so cannot say whether the exclusivity reading of the statute is more of a threat to the popularity of arbitrators or to that of courts. But whatever the consequences of our holding, the statutory text gives us no business to expand the statutory grounds.

While it is true that the agreement does not expressly invoke FAA § 9, § 10, or § 11, and none of the various motions to vacate or modify the award expressly said that the parties were relying on the FAA, the District Court apparently thought it was applying the FAA when it alluded to the Act in quoting *LaPine*, 130 F.3d at 889, for the then-unexceptional proposition that "'[f]ederal courts can expand their review of an arbitration award beyond the FAA's grounds, when . . . the parties have so agreed.'"

Although we agree with the Ninth Circuit that the FAA confines its expedited judicial review to the grounds listed in 9 U.S.C. §§ 10 and 11, we vacate the judgment and remand the case for proceedings consistent with this opinion.

It is so ordered.

Comment

As noted in the case introduction, *Hall Street* has two distinct parts: exclusivity and manifest disregard. We consider each in turn.

I. Should the Grounds for Arbitration Review Be Exclusive?

Arbitration is a continual back and forth dance between the courts and the arbitrator(s). The dance is particularly involved at the beginning and, as we now reach, the end. Court involvement is required in the beginning of the process where a party does not cooperate in commencing the arbitration, and so, as we have seen, Sections 3, 4 and 5 provide mechanisms to force the arbitration to take place. Where, however, parties cooperate in setting up and running their arbitration, there is no need at all for judicial involvement at the start. Many arbitrations commence and hum along without a court even knowing.

At the end, though, judicial involvement of at least some level is both required and prudent. Unless the losing party pays virtually on demand, it is wise to seek judicial confirmation of the award through Section 9, as reviewed in Chapter 13, before the one year to do so expires (and even long before), so the winning party has a judgment on record.

That means that the end-stage of arbitration creates at least an administrative burden for courts. This may be the sentiment behind *Hall Street*. The Supreme Court may have been protective of the lower courts in not wanting to expand this burden. Or, at a more exalted level, the Court may simply have not wanted to transform arbitration into what would ultimately be a court-controlled judicial exercise as to result. It again bears repeating that with limited exceptions, the "one-and-done" model is one of the distinctive features of arbitration versus litigation.

Problem

Would the result have been the same in *Hall Street* if the parties had agreed to a *lower* standard of judicial review of arbitration awards, rather than a heightened one? Consider, for example, the following provision:

> Notwithstanding anything to the contrary in federal or state law, including but not limited to Section 10 of the Federal Arbitration Act, the arbitrator's decision shall be final and no party shall object to its confirmation and enforcement.

Parties who agreed to this standard would be at the opposite end of the spectrum from those in *Hall Street*. Rather than wanting protection from legal error, they would have elected to insulate themselves from virtually any further proceedings at all. Other than the rubber stamp of confirmation, parties who agreed to the above language express in clear terms that they do not want judges mucking about in their private arbitration, and when it is over it is *truly* over. Rather than impose a higher ceiling (as in *Hall Street*) they would be lowering the floor. Why should this not be permissible? What in Hall Street *would* bar this? What in Hall Street *should* bar this?

A. *Hall Street* and Manifest Disregard: "Maybe"

Smack in the middle of deciding whether parties can create "legal error" as an additional standard of review under Section 10, the *Hall Street* court veered into discussion of a different standard: manifest disregard. Oddly, after floating the idea that manifest disregard might itself be a standard for review, the Court dropped the question without answering it:

> Maybe the term "manifest disregard" was meant to name a new ground for review, but maybe it merely referred to the § 10 grounds collectively, rather than adding to them. *See, e.g., Mitsubishi Motors Corp. v. Soler Chrysler-Plymouth, Inc.,* 473 U.S. 614, 656 (1985) (Stevens, J., dissenting) ("Arbitration awards are only reviewable for manifest disregard of the law, 9 U.S.C. §§ 10, 207"). Or, as some courts have thought, "manifest disregard" may have been shorthand for § 10(a)(3) or § 10(a)(4), the paragraphs authorizing vacatur when the arbitrators were "guilty of misconduct" or "exceeded their powers." We, when speaking as a Court, have merely taken the *Wilko* language as we found it, without embellishment.

For those who thought the "maybe" was less than clear, the Court's next opinion on the subject made things even murkier.

Two terms after *Hall Street,* the Supreme Court returned to the standards governing review of arbitration awards. This time, in *Stolt-Nielsen S.A. v. AnimalFeeds Int'l Corp.,* 559 U.S. 662 (2010), the Court revisited the *Greentree v. Bazzle* issue, *see* Chapter 3, of whether silence in an arbitration clause precluded or permitted a class action arbitration. There, the arbitrator had construed the parties' contract and found that an arbitration class action would be consistent with that contract. In the course of finding that the ultimate award violated Section 10(a), as reviewed in the last chapter, the Court dropped the following footnote: "We do not decide whether 'manifest disregard' survives our decision in *Hall Street Associates, L.L.C. v. Mattel, Inc.,* 552 U.S. 576, 585 (2008), as an independent ground for review or as a judicial gloss on the enumerated grounds for vacatur set forth at 9 U.S.C. sec. 10."

Not content with merely leaving this unresolved question wide open, the Court then added to the confusion by giving an example of when manifest disregard might apply *if* it existed: "*AnimalFeeds* characterizes that standard as requiring a showing that the arbitrators knew of the relevant [legal] principle, appreciated that this principle controlled the outcome of the disputed issue, and nonetheless willfully flouted the governing law by refusing to apply it. Assuming, arguendo, that such a standard applies, we find it satisfied for the reasons that follow." *Stolt-Nielsen,* 559 U.S. 672 at n.3.

That one-two punch has left the circuit courts reeling. The combination of the *Hall Street* opaque language on manifest disregard and *Stolt-Nielson*'s deliberate refusal to clarify that uncertainty has led to a full-blown, three-way circuit split. Some circuits consider manifest disregard dead, some consider it to thrive as an independent ground for vacatur, and some consider it alive, but merely a supplementary gloss on the exclusive statutory grounds.

B. Manifest Disregard Is Dead

The Fifth Circuit, which had previously been a manifest disregard jurisdiction, expanded on why this was no longer the case.

Citigroup Global Mkts. Inc. v. Bacon

562 F.3d 349 (5th Cir. 2009)

JOLLY, Circuit Judge:

An arbitration panel ordered Citigroup Global Markets to pay Debra Bacon $256,000. Citigroup moved the district court to vacate the award, and the district court obliged on the basis that the arbitrators had manifestly disregarded the law. On appeal, we consider whether manifest disregard of the law remains a valid ground for vacatur of an arbitration award in the light of the Supreme Court's recent decision in *Hall Street Associates, L.L.C. v. Mattel, Inc.*, 128 S. Ct. 1396, 1403 (2008). We conclude that *Hall Street* restricts the grounds for vacatur to those set forth in § 10 of the Federal Arbitration Act (FAA or Act), 9 U.S.C. § 1 *et seq.*, and consequently, manifest disregard of the law is no longer an independent ground for vacating arbitration awards under the FAA. *Hall Street* effectively overrules our previous authority to the contrary, so we must VACATE the district court's judgment and REMAND for reconsideration in accord with the exclusivity of the statutory grounds.

I.

Debra Bacon's quarrel with Citigroup began in 2002 when she discovered that her husband had withdrawn funds from her Citigroup Individual Retirement Accounts without her permission. By forging her signature, he made five withdrawals totaling $238,000. As soon as Bacon discovered the unauthorized withdrawals, she notified Citigroup. In 2004, Bacon submitted a claim in arbitration against Citigroup seeking reimbursement for the unauthorized withdrawals.

The arbitration panel granted Bacon $218,000 in damages and $38,000 in attorneys' fees. Citing § 10 of the FAA, Citigroup made an application to the district court requesting vacatur of the award.

The district granted the motion to vacate, holding that the award was made in manifest disregard of the law. The court based its holding on three grounds: (1) Bacon was not harmed by the withdrawals because her husband used the money for her benefit and subsequently promised to pay her back; (2) Bacon's claims were barred by Texas law, which permits such claims only if the customer reports the unauthorized transaction within thirty days of the withdrawal; and (3) Texas law requires apportionment among the liable parties, which, in this case, includes Bacon's husband.

Bacon appeals. We review *de novo* the vacatur of an arbitration award. *Kergosien v. Ocean Energy, Inc.*, 390 F.3d 346, 352 (5th Cir. 2004).

II

A.

Although *Hall Street* clearly has the effect of further restricting the role of federal courts in the arbitration process, there is nothing revolutionary about its holding.

Even when a submission agreement did not contain an express agreement to adhere to the decision of the arbitrators, courts implied such an agreement and enforced the awards as binding. *See Smith v. Morse,* 76 U.S. 76, 82 (1869) ("The law implies an agreement to abide the result of an arbitration from the fact of submission."). Although arbitration was binding and final, awards could be set aside in the following circumstances: (1) where the arbitrators engaged in fraud, corruption, or improper conduct; (2) where the arbitrators failed to decide all of the issues submitted; (3) where the arbitrators exceeded their powers by deciding issues not submitted; and (4) where the award was not certain, final, and mutual. *See Burchell,* 58 U.S. at 351 ((1) and (3)); *Carnochan v. Christie,* 24 U.S. 446, 460–67 ((2), (3), and (4)). These limited grounds are akin to the provisions of § 10 of the FAA.

III.

A.

The question before us now is whether, under the FAA, manifest disregard of the law remains valid, as an independent ground for vacatur, after *Hall Street.* The answer seems clear. *Hall Street* unequivocally held that the statutory grounds are the exclusive means for vacatur under the FAA. Our case law defines manifest disregard of the law as a *nonstatutory* ground for vacatur. *See Kergosien,* 390 F.3d at 353; *Prestige Ford,* 324 F.3d at 395; *Harris v. Parker Coll. of Chiropractic,* 286 F.3d 790, 792 (5th Cir. 2002). Thus, to the extent that manifest disregard of the law constitutes a nonstatutory ground for vacatur, it is no longer a basis for vacating awards under the FAA.

Four other circuits have considered this issue. The First Circuit, in dictum and with little discussion, concluded that *Hall Street* abolished manifest disregard of the law as a ground for vacatur. *See Ramos-Santiago v. United Parcel Serv.,* 524 F.3d 120, 124 n.3 (1st Cir. 2008) ("We acknowledge the Supreme Court's recent holding in *Hall Street Assocs., L.L.C. v. Mattel* that manifest disregard of the law is not a valid ground for vacating or modifying an arbitral award in cases brought under the [FAA]." (citations omitted)). The Sixth Circuit, in an unpublished opinion, reached the opposite conclusion by narrowly construing the holding of *Hall Street* to apply only to contractual expansions of the grounds for review. *Coffee Beanery, Ltd. v. WW, L.L.C.*, 300 Fed. Appx. 415, 418–19 (6th Cir. 2008). The Second Circuit has also held that manifest disregard survives *Hall Street*. *Stolt-Nielsen SA v. AnimalFeeds Int'l Corp.*, 548 F.3d 85, 93–95 (2d Cir. 2008). The court, however, recognized that *Hall Street's* holding was in direct conflict with the application of manifest disregard as a nonstatutory ground for review, but resolved the conflict by recasting manifest disregard as a shorthand for § 10(a)(4). *Id.* Finally, the Ninth Circuit has concluded that *Hall Street* did not abolish manifest disregard because its case law defined manifest disregard as shorthand for § 10(a)(4). *See Comedy Club Inc. v. Improv West Assocs.*, 553 F.3d 1277, 1290 (9th Cir. 2009) ("*Comedy Club II*"). We now turn to discuss the opinions of the Sixth, Second, and Ninth Circuits.

1.

Coffee Beanery only briefly considered the effect of *Hall Street* on manifest disregard of the law. 300 Fed. Appx. at 418–19. In what we view as an understatement, the Sixth Circuit acknowledged that *Hall Street* "significantly reduced the ability of federal courts to vacate arbitration awards for reasons other than those specified in 9 U.S.C. § 10." *Id.* at 418. Citing *Hall Street*'s discussion of *Wilko*, which *Coffee Beanery* thought demonstrated a "hesitation to reject the 'manifest disregard' doctrine," and noting the acceptance of the standard by each and every court of appeals, the court concluded that it would be imprudent to cease vacating arbitration awards made in manifest disregard of the law. *Id.* at 419.

This decision suffers from two significant flaws. First, the opinion utterly fails to address *Hall Street*'s express holding that the grounds for vacatur found in § 10 are exclusive. Instead, the court narrowly construed *Hall Street* as applying only to contractual expansions of the grounds for vacatur. *Id.* In the light of *Hall Street*'s repeated statements that "*We hold* that the statutory grounds are exclusive," we think it incorrect so narrowly to construe *Hall Street's* holding. 128 S. Ct. at 1400 (emphasis added).

Second, we believe that *Coffee Beanery* misread *Hall Street*'s discussion of *Wilko*. We do not see hesitation by *Hall Street* to reject manifest disregard of the law as an independent ground for vacating an award under the FAA; instead, *Hall Street*'s discussion of *Wilko* demonstrates the Supreme Court's unwillingness to give any significant meaning to *Wilko*'s vague language. *Hall Street* observed that *Wilko* dealt with an entirely separate issue and, noting the vagueness of *Wilko*'s statement, concluded that: "When speaking as a Court, we have taken the *Wilko* language as we found it, without embellishment, and now that its meaning is implicated, we see no reason to accord it the significance that [the petitioner] urges." *Id.* at 1404.

2.

Unlike *Coffee Beanery,* the Second Circuit in *Stolt-Nielsen* did not shy from *Hall Street's* holding. The court acknowledged that *Hall Street* "held that the FAA sets forth the 'exclusive' grounds for vacating an arbitration award." *Stolt-Nielsen,* 548 F.3d at 94. The court also recognized that this holding was in conflict with its own prior statements regarding manifest disregard, which the court discounted as dicta. *Id.* ("[*Hall Street*'s] holding is undeniably inconsistent with some dicta by this Court treating the 'manifest disregard' standard as a ground for vacatur entirely separate from those enumerated in the FAA."). Instead of directly concluding that *Hall Street* eliminated manifest disregard as a ground for vacatur under the FAA, the court reasoned that manifest disregard of the law should be "reconceptualized as a judicial gloss on the specific grounds for vacatur enumerated in section 10 of the FAA. . . ." *Id.*

Describing its "reconceptualization," the court stated:

> We must therefore continue to bear the responsibility to vacate arbitration awards in the rare instances in which "the arbitrator knew of the relevant [legal] principle, appreciated that this principle controlled the outcome of the disputed issue, and nonetheless willfully flouted the governing law by refusing to apply it." *Westerbeke,* 304 F.3d at 217. At that point the arbitrators have "failed to interpret the contract at all," *Wise,* 450 F.3d at 269, for parties do not agree in advance to submit to arbitration that is carried out in manifest disregard of the law. Put another way, the arbitrators have thereby "exceeded their powers, or so imperfectly executed them that a mutual, final, and definite award upon the subject matter submitted was not made." 9 U.S.C § 10(a)(4).

Stolt-Nielsen, 548 F.3d at 95. Thus, the court seems to conclude that manifest disregard—as the court describes it—does not add to the statutory grounds. The court simply folds manifest disregard into § 10(a)(4). In the full context of the Second Circuit's reasoning, this analysis is not inconsistent with *Hall Street's* speculation that manifest disregard may, among other things, "have been shorthand for § 10(a)(3) or § 10(a)(4) . . ." *Hall Street,* 128 S.Ct. at 1404.

We should be careful to observe, however, that this description of manifest disregard is very narrow. Because the arbitrator is fully aware of the controlling principle of law and yet does not apply it, he flouts the law in such a manner as to exceed the powers bestowed upon him. This scenario does not include an erroneous application of that principle.

B.

In the light of the Supreme Court's clear language that, under the FAA, the statutory provisions are the exclusive grounds for vacatur, manifest disregard of the law as an independent, nonstatutory ground for setting aside an award must be abandoned and rejected. Indeed, the term itself, as a term of legal art, is no longer useful in actions to vacate arbitration awards. *Hall Street* made it plain that the statutory language means what it says: "courts *must* [confirm the award] unless the award is vacated, modified, or corrected as prescribed in sections 10 and11 of this title," 9 U.S.C. § 9 (emphasis added), and there's nothing malleable about "must." *Hall Street*, 128 S. Ct. at 1405. Thus from this point forward, arbitration awards under the FAA may be vacated only for reasons provided in § 10.

To the extent that our previous precedent holds that nonstatutory grounds may support the vacatur of an arbitration award, it is hereby overruled.

CASE PREVIEW. The manifest disregard debate made its way into the dispute about Prince's estate after his untimely death. The district court, sitting in the Eighth Circuit, left no doubt that it considered the doctrine dead.

Paisley Park Enters. v. Boxill

371 F. Supp 3d 578 (D. Minn. 2019)

WRIGHT, District Court Judge:

Before the Court are cross motions to vacate and to confirm an arbitration award that was issued by Arbitrator Hon. Kathleen A. Blatz on August 31, 2018. Defendant George Ian Boxill moves to vacate the award, (Dkt. 365), and Plaintiffs move to confirm the award and enter final judgment, (Dkt. 397). For the reasons addressed below, the Court confirms the arbitration award and enters final judgment as described herein.

BACKGROUND

This matter pertains to the previously unreleased recordings of Prince Rogers Nelson (Prince), who died in April 2016. Plaintiffs are Paisley Park Enterprises, Inc., and Comerica Bank & Trust, N.A., as Personal Representative of the Estate of Prince Rogers Nelson. Defendant Boxill is a sound engineer who worked with Prince during his recording career. The other Defendants include Rogue Music Alliance, LLC; Deliverance, LLC; David Staley; Gabriel Solomon Wilson; and Sidebar Legal, PC. Plaintiffs contend that Defendants unlawfully possess and have attempted to exploit commercially several sound recordings of Prince.

Plaintiffs initiated this lawsuit in April 2017, asserting breach-of-contract, conversion, and copyright claims. Plaintiffs filed a demand for arbitration of the breach-of-contract and conversion claims, which correspond to Counts 2 and 3 of Plaintiffs' third amended complaint. Boxill moved to enjoin the arbitration, arguing that copyright law preempted arbitration of the breach-of-contract and conversion claims. But the Court denied Boxill's motion to enjoin the proceedings. The Arbitrator conducted an evidentiary hearing and determined that copyright law did not preempt the matter. The Arbitrator issued an interim award in favor of Plaintiffs as to their breach-of-contract and conversion claims and held that the Prince Estate was entitled to damages and the return of the disputed recordings. The final award, issued on August 31, 2018, includes additional relief to Plaintiffs for reasonable attorneys' fees and costs. Now pending before the Court are cross motions to vacate and confirm the arbitration award.

ANALYSIS

I. Arbitration Award

Boxill seeks to vacate, and Plaintiffs seek to confirm, the arbitration award. When reviewing an arbitration award, a district court affords "an extraordinary" degree of deference to the underlying award. Even if an arbitrator makes an error of law or fact, the error does not constitute an arbitrator exceeding her powers. When a district court does not vacate or modify the arbitration award, the court must confirm the award. 9 U.S.C. § 9.

Section 10 contains the *exclusive* bases for vacating an arbitration award. *See Hall Street.* After the decision of the Supreme Court of the United States in *Hall Street,* the Eighth Circuit no longer recognizes the judicially created "manifest disregard" basis for vacatur, which allowed a district court to vacate an arbitration award when an arbitrator exhibited a manifest disregard of the law.

Boxill first asserts that the Arbitrator manifestly disregarded copyright law when she decided Plaintiffs' claims on the merits. But because a district court lacks the authority to vacate an arbitration award based on an arbitrator's manifest disregard of the law, Boxill's argument is unavailing.

Comment

Agreeing with the Fifth Circuit, the Seventh, Eighth, and Eleventh Circuits also interpret *Hall Street* to mean that manifest disregard is no longer a valid basis for vacatur. *See Quezada v. Bechtel OG & C Constr. Servs.*, F.3d 837 (5th Cir. 2020); *Crosby v. Sears Holding Corp.*, No. 15 C 6396, 2018 U.S. Dist. LEXIS 45182 (N.D. Ill. Mar. 20, 2018); *Med. Shoppe Intern., Inc. v. Turner Invs., Inc.* 614 F.3d 485 (8th Cir. 2010); *Frazier v. Citifinancial Corp., LLC*, 604 F.3d 1313 (11th Cir. 2010) ("We hold that our judicially-created bases for vacatur are no longer valid in light of *Hall Street*.").

C. Manifest Disregard Is Alive

Some circuits, in the wake of *Hall Street*, still consider manifest disregard to be a basis for vacating an arbitration award. These courts generally describe manifest disregard as a judicial gloss on § 10(a).

We begin with these courts' struggle to define manifest disregard.

ExxonMobil Oil Corp. v. TIG Ins., Co.

2020 U.S. Dist. LEXIS 87407 (S.D.N.Y. May 18, 2020)

RAMOS, District Judge:

Over three years after the Court stayed this action and ordered the parties to arbitration, the Court is now faced with ExxonMobil Oil Corporation's ("Mobil") motion to lift the stay and confirm the arbitral award, and TIG Insurance Company's ("TIG") cross-motion to vacate that award.

Mobil's motion asks the Court to confirm the award and to enter a final judgment that includes pre-judgment interest.

TIG moves to vacate the arbitral tribunal's decision on the grounds that in defining a key term in the underlying insurance agreement, the arbitral tribunal stated that its analysis was "guided by applying common speech and the reasonable expectation and purpose of the ordinary businessman to determine the intent of the parties," an interpretive method long-used by New York courts in interpreting insurance agreements. TIG claims this interpretive principle is based on *contra proferentum* and is therefore contrary to the dictates in parties' contract that the policy be construed in an "evenhanded" manner.

For the reasons stated below, Mobil's motion is GRANTED and TIG's is DENIED.

I. BACKGROUND

The underlying dispute arises out of a number of lawsuits against Mobil seeking damages for contamination involving methyl tertiary butyl ether ("MTBE"), a gasoline additive Mobil once used. At least some of the alleged contamination arose from leaks from underground storage tanks at service stations.

II. LEGAL STANDARD

The Federal Arbitration Act provides a "streamlined" process for a party seeking "a judicial decree confirming an award, an order vacating it, or an order modifying or correcting it." *Hall St. Assocs., L.L.C. v. Mattel, Inc.*, 552 U.S. 576, 582 (2008). District courts "treat a petitioner's application to confirm or vacate an arbitral award as akin to a motion for summary judgment." *City of New York v. Mickalis Pawn Shop, LLC*, 645 F.3d 114, 136 (2d Cir. 2011) (quotation marks omitted).

Under the FAA, a court "must grant" a petition to confirm an arbitral award "unless the award is vacated, modified, or corrected as prescribed in [the FAA]."

Confirmation of an arbitration award is thus "a summary proceeding that merely makes what is already a final arbitration award a judgment of the court." This "severely limited" review promotes the twin goals of arbitration, namely to settle disputes efficiently and avoid long and expensive litigation.

Conversely, the showing required to avoid confirmation is very high. The party moving to vacate an award bears "the heavy burden of showing that the award falls within a very narrow set of circumstances delineated by statute and case law."

In addition, as "judicial gloss" on these specific [FAA] grounds for vacatur, the Second Circuit has held that "the court may set aside an arbitration award if it was rendered in manifest disregard of the law." *Schwartz v. Merrill Lynch & Co., Inc.*, 665 F.3d 444, 451 (2d Cir. 2011) (internal quotation marks omitted). "A litigant seeking to vacate an arbitration award based on alleged manifest disregard of the law bears a heavy burden, as awards are vacated on grounds of manifest disregard only in those exceedingly rare in stances where some egregious impropriety on the part of the arbitrator is apparent." *Weiss v. Sallie Mae, Inc.*, 939 F.3d 105, 109 (2d Cir. 2019) (quoting *T.Co Metals, LLC v. Dempsey Pipe & Supply, Inc.*, 592 F.3d 329, 339 (2d Cir. 2010). An arbitral award will be upheld under this standard "so long as 'the arbitrator has provided even a barely colorable justification for his or her interpretation of the contract.'" *Id.* (quoting *Schwartz v. Merrill Lynch & Co.*, 665 F.3d at 452).

III. DISCUSSION

A. TIG's Motion to Vacate

TIG argues the Award should be vacated because the Tribunal "manifestly disregarded the law."

The Second Circuit has adopted a three part test to analyze such a claim: (1) the Court "must consider whether the law that was allegedly ignored was clear, and in fact explicitly applicable to the matter before the arbitrators;" (2) the Court considers whether "the law was in fact improperly applied, leading to an erroneous outcome;" and (3) once the two previous inquiries are satisfied, the Court looks to "a subjective element, that is, the knowledge actually possessed by the arbitrators," and whether the arbitrator knew of the existence of the law and its "applicability to the problem before him" *Duferco Int'l Steel Trading v. T. Klaveness Shipping A/S*, 333 F.3d 383, 389–90 (2d Cir. 2003) (internal citations omitted).

To briefly summarize the issue here, the Tribunal was tasked with deciding whether the activity Mobil sought coverage for, leaks from underground storage tanks at service stations, "aros[e] out of the end-use of goods or products manufactured, sold, tested, handled or distributed by [Mobil]." (Award ¶¶ 97–118 .) The parties provided the Tribunal with different meanings of the term "end-use," one, proposed by Mobil, that included the relevant activity and one, proposed by TIG, that excluded it. The Tribunal rejected the interpretation offered by both parties, deciding "end-use" "to be the instant when the product, MTBE-treated gasoline, has made its way to the end of its distribution process and is the ultimate finished product available for purchase and use by an end user," a definition which would include the leaks from the service stations at issue here and lead to a result in Mobil's favor. (Award ¶103.)

TIG objects to this decision because the Policy provides that "its terms are to be construed in an 'even-handed' fashion, with no presumptions in favor of either party," an interpretive methodology which, TIG argues, the Tribunal did not follow. Specifically, TIG argues that in interpreting "end-use," the Tribunal stated that its analysis was "guided by applying common speech and the *reasonable expectation and purpose of the ordinary businessman*" (emphasis in TIG's brief). TIG contends that this principle "is based on law that adopts *contra proferentum* as a means of interpreting ambiguous language in a contract" and is therefore not "evenhanded."

TIG's argument has no merit.

CASE PREVIEW. The Fourth Circuit considered manifest disregard in the particular context of an arbitrator's interpretation of a release and found that the award manifestly disregarded that document.

Dewan v. Walia

544 Fed. App'x 240 (4th Cir. 2013)

PER CURIAM:

Kiran Dewan and his close corporation, Kiran M. Dewan, CPA, P.A. ("the Company") (collectively, "Appellants"), appeal from the district court's confirmation of an arbitral award in favor of the Company's former employee, Appellee Arun Walia. Walia came to the United States from Canada in 2003 on an employment visa to work for the Company as an accountant. By 2009, the parties agreed to a parting of the ways, in connection with which Walia executed a broadly worded Release Agreement ("the Release") in consideration for the Company's payment of $7,000.

The parting proved less than amicable. In January 2010, Appellants filed a demand for arbitration against Walia, alleging that Walia breached the noncompetition/non-solicitation provisions in his employment agreement. Despite the Release, Walia asserted numerous counterclaims in the arbitral forum, primarily alleging that the Company had underpaid him during his employment and that Appellants had run afoul of federal immigration law attendant to the visa program. The Arbitrator found in favor of Walia on Appellants' original claims. She also concluded, however, that the Release was valid and enforceable, but nevertheless made a substantial monetary award in Walia's favor, holding Appellants jointly and severally liable.

In due course, the parties filed opposing petitions to vacate and to confirm/enforce the award in federal district court. The district court confirmed the award and granted Walia's motion for attorney's fees and costs.

For the reasons that follow, we hold that the award in favor of Walia is the product of a manifest disregard of the law by the Arbitrator. Accordingly, we vacate the judgment and remand to the district court with instructions to vacate the award.

I.

A.

Walia, a Canadian national, came to the United States in 2003 on an employment visa to work for the Company as an accountant. He entered into a three-year employment agreement. In 2006, Walia and the Company entered into a second three-year employment agreement ("the 2006 Employment Agreement") extending through March 23, 2009. The 2006 Employment Agreement included nonsolicitation and noncompetition provisions, as well as a broad arbitration provision. Dewan signed it in his capacity as president of the Company.

In February and March 2009, Walia underwent treatment for thyroid cancer. On approximately March 14, 2009 (as the termination date for the 2006 Employment Agreement approached), the Company's office manager, Veena Sindwani (who was also Dewan's wife), went to the intensive care unit to see Walia. The parties dispute the events occurring in the hospital. Walia contended (and the Arbitrator later found) that Sindwani presented him with a new employment agreement, which he signed. Appellants contended that no such agreement existed.

In any event, Walia continued to work for the Company through at least August 21, 2009. The parties vigorously dispute the circumstances surrounding the termination of Walia's employment. This much is undisputed: Though no termination letter was ever sent to Walia, on November 3, 2009, Walia executed the Release, which "release[d] and discharge[d]" Appellants from claims related to Walia's employment in exchange for $7,000. The Release provided for "binding arbitration" should a dispute arise concerning the Release or its performance. As with the 2006 Employment Agreement, Dewan signed it in his capacity as president of the Company.

B.

Less than three months after Walia executed the Release, on January 29, 2010, Dewan initiated arbitration proceedings against Walia with the American Arbitration Association. Dewan asserted that Walia "breached an employment agreement by competing with and soliciting the clients of the employer," and "breached a settlement and release agreement by making various claims against the Employer (Claimant)."

Walia asserted several counterclaims. He alleged, among other things, that (1) based on his years of accounting experience he was underpaid (in apparent violation of the relevant immigrant work visa regulations) during his time at the Company; (2) the Company breached the profit-sharing terms of the 2006 Employment Agreement; and (3) Dewan, Walia's immigration attorney of record, fraudulently sought to withdraw Walia's employment authorization.

On November 18, 2011, the Arbitrator issued a final award ("the Final Award"). The Arbitrator first recounted a series of developments since the Interim Award. These included a finding that Dewan "was a party to fraud" based on the differences between documents obtained by Walia through FOIA requests and documents provided in discovery. The Arbitrator then awarded Walia $387,108.20 in compensatory damages and $70,000 in punitive damages, and found that Dewan and the Company were jointly and severally liable for the combined $457,108.20.

On December 16, 2012, Appellants filed an amended complaint in their previously filed federal court action challenging the Final Award. Eventually thereafter, Walia filed a petition to confirm and enforce the Final Award.

On appeal from the district court's evaluation of an arbitral award, "[w]e review the district court's findings of fact for clear error and its conclusions of law, including its decision to vacate [or confirm] an arbitration award, de novo." *Raymond James Fin. Servs., Inc. v. Bishop*, 596 F.3d 183, 190 (4th Cir. 2010).

Appellants argue, among other things, that the arbitration award must be vacated because it is the product of the Arbitrator's manifest disregard of the law. Specifically, they contend that the Arbitrator could not find the Release valid and enforceable but nevertheless make an award to Walia on claims arising out of his employment with the Company. We are constrained to agree.

"The permissible common law grounds for vacating such an award 'include those circumstances where an award fails to draw its essence from the contract, or the award evidences a manifest disregard of the law.'" *MCI Constructors*, 610 F.3d at 857. "Under our precedent, a manifest disregard of the law is established only where the 'arbitrator[ ] understand[s] and correctly state[s] the law, but proceed[s] to disregard the same.'" *Patten v. Signator Ins. Agency, Inc.*, 441 F.3d 230, 235 (4th Cir. 2006). Merely misinterpreting contract language does not constitute a manifest disregard of the law. *Id.* An arbitrator may not, however, disregard or modify unambiguous contract provisions. *Id.* "Moreover, an award fails to draw its essence from the agreement if an arbitrator has 'based his award on his own personal notions of right and wrong.' . . . In such circumstances, a federal court has 'no choice but to refuse enforcement of the award.'" *Id.* (citations omitted).

Here, Walia agreed to "release and discharge" Appellants from claims related to Walia's employment in exchange for $7,000. The expansive breadth and scope of the Release are plainly reflected in its plain language, which we set forth in full:

> 3. Release. EMPLOYEE, on behalf of himself and his representatives, spouse, agents, heirs and assigns releases and discharges COMPANY and COMPANY'S former, current or future officers, employees, repre-

> sentatives, agents, fiduciaries, attorneys, directors, shareholders, insurers, predecessors, parents, affiliates, benefit plans, successors, heirs, and assigns from any and all claims, liabilities, causes of action, damages, losses, demands or obligations of every kind and nature, whether now known or unknown, suspected or unsuspected, which EMPLOYEE ever had, now has, or hereafter can, shall or may have for, upon or by reason of any act, transaction, practice, conduct, matter, cause or thing or any kind whatsoever, relating to or based upon, in whole or in part, any act, transaction, practice or conduct prior to the date hereof, including but not limited to matters dealing with EMPLOYEE'S employment or termination of employment with the COMPANY, or which relate in any way to injuries or damages suffered by EMPLOYEE (knowingly or unknowingly). This release and discharge includes, but is not limited to, claims arising under federal, state and local statutory or common law, including, but not limited to, the Age Discrimination in Employment Act ("ADEA"), Title VII of the Civil Rights Act of 1964, claims for wrongful discharge under any public policy or any policy of the COMPANY, claims for breach of fiduciary duty, and the laws of contract and tort; and any claim for attorney's fees. EMPLOYEE promises never to file a lawsuit or assist in or commence any action asserting any claims, losses, liabilities, demands, or obligations released hereunder.
>
> 4. Known or Unknown Claims. The parties understand and expressly agree that this AGREEMENT extends to all claims of every nature and kind, known or unknown, suspected or unsuspected, past, present, or future, arising from or attributable to any conduct of the COMPANY and its successors, subsidiaries, and affiliates, and all their employees, owners, shareholders, agents, officers, directors, predecessors, assigns, agents, representatives, and attorneys, whether known by EMPLOYEE or whether or not EMPLOYEE believes he may have any claims and that any and all rights granted to EMPLOYEE under the Annotated Code of Maryland or any analogous state law or federal law or regulations, are hereby expressly WAIVED.

As noted above, the Release provided for "binding arbitration" should a dispute arise concerning the Release or its performance.

In the Interim Award, the Arbitrator rejected Walia's argument that the Release was unconscionable. She then found that Walia

> knew he was signing a release and chose to sign it. However, he did not know the legal consequences nor the significance of his signature. However, he voluntarily signed it but without consulting an attorney and is now legally bound. Accordingly, all [Walia's] rights for all tort and contractual claims in federal or state courts as well as attorney's fees are now waived.

The Arbitrator also found that Walia had negotiated the checks "for the composite amount of the Release . . . J.A. 66; *see also* J.A. 69 ("All claims involving Solicitation, Covenant not to Compete and unauthorized release of Confidential Data from the Claimant's CPA firm are dismissed except for the valid execution of the Release (2009) based on Maryland law. Accordingly, [Walia] is precluded from bringing all tort and contractual claims in state and federal courts as well as being precluded from receiving attorney's fees.").

In sum, the Arbitrator appears to have concluded that the Release sufficed to extinguish Walia's common law and state and federal statutory claims if they were brought in state or federal court, but did not extinguish some or all of such claims if they were brought in an arbitral forum. We find untenable the Arbitrator's attempt to parse the language of the Release so finely.

We agree with Appellants that in purporting to construe "the release and waiver provision to apply only to tort and contractual claims Walia might file in federal or state court," the Arbitrator "rewr[ote] the release, which expressly 'includes, but is not limited to, claims arising under federal, state and local statutory or common law,' and imposes no qualifications whatsoever concerning the forum in which those released claims could have been brought." We have no doubt that Maryland law accords with Appellants' contentions. *See Herget v. Herget*, 319 Md. 466, 573 A.2d 798, 801 (Md. 1990) (stating that a broad settlement agreement purporting to release all claims, whether known or unknown, is enforceable); *Bernstein v. Kapneck*, 290 Md. 452, 430 A.2d 602, 606 (Md. 1981).

The Arbitrator's finding that the Release was valid and enforceable forecloses all of Walia's arguments on appeal that the Release was unconscionable. We do not know how the Arbitrator reached her interpretation of the Release. However, it is clear to us that neither linguistic gymnastics, nor a selective reading of Maryland contract law, could support her conclusion that the Release was enforceable but that Walia's claims were arbitrable anyway.

Objectively viewed, the language of the Release could not be more expansive, clear, or unambiguous. The plain language of the Release fatally undermines the suggestion that Walia retained the right to bring any of his counterclaims in arbitration. The Release waived all claims stemming from his employment relationship with the Company, regardless of forum. Accordingly, we hold that the Arbitrator manifestly disregarded the law by holding the Release valid and enforceable but nevertheless arbitrating Walia's counterclaims arising out of his employment with the Company.

IV.

For the reasons set forth, we vacate the judgment and remand with instructions that the district court vacate the award.

Notes and Questions

1. The Fourth Circuit found it too much to bear that the arbitrator did not honor a broad release. The Fourth Circuit also found unacceptable the apparent distinction that the release permitted claims in arbitration but not in any other forum. Assume that the release was in fact deserving of as broad enforcement as the majority in *Dewan* found, but that you find yourself litigating this question in a circuit where manifest disregard is dead after *Hall Street* (*see* below). Would you have any arguments for vacatur on these facts under the four subsections of FAA Section 10(a)? As we have seen, most merits challenges such as this one end up being shoehorned under Section 10(a)(4)'s "exceeded his powers" language—would *Dewan* so qualify?

2. Did the arbitrator really "disregard" the release? Or was the release very much part of the arbitration award? The arbitrator found factual issues of concern, finding that the employee "did not know the legal consequences nor the significance of his signature." One could have proceeded from that finding to overturn the binding nature of the release on the basis of classic contract arguments, such as capacity or adhesion. The arbitrator's mistake was in not doing so but instead in finding the release enforceable and binding anyway, as a matter of contract law, but then trying an end run around this by allowing actions in tort. The reviewing court properly squelched that on a manifest disregard basis—but what if the arbitrator had not tried the end run and simply held the release invalid and unenforceable? Would that rise to manifest disregard? Or would that simply be a contract ruling entirely within the arbitrator's mandate?

3. Assume that the arbitrator had simply stated, "I don't like this release and have decided not to enforce it." Assume further a no-manifest disregard jurisdiction. Would there be any opportunity to challenge the award?

CASE PREVIEW: *Dewan* rests on contract law and what the Fourth Circuit considered to be plain language. As the majority in *Dewan* held, "neither linguistic gymnastics, nor a selective reading of Maryland contract law, can support the arbitrator's finding." What if, beyond an arbitrator simply reading a contract incorrectly as in *Dewan*, the arbitrator's ruling ran directly against public policy? The Ninth Circuit considered this situation post-*Hall Street* in the next case.

Comedy Club, Inc. v. Improv West Assocs.

553 F.3d 1277 (9th Cir. 2009)

GOULD, Circuit Judge:

On June 13, 1999, Comedy Club, Inc. and Al Copeland Investments, Inc. (collectively "CCI") executed a Trademark License Agreement ("Trademark Agreement") with Improv West Associates ("Improv West") that granted CCI an exclusive nationwide license to use Improv West's trademarks. A few years later, CCI breached the agreement and sought to protect its interests in the trademarks in federal district court by filing a declaratory judgment action. After a complex procedural history, the parties were left with an arbitration award and two district court orders, one order compelling the parties to arbitrate, and another order confirming the arbitration award. CCI appealed both district court orders. We have jurisdiction under 28 U.S.C. § 1291.

In a prior opinion, published at 514 F.3d 833, we determined that we lacked jurisdiction to review the district court's order compelling arbitration. We affirmed in part and vacated in part the district court's order confirming the arbitration award. The Supreme Court vacated that opinion and remanded this case to us for reconsideration in light of *Hall Street Associates L.L.C. v. Mattel, Inc.*, 128 S. Ct. 1396 (2008). We determine that *Hall Street Associates* does not undermine our prior precedent, *Kyocera Corp. v. Prudential-Bache T. Servs,* 341 F.3d 987 (9th Cir. 2003) (en banc). As a result, in this circuit, an arbitrator's manifest disregard of the law remains a valid ground for vacatur of an arbitration award under § 10(a)(4) of the Federal Arbitration Act. Therefore, we adhere to the outcome in our prior decision.

I.

Improv West is the founder of the Improv Comedy Club and the creator and owner of the "Improv" and "Improvisation" trademarks ("Improv marks"). CCI owns and operates restaurants and comedy clubs nationwide. On June 13, 1999, CCI and Improv West entered a Trademark Agreement that provided, *inter alia:* (1) that Improv West granted CCI an exclusive nationwide license to use the Improv marks in connection with the opening of new comedy clubs; (2) that, according to a development schedule, CCI was to open four Improv clubs a year in 2001 through 2003; and (3) that CCI was prohibited from opening any non-Improv comedy clubs during the term of the Trademark Agreement. The Trademark Agreement also had an arbitration clause:

> All disputes relating to or arising under this Agreement or the Asset Purchase Agreement shall be resolved by arbitration in Los Angeles, California in accordance with the commercial arbitration rules of the American Arbitration Association. In any such arbitration, the parties shall be entitled to discovery in the same manner as if the dispute was being litigated in Los Angeles Superior Court. Notwithstanding this agreement to arbitrate, the

> parties, in addition to arbitration, shall be entitled to pursue equitable remedies and agree that the state and federal courts shall have exclusive jurisdiction for such purpose and for the purpose of compelling arbitration and/or enforcing any arbitration award. The parties agree to submit to the jurisdiction of such courts and agree that service of process in any such action may be made by certified mail. The prevailing party in any arbitration or action to enforce this Agreement or the Asset Purchase Agreement shall be entitled to its costs, including reasonable attorneys fees.

CCI concedes that it failed to open eight Improv clubs by 2002, and that it was in default of amended § 12.a. of the Trademark Agreement. Consistent with Improv West's sole remedy, as stated in § 13.b., Improv West sent CCI a letter asserting that CCI was in default of the Trademark Agreement, withdrawing CCI's license to use the Improv marks and rights to open more Improv clubs, and informing CCI that Improv West intended to begin opening its own Improv clubs.

In response to Improv West's letter, CCI filed a complaint in federal district court seeking declaratory relief. CCI's complaint sought a declaration that the covenant that CCI could not open any non-Improv comedy clubs was void under California Business and Professions Code ("CBPC") § 16600, and that CCI's failure to meet the development schedule did not revoke CCI's license to the Improv marks or right to open Improv clubs. Improv West then filed a demand for arbitration seeking damages.

On August 2, 2004, the district court ordered the parties to arbitrate their dispute. CCI did not appeal that order until May 16, 2005. On February 28, 2005, the arbitrator entered a Partial Final Arbitration Award that stated: (1) that CCI defaulted on the Trademark Agreement by failing to adhere to the development schedule listed in amended § 12.a.; (2) that CCI forfeited its rights to open Improv clubs and its use of the Improv marks license in connection with any clubs not open or under construction as of October 15, 2002; (3) that Improv West could open or license to third parties new Improv clubs; (4) that § 9.j. of the Trademark Agreement was "a valid and enforceable in-term covenant not to compete" and remained valid "for the remaining term of the Agreement"; (5) that CCI and its "Affiliates" were enjoined from opening or operating any other comedy clubs other than those open or under construction as of October 15, 2002 for the duration of the Trademark Agreement; (6) that neither CCI nor its Affiliates could change the name on any of its current clubs; and (7) that Improv West was entitled to attorneys fees and costs. On April 14, 2005, the district court confirmed the Partial Award. CCI timely appealed, tendering to us the issues addressed in this opinion.

In an opinion filed on September 7, 2007 and amended on January 23, 2008, we held that we did not have jurisdiction to review the district court's order compelling the parties to arbitrate; that the arbitrator did not exceed his authority by arbitrating the equitable claims; that the arbitrator did exceed his authority by issuing permanent injunctions that enjoined relatives who were not parties to the agreement; that the arbitrator's award was not completely irrational; and that the arbitrator's enforcement of the covenant not to compete was a manifest disregard for the law. The Supreme Court granted a petition for a writ of certiorari, vacated our prior opinion, and remanded this case to us to reconsider our decision in light of *Hall Street Associates v. Mattel.*

Both parties agree that this remand only affects the portion of the prior opinion in which we found the arbitrator acted with a "manifest disregard of the law." Therefore, we continue to hold that we do not have jurisdiction over the district court's order compelling arbitration. We also determine that the arbitrator did not exceed his authority when he arbitrated the equitable claims, but that he exceeded his authority regarding the permanent injunction that enjoined non-parties to the agreement. We also decide that the arbitrator's award was not completely irrational. Finally, addressing the issue raised by the Supreme Court's remand, we conclude that *Hall Street Associates* did not undermine the manifest disregard of law ground for vacatur, as understood in this circuit to be a violation of § 10(a)(4) of the Federal Arbitration Act, and that the arbitrator manifestly disregarded the law.

III.

We address CCI's claim that the partial arbitration award should be vacated because it is in violation of CBPC § 16600. CCI argues that the arbitrator's validation of § 9.j. is in manifest disregard of the law. Improv West counters that after the recent Supreme Court case, *Hall Street Associates,* 128 S. Ct. 1396 (2008), manifest disregard of the law is not a valid ground for vacatur. In *Hall Street Associates,* the Supreme Court held that the FAA provided exclusive grounds to modify or vacate an arbitration award. *Id.* at 1404. Improv West argues that manifest disregard of the law is not among the statutory grounds for vacatur, and therefore we must amend our prior opinion that vacated this part of the arbitrator's award for that reason.

We have already determined that the manifest disregard ground for vacatur is shorthand for a statutory ground under the FAA, specifically 9 U.S.C. § 10(a)(4), which states that the court may vacate "where the arbitrators exceeded their powers." *Kyocera Corp. v. Prudential-Bache TServs.,* 341 F.3d 987, 997 (9th Cir. 2003) (en banc) (holding that "arbitrators 'exceed their powers' . . . when the award is 'completely irrational,' or exhibits a 'manifest disregard of law'") (citations omitted). The Supreme Court did not reach the question of whether the manifest disregard of the law doctrine fits within §§ 10 or 11 of the FAA. *Hall Street Associates,* 128 S. Ct. at 1404. Instead, it listed several possible readings of the doctrine, including our own. We cannot say that *Hall Street Associates* is "clearly irreconcilable" with Kyocera and thus we are bound by our prior precedent. Therefore, we conclude that, after *Hall Street Associates,* manifest disregard of the law remains a valid ground for vacatur because it is a part of § 10(a)(4). We note that we join the Second Circuit in this interpretation of *Hall Street Associates. Stolt-Nielsen Transportation,* 548 F.3d 85, 96 (2d Cir. 2008). *But see Ramos-Santiago v. UPS,* 524 F.3d 120, 124 n.3 (1st Cir. 2004).

We have stated that for an arbitrator's award to be in manifest disregard of the law, "[i]t must be clear from the record that the arbitrator[ ] recognized the applicable law and then ignored it." *Mich. Mut. Ins. Co. v. Unigard Sec. Ins. Co.*, 44 F.3d 826, 832 (9th Cir. 1995).

Under CBPC § 16600, it is well established that broad covenants not to compete are void unless they involve a situation where a person sells the goodwill of a business [or] where a partner agrees not to compete in anticipation of dissolution of a partnership," *see Kelton v. Stravinski*, 138 Cal. App. 4th 941, 946 (2006), CBPC §§ 16601, 16602, or "they are necessary to protect . . . trade secrets." *Whyte v. Schlage Lock Co.*, 101 Cal. App. 4th 1443, 1462 (2002). Neither party alleges any of the above exceptions apply in this case.

The majority of cases interpreting CBPC § 16600 under California law deal with postcontract or post-employment covenants not to compete. *See e.g., Whyte v. Schlage Lock Co.*, 101 Cal. App. 4th at 1443; *Thompson v. Impaxx, Inc.*, 113 Cal. App. 4th 1425, 1427–29 (2003). In this case, the Trademark Agreement has not been terminated or canceled; rather the contractual relationship between CCI and Improv West is ongoing and § 9.j. can be viewed as an in-term covenant not to compete.

We have not found, and the parties do not cite, any Ninth Circuit or California cases holding that in-term covenants not to compete of any scope are necessarily valid. There are, however, cases addressing in-term covenants not to compete, and we discuss several of those cases here because of the limitations that we believe they impose under § 16600, even in the context of a continuing covenant not to compete.

CCI's "business" is operating full-service comedy clubs. CCI currently operates at least seven Improv clubs. As interpreted by the arbitrator, the § 9.j. covenant not to compete applies geographically to the contiguous United States, and does not end until 2019. Thus, the covenant not to compete has dramatic geographic and temporal scope. Combined with the arbitrator's ruling that CCI forfeited its rights to use the Improv marks license in any new location, the practical effect of the arbitrator's award enforcing § 9.j. is that for more than fourteen years the entire contiguous United States comedy club market, except for CCI's current Improv clubs, is off limits to CCI. This "foreclose[s] competition in a substantial share" of the comedy club business. *Dayton Time Lock*, 52 Cal. App. 3d at 6; *see also Gen. Commercial*, 126 F.3d at 1134 (reasoning that a contract cannot place "a substantial segment of the market off limits").

In ruling on CCI's motion for reconsideration the arbitrator reasoned as follows: *Dayton Time Lock* is inapplicable. That case involved an attack on an exclusive dealing contract under the *antitrust laws*. The cases cited in the portion of the *Dayton* opinion involved validity of exclusive dealing contracts under the federal Sherman Act. The type of "rule of reason" analysis applied in antitrust cases—involving the determination whether a particular agreement unreasonably restricts competition generally in a defined geographic and product market—is not applicable to a determination of illegality under Section 16600. California's antitrust statute, the Cartwright Act, is separate and distinct from § 16600 of the Business & Professions Code.

The arbitrator's award, while aware of *Dayton Time Lock*, interpreted it in a way to render it inapplicable to this case. However, as we have explained, *Dayton Time Lock* established that under CBPC § 16600 in-term covenants not to compete cannot prevent a party from engaging in its business or trade in a substantial section of the market. The arbitrator's award effectively quarantines CCI from engaging in its business in forty-eight states until 2019 and does not follow well-established California law. Even under the permissive standard with which we view arbitral decisions, the economic restraint of § 9.j. on competition is too broad to be countenanced in light of the clear prohibition of § 16600, as interpreted by the California courts. The grounds given by the arbitrator for disregarding *Dayton Time Lock* are fundamentally incorrect. We hold that the arbitrator's ruling that § 9.j. is a valid covenant not to compete ignores CBPC § 16600 and thus is in manifest disregard of the law. To comply with § 16600, the covenant not to compete must be more narrowly tailored to relate to the areas in which CCI is operating Improv clubs under the license agreement.

We conclude (1) that the arbitrator properly arbitrated the equitable claims; (2) that the arbitrator's award is not completely irrational; (3) that the arbitrator exceeded the scope of his authority by enjoining the non-party Affiliates; and (4) that the arbitrator's award violates CBPC § 16600. We vacate the district court's order confirming the arbitration award and remand to the district court with instructions to vacate the Partial Final Arbitration Award in so far as it enjoins CCI's Affiliates, unless they are agents or otherwise acting for CCI, and to the extent it prevents CCI from opening or operating non-Improv clubs in counties in which CCI does not now operate or own an Improv club.

Notes and Questions

The arbitrator imposed injunctions that were proscribed by both common and statutory California law. Assume this fact pattern in circuits that do not acknowledge any post-*Hall Street* life in manifest disregard. This takes us to a substantial difference in the enforcement regime governing domestic versus international arbitrations. The United Nations Convention on the Recognition and Enforcement of Arbitration Awards, more popularly known as the "New York Convention," 330 UNTS 38; 21 UST 2517; 7 ILM 1046 (1968), forms the entirety of Chapter II of the FAA and is therefore incorporated into U.S. law. (For a complete treatment of the New York Convention, which serves as the foundation of modern U.S. international arbitration practice, see Gary Born, International Commercial Arbitration (2014); *see also* Albert Jan van den Berg, The New York Arbitration Convention of 1958 (1994).) See also infra Chapter 16. Article V of the New York Convention provides grounds for refusing enforcement of an international arbitration award made in another country. Article V(2)(b) states that one such ground for refusing enforcement is where "the recognition or enforcement of the award would be contrary to the public policy of that country." *See generally* Ronald A. Brand, *Enforcement of Foreign Money-Judgments in the United States: In Search of Uniformity and International Acceptance*, 67 NOTRE DAME L. REV. 253 (1991). Under a New York Convention standard, a case like *Comedy Club* might not be enforced in another country if the remedy was, as here, contrary to a system of laws in the enforcing country. But there is no corresponding "public policy" exception in the domestic portion of the FAA. Should there be, by amendment or by implication? Does manifest disregard impose that standard? If no to either (or both) of the last two questions, then how should arbitration awards contrary to law be handled? Start here

Barzelatto v. Spire Sec., LLC

Case No. 19 Civ. 6238 (CM), 2019 U.S. Dist. LEXIS 231274 (S.D.N.Y. Nov. 5 2019)

McMAHON, C.J.

The Panel Did Not Engage in Manifest Disregard of Controlling Law

Neither the FAA nor the CPLR assigns manifest disregard for the law as a basis for vacatur of an arbitral award, and while the Second Circuit has long recognized manifest disregard as a basis for vacatur, its position has been criticized by many, including the Supreme Court, *see Hall St. Assocs, L.L.C. v. Mattel, Inc.*, 552 U.S. 576, 584 (2008), and may not be good law. *See* Annie Chen, Note, *The Doctrine of Manifest Disregard of the Law after Hall Street: Implications for Judicial Review of International Arbitrations in U.S.*, 32 FORDHAM INT'L L.J. 1872, 1885–89 (2008) (collecting critiques). However, criticism is not the same as overruling; and as recently as September of this year, the Second Circuit has recognized that a "court may set aside an arbitration award if it was rendered in manifest disregard of the law." *Weiss v. Sallie Mae, Inc.*, 939 F.3d 105, 109 (2d Cir. 2019) (internal citation omitted).

That said, it is difficult to explain what "manifest disregard" might be—especially since the arbitrators are not required to write an opinion explaining its reasoning, *see, e.g., Singh v. Raymond James Fin. Servs., Inc.*, 633 F. App'x 548, 551 (2d Cir. 2015) —which, as a purely logical matter, would seem to be the only way that a district court could be sure that an arbitral panel "manifestly disregarded" controlling law.

It is easier to say what manifest disregard is not. Arbitrators who get the law wrong, or who issue a decision that is not in accordance with law that would be controlling in a courtroom, do not "manifestly disregard" it. One thing is crystal clear: a federal district court does not sit as a court of appeals over an arbitration panel to correct errors of law.

Rather, manifest disregard means there is some apparent and egregious impropriety on the part of the arbitrator. *Weiss*, 939 F.3d at 109 (quoting *T.Co Metals, LLC v.*

Dempsey Pipe & Supply, Inc., 592 F.3d 329, 339 (2d Cir. 2010)). To establish manifest disregard, Respondents must show that: "(1) the arbitrators knew of a governing legal principle yet refused to apply it or ignored it altogether," *and* (2) "the law ignored by the arbitrators was well defined, explicit, and clearly applicable to the case." *KT Corp. v. ABS Holdings, Ltd.*, No. 18-2300, 784 Fed. Appx. 21, 2019 WL 4308992, at *2 (2d Cir. Sept. 12, 2019) (quoting *Zurich Am. Ins. Co. v. Team Tankers A.S.*, 811 F.3d 584, 589 (2d Cir. 2016)).

For a panel to engage in manifest disregard of the law, the law must be well defined, explicit, and clearly applicable to the case. "A legal principle clearly governs the resolution of an issue before the arbitrator if its applicability is obvious and capable of being readily and instantly perceived by the average person qualified to serve as an arbitrator." *Westerbeke Corp. v. Daihatsu Motor Co.*, 304 F.3d 200, 209 (2d Cir. 2002) (internal quotation and citation omitted). This Court may not vacate an award on this ground where the award "rests on the application of an unclear rule of law to a complex factual situation," *GMS Grp., LLC v. Benderson*, 326 F.3d 75, 82 (2d Cir. 2003) (internal quotations and citations omitted); the allegedly controlling case law is factually distinguishable from the arbitration case in a material respect, *In re Arbitration Between Atherton & Online Video Network, Inc.*, 274 F. Supp. 2d 592, 595–96 (S.D.N.Y. 2003); or there is "an arguable difference regarding the meaning or applicability of laws urged upon [the panel]," *Merrill Lynch, Pierce, Fenner & Smith, Inc. v. Bobker*, 808 F.2d 930, 934 (2d Cir. 1986).

D. Some Courts Are Just Undecided

Nothing shows the uncertainty left in *Hall Street*'s wake than the subsequently expressed uncertainty in the lower courts as to whether the manifest disregard standard exists or not.

Prospect CCMC, LLC v. CCNA/Pa. Ass'n of Staff Nurses & Allied Prods.

Civ. Action No. 18-174, 2019 U.S. Dist. LEXIS 12714 (E.D. Pa. Jan. 28, 2019)

McHUGH, J., District Judge.

This action follows an arbitration award ("Award") resolving a labor dispute. The prevailing party seeking to enforce the Award is the Pennsylvania Association of Staff Nurses and Allied Professionals ("PASNAP") a labor organization representing nurses employed by Crozer-Chester Medical Center ("CCMC"). The losing party seeking to vacate the Award (Civil Action No. 18-174) is the owner of CCMC's hospital system, Prospect Medical Holdings ("Prospect"). PASNAP has filed a separate suit to enforce the Award (Civil Action No. 184039). The separately filed suits concern the vacation or confirmation of the same arbitration award and therefore were consolidated by order of this Court.

As a threshold issue, whether manifest disregard of federal law exists as a judicially created extension of 9 U.S.C. § 10(a)(4) for vacatur of an arbitration award in the Third Circuit remains an open question. This ground for vacatur can be traced to *Wilko v. Swan*, 346 U.S. 427, 436–37 (1953), where the Supreme Court seemed to create an additional basis for vacatur when it contrasted erroneous interpretations of the law by arbitrators—not subject to judicial review—with "manifest disregard" of the law that would ostensibly trigger Section 10 of the FAA. Circuit courts, including the Third Circuit, initially acknowledged such a judicially created extension of § 10(a)(4). *Local 863 Int'l Bhd. of Teamsters, Chauffeurs, Warehouseman and Helpers of Am. v. Jersey Coast Egg Producers, Inc.*, 773 F.2d 530, 534 (3d Cir. 1985). Subsequent Supreme Court decisions in *Hall Street Assocs. LLC v. Mattel, Inc.*, 552 U.S. 576, 585 (2008), and *Stolt-Nielsen S. A. v. AnimalFeeds Int'l Corp.*, 559 U.S. 662, 672 n.3 (2010), made clear that *Wilko* did not create a general expansion of vacatur authority applicable to arbitration awards based on contract. However, the Court has not decided whether manifest disregard nonetheless survives as an independent ground for review.

Circuit courts have since split on this issue, with the Third Circuit not yet taking a position. *See e.g., Whitehead v. Pullman Grp., LLC,* 811 F.3d 116, 120 (3d Cir. 2016) (whether the manifest disregard of the law standard survived *Hall Street* "is an open question"). As I did in a prior case, *Knabb P'ship v. Home Income Equity, LLC,* 2017 U.S. Dist. LEXIS 59485, 2017 WL 1397247 (E.D. Pa. April 19, 2017), I will again assume without deciding that manifest disregard of the law remains a viable basis for vacatur. Applying the test formulated by the Third Circuit before the Supreme Court's decision in *Hall Street,* I find that Prospect has not carried its burden of proving that Miller willfully ignored controlling law.

Notes and Questions

While there is no clear definition of manifest disregard, the above cases suggest several requirements for a successful manifest disregard challenge in a jurisdiction still applying this doctrine. First, the law must be clear. Second, petitioner must show that the arbitrator was aware of this law yet chose to ignore it and apply a different standard: that he literally made manifest his disregard of the undisputed legal standard.

Does this reward the stupid or ignorant arbitrator? The subjective element—as one court above phrased it, "the knowledge actually possessed by the arbitrators"—is particularly difficult to apply should manifest disregard prove to have a longer life.

It suggests that an arbitrator who is too unskilled to take note of governing precedent in his award might withstand review of that award, since his disregard was not "manifest" —but that, by contrast, an arbitrator who took note of a statute and then explained why he was ignoring it in this case would have put his contempt for the law front and center and would be said to have disregarded the law in the most "manifest" way possible.

This sets up any number of questions as to the impact of arbitrator ignorance in a manifest disregard jurisdiction:

Problem 1.

The parties' contract adopts as governing law a state with a four-year statute of limitations for contract claims. The arbitrator acknowledges this law, finds that the dispute was not brought until year 5, but finds that the defendant's action was so unfair that he will disregard the otherwise binding effect of the limitations period. Is this manifest disregard?

Problem 2.

What if the parties addressed the statute of limitations issue in their briefing, but the arbitrator ignored it in his final award in which he does not dismiss the action as time-barred? Is the disregard any less manifest for not being mentioned?

Problem 3.

What if the parties address the limitations period argument, and the arbitrator finds that the period does not apply because of the fraudulent concealment exception to the limitations period (by which the period is deemed tolled until the plaintiff had actual notice of the claim once the concealment ended)? How strong must the evidence of concealment be to tolerate the limitations period not being applied? Is the answer different in a manifest disregard jurisdiction versus a strict Section 10-only jurisdiction?

E. *Daesang Corp. v. NutraSweet:* Manifest Disregard Comes to Life—Briefly

In 2017, manifest disregard did not merely flicker to life—it burst onto the scene in a case that received national and international attention. A New York court, in a high-profile case, vacated part of an arbitrator's order on the ground that the arbitration had "manifestly disregarded" New York law regarding the intersection between contract and fraud claims.

NutraSweet had agreed to buy a part of Daesang's business for just under $80 million. The asset purchase agreement contained an arbitration clause. After making two payments of $5 million each, NutraSweet ceased making the payments on the grounds that Daesang had violated antitrust laws. The underlying arbitration went on for years. The tribunal ultimately found for Daesang, including on the ground of fraudulent inducement, which allowed equitable rescission of the contract.

On cross-petitions to confirm and to vacate, the New York Supreme Court (the trial-level court in New York State) granted NutraSweet's vactur motion in part, on the basis of manifest disregard. This caused no small amount of consternation in the New York arbitration community; as the appellate division recognized on appeal, "we are cognizant, in deciding this appeal, of the following caution issued by The Association of the Bar of the City of New York in the amicus curiae brief it has submitted in support of this appeal: 'Any suggestion that New York courts will review the arbitrators' factual and legal determinations, as if on appeal. . .will discourage parties from choosing New York as the place of arbitration.'"

The N.Y. Appellate Division reversed, in the following opinion.

Matter of Daesang Corp. v. NutraSweet Co.

167 A.D.3d 1 (N.Y. App. Div. 1st Dept. 2018).

FRIEDMAN, Justice of the Peace.

This appeal, arising from a bitter international commercial dispute between producers of an artificial sweetener, raises the question of whether, under the Federal Arbitration Act (9 USC §1 *et seq.*) (FAA), grounds exist to deny confirmation to an arbitration award rendered in New York. In the order under review, Supreme Court vacated the award in substantial part and remanded to the arbitrators, for their redetermination, certain defenses and counterclaims that they had dismissed (55 Misc 3d 1218[A], 58 NYS3d 873, 2017 NY Slip Op 50646[U] [2017]). The court took this action, albeit "reluctant[ly]" (as it told the parties at oral argument), based on its view that the arbitrators, in disposing of these defenses and counterclaims, had manifestly disregarded the law and had misconstrued the procedural record. This was error.

The order vacating the award in part cannot be justified under the "emphatic federal policy in favor of arbitral dispute resolution" embodied in the FAA, a policy that "applies with special force in the field of international commerce" (*Mitsubishi Motors Corp. v Soler Chrysler- Plymouth, Inc.*, 473 US 614, 631 [1985]). Under the FAA, even if an arbitral tribunal's legal and procedural rulings might reasonably be criticized on the merits, an award is not subject to vacatur for ordinary errors of the kind the court identified in this case, as opposed to manifest disregard of the law, a concept that, as more fully discussed below, means "more than a simple error in law" (*Wien & Malkin LLP v Helmsley-Spear, Inc.*, 6 NY3d 471, 481, 846 NE2d 1201, 813 NYS2d 691 [2006] [internal quotation marks omitted]). "The potential for . . . mistakes [by the arbitrators] is the price for agreeing to arbitration" (*Oxford Health Plans LLC v Sutter,* 569 US 564, 572–573 [2013]), and, "however disappointing [an award] may be," parties that have bargained for arbitration "must abide by it" (*Matter of Wilkins,* 169 NY 494, 497, 62 NE 575 [1902]; *see also Matter of Pine St. Realty Co., Inc. v Coutroulos,* 233

App Div 404, 407, 253 NYS 174 [1st Dept 1931] ["Errors, mistakes, departures from strict legal rules, are all included in the arbitration risk"], *lv denied* 258 NY 609, 180 NE 354 [1932]). Accordingly, we reverse, grant the petition to confirm the award, and deny the cross motion to vacate it.

In 2002, petitioner Daesang Corporation and respondent The NutraSweet Company, the world's largest producer of the artificial sweetener aspartame, began to discuss NutraSweet's potential acquisition of Daesang's aspartame business. In connection with these discussions, Daesang and NutraSweet entered into a December 2002 joint defense and confidentiality agreement (JDA). Section 10 of the JDA provides, inter alia, that NutraSweet is entitled to rescind any transaction ultimately agreed upon in the even legal proceedings challenging the deal as an antitrust violation are instituted "by any customer with annual worldwide aspartame requirements in excess of 1,000,000 pounds."

On April 30, 2003, Daesang and NutraSweet entered into an asset purchase agreement (APA), pursuant to which Daesang sold all of its aspartame assets to NutraSweet for $79,250,000, $5 million of which was to be paid at closing and the remainder in five annual installment payments. In connection with the APA, the parties also entered into a processing agreement, dated May 13, 2003, pursuant to which NutraSweet engaged Daesang to provide aspartame production services at the Korean manufacturing facilities that NutraSweet was acquiring. The APA and the processing agreement each provides that it is governed by New York law and that disputes are to be resolved through arbitration by a three-member tribunal in New York under the rules of the International Chamber of Commerce. In this regard, the APA provides that "[t]he resolution of disputes by the arbitrators . . . shall be conclusive and binding upon and non- appealable by the Parties."

The APA and the processing agreement contain a number of representations and warranties by Daesang that are relevant to this appeal. Among these is Daesang's representation in the APA that it "has complied in all material respects with all applicable laws" in operating its aspartame business (the compliance-with-law warranty). Also pertinent are Daesang's representations and warranties in the APA and the processing agreement concerning its product quality, manufacturing processes, production capacity, and production costs, and concerning the absence of customer complaints. However, another provision of the APA bars either party from seeking rescission based solely on the other party's breach of its representations and warranties in the APA or the processing agreement.

After the transaction closed in May 2003, NutraSweet made the 2004 and 2005 annual installment payments of the purchase price under the APA, each in the amount of $5 million. Nutrasweet failed, however, to remit the third installment payment of $9.25 million, which became due in June 2006. In December 2006, after the requisite period of time had passed without cure of the default, Daesang exercised its right under the APA to accelerate the $55 million balance of the purchase price. In March 2007, Daesang notified NutraSweet that, pursuant to Daesang's rights under the APA in the event of a default, Daesang would resume manufacturing aspartame for its own account at the Korean plant NutraSweet had purchased.

Five days later, NutraSweet notified Daesang that it was rescinding the transaction pursuant to section 10 of the JDA, based on an antitrust class action that several industrial aspartame customers had commenced against NutraSweet and Daesang (among other aspartame producers) in June 2006.

After a full day of oral closing argument was heard in New York on October 20, 2011, the tribunal issued a 34-page "Partial Final Award," dated December 21, 2012 (the partial award), unanimously finding in favor of Daesang on all of its claims and dismissing all of NutraSweet's defenses and counterclaims.

The tribunal issued a final award, dated June 14, 2016, awarding Daesang damages in the total amount of $100,766,258, which included, among other elements, the $64.25 million unpaid balance of the purchase price under the APA and interest through June 10, 2016. The tribunal stood by its dismissal of all of NutraSweet's defenses and counterclaims, including the dismissal of the counterclaim for damages for breach of contract.

After hearing argument in December 2016, Supreme Court issued an order, entered May 15, 2017, granting NutraSweet's motion to vacate the awards to the extent of vacating the dismissals of the second and third counterclaims seeking equitable rescission based on fraudulent inducement and of the fourth counterclaim for breach of contract, and remanding the matter to the arbitration tribunal for a "redetermination" of those claims. Daesang's petition for confirmation was held in abeyance pending the tribunal's redetermination of the remanded claims.

In its decision, Supreme Court recognized that the enforceability of the partial award and final award is governed by the FAA, that judicial review of an arbitration award under the FAA (as under New York law) is extremely limited, and that the doctrine of manifest disregard of the law does not authorize a court to vacate an arbitration award based simply on the arbitrators' arguable error or misunderstanding of the applicable law. Applying these principles, the court concluded that it could not vacate the tribunal's dismissal of NutraSweet's counterclaim for rescission under section 10 of the JDA. The court reached a different conclusion, however, with regard to the dismissal of the counterclaims for equitable rescission and for breach of contract.

Concerning the counterclaims for equitable rescission, the court found that "the Tribunal chose to disregard the well-established principle [invoked by NutraSweet during the arbitration] that a fraud claim can be based on a breach of contractual warranties where the misrepresentations are of present facts (in contrast to future performance) and cause the actual losses claimed." As to the counterclaim for breach of contract, the court found that "a careful reading of the transcript utterly fails to demonstrate that there was a waiver by Nutra[S]weet of its breach of contract counterclaim at the October 20, 2011 [closing argument] hearing." The court opined that "[t]he portion of the transcript relied upon by the Tribunal was a dialogue concerning [counterclaim] III, rescission, not [counterclaim] IV, breach of contract. Thus, there was no basis to conclude that there was a waiver by NutraSweet." Therefore, the court concluded, "The refusal to consider the merits of NutraSweet's breach of contract counterclaim and the baseless determination of waiver goes beyond mere error in law or facts, and amounts to an egregious dereliction of duty on the part of the Tribunal." The court did not reach NutraSweet's argument that enforcement of the awards would be contrary to public policy. This appeal by Daesang ensued.

The parties agree that the enforcement of the arbitration awards rendered in this international commercial dispute is governed by the Convention on the Recognition and Enforcement of Foreign Arbitral Awards (21 UST 2517, TIAS No. 6997 [1958]) (the Convention) and by the FAA (*see Yusuf Ahmed Alghanim & Sons v Toys "R" Us, Inc.*, 126 F3d 15, 18–19 [2d Cir 1997], *cert denied* 522 US 1111 [1998]). Because the awards were rendered in the United States, the FAA governs (pursuant to the Convention, art V, § 1 [e], and 9 USC § 208) whether the awards may be set aside or vacated in this proceeding brought within the United States (*Yusuf Ahmed Alghanim & Sons*, 126 F3d at 2023). The Convention and the FAA mandate, however, that a court "shall confirm [an arbitral] award unless it finds one of the grounds for refusal or deferral of recognition or enforcement of the award specified in the said Convention" (9 USC § 207; Convention, art V, §§ 1, 2).

The FAA expressly provides four grounds on which a court, upon application by a party, may vacate an arbitration award (9 USC § 10 [a]). Of these four express statutory grounds for vacatur, only one is invoked by NutraSweet here—a situation "where the arbitrators exceeded their powers, or so imperfectly executed them that a mutual, final, and definite award upon the subject matter submitted was not made" (9 USC § 10 [a] [4]). In addition, NutraSweet argues that the subject awards are subject to vacatur on the implied ground of manifest disregard of the law (*see Wilko v Swan*, 346 US 427, 436–437 [1953]), of which the Court of Appeals has written:

> [A]n award may be vacated under federal law if it exhibits a "manifest disregard of law" (*Duferco Intl. Steel Trading v T. Klaveness Shipping A/S*, 333 F3d 383, 388 [2d Cir 2003]; *Goldman v Architectural Iron Co.*, 306 F3d 1214, 1216 [2d Cir 2002], citing *DiRussa v Dean Witter Reynolds Inc.*, 121 F3d 818, 821 [2d Cir 1997]). But manifest disregard of law is a 'severely limited' doctrine (*Matter of Arbitration* No. AAA13-161-0511-85 Under Grain Arbitration Rules, 867 F2d 130, 133 [2d Cir 1989]). It is a doctrine of last resort limited to the rare occurrences of apparent 'egregious impropriety' on the part of the arbitrators, "where none of the provisions of the FAA apply" (*Duferco*, 333 F3d at 389). The doctrine of manifest disregard, therefore, "gives extreme deference to arbitrators" (*DiRussa*, 121 F3d at 821). The Second Circuit has also indicated that the doctrine requires "more than a simple error in law or a failure by the arbitrators to understand or apply it; and, it is more than an erroneous interpretation of the law" (*Duferco*, 333 F3d at 389). We agree with that premise. To modify or vacate an award on the

> ground of manifest disregard of the law, a court must find "both that (1) the arbitrators knew of a governing legal principle yet refused to apply it or ignored it altogether, and (2) the law ignored by the arbitrators was well defined, explicit, and clearly applicable to the case" *(Wallace v Buttar,* 378 F3d 182, 189 [2d Cir 2004], quoting *Banco de Seguros del Estado v Mutual Mar. Off., Inc.,* 344 F3d 255, 263 [2d Cir 2003])" *(Wien & Malkin,* 6 NY3d at 480–481 [footnotes omitted]).[1]

We turn first to the arbitrators' dismissal of NutraSweet's second and third counterclaims for equitable rescission of the transaction based on fraud in the inducement. As previously noted, Supreme Court set aside this determination, and remanded the two equitable rescission counterclaims to the arbitrators for redetermination, on the ground that the tribunal had manifestly disregarded the law in holding that these claims, based on allegedly false representations made by Daesang in the APA and the processing agreement, were contractual in nature and therefore could not be pursued by NutraSweet on a theory of fraud. In so doing, Supreme Court plainly erred. At most, the tribunal "state[d] an intention to apply a law, and then misapplie[d] it," which constitutes nothing more than a mere error of law for which "[an] award will not be set aside" (*Matter of Sprinzen [Nomberg],* 46 NY2d 623, 629, 389 NE2d 456, 415 NYS2d 974 [1979]).

To recapitulate, NutraSweet, in its second and third counterclaims, alleges that Daesang's compliance-with-law warranty in the APA, and several other representations and warranties concerning Daesang's aspartame business in the APA and the processing agreement, were materially false when made. Before the arbitrators, NutraSweet contended that, because these allegedly false contractual representations fraudulently induced it to enter into the transaction, it was entitled to rescission of the entire transaction on equitable grounds. The parties disputed, among other issues relating to these counterclaims, whether claims that contractual representations had been false when made could be pursued on a fraud theory (as opposed to a theory of breach of contract) under New York law.

In debating whether the second and third counterclaims could be maintained on a theory of fraud, each side relied on an opposing line of decisional authority. One of the cases on which NutraSweet placed primary reliance was *Merrill Lynch & Co. Inc. v Allegheny Energy, Inc.* (500 F3d 171 [2d Cir 2007]). In dismissing the equitable rescission counterclaims in the partial award, the arbitrators quoted and applied

1. Since Wien & Malkin was decided, the Second Circuit has clarified, in light of Hall Street Associates, L.L.C. v. Mattel, Inc. (552 US 576 [2008]), that it regards the doctrine of manifest disregard of the law as "a judicial gloss on the specific grounds for vacatur enumerated in section 10 of the FAA," rather than as "a ground for vacatur entirely separate from those enumerated in the FAA" (Stolt-Nielsen SA v AnimalFeeds Intl. Corp., 548 F3d 85, 94 [2d Cir 2008], rev'd on other grounds, 559 US 662 [2010]).

(whether correctly or incorrectly) the following standard set forth in *Merrill Lynch* for resolving the issue presented:

> "[U]nder New York law, parallel fraud and contract claims may be brought if the plaintiff (1) demonstrates a legal duty separate from the duty to perform under the contract; (2) points to a fraudulent misrepresentation that is collateral or extraneous to the contract; or (3) seeks special damages that are unrecoverable as contract damages" (*id.* at 183).

The tribunal went on to discuss the facts of *Merrill Lynch,* observing that the fraud claim in that case was allowed to proceed because it was "based on misrepresentations regarding the financial statements delivered to Allegheny *before* the parties entered into their contract. This involved a legal duty separate from the duty to perform under the contract and also involved a misrepresentation that was collateral or extraneous to the contract. Thus, the misrepresentations with respect to the financial statements could give rise to a claim for fraud wholly apart from any claim for breach of contract" (citation and internal quotation marks omitted).

The tribunal concluded that *Merrill Lynch* was distinguishable from the instant matter because NutraSweet

> "rel[ies] only on the language of the representations in the APA to support [its] claim of fraud in the inducement. However, the contract provision does not create a legal duty separate from the contract; it is not a provision collateral or extraneous to the contract.... Thus, [NutraSweet's] reliance on the *Merrill Lynch* decision is misplaced."

The tribunal further opined that "[t]he facts of this case are much more similar to the cases relied on by Daesang," citing, inter alia, *DynCorp v GTE Corp.* (215 F Supp 2d 308, 324 [SD NY 2002] [dismissing "fraud claims based on the breach of contractual warranties and representations . . . as duplicative of (the party's) claim for breach of contract"]).

The foregoing suffices to show that the resolution in the partial award of the issue of the viability of NutraSweet's fraud counterclaims—whether or not that resolution was correct (a question on which we express no opinion)—does not meet the high standard required to establish manifest disregard of the law, namely, a showing that "the arbitrator[s] knew of the relevant principle, appreciated that this principle controlled the outcome of the disputed issue, and nonetheless willfully flouted the governing law by refusing to apply it" (*Westerbeke Corp. v Daihatsu Motor Co., Ltd.,* 304 F3d 200, 217 [2d Cir 2002]). On the contrary, the tribunal accepted the authority of the decision on which NutraSweet primarily relied (*Merrill Lynch*) and, "after analyzing [the] case law offered by both sides" (*Cheng v Oxford Health Plans, Inc.,* 45 AD3d 356, 357, 846 NYS2d 16 [1st Dept 2007]), made a good faith effort to apply to the facts of this case the *Merrill Lynch* standard proffered by NutraSweet. That the arbitrators did not accept NutraSweet's view of how the relevant legal principle applies to the facts of this case does not amount to "refus[ing] to apply [the principle] or ignor[ing] it altogether" (*Wien & Malkin,* 6 NY3d at 481 [internal quotation marks omitted]). The arbitrators' ruling, whether or not we agree with it on the merits, more than meets the requirement that there be at least "a barely colorable justification for the outcome reached" (*id.* at 479 [internal quotation marks omitted]). Even if a thorough analysis of the underlying legal issue (which we do not propose to undertake here) would lead us to conclude that NutraSweet was correct on the merits, a finding of manifest disregard of the law "requires more than a simple error in law or a failure by the arbitrators to understand or apply it" (*id.* at 481 [internal quotation marks omitted]). On this record, NutraSweet can show nothing more than this.

Notes and Questions

1. The end result is not as confused as *Hall Street* left matters but is still far more confused that it should be. *Daesang v. Nutrasweet* showed what the beast unleashed could be, and courts shrank back. Unless and until the Supreme Court clarifies that which it has now twice left muddled, there remains uncertainty on the most important of all topics in this Unit III: what is the standard of review for legal error in arbitration?

   One answer is that of conscious disregard. In this sense, the venal are penalized more than the ignorant. The arbitrator must not only apply the law incorrectly: he must consciously apply it incorrectly. Consider Arbitrator A and Arbitrator B. Both are faced with arbitrations in which the statute of limitations is four years for a contract action. Both are considering cases not filed until five years have passed from the running of the limitations period. Arbitrator A acknowledges the statute of limitations but states that he does not believe it would be "fair" to apply it. Arbitrator B never acknowledges the limitations period at all, and simply awards damages.

   On the basis of the Second Circuit test, Arbitrator A would be held to have manifestly disregarded the law, since he took note of it but then did not apply it. Arbitrator B, laboring away in blissful ignorance, would apparently be protected from vacatur. Is this the right way to proceed? Should manifest disregard mean something else? Or should it just be replaced with a different standard of legal error—or, at the opposite end, simply fade away post-*Daesang v. Nutrasweet*?

2. *Manifest Disregard and "Manifest Injustice."* Before repudiating manifest disregard, the Fifth Circuit added an "injustice" element to the test: "Even if the arbitrator did manifestly disregard the law, a second step of the manifest disregard analysis requires that before an arbitrator's award

can be vacated, the court must find that the award resulted in a 'significant injustice.'" *Kergosien v. Ocean Energy,* 390 F.3d 346, 355 (5th Cir. 2004) (citing *Williams v. CIGNA Financial Advisors,* 197 F.3d 752, 762 (5th Cir. 1999), *cert. denied,* 259 U.S. 1099 (2000)).

PRACTICE POINTER. Given both the uncertainty and circuit split that characterizes manifest disregard, lawyers negotiating the choice-of-law clause in a contract containing an arbitration provision should consider whether they want the award to be subject to this standard, or not. Until the Supreme Court elects to clarify what it has left in chaos, choice of law matters.

Chapter 16

International Commercial Arbitration

Up until this chapter, the parties in the cases we have studied have all been from the United States. The cases have been based in the United States. The governing law has been that of the United States. The enforcement mechanisms we have studied have assumed that the losing party and its assets have been located in the United States and that, since the award was rendered in the United States, the applicable enforcement law was that found in Sections 9 through 11 of the FAA and the cases interpreting those sections.

But what happens when at least one of the parties is located outside of the United States? How does arbitration change? Are there different rules, and should there be? What special features should practitioners understand in order to best advise their clients in the crafting of an arbitration clause with a non-U.S. party? What should practitioners know about how to arbitrate against, or on behalf of, a non-U.S. party? How does one find the money if it isn't in the United States?

It is impossible to address all these issues and the others that make international arbitration unique in a single chapter. The scope of the issues can and do support an entire law school course confined to arbitration between parties of different countries, and there are excellent casebooks on the subject. See, for example, Gary B. Born, International Commercial Arbitration (2014), and Nigel Blackaby, et al., Redfern and Hunter on International Arbitration (2015). This chapter will focus on those areas in which international arbitration differs most from the basics of commercial arbitration law in the United States.

We begin, though, with the similarities between domestic and international arbitration. Both share the fundamental basics of party consensus and arbitrator mandate. As with domestic arbitration, international arbitration requires a clear agreement between the parties to arbitrate their dispute. As with domestic arbitration, without a clear mandate the arbitrator is powerless, and with a clear mandate the arbitrator is afforded discretion to act under those instructions. As with domestic arbitration, the national court system in international arbitration is most likely to be called upon at the beginning (to enforce the arbitration agreement) and the end (to enforce the arbitration award) and will most often be involved least in the middle phase (the arbitration itself). That much remains the same.

It is the manner in which those basics play out that differs. The best way to study those differences is to follow the same three-stage model that otherwise frames this book: the formation of the arbitration agreement, the conduct of the arbitration itself, and the enforcement of the arbitration award.

We start by looking at why international arbitration exists at all.

I. The Trend Toward International Arbitration

The growth of international arbitration is at first blush a simple proposition: as the volume of international trade increased, so has the amount of international arbitration. *See, e.g.*, Mark Bezant, James Nicholson, & Howard Rosen, *Trends in International Arbitration*, FTI Journal (Feb. 2015), https://ftijournal.com/article/trends-in-international-arbitration. (Query whether this trend will continue in the present decade given more nationalistic governments, and whether that will have an impact on international arbitration—both topics for another course.) But why would the one necessarily lead to the other? Why, for example, would there not instead be an increase in the amount of national court cases in which one of the parties was from a different country than the other? Why have the parties chosen instead to create their own dispute resolution procedure just like the parties in the previous chapters of this book?

In addition to the advantages you have already studied about arbitration, including confidentiality, speed, and supposed efficiency, there are at least three reasons why parties choose international arbitration as their means of dispute resolution in cross-border contracts: jurisdiction, neutrality, and enforcement.

1. *Jurisdiction.* Consent to arbitration by definition creates personal jurisdiction. In international court litigation—cases between parties from different countries, normally heard in the national courts of one or the other— jurisdictional questions can predominate. Merely sending goods abroad does not necessarily create jurisdiction in the court where the goods arrive, and merely sending money back to the United States for those goods does not necessarily create U.S. jurisdiction. Parties can, of course, take the suspense out of this issue without agreeing to arbitration by instead agreeing in their contract's dispute resolution clause that any dispute between them will be heard in the home courts of one party—but the price of creating jurisdiction that way is to land one party in another party's national court system. International arbitration provides jurisdictional certainty without jeopardizing neutrality.
2. *Neutrality.* The advantage of arbitration, both domestic and international, is that neither party gets to play a "home game"—instead, the arbitration usually takes place in a neutral location. That feature can be especially important when the alternative is having to litigate in an entirely

different country, with different languages, legal rules, and customs. The privatization of dispute resolution that arbitration permits allows parties doing business internationally to avoid unfamiliar procedures.

3. *Enforcement.* International arbitration has been advanced significantly by a treaty popularly referred to as the New York Convention, which permits the enforcement of international arbitration awards in any country that is a party to that treaty. Convention on the Recognition and Enforcement of Foreign Arbitral Awards, 91 Pub. L. 368, 84 Stat. 692. That means that an English company which wins an arbitration held in Paris against an Italian company can enforce the arbitration award against the Italian company's assets in Italy, England, or a third country such as Germany—or in any other one of the over 160 countries that are signatories to the New York Convention.

Each of these features makes international arbitration attractive as a means of dispute resolution between commercial actors from different countries.

II. Getting the Arbitration Started

A. The International Arbitration Clause

As with domestic arbitration, the agreement to arbitrate is most often found in the dispute resolution clause in the contract between the parties and the agreement can also arise (or be modified) after the dispute arises.

An illustrative international arbitration clause in a contract looks like this:

> Any dispute arising out of or in connection with this contract, including any question regarding its existence, validity or termination, shall be referred to and finally resolved by arbitration under the LCIA Rules, which Rules are deemed to be incorporated by reference into this clause.
>
> The number of arbitrators shall be one.
>
> The seat, or legal place, of arbitration shall be Frankfurt, Germany.
>
> The language to be used in the arbitral proceedings shall be English. The governing law of the contract shall be the substantive law of the state of Delaware in the United States of America.

Model Arbitration Clause from the London Court of International Arbitration ("LCIA").

An effective international arbitration clause will, like an effective domestic clause, express the parties' election to arbitrate their disputes in clear and mandatory language, ideally using the word "shall." The parties are likely to pay particular attention here to the place of arbitration (the "forum"), which frequently will be in a city located in a country where neither of the parties are from.

Language. The LCIA model clause above is careful to select a governing language. Parties to an international arbitration who neglect this issue in their arbitration clause can quickly find themselves with a host of logistical problems. In which language should the arbitration be conducted? In which language shall the award be rendered? If one party speaks only Chinese and the other party only English, is it fair for the official language to be either Chinese or English? If documents were translated during the lifetime of the case, which version—original or translated—is official? How should translation differences be treated? How should translation services work at the hearing, how should the translators be selected, and who should pay the cost of the translation? Institutional arbitration services can provide neutral answers to many of these questions. Parties are well served to address these questions in advance of finalizing their arbitration clause or, at the latest, before the hearing.

PRACTICE POINTER. Are there issues other than language that you should address in the international arbitration clause? Would your concerns be different if you were representing the United States party, rather than the non-U.S. party, to the contract? What if you were the buyer rather than the seller? Return to the checklist in Chapter 1. How would you change this list if you were drafting the arbitration clause for an international transaction?

B. Institutions in International Arbitration

As with domestic arbitration, the parties have the option of running their arbitration under the auspices of an arbitration institution, or else proceeding *ad hoc*, meaning institution-free. The advantages and disadvantages of institutional arbitration are the same as between domestic and international arbitration, in that institutions add a level of cost while providing a process, a structure of rules, and in some cases, a roster of skilled and experienced arbitrators from which the parties can choose.

Despite their increased cost, institutions may be more frequently used in international than domestic arbitration because the parties are venturing into a dispute without a particular national border. National arbitration statutes still exist, as discussed below, but to the parties it may appear that more structure is needed from the beginning. Accordingly, there exists a host of international arbitration institutions. Some are wholly international in scope and are used by parties irrespective of where their dispute arises. These include the Paris-based International Chamber of Commerce ("ICC"), the International Center for Dispute Resolution ("ICDR," which is the international arm of the American Arbitration Association), and the London-based London Court of International Arbitration ("LCIA"). Despite their names, the Paris organization is not a standard chamber of commerce and the London organization is not a court. Both are institutions which administer arbitrations pursuant to their distinct procedural rules.

There are also regional arbitration organizations that parties can select when they decide to site their arbitration in a particular area. Leading regional arbitration institutions include the Stockholm Chamber of Commerce, as Sweden has become a preferred destination for arbitrations between Western investors and Russian companies, and the Singapore International Arbitration Centre, as Singapore has become a leading locale for commercial disputes in Asia. The Dubai International Arbitration Centre ("DIAC") and the China International Economic Trade and Arbitration Commission ("CIETAC") are also popular for use in Dubai and China-based arbitrations, respectively.

C. The Law of the Seat

Whether they realize it or not, parties to an international arbitration choose not one but two sources of law to govern their dispute. The first, with which they would usually be aware, is that of the substantive law governing their contract. International arbitration lawyers refer to this as the *lex loci contractus*. An example would be "this contract shall be governed by the laws of the United Kingdom of England and Wales." The second is that of the law governing the jurisdiction where the arbitration takes place. This is the seat of their arbitration, also referred to as the *lex loci arbitri*.

The law of the seat governs precisely the type of procedural questions that we have seen up until now governed by the Federal Arbitration Act. Questions about a party's obligation to arbitrate, or about the enforcement of the award or its propriety, are resolved first by applications to the courts in the jurisdiction where the arbitration takes place. For arbitrations that take place in the United States, the Federal Arbitration Act is the law of the seat. Similarly, an arbitration taking place in India would be governed by the Arbitration and Conciliation Act. An arbitration taking place in London would be governed by the English Arbitration Act. Each of these are national laws that these countries have enacted regarding arbitration. An arbitration occurring within those borders will be governed, at least *procedurally*, by those national laws.

The law of the seat and the law governing the contract need not, of course, always be different. A party, especially one with sufficient bargaining power, may want very much to deal only with familiar law. Thus, for example, an Indian developer doing business with a Chinese investor may agree to arbitrate disputes, but only if that arbitration is heard in New Delhi (which would make India's Arbitration and Conciliation Act the law of the seat) under Indian law (which would also make Indian law the law of the contract). Because the law of the seat and law of the contract do not have to be the same, practitioners of international arbitration must be keenly aware of which law they are referencing and at which phase when discussing or addressing the law of their case. Anything going to the merits of the dispute is governed by the law of the contract, but everything else is governed by the law of the seat.

Example

Canadian company buys pharmaceutical manufacturing equipment from Indian seller with offices in Mumbai, India. The parties elect Indian law as the law of the contract but agree to arbitrate in London under the rules of the London Court of International Arbitration ("LCIA"). When payment and performance disputes develop, Indian company sues Canadian company in Indian court in Mumbai. Canadian company responds by instituting LCIA arbitration in London. Indian company claims that this is contempt of Indian court rulings setting Mumbai as the forum and brings an "anti-suit injunction," demanding Canadian company to halt any other lawsuit or proceedings. Where should the Indian company's anti-suit injunction be heard? In English court as the seat? In Indian court as the forum? In both? What should be the reach of the juridical seat to anti-suit injunctions? For more on anti-suit injunctions in international arbitration, see, for example, S. I. Strong, *Border Skirmishes: The Intersection Between Litigation and International Commercial Arbitration*, 2012 J. DISP. RESOL. 1 (2012); Julian D. M. Lew, *Does National Court Involvement Undermine the International Arbitration Process?*, 24 AM. U. INT'L L. REV. 489 (2009).

The following article by a leading international arbitration scholar examines not only the areas where local law can collide with the parties' choice of law, but the different ways in which different nations (and commentators) would treat this clash.

William W. Park, *The* Lex Loci Arbitri *and International Commercial Arbitration*

32 INT'L & COMP. L.Q. 21 (Jan. 1983)

Luke's gospel reports that Jesus once declined to arbitrate a family dispute over an inheritance by asking a disgruntled sibling, "Who set me over you to arbitrate?" Private resolution of business disputes raises a related question: whence springs the arbitrator's authority to render a binding award? A company that submits a controversy to arbitration may later regret having abandoned recourse to the courts. On the day of reckoning, the sage chosen to decide the dispute may no longer seem so wise to the losing party, and the loser might consider refusing to comply with the arbitrator's decision. Some legal system, therefore, must legitimise the arbitrator's authority. Otherwise, the award remains an unenforceable conciliation attempt that the parties are free to treat as mere foreplay to litigation.

The country where the award is rendered traditionally has legitimised arbitral authority subject to conditions, in the form of mandatory procedural rules imposed on the arbitral proceedings. The proper scope of these local curial norms—commonly known as the *lex loci arbitri—has* been problematic.

* * *

The author concludes that control of international commercial arbitration by the *lex loci arbitri* commends itself if the local judge limits his role to ensuring the integrity of the arbitral proceedings and respect for the interests of third parties.

* * *

[A]rbitration is controlled by some national law, a *lex arbitri*. The *lex arbitri* is not necessarily the law governing the substance of the dispute, nor the procedural rules applied by the arbitrators. Rather, the *lex arbitri* governs the validity of the arbitral process itself.

* * *

The law of the arbitration is the law of the place of the proceedings: the *lex arbitri* is the *lex loci arbitri*. Thus an arbitrator must bow to mandatory norms of the country in which he sits. Parties may choose the law governing the contract. They may even choose some of the procedural rules applied by the arbitrator to a matter such as cross-examination of witnesses. They do not, however, choose the law governing the arbitration, except indirectly through choice of its *situs*.

F.A. Mann has articulated this traditional view with force, arguing that the pronouncements of an arbitral tribunal are not binding unless linked to a specific system of national law:

> Every right or power a private person enjoys is inexorably conferred by or derived from a system of municipal law which may conveniently and in accordance with tradition be called *lex fori*, though it would be more exact (but also less familiar) to speak of the *lex arbitri*.

The mandatory rules imposed by the *lex loci arbitri* do not yield to neat classification. Many legal systems prohibit arbitration of disputes involving sensitive public interests, such as the protection of investors in corporate securities or contracts with state agencies. Some require arbitrators to state the reasons for their awards, or provide for the removal of arbitrators who are inept or unfair. A few legal systems have provided for appeal from arbitrator error on matters of law.

English judges traditionally have given the *lex loci arbitri* greater significance than their French or American brethren. One Court of Appeal decision held that the selection of London as a *situs* for arbitration implied that English substantive law governed the issue of contract damages. This decision contrasts with American and French cases that have minimised the influence of the law of the place of arbitration.

The traditional role of the *lex loci arbitri* has been questioned by scholars and practitioners who suggest that an international commercial arbitral award may "float" free from the constraints of the national law of the place of the proceedings. Such denationalised arbitration, producing an "a-national" arbitral award, marries well with the commercial motive behind the trend toward greater arbitral autonomy in modern arbitration law: to increase a country's attractiveness as a *situs* for arbitral proceedings. This approach also permits national tribunals to concern themselves less with disputes not implicating national interests, and accommodates international business transactions in which the parties' divergent nationalities create a special need for a neutral and private forum for dispute resolution.

"Denationalised" arbitration, however, has come to mean more than self-restraint by the country of the proceedings in the imposition of local procedural law. "Floating" awards, it has been argued, are and should be enforceable outside the country of proceedings despite annulment where rendered. For example, suppose arbitration is conducted in Azania, where the award is set aside on the ground that the parties did not validly consent to arbitration. Should a court in Ruritania, where the loser has assets, nevertheless enforce the award if it comes to a different conclusion about the validity of the arbitration agreement? What if Azanian courts set aside the award for error of law, a ground for annulment unknown to Ruritanian law?

Varying degrees of floating arbitration might be contemplated. For instance, Ruritania might take the position that annulment in Azania is never relevant to enforcement in Ruritania. A less extreme position might take annulment of an award in Azania as an impediment to enforcement in Ruritania if the annulment was made for reasons considered appropriate under Ruritanian law. For example, Ruritania might accept annulment for arbitrator corruption, but not for arbitrator error of law.

Ruritanian courts, of course, may always deny recognition to an arbitration defective under their own standards. So much is accepted by both traditionalists and proponents of floating arbitration. The divisive issue is whether Ruritanian courts should also defer to Azanian nullification for violation of the latter's procedural norms.

Critical to the viability of "a-national" arbitration is the legal effect of an arbitral award not linked to a national legal system. The distinguished arbitration lawyer, Jan Paulsson, has written recently that "the binding force of an international award may be derived . . . without a specific legal system serving as its foundation." Focusing on the French case of *Gotaverken v. Libyan General National Maritime Transport Co.*, Paulsson demonstrates that an international arbitral award may be enforced even if not subject by the *lex loci arbitri* to the same appeal procedures as a domestic award.

The arbitration in *Gotaverken* involved three tankers constructed by a Swedish shipyard for a Libyan government agency. The Libyans refused delivery, inter alia, on the ground that ship components had been made in Israel in violation of Libyan boycott law. The arbitrators ordered the Libyans to take delivery of the vessels and to pay the outstanding portion of the price. The Libyans challenged the award, arguing that it violated the public policy (ordre public) of France because of its failure to respect Libyan boycott law. The Paris Cour d'Appel refused to hear the challenge on the ground that the award was not French. Such an award, Paulsson maintains, is enforceable "without a specific legal system serving as its foundation."

The paradox of a legal obligation independent of a legal order suggests Athena springing full-blown from the head of Zeus: a binding commitment, free from any municipal law, just appears. Grasp of Paulsson's thesis requires a conceptual leap to a document labelled "obligation" enforced without respect to whether the document constitutes a valid obligation under the legal system normally selected by the enforcement forum's choice of law principles. In other words, the document receives contractual force from the enforcement forum itself regardless of the otherwise governing law. An international arbitration, rather than being "detached from its country of origin," receives substantially greater autonomy, and is subject to fewer constraints, than a domestic arbitration.

* * *

The second situation in which one might approve enforcement of an award annulled in its country of origin is where the local judiciary is corrupt or biased. For example, a judge of a country without a tradition of judicial independence might set aside an award rendered against its own government merely to please the bureaucracy, without regard to the fairness of the proceedings. Enforcement of such an award by a country where the debtor government has assets would seem neither improper nor inappropriate.

The 1958 New York Arbitration Convention leaves open the theoretical possibility that the *lex arbitri* may be other than the law of the place of the proceedings. Under Article V(l)(e), a non-domestic arbitral award may be refused recognition on proof that it has been set aside by "a competent authority of the country in which, or *under the law of which*, that award was made." Annulment by an authority of the country "under the law of which" an award is made could be construed as a supplementary, rather than substitute, ground for refusal of recognition.

Debate over the nationality of awards is more than an academic quibble. The critical importance of the *lex loci arbitri* was strikingly illustrated by the saga of *Societe Europeenne d'Etudes et d'Entreprise (S.E.E.E.) v. Yugoslavia*. Before World War II S.E.E.E. built a railroad in Yugoslavia for which it was paid in devalued French francs. A panel of two arbitrators found an implicit currency stabilisation provision and rendered an ex parte arbitral award in favour of S.E.E.E. in Lausanne on July 2, 1956. In an action before the cantonal court of Vaud, Yugoslavia argued that an even number of arbitrators violated mandatory dispositions of local law. The Swiss court, reasoning that the arbitration| was not governed by Vaud cantonal law, refused deposit of the award and returned it to the parties.

In a subsequent action in the Netherlands to enforce the award, the Dutch Supreme Court rejected the Yugoslav argument that the award was invalid because it was not linked to any national legal system. The victory of the "floating award," however, was short-lived. In a second decision the Dutch Supreme Court held that the Swiss refusal to hear the Yugoslav challenge had the same consequence as annulment of the award, which therefore was refused recognition. The Dutch court considered the arbitrator's decision to constitute a Swiss award notwithstanding the Swiss court's contrary view.

B. Scope of Application of the Lex loci arbitri

A legal system that subjects international arbitration to its judicial control must decide which procedural norms are to be applicable. Judicial intervention might be limited to ascertaining the award's basic integrity, breached by an arbitrator who is not impartial, or who decides matters that the parties never entrusted to his adjudication. On the other hand, the courts also might concern themselves with the legal merits of the dispute. The extent of judicial control will depend upon conclusions as to whether it is more important that an arbitral award be correct, or that it be final.

* * *

[T]he judiciary need not concern itself with the correctness of an arbitrator's conclusions merely to ensure a correct interpretation of the parties' contract. Court intervention on the merits of a dispute voluntarily submitted to arbitration is required only if an arbitrator's decision directly implicates national or third party interests. Intervention may be justified, for example, if an arbitrator's misinterpretation of an oil supply contract would result in injury to the consumers of the fuel, or when an arbitrator's interpretation of company law frustrates a national policy of protecting the integrity of the market for corporate securities. If national policies are not implicated, courts should limit their role to ensuring that the award is not obtained through violation of fundamental norms of procedural fairness, such as arbitrator fraud, partiality or excess of authority.

International arbitration is less likely than domestic arbitration to involve such disputes. Even if it does, a national legal system still may accommodate the needs of international trade and investment by refraining from exercising supervision over the legal merits of the arbitration. The United States Supreme Court adopted such an attitude in *Scherk v. Alberto-Culver*, a case involving allegedly fraudulent misrepresentations in the sale of stock, normally a non-arbitrable issue in the United States. The policy in favour of permitting a neutral private forum to settle international business disputes outweighed the competing consideration of protecting investors from fraud in the sale of investment securities.

Judicial control over the substantive legal issues of an international arbitration should be minimal. Parties to the dispute should have the privacy for which they bargained. In addition, arbitrators should be free of the threat of being overruled because of errors in their analysis, so that reasoned awards will be rendered more frequently, thereby contributing to the development of a modern "law merchant."

Complete lack of judicial control, however, is undesirable. Even if the arbitration involves neither citizens nor interests of the forum State, national courts should ensure the integrity of awards rendered within national borders. Such awards may benefit from recognition and enforcement under the 1958 New York Convention. Some parties to the Convention, including the United States, limit its application to awards rendered in the territory of another contracting State. By allowing an award rendered on its territory to become binding, a State facilitates enforcement of an award, and therefore should provide a mechanism for challenging the award's procedural deficiencies.

Deficiencies in the award's integrity should be dealt with by the legal system of the place of the proceedings. Otherwise, the losing party must attack an invalid award in each of the many States where the award might be enforced against its property. The contesting party should have an opportunity to expose procedural irregularities at the place of the arbitration, which will normally have as great a claim as any other forum to being mutually convenient to the parties.

* * *

"The test of a first-rate intelligence," wrote the American novelist F. Scott Fitzgerald, "is the ability to hold two opposed ideas in the mind at the same time, and still retain the ability to function." Elaboration of an appropriate standard of interaction between judge and arbitrator requires a similar capacity to accept seemingly inconsistent principles: the law must be applied correctly; yet adjudication must be binding. The commercial community's need for finality in private dispute resolution competes with the desirability of uniform application of law.

Wisdom dictates that the State of arbitration exercise some control over the integrity of the proceedings and the interests of third parties. *Prima facie* validity is accorded foreign arbitral awards under the 1958 New York Arbitration Convention. Fairness requires that a procedurally defective arbitration be susceptible to being annulled at the place where rendered. The loser should not be forced to litigate issues such as arbitrator corruption in all States where it has assets. Nor should an award benefit from the presumptive validity accorded by the New York Convention when there exists a fundamental disaccord between how the arbitrator decided and how the parties to the dispute authorised him to decide. Control by the *lex loci arbitri*, however, should be limited to ensuring respect for traditional standards of fairness, the limits of the arbitral mission and the rights of third parties.

D. Arbitrator Selection in International Arbitration

Arbitrators are selected, as in domestic arbitration, in one of (or a combination of) three ways: directly by the parties, by the arbitration institution, or, in the case of the chair of a three-arbitrator panel, by the two party-appointed arbitrators.

The parties may wish to preserve more control over the appointment process than the following institutional rules (from the LCIA and ICC, respectively) provide them, in which case they need to draft expressly—especially if they otherwise choose institutional arbitration.

1. Institutional Rules

LCIA, Article 5. Formation of Arbitral Tribunal

5.1 The formation of the Arbitral Tribunal by the LCIA Court shall not be impeded by any controversy between the parties relating to the sufficiency of the Request or the Response. The LCIA Court may also proceed with the arbitration notwithstanding that the Request is incomplete or the Response is missing, late or incomplete.

5.2 The expression the "Arbitral Tribunal" includes a sole arbitrator or all the arbitrators where more than one.

5.3 All arbitrators shall be and remain at all times impartial and independent of the parties; and none shall act in the arbitration as advocate for or representative of any party. No arbitrator shall advise any party on the parties' dispute or the outcome of the arbitration.

5.4 Before appointment by the LCIA Court, each arbitral candidate shall furnish to the Registrar (upon the latter's request) a brief written summary of his or her qualifications and professional positions (past and present); the candidate shall also agree in writing fee-rates conforming to the Schedule of Costs; the candidate shall sign a written declaration stating: (i) whether there are any circumstances currently known to the candidate which are likely to give rise in the mind of any party to any justifiable doubts as to his or her impartiality or independence and, if so, specifying in full such circumstances in the declaration; and (ii) whether the candidate is ready, willing and able to devote sufficient time, diligence and industry to ensure the expeditious and efficient conduct of the arbitration. The candidate shall furnish promptly such agreement and declaration to the Registrar.

5.5 If appointed, each arbitral candidate shall thereby assume a continuing duty as an arbitrator, until the arbitration is finally concluded, forthwith to disclose in writing any circumstances becoming known to that arbitrator after the date of his or her written declaration (under Article 5.4) which are likely to give rise in the mind of any party to any justifiable doubts as to his or her impartiality or independence, to be delivered to the LCIA Court, any other members of the Arbitral Tribunal and all parties in the arbitration.

5.6 The LCIA Court shall appoint the Arbitral Tribunal promptly after receipt by the Registrar of the Response or, if no Response is received, after 35 days from the Commencement Date (or such other lesser or greater period to be determined by the LCIA Court pursuant to Article 22.5).

5.7 No party or third person may appoint any arbitrator under the Arbitration Agreement: the LCIA Court alone is empowered to appoint arbitrators (albeit taking into account any written agreement or joint nomination by the parties).

5.8 A sole arbitrator shall be appointed unless the parties have agreed in writing otherwise or if the LCIA Court determines that in the circumstances a three-member tribunal is appropriate (or, exceptionally, more than three).

5.9 The LCIA Court shall appoint arbitrators with due regard for any particular method or criteria of selection agreed in writing by the parties. The LCIA Court shall also take into account the transaction(s) at issue, the nature and circumstances of the dispute, its monetary amount or value, the location and languages of the parties, the number of parties and all other factors which it may consider relevant in the circumstances.

5.10 The President of the LCIA Court shall only be eligible to be appointed as an arbitrator if the parties agree in writing to nominate him or her as the sole or presiding arbitrator; and the Vice Presidents of the LCIA Court and the Chairman of the LCIA Board of Directors (the latter being ex officio a member of the LCIA Court) shall only be eligible to be appointed as arbitrators if nominated in writing by a party or parties—provided that no such nominee shall have taken or shall take thereafter any part in any function of the LCIA Court or LCIA relating to such arbitration.

ICC, Article 12. Constitution of the Arbitral Tribunal

Number of Arbitrators

1) The disputes shall be decided by a sole arbitrator or by three arbitrators.

2) Where the parties have not agreed upon the number of arbitrators, the Court shall appoint a sole arbitrator, save where it appears to the Court that the dispute is such as to warrant the appointment of three arbitrators. In such case, the claimant shall nominate an arbitrator within a period of 15 days from the receipt of the notification of the decision of the Court, and the respondent shall nominate an arbitrator within a period of 15 days from the receipt of the notification of the nomination made by the claimant. If a party fails to nominate an arbitrator, the appointment shall be made by the Court.

Sole Arbitrator

3) Where the parties have agreed that the dispute shall be resolved by a sole arbitrator, they may, by agreement, nominate the sole arbitrator for confirmation. If the parties fail to nominate a sole arbitrator within

30 days from the date when the claimant's Request for Arbitration has been received by the other party, or within such additional time as may be allowed by the Secretariat, the sole arbitrator shall be appointed by the Court.

Three Arbitrators

4) Where the parties have agreed that the dispute shall be resolved by three arbitrators, each party shall nominate in the Request and the Answer, respectively, one arbitrator for confirmation. If a party fails to nominate an arbitrator, the appointment shall be made by the Court.
5) Where the dispute is to be referred to three arbitrators, the third arbitrator, who will act as president of the arbitral tribunal, shall be appointed by the Court, unless the parties have agreed upon another procedure for such appointment, in which case the nomination will be subject to confirmation pursuant to Article 13. Should such procedure not result in a nomination within 30 days from the confirmation or appointment of the co-arbitrators or any other time limit agreed by the parties or fixed by the Court, the third arbitrator shall be appointed by the Court.
6) Where there are multiple claimants or multiple respondents, and where the dispute is to be referred to three arbitrators, the multiple claimants, jointly, and the multiple respondents, jointly, shall nominate an arbitrator for confirmation pursuant to Article 13.
7) Where an additional party has been joined, and where the dispute is to be referred to three arbitrators, the additional party may, jointly with the claimant(s) or with the respondent(s), nominate an arbitrator for confirmation pursuant to Article 13.
8) In the absence of a joint nomination pursuant to Articles 12(6) or 12(7) and where all parties are unable to agree to a method for the constitution of the arbitral tribunal, the Court may appoint each member of the arbitral tribunal and shall designate one of them to act as president. In such case, the Court shall be at liberty to choose any person it regards as suitable to act as arbitrator, applying Article 13 when it considers this appropriate.

Article 13: Appointment and Confirmation of the Arbitrators

1) In confirming or appointing arbitrators, the Court shall consider the prospective arbitrator's nationality, residence and other relationships with the countries of which the parties or the other arbitrators are nationals and the prospective arbitrator's availability and ability to conduct the arbitration in accordance with the Rules. The same shall apply where the Secretary General confirms arbitrators pursuant to Article 13(2).

. . .

5) The sole arbitrator or the president of the arbitral tribunal shall be of a nationality other than those of the parties. However, in suitable circumstances and provided that none of the parties objects within the time limit fixed by the Court, the sole arbitrator or the president of the arbitral tribunal may be chosen from a country of which any of the parties is a national.

———

Comment

International arbitration institutions frequently have a so-called "roster" of arbitrators from each member country. The presumption is that to be included in this roster, a lawyer must have established his or her legal acumen, trustworthiness and integrity, and ability to fairly and efficiently administer an international proceeding. Parties may attempt the best of both worlds by selecting their own party-appointed arbitrator and then leaving the selection of the neutral chair to come from the institution's roster.

2. Nationality of International Arbitrators

ICC Article 13(5), which you have just reviewed, shows that international arbitration adds an entirely new dimension to arbitrator selection. In addition to looking at an arbitrator's experience, the parties may focus on her nationality. Article 13(5) demonstrates that parties may be particularly wary of an arbitrator, especially the neutral chair, of the same nationality as that party's opponent. But there are also times when a party may *want* to elect an arbitrator from the other side's country, particularly given choice-of-law issues. While forums may be neutral, the choice of law may not always be divorced from the parties' contract.

Example

Consider a shipping contract between a U.S. buyer and a Greek merchant marine company. Assume further that the contract provides for arbitration in London but for Greek law to govern. The U.S. party may be tempted to select a U.S. arbitrator, but if the Greek respondent selects a Greek arbitrator and then the two of them select a German chair, what happens when particular issues of Greek law arise? Will the German arbitrator give greater weight to the views of the Greek arbitrator since that is "his" law? Or is it safe to rely on submissions from Greek law experts (see discussion below of legal opinions as evidence)? Assuming you could not change the choice-of-law provision, what would you counsel your client as to the nationality of your preferred party-appointed arbitrator? What would you counsel your client with respect to the preferred nationality of the neutral arbitrator?

3. Conflicts of Interest in International Arbitrator Selection

The selection process is also tempered by conflicts of interest. This is a particularly acute problem in international arbitration because conflicts of interest require rules of engagement in order to assess whether a particular fact pattern is or is not a conflict. In national arbitration, those rules come from cases or statutes. Recall from Chapter 6 the interplay between the rules of the American Arbitration Association and the courts, with the final decisions made by the court rulings in such cases as the Supreme Court's ruling in *Commonwealth Coatings* and the Texas Supreme Court's ruling in *Americo Life, Inc. v. Myer*, 440 S.W.3d 18, 20 (Tx. 2014).

What is the source of such rules in a system that is by definition separate from national guidelines? And if different cultures and legal systems react differently to what constitutes a conflict, which standard governs?

In international arbitration, this problem (as well as that of diversity, considered *infra*) was exacerbated by the repeat appointments of particularly well-regarded arbitrators whose very appointment could be deemed a conflict in a future case involving the same party that selected them in a previous proceeding. The conflict issue was also complicated by the fact that in the United States and abroad, most arbitrators are working lawyers who, both individually and through their law firms, have contacts with a broad group of persons. This in turn was exacerbated by still a third factor, the emergence of the 1,000-lawyer plus mega firm. A potential arbitrator in Paris may have never met his Cape Town partner, much less realize that the Cape Town lawyer represents the offshore Mauritius subsidiary of a Dutch entity that the Paris partner is about to proceed against. Law firms need sophisticated conflict-checking mechanisms, and the arbitration bar needs to decide what contacts are recusal-causing conflicts.

The International Bar Association stepped admirably into this subject in 2014, issuing a set of detailed guidelines for parties and arbitrators. *See Guidelines on Conflicts of Interest in International Arbitration* (2014), https://www.ibanet.org/Publications/publications_IBA_guides_and_free_materials.aspx.

As discussed in Chapter 6, the IBA has divided the potential contacts into a so-called green, orange, and red list, in increasing level of disqualification-causing conflict. The IBA is a voluntary lawyers' organization akin to the U.S.-based American Bar Association, and so there is nothing mandatory under *any* system of law requiring parties to abide by these guidelines. Their use is as consensus-based as anything else in arbitration, and so parties desiring to use them should so state in their dispute resolution clause. The *IBA Guidelines* go into great detail on the potential situations that can arise and suggest a traffic light system of caution, in which green is acceptable, orange suggests a need for review, and red is not allowed at all or allowed only if expressly waived.

Class Problems

1. Arbitrator Jones is selected by Party A and Party B's lawyers. It turns out that Jones was in a study group with A's lawyer while the two were in law school. Jones discloses this contact. Does it qualify as a conflict?
2. Arbitrator Jones is selected by Party A and Party B's lawyers. Two months later, her law firm acquires a Paris office, where one of the partners there represents party B. Jones has never met that French partner nor has she done any work for party B. Must Jones withdraw as arbitrator?
3. Arbitrator Jones is selected by party A and party B's lawyers. Party B himself has a very wealthy uncle who controls cellular telephone contract distribution. Uncle uses Arbitrator Jones' New York office for that work. Arbitrator Jones does not do cell phone work, but her office is on the same floor as the partner who does. Is this a conflict under the IBA rules?

Comment

Interviewing the Arbitrator. As parties engage in the arbitrator selection process, including vetting contacts as to potential red/orange/green lists, particular skills and qualifications, and availability, they will require information. The best source of this information is the candidate herself. It is not uncommon, and not disfavored, for parties to speak with their potential candidates. The norm is that the lawyer interviewing the arbitrator candidate may disclose, but not argue, the specifics of the case. Different lawyers obviously strike this balancing act in different manners. Once an arbitrator is selected, any further conversation would be ex parte and is usually prohibited by operative rules. Exceptions can be made by party agreement where the two party-appointed arbitrators are selecting the neutral arbitrator and may wish to receive instructions on preferences from the party appointing them. *See* LCIA Rules 13.4, 13.5.

4. Diversity in International Arbitration

The same pressures for greater diversity in the composition of domestic arbitration tribunals that you studied in Chapter 5 exist now in international arbitration as well. As with domestic arbitration, there is no lack of pressure for diversity, and no lack of statements of support by the relevant institutions. The ICC, for example, states:

> The ICC International Court of Arbitration continues its concerted efforts to narrow gender and cultural disparities. We do this in the belief that more

> diversity will enhance the arbitration process in the long term and give users of our services access to the very best minds and talents available.

Diversity in Arbitration, ICC, https://iccwbo.org/global-issues-trends/diversity/diversity-in-arbitration/.

Some progress is being made, though much still remains, on both gender and race. "It's clear that a lot has been done to promote gender diversity in international arbitration—but it's also clear that more needs to be done if we are to achieve the goal of gender equality in arbitration." Victoria Clark, *Diversity in Arbitration: A Call to Action*, LEXOLOGY (March 6, 2020), https://www.lexology.com/library/detail.aspx?g=397c0316-d45d-4654-8cc9-4f0ebc878644. *See also* LLP Jocelyn Turnbull Wallace & Ripple Kaila, *"Diversity"—More than Just a Buzzword—Diversity in International Arbitrator Selection is Necessary*, LEXOLOGY (July 2020), https://www.lexology.com/library/detail.aspx?g=597b5ad6-d9bc-4478-8eca-d67754a15e10.

III. Presenting the Case in International Arbitration

The hard-charging American lawyer who whips into his first London-based international arbitration, expecting to demand boatloads of documents and then put on his case mostly through examining live his own witness, is in for several surprises. There is generally less discovery and less direct testimony in international arbitration. On the flip side, self-executing disclosures and cross-examination take on greater roles.

A. Pre-Hearing Discovery and Disclosure in International Arbitration

The scope of discovery in international arbitration is affected not merely by different rules but by different norms. Depositions, for example, are a particularly American form of discovery. They are rarely used in foreign national courts, and so it is no surprise that depositions are infrequently ordered in arbitrations featuring at least one non-U.S. party. What a U.S. lawyer might call "document production requests" are also more unilateral and self-executing than an American lawyer might be used to; rather than produce documents on demand, most international arbitration rules require parties to produce documents they believe relevant to their case. This again reflects non-U.S., and especially continental European, practice. There are obvious advantages and disadvantages. On the one hand, the opposing party obtains documents early in the case with a clear sense of what documents its opponent will be relying upon. On the other, the documents are self-selected and run the risk of eliminating documents that are unfavorable or, less sinister, are simply not deemed to be as relevant by the producing party as they are by the party who may be attacking the producer's case.

With the increasing emergence of London as an international arbitration center, and the increasing prevalence of U.S. parties generally to engage in international arbitration as U.S. foreign trade expands, there is a developing controversy regarding how much international arbitration practice should reflect more aggressive U.S. (and to some degree English) discovery/disclosure practices. This controversy is exacerbated by the increased level of detail brought to discovery by electronic discovery (ESD) procedures. In a system that is not set up for detailed document disclosures in the first place, how much should parties be held to, for example, particular electronic search terms? *See, e.g.*, Eric Bergsten, *Americanization of International Arbitration*, 18 Pace Int'l L. Rev. 289 (2006); Roger P. Alford, *The American Influence on International Arbitration*, 19 Ohio St. J. on Disp. Resol. 69 (2003–2004).

Most modern institutional arbitration rules allow for arbitrator *discretion* in permitting pre-hearing discovery. It is not a given. The case for document disclosures—which is as much discovery as you are likely to get, as it is worth repeating that interrogatories and requests for admission [and depositions?] do not exist—must be made to the arbitrator.

This offers a U.S. lawyer an opportunity and a challenge. U.S. lawyers are especially experienced in pre-hearing discovery. It forms a fundamental part of U.S. practice and drives much of the expense and timelines of U.S. litigation. But for those same reasons, non-U.S. practitioners—and especially neutral arbitrators from outside of the United States—can be wary of what they might regard (based on their own experience and court systems) as an excess of discovery sought. How to best balance that?

Class Problem

You represent a U.S. seller of electronic parts to a Singapore-based precision machinery manufacturer. Your client's technology is novel and has not heretofore been used in sophisticated machinery. Your client (Seller) and Buyer have agreed upon a specific set of pre-delivery tests that the components and machines must pass before the first payment is due. The actual testing must be done at Buyer's factory site, and so Buyer has a great deal of control over the environment for these tests. Buyer is also in a great hurry to receive the parts and sell its finished product to the market. The test results are announced as a success and shipment starts. After three months, Buyer informs your client that the parts are defective and not integrating properly with Buyer's machinery. Your client informs you that he doubts that the pre-payment tests were done correctly. You want all documents related to the testing, as these will not all be in your client's possession since they were not done at your client's facility. How do you best obtain these documents? Under what rules would you wish to proceed? Assume you have not addressed disclosures or discovery in the dispute resolution clause itself.

B. Witness Statements

Evidence in international commercial arbitration usually comes in at the discretion of the party providing it, rather than by compulsion of the other side. The initial manner of presenting evidence usually comes in the form of "witness statements," which a U.S. attorney would recognize as akin to an affidavit presented at the summary judgment stage. The witness statement is accompanied by documents. The witness statement is not only a vehicle for presenting this documentary evidence but usually supplants the need for direct examination. The presumption is that anything the witness has to say is set out in her statement. At the hearing, the "direct" portion of the witness's testimony may therefore amount to little more than affirming that this was her statement—unless there are new developments to relay to the tribunal. Most institutional international arbitration rules account for witness statements and require them as part of a party's initial submissions of evidence. *See, e.g.*, London Court of International Arbitration (LCIA), Article 15 ("Written Statements"); Arbitration Institute of the Stockholm Chamber of Commerce (SCC), Article 29 (Expert "Legal" Opinions).

Because arbitrators may have to make rulings on the law of a system other than that with which they are most familiar, it is not uncommon for international arbitration submissions to contain legal opinions from persons considered experts in the governing law on the subject of the case. In domestic U.S. legal practice, legal opinions from any person other than the judge are frowned upon. A notable exception in U.S. courts is made for foreign law: Fed. R. Civ. P. 44.1 permits a party to support a contention of foreign law by "any relevant material or source, including testimony." Such testimony is a matter of routine in international arbitration. A case featuring, for example, a contested point of Swedish taxation law or Indian land use regulation may come with an expert witness statement from a Swedish tax law professor or Indian land use lawyer.

C. Due Process Paranoia and the Prague Rules

In recent years, there was criticism that complex international arbitrations were becoming too "Western" in the sense of overly long, expensive, and dragged down by discovery fights. Arbitrators, concerned about the potential of their award not being enforced, would admit everything and allow most requests for further disclosures. This has become known, and criticized, as "due process paranoia"—a concern for enforcement that outweighs a concern for efficiency. *See, e.g.*, K Berger & J. Ole Jensen, *Due Process Paranoia and the Procedural Judgment Rule: A Safe Harbour for Procedural Management Decisions by International Arbitrators*, 32 ARB. INT'L 415, 416 (2016).

In partial reaction to due process paranoia, a group of arbitration practitioners and scholars, primarily Russian and Eastern European, promulgated a new set of rules that would give arbitrators far more discretion in moving things along and refusing discovery/disclosure demands. These are known as the "Prague Rules." The Prague Rules are aimed at creating an interventionist arbitration panel. They give discretion to the arbitrators to take control of the case, early and often. This is in marked contrast to the "party autonomy" approach by which the arbitrators essentially sit back while the parties present their case as they see fit. The following are some examples of these rules:

Article 2. Proactive Role of the Arbitral Tribunal.

2.4. The arbitral tribunal may at the case management conference or at any later stage of the arbitration, if it deems it appropriate, indicate to the parties:

a. the facts which it considers to be undisputed between the parties and the facts which it considers to be disputed;

b. with regard to the disputed facts—the type(s) of evidence the arbitral tribunal would consider to be appropriate to prove the parties' respective positions;

c. its understanding of the legal grounds on which the parties base their positions; d. the actions which could be taken by the parties and the arbitral tribunal to ascertain the factual and legal basis of the claim and the defence.

e. its preliminary views on:

   i. the allocation of the burden of proof between the parties;

   ii. the relief sought;

   iii. the disputed issues; and

   iv. the weight and relevance of evidence submitted by the parties.

Article 3. Fact Finding.

3.1. The arbitral tribunal is entitled and encouraged to take a proactive role in establishing the facts of the case which it considers relevant for the resolution of the dispute. This, however, shall not release the parties from their burden of proof.

3.2. In particular, the arbitral tribunal may, after having heard the parties, at any stage of the arbitration and at its own initiative:

a. request any of the parties to submit relevant documentary evidence or make fact witnesses available for oral testimony during the hearing;

b. appoint one or more experts, including on legal issues;

c. order site inspections; and/or

d. for the purposes of fact finding, take any other actions which it deems appropriate.

3.3. The arbitral tribunal shall consider imposing a cut-off date for submission of evidence and not accepting any new evidence after that date, save for under exceptional circumstances.

Article 5. Fact Witnesses.

. . .

5.2. The arbitral tribunal, after having heard the parties, will decide which witnesses are to be called for examination during the hearing in accordance with Articles 5.3–5.9 below.

5.3. The arbitral tribunal may decide that a certain witness should not be called for examination during the hearing, either before or after a witness statement has been submitted, in particular if it considers the testimony of such a witness to be irrelevant, immaterial, unreasonably burdensome, duplicative or for any other reasons not necessary for the resolution of the dispute.

. . .

5.6. If a written witness statement is submitted by a party by virtue of Article 5.4 or at the invitation of the arbitral tribunal by virtue of Article 5.5, the arbitral tribunal, upon having heard the parties, may decide that such witness nonetheless should not be called for examination at the hearing.

5.7. However, if a party insists on calling a witness whose witness statement has been submitted by the other party, as a general rule, the arbitral tribunal should call the witness to testify at the hearing, unless there are good reasons not to do so.

Article 6. Experts.

6.1. At the request of a party or on its own initiative and after having heard the parties, the arbitral tribunal may appoint one or more independent experts to present a report on disputed matters which require specialised knowledge.

Article 8. Hearing.

8.1. In order to promote cost-efficiency and to the extent appropriate for a particular case, the arbitral tribunal and the parties should seek to resolve the dispute on a documents only basis.

Article 11. Allocation of Costs.

When deciding on the allocation of costs in an award, the arbitral tribunal may take into account the parties' conduct during the arbitral proceedings, including their co-operation and assistance (or the lack thereof) in conducting the proceedings in a cost-efficient and expeditious manner.

These rules are quite different from the present standards in international arbitration. Consider, for example, Rule 5.3. It is one thing to present direct evidence by written statement rather than presenting it live; as noted above, that is common feature of international arbitration and one which differs from domestic practice in the United States. But generally, where one side elects to submit that witness statement, the other party is entitled to cross-examine that witness. The Prague Rules remove that right and leave the decision instead to the arbitrators.

Comment

If due process paranoia and overbroad discovery/disclosure stages are at one extreme, do the Prague Rules swing too far toward the other extreme and ignore party autonomy (choice)? Can we cure inefficient arbitrations while still promoting party autonomy? Does paranoia require Prague? The question is particularly cogent since the Prague Rules have not been received with complete enthusiasm. *See* Laurence W. Newman & David Zaslowsky, *The Russians Are Coming, and They Want to Change How We Conduct International Arbitration*, N.Y. LAW JOURNAL (May 23, 2018) ("Commentators on arbitration have regularly hailed as one of its valued attributes that it affords greater autonomy to the parties than do national courts. Moreover, consciously and deliberately undercutting the adversary system as the Prague Rules do, is counter to what most of the world, not just the common-law world, regards as of great value. The Prague Rules would replace the adversary system with a more paternalistic or authoritarian approach with which the drafters, most of them from Central and Eastern Europe, may be comfortable, but others may not.").

D. Investment Arbitration: The Special Case of Suing the Sovereign

Not all international commercial arbitration is between private parties. There is a specific and active part of international arbitration law that concerns disputes between private parties and sovereign nations. Because these disputes arise out of investments that outside investors have made in a foreign country, this strain of international arbitration is referred to as "investment arbitration."

Example

Assume a Chilean investor who observes the boom in Malbec wine exports from Argentina elects to put money into a winery in Argentina. He buys a 51% share in Malbecia Ltd., a winery located in the heart of the Malbec-producing region in Argentina. The following year, Argentina is in a financial crisis. Looking for ways to raise money that will have the least political and financial impact on its own citizens, the Government of Argentina imposes a tax on all foreign investors in Argentinian agricultural enterprises. Does the Chilean investor have rights against the winery? Against the Argentine government? What role does the Chilean government properly have here? How involved should it get on behalf of its private sector national investor?

The above example is one of alleged discriminatory treatment. Concerns about such treatment have been a consistent worry of foreign investors and understandably so, since their money and energies are directed to a legal system and country foreign to their own. They are casting their bread upon waters where they may lack the same political and economic influence they have in their own country. Their motives, to be sure, are not altruistic. Very often their rates of return are expected to be higher than if they had kept their money in their own country. They are, then, playing a risk/reward game.

That risk has been capped over time by so-called "investment treaties." These treaties provide that the country in which the investment is made will not accord disparate, or discriminatory, treatment to foreign investors. In the above example, if the Argentinian tax was made on all wineries instead of only on foreign investors in Argentinian wineries, it would be less discriminatory and arguably not at all.

This ties back to arbitration, as these investment treaties create a system of dispute resolution. The host states promise not only to avoid discriminatory treatment but to make themselves available to arbitrate any such disputes. This is a particularly important point because of the international law doctrine of sovereign immunity, by which a nation is deemed immune from private suit for actions that nation takes in its sovereign capacity. Arbitration clauses in international investment treaties are a qualified waiver of sovereign immunity.

The modern term for an investment treaty is a bilateral investment treaty, usually referred to by the shorthand "BIT." As an example, the United States has a BIT with Poland. 1990 U.S.T. LEXIS 237. This BIT, as with most modern BITs, has an arbitration clause. Disputes under it are referred to arbitration before a body called ICSID, which is the International Centre for the Settlement of Investment Disputes. *See* 1990 U.S.T. LEXIS 237, *41–42. ICSID is a body administered under the auspices of the World Bank in Washington, D.C. Specialized ICSID arbitration tribunals resolve investment disputes under BITs. Because these disputes are by definition with public entities, the usual confidentiality of arbitration does not apply, and so these decisions frequently are published. The following is an arbitration award in an ICSID investment case brought by a foreign investor against the Government of Venezuela.

Rusoro Mining Ltd. v. Bolivarian Republic of Venezuela

ICSID Case No. ARB(AF)/12/5 (August 22, 2016)

In August 2016, the International Centre for Settlement of Investment Disputes (ICSID) ordered Venezuela to pay US$966.5 million plus interest to Canadian company Rusoro Mining Limited (Rusoro) for unlawfully expropriating its mining investment.

From 2006 to 2008, Rusoro acquired fifty-eight mining concessions and contracts to explore and produce gold in Venezuela. During that time, Venezuela already had restrictions on the exportation of gold. The rules fluctuated over several years until August 2011, when then-president Hugo Chávez nationalized the gold mining industry. Following intense negotiations, Rusoro and Venezuela could not reach an agreement on the amount of compensation to be paid to Rusoro. On July 17, 2012, Rusoro initiated arbitration proceedings, claiming that Venezuela expropriated its investment, among other breaches of the Venezuela–Canada bilateral investment treaty (BIT). Rusoro asked for a compensation of roughly US$2.3 billion plus interest.

XI. DECISION

904. For the foregoing reasons, the Tribunal unanimously rules as follows:

1. Declares that any alleged breach of the Treaty committed by Bolivarian Republic of Venezuela and based on the 2009 Measures is time-barred.
2. Declares that the Tribunal lacks jurisdiction to adjudicate the counterclaim submitted by the Bolivarian Republic of Venezuela.
3. Declares that the Bolivarian Republic of Venezuela breached Art. VII of the BIT by expropriating Rusoro's investment in Venezuela without payment of compensation.
4. Declares that the Bolivarian Republic of Venezuela breached paragraph 6 of the Annex to the BIT by issuing the 2010 BCV Resolution and imposing additional restrictions on the export of gold.
5. Orders the Bolivarian Republic of Venezuela to pay Rusoro USD 966,500,000 as compensation for the expropriation of its investment.
6. Orders the Bolivarian Republic of Venezuela to pay Rusoro USD 1,277,002 as damages suffered as a consequence of the breach of paragraph 6 of the Annex to the BIT.
7. Orders the Bolivarian Republic of Venezuela to pay Rusoro interest on the amounts of compensation and damages awarded in the two preceding paragraphs, accrued between 16 September 2011 and the date of actual payment, calculated at an interest rate p.a. equal to USD LIBOR for one year deposits, plus a margin of 4%, with a minimum of 4% p.a., to be compounded annually.
8. Orders the Bolivarian Republic of Venezuela to pay Rusoro USD 3,302,500 as costs of this arbitration.
9. Declares that the compensation, damages and interest granted in this Award are net of any taxes imposed by the Bolivarian Republic and orders the Bolivarian Republic to indemnify Rusoro with respect to any Venezuelan taxes imposed on such amounts.
10. Dismisses all other claims or counter-claims.

Comment

Not all investment disputes are resolved by ICSID procedures, and not all are the product of a one-off regulation, as in our Argentinian wine example, with respect to a particular industry. Commerce frequently becomes swept up in politics and history. There may, for example, be a particular nationalization campaign carried out by developing countries to seize control of their resources. This occurred in the 1970s when a number of Middle Eastern countries took control of, or "expropriated," oil refineries and related petroleum extraction businesses in their countries. This has led to the development of a fascinating tension in international law between the rights of investors and the rights of sovereign countries to the fruits of the development of those resources. The development of this law took place against the background of the post-colonialism debates of the post-World War II period.

Sometimes the political events are entirely destructive of foreign investment in a particular country—and especially of investors from a particular country. Such was the case in the wake of the Iranian Revolution of 1979. For over two decades, Iran had been a key pillar in U.S. foreign policy in the Middle East. The Shah of Iran was a leading consumer of U.S. military exports. Hundreds of private investments in Iran followed, from helicopter service contracts to travel agencies. There was a high degree of integration and investment levels. All of that changed with the return to Iran of the Ayatollah Khomeni in February 1979. The United States, a longtime supporter of the Shah, was deemed an enemy, U.S. diplomatic personnel at the embassy in Tehran were seized soon afterwards and held for over one year, and the government of Iran expropriated U.S. investments in Iranian business—especially, but not exclusively, the investments in the Iranian petroleum industry, among the largest in the world.

U.S. investors responded with suits in the United States against Iran. These suits complicated efforts of the U.S. government to secure release of the embassy hostages. Ultimately, the U.S. Supreme Court held in *Dames & Moore v. Regan* that the U.S. government had the ability under the Fifth Amendment's takings clause to compel U.S. litigants to resolve their suits against Iran in a different forum. *See* 453 U.S. 654, 101 S. Ct. 2972 (1981). The United States and Iran agreed, as part of the agreement releasing the hostages, to create a specialized arbitration tribunal, the Iran-United States Claims Tribunal, to resolve all such disputes arising from the Iranian Revolution. Remarkably, as of 2020, 41 years after the revolution, that tribunal is still functioning, and has finalized nearly all of the approximately 4,700 claims filed. *See Iran-U.S. Claims Tribunal*, U.S. DEP'T OF STATE, https://www.state.gov/iran-u-s-claims-tribunal/.

The awards are paid without the need for any execution proceedings by a fund that Iran has agreed to keep available for payment. *See, e.g.*, Award No. 602-A15(IV)/A24-FT, http://www.iusct.net/General%20Documents/AWARD/1-A-AWARD%20NO.%20602-A15%20(IV)A24-FT-EN.pdf); *see also* David Caron, *The Nature of the*

Iran-United States Claims Tribunal and the Evolving Structure of International Dispute Resolution, 84 Am. J. Int'l L. 104 (1990).

IV. Enforcement of International Arbitration Awards

A. The New York Convention

A consistent theme of this book has been the required interplay at several stages of the arbitration process between arbitration and the courts. Arbitration supplants the courts as the forum for resolving selected disputes, but the courts are still needed at the beginning and the end of the process—at the beginning to order recalcitrant parties to honor their agreements to arbitrate their dispute, and at the end to afford victorious parties a means to execute their awards against losing parties otherwise predisposed not to pay.

That makes perfect sense when the parties are all within the same court system. National arbitration acts, including the FAA, contain sections that require courts to enforce duly rendered arbitration awards subject to stated exceptions. We studied in Chapters 13 and 14 Sections 9, 10, and 11 of the FAA as establishing an enforcement regime in the United States by which U.S. courts are instructed to uphold arbitration awards unless they fall within highly narrow exceptions, and we have seen the rigor with which courts follow that mandate. Domestic arbitration enforcement in the United States thus involves national courts looking to a national statute in order to enforce an arbitration rendered within the United States.

But how can an international arbitration award be enforced? If the award is rendered in Paris rather than New York, what role would Section 9 of the FAA have? If the losing party is located in Indonesia and the award is rendered in Singapore, what role then for Section 9? How does the law provide for enforcement of arbitration awards across national borders, and without any such mechanism, what possible sense does international arbitration make in the first place?

The answers to these questions are provided by a treaty called the Convention on the Recognition and Enforcement of Foreign Arbitral Awards (1958), commonly known as the New York Convention.

There are two critical parts to the New York Convention: recognition and enforcement. Recognition is set out in Article III: "Each Contracting State shall recognize arbitral awards as binding and enforce them in accordance with the rules of procedure of the territory where the award is relied upon, under the conditions laid down in the following articles."

Recognition is not automatic. There are exceptions. But these exceptions are sharply limited in Article V and, as with the FAA, do not contain a merits basis for review.

New York Convention, Article V

1. Recognition and enforcement of the award may be refused, at the request of the party against whom it is invoked, only if that party furnishes to the competent authority where the recognition and enforcement is sought, proof that:

(a) the parties to the agreement referred to in article II were, under the law applicable to them, under some incapacity, or the said agreement is not valid under the law to which the parties have subjected it or, failing any indication thereon, under the law of the country where the award was made; or

(b) the party against whom the award is invoked was not given proper notice of the appointment of the arbitrator or of the arbitration proceedings or was otherwise unable to present his case; or

(c) the award deals with a difference not contemplated by or not falling within the term of the submission to arbitration, or it contains decisions on matters beyond the scope of the submission to arbitration, provided that, if the decisions on matters submitted to arbitration can be separated from those not so submitted, that part of the award which contains decisions on matters submitted to arbitration may be recognized and enforced; or

(d) the composition of the arbitral authority or the arbitral procedure was not in accordance with the agreement of the parties, or failing such agreement, was not in accordance with the law of the country where the arbitration took place; or

(e) the award has not yet become binding on the parties, or has been set aside or suspended by a competent authority of the country in which, or under the law of which, that award was made.

2. Recognition and enforcement of an arbitral award may also be refused if the competent authority in the country where recognition and enforcement is sought finds that: (a) the subject matter of the difference is not capable of settlement by arbitration under the law of that country; or (b) the recognition or enforcement of the award would be contrary to the public policy of that country.

The New York Convention has proven to be hugely popular: over 160 countries have signed and ratified the Convention, and the United States is among those countries. *See Contracting States*, N.Y. Arb. Convention, http://www.newyorkconvention.org/countries (as of August 2020, 164 countries are parties to the convention). It is popular because it is effective, and it is effective because it is popular. The more countries that sign on, the greater the reach of international arbitration enforcement.

The result is that as international trade has increased dramatically over the past half century, so has the use of international arbitration.

The United States was one of the first countries to execute the Convention, and it has been incorporated expressly into U.S. law: the New York Convention makes up the entirety of Chapter II of the Federal Arbitration Act. *See* 9 U.S.C. secs. 201–208.

B. The New York Convention in United States Courts

International arbitration enforcement plays out in national courts, including in U.S. courts. The fundamental issue is generally whether any of the limited Article V exceptions to enforcement apply, but U.S. courts may also find themselves navigating whether they are proceeding under the domestic (FAA) part or the international (N.Y. Convention) part of Section 9 of the U.S. Code. The following case is an example:

Yusuf Ahmed Alghanim & Sons, W.L.L. v. Toys "R" Us, Inc.

126 F.3d 15 (2d Cir. 1997)

MINER, Circuit Judge:

Appeal from a judgment entered in the United States District Court for the Southern District of New York (McKenna, J.) denying respondents' cross-motion to vacate or modify an arbitration award and granting the petition to confirm the award. The court found that while the petition for confirmation was brought under the Convention on the Recognition and Enforcement of Foreign Arbitral Awards, respondents' cross-motion to vacate or modify the award was properly brought under the Federal Arbitration Act, and thus those claims were governed by the Federal Arbitration Act's implied grounds for vacatur. Nonetheless, the court granted the petition to confirm the award, finding that respondents' allegations of error in the arbitral award were without merit.

For the reasons that follow, we affirm.

BACKGROUND

In November of 1982, respondent-appellant Toys "R" Us, Inc. (collectively with respondent-appellant TRU (HK) Limited, "Toys 'R' Us") and petitioner-appellee Yusuf Ahmed Alghanim & Sons, W.L.L. ("Alghanim"), a privately owned Kuwaiti business, entered into a License and Technical Assistance Agreement (the "agreement") and a Supply Agreement. Through the agreement, Toys "R" Us granted Alghanim a limited right to open Toys "R" Us stores and use its trademarks in Kuwait and 13 other countries located in and around the Middle East (the "territory"). Toys "R" Us further agreed to supply Alghanim with its technology, expertise and assistance in the toy business.

From 1982 to the December 1993 commencement of the arbitration giving rise to this appeal, Alghanim opened four toy stores, all in Kuwait. According to Toys "R" Us, the first such store, opened in 1983, resembled a Toys "R" Us store in the United States, but the other three, two of which were opened in 1985 and one in 1988, were small storefronts with only limited merchandise. It is uncontested that Alghanim's stores lost some $6.65 million over the 11-year period from 1982 to 1993, and turned a profit only in one year of this period.

Following the Gulf War, both Alghanim and Toys "R" Us apparently concluded that their relationship needed to be altered. Representatives of Alghanim and Toys "R" Us's International Division met in September of 1991 and February of 1992. Alghanim expressed a desire for Toys "R" Us to contribute capital toward Alghanim's expansion into other countries. Alghanim advised that it would be willing to proceed in the business only under a new joint venture agreement that would shift a substantial portion of responsibility for capital expenditures to Toys "R" Us. Toys "R" Us was unwilling to take on a greater portion of this responsibility.

On July 20, 1992, Toys "R" Us purported to exercise its right to terminate the agreement. On December 20, 1993, Toys "R" Us invoked the dispute resolution mechanism in the agreement, initiating an arbitration before the American Arbitration Association. Toys "R" Us sought a declaration that the agreement was terminated on December 31, 1993. Alghanim responded by counterclaiming for breach of contract.

On May 4, 1994, the arbitrator denied Toys "R" Us's request for declaratory judgment. The arbitrator found that, under the termination provisions of the agreement, Alghanim had the absolute right to open toy stores, even after being given notice of termination, as long as the last toy store was opened within five years. The parties then engaged in substantial document and expert discovery, motion practice, and a 29-day evidentiary hearing on Alghanim's counterclaims.

On July 11, 1996, the arbitrator awarded Alghanim $46.44 million for lost profits under the agreement, plus 9 percent interest to accrue from December 31, 1994. The arbitrator's findings and legal conclusions were set forth in a 47-page opinion.

Alghanim petitioned the district court to confirm the award under the Convention on the Recognition and Enforcement of Foreign Arbitral Awards of June 10, 1958 ("Convention"), 21 U.S.T. 2517, 330 U.N.T.S. 38, *reprinted at* 9 U.S.C. § 201. Toys "R" Us cross-moved to vacate or modify the award under the Federal Arbitration Act ("FAA"), 9 U.S.C. § 1 *et seq.*, arguing that the award was clearly irrational, in manifest disregard of the law, and in manifest disregard of the terms of the agreement. The district court concluded that "the Convention and the FAA afford overlapping coverage, and the fact that a petition to confirm is brought under the Convention does not foreclose a cross-motion to vacate under the FAA, and the Court will consider [Toys "R" Us's] cross-motion under the standards of the FAA." By judgment entered December 20, 1996, the district court confirmed the award, finding Toys "R" Us's objections to the award to be without merit. This appeal followed.

DISCUSSION

I. Availability of the FAA's Grounds for Relief in Confirmation Under the Convention

Toys "R" Us argues that the district court correctly determined that the provisions of the FAA apply to its cross-motion to vacate or modify the arbitral award. In particular, Toys "R" Us contends that the FAA and the Convention have overlapping coverage. Thus, Toys "R" Us argues, even though the petition to confirm the arbitral award was brought under the Convention, the FAA's implied grounds for vacatur should apply to Toys "R" Us's cross-motion to vacate or modify because the cross-motion was brought under the FAA. We agree that the FAA governs Toys "R" Us's cross-motion.

A. Applicability of the Convention

Neither party seriously disputes the applicability of the Convention to this case and it is clear to us that the Convention does apply. The Convention provides that it will

> apply to the recognition and enforcement of arbitral awards made in the territory of a State other than the State where the recognition and enforcement of such awards are sought, and arising out of differences between persons, whether physical or legal. It shall also apply to arbitral awards *not considered as domestic awards* in the State where their recognition and enforcement are sought.

Convention art. I(1) (emphasis added). The Convention does not define nondomestic awards. *See Bergesen* v. *Joseph Muller Corp.*, 710 F.2d 928, 932 (2d Cir. 1983). However, 9 U.S.C. § 202, one of the provisions implementing the Convention, provides that an agreement or award arising out of such a relationship which is entirely between citizens of the United States shall be deemed not to fall under the Convention unless that relationship involves property located abroad, envisages performance or enforcement abroad, or has some other reasonable relation with one or more foreign states.

In *Bergesen*, we held "that awards 'not considered as domestic' denotes awards which are subject to the Convention not because made abroad, but because made within the legal framework of another country, e.g., pronounced in accordance with foreign law or involving parties domiciled or having their principal place of business outside the enforcing jurisdiction." 710 F.2d at 932 (quoting 9 U.S.C. § 201). The Seventh Circuit similarly has interpreted § 202 to mean that "any commercial arbitral agreement, unless it is between two United States citizens, involves property located in the United States, and has no reasonable relationship with one or more foreign states, falls under the Convention." *Jain* v. *de Mere*, 51 F.3d 686, 689 (7th Cir.), *cert. denied*, 516 U.S. 914, 133 L. Ed. 2d 206, 116 S. Ct. 300 (1995).

The Convention's applicability in this case is clear. The dispute giving rise to this appeal involved two nondomestic parties and one United States corporation, and principally involved conduct and contract performance in the Middle East. Thus, we consider the arbitral award leading to this action a non-domestic award and thus within the scope of the Convention.

We have held that the FAA and the Convention have "overlapping coverage" to the extent that they do not conflict. However, by that same token, to the extent that the Convention prescribes the exclusive grounds for relief from an award under the Convention, that application of the FAA's implied grounds would be in conflict, and is thus precluded.

In *Parsons & Whittemore Overseas Co.* v. *Societe Generale de L'Industrie du Papier (RAKTA)*, 508 F.2d 969 (2d Cir. 1974), we declined to decide whether the implied defense of "manifest disregard" applies under the Convention, having decided that even if it did, appellant's claim would fail. *See id.* at 977. Nonetheless, we noted that "both the legislative history of Article V and the statute enacted to implement the United States' accession to the Convention are strong authority for treating as exclusive the bases set forth in the Convention for vacating an award." *Id.* (citation and footnote omitted).

There is now considerable caselaw holding that, in an action to confirm an award rendered in, or under the law of, a foreign jurisdiction, the grounds for relief enumerated in Article V of the Convention are the only grounds available for setting aside an arbitral award. *See, e.g., M & C*, 87 F.3d at 851 (concluding that the Convention's exclusive grounds for relief "do not include miscalculations of fact or manifest disregard of the law"); *International Standard Elec. Corp.* v. *Bridas Sociedad Anonima Petrolera, Industrial y Comercial*, 745 F. Supp. 172, 181–82 (S.D.N.Y. 1990) (refusing to apply a "manifest disregard of law" standard on a motion to vacate a foreign arbitral award); *Brandeis Intsel Ltd.* v. *Calabrian Chems. Corp.*, 656 F. Supp. 160, 167 (S.D.N.Y. 1987) ("In my view, the 'manifest disregard' defense is not available under Article V of the Convention or otherwise to a party . . . seeking to vacate an award of foreign arbitrators based upon foreign law."); *see also* Albert Jan van den Berg, *The New York Arbitration Convention of 1958: Towards a Uniform Judicial Interpretation* 265 (1981) ("*the grounds mentioned in* Article V *are exhaustive*"). This conclusion is consistent with the Convention's pro-enforcement bias. *See, e.g., Scherk* v. *Alberto-Culver Co.*, 417 U.S. 506, 519–20 & n.15, 41 L. Ed. 2d 270, 94 S. Ct. 2449 (1974); *Parsons*, 508 F.2d at 973. We join these courts in declining to read into the Convention the FAA's implied defenses to confirmation of an arbitral award.

2. Nondomestic Award Rendered in the United States

Although Article V provides the exclusive grounds for refusing confirmation under the Convention, one of those exclusive grounds is where "the award . . . has been set aside or suspended by a competent authority of the country in which, or under the law of which, that award was made." Convention art. V(1)(e). Those courts holding that implied defenses were inapplicable under the Convention did so in the context of petitions to confirm awards rendered abroad. These courts were not presented with the question whether Article V(1)(e) authorizes an action to set aside an arbitral award under the domestic law of the state in which, or under which, the award was rendered. We, however, are faced head-on with that question in the case before us, because the arbitral award in this case was rendered in the United States, and both confirmation and vacatur were then sought in the United States.

We read Article V(1)(e) of the Convention to allow a court in the country under whose law the arbitration was conducted to apply domestic arbitral law, in this case the FAA, to a motion to set aside or vacate that arbitral award.

Indeed, many commentators and foreign courts have concluded that an action to set aside an award can be brought *only* under the domestic law of the arbitral forum, and can never be made under the Convention. There is no indication in the Convention of any intention to deprive the rendering state of its supervisory authority over an arbitral award, including its authority to set aside that award under domestic law.

From the plain language and history of the Convention, it is thus apparent that a party may seek to vacate or set aside an award in the state in which, or under the law of which, the award is rendered. Moreover, the language and history of the Convention make it clear that such a motion is to be governed by domestic law of the rendering state, despite the fact that the award is nondomestic within the meaning of the Convention as we have interpreted it in *Bergesen*, 710 F.2d at 932.

In sum, we conclude that the Convention mandates very different regimes for the review of arbitral awards (1) in the state in which, or under the law of which, the award was made, and (2) in other states where recognition and enforcement are sought. The Convention specifically contemplates that the state in which, or under the law of which, the award is made, will be free to set aside or modify an award in accordance with its domestic arbitral law and its full panoply of express and implied grounds for relief. *See* Convention art. V(1)(e). However, the Convention is equally clear that when an action for enforcement is brought in a foreign state, the state may refuse to enforce the award only on the grounds explicitly set forth in Article V of the Convention.

CONCLUSION

For the foregoing reasons, the judgment of the district court is affirmed.

Notes and Questions

1. In the above case, the award survived scrutiny on both standard FAA *and* manifest disregard grounds. Should there be anything different about international arbitration cases that invokes (or precludes) manifest disregard analysis?
2. Did the U.S. court apply U.S. law or international law to the review under the New York Convention? Which law should the reviewing court

apply? Is your answer affected by the incorporation of the New York Convention into Chapter II of the FAA?

We come again, as in domestic arbitration, to the "how low does it have to go?" question. Just how bad, how abusive, how wrong, must an international arbitration award be in order to be denied confirmation by a U.S. court? The following case, which originated as an arbitration before the Iran-US Claims Tribunal, suggests that rampant procedural unfairness will not be tolerated—but that it helps to have a strong dissent from a U.S. arbitrator.

Iran Aircraft Industries v. Avco Corp.

980 F.2d 141 (2d Cir. 1992)

LUMBARD, Circuit Judge:

Iran Aircraft Industries and Iran Helicopter Support and Renewal Company (collectively the "Iranian parties"), both agencies and instrumentalities of the Islamic Republic of Iran, appeal from the December 10, 1991 order of the District Court for the District of Connecticut, Daly, J., granting defendant Avco Corporation's motion for summary judgment.

In granting Avco's motion, which was not timely opposed by the Iranian parties, the district court declined to enforce an award of the Iran-United States Claims Tribunal which resulted in a net balance of $3,513,086 due from Avco to the Iranian parties (the "Award"). The Iranian parties argue that the district court erred in declining to enforce the Award because, as claimed by the Iranian parties, the Tribunal's awards are "directly" enforceable in United States courts. In the alternative, the Iranian parties contend that the Award is enforceable under the United Nations Convention on the Recognition and Enforcement of Foreign Arbitral Awards, June 10, 1958, 21 U.S.T. 2517 (the "New York Convention"). Because we find that the district court properly denied enforcement of the Award, we affirm.

Beginning in 1976, Avco entered into a series of contracts whereby it agreed to repair and replace helicopter engines and related parts for the Iranian parties. After the Iranian Revolution of 1978–79, disputes arose as to Avco's performance of, and the Iranian parties' payments under, those contracts. On January 14, 1982, the parties' disputes were submitted to the Tribunal for binding arbitration.

The Tribunal was created by the Algiers Accords (the "Accords"), an agreement between the United States and Iran, through the mediation of Algeria, which provided for the release of the 52 hostages seized at the American Embassy in Tehran on November 4, 1979. In addition to providing conditions for the release of the hostages, the Accords established the Tribunal to serve as a forum for the binding arbitration of all existing disputes between the governments of each country and the nationals of the other. Accordingly, the Tribunal was vested with exclusive jurisdiction over claims by nationals of the United States against Iran, claims by nationals of Iran against the United States, and counterclaims arising from the same transactions. *See* Claims Settlement Declaration, Art. II(1).

On May 17, 1985, the Tribunal held a pre-hearing conference to consider, *inter alia,* "whether voluminous and complicated data should be presented through summaries, tabulations, charts, graphs or extracts in order to save time and costs." *See Avco Corp. v. Iran Aircraft Indus.,* Case No. 261, 19 Iran-U.S. Cl. Trib. Rep. 200, 235 (1988) (Brower, J., concurring and dissenting). At the conference, Avco's counsel, Dean Cordiano, requested guidance from the Tribunal as to the appropriate method for proving certain of its claims which were based on voluminous invoices, stating:

> In the interest of keeping down some of the documentation for the Tribunal we have not placed in evidence as of yet the actual supporting invoices. But we have those invoices and they are available and if the Tribunal would be interested in seeing them we can obviously place them in evidence or we can use a procedure whereby an outside auditing agency, uh, certifies to the amounts of the, uh, summaries vis-a-vis the underlying invoices. Both of those approaches can be taken. But I want to assure the Tribunal that all of the invoices reflected in our exhibits to the memorial . . . exist and are available.

Id. at 235–36. After noting that the Iranian parties "obviously have had those invoices all along," Cordiano stated that he would:

> like the Tribunal's guidance as to whether, uh, you would like this outside certifying agency to go through the underlying invoices and certify as to the summary amounts or that the Tribunal feels at this point that the, uh—that you would rather have the, uh, raw data, so to speak—the underlying invoices. Oh, we're prepared to do it either way.

Id. at 236.

The Chairman of Chamber Three, Judge Nils Mangard of Sweden, then engaged in the following colloquy with Cordiano:

> Mangard: I don't think we will be very, very much enthusiastic getting kilos and kilos of invoices.
>
> Cordiano: That, that's what I thought so . . .
>
> Mangard: So I think it will help us . . .
>
> Cordiano: We'll use . . .
>
> Mangard: to use the alternative rather.
>
> Cordiano: Alright . . .
>
> Mangard: On the other hand, I don't know if, if any, if there are any objec-

tions to any specific invoices so far made by the Respondents. But anyhow as a precaution maybe you could . . .

Cordiano: Yes. sir.

Mangard: Get an account made.

Id. at 236. Neither counsel for the Iranian parties nor the Iranian Judge attended the pre-hearing conference.

On July 22, 1985, Avco submitted to the Tribunal a Supplemental Memorial, which stated in part:

> In response to the Tribunal's suggestion at the Pre-hearing Conference, Avco's counsel has retained Arthur Young & Co., an internationally recognized public accounting firm, to verify that the accounts receivable ledgers submitted to the Tribunal accurately reflect the actual invoices in Avco's records.

Attached to the Supplemental Memorial was an affidavit of a partner at Arthur Young & Co. which verified that the accounts receivable ledgers submitted by Avco tallied with Avco's original invoices, with the exception of one invoice for $240.14. *Id.* at 237.

The Tribunal held its hearing on the merits on September 16–17, 1986. By that time, Judge Mangard had resigned as Chairman of Chamber Three and had been replaced by Judge Michel Virally of France. At the hearing, Judge Parviz Ansari of Iran engaged in the following colloquy with Cordiano:

Ansari: May I ask a question? It is about the evidence. It was one of the first or one of the few cases that I have seen that the invoices have not been submitted. So what is your position on this point about the substantiation of the claim?

Cordiano: Your Honor, this point was raised at the pre-hearing conference in May of last year.

Ansari: I was not there.

Cordiano: I remember that you weren't there. I think we were kind of lonely that day. We were on one side of the table, the other side was not there. . . . We could have produced at some point the thousands of pages of invoices, but we chose to substantiate our invoices through . . . the Arthur Young audit performed specifically for this tribunal proceeding.

Id. at 237.

The Tribunal issued the Award on July 18, 1988. Of particular relevance here, the Tribunal disallowed Avco's claims which were documented by its audited accounts receivable ledgers, stating, "The Tribunal cannot grant Avco's claim solely on the basis of an affidavit and a list of invoices, even if the existence of the invoices was certified by an independent audit." *Id.* at 211 (majority opinion).

Judge Brower, the American judge and the only judge of the panel who was present at the pre-hearing conference, filed a separate Concurring and Dissenting Opinion in which he stated:

> I believe the Tribunal has misled the Claimant, however, unwittingly, regarding the evidence it was required to submit, thereby depriving Claimant, to that extent, of the ability to present its case . . .
>
> * * *
>
> Since Claimant did exactly what it previously was told to do by the Tribunal the denial in the present Award of any of those invoice claims on the ground that more evidence should have been submitted constitutes a denial to Claimant of the ability to present its case to the Tribunal.

Id. at 231, 238.

A. "Direct" Enforceability of the Award

The Iranian parties contend that the district court erred in refusing to enforce the Award because the Tribunal's awards are "directly" enforceable in United States courts, irrespective of the defenses to the enforcement of foreign arbitral awards provided for in the New York Convention. The Iranian parties do not, and cannot, point to any mechanism in the Accords for direct enforcement of Tribunal awards issued against United States nationals. Nevertheless, the Iranian parties argue that Tribunal awards must be "directly" enforced because the Accords state that "All decisions and awards of the Tribunal shall be final and binding." *See* Claims Settlement Declaration, Art. IV(1).

The Tribunal's own interpretation of the Accords reveals the lack of merit in the Iranian parties' position. In *Islamic Republic of Iran v. United States,* Case No. A/21, 14 Iran-U.S. Cl. Trib. Rep. 324 (1987), the Tribunal considered whether the Accords obligated the United States to satisfy awards issued in favor of Iran or its nationals upon the default of United States nationals. The Tribunal ruled that while the United States had no such obligation under the Accords, it had assumed a treaty obligation to provide an enforcement mechanism for the Tribunal's awards, stating:

> It is therefore incumbent on each State Party to provide some procedure or mechanism whereby enforcement may be obtained within its national jurisdiction, and to ensure that the successful Party has access thereto. If procedures did not already exist as part of the State's legal system they would have to be established, by means of legislation or other appropriate measures. Such procedures must be available on a basis *at least as favorable* as that allowed to parties who seek recognition or enforcement of foreign arbitral awards.

Id. at 331 (emphasis added). Accordingly, the Accords require only that we grant the Award "at least as favorable" treatment as we grant other "final and binding" foreign arbitral awards.

The Iranian parties argue that where parties agree to "final" or "binding" arbitration, the resulting arbitral award must be treated as a final, res judicata judgment against the non-prevailing party. We disagree. The terms "final" and "binding" merely reflect a contractual intent that the issues joined and resolved in the arbitration may not be tried de novo in any court. *See I/S Stavborg v. National Metal Converters, Inc.,* 500 F.2d 424, 427 (2d Cir. 1974). Furthermore, we have held that even a "final" and "binding" arbitral award is subject to the defenses to enforcement provided for in the New York Convention. *See Fotochrome, Inc. v. Copal Co., Ltd.,* 517 F.2d 512, 519 (2d Cir. 1975). Accordingly, the "final and binding" language in the Accords does not bar consideration of the defenses to enforcement provided for in the New York Convention.

B. The New York Convention

Avco argues that the district court properly denied enforcement of the Award pursuant to Article V(1)(b) of the New York Convention because it was unable to present its case to the Tribunal. The New York Convention provides for nonenforcement where:

> The party against whom the award is invoked was not given proper notice of the appointment of the arbitrator or of the arbitration proceedings or was *otherwise unable to present his case* . . .

New York Convention, Art. V(1)(b) (emphasis added).

We have recognized that the defense provided for in Article V(1)(b) "essentially sanctions the application of the forum state's standards of due process," and that due process rights are "entitled to full force under the Convention as defenses to enforcement." *Parsons & Whittemore Overseas Co., Inc. v. Societe Generale de L'Industrie du Papier (RAKTA),* 508 F.2d 969, 975–76 (2d Cir. 1974). Under our law, "the fundamental requirement of due process is the opportunity to be heard 'at a meaningful time and in a meaningful manner.'" *Mathews v. Eldridge,* 424 U.S. 319, 333, 47 L. Ed. 2d 18, 96 S. Ct. 893 (1976) (quoting *Armstrong v. Manzo,* 380 U.S. 545, 552, 14 L. Ed. 2d 62, 85 S. Ct. 1187 (1965)). Accordingly, if Avco was denied the opportunity to be heard in a meaningful time or in a meaningful manner, enforcement of the Award should be refused pursuant to Article V(1)(b).

At the pre-hearing conference, Judge Mangard specifically advised Avco not to burden the Tribunal by submitting "kilos and kilos of invoices." Instead, Judge Mangard approved the method of proof proposed by Avco, namely the submission of Avco's audited accounts receivable ledgers. Later, when Judge Ansari questioned Avco's method of proof, he never responded to Avco's explanation that it was proceeding according to an earlier understanding. Thus, Avco was not made aware that the Tribunal now required the actual invoices to substantiate Avco's claim. Having thus led Avco to believe it had used a proper method to substantiate its claim, the Tribunal then rejected Avco's claim for lack of proof.

We believe that by so misleading Avco, however unwittingly, the Tribunal denied Avco the opportunity to present its claim in a meaningful manner. Accordingly, Avco was "unable to present [its] case" within the meaning of Article V(1)(b), and enforcement of the Award was properly denied.

Affirmed.

Notes and Questions

Public Policy. Article V(2) of the New York Convention contains an exception for an award that would be "contrary to the public policy of that country." There is no such contrary exception in Section 10 of the Federal Arbitration Act. Public policy is a "softer," more subjective standard—or it can be in the hands of imaginative practitioners—than concepts such as arbitrator jurisdiction. *See, e.g.*, Anton G. Maurer, The Public Policy Exception Under the New York Convention (2012); *Report on the Public Policy Exception in the New York Convention—A Report by the IBA Subcommittee on Recognition and Enforcement of Foreign Arbitral Awards dated October 2015*, N.Y. ARB. CONVENTION (Dec. 15, 2015), http://www.newyorkconvention.org/news/report+on+the+public+policy+exception+in+the+new+york+convention+-+a+report+by+the+iba+subcommittee+on+recognition+and+enforcement+of+foreign+arbitral+awards+dated+october+2015. A party could argue that it violates public policy to let the other party breach a contract, which could take the parties right back into a substantive argument on breach, this time raised at the enforcement stage. Should public policy be a strictly regulated and rarely applied basis for denying enforcement lest it become the exception swallowing the rule, or in the alternative, should it be encouraged in order to keep international consensus regarding arbitration enforcement? Why do you think public policy exists as a basis for denying enforcement in international but not domestic arbitration?

Aggarao v. MOL Ship Mgmt. Co.

No. CCB-09-3106, 2014 U.S. Dist. LEXIS 108692 (D. Md. Aug. 7, 2014)

BLAKE, United States District Judge.

MEMORANDUM

Plaintiff Potenciano Aggarao, a citizen of the Philippines, brought this lawsuit against defendants MOL Ship Management Co., Ltd., Nissan Motor Car Carrier Co., Ltd., and World Car Carriers, Inc. (collectively, "the Vessel Interests") after he sustained severe injuries aboard the M/V Asian Spirit. On September 30, 2010, this court dismissed Mr. Aggarao's complaint for improper venue, reasoning that, pursuant to the Philippine Overseas Employment Administration Contract of Employment ("the POEA Contract"), his exclusive remedy against the Vessel Interests was arbitration in the Philippines.

This court directed Mr. Aggarao to initiate arbitration in the Philippines within sixty days. Mr. Aggarao complied with the order and filed a complaint with the Philippine National Labor Relations Commission ("NLRC"). Leading up to Labor Arbiter Romelita N. Rioflorido's decision, six mandatory conferences were scheduled between September 2012 and January 2013. Both sides filed position papers and memoranda in reply, and hearings were held on March 19, 2013, and April 4, 2013. The arbiter rendered a decision on April 25, 2013.

Now pending before the court are Mr. Aggarao's motion to vacate the Philippine arbitration decision[1] and, conversely, the Vessel Interests' motion to confirm that decision. The issues in this case have been fully briefed, and a hearing was held on July 14, 2014. For the reasons stated below, the court will grant Mr. Aggarao's motion and deny the Vessel Interests' motion.

B. Arbitration Decision

The arbiter's April 25, 2013, decision purported to address Mr. Aggarao's claims for unpaid wages and contractual compensation benefits, lost future wages, maintenance and cure, moral and exemplary damages, and attorney's fees and interest.

As a preliminary matter, the arbiter determined that U.S. law did not apply to any of the above claims, citing both Section 10 of Philippine Republic Act No. 8042 and the POEA Contract. Noting that there was "no question" that Mr. Aggarao's claims against MOL stemmed from their employment relationship, the arbiter reasoned that the claims against Nissan and World Car would not have existed had

1. Although Mr. Aggarao moves to vacate the Philippine arbitration award, the court is only empowered to refuse to recognize and enforce a foreign arbitration award. *See* Convention, art. V(1) (emphasis added) ("**Recognition and enforcement of the award may be refused, at the request of the party against whom it is invoked**, only if that party furnishes to the competent authority where the recognition and enforcement is sought, [the appropriate] proof. . . ."); *id.* (V)(2) (providing additional grounds for refusal to recognize and enforce a foreign arbitration award); *see also* 9 U.S.C. § 207 (emphasis added) ("The court shall confirm [a foreign arbitration] award unless it finds one of the grounds for *refusal or deferral of recognition or enforcement of the award* specified in the . . . Convention."). To the extent Article V contemplates vacatur of a foreign arbitration award, it contemplates that the "competent authority of the country in which . . . [the] award was made" may set aside the award. *See* Convention, art. V(1)(e); *see also* Zeiler v. Deitsch, 500 F.3d 157, 165 n.6 (2d Cir. 2007) (explaining that neither the Convention nor its enabling statute gives the district court power to vacate a foreign arbitration award, rather the court should refuse to enforce the award); M & C Corp. v. Erwin Behr GmbH & Co., KG, 87 F.3d 844, 849 (6th Cir. 1996) (reasoning that, under the Convention, a motion to vacate a foreign arbitration award "may be heard only in the courts of the country where the arbitration occurred or in the courts of any country whose *procedural* law was specifically invoked in the contract calling for arbitration of contractual disputes").

the employment-related accident not occurred. In addition to upholding the POEA Contract's choice-of-law provision, the arbiter explained that, in the absence of proof to the contrary, "foreign law is presumed the same as Philippine law." Thus, according to the arbiter, she could not simply take judicial notice of foreign law; rather, Mr. Aggarao had the burden of showing that foreign law controlled. Because Mr. Aggarao did not provide sufficient proof that U.S. law applied, the arbiter applied Philippine law to all of his claims against the Vessel Interests.

ANALYSIS

Mr. Aggarao claims that, because of the arbiter's decision to apply Philippine law, he was deprived of the opportunity to vindicate U.S. general maritime rights and denied an adequate remedy. He argues that the arbiter's failure to address his legitimate interest in the enforcement of U.S. general maritime law empowers this court to refuse to recognize and enforce the arbitration award as violative of U.S. public policy.

Before the court may decide whether Mr. Aggarao's arbitration award violates public policy by depriving him of the opportunity to pursue the remedies to which he was entitled as a seafarer, it must establish what remedies were available to Mr. Aggarao under U.S. law. Accordingly, the court will first determine Mr. Aggarao's rights under U.S. general maritime law, and then determine whether he was able to effectively vindicate those rights during the arbitration proceedings in the Philippines.

A. Mr. Aggarao's Rights Under U.S. General Maritime Law

Mr. Aggarao argues that, under U.S. general maritime law, MOL and World Car are liable for maintenance and cure, World Car is liable for the unseaworthiness of the vessel and its appurtenances, and Nissan is liable for negligence. As a threshold matter, the court determines that U.S. law is applicable to Mr. Aggarao's claims under a *Lauritzen-Rhoditis* analysis. Although the Supreme Court has acknowledged a "tendency" to apply the law chosen by parties under the terms of their contract, it has indicated that "a quite different result would follow if the contract attempted to avoid applicable law, for example, so as to apply foreign law to an American ship." *Lauritzen v. Larsen*, 345 U.S. 571, 588–89, 73 S. Ct. 921, 97 L. Ed. 1254 (1953). Here, Mr. Aggarao's POEA Contract attempts to apply Philippine law to a Liberian-flagged ship. Thus, rather than simply apply the choice-of-law provision in Mr. Aggarao's contract, the court proceeds to the choice-of-law inquiry set forth by the Supreme Court for maritime injury cases.

Applying the above principles here, even if Mr. Aggarao was fit for repatriation as of December 8, 2008, he was still entitled to maintenance and cure if he had not reached maximum cure or if palliative care would have improved his condition. Any ambiguity as to Mr. Aggarao's right to maintenance and cure was to be resolved in his favor, and he was entitled to maintenance and cure regardless of whether MOL or World Car—assuming World Car may be held liable for maintenance and cure—acted negligently or were otherwise at fault.

In addition to seeking maintenance and cure, a seafarer may pursue claims for negligence and unseaworthiness. *See Norfolk Shipbuilding & Drydock Corp. v. Garris*, 532 U.S. 811, 813, 121 S. Ct. 1927, 150 L. Ed. 2d 34 (2001) (citations omitted) ("It is settled that the general maritime law imposes duties to avoid unseaworthiness and negligence . . . [and] that nonfatal injuries caused by the breach of either duty are compensable. . . .").

Thus, applying the above concepts here, U.S. general maritime law affords Mr. Aggarao potential causes of action against Nissan and World Car for negligence and unseaworthiness, respectively.

B. Mr. Aggarao's Arbitration Award Violates U.S. Public Policy

Mr. Aggarao next claims that the arbiter's decision failed to address the Vessel Interests' accountability for maintenance and cure, negligence, and unseaworthiness. The court's role in reviewing a foreign arbitration award is limited. *See Int'l Trading and Indus. Inv. Co. v. DynCorp Aerospace Tech.*, 763 F. Supp. 2d 12, 20 (D.D.C. 2011); *see also Ministry of Def. and Support for the Armed Forces of the Islamic Republic of Iran v. Cubic Def. Sys., Inc.*, 665 F.3d 1091, 1098 (9th Cir. 2011) (indicating that there is a strong public policy favoring confirmation of foreign arbitration awards); *Europcar Italia, S.p.A. v. Maiellano Tours, Inc.*, 156 F.3d 310, 316 (2d Cir. 1998) (stating that, under the Convention, "an arbitration award cannot be avoided solely on the ground that the arbitrator may have made an error of law or fact"). Pursuant to 9 U.S.C. § 207, "[t]he court shall confirm [a foreign arbitration] award unless it finds one of the grounds for refusal or deferral of recognition or enforcement of the award specified in the . . . Convention." Article V(2)(b) of the Convention specifies that "[r]ecognition and enforcement of an arbitral award may . . . be refused if the competent authority in the country where recognition and enforcement is sought finds that . . . recognition or enforcement of the award would be contrary to the public policy of that country." *See Europcar Italia, S.p.A.*, 156 F.3d at 315 (explaining that the public policy exception is to be construed narrowly).

Mr. Aggarao was denied the opportunity to pursue the remedies to which he was entitled as a seaman and, as a result, was deprived of an adequate remedy. First, Mr. Aggarao was unable to effectively vindicate his claim for maintenance and cure. The Fourth Circuit has made clear that "a seaman's fitness for repatriation is not determinative of his right to maintenance and cure." *Aggarao*, 675 F.3d at 377 n.22. Rather, a seafarer is entitled to maintenance and cure until he achieves maximum cure, "'defined as the point at which he is either cured or his condition is diagnosed as permanent and incurable.'" *Id.* (quoting *Kopacz*, 584 F.3d at 632). Moreover, even when the seafarer is permanently disabled, "maintenance and cure is required where palliative care would improve [his] condition." *Id.* The arbiter in Mr. Aggarao's case, however, made absolutely no attempt to ascertain whether he had reached maximum cure, or whether he would benefit from palliative care. Instead, finding that Mr. Aggarao was fit for repatriation, she decided that he had no right to maintenance and cure.

The Vessel Interests argue that the public policy exception is not satisfied simply because the remedies available under foreign law are less favorable than U.S. legal remedies. While the court agrees with this statement, that is not the basis for today's decision. As in *Asignacion*, the arbiter did not simply provide less favorable remedies than those available under U.S. law: she provided no such remedies. The POEA Contract destroyed Mr. Aggarao's right to maintenance and cure, and cut off any potential cause of action against Nissan and World Car. In limiting Mr. Aggarao's remedies to those allowed by the POEA Contract, the arbiter transgressed this country's strong and longstanding policy of protecting injured seafarers and providing them special solicitude. *See, e.g., Am. Export Lines, Inc. v. Alvez*, 446 U.S. 274, 285, 100 S. Ct. 1673, 64 L. Ed. 2d 284 (1980) (quoting *Moragne v. States Marine Lines*, 398 U.S. 375, 387, 90 S. Ct. 1772, 26 L. Ed. 2d 339 (1970)) (explaining that "[a]dmiralty jurisprudence has always been inspirited with a 'special solicitude for the welfare of those men who under[take] to venture upon hazardous and unpredictable sea voyages'"); *see also Asignacion*, 2014 U.S. Dist. LEXIS 24472, 2014 WL 632177, at *9. Accordingly, the court will not recognize or enforce Mr. Aggarao's arbitration award.

CONCLUSION

For the reasons set forth above, Aggarao's motion will be granted, and the Vessel Interests' motion will be denied. A separate order follows.

PRACTICE POINTER. The above cases show the same pro-enforcement and pro-arbitration bias in international arbitration as those you studied in previous chapters in domestic arbitration. The *Iran Air* case is a distinct outlier in which the bait and switch tactics by the arbitration tribunal, called out in a strong dissent by the U.S. arbitrator, were too much to bear. As a more general rule and practice pointer, be aware that it is difficult to overturn international arbitration awards. The fact patterns in such rare cases are generally extreme.

This takes us to a key practice pointer: *in international business, when representing a U.S. party, elect arbitration over litigation.* For United States parties to an international transaction, an arbitration clause is usually the only responsible choice. This is because there is no corresponding treaty between the United States and any other country by which *court* judgments are given the presumption of enforcement by another country. There is no equivalent of the New York Convention on the litigation side. An arbitration award rendered in New York against a French company is enforceable in France without the need to re-litigate the merits of the dispute, but a court judgment rendered down the street by the Southern District of New York does not enjoy the same presumption of enforceability.

That concept may at first seem counterintuitive. One might instinctively think that governments will enforce a result that comes out of another government's system more easily than it will enforce a privately rendered result like arbitration. The logical thought is that a court will be comfortable with the result from another court, even one from a different country, than with a privately rendered, consensual award. Experience has proven otherwise. While there are regional treaties by which countries in, for example, Europe and South America have agreed to enforce one another's court judgments, the United States is not party to a single such treaty. *See, e.g.*, 1968 Brussels Convention on Jurisdiction and the Enforcement of Judgments in Civil and Commercial Matters; Lugano Convention of 30 October 2007 on Jurisdiction and the Enforcement of Judgments in Civil and Commercial Matters; Inter-American Convention on International Commercial Arbitration. The United States has not joined any regional judgment enforcement convention, nor has it been able to conclude even a bilateral treaty, with a single country, by which the United States and the other country would agree to enforce court judgments rendered in the territory of the other.

This is not from lack of trying. The United States has sought continually to conclude such a treaty by which its court judgments would be subject to a presumption of enforcement abroad, but it has largely been unable to do so. Among the concerns voiced by other nations has been a reluctance to have their citizens effectively "buy in" to the high jury awards and treble damages awards existing in the U.S. court system. One potential exception has been in business-to-business contracts, where the U.S. and 16 other nations have concluded a judgment enforcement treaty, but that treaty has to date had limited acceptance and even less use. *See* Convention of 30 June 2005 on Choice of Court Agreements ("Hague choice of court convention"). For a further discussion of this treaty, see Matthew H. Adler & Michele Crimaldi Zarychta, *The Hague Convention on Choice of Court Agreements: The United States Joins the Judgment Enforcement Band*, 27 Nw. J. Int'l Law & Bus. 1 (2006).

That leaves arbitration in the lead role in *international* dispute resolution. A U.S. lawyer negotiating a contract on her client's behalf with a non-U.S. party—let's assume one in which the U.S. party is the buyer of goods and the French party is the seller—has five choices before her:

a. disputes to be resolved in French court
b. disputes to be resolved in U.S. court
c. disputes to be resolved by arbitration in the United States
d. disputes to be resolved by arbitration in France
e. disputes to be resolved by arbitration in a neutral territory

The litigation alternatives have distinct disadvantages. Option (a), litigation in France, would provide "one-stop shopping," as it would eliminate the need to establish jurisdiction over the defendant and presumably would be situated where the defendant's assets are located. It would, however, require the U.S. litigant to establish merits in a court system that is foreign in every sense of the term. Option (b), litigation in the United States, affords familiarity with the law and legal system of the client's own country, and if included as a contract clause, likely eliminates any jurisdictional objection by the French company since agreement to resolve disputes in U.S. courts is a consent to personal jurisdiction. It is generally unlikely, however, absent an extreme imbalance in bargaining power, that a non-U.S. company would agree to be sued in the United States—and even if the French company were to agree, that would only be stage 1. If the U.S. client prevailed in the U.S. court action, then, unless the French party had assets in the United States against which to execute, the U.S. client would have to take the U.S. judgment to a French court and seek, under French law, execution against the French company's assets there. Absent the presumption of validity afforded arbitration awards by the New York Convention, the court judgment could be subject to collateral attack on the merits with the result that the client would have to litigate merits twice.

If the U.S. lawyer instead chooses arbitration in drafting the dispute resolution clause, the risk of having to re-litigate the merits of the case at the enforcement stage, after winning at the arbitration stage, recedes significantly. The enforcement provisions of Article III take over. Owing to the territorial application of the New York Convention, this is the case irrespective of which particular place the parties choose. Thus, whether the parties elect option c (arbitration in the United States), d (arbitration in France), or e (arbitration at a neutral site, perhaps the easiest to negotiate)—the second phase, the *enforcement* phase (where the client gets the money), is generally substantially easier.

It is, therefore, this author's considered opinion that for international commercial transactions, arbitration should be the preferred means of dispute resolution. The only reasonable exception to this general rule would be where the non-U.S. party consents to the jurisdiction of U.S. courts *and* has assets (such as U.S. bank accounts or real property) that are readily executable against in the States.

Final Practice Problem

Having now reviewed the similarities and differences between domestic and international arbitration, consider the following situation. Your client, SpeedBoard, is a Silicon Valley startup manufacturer of high-end circuit boards used for prototype testing by large electronic companies. Before any manufacturer will go to market on a new circuit board, your client is expected to build a prototype of it so that detailed tests can be run. Speed is everything, because your client's clients are anxious to go to market with new designs. Your client has an in-house manufacturing facility so that it can best manage pace, but it has to import a particular grade of industrial wire used for the circuits it builds. SpeedBoard concludes a supply contract with WireCo, an Israeli company. Keeping in mind that interruption of supply could cripple your client's nascent business, what dispute resolution clause would you design? Litigation in California? In Tel Aviv? Arbitration? With an injunction carve-out? Why?

Index

A

Adhesion Contract, 5, 84, 105, 156
American Arbitration Association, 194
  Appellate rules, 573
  Choosing arbitrators under, 201–203, 206
  Class action statistics and, 157
  Delegation clauses under, 120
  Discovery under, 260–261, 280, 289, 469–470, 570
  Dispositive motions under, 474
  Disqualification of arbitrators under, 226–227
  Diversity and, 207, 213
  Electronically stored information under, 263
  Emergency injunctions under, 403
  Impartiality rule for arbitrators, 223
  Mediation and, 18–19
  Virtual hearings under, 536, 541–542
Antitrust laws, 56, 174, 182, 492, 607
Appeal (see "Vacatur of arbitration awards")
Arbitrability (see also "Severability") 40–41, 52, 97–98, 113, 120, 138, 150, 155–156, 431
  Class actions and, 132 (see also "Class Actions")
  Consolidation and, 423, 431
  Gateway issues and, 399 (see also "Gateway Issues")
  Injunctions and, 391
Arbitration
  Affordability, 20
  Claim, 27
  Compelling, 11, 23, 52, 327–328, 336, 338, 339, 356, 358, 446
  Consensus, 4–6, 39–40, 73, 172–173, 191, 198, 327, 391, 427–428
  Defined, 6–7
  Failure to, 91–95
  Hearing, 457
  Injunctions (see "Injunctions")
  Institutional, 29–31, 194, 202, 259, 442 (see also "Arbitration Institutions")
  Jurisdictional allegation
  Limitations on, 52
  Mediation, distinguished from, 17
  Presumption in favor of, 39–41, 45, 91, 106, 487, 496
  Response, 92
  Seat, 619–620
  Waiver, 83, 246, 423, 445–446
Arbitration, Institutional (see "Institutional Arbitration")
Arbitration Clause
  Choice of Law, 33, 73, 614, 629

Choice of law and discovery, 632
Class actions 153, 184 (see also "Class Actions")
Consolidation and, 444–445 (see also "Consolidation")
Discovery covered by, 258–259
Drafting, 25–26
Enforcement and, 7, 40, 73
Evolution of post–Concepcion, 168, 184, 192–193
Injunctions and, 391, 394, 401–404, 419, 421
Post dispute clauses, 35–36
Qualifications of arbitrator in, 199
Sample arbitration clauses, 26–27, 32
Scope, 44, 89
Third Parties and, 327–328 (see also "Third Parties")
Waiver, 423, 445

Arbitrators
Appointment, 28–30, 202, 223, 463–464
Challenge to, 221, 245
Conflicts, 223, 244
"Evident partiality," 506 (see also "Vacatur")
Disclosure rules, 223, 226–227, 236, 241–242
Diversity among, 206–213
Federal Arbitration Act and, 222
International arbitration and, 625, 627, 642
Law firms and, 225, 233–234
Non–lawyers, 34
Number, 29, 202, 627
Researching choice, 203–204

Attorney's Fees, 168, 534
Award, 33, 465, 484

B

Bifurcation, 465, 467
Bilateral Investment Treaty, 638

C

Class actions, 132, 153–157
Arbitration clauses and, 153, 155–157
Consent and, 184
Consumer Financial Protection Bureau and, 156, 195
Defined, 154
Effective vindication and, 154, 170, 173–174, 182
Suitability to arbitration, 132

Confidentiality, 22, 567
Confirmation of Arbitration Awards, 479–480, 490–491
Consensus, 4–5, 39, 73, 172–173, 191, 291, 427
Consolidation, 423–425, 427, 431, 442–445
Consumer Financial Protection Bureau, 156, 195
Contract law, 191, 331, 378, 446, 597
Deference to arbitrator on, 597
State law and, 345, 82
Third parties and, 327, 331, 358

Convention on the Recognition and Enforcement of Foreign Arbitral Awards (see New York Convention)
Cooling off periods, 23–24
COVID-19, 535, 541–542 (see "Virtual Hearings")
CPR, 215, 259

D

Default, 28, 92–93
Delegation Clauses, 113, 117–120, 124, 131
Class actions and, 132
Clause within clause, 118
Consolidation and, 431

Discovery, 255, 258, 284, 288
Arbitration clause and, 258
Choice of law, 258–261
Depositions, 258, 260, 264, 278–279

Electronically stored information, 263, 284
Former employees and, 225, 506
Institutional arbitration and, 259
Motions for, 278, 283
Of arbitrator bias/contacts, 226–227
Prehearing circuit split, 310
Sample clause, 32
Sample order on, 469
Subpoenas, 313
Third Parties and, 291–294, 324
Dispositive Motions, 458, 472–473
Diversity in Arbitration, 206–208, 213, 216–217, 219, 631–632
Dodd-Frank Act, 195

E
Effective Vindication rule, 154, 170, 173–174, 182
Electronically stored information ("ESI"), 263, 276, 284
Evidence, 291–293, 313
Expert witness/reports, 281, 556, 634

F
Federal Arbitration Act 3, 10, 40, 69, 91, 105 222, 291, 327, 619
Arbitrator bias and, 222
Confirmation and, 490–49, 567
Consolidation and, 428 (see also "Consolidation")
Consumers and, 43–44, 168
Institutional rules and, 222 (see also "Institutional Rules")
Interlocutory appeal and, 253
Presumption in favor of arbitration in, 40–41, 56, 91, 153
Purpose of, 3, 73, 253
Section 2, 6–7, 45, 106, 167
Section 3, 92–94 382–383 (see also "Default")
Section 4, 11, 52, 92
Section 5, 29, 92–93, 463
Section 7, 291 (see also "Discovery")
Section 9, 490
Section 10, 221, 245–246, 479, 491, 575, 653
Section 11, 545, 558
Substantive law, 52, 56
Federal Rules of Civil Procedure
Rule 1, 397
Rule 26, 261
Rule 42, 424
Rule 45, 313
Rule 81, 429
Federal Rules of Evidence, 458, 482
Federalism, 52, 173, 183
and Moses Cone, 52
preemption and, 183–184
severability and, 108
state law and, 167
Fraud, 105–107, 496, 506
Confirmation and, 491, 496
Functus officio, 545, 560

G
Gateway Issues, 97, 138, 431
Consolidation and, 440

I
IBA Guidelines, 223, 630
ICDR, 217, 404, 443, 618
Injunctions, 33, 381–382, 391, 394–395, 400, 402, 404, 419, 462
and Arbitration clause, 391, 402
Appeal of, 404
Carve out for, 391, 394, 397, 404
Emergency in arbitration, 394, 396, 403, 413
Halting arbitration, 246, 509
"Hollow formality" theory, 382, 394, 402
Mandatory vs. Permissive, 400–402
Litigation vs Arbitration injunctions distinguished, 381–382, 458
Orders, 403, 404
Section 3 of FAA and, 402
Timing, 245

Institutional Arbitration, 29–31, 618
  Arbitrator selection and, 35, 202, 625
  Consumer arbitration clauses in, 194
  Consolidation and, 442–444
  Discovery and, 32, 259, 265, 633
  Diversity and, 206–207
  Electronically stored information, 263
  Injunctions and, 403
  International institutions, 618 (see also "International Arbitration")
  Rules, generally, 31, 120, 202, 260, 262, 570
  Severability and, 118–120, 123
Interim Measures of Protection, 403–404 (see also "Injunctions")
Interlocutory appeal, 253
International Arbitration, 615–618
  Arbitrator selection, 625–629, 631
  Conflicts of interest in, 630–631 (see also "IBA Guidelines")
  Discovery, 632–634, 634–635
  Distinguished from Litigation, 657–658
  Diversity in, 631–632
  Enforcement, 617, 641–643
  Evidence, 632
  Institutions and, 618–619, 626 (see also "Institutional Arbitration")
  International Investment arbitration (see "Investment Arbitration")
  Nationality, 629
  Popularity, 616–617
  Sample clause, 617
  Seat, 619–620
  Third Parties in, 540
International Bar Association, 223, 630
International Chamber of Commerce (ICC), 618, 627, 629, 631
International Commission for the Settlement of Investment Disputes (ICSID), 638, 640
Investment Arbitration, 637–638

J
JAMS
  Arbitrator selection, 30, 250
  Consolidation, 442
  Control, 263–264
  COVID-era hearings, 536, 542
  Discovery, 259–260, 262
  Diversity, 207
  Injunctions, 404
  Interim measures of protection (see "Injunctions")
Jurisdiction
  Lex loci, 619, 620

L
Litigation
  Distinguished from Arbitration, 457–458, 657–658
London Court of International Arbitration ("LCIA"),
  Arbitrator selection, 626–627, 631
  Disclosures, 634
  Model clause, 617–618

M
Manifest Disregard, 575, 584, 590
  Circuit split, 583, 584, 590, 605
  Defined, 575–576
  Exceeded powers test, 523–524
  Exclusivity and, 582–583
  International arbitration and, 603, 605
  "Judicial Gloss" theory and, 590
  "Manifest injustice" and, 613
  SCOTUS uncertainty and, 583–584
Mediation 13, 17,
  Distinguished from Arbitration, 17, 21, 22
Mistake, 545, 556–557
Motions, 93–94, 446, 492, 516

N

New York Convention (Convention on the Recognition and Enforcement of Foreign Arbitral Awards), 603–604, 617, 641–643, 653

O

Organizational Conference, 442

P

Preemption (see "Federalism")
Public Policy, 46, 51, 65, 153–157, 603, 653

S

Sexual harassment and discrimination, 65
Singapore International Arbitration Commission, 619
State Law, 52–53, 57, 62, 64, 153, 168, 184, 191, 322, 342
Statutes of Limitation, 606, 613
Subpoena, 294, 313–315, 320, 322

T

Testimony, 292, 536, 634
Third Parties, 327
  Agency, 345
  Assumption, 342
  Estoppel, 338
  Evidence, 291–294, 309–312, 313–314
  Incorporation by reference, 339
  Severability, 378
  Third party beneficiary, 358
  Veil piercing, 356

U

Unconscionability, 51, 167

V

Vacatur (of arbitration awards), 491, 495–496
  Choice of law in, 614
  Drafting and, 490
  "Essence test," 524–525
  Evidence as basis, 516, 519–521
  Evident Partiality as grounds, 505–506
  Exceeded Powers and, 523–524, 534
  Federal Arbitration Act and, 491–492
  Fraud as grounds, 496, 502
  Limited Nature of, 495–496
  Manifest disregard (see "Manifest Disregard")
  Misconduct, 491
  Time Limits, 490
Virtual hearings, 535–536, 540–541, 543–544

W

Waiver, 423, 245–246, 445–446